Marketing Today
Fourth Edition

John T. Mentzer
Virginia Polytechnic Institute and State University

David J. Schwartz
Georgia State University

Harcourt Brace Jovanovich, Publishers
San Diego   New York   Chicago   Atlanta   Washington, D.C.
London   Sydney   Toronto

To
Brenda,
Minnie,
and the memory of
Tom, Sr.

Cover design by HumanGraphics.

Title page photo © Karen Kent.
Copyrights and Acknowledgments and Illustration Credits appear on pages
822–23, which constitute a continuation of the copyright page.

ISBN: 0-15-555093-4

Library of Congress Catalog Card Number: 84-81509

Printed in the United States of America

Marketing in Action

For more than 30 years New York Twist Drill made a better industrial bit and the world beat a path to its doorstep. Sales doubled every five years until 1980, when the recession dried up business. During the next two years orders fell by 40 percent, and management searched frantically for a cure. After weeks of early-morning "skull" sessions, they finally found the answer—marketing. With the sales manager doubling as the marketing director and the salesmen providing the market research, the company quickly recruited customers for a new line of products. Since then, the massive machine-tool lathes and grinders that once produced reamers and bits used to make airplanes and tractors have been sculpting delicate stainless-steel surgical drills and grinding out 13-piece drill sets for consumers. "We used to say, 'Who needs a marketing program?'" confesses vice president of sales C. J. Sirignano, who is happy to report that sales have jumped 30 percent since June. "Now, we're true believers."

"To Market, To Market," *Newsweek*, January 9, 1984.

Preface

Marketing Today, Fourth Edition, represents a major departure from the previous editions. With John Mentzer as a co-author we have made a significant effort to raise the level of discussion and update the book while maintaining its traditional managerial approach and focusing on product, place, promotion, and pricing decisions. The broad objective, as before, is to present the fundamentals of marketing in an interesting, challenging, and rewarding way.

Each chapter includes a Marketing Strategy and a Marketing Milestone. In most chapters the Strategy compares the ways two different companies approach a similar marketing decision. Some examples include Gallo versus Taylor Wine, IBM versus Apple, Coca-Cola versus Dad's Root Beer, and Kodak versus Polaroid. These strategies have always been a popular feature and continue to illustrate the variety and creativity with which marketing managers attempt to reach their goals.

Marketing Milestones, also popular in the past, have been retained as well, with some more recent Milestones, such as Cable Television and Telemarketing, added.

Students in the past have found the people in the Marketing Profiles both interesting and inspiring. Among those profiled are Diane Von Furstenberg, the fashion marketer; Berry Gordy, one of the recording industry's great marketers; and the late Ray Kroc, founder of the McDonald's franchising empire. Each major section of the book begins with a Profile of an individual whose career has followed that area of marketing.

In this edition we have attempted to raise the quality and level of the cases at the end of each chapter. Each case is based on the experiences of an actual company (in most cases the company is identified), and students should find these real-world marketing situations both challenging and interesting.

Structurally, the Fourth Edition differs considerably from preceding editions: We have reorganized the second section in order to more accurately reflect current thought on markets and customers, combined the chapters on the legal aspects and social responsibility of marketing, and added a final chapter on strategic marketing planning. A computerized test bank is a new feature available to instructors using the text. Also available is an instructor's manual; and a *Study Guide to Marketing Today* is available for students. Additionally, we have compiled a new readings book, *Readings in Marketing Today*, as part of the overall *Marketing Today* package.

No project of this magnitude is the sole effort of one or even two individuals. We wish to thank the editorial staff of Harcourt Brace Jovanovich for its invaluable assistance. In addition we would like to thank Joe Chapman, Satya Chattopadhyay, Nancy Jones, Natalie Marker-Gates, Mike Martino, and David Pack—research assistants at Virginia Polytechnic Institute and State University—for their help in researching this edition. Special appreciation goes to Ms. Wanda Belcher for her outstanding job typing the first draft of this edition and for pleasantly tolerating the work load Dr. Mentzer placed upon her. We are also indebted to Robert E. Krapfel of the University of Maryland; Douglas M. Lambert of Michigan State University; Kenneth D. Bahn, Stephen W. Clopton, Kent B. Monroe, and David J. Roberts of Virginia Tech; and two anonymous reviewers for their suggestions on improving the first draft. Special thanks goes to Brenda Mentzer, who not only read every page of this edition several times, but without whose love and support this edition would never have been completed.

Although we live in a time of increasingly rapid change and uncertainty, particularly in business and marketing, we hope *Marketing Today*, Fourth Edition, will help students appreciate and understand the role of marketing not only in business and other organizations but in society as well.

John T. Mentzer

David J. Schwartz

CONTENTS

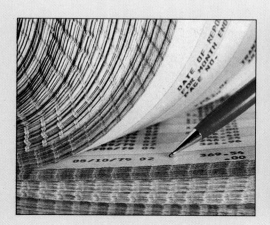

PART TWO
Understanding the Marketplace   103

5 Consumer Behavior 137

6 Organizational Buyers 177

PART THREE
Product Decisions   237

9 Product Management 275

10 Marketing Services and Nonprofit Products 313

13 Retailing 407

14 Physical Distribution 441

ONE

Introduction
To Marketing

1 Marketing: An Overview

STUDY OBJECTIVES

After studying this chapter, you should be able to

1. Define marketing and discuss the activities it involves.
2. Trace the evolution of marketing to its present state and define the marketing concept.
3. Discuss the importance and scope of marketing.
4. Define marketing mix, the marketing controllable variables, and the role of marketing information systems and marketing research.
5. Describe the relationship between marketing and business, economics, sociology, and psychology.

Many definitions of marketing exist, of which Figure 1-1 gives but a few. Obviously, marketing means different things to different people. At its most basic level marketing refers to the efforts of a producer to convince potential customers to buy a product.

To have a common ground from which to work, we will define marketing as follows:

Marketing consists of the activities performed by individuals or organizations for commercial or noncommercial objectives,

---

Figure 1-1

Definitions of Marketing

Marketing is:
"the exchange taking place between consuming groups on the one hand and supplying groups on the other."*

"the performance of business activities that direct the flow of goods and services from producer to consumer to user."†

"the process in a society by which the demand structure for economic goods and services is anticipated or enlarged and satisfied through the conception, promotion, and physical distribution of such goods and services."‡

"the process in a society by which the demand structure for economic goods and services is anticipated or enlarged and satisfied through the conception, promotion, exchange, and physical distribution of such goods and services."§

"concerned with regulating the level, timing, and character of demand for one or more products of an organization."**

"human activity directed at satisfying needs and wants through exchange processes."††

---

* Wroe Alderson, *Marketing Behavior and Executive Action* (Homewood, Ill.: Richard D. Irwin, 1957), p. 42.
† Ralph S. Alexander, chairman, "Report of the Definitions Committee," *Journal of Marketing*, October 1948, pp. 207–217. This definition was not altered in, Committee on Definition, *Marketing Definitions: A Glossary of Marketing Terms* (Chicago: American Marketing Association, 1960), p. 15.
‡ Statement of the Philosophy of the Marketing Faculty, The Ohio State University, College of Commerce and Administration (Columbus, Ohio, 1964), p. 2.
§Marketing Staff of the Ohio State University, "A Statement of Marketing Philosophy," *Journal of Marketing*, January 1965, p. 43.
** Philip Kotler, "The Major Tasks of Marketing Management," *Journal of Marketing*, October 1973, p. 42.
†† Philip Kotler, *Marketing Management: Planning, Analysis, and Control*, 4th ed. (Englewood Cliffs, N.J.: Prentice-Hall, 1980), p. 19.

aimed at satisfaction through the exchange process of buyers'
demand for products, services, people, and ideas.

To begin our understanding of marketing, we will examine each component of this definition.

WHAT IS MARKETING?

First, *marketing involves specific activities.* Although we will examine these
activities in detail throughout the book, an example should suffice for now.
Consider just a few of the marketing activities performed by automobile
manufacturers to persuade you to exchange your dollars for their cars:

1. Conducting research on product design, styling, and demand.
   (Thus, marketing begins before the production process.)
2. Setting prices at both the manufacturer and retailer (dealer) levels.
3. Transporting and storing the finished cars, first by the manufacturer and later by the retailer.
4. Advertising in magazines, on radio and television, in newspapers,
   on billboards, and through other media. (Demand is not just satisfied; it is often created or directed.)
5. Providing sales tools and promotional aids to dealers. (Educating
   dealer personnel is a major marketing activity in this and many
   other industries.)
6. Managing franchised dealers to make sure customers receive adequate service; establishing sales quotas, policies, plans, and controls.
7. Coaching dealer personnel in personal selling.
8. Financing dealer inventories and, perhaps, customer purchases.
9. Providing postpurchase services to ensure customer satisfaction.

Second, *marketing is performed by both individuals and organizations.* Marketing by large organizations is much more conspicuous because of its
heavy emphasis on promotion. But small businesses must also market successfully to survive and prosper. The sole proprietor of a small sandwich
shop performs marketing activities by displaying cold cuts in a glass-fronted cooler or painting a menu on the front window. When a student
places an ad in the school paper to sell some books or a bicycle, he or she is
also engaged in marketing.

Third, our definition also states that *marketing is intended to meet either
commercial or noncommercial objectives.* Although this book focuses on the
commercial objectives of profit-seeking firms, nonprofit-seeking enterprises must also perform marketing activities to survive. Many universities
use advertising and other promotional techniques to market continuing

Hiroaki Aoki
(b. 1939)

A Japanese-American with a flair for promotion, Hiroaki (Rocky) Aoki introduced a new concept in dining: Benihana of Tokyo is one of the most successful restaurant chains in America, consisting of both company-owned and franchised Japanese steak-houses.

Rocky Aoki first visited New York City at the age of 20 when he toured America with the Keio University wrestling team. He decided to stay and enrolled in the city's Community College School of Hotel and Restaurant Management. By working 15 hours a day, 7 days a week as an ice-cream vendor in Harlem, Aoki more than made ends meet. When he graduated in 1965, he had saved $10,000.

With his savings plus a loan of $20,000, he opened a small restaurant in Manhattan. From his father's restaurant in Japan he borrowed the name Benihana, which means "red flower," and the idea of the hibachi table. The hibachi table consists of a cooking center fired by gas jets, surrounded by a wooden surface on which food is served to guests.

The restaurant paid for itself in less than six months. Aoki opened a larger one three blocks away. That, too, was paid for in less than a year.

Japanese-styled food modified for American palates, authentic Japanese "country inn" decor, and a preponderance of imported first-generation Japanese employees are the hallmarks of Benihana's success. Patrons watch as chefs theatrically wield razor-sharp knives to cut shrimp, beef, and chicken

education programs; the United Way and other charitable organizations perform marketing activities to win public support and generate needed funds; and mounting an evangelical crusade requires careful marketing planning and execution.

Fourth, *marketing is concerned with more than physical products,* such as appliances, food, or tennis balls. Services, such as health care, hair styling, and entertainment, are intangible "products" that must be marketed as well. Marketing activities are needed to bring about the exchange of concepts and ideas. Certainly, politicians use marketing techniques to obtain

into bite-sized pieces, then cook them with vegetables in the Japanese "teppen-yaki" manner. The menu is kept simple to reduce waste and increase profit.

Each restaurant—there were 44 in the United States in 1983—is constructed of materials purchased from old houses in Japan and is put together without nails by imported Japanese craftsmen and architects. Woodblock prints, caligraphic drawings, and ceramics add interior atmosphere.

Aoki is chairman of both Benihana of Tokyo (the restaurant chain) and Benihana National Corporation. The latter company owns 14 of the Benihana of Tokyo restaurants and markets a line of oriental frozen foods.*

Aside from his restaurants, Rocky Aoki's interests are varied. He collects art objects and antique cars. He has promoted sporting events and Broadway plays. He has sponsored Japanese artists in the United States and has produced films about them for release in Japan. He broke a 3314-mile ballooning record when he crossed the Pacific from Japan to California in 1981.

Aoki maintains that only in America could he have become so successful.

> If I had tried to start Benihana or any business in Japan, I'd never have gotten off the ground. The opportunities there are so few and far between, I'd never have been able to start, much less build up, a $15 million business in ten short years.
>
> I would advise a marketing student, or any business student for that matter, to pay attention to your school work, to the overall basic concepts and techniques; the details of how-to-do-it will come later, with experience. But be prepared, when the time comes for execution of your ideas and programs, to produce at least as much as, if not more than, you promise. To my mind, there is nothing worse than a product or service which does not live up to its advertising promise. Be honest and you can't miss.

* "Benihana Tries to Put More Sizzle in Its Stock," *Business Week*, November 28, 1983, p. 113.

votes in exchange for their promises, as the massive TV ad campaigns mounted by political candidates plainly illustrate. Various kinds of social movements seem to succeed or fail according to how effectively they are marketed.

Finally, *marketing revolves around the exchange process.* The marketing process is not complete until the buyer exchanges something of value for what he or she consumes. Although we often think of that exchange as money or the promise of money (credit) for consumption, consumers may "pay" with their votes for a political candidate or support for an organization or movement. In fact a growing segment of our economy utilizes marketing in the exchange of one product or service for another (barter), with no money actually changing hands.[1]

Marketing Involves More than Selling and Advertising

Students and many business people often feel that marketing is synonymous with personal selling and advertising. Unquestionably, selling and advertising are two key activities in marketing many products and services. But marketing includes much more. For example, a retailer of tape recorders and related merchandise must decide which target market to reach, where to locate the store, the hours of operation, what specific items and how many to stock, where and how to display them, how to price them, and how to handle credit. All are marketing-related issues.

EVOLUTION OF MARKETING

The evolution of marketing is the evolution of the exchange process. Unless two or more individuals or organizations have something to exchange, there is no need for marketing. The desire to exchange occurs only when someone produces more than he/she can consume (a surplus). This surplus is exchanged for surplus someone else produced. Possibly the first marketing transaction took place when one cave-dweller, who enjoyed making arrows but did not like to hunt, persuaded a fellow cave-dweller, who liked to hunt but did not enjoy making arrows, to accept some arrows in exchange for some animal skins and meat. Since that primitive time, marketing has become very sophisticated indeed.

As elementary civilization spread, one tribe learned to trade goods with another tribe. The invention and acceptance of money, a medium of exchange, was a giant step forward. Gradually, people began to learn that they could live better if they specialized in producing one good and traded their surplus to people who specialized in producing something else. The interdependency of human beings, which is inherent in the civilizing process, continued to grow.

The Egyptians, Phoenicians, Greeks, and Romans all had well-developed trade systems. The Old Testament contains many references to such marketing topics as money, wealth, credit, products, international trade,

---

[1] "Using Barter as a Way of Doing Business," *Business Week,* August 4, 1980, p. 57.

government regulation, middlemen, taxation, poverty, welfare, pricing, trade fairs, and business ethics.

During the Middle Ages trade declined. However, it picked up again during the Age of Discovery (roughly 1400–1760 A.D.) as merchants sought to extend their reach over much of the world. As you no doubt recall, Columbus made his first voyage to America in an effort to find a more direct trade route to Asia and the Far East.

In the late 1700s the Industrial Revolution began, and as it continued, marketing grew in importance. This latter-day development can be divided into three periods—the production era, the sales era, and the marketing era.

Production Era

By the late 1800s the Industrial Revolution had brought technology to a point where mass production was a reality. The high level of employment created by all this economic activity also created more disposable income for consumers and more consumer demand than production capacity could produce. This, combined with little competition, allowed companies to sell all that they could produce. Thus little need existed for marketing research or consumer-oriented marketing plans. Consumers already bought whatever was available. Management was chiefly concerned with achieving production efficiency, and marketing activities were confined mainly to the efficient physical distribution of products.

Sales Era

In the early twentieth century consumer demand had leveled off and more competition in the form of new companies had entered the marketplace. Companies realized that to continue production at the same high, efficient levels, customers would have to have products "sold" to them. That is, consumers would have to be convinced that what a producer had to sell was what they really wanted. For the first half of this century business used sales efforts to maintain and increase profits, and marketing consisted mainly of personal selling and advertising.

Marketing Era

By the 1950s consumers had a higher level of income and a diversity of product offerings available to them. As a result they could be discriminating in what they bought. Businesses began to realize that sales and advertising could not sell a product if it was not what the consumer wanted. Thus it became important to first find out what the consumer wanted or needed and then produce a product to satisfy that want or need. This attitude led to the development of the **marketing concept.** In 1957 the president of General Electric, John B. McKitterick, formally defined the marketing concept as a consumer-oriented, integrated, profit-oriented philosophy of business.[2]

Over the years the marketing concept has evolved into a philosophy aimed at pursuing organizational goals by identifying the wants and needs of the organization's consumers (the organization's target markets) and designing an integrated product/service offering to fill those wants and needs. An integrated offering implies that *all* organizational activities are aimed at this consumer orientation. The organization's goals may be profit, in the case of commercial organizations, or nonprofit, in the case of organizations such as churches or political parties.

It is important to note the difference between this marketing attitude and that of the Sales Era. The sales orientation emphasizes convincing consumers to buy what the company already produces. The marketing concept advocates gathering information from consumers, then using it to develop the company's product/service offering. The aspect of consumer feedback is crucial to the marketing concept. Thus the marketing concept dictates that organizations be people-oriented rather than product-oriented.

IMPORTANCE AND SCOPE OF MARKETING

Marketing affects our economy in a number of ways: It stimulates demand, employs much of our labor force, accounts for more than half of each dollar spent by consumers, and is essential to business. Its scope is virtually all-pervasive.

Demand Stimulation

It is the responsibility of those engaged in marketing to discover the wants and needs of consumers and to stimulate and fulfill this demand. In 1980 American companies spent more than $66,580 million[3] (more than the combined GNP of Kenya, Bangladesh, Chile, Ethiopia, and Egypt) for advertising—just one of many marketing activities.[4] This enormous sum

---

[2] John B. McKitterick, "What Is the Marketing Concept?" in Frank M. Bass, ed., *The Frontiers of Marketing Thought and Action* (Chicago: American Marketing Association, 1957), pp. 71–82.

[3] U.S. Department of Commerce, Bureau of the Census, *Statistical Abstract of the United States*, 104th ed., 1984, p. 567.

[4] Ibid., p. 865.

of money leaves no doubt that American businesses intentionally seek to create and stimulate demand.

Demand stimulation is a key not only to consumption, but also to income and employment. Consider what happens when just one family buys a new television set. This transaction generates income for the salesperson (who gets a commission), for the retailer (who presumably earns a profit), and for the manufacturer (who also presumably makes a profit). The retailer and manufacturer are encouraged to stay in business and to continue to provide employment. There are also many indirect beneficiaries of this marketing transaction—the businesses that supply components to the television manufacturer, the transportation companies that handle the shipping of parts and finished products, the utility company that sells the energy to power the set, warehousemen, advertising agencies, merchants who sell to the employees of the television manufacturer, plus countless other people and firms. When people buy (consume), they help create employment. Employment creates more purchasing power, which in turn creates more consumption. This increased consumption creates further employment, thus establishing an economic chain reaction.

Marketing Employment

This economic chain reaction creates considerable employment in marketing activities. Of the 1982 U.S. labor force, 14 million persons were employed in retailing, 5.4 million in wholesaling, and 3 million in distribution.[5] This 22.2 percent of the labor force does not include the millions of people employed in industries that support marketing activities. For instance, advertising and marketing research firms constitute entire marketing industries with billions of dollars in annual billings.

Dollars Spent on Marketing

Although an exact figure is difficult to determine, marketing accounts for at least 50 cents of every dollar spent by the consumer.[6] Just the distribu-

---

[5] Ibid., p. 798.

[6] Reavis Cox, *Distribution in a High Level Economy* (Englewood Cliffs, N.J.: Prentice-Hall, 1965), p. 149; Paul W. Stewart and J. Frederick Dewhurst, *Does Distribution Cost Too Much?* (New York: Twentieth Century Fund, 1963), pp. 117–18; and Jules J. Schwartz, *Corporate Policy: A Casebook* (Englewood Cliffs, N.J.: Prentice-Hall, 1978), pp. 6–7.

Money is one of the most used, most abused, and least understood commodities developed by man. The development of money is also the most important of all milestones for marketers.

Economists define money as "something generally accepted as a medium of exchange, a measure of value, and means of holding wealth." The "something" changes in form and content from society to society and era to era, but its reason for being is always the same: It provides a convenient system of accounting.

Originally, man bartered his own surplus goods for other commodities he wished to own. Gradually, through the centuries, this unwieldy, time-consuming procedure was replaced by the exchange of a commodity that had a standard value as a medium of exchange or a measure of wealth. Historically, as societies became more economically sophisticated, they relinquished the bulky barter currency (such as cattle and grain) and adopted more convenient commodity metals (such as gold and silver). Egyptians, for example, used a copper unit as early as 5,000 B.C.

Coinage was a further refinement of this system. It was in the seventh century B.C. that King Gyges of Lydia stamped his seal on a piece of metal and ushered in the age of state-issued currency. Bimetalism was introduced in the fourteenth century A.D., when the ratio between gold and silver was defined. For Europeans, further ease of handling came about when Florentine bankers printed paper money during the Middle Ages. (Paper money was used by the Chinese as early as the ninth century A.D.)

tion activity of marketing costs at least 25 cents out of every consumer dollar.[7]

Many critics claim this cost is too high. However, when you consider how difficult, if not impossible, it would be to maintain our life-style and present level of consumption without marketing, the money seems well spent. Without marketing, we would literally return to a society in which each individual consumed only what he or she could produce.

---

[7] *Physical Distribution Management—Career Information* (Chicago, Ill: National Council of Physical Distribution Management, 1982), p. 1.

The ideal monetary unit is useful, portable, comparatively indestructible, and homogeneous. Its value is stable and can be easily calculated in terms of the currencies used by other nations. It is easily divisible, in order to simplify calculations, and it is easily recognizable (yet hard to counterfeit). Over the years, national currencies have gradually developed many of these characteristics.

Adoption of the dollar as the unit of money and the decimal system as the method of reckoning greatly facilitated trade in the young United States. The move eliminated considerable confusion from commercial transactions caused by the English shillings, French Louis d'or and Spanish doubloons then in circulation. (It is ironic, though, that Americans accepted money on the metric system, yet rejected metrication of all other measurements.)

Congress authorized the first coins in 1792, to be minted of gold, silver, and copper. Paper currency issued by banks came into common use, but the U.S. government did not issue Treasury demand notes until 1862. United States notes, popularly known as "greenbacks," were also issued in that year.

The last U.S. gold coin was struck in 1933. Today, many leading countries use their gold reserves in international trade and do not allow their private citizens to redeem paper currency for gold, to hoard gold, or to use it as money.

Checking accounts (or demand deposits) are a modern form of money used in addition to coins and paper money. In the U.S. today, coins make up about 1 percent of the money supply, paper money accounts for about 20 percent, and nearly 80 percent is attributable to individual and corporate checking accounts.

Modern societies are moving toward electronic transference of money and credit, sometimes described as a "cashless, checkless" settlement of obligations. Yet for many centuries, commerce and marketing in our densely populated world would have been virtually impossible without the tangible, officially issued coins and paper known as money.

Business Needs Marketing

Our economy depends on marketing activities. Without marketing, companies could not maintain the efficiencies of production and distribution necessary to survive. Efficient production and delivery at a reasonable price allow corporations to make the profits necessary to maintain operations, provide employment, and attract capital. Without this success the companies—and eventually the economy—and our way of life would fail. In addition the customer feedback generated by marketing is essential in allocating resources and production to best satisfy the needs and goals of society.

Scope of Marketing

Marketing is everywhere. Businesses engage in such varied marketing activities as buying, selling, advertising, sales force management, forecasting, pricing, packaging, branding, warehousing, transporting, order processing, location analysis, customer analysis, wholesaling, retailing, supplier selection, marketing research, public relations, establishing warranty offers, attending trade shows, and planning and development of marketing channels. All organizations—and many individuals—pursue at least some of these activities. In fact even such traditionally nonmarketing institutions as banks are now allowed to engage more actively in marketing research, target identification, new product development, pricing, advertising, and promotion.[8]

Marketing and the marketing concept are also applied by numerous organizations and individuals engaged in nonbusiness pursuits. These include churches, charities, political candidates, political action groups, museums, concert halls, and federal, state, and local governments. Whether they realize it or not, they all are attempting to identify and satisfy the demands of some segment of our society. Truly, marketing touches our lives many times every day.

MARKETING MANAGEMENT

A convenient way to study marketing is to separate its various activities into four decision areas—product decisions, place decisions, promotion decisions, and price decisions. Once a marketing manager has decided on the group of customers—the target market—to which a product or service will be offered, he or she must make the product, place, promotion, and price decisions to reach the target market. Because the manager has the power to make these decisions, we often refer to them as the **marketing controllable variables.**

In addition the marketing manager is responsible for gathering information about the target market and the uncontrollable aspects of the marketing environment. This information is used to adjust the marketing controllable variables to best accomplish organizational goals while meeting the wants and needs of the target market and adapting to the dynamic nature of the environment. Figure 1-2 illustrates these relationships.

Corporate Management and Marketing Management

Many decisions made by a company's corporate management affect the environment in which its marketing management operates. Because it is

---

[8] "Now Bankers Turn to a Hard Sales Pitch," *Business Week*, September 21, 1981, p. 62.

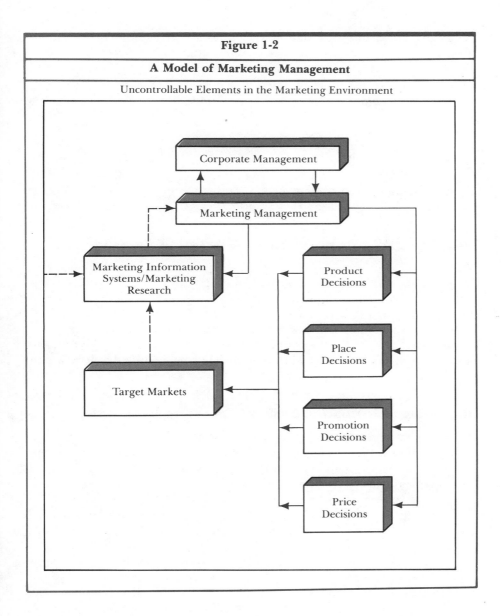

Figure 1-2

A Model of Marketing Management

Uncontrollable Elements in the Marketing Environment

Corporate Management

Marketing Management

Marketing Information Systems/Marketing Research

Product Decisions

Place Decisions

Promotion Decisions

Price Decisions

Target Markets

corporate management that makes these decisions, we refer to them as the **controllable elements** in the marketing environment. Foremost among these controllable elements is the determination of organizational goals. For example, two different companies may both make power hand tools. However, the corporate management of Company A has decided that the company will sell its products only to manufacturing firms, making industrial markets the only target markets that Company A's marketing management can pursue. On the other hand Company B's corporate management is after the do-it-yourself consumer. Marketing is restricted to consumer channels and markets. As a result Company B's marketing managers may try to make the company a sole supplier to a large retail chain such as Sears, an option not open to Company A. As we can see two similar companies end up with different marketing missions because of the goals of corporate management.

Corporate management decisions concerning organization, staffing, control, and the role of marketing and other business functions in the corporation also affect marketing management. We will discuss the controllable elements of the marketing environment in more detail in Chapter 2.

Uncontrollable Elements in the Marketing Environment

There are various elements in the marketing environment over which corporate managers have little or no control. They include competitors' actions, government actions, consumer choice, economic conditions, social change, and technological change. Although corporate management cannot control these elements, marketing management must constantly monitor them in order to be aware of any potential changes and to be ready to react to these changes. We will discuss these **uncontrollable elements** in greater detail in Chapter 2.

Marketing Information System/Marketing Research

As we just mentioned, marketing management must know about environmental changes before it can react. In addition the marketing concept dictates that the wants and needs of the target customers must be identified before a product/service offering can be developed. Thus, marketing managers need some system through which to gather information about the uncontrollable environment and the company's target markets. Both the marketing information system and marketing research are information-gathering activities. The marketing information system is a formal corporate activity devoted to gathering information about environmental elements that may affect marketing plans. Market research is usually a problem-oriented effort aimed at the target market; that is, information is gathered to help solve a particular marketing problem. To illustrate the difference, note the following examples: Subscribing to a monthly publication that summarizes recent court decisions in the marketing area is a marketing information system activity aimed at the legal element of the environment. Determining what quantities of a new product consumers will purchase at three possible introductory prices is a marketing research effort. We will discuss both of these marketing areas in more detail in Chapter 3.

Marketing Controllable Variables

Marketing managers should aim all their decisions at satisfying target customers. The goals of marketing managers and their organizations cannot be met by marketing products that customers do not want or by trying to sell desirable products at undesirable locations, through ineffective promotional means, or at the wrong price. Marketing managers must design the proper mix of the marketing controllable variables based on their assessment of the environment and the target market and subject to the dictates of corporate management.

Product Decisions   Product-related decisions include the kind of product to make, how to package it, and what to call it. Remember, everything sold, whether tangible or intangible, is a product.

Product decisions are risky. In fact many new products fail. Consider Appleasy, a Pillsbury product that failed despite three years of extensive research.

> Appleasy went the way of most new food products—down the drain. The failure rate has always been enough to give food-company executives indigestion, and it is getting worse. More than 60 percent of all new grocery products introduced into test markets in 1977 failed, compared with about 50 percent in 1971, according to A.C. Nielsen Co. And the failure rate is well over eight in ten, counting all the products scrapped in the test kitchen before they are marketed.
>
> Batteries of tests and surveys are conducted to discern what

shoppers want, to develop and refine recipes, to choose brand names and even to design packages for new products, but all these efforts have been to little avail. There still isn't a foolproof method of telling what will succeed. "If anybody really knew, the failure rate wouldn't be so high," says Edward Tauber, research director at the Dancer Fitzgerald Sample, Inc., advertising agency.[9]

Place Decisions   Place decisions concern selecting product locations that are convenient to customers, maintaining an adequate inventory, selecting wholesalers and retailers, and maintaining distribution centers. Place decisions also involve selecting transportation companies and arranging storage or warehousing for the product. Although it is easy to lose sight of the marketing goals when discussing place decisions, keep in mind that place decisions create what one executive referred to as the five rights of distribution: "The right product at the right place at the right time in the right condition for the right cost."

Innovative place decisions can have a major effect on the success of a marketing effort. Consider how Gould Corporation tried to gain a competitive advantage in the retail automotive battery market:

Gould's marketing plans call for it to establish an aid service to stranded motorists by leasing 24 vans in the seven-county Chicago area and equipping them with a stock of batteries. A

---

[9] Laurence Ingrassia, "There's No Way to Tell If a New Food Product Will Please the Public," *Wall Street Journal,* February 26, 1980, p. 1.

motorist having trouble starting his car can dial a toll-free number (800 BATTERY) and Gould will dispatch a repair van within the hour. If tests show the battery is faulty, the van driver sells and installs a replacement on the spot, at a price ranging from $40 to $70. If only a jump start is needed, a flat fee of $15 is charged. Customers can pay by cash, check, or credit card.

Gould began experimenting with the van program last October in the Wilkes-Barre/Scranton (Pa.) area. In eight months, it grabbed 5% of the market. Encouraged, the company is now running a major test in the Chicago area.[10]

Promotion Decisions   Promotion decisions facilitate the exchange process by communicating with and persuading the target market to buy a product. After all, customers cannot buy products they are not aware of. Consumers also will not buy products whose features they are uninformed about. The old adage "If a man builds a better mousetrap, the world will beat a path to his door," overlooks the fact that the world will not come knocking if it does not know you have the mousetrap.

Often a corporation finds it necessary not only to inform consumers of its product, but also to persuade them to purchase it. Although this persuasion may take a logical approach, it often appeals to our emotions.

> As the young mother gently nestles her newborn child into a crib, her worried five-year-old son asks: "Who do you like better?" Mom replies: "I love you both." Says an off-camera announcer: "He's got a new baby brother. Now he has to share your attention. You try to reassure him. . . . You give him lots of love."
>
> This is how Coca-Cola Co. advertises Minute Maid orange juice these days. No more Bing Crosby touting it as "the best there is," no comparison with other brands, not even much talk about taste, freshness or ingredients. Just an unabashed yank of the heartstrings—what Marschalk Co., Minute Maid's ad agency, calls "emotional hard sell."
>
> Sentimentality—a device usually associated with such advertisers as Hallmark and Eastman Kodak—is being put to work on a growing list of products that most folks would find decidedly unemotional.
>
> Procter & Gamble uses it to sell White Cloud toilet paper, Sterling Drug for Lysol disinfectant, General Foods for Maxwell House coffee and Jell-O, Cannon Mills for towels and sheets and General Electric for light bulbs and toasters.
>
> Many advertisers have turned to sentiment because they've

---

[10] "Gould Gets a Jump on Roadside Battery Service," *Business Week,* June 15, 1981, p. 132.

run out of compelling appeals to logic. Their own sales pitches have lost their punch and, for the increasing number of products that don't differ markedly from their competitors, new arguments are hard to find.

You're playing with something that can be absolute garbage, sentimental slop, says John Bergin, president of McCann-Erickson, the agency that doles out emotion for Coca-Cola soft drinks. "Everyone will start throwing up if it's overdone."[11]

The main promotional tools at the disposal of marketing management are personal selling, advertising, sales promotion, and public relations. Marketing managers must decide which of these tools to use and how much money to spend on each. Promotion decisions can be very complex. For example, if you are an advertising manager with $10,000,000 to spend, how would you divide it among the various print and broadcast media? Would you spend more of your budget during the summer than during the winter? Would you advertise on television during the day or at night? Which magazine would be more appropriate for your product and your target market—Reader's Digest or Rolling Stone?

Price Decisions   Everything of commercial value commands a price. In part, the price is marketing management's statement about the value of the other three marketing controllable variables. However, consumers often perceive the price itself as part of the product's value. Many products—mattresses, raincoats, sweaters, shoes, tires, batteries, and so on—are made by the same manufacturer according to identical specification, but sold under different brand names at different prices. Often one brand is higher priced because consumers expect it to be—whether the quality is any better or not.

At Merns, Inc., near the World Trade Center in the financial district of Lower Manhattan, silk ties with the Ted Lapidus label sell for $6.99. In the chrome and glass Ted Lapidus boutique on Fifth Avenue uptown, Ted Lapidus silk ties go for $55. Arnaud Thieffrex, president of Ted Lapidus, says the Merns ties are fakes. Yet Steve Manko, whose Davan Enterprises, Inc., manufactured the Merns ties with the Ted Lapidus label (but no longer makes Lapidus ties), says they aren't; he's been dumping his unsold stock of Lapidus ties to Merns and others, and Merns says its ties are genuine.[12]

---

[11] Bill Abrams, "If Logic in Ads Doesn't Sell, Try a Tug on the Heartstrings," *Wall Street Journal,* April 8, 1982, p. 27.

[12] "Location, Volume, Marketing Make Prices Vary Widely in New York City," *Wall Street Journal,* December 3, 1981, p. 31.

It is clear that the customers at the Ted Lapidus boutique are willing to pay almost eight times as much because of the boutique's quality image.

Finally, the cost structure for marketing a product to its target market provides a standard from which to determine its minimum acceptable price. Thus, understanding costs is necessary before discussing price.

The Target Market Determines the Marketing Mix

The marketing concept dictates that the demands of the target market determine the marketing mix (particular decisions on the marketing controllable variables). Figures 1-3 and 1-4 demonstrate how two different target markets drastically change the marketing strategy manifested in the marketing mix. Because the target market in Figure 1-3 is high-income, quality-oriented people, the marketing mix emphasizes quality products and outlets as well as the higher prices expected to accompany quality products. Promotion is aimed at reaching only that target market.

On the other hand the marketing mix in Figure 1-4 presents a bargain image to a bargain-conscious target market. Figure 1-5 further illustrates how the market concept is applied and not applied through the marketing controllable variables.

Target market decisions are by no means simple to make. Sears, the nation's largest retailer, originally selected the American middle class as its target market. Promotion centered on good product quality at low prices. In the early 1970s, however, Sears decided to appeal to more affluent, fashion-conscious consumers. When this strategy failed, Sears elected to again appeal to its original target market by concentrating on retailing to middle-class consumers and enforcing more consistent pricing by its retail stores. This uncertainty in what represented Sears' target market and what marketing mix this target market would respond to caused serious corporate setbacks.

> Revenues in Sears' $18 billion retailing business have stagnated, and profits have tumbled since 1977 as the company has wrestled with high overhead, tough competition, and its own loss of direction in picking demographic markets (target markets) in which to concentrate.[13]

Competition for Differential Advantage   Marketing managers try to develop a marketing mix that their target customers will prefer, that is, the marketing mix that has some "differential advantage" over competitive offerings. For example, if two companies offer identical products at the

---

[13] "The New Sears," *Business Week*, November 16, 1981, pp. 140–46.

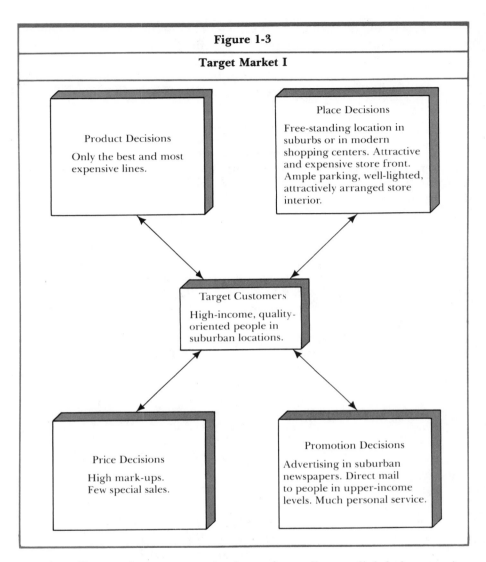

Figure 1-3

Target Market I

Product Decisions

Only the best and most expensive lines.

Place Decisions

Free-standing location in suburbs or in modern shopping centers. Attractive and expensive store front. Ample parking, well-lighted, attractively arranged store interior.

Target Customers

High-income, quality-oriented people in suburban locations.

Price Decisions

High mark-ups. Few special sales.

Promotion Decisions

Advertising in suburban newspapers. Direct mail to people in upper-income levels. Much personal service.

same retail stores but one company's product sells at a slightly lower price and is backed by superior promotional effort, that product clearly will have a competitive advantage. Developing this differential advantage is not always so simple or obvious. Companies constantly compete to find the marketing mix that will convince target customers of their product's superiority—its differential advantage—to the competition. This differential advantage, which marketing managers are always trying to achieve and keep, influences all marketing mix decisions and is fundamental to everything we will discuss in this book.

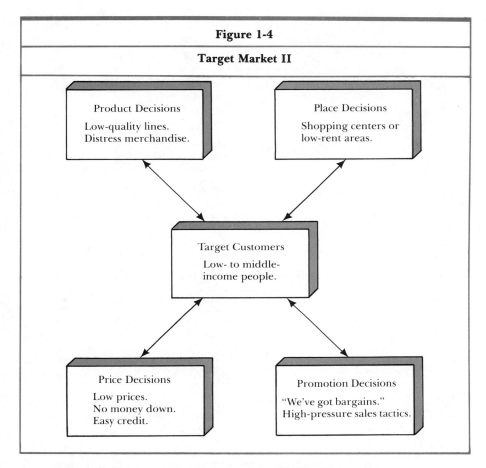

Figure 1-4

Target Market II

Product Decisions
Low-quality lines.
Distress merchandise.

Place Decisions
Shopping centers or
low-rent areas.

Target Customers
Low- to middle-
income people.

Price Decisions
Low prices.
No money down.
Easy credit.

Promotion Decisions
"We've got bargains."
High-pressure sales tactics.

MARKETING AND OTHER DISCIPLINES

As a final area of discussion in this introductory look at marketing, we will examine some of the other academic areas to which marketing is related and from which marketing has borrowed concepts and techniques. Business, economics, sociology, and psychology are extremely relevant to marketing. As such, they are helpful to anyone entering the field.

Marketing and Business

Marketing is directly related to business policy, quantitative methods, accounting, finance, and business communications. The relationship of marketing to management is especially close. Much of this book shows how the management function leads to the development and implementation of marketing plans.

Figure 1-5

The Marketing Concept Applied and Not Applied

Applied	Not Applied
PRODUCT DECISIONS • Product quality is consistent. • Design, style, color, size, taste, and other characteristics are matched with consumer preferences as determined through market research. • Product is offered in as many varieties as can be profitably marketed. • Product warranties are fulfilled, and consumer complaints are adjusted as quickly and efficiently as possible.	**PRODUCT DECISIONS** • Product quality is inconsistent. • Product characteristics are based on what is easiest to produce or on subjective whims of management. • Product varieties are determined by convenience in production and shipping. • Attempts are made to "get around" warranties and thus save money.
PLACE DECISIONS • The product is made easily accessible to the consumer. • The product is delivered on time and in good condition. • The product is in inventory when the consumer wants it. • The product is sold in attractive, clean surroundings.	**PLACE DECISIONS** • The product is sold in hard-to-find locations. • Delivery of the product is strictly at the convenience of the seller. • The product is frequently out of stock. • No attention is paid to the attractiveness of the locations where the product is sold.
PROMOTION DECISIONS • Avoid exaggerated claims. • Aim at clearly identified target markets. • Stress desired product benefits. • Salespeople serve as consultants and problem solvers.	**PROMOTION DECISIONS** • Use exaggerated or misleading product claims. • Use a "shotgun" approach aimed at everyone rather than specific targets. • Tell consumers what they want to hear. • Salespeople use pressure, not advice, to make sales.
PRICE DECISIONS • Price is related to product quality or perceived value. • Special sales are, in fact, special sales. • Price policies encourage repeat patronage. • The total price including cost of extras and service contracts is explained.	**PRICE DECISIONS** • Gouge consumer, falsify value. • Price reductions are made by marking down a grossly inflated original markup. • The product is priced to maximize short-run profits. • The price seems to include extras when it does not.
LIKELY RESULTS • Firm credibility. • Repeat business. • Significant profit success.	**LIKELY RESULTS** • Weakened consumer confidence in firm. • Consumers likely to patronize another product or store. • Limited profit success.

Strategy

K Mart Versus Zayre

When two merchandisers select identical target markets and employ highly similar strategies to reach them, what makes one more successful than the other? Find the clue in the following examination of the marketing strategies used by K Mart and Zayre, two of the nation's largest discount store operations.

K Mart and Zayre have long and fairly complex family trees. At the turn of the century Sebastian S. Kresge bought a half-interest in a Memphis, Tennessee store with $8,000 saved from his earnings as a traveling salesman. Only one year later he opened a second store in Detroit, Michigan. By 1917 there were 150 variety stores in the northern states, and in the 1920s Kresge expanded into Canada.

The dimestore-variety format was successful for the S.S. Kresge Corporation, named for its founder. Sebastian Kresge's spirit of adventure was evident throughout his long career and left a strong imprint on his successors. When discount retailing, now known as **mass merchandising,** came into vogue in the 1950s, Kresge knew it was the way his company must go. He began phasing out the variety stores and replaced them with new discount stores called K Marts. Kresge guided his firm toward becoming a company of discount stores with a variety store division, rather than vice versa. In 1977 the company name was officially changed to the K Mart Corporation.

The Zayre Corporation began as a retail outlet for ladies' hosiery in 1929, after 10 years in business as the New England Trading Company. Until 1956 apparel dominated Zayre's merchandise offerings through a chain of specialty stores called Bell Shops and Nugents. That year Zayre management also recognized the coming importance of the self-service discount store. Two Zayre discount stores were opened in Massachusetts, the first of more than 260 now operating in more than 70 cities throughout the eastern United States.

The similarities between Zayre and K Mart are striking.

Target Market   Traditionally both companies have singled out the average middle-income suburban family. K Mart is now pursuing the higher-income shopper by being more fashion conscious, renovating old stores, and concentrating on merchandise display. K Mart hopes "to get the customer to stay longer and buy more."* Zayre has also taken steps to improve its image by renovating stores and treating certain departments like specialty shops or

continued

continued

boutiques. Both companies hope to gain some of the higher-income market without losing any of their traditional customer base.

Product Lines   K Mart expects its 65,000 different items "to supply 90 percent of what's needed on the shopper's list."† Consequently 55 percent of its sales are from hard goods. Zayre has made a product decision to "deepen and expand" its offerings in fashion apparel.‡ These soft goods account for up to 65 percent of sales in some Zayre stores. Both K Mart and Zayre have turned to more and better brand-name items in order to match American shoppers' recent desire for famous brands and designers. They also both use computerized point-of-sale registers and distribution systems to ensure that adequate merchandise is on hand to meet customer demand.

Location   The stores are typically free-standing or in small neighborhood shopping centers. By having several stores in a city or community, advertising costs can be spread over more than one outlet, allowing them to generate the massive customer traffic needed to succeed. Both companies prefer large metropolitan areas, but K Mart tends to choose more suburban locations and in recent years has moved into communities with populations of less than 8,000. Zayre prefers inner-city urban locations. It now has over half its stores in these locales and plans to open more.

Promotion   Newspapers, radio, and television play a large role in attracting heavy store traffic for both companies. Once customers are in the stores, Zayre's specialty-store concept helps them relate their needs to its products. K Mart is in the process of improving its merchandise displays. Full-view garment display racks and high-ticket items, like cameras and jewelry, displayed in the front of the store are two of the changes being made to encourage impulse buying. Both stores are remodeling facilities and developing more sophisticated advertising to improve their customer image.

Credit   After releasing $23 million in customer receivables to General Electric some years back, Zayre now offers a revolving charge plan. K Mart discontinued its credit card in 1975 after learning that only 9 percent of its

In addition, marketing considerations frequently affect the technical decisions of engineers and other specialists in the physical sciences. Marketing executives make many of the decisions about physical characteristics or chemical properties of a product, because "Will it sell?" is just as important a question as "Will it work?"

A number of issues in business law affect marketing practices. Although we will discuss these in more detail in Chapters 2 and 21, it should be noted that numerous laws have been passed (and some repealed) that affect marketing practices. Many administrative agencies also have the au-

customers used the card. Tying up about $100 million in a credit operation servicing so few customers proved highly unprofitable. K Mart reasoned that its customers associated bargains with cash payment. Major credit cards are accepted by the stores, however, as a convenience to customers.

Pricing The move to carry more brand names has increased prices on many items, especially apparel, in both companies' stores. Private or house brands are still important for both as they offer a good dollar value. Zayre typically narrows its brand-name offerings to the most popular fashion items in order to increase profits and speed up turnover. K Mart carries high-priced brand-name items at a 10–15 percent discount in most merchandise categories, hoping to attract the upper- and middle-income shopper.

Evidently, then, the similarities between the marketing approaches used by Zayre and K Mart outweigh the differences. So what is the bottom line? K Mart is far more successful. As a point of comparison K Mart reported 1982 earnings in excess of $222,000,000§; Zayre's earnings came to $22,147,000.**

Why this vast difference between firms that entered the mass merchandising field almost simultaneously? Most observers point to the quality of K Mart's management. It is, they say, superior by length and intensity of its training. K Mart lets each store manager make the product, place, promotion and pricing decisions necessary to make that store more competitive. The majority of Zayre's decisions are made at the corporate level. It may be K Mart's flexibility in adapting to the needs of each particular target market that has brought it success.

---

* Jeremy Main, "K Mart's Plan to be Born Again, Again," *Fortune,* September 21, 1981, pp. 74–85.
† Eleanor Carruth, "K Mart Has to Open Some New Doors on the Future," *Fortune,* July 1977, p. 154.
‡ "How Zayre Utilizes Specialty Retailing," *The Discount Merchandiser,* January 1982, pp. 64–68.
§ *Standard and Poor's Standard Corporate Descriptions,* November 1982, p. 5978.
** Ibid., June 1983, p. 8525.

thority to rule on various marketing activities. Besides asking "Will it sell?" and "Will it work?", the marketing manager must often also ask, "Is it legal?"

Marketing and Economics

Marketing is closely related to economics, the social science concerned with the production, distribution, and consumption of useful goods and services. In traditional economic thought economic activity creates utilities of form, place, time, and possession. To marketers the form created is the product; place and time refer to having the product available where and when it is needed; and possession relates to ownership or transfer of title. Marketing is a part of the broad field of economics and helps to create these four all-important utilities.

Marketing and Sociology

Marketing is also related to other social sciences. It draws freely from sociology, the scientific analysis of social institutions as a functioning whole and as they relate to the rest of society. As we move along, it will become clear that marketing studies people in a social context, as members of different groups. Advertisers, for example, aim their appeals at particular market segments, such as the youth market, the urban market, the black market, or the farm market.

Sociology helps us understand the differences not only between our society and those of other nations but also between various subcultures within our own country—Mexican-American versus Chinese-American, for example.

Marketing and Psychology

Psychology is the study of the mental, attitudinal, motivational, or behavioral characteristics of an individual or a group of individuals. Marketing practitioners find a knowledge of psychology helpful in formulating advertising and sales campaigns. How do people think? What motivates them to buy? How can we change their buying habits? What price will have the strongest appeal? Psychological research has become a major tool of marketing analysts.

ORGANIZATION OF THIS BOOK

Marketing Today is divided into seven parts. Part One is an introduction to marketing and covers the controllable and uncontrollable elements in the marketing environment as well as marketing information systems and marketing research techniques used to study the environment and target markets. Part Two revolves around the study of purchasers. It investigates the particulars of individual and organizational consumers and how they are typically identified, and concludes with a discussion of how this knowledge is used to group markets into market segments and select target markets. Parts Three, Four, Five, and Six address, respectively, the issues of developing product, place, promotion, and price strategies to reach selected target markets, whereas Part Seven considers international marketing, the social responsibility of marketing, and strategic market planning. Finally, we have provided some discussion of career opportunities in marketing and marketing math in the appendices.

SUMMARY

- Marketing involves much more than advertising and selling. It includes all activities required to satisfy target customer demand for products, services, people, or ideas.
- Marketing is a vital and virtually all-pervasive element in our economy.
- Marketing is a part of and has evolved with the exchange process.
- The marketing mix includes four decision areas: product decisions, place decisions, promotion decisions, and price decisions.
- Product, place, promotion, and price decisions are largely under the control of the marketing manager.
- There is no one "right" marketing mix. Product, place, promotion, and price decisions must be made with the target customer in mind.
- Marketing managers do not have full control over the marketing environment.
- Marketing information systems and marketing research help the marketing manager learn about the marketing environment and the target customers, which in turn helps in the design of the marketing mix.
- Business, economics, sociology, and psychology have made important contributions to our understanding of marketing.

DISCUSSION QUESTIONS

1. What are some of the activities involved in marketing jogging shoes? Tennis racquets? Farm machinery? Airplanes? What do these products have in common with regard to marketing?
2. "Marketing involves much more than selling and advertising." Explain.
3. "The production and sales eras were product oriented, but marketing is people oriented." Explain.
4. How does profit relate to the marketing concept?
5. Give some examples of product decisions marketing managers make. Place decisions. Promotion decisions. Price decisions.
6. How do target customers affect decisions made by marketing managers?
7. How does the study of marketing relate to economics? Sociology? Psychology?
8. Marketing stimulates demand. How does this fact affect our economy?
9. How does marketing affect a firm's chances for survival and prosperity?
10. Explain the term "marketing concept." Cite three examples you have seen in

which the marketing concept was applied and three examples in which it was not applied.

APPLICATION EXERCISES

1. John Washington wants to open a sandwich shop. He knows you are studying marketing and comes to you for advice. Prepare two questions for him to answer about each of the following—target customers, product offering, place, promotion, and price—before he goes ahead.
2. Select a firm you feel does a good job of applying the marketing concept. In terms of its product, place, promotion, and price decisions, explain why you think the firm is successful.
3. Assume you plan to go into business for yourself. After choosing the type of business, develop five key questions you should answer with regard to (a) target customers, (b) products, (c) place, (d) promotion, and (e) price.

CASE 1
Ski Resorts on the Slide[14]

Throughout the 60s and 70s skiing, characterized by high price tags on travel, lodging, equipment, and lift tickets, was stereotyped as a trendy sport for the young and wealthy. During that period World War II veterans of the Army's Tenth Mountain Division operated most ski areas. These avid skier–managers did very well then, because the key marketing ingredient for success was simply having a mountain with lifts and snow.

The industry faces a much tougher marketing task now, however, with the popularity of the sport apparently on the downswing, especially in the West. In Colorado alone, skier days declined from 7.9 million in 1979–80 to 7.6 million in 1981–82.[15] The figures for 1980–81 were even worse because of persistently poor snow conditions. Similar problems have beset the ski equipment manufacturing industry, which has seen its growth decline 40 percent from the boom years of the 70s. This slide has occurred even though the number of skiers has continued to grow (A. C. Nielson Co. estimates there are now 19 million skiers in the U.S.). How can this be?

A look at the ski market over the past 10 years shows that the average age of skiers has jumped from 23 to 28. Although this aging process appears insubstantial,

---

[14] "Restyling Skiing's Trendy Image," *Business Week,* November 29, 1982, pp. 107–108.
[15] A skier day is defined as 1 skier per 1 day of operation.

it has propelled the industry's target market out of the free-spending days of its youth and into the age of parenthood, an age marked by less vacation time and a higher degree of cost-consciousness.

The task facing the industry, then, is to shake an image traditionally appealing to the young and wealthy, because they represent an increasingly smaller percentage of the target market. Most resorts have dropped lift and lodging rates and added features appealing to families. As an example, many resort ads now picture families, not glamorous models, enjoying the snow. In addition large corporations with vast marketing expertise, lured by the real-estate and market potential in a sport that combines image with money, have replaced the traditional skier–manager.

Aspen, Colorado, is one ski resort traditionally stereotyped as trendy, jet-set, and high-priced. Now owned jointly by Twentieth Century-Fox and Aetna Life and Casualty Company, Aspen Skiing Company is aggressively using product, place, promotion, and pricing decisions to appeal to the changing market. In two years the resort has tripled its marketing budget to $2 million. It also is actively pursuing groups it spurned in the past. For example, this winter Aspen offered skiers a 30 percent discount on lodging, skiing, and air fare if they booked on Tuesday for the following weekend, attracting cost-conscious Denver skiers. Another strategy, aimed at competing with East Coast and European resorts, revolves around a $638, eight-day ski package that includes lodging, car rental, lift tickets, and round-trip air fare from New York City. Car rental companies, airlines, and lodging chains have been willing participants in these packages, because ski vacations account for a significant percentage of their revenues.

Aspen is utilizing the marketing expertise of its parent corporations in other ways. Twentieth Century-Fox is using its entertainment contacts to line up celebrity races and finance a promotional film on the resort. Aetna is using its investment and land development interests to finance the much-needed revitalization of Aspen's lodging and convention facilities.

It remains to be seen whether Aspen's management can use its increased awareness of the marketing mix to reverse the 15-percent-per-year slide in skier days that has plagued the resort for the past few years.

Discussion Questions

1. What are Aspen's target markets?
2. If you were responsible for developing a marketing strategy for Aspen, how would you describe its product? How about the place variable? What promotional and pricing recommendations would you make?
3. How would the marketing controllable variables mentioned in Question 2 differ if the target market was still 23-year-old, affluent singles?

2 The Marketing Environment

STUDY OBJECTIVES

After studying this chapter, you should be able to

1. Discuss the influence of corporate planning and organization on marketing management.
2. Explain the importance of consumer choice and competitive strategies to marketing.
3. Discuss the effect of various laws, regulatory agencies, and courts on marketing activities.
4. Describe how economic conditions can change marketing plans.
5. Discuss the importance of technological and social change to marketers.

M arketing operates in an environment containing both controllable and uncontrollable elements. The controllable elements are corporate management decisions that affect marketing and other business areas that interact with marketing. The uncontrollable elements are all the outside activities that may affect the success of the corporation's marketing effort. The controllable elements constrain what marketing management can do. The uncontrollable elements, to a large degree, determine whether marketing management and the corporation succeed or fail.

Nonetheless, these elements are not independent. Excessive uncertainty in the uncontrollable environment may lead management to change corporate goals (a controllable element). By the same token corporate management's goals may change certain uncontrollable elements. For example, a corporation that does not concern itself with social responsibility may quickly find itself incurring the wrath of consumer groups and legislators.

Both elements of the marketing environment must be understood to plan the marketing mix. For this reason all of Chapter 2 will be devoted to discussing the controllable and uncontrollable elements of the marketing environment.

CONTROLLABLE ELEMENTS

The controllable elements of the marketing environment revolve around corporate planning and organization. Although marketing management must plan and organize marketing activities, here we are concerned specifically with corporate management activities.

Planning

Planning involves determining the direction of the company, its objectives, and the strategies to accomplish those objectives.

Direction refers to such company decisions as the line of business, geographic target regions, product/service categories, and customers. For example, Anheuser-Busch and Schlitz both produce and market beer. Both sell to tavern owners and in-home customers. Because Anheuser-Busch has been able to maintain its prominence as the number-one national distributor of beer, however, Schlitz decided not to compete directly with its better financed rival (in 1982 Anheuser-Busch spent $193.9 million dollars on advertising alone—more than twice the amount spent by Schlitz) and changed the company's direction from a national to a regional marketer of beer. Following corporate management's lead, Schlitz' marketing management now concentrates on the company's strongest target markets. As Robert A. Rechholtz, Senior Vice-President of Marketing at Schlitz, put it, "We're going to spend our money where the business is."[1] Clearly, the different directions chosen by the two corporations have greatly influenced the goals and strategies of marketing management.

Objectives are the mileposts for a corporation—the goals that measure how well the corporation is moving in its chosen direction. The degree of the corporation's success or failure is determined by comparing its actual performance with these objectives. Sales, profits, return on investment, and market share are but a few of the objectives corporate management may set.

Strategies are the methods management uses to accomplish its objectives. In the case of Ford and General Motors you could say their objectives are to maintain dominance in the U.S. auto market by offering a more cost-competitive car. Their strategies for accomplishing this objective are reducing administrative overhead, increasing productivity, and obtaining labor cost concessions while maintaining product quality levels.

Although corporate management formulates these strategies, they greatly affect marketing management. Corporate planning defines not only the direction the corporation will take, but also the role marketing will play in achieving the objectives set by that direction. The importance of marketing in the corporation depends on that role.

Teleprompter was one of the original cable TV franchisors. However, its lack of marketing orientation almost led to bankruptcy. Because corporate management did not consider marketing important, it left marketing management little opportunity to develop a customer base. Since the company's purchase by Westinghouse, marketing management figures more prominently in corporate plans. As Teleprompter's chief executive put it, "We are really changing our focus from one of a supplier of hardware and basic services to an aggressive, marketing-oriented company." One indication of this commitment is the growth of corporate direct sales staff from 175 in 1981 to 1200 in 1982.[2] Marketing will receive more support as a direct result of major changes in corporate management's direction, objectives, and strategies.

Organizing

It is corporate management that decides the structure of the functional areas (finance, production, personnel, and marketing) and how they relate

---

[1] "Schlitz's Brew of Old and New," *Business Week*, May 12, 1980, pp. 31–32.
[2] Laura Landro, "Struggling Teleprompter Gets a New Name and Strategy, and Hopes for New Successes," *Wall Street Journal*, April 21, 1982, pp. 31–40.

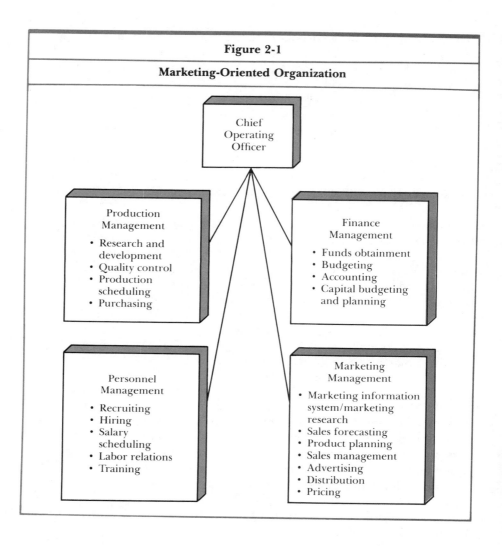

Figure 2-1

Marketing-Oriented Organization

Chief Operating Officer

Production Management
- Research and development
- Quality control
- Production scheduling
- Purchasing

Finance Management
- Funds obtainment
- Budgeting
- Accounting
- Capital budgeting and planning

Personnel Management
- Recruiting
- Hiring
- Salary scheduling
- Labor relations
- Training

Marketing Management
- Marketing information system/marketing research
- Sales forecasting
- Product planning
- Sales management
- Advertising
- Distribution
- Pricing

to each other. These decisions include the designation of units (divisions, departments, branches, and so on), to whom each unit reports, and what authority each unit possesses.

Organizations are typically production, sales, or marketing oriented. Production-oriented organizations view their products from an engineering standpoint. They emphasize technical innovation and efficiency, and often assign product development to the production manager. Marketing is usually a staff function fragmented in different areas of the corporation and performed on an occasional basis, with no direct authority to make decisions.

In a sales-oriented organization the primary marketing units are sales and advertising. Although they are often distinct organizational units, their primary responsibility is to support production. Marketing research reports to advertising, distribution reports to sales or purchasing, and product development is still part of production.

A marketing-oriented organization (illustrated in Figure 2-1) views marketing as a distinct corporate area with authority equal to production, finance, and personnel. Marketing has direct decision-making responsibility in its area. It deals with the other business areas as an equal.

In summary, corporations that consider marketing important give it decision-making authority and allow it to interact with (rather than be dictated by) production and finance. Companies that do not consider marketing important subordinate it to finance and production and consider it the same thing as sales. Resources necessary to carry out such marketing activities as research or advertising are often considered unnecessary and not allocated.

Marketing Often Conflicts with Production and Finance　Because production and finance managers often view the corporation from a different perspective than marketing managers, conflicts between marketing, finance, and production often occur.

Due to economies of scale, production prefers to produce large quantities of one product at a time, with few variations in the product line, limited options, and few style changes. Long production runs normally create excessive inventory buildup with which marketing must cope. In addition the production approach of few product variations runs counter to the marketing approach of designing particular products and options to meet the wants and needs of each target market.

Marketing has often been characterized by the philosophy, "You have to spend money to make money." Such a concept makes many finance managers cringe, because they are responsible for controlling spending and, therefore, may advocate low inventory levels, low advertising and promotional budgets, strict control of salesperson spending, and quick collection of bills. Marketing not only wants higher inventory levels to meet demand but also easy credit terms, advertising, promotion, and liberal salesperson expenditures to stimulate demand.

Compromise can be reached on these conflicts. However, such compromise is not likely if marketing is not a corporate equal to finance and production.

UNCONTROLLABLE ELEMENTS

Although management can directly determine how marketing fits into corporate plans and organization, it cannot control much of the environment marketing faces. Thus marketing management must understand and mon-

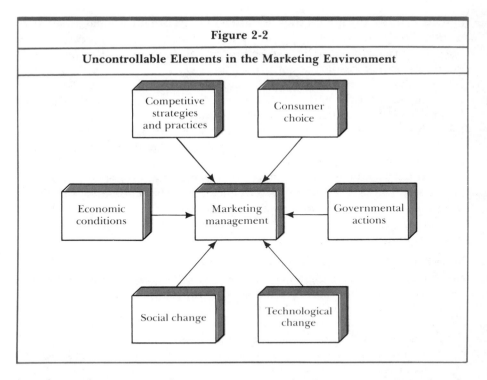

Figure 2-2

Uncontrollable Elements in the Marketing Environment

itor the environment, so it can react appropriately. Many a well-laid marketing plan has failed due to unexpected reactions in the uncontrollable elements of the environment. Figure 2-2 points out the various uncontrollable elements of the environment that affect marketing decisions. We will discuss each element separately.

Consumer Choice

Although marketing managers spend a great deal of their time trying to influence and anticipate consumer decisions, they have little control over when, where, and how much of the corporate products consumers will choose to buy. It does a company little good to advertise and distribute a new product in Baltimore if the only demand for the product is in Los Angeles.

Freedom to spend gives consumers unusual power. Just as individuals who cast votes for or against various candidates control our political system, so, too, individuals who "cast votes" for or against various products or sellers of those products control our economic system. Each consumer purchase is an economic vote. When consumers purchase Buick cars, they cast their economic votes for Buick and, indirectly, against Buick's competitors. Purchase of a certain brand is an endorsement of that brand. By the same line of reasoning, when people do not buy a certain product, in effect they are saying, "There is something about your product—its quality, appeal, package, location, advertising, or price—that we do not like." If too few consumers buy a certain brand or patronize a certain store, that brand or store will fail.

One grocery store located on a major commuter route to a large city learned this lesson the hard way. Although a well-promoted, national chain store, it was located on the left side of the road when commuters were going home (the time when they stopped for groceries). Drivers did not want to make a left turn across a busy thoroughfare, so they did not patronize the store. In spite of much advertising and sales promotions this seemingly small aspect of the location decision made consumers cast their economic votes for the more convenient competitors. The store eventually went out of business.

The way consumers decide to spend their money determines what goods and services our economy produces, their quality and quantity, and, to some extent, their prices. The freedom of consumers to make whatever purchases they wish and can afford not only serves to keep businesses on their toes and eager to improve their existing products and services in order to maintain consumer loyalty, it also serves as a prime incentive for the formation of new businesses and the introduction of new products and services by existing businesses. Business people reason thusly: "Consumers have money. This money is not permanently committed to certain products or services or stores. If we can come up with something new or better or different, we should be able to attract some of those dollars." In this way new businesses and new products and services are born.

The effect of consumer choice is evident in the rate at which new products are developed and fail. Even conservative estimates put the new product failure rate at 33 percent, that is, consumers reject one out of every three new products offered to them by marketing managers.[3]

Although marketing managers cannot control consumer choice, they must constantly try to understand, anticipate, and influence the choice process. You cannot design a product to satisfy the wants and needs of your target market if you do not know what those wants and needs are.

Competitive Strategies and Practices

Although consumers' actions cannot be controlled, they are not malicious. Competitors, on the other hand, take action to benefit themselves at the expense of other companies.

Because one firm cannot control the marketing mix of a competing firm—that is, one business cannot control the products its competitor

---

[3] David Hopkins, "Survey Finds 67% of New Products Succeed," *Marketing News,* February 8, 1980, p. 1.

makes, the places these products are marketed, the promotional strategies used, or the prices charged—companies often keep new products and marketing strategies closely guarded secrets. Therefore, when it introduces a new product or implements a new marketing plan, the competition may not be able to match the change for weeks, months, or even years. For example, when a toothpaste manufacturer introduces a new flavor or makes a new premium offer, its competitors may be forced to revise their own products or strategies to avoid losing some portion of their market share.

In football each team knows the possible plays the other team may use; nevertheless, one team is often caught off guard concerning what play will be used in a specific situation. So it is in marketing. Although alert business people know most of the strategies their competitors may use, they often do not know what strategy will be used in specific circumstances.

To analyze the actions of a competitive firm, the marketing manager must first determine the competitor's structure. Companies typically operate in one of four ways—as a monopoly, as an oligopoly, under monopolistic competition, or under pure competition.

A **monopoly** exists when only one company offers a certain product or service. Among the most familiar monopolies are our local power and telephone companies, which the government allows to be the only seller in a particular area and which are called **regulated monopolies**, because the government regulates and approves their marketing plans.

An **unregulated monopoly** typically describes a company that has a

patent (exclusive right to market an invention for 17 years) on a particular product. Due to the unique nature of the product the monopolist does not need to consider competitors when formulating its marketing plans. These plans must provide a means for maintaining that product uniqueness, however, so competitors can be kept out of the market.

An **oligopoly** exists when only several (usually large) companies sell most of a particular product. For example, Whirlpool, General Electric, and Frigidaire account for a large percentage of total refrigerator sales. Many industries in the United States are oligopolistic.

Oligopolistic industries typically have few sellers, because the cost of entering the industry is so high. Take General Motors. To build just one of the more than 20 GM plants in the United States that do nothing but assemble cars (other plants make the parts) would probably cost in excess of $100 million. Few companies can come up with this minimum amount to "get in the business." John DeLorean, a former GM vice president, discovered this difficulty when he designed the DeLorean automobile and started a new company to produce and market it. His company is now in bankruptcy partly because of the enormous amount of money needed just to produce the first car.[4]

Because an oligopolistic industry consists of so few companies, the consumer can easily scan all competitive prices, thus creating a kinked demand curve: Demand for one company's product will drop sharply if its price is raised (everyone else's price is lower) and increase only slightly as its price is dropped (everyone else will also drop their prices). For this reason oligopolies try to avoid price competition. Rather, marketing efforts attempt to create a differential advantage through superior products, distribution, or promotion.

Monopolistic competition occurs when an oligopoly succeeds in differentiating its product offering from those of other companies within its industry. Customers perceive its product as different from the others, come to prefer and even demand it, and will accept no substitutes. Within the industry that company has created a monopolistic pocket where there is only one seller. Campbell's Soup has long enjoyed such a situation. Whether Campbell's makes a superior soup or not, many customers perceive it to be superior and will buy nothing but Campbell's.

Differential advantage is created through the marketing controllable variables. Unique product quality and design, appropriate outlets, and a superior promotional message typically differentiate one product from its competitors. The relative monopoly status normally allows the company to charge a higher price to recoup the extra expenditures on product, place, and promotion. However, other companies are trying to establish a differ-

---

[4] "U.S. Investor May Help Save DeLorean Unit," *Wall Street Journal,* April 23, 1982, p. 4.

Strategy

Amateur Photography's Giant Duopolists: Kodak and Polaroid

Eastman Kodak and Polaroid Corporation, the Goliaths of their industry, share a majority of the market for cameras, film, and other equipment purchased by amateur photographers. For decades peaceful coexistence was their motto. They were not in direct competition with each other, because they marketed products based on different concepts. Then in April 1976 Kodak introduced an instant photo camera, a product line that had been Polaroid's exclusively. The big question in marketing circles was whether Kodak's technical and marketing skills could match or surpass those of the undisputed king of instant photography, Polaroid. The following discussion of their approaches offers some clues.

So great is Eastman Kodak's expertise in the production of photographic materials and equipment that it is known to professional photographers as "The Great Yellow Father." Originally, Kodak designed the bulk of its products for the professional, who represented only 20 percent of the total market. Kodak's success with amateurs was severely limited until market research in the 1960s indicated that most Americans wanted to take photographs, but were hindered by two obstacles—loading and unloading the camera. Kodak immediately responded to this consumer concern by designing a drop-in film cartridge that eliminated threading and rewinding of the film. The company steered clear of direct competition with Polaroid, however, because of a veritable wall of patents on cameras that printed their own photos.

Thirteen years later Kodak saw that the time was right to break Polaroid's monopoly and introduced its EK-6 and EK-4 instant cameras.

Polaroid's first instant photo camera was sold in 1948. Headed by Dr. Edwin H. Land, Polaroid Corporation was strongly oriented toward turning scientific advances into excellent, marketable products: Its SX-70 instant camera, introduced in 1972, was one of the longest-lived and best-received series of instant cameras. Since its inception, Polaroid followed Edwin Land's love-

ential advantage, and entry into the industry is not always difficult. To continue in a differentiated position, the company must continually revise and update its marketing strategy.

Pure competition exists when many companies in an industry make the same or very similar products and no company commands a very large

it-or-leave-it strategy toward the consumer. For years Polaroid had "handed down novel technological wizardry to a market who responded with awe and orders."* In a more competitive market this attitude could not continue. In anticipation of the competitive challenge Kodak presented, Polaroid introduced the Pronto one month before the EK-6 and EK-4 were in the stores. The Pronto, a modification of the SX-70, was feature- and price-competitive with Kodak's line.

Both companies experienced problems right from the beginning of the contest. For Polaroid it was the discovery that its film had a short shelf-life and the camera itself had a battery problem. Kodak was plagued with slow deliveries. Although they were intrigued by the huge press and advertising campaign Kodak's instant cameras had been given, potential customers were often unable to find the product in stores. Once the smoke cleared in the instant camera market, Polaroid came out ahead with a 65-percent market share compared to Kodak's 35-percent.†

Uncontrollable changes are presently taking place in the photography industry. The growth of photography in the U.S. has fallen from 12 percent in 1979 to only 4 percent in 1981.‡ New technologies have vastly simplified the 35 mm camera and brought about the development of new amateur photographic methods, like the video and electronic cameras. Both companies have responded to these encroachments by not only developing plans to diversify and concentrate on the industrial market, but also developing industrial products based on technologies used in their successful consumer products. They have also changed their internal organizations. Kodak has implemented a team of strategic planners and market researchers to seek new growth areas outside their traditional business.§ At Polaroid upper and middle management were regrouped into a product-oriented organization with a greater emphasis on marketing.**

The change in consumer habits and new technology are two uncontrollable elements impacting Kodak and Polaroid's business. Both companies are controlling and adapting their internal organizations and marketing strategies to meet these changes. It will be interesting to see how successful their new courses will be.

* Philip Maher, "Polaroid Seeks Business Focus," *Industrial Marketing*, October 1981, pp. 8, 31, 33, 35, 36, 38.
† Louis Fanelli, "Polaroid Needs Brighter Image," *Advertising Age*, May 4, 1981, p. 4.
‡ "Kodak Fights Back," *Business Week*, February 1, 1982, pp. 48–54.
§ Ibid.
** "Polaroid Seeks Business Focus."

market share. Because everyone sells the same product, demand is quite elastic (a price rise will drastically reduce sales, and a price drop will drastically increase sales). Limited control over product, place, and promotion marketing variables (products are identical) forces most companies to concentrate on minimizing costs and keeping prices competitively low.

	Figure 2-3	
	Antitrust Laws	
Legislation	**Year Enacted**	**Primary Purpose**
Sherman Act	1890	Prohibits monopolies and maintains competition
Clayton Act	1914	Prohibits price discrimination, exclusive agreements, and tie-in sales. Also prohibits interlocking directorates and stock purchase by competing firms.
Federal Trade Commission (FTC) Act	1914	Created FTC to enforce previous acts and to prohibit "unfair methods of competition in commerce."
Robinson–Patman Act	1936	Prohibits price discrimination.
Miller–Tydings Act (repealed in 1976 by Consumer Goods Price Act)	1937	Permits retail price maintenance to protect small retailers from chains.
Wheeler–Lea Amendment	1938	Revised FTC Act to include unfair or deceptive practices.
Lanham Trademark Act	1946	Protects and regulates trademarks and brand names.
Reed–Bulwinkle Act	1948	Exempts transportation rate bureaus from antitrust laws.
Celler–Kefauver Antimerger Act	1950	Limits acquisition of competitors if effect would lessen competition.

Each of the four industry types we have discussed suggests which general marketing strategies to use. Of course, specific strategies require an analysis of each competitor, of the strategies of that competitor, and how that competitor will react to changes in other companies' marketing strategies. The competition's retaliation to keep or gain customer loyalty greatly affects the success of any marketing effort.

Governmental Actions

Few aspects of marketing are exempt from some form of regulation by federal, state, or local governments. Governmental responsibility in these matters is twofold. First, it must maintain competition and prevent or regulate monopolies. Second, it is expected to protect consumers from such things as dangerous products, deceptive selling practices, and exploitation.

To achieve these two goals, various levels of government regulate all aspects of the marketing mix. For example, in making product decisions marketing managers must conform to regulations concerning product safety; place decisions are shaped by zoning regulations; promotion decisions in product advertising must comply with regulations concerning the use of false or misleading statements; and price decisions, especially those made by public utilities and transportation companies, must be approved by public regulating agencies.

Marketing activities are regulated primarily by federal legislation, federal regulatory agencies, federal courts, and state and local governments.

Federal Legislation   Since the late 1800s Congress has passed many laws aimed at preventing any one company from controlling a market or industry, or severely limiting competition. Figure 2-3 summarizes these various **antitrust laws**. Often referred to as the **Sherman Acts**, this body of legislation prohibits numerous "anticompetitive" activities and created the **Federal Trade Commission (FTC)** to act as a watchdog agency. Figure 2-4 summarizes a number of these anticompetitive activities.

Figure 2-4
Ten Don'ts of Antitrust
Warnings that companies most frequently issue to employees to keep them in compliance with antitrust laws: <ol><li>***Don't*** discuss with customers the price your company will charge others.</li><li>***Don't*** attend meetings with competitors (including trade association gatherings) at which pricing is discussed. If you find yourself in such a session, walk out.</li><li>***Don't*** give favored treatment to your own subsidiaries and affiliates.</li><li>***Don't*** enter into agreements or gentlemen's understandings on discounts, terms or conditions of sale, profits or profit margins, shares of the market, bids or the intent to bid, rejection or termination of customers, sales territories or markets.</li><li>***Don't*** use one product as bait for selling another.</li><li>***Don't*** require a customer to buy a product only from you.</li><li>***Don't*** forget to consider state antitrust laws as well as the federal statutes.</li><li>***Don't*** disparage a competitor's product unless you have specific proof that your statements are true. This is an unfair method of competition.</li><li>***Don't*** make either sales or purchases conditional on the other party making reciprocal purchases from or sales to your company.</li><li>***Don't*** hesitate to consult with a company lawyer if you have any doubt about the legality of a practice. Antitrust laws are wide-ranging, complex, and subject to changing interpretations.</li></ol>
SOURCE: "How to Avoid Antitrust," *Business Week*, January 27, 1975, p. 84.

In this century Congress has passed a great deal of legislation to protect the consumer from unfair or deceptive marketing practices. These laws are too numerous to explain in detail, but Figure 2-5 provides a list. Clearly, marketing practices are constrained in many ways by a multitude of federal statutes. However, if many past marketing practices had not been abusive, this myriad of laws probably would not have been enacted.

Figure 2-5	
Consumer-Oriented Legislation	
Year	**Legislation**
1906	Food and Drug Act
1906	Meat Inspection Act
1914	FTC Act
1938	Wheeler–Lea Act
1939	Wool Products Labeling Act
1951	Fur Products Labeling Act
1953	Flammable Fabrics Act
1958	Food Additives Amendment
1958	Automobile Information Disclosure Act
1959	Textile Fiber Identification Act
1960	Federal Hazardous Substances Labeling Act
1962	Kefauver–Harris Drug Amendment
1965	Drug Abuse Control Amendment
1966	Fair Packaging and Labeling Act
1966	National Safety and Motor Vehicle Safety Act
1966	Child Protection Act
1967	Cigarette Labeling Act
1967	Wholesome Meat Act
1968	Consumer Credit Protection Act
1968	Wholesome Poultry Products Act
1968	Hazardous Radiation Act
1969	Child Protection and Toy Safety Act
1969	Public Health Smoking Cigarette Act
1969	National Environmental Policy Act
1970	Fair Credit Reporting Act
1970	Council on Environmental Quality
1970	Poison Prevention Labeling Act
1971	Federal Boat Safety Act
1972	Drug Listing Act
1972	Consumer Product Safety Act
1974	Motor Vehicle Information and Cost Savings Act
1974	Transportation Safety Act
1975	Magnuson–Moss Warranty/FTC Improvement Act
1978	National Consumer Cooperative Bank Act
1978	Fraudulent Solicitations Through the Mails Act
1980	FTC Improvements Act

Federal Regulatory Agencies   In addition to federal laws many federal agencies have been created to regulate marketing activities. As Figure 2-6 illustrates, every aspect of marketing is subject to some federal agency.

The Federal Trade Commission (FTC), created in 1914, is the chief governmental agency responsible for regulating competitor-oriented marketing activity. The commission was originally designed to halt the growth

Figure 2-6	
Federal Agencies Regulating Marketing Activities	
Agency	**Effect on Marketing**
Civil Aeronautics Board (CAB)	Regulates airlines.
Consumer Product Safety Council (CPSC)	Sets and enforces (can direct recalls) product safety standards.
Environmental Protection Agency (EPA)	Develops and enforces environmental standards for products.
Federal Communications Commission (FCC)	Regulates print, radio, and television media.
Federal Maritime Commission (FMC)	Regulates water-bound carriers.
Federal Power Commission (FPC)	Regulates natural gas producers and pipelines.
Federal Trade Commission (FTC)	Enforces laws and regulations concerning unfair business practices and false or deceptive advertising and labeling.
Food and Drug Administration (FDA)	Education and standards regarding food, drug, and cosmetic products, packages, and labels.
Food Safety and Quality Service (FSQS)	Sets standards and certifies quality of dairy, meat, poultry, and egg products.
Interstate Commerce Commission (ICC)	Regulates railroads and motor carriers.
Office of Consumer Affairs (OCA)	Assists consumers (especially disadvantaged) with complaints and problems.
Postal Service	Petitions for postal rates and services and regulates flow of deceptive or fraudulent material through the mail.
Securities and Exchange Commission (SEC)	Regulates marketing of securities.
U.S. Tariff Commission	Regulates unfair practices concerning products imported to the United States.

Figure 2-7

Primary Statutes under FTC Jurisdiction

Legislation	Year Enacted	Primary Purpose
Clayton Act	1914	Deals with situations that tend to lessen competition or create monopolies.
Webb–Pomerene Export Trade Act	1918	Permits certain cooperative activities in support of export trade.
Wool Products Labeling Act	1939	Governs the disclosure and use of substitutes and mixtures in manufactured wool products.
Lanham Trade Mark Act	1946	Protects trademarks used in commerce.
Fur Products Labeling Act	1951	Governs the branding, advertising, and invoicing of furs and fur products.
Textile Fiber Products Identification Act	1958	Oversees the branding and advertising of fiber content of textile fiber products.
Fair Packaging and Labeling Act	1966	Seeks to prevent unfair or deceptive packaging or labeling of certain consumer products.
Truth in Lending Act	1969	Deals comprehensively with consumer credit.
Fair Credit Reporting Act	1970	Protects consumers from inaccurate credit reporting.
Magnuson–Moss Warranty—Federal Trade Commission Improvement Act	1975	Expands the Commission's authority in several areas, among them enabling the agency to pursue any unlawful act "affecting commerce" rather than only those acts defined as "in commerce."
Fair Credit Billing Act	1975	Helps consumers to correct inaccurate reports made by creditors.
Equal Credit Opportunity Act	1975	Prevents the denial of credit to consumers on the basis of sex, marital status, age, race, religion, or national origin.

SOURCE: "Your FTC. What It Is and What It Does," Federal Trade Commission, U.S. Government Printing Office, 1977, pp. 6–8.

of monopolies as defined by the Sherman Antitrust Act, but since that time its authority has expanded to include the prevention of deceptive practices (especially in advertising and labeling), concentration of power within a given industry, fixing of prices and quotas, and violations of product-safety requirements.

Until 1938 the FTC could act only when it received a complaint by a consumer, a competitor, or another branch of government, and when injury to competition was involved. The Wheeler–Lea Amendment not only empowered the commission to issue its own complaints and to act in cases not necessarily involving injury to competition, but it specifically banned "unfair or deceptive acts or practices" as well.

Besides the Wheeler–Lea Amendment, the FTC is also responsible for enforcing the Wool, Textile, Fur, and Flammable Fabrics Acts. In the field of food and drugs it shares enforcement responsibility with the Food and Drug Administration and the Meat Inspection Branch of the Agriculture Research Service (part of the Department of Agriculture). Figure 2-7 outlines the primary statutes under FTC jurisdiction.

Though not a regulatory agency, the Justice Department is another important governmental branch that governs corporate activity. The assistant attorney general in charge of the Antitrust Division of the Justice Department is responsible for the enforcement of the federal antitrust laws. The division investigates possible antitrust violations, conducts grand-jury proceedings, prepares and tries antitrust cases, prosecutes appeals, and negotiates and enforces final judgments. The Justice Department routinely seeks jail terms in price-fixing cases, because that offense is a felony. Furthermore, the Antitrust Division represents the United States in judicial proceedings to review certain orders of the Interstate Commerce Commission, the Federal Maritime Commission, and the Federal Communications Commission. It also directly represents the Secretary of the Treasury and the Civil Aeronautics Board in certain review proceedings, and helps prosecute FTC cases before the Supreme Court. Finally, it is responsible for supporting competitive policies within federal departments and agencies and will advise other agencies on the competitive effects of activities within their jurisdiction.

Federal Courts   In suits brought by consumers, the Justice Department, or regulatory agencies, the federal courts hand down rulings that often significantly affect corporate activities.[5] Court views have changed drastically over the years. At one time their philosophy toward product liability was *caveat emptor,* or "let the buyer beware." This attitude eventually evolved into the belief that the manufacturer should be responsible for any

---

[5] For a review of the Supreme Court rulings from 1975 through 1981 that affected marketing, see: Ray O. Werner, "Marketing and the United States Supreme Court, 1975–1981," *Journal of Marketing,* Spring 1982, pp. 73–81.

damages or injuries resulting from the proper use of its products. Recently, the courts have held the manufacturer responsible even when the consumer *misused* the product. For instance, the wheels on certain 1960–65 General Motors trucks collapsed when the truck load limit was exceeded by overweight campers. GM argued that the overloading, which was warned against in the owner's manual, constituted owner abuse. The court ruled there was abuse, but it was "reasonably foreseeable"—everyone realized trucks often will be overloaded. Only "unforeseeable abuse" might have excused GM.[6]

Court cases can drag on for years and cost companies millions of dollars. The Justice Department's antitrust suit against IBM continued for 13 years before Assistant Attorney General William Baxter dropped the case as "without merit." Even then, the case was not dead. Chief Judge David N. Edelstein, who presided over the case, declared Baxter had a conflict of interest and, in an unprecedented test of the courts' power, attempted to order the case continued.[7]

State and Local Governments   What does not come under federal jurisdiction is subject to the laws and regulations of the various state and local governments. Marketers must be aware of how widely laws vary from state to state. In 36 states statutes exist that hold not only the manufacturer of a defective product liable for product-related injuries, but also all sellers of that product. Voss Equipment Company in Illinois paid $165,000 in damages to a steel company employee who was injured after improperly loading a truck the steel company had leased from Voss. Said company president, Peter Voss, Jr., "We do not make the trucks we sell or lease; we cannot drive them for our customers; and we cannot keep a constant watch over their use."[8] Ironically, in 14 other states the government agrees with Mr. Voss—only the manufacturer is liable for product injury.

Similar variations in state antitrust laws also exist. Companies must be aware of these differing state laws affecting marketing practices to protect themselves from legal action.

The chief state-level regulatory agency is the **public service commission.**[9] Typically, voters elect the members of state regulatory commissions,

---

[6] Walter Guzzardi, Jr., "The Mindless Pursuit of Safety," *Fortune,* April 9, 1979, pp. 54–64.

[7] Bro Uttal, "Life After Litigation at IBM and AT&T," *Forbes,* February 8, 1982, pp. 59–61; "The Case That Won't Die," *Wall Street Journal,* April 8, 1982, p. 24; "IBM Cautions Court Against Usurpation of Executive Power," *Wall Street Journal,* April 9, 1982, p. 36; "When Judges Object to Antitrust Dismissals," *Business Week,* April 19, 1982, p. 42; and Robert E. Taylor, "Antitrust Chief Who Dropped IBM Case Owns Small Holdings in 3 Computer Firms," *Wall Street Journal,* April 20, 1982, p. 5.

[8] Beth Brophy, "Who, and Where, Do I Sue?," *Forbes,* April 12, 1982, pp. 64–66.

[9] Public Service Commissions are sometimes known by other names, for example, as Corporation Commissions (Arizona), Commerce Commissions (Arkansas), or Public Utilities Commissions (California).

who have extensive power over the marketing operations of many industries, such as railroads, truck and bus lines, telephone companies, electric power and gas utilities, terminal companies, and dock and wharf companies. In fixing the rates or prices these companies can charge, the commissions conduct investigations and public hearings. In addition to fixing rates, public service commissions determine such matters as how much and what type of services regulated industries must provide. State law regulates the authority of all public service commissions. In practice the commission acts as an umpire between the consumer and regulated industries. Although its sole purpose may appear to be consumer protection, it also functions to safeguard the financial stability of regulated industries so that they can maintain or expand their services as needed.

Government Action in Perspective   Our various federal, state, and local government systems are so pervasive and powerful that they affect almost all decisions marketing managers make. When planning the marketing mix, marketers should make sure they have not violated any laws or regulations. Even so, companies may still find themselves in court. It is important, therefore, that they be prepared for such a possibility and that they not only understand the potential government actions surrounding marketing activities, but also have documented that they violated no laws or regulations.

Many companies see government not as an adversary, but as an ally in successfully fulfilling the corporate mission. When a product or service offered benefits the target market and society at large, a viable marketing strategy is **marketing by mandate.** Under this strategy marketers convince the appropriate governmental agency to require (mandate) the use of the company's product. For example, in 1980 the California Public Utilities Commission ordered the state's four largest utilities to finance 375,000 residential solar hot water installations at 6 percent interest. Further, San Diego County requires all new homes to be equipped with solar hot water systems.[10] Clearly, the solar heating industry's efforts to work with local governments have paid off in a sizeable, mandated target market. Marketers and governments can work together for the benefit of all.

Economic Conditions

The rate of inflation, business activity (recession or growth), and shortages affect marketing in all businesses. When the rate of inflation is high, the price of many goods and services may move out of some consumers' reach. In 1982, for example, mortgage rates rose to over 17 percent, and many couples gave up hope of ever owning a house. A high rate of inflation also encourages consumers to spend money today rather than save: "If the

---

[10] Robert E. Krapfel, "Marketing by Mandate," *Journal of Marketing*, Summer 1982, pp. 79–85.

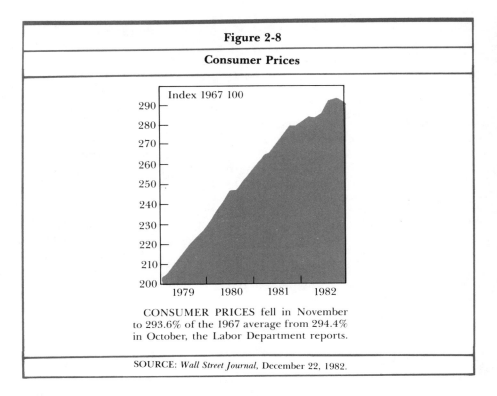

Figure 2-8

Consumer Prices

Index 1967 100

CONSUMER PRICES fell in November to 293.6% of the 1967 average from 294.4% in October, the Labor Department reports.

SOURCE: *Wall Street Journal*, December 22, 1982.

money will be worth less tomorrow, why should I save it?" Lack of savings results in less investment money available for companies to borrow, which drives interest rates even higher. In marketing inflation makes the job of setting prices especially difficult. Figure 2-8 graphs the rise in the Consumer Price Index, a measure of inflation, over a four-year period. With prices rising at such a rapid rate, marketers had difficulty predicting what price consumers would pay and what the costs to offer a product would be in even the near future. Conversely, in years such as 1983 and 1984 when inflation was at a low level, companies had difficulty justifying any cost-induced price increases.

Concerning inflation, the issue is whether real income has increased or decreased. If inflation rises at a rate faster than a consumer's disposable income, that consumer's real income has decreased. The cost of products has risen faster than the consumer's ability to purchase them. When this occurs, consumers typically save less and buy fewer luxuries and more necessities (like food). Thus, marketers of more expensive durable goods (cars) and luxuries (vacations) face a tougher task in selling their products.

The amount of economic activity—or growth—is measured by the increase in the gross national product, or **GNP** (volume of goods and

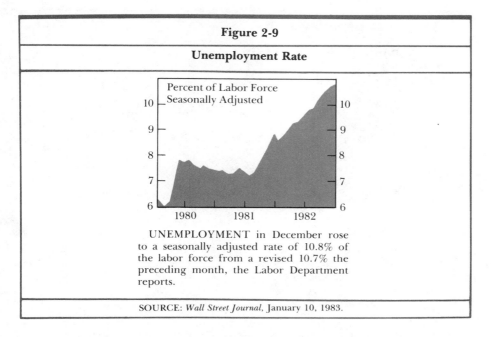

Figure 2-9

Unemployment Rate

Percent of Labor Force
Seasonally Adjusted

UNEMPLOYMENT in December rose to a seasonally adjusted rate of 10.8% of the labor force from a revised 10.7% the preceding month, the Labor Department reports.

SOURCE: *Wall Street Journal*, January 10, 1983.

services produced), over a given period of time. When economic activity is high, many people are working (low unemployment) and earning income. High income creates savings for investment and more demand for goods and services. When economic activity is low **(recession)**, many people are out of work, savings and investment are low, and demand falls off. These two scenarios create very different challenges for marketers. In active times marketers can expand their product line and distribution channels. In recessions it is often difficult to maintain product lines and channels, and creative advertising and promotion are needed to protect company sales.

In recent years our economy has been plagued by recessions accompanied by high inflation rates, a particularly dangerous phenomenon known as **stagflation.** From 1980 to 1982, for example, high unemployment rates (Figure 2-9) combined with high inflation rates (Figure 2-8), so that consumer disposable income fell (due to unemployment), while prices rose (due to inflation). Such a situation creates a devastating effect on consumers, businesses, and the economy. Retailers' sales often most clearly reflect these economic conditions. In 1981, when the inflation rate was double-digit and unemployment was rising, Sears sales grew only 2.1 percent. Penney's fell 0.4 percent, Woolworth's fell 1.8 percent, and Montgomery Ward's fell 9.2 percent.[11] Falling sales at the retail level eventually mean falling sales for all of the companies that supply products to them.

---

[11] "No Sunshine at the Sales Counter," *Business Week,* April 26, 1982, pp. 30–31.

The Development of Consumer Credit

Americans have come a long way from adherence to the saying, "In God we trust; all others must pay cash." Today payment practices based on the Latin word *credere,* meaning "to trust or to believe," are more common than cash transactions.

Actually, the first example of consumer credit in the New World was furnished by the Mayflower pilgrims. A wealthy London merchant, Thomas Weston, "trusted" the determined, courageous group of 102 who formed a colony on Cape Cod. He extended open credit to them for all they needed to buy. When they could not repay their debt within the specified seven years, he arranged for nine additional years of credit. Again they defaulted. It was 25 years before America's best-known colonists made their final payment to Weston and his associates.

During America's developmental period merchants commonly extended credit to regular customers. Farmers could scarcely have survived without open accounts during the planting and growing seasons. As America grew in population, however, most people conducted business with cash.

The wealthy were able to enjoy the convenience of credit. By obtaining "letters of credit" or recommendations from the banks that kept their large deposits, people of means were able to travel without carrying along large amounts of cash. Their bankers, after all, practically guaranteed that payment would be made for whatever goods the bearers of the letters purchased. Less affluent people had no such pull, however, until the twentieth century brought changing attitudes toward deferred payment and efficient techniques for bolstering the "trust" extended to consumers by creditors.

Consumer credit, which includes all credit extended for personal use, such as personal loans, installment sales, charge accounts, and credit cards, is a marketing function that facilitates consumer buying. As such, it has played an important role in expanding the economy, particularly since World War II.

Shortages of goods and raw materials recently have become a problem for the U.S. economy. Since 1970 the United States has experienced several oil shortages, a steel shortage, and numerous other materials shortages. These shortages often cause prices to skyrocket (in 1970 it was possible to purchase gasoline for 20 cents a gallon) and can seriously disrupt corporate operations. Marketers face the difficult task of allotting limited

In 1948 consumer credit in the United States exceeded $18 million. By 1984 consumer credit exceeded $400 billion and is still growing.

The United States government, which encourages but tries to closely scrutinize and regulate consumer credit, says that a business which extends credit believes that:

1. The customer intends to pay for his purchase.
2. The customer is able to pay for it.
3. Nothing will happen to prevent the customer from making payment when it is due.
4. The customer is of good character and integrity.

Credit cards gave merchants an opportunity to express these beliefs by extending credit to selected individuals. Plastic credit cards as we know them today evolved from Charge-Plates issued by the Farrington Manufacturing Company in 1928. Despite its name the plate was really used for identification purposes, not for charging purchases to accounts. Credit cards in various forms had been used earlier, however, beginning with those issued by gasoline companies in 1914. American Telephone and Telegraph, the railroads, and the airlines were pioneers of credit cards during the thirties and forties. Of course, many department stores issued their own limited-use cards to favored customers. A new dimension was added to consumer credit in 1949 with the introduction of the Diner's Club Card. With his brainchild, Frank McNamara ushered in the era of the travel and entertainment (T & E) card, a credit device that could be used at numerous establishments. The next stage in the evolution of consumer credit came in the late fifties and mid-sixties with credit cards issued by banks. This development led to the establishment of major credit card companies, such as MasterCard and Visa, whose cards are recognized and accepted worldwide. With these cards average consumers can spend with their own "letters of credit."

Consumer credit is moving along a continuum leading to the cashless, checkless society. Already, some stores and banks are using point-of-purchase devices to instantly record purchases in a central computer, which keeps track of the consumer's deposits and debits. In these instances the "promise to pay" relies less on trust and belief in personal integrity than on confidence in advanced computer technology.

Whatever the method, consumer credit facilitates the exchange process and thus aids companies in the marketing of their goods.

supplies of products and pricing when only a limited amount of a product can be sold.

There is little doubt that economic activity affects marketing plans. The 1982 recession led many companies to change their advertising themes. Heublein, Inc., for example, began suggesting their A.1. Steak Sauce was no longer solely for use on steaks, but also suitable for use on hamburger (a recession staple). Dow Chemical, the maker of Ziploc food bags, began emphasizing that its product's airtight seal was even more important in preserving leftovers since food prices had risen so high.[12]

Technological Change

Because new products and modifications in existing products depend on technology, marketing is affected by technological change, over which it generally lacks control. This change has been rapid. In 1980 there were more than 24 million Americans aged 65 or older, 11 percent of the total population, all of whom were born in 1915 or before. Consider just a few of the technological changes that have occurred during their lives. In 1915 there were very few cars and fewer paved roads. Hardly anyone had electricity, telephones, or indoor plumbing. There were no radios, televisions, talking pictures, lasers, electronic computers, Polaroid cameras, air conditioning, jet aircraft, or frozen foods, all of which we now take for granted as everyday elements of our environment. These basic technological developments have had far-reaching effects on our lives. Take computers, for example. The first computer designed for commercial use appeared in 1951. For a number of years only large corporations could afford the millions of dollars required to own one. Technological advances, however, have made today's computers affordable even to private consumers. In 1982 Timex introduced a personal computer that sold for $99.95 and weighed 12 ounces! A complete system, with printer and expanded memory capacity, cost $250.[13] By the end of 1982 this cost had been discounted to $225.[14] The price of the Timex computer eventually fell to $49.95. The analytical power of computers and the sophistication it lends to management are now not only available to companies of all sizes, but also to individuals.

Technological change does not merely add to the list of products available to consumers. It also affects the nature of previously available products. The invention of movable type is a classic example. Prior to the mid-fourteenth century, all documents—books, legislation, contracts—had to be laboriously copied by hand. The cost of hand copying was so great that only the clergy and the nobility could afford to buy written information. With the invention of movable type, however, books became so inexpensive that the general public could afford them. The creation of a new product, the mass-produced book, made the old hand-copied tracts obsolete, which

---

[12] Dennis Kneale, "Many Advertisers Alter Campaigns to Account for Recession Strategy," *Wall Street Journal,* August 10, 1982, pp. 1, 22.

[13] A Low-Priced Computer," *Business Week,* May 3, 1982, p. 42.

[14] Jeremy Main, "Products of the Year," *Fortune,* December 27, 1982, pp. 42–45.

in turn virtually eliminated the demand for animal-product parchment while simultaneously creating a new market for cheap rag-product paper. More importantly, movable type led to the standardization of spelling, punctuation, and grammar. Most importantly, it facilitated the passage of knowledge from the ruling monied classes to the previously uneducated lower classes. It was this aspect of technological change that led to the general proliferation of knowledge we now refer to as the Renaissance. You need only think of the mass production of automobiles or the synthesizing of plastics from petroleum products to realize that technological changes lead naturally to social changes.

For marketers it is important to be aware of new developments and not let the industry "pass you by" technologically. Most companies do not manage technology well. As Richard N. Foster of McKinsey and Company put it,

> The record is uncomfortably clear. Technology leaders tend to become technology losers. A few companies manage transitions to new technological fields effectively, but many others are unable even to begin the process, and most find it impossible to complete the move successfully.

To manage technology effectively, Foster suggests companies must decide:

1. Which technology to pursue and when to pursue it.
2. How to manage the transition from one technology to another, and
3. How to prepare the corporation for technological change.[15]

No one knows for certain what life—and marketing—will be like in the years ahead, but if previous developments are a guide, it is reasonable to assume that the process of change will continue to accelerate. Many forces are at work that are certain to dramatically alter today's world. New sources of energy and still faster means of communication are likely to substantially change the marketing environment. There will also be new products to which the marketing system must adapt. It seems probable, in fact, that our economic and social lives will change more in the next 40 years—roughly the working lifetime of today's college student—than they have changed in the last 100 years.

---

[15] Richard N. Foster, "A Call for Vision in Managing Technology," *Business Week*, May 24, 1982, pp. 24—33.

Social Change

Although marketing practices may influence social change—as in the case of Henry Ford's mass production of the automobile—such practices do not directly control social change. In most cases it is social change that affects marketing practices. Consider just a few comparatively recent social changes and their general impact on marketing.

- The ever-increasing number of working women has resulted in not only an expanded work force, but also a larger amount of money available for spending.
- A reduced birth rate has lowered the demand for large houses.
- Increased concern for the environment has prompted many states to pass laws banning throwaway cans and bottles.
- Consumerism has encouraged more people to speak out about products and services they feel are overpriced, dangerous, or falsely advertised.
- The millions of people who have taken up jogging have created a huge demand for appropriate shoes and apparel.
- A decline in the work ethic has greatly expanded the demand for recreational facilities and products.

Social change is certain. Marketing managers can either view it as a threat and be hurt or view it as an opportunity and benefit. General Electric

recognized the recent reactions from parents against television programs unsuitable for children as an opportunity. In 1982 GE announced the introduction of a television that parents can program to censor (block out) certain shows.[16] Positive reaction to social pressure is vital to the success of any company's marketing efforts.

Dealing With Uncontrollable Elements

If individual businesses have only limited control over such factors as competition and governmental actions, how can they prepare to deal with them? How can a firm protect itself from the harmful effects of a change in government policy, a switch in consumer preferences, or the introduction of a new and effective strategy by the competition?

Although there is no foolproof system for dealing with these uncontrollable factors, there are guidelines that help the marketing manager operate successfully.

First, anticipate change. A marketing manager who expects changes in the environment is less likely to be caught off guard. The firms that corner the market with a new product or service are often the ones that anticipate change in advance of their competitors. Anticipating change is a role of the marketing information system. Without proper information we cannot anticipate anything.

Second, remain flexible. Marketing managers should design their plans and policies so that they can modify them in a relatively short time. Advertising strategists, product and package designers, sales executives, and other key marketing personnel should all be able to revise their plans quickly in response to environmental changes.

Third, act progressively. Businesses that do extensive marketing research, encourage managers to attend special seminars, keep up with current literature, make a deliberate effort to keep abreast of changing times, and generally emphasize "staying alert" are better prepared to adjust to uncontrollable changes than businesses that ignore such opportunities.

By anticipating change, maintaining flexible viewpoints, and acting progressively in response to changes, management can greatly increase its effectiveness in our highly competitive society.

---

[16] Tim Metz, "Thanks to GE, a Little More Fun is About to Go Out of Being a Kid," *Wall Street Journal,* April 13, 1982, p. 37.

SUMMARY

- The marketing environment involves controllable and uncontrollable elements.
- The corporate management functions of planning and organizing constitute the controllable elements of marketing.
- Corporate direction, objectives, and strategies influence the role and importance of marketing in the company.
- Marketing's place in the corporate organization affects its ability to carry out its responsibilities and to resolve conflicts with production and finance.
- Consumer choice, competitive actions, governmental actions, economic conditions, technological change, and social change constitute the uncontrollable elements of the marketing environment.
- Consumer choice represents the "economic votes" by which consumers approve or disapprove of a company and its marketing offering.
- Competitive actions are affected by the number of companies in an industry and the strategies of each.
- Marketing actions are governed by a myriad of federal, state, and local laws, regulations, and court decisions.
- Inflation, business activity, and shortages are economic conditions that affect the way in which products should be marketed.
- Technology changes at a phenomenal pace. Marketers must be aware of new technological developments to maintain a differential advantage.
- Social change affects consumer attitudes and therefore influences marketing activities.
- Marketing managers can best deal with uncontrollable elements by anticipating change, remaining flexible, and acting progressively.

DISCUSSION QUESTIONS

1. Discuss the relationship between planning, objectives, and strategies and the role of each in an organization.
2. Discuss the functional role of marketing in various types of organizations. Why is it necessary for marketing to be on an "equal footing" with the production and finance functions?

3. Explain the difference between controllable and uncontrollable variables. Give examples of each. What implications do these variables pose for the marketing manager?
4. "Freedom to spend gives consumers unusual power." Explain this statement and its implications for the marketing concept.
5. What does *caveat emptor* mean? How has the concept of consumerism changed its applicability? What are the implications of this change for the firm?
6. The actual inflation rate for 1984 (5.1%) was much lower than the forecasted rate (7–8%). How could this fact affect a company's marketing objectives and strategies for 1985?
7. What impact will future technological change have on the marketing-oriented company and how might the marketing-oriented company cope with such change?
8. "Marketing managers can either view social change as a threat and be hurt, or they can view it as an opportunity and benefit." G.E. was used earlier as an example of the latter. Give an example of a company that has been hurt by social change. How might they have altered their marketing strategy to benefit from this change?
9. How might the various industry structures discussed affect marketing strategy?
10. Several guidelines for dealing with uncontrollable elements were discussed. How has the American automobile industry failed to follow these guidelines? How might they successfully cope with these elements in the future?

APPLICATION EXERCISES

1. In recent years Japanese auto manufacturers have been very successful at making inroads in the U.S. automobile market. How have the Japanese utilized the concepts of controllable and uncontrollable variables in establishing differential advantages for their products? If you were the president of G.M., how would you alter your strategy and marketing mix to meet the Japanese challenge? Prepare a report outlining this strategy and mix.
2. Suppose you were the marketing manager for your local telephone company. Outline how the breakup of AT&T by the Justice Department will influence your current and future marketing strategies.
3. Historically, the regulatory environment has prohibited banks from competing on a price (interest-rate) basis. The major marketing thrust of most banks has been on the advertising and promotional aspects of their marketing mix. Recent regulatory changes have relaxed the restrictions on interest-rate ceilings and thus affected the competitive environment of banks. List some changes you have observed in the marketing strategies of banks.

CASE 2
Apple Computer, Inc.[17]

After its public debut in 1980 Apple Computer, Inc. experienced 200 percent to 300 percent annual growth. Recent events, however, suggest the young company's wildfire growth may be on the wane. Although many companies might envy Apple's gains in revenues and income for 1982, the numbers clearly indicate a quarter-to-quarter flattening trend in the company's growth. In 1982 sales grew 69 percent—healthy, but certainly slower than in previous years. Analysts readily concede that this flattening can be attributed partially to factors beyond the company's control. For one thing the effect of the 1981–82 recession should be considered. No company can reasonably be expected to sustain 200–300 percent growth figures during a recession.

Many analysts, however, feel that the slowing growth trend reflects greater problems. Chief among these is Apple's apparent inability to keep pace with changing technology. An old product line makes flattening sales inevitable, particularly because technological change is a way of life in the computer industry. Apple's product-line mainstay, the Apple II, was founder Steven Jobs' initial market introduction in 1977. Although this technological breakthrough virtually created the personal computer industry, it now faces challenges from all sides. Analysts consider it a remarkable accomplishment that a product designed in 1977 has done so well for so long in the face of rapidly changing technology.

To Apple's credit, the company has taken steps to keep pace with changing technology. Its initial try, however, a model called the Apple III, had a disastrous debut in 1980. Critics claim that Apple introduced the machine prematurely, and in fact many machines were delivered "dead on arrival," that is, nonfunctional. Apple spent the better part of one year correcting the bugs and in 1982 pulled off a surprisingly successful reintroduction of the Apple III. Also in 1982, the company introduced a "souped-up" version of the Apple II. This model, the Apple IIE, along with products developed by other companies that increased the capacity of the Apple II and the Apple III, kept Apple Computer in the tentative position of market leader.

However, at the end of 1982 industry analysts generally agreed that Apple had failed to keep pace with IBM and Tandy in developing and marketing a machine powered by a 16-bit microprocessor. In addition, the same technological advances by peripheral companies that prolonged the competitiveness of the Apple II had made possible the duplication of many Apple functions on IBM and Tandy machines.

Some analysts have defended Apple's lagging innovations by insisting that the company had little incentive to move faster until 1982, when competition increased so dramatically. Nonetheless, the days of little competition have long since passed.

---

[17] Marilyn Chase, "Apple Computer's Slowed Growth Signals Tough Year for a Competitive Industry," *Wall Street Journal,* April 16, 1982, p. 14; Marilyn Chase, "Apple Computer has a Lot Riding on 'Lisa,' Two Other New Models," *Wall Street Journal,* January 4, 1983, pp. 31, 34; and Ann M. Morrison, "Apple Bites Back," *Fortune,* February 20, 1984, pp. 86–100.

In 1981 the personal computer industry reaped $1.4 billion in revenues. Apple led the market with a 20-percent share, and the top three suppliers—Apple, Tandy Corporation's Radio Shack, and Commodore International, Ltd.—together controlled 50 percent of the market. IBM entered the industry in October of 1981. By 1984 it had captured 26 percent of the industry's revenues, whereas Apple tentatively held on to a 21-percent share. This increased competition led Apple to introduce the Lisa (a sophisticated model initially selling for $10,000) and the McIntosh ($2,495). Many industry analysts, however, now view IBM, not Apple, as the technology leader.

On the regulatory front, Apple is awaiting the fate of a Congressional bill to give it a tax break for donating an Apple computer to every public school in the country. The passage of this bill would greatly enhance Apple's exposure to the newest generation of personal computer users—precollege students. IBM has countered by offering special prices on its PC and PCJr to colleges and their students.

Some have been impressed with Apple's attempts to remain a viable market force in a highly competitive environment. They point to the fact that Apple is undertaking an enormous development job for so young a company. Skeptics remain, however. One critic feels that Apple is taking the wrong approach. He says, "Apple's in a short-term tactical mode while their next competitor, IBM, is thinking 1990." If the skeptics are right, the implication is that in the tremendously competitive, high technology industry of personal computers, planning a model a year at a time is not enough.

Discussion Questions

1. Describe the various environmental forces affecting Apple Computer, Inc.
2. What mixture of marketing controllable variables would you use to combat the threat from IBM?
3. Do you think the idea of giving an Apple to every school is a good idea?

3

Marketing Information Systems, Marketing Research, and Forecasting

STUDY OBJECTIVES

After studying this chapter, you should be able to

1. Describe the Marketing Information System, its components, and what each component tries to accomplish.
2. Discuss marketing research and how it contributes to marketing management.
3. Discuss the various stages in a marketing research project.
4. Define the terms primary data and secondary data and explain the advantages and disadvantages of each.
5. List the characteristics and uses of the experimental method, survey method, and observational method in conducting marketing research.
6. Define sales forecasting and explain why forecasts are necessary and how they are made.

I nformation is vital to the plans of marketing management. How can marketing managers plan the marketing mix if they know nothing about what the target market wants, what the competition will do, what the laws affecting the company are, and so on?

To develop marketing plans, accurate, up-to-date information about the target market and the uncontrollable elements of the marketing environment must be available to the marketing manager. To accomplish this, most companies have a formal or informal method of gathering information called a Marketing Information System. Without realizing it, all companies have at least an informal information-gathering system. Each time an executive reads a newspaper or magazine, for example, he or she is gathering information about the company's environment.

MARKETING INFORMATION SYSTEMS

A **Marketing Information System (MIS)** has been defined as "a structured, interacting complex of persons, machines, and procedures designed to generate an orderly flow of pertinent information collected from both intra- and extra-firm sources for use as the bases for decision-making in specific responsibility areas of marketing management."[1] *The basic function of a Marketing Information System is to help marketing managers make better decisions.* A properly designed system should provide data to aid in making product, place, promotion, and price decisions. It should also provide continuing information on sales results and costs incurred.

The well-designed system provides immediate updates on critical information. For example, many hotels, car rental agencies, and airlines have systems that monitor the availability, location, and price of rooms, autos, and airline seats at any given time. This information is not only convenient for customers, but it also keeps managers aware of their firms' status.

Another system that provides immediate information to marketing managers is tied to the use of the **Universal Product Code (UPC).** Designed for the food retailing industry, the code is printed on a product label. A machine at the checkout stand reads the type of product sold and its price and immediately relays this information to a computer. The computer can provide marketing personnel with second-by-second inventory and sales information.

---

[1] Richard H. Brien and James E. Stafford, "Marketing Information Systems: A New Dimension for Marketing Research," *Journal of Marketing,* July 1968, p. 21.

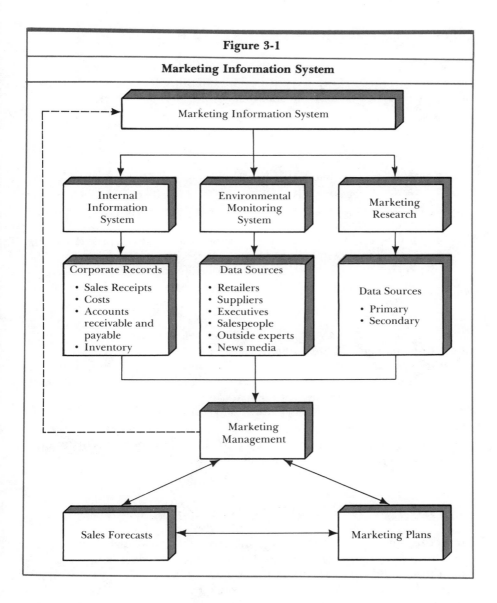

Figure 3-1

Marketing Information System

Marketing Information System

Internal Information System

Environmental Monitoring System

Marketing Research

Corporate Records
- Sales Receipts
- Costs
- Accounts receivable and payable
- Inventory

Data Sources
- Retailers
- Suppliers
- Executives
- Salespeople
- Outside experts
- News media

Data Sources
- Primary
- Secondary

Marketing Management

Sales Forecasts

Marketing Plans

As Figure 3-1 depicts, *a complete MIS is composed of an internal information system, an environmental monitoring system, and marketing research.* In this chapter we will be concerned primarily with these three components and the use of the information obtained to develop sales forecasts. Later chapters will deal with marketing plans.

INTERNAL INFORMATION SYSTEM

Much of the information that a marketing manager can use to make decisions exists in the corporate records. The following list provides but a few of the sources and uses of internal data.

1. Quantity of sales attributable to particular salespeople (by geographic territory) can be monitored by compiling regional sales from the addresses on orders.
2. Forecast accuracy can be determined from sales data.
3. Accounts receivable is a measure of how liberal credit terms are. (It can be compared to sales to see if a relationship exists between easier credit and higher sales.)
4. How often inventory runs out (called a **stockout**) helps determine the effectiveness of the "place" marketing controllable variable. (Again, this can be compared to sales to determine whether customers are annoyed by stockouts and start to buy from competitors.)

These are only a few of the possible internal information sources the marketing manager should investigate. In fact the entire corporate accounting system is an excellent source for gathering marketing information. Accounting, as an information-gathering area of business, has become quite sophisticated over the last 50 years.

Because much of the information marketing managers need is available in the corporate Internal Information System, it makes little sense for marketing to spend money gathering information outside the corporation when it is available, for free, internally.

ENVIRONMENTAL MONITORING SYSTEM

Marketing managers need an ongoing stream of information about the uncontrollable environmental elements they face. To obtain this information, they should regularly query the company's retailers, suppliers, executives, and salespeople on their impressions of recent competitive and governmental actions, as well as any changes in technology, social attitudes, and economic conditions. Outside experts should be approached for information in specific areas. For example, lawyers can provide valuable information concerning new laws, regulations, and court rulings. Economists and business consultants provide information on economic conditions and competitive actions. Finally, a methodical search of newspapers, trade journals, magazines, and television can inform the marketing manager of new developments and provide a general impression of the environment in which marketing must function. In addition many universities and business service organizations offer regular seminars to provide information updates for business people.

Although this process may sound rather haphazard, it is marketing management's responsibility to gather, in an understandable form, all possible relevant information about the environment and communicate it to the proper decision makers.

MARKETING RESEARCH

Probably the most visible aspect of a Marketing Information System is marketing research. *Marketing research is defined as "the systematic gathering, recording, and analyzing of data about problems relating to the marketing of goods and services."* It "may be undertaken by impartial agencies or by business firms or their agents for solution of marketing problems."[2] Generally, marketing research consists of a formal procedure for collecting and analyzing information, which is normally used to help solve one-of-a-kind problems or special situations. The overall Marketing Information System, in contrast, is intended to supply continuous data about internal operations and the external environment. For example, a marketing manager might use marketing research to forecast sales, determine why a product is not selling as planned, choose the location of a new store, or select an advertising campaign. In contrast, he might use a Marketing Information System to supply him with data about inventory levels, sales of specific products in specific stores, marketing expenses, recent legal developments, and so on. The basic rationale for research is that it increases the probability of making correct, or at least better, decisions. Obviously, a business that applies the marketing concept will rely heavily on marketing research. Not all questions facing marketing management can be researched, of course. Moreover, if the cost of obtaining the information exceeds the expected value of the data, research is not justified.

To be successful, good marketing research projects require as much careful planning as a well-designed product. Before launching a research project, the marketing research director should design a step-by-step plan for obtaining the information needed to answer questions pertinent to the problem.

Figure 3-2 presents a general procedure for conducting a marketing research project. We will deal with each step separately.

---

[2] Committee on Definitions, *Marketing Definitions: A Glossary of Marketing Terms* (Chicago: American Marketing Association, 1960), pp. 16–17.

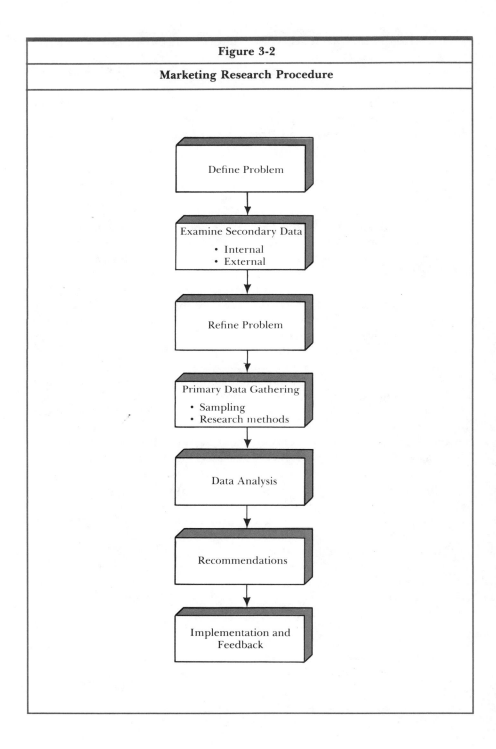

Figure 3-2

Marketing Research Procedure

Define Problem

Examine Secondary Data
- Internal
- External

Refine Problem

Primary Data Gathering
- Sampling
- Research methods

Data Analysis

Recommendations

Implementation and Feedback

Define Problem

Most marketing research is oriented toward problem solving. To gather useful information to solve a problem, we must first define *specifically* what the problem is. For example, the research question, "Why aren't we selling more?" is probably asked by every marketing manager at some time. It is impossible to design a marketing research study to answer that question, however, because it does not specify what information we need. A more workable question would be, "Why are there falling Product K sales through chain retail stores in our Cleveland market?" Stated as a research question, this problem gives us some guidelines to use in designing a research study. Specifically, we are only concerned with target customer opinions of Product K, our target customers are in Cleveland, and they shop in retail chain stores (K Mart, for instance).

Examine Secondary Data

Often it is unnecessary to conduct a formal research study to answer our questions. Either partially or completely, someone else (or previous marketing research) may have already gathered the information, and it is available to marketing management. Such information is called **secondary data.** Data gathered directly by a marketing research project is called **primary data.** If a motel chain questioned consumers about its service, the information it collected would be considered primary data. If the same motel chain obtained similar data from material published by a motel trade association, the information would be considered secondary data.

Internal Secondary Data   Secondary data from within the corporation is typically obtained from the Internal Information System of the MIS. Such information includes inventory levels, costs, sales by region, accounts receivable and payable, and prior research results.

In the case of internal secondary data the questions to be answered are simply, "Who has the data?" (accounting, for example) and "In what form can they make it available to us?"

External Secondary Data   If the information the marketing manager needs is not available internally, it may be available from governmental or several nongovernmental sources.[3]

---

[3] Several overviews of available secondary data sources are: S.H. Britt and I.A. Shapiro, "Where to Find Business Facts," *Harvard Business Review,* September–October 1973, pp. 44–50; C.R. Goeldner and Laura M. Dirks, "Business Facts: Where to Find Them," *MSU Business Topics,* Summer 1976, pp. 23–26; and A.C. Samli and J.T. Mentzer, "An Industrial Analysis Market Information System," *Industrial Marketing Management,* Spring 1980, pp. 237–45. Reference guides to available information include the *Business Periodicals Index, Marketing Information Guide, Monthly Catalog of U.S. Government Publications,* and the *Readers' Guide to Periodical Literature.*

Figure 3-3

Some Governmental Information Sources

Agency	Publication(s)
Bureau of Census	*Catalog of U.S. Census Publications; Census of Manufacturers; Census of Population; Census of Retail Trade, Wholesale Trade, and Selected Service Industries; Census of Transportation*
Bureau of Labor Statistics	*Monthly Labor Review; Monthly Urban Review*
Congressional Information Service	*American Statistical Index*
Department of Agriculture	
Department of Commerce	*Annual Survey of Manufacturers; County and City Data Book; Statistical Abstract of the United States*
Department of Labor	
Federal Communications Commission	
Federal Maritime Commission	*National Cargo Analysis System*
Federal Reserve System	*Federal Reserve Bulletin*
Federal Trade Commission	
Food and Drug Administration	
Interstate Commerce Commission	
National Center for Educational Statistics	
National Center for Health Statistics	
National Technical Information Service	
Office of Business Economics	*Business Statistics; Survey of Current Business*
Small Business Administration	
Statistical Reporting Service	
U.S. Postal Service	

The federal government gathers and publishes a great deal of information concerning marketing, markets, and consumers. Figure 3-3 lists some of the agencies that gather information as well as government publications of interest to marketers.

In addition there are many nongovernmental sources of useful secondary data, such as professional associations that publish material pertinent to marketing (the American Marketing Association is the most prominent of these), periodicals, and professional research companies. Figure 3-4 is a sample of the periodicals and professional research firms that gather and sell secondary data. A business library will contain numerous other sources

---

Figure 3-4

Periodicals and Research Companies

Periodical	Company*
Advertising Age	A.C. Nielsen
Business Horizons	Arbitron
Business Week	Audit Bureau of Circulation
California Management Review	Audits and Surveys
Chain Store Age	Chase Econometrics
Columbia Journal of World Business	Dun and Bradstreet
Forbes	Gallup and Robinson
Fortune	IMS
Graphic Guide to Consumer	Market Research Corporation of
Markets	America
Industrial Marketing Management	National Family Opinion
Journal of the Academy of	National Purchase Dairy Panel
Marketing Science	R.L. Polk
Journal of Advertising	Selling Area—Marketing Inc.
Journal of Advertising Research	(SAMI)
Journal of Business	Simmons
Journal of Business Logistics	Standard Rate and Data Service
Journal of Business Research	Starch
Journal of Consumer Research	
Journal of International Business	
Studies	
Journal of Marketing	
Journal of Marketing Research	
Journal of Retailing	
Marketing News	
Nielsen Researcher	
Progressive Grocer	
Rand McNally Commercial Atlas	
and Marketing Guide	
Sales and Marketing Management	
Stores	
Wall Street Journal	

* For a more exhaustive coverage of research companies, see Donald R. Lehmann, *Market Research and Analysis*, (Homewood, Ill.: Richard D. Irwin, 1979), pp. 208–245.

---

of secondary data, and many other research companies exist. The appendix following this chapter provides an extensive, annotated list of both governmental and nongovernmental sources of secondary data.

Secondary data purchased from a research company is different from hiring a research company to gather primary data. Primary data is gathered to solve a particular problem for a company and often is quite expensive. Many research companies conduct ongoing studies of a more general nature. Clients can purchase this information at a lower cost than a specific research project.

It is important to note that much existing secondary data is *free*. Many other sources are fairly low in cost. For example, you can purchase U.S. Census data results from a two-page survey of over 80 million households and a six-page survey of 16 million households for $10,000.[4] For the typical marketing research budget this is a great deal of information for a relatively small expenditure.

Secondary Data Advantages   As indicated previously, one advantage of secondary data is its *low cost*. It is much less expensive to go to the library for documents or contact an appropriate government agency than it is to launch a full-scale primary data research project. In addition secondary data is often both *easier and less time-consuming to obtain* than primary data. Finally, some data, such as that compiled by the Bureau of the Census and other governmental agencies, may be available only from secondary sources.

Secondary Data Disadvantages   A major drawback of secondary data is its *limited applicability,* for it rarely fits a company's exact intelligence needs. Second, such data is frequently *out of date*. For many research projects information must be current, because consumers' incomes, attitudes, and circumstances are constantly changing. Information that was useful five years ago may be worthless today. A third disadvantage of data from secondary sources is its *limited credibility*. There is often an element of doubt regarding the validity of secondary data. "Who collected it?", "Why did they collect it?", and "How was it collected?" are questions that should be considered before placing too much reliance on secondary data.

Refine Problem

After all available secondary data has been studied, it is important to re-examine the problem to be certain it has not changed. Obviously, primary data need not be gathered if the secondary data provides enough information to solve the problem. Even if primary data is still needed, the new information gained from the secondary data may allow a more specific or slightly different problem statement (refinement) that acts as a guide in the rest of the research procedure, as the experience of one company illustrates.[5]

Company X manufactures a particular brand of diet aids, which it sells in numerous independent and chain retail stores. Sales of the product in one large chain (X's largest customer) had fallen drastically. Company X stated the research question as, "Why are our customers in this retail chain no longer buying our product?"

---

[4] Peter K. Francese, "Bargained-Priced Census Data a Boon to Consumer, Market Researchers," *Marketing News*, May 15, 1981, p. 14.
[5] Company name withheld upon request.

Before conducting a large and costly survey of customers in this chain, X requested some secondary data from the chain: the amount of the product on the shelf in each store. Results of this investigation showed that in over half of the chain's stores the product was out of stock (none on the shelf)! Thus, consumers in those stores had stopped buying the product, because it was not available. The research question was refined to, "Why are these particular stores no longer stocking our product?"

Subsequent investigation through a primary data research project revealed that stockpeople had simply forgotten the store carried the product. Company X solved the problem by a promotional campaign aimed at reminding the stockpeople to keep its product in stock. Without this effective use of secondary data Company X could not have refined the problem and would have spent thousands of dollars gathering unnecessary primary data.

Gather Primary Data

The gathering of primary data, which is what most people think of as marketing research, consists of conducting a study (either by the corporate marketing research people or by another company paid to do the research) to gather particular information to solve a problem. To gather primary data, marketing management must first develop a research design. The **research design** is a specific procedure for gathering data and answers the questions, "Who should be studied?" and "How will we study them?" Answering the first question is called **sampling** and the second is called **research methods.**

Sampling   A company can seldom afford to ask questions of every potential customer. For many companies that would mean questioning over 200 million people! Thus, most marketing researchers try to select a small portion (called a **sample**) of all the possible target customers and draw some conclusions about the larger market (called the **population**) based on what this sample has to say.

Marketing researchers can use either a probability sample or a nonprobability sample to select respondents. In a **probabilty sample** each member of the population has a known probability of being chosen for the research, whereas in a **nonprobability sample** members are chosen according to the researcher's judgment. Probability samples are usually more accurate representations of the population. To provide an overview of sampling, we will briefly discuss seven different types of samples (three probability and four nonprobability).

1. **Simple random sample** (probability). Every member of the population has a known and equal chance of being selected. Example: The names of 1,000 people are randomly selected from a mailing

Strategy

A.C. Nielsen versus Information Resources

Sound consumer marketing strategies are based on an understanding of consumer behavior. Determining the characteristics of consumers and their buying habits requires a vast amount of consumer and market information. Generating and supplying this type of information in a form useable to marketers is the sole purpose of some businesses.

The A.C. Nielsen Company pioneered the consumer marketing research industry. Its data collection philosophy grew out of a mistake made by its founder, Arthur C. Nielsen, Sr. In the 1930s Nielsen based sales forecasts for two soap products on interviews he had with housewives. His forecasts proved to be the exact opposite of actual sales. Nielsen concluded that consumer interviews did not produce accurate information, because the interviewees often said one thing and did another. From then on Nielsen proceeded with the idea that quantitative measurements of consumers' actions are the best indicator of what their future actions will be.

The firm grew by using machines, not personal interviews, to collect data. In 1942 Nielsen installed its first electronic meters to accurately measure radio audiences. Nielsen expanded the same electronic coverage to television in 1949, whereas others were still weighing mail bags to determine audience size.

As soon as electronic computers were commercially available, Nielsen began using them to compile the numerical results of its research. This early use of computers allowed Nielsen to become the present-day leader in the $9.8 billion marketing-information industry.*

Today Nielsen electronically monitors the television-viewing patterns of 2,900 individuals, with an additional 2,400 homeowners writing diaries to help establish demographic profiles. Nielsen also monitors supermarket purchases in over 100 stores around the country. Furthermore, Nielsen has branched out and now not only supplies consumer information about grocery purchases and television viewing but also collects information for the computer and petroleum industries.

To remain the market leader, Nielsen continues to spend money on state-of-the-art equipment and research. For example, it is taking advantage of information provided by the new scanning cash registers by purchasing the scanner tapes to supplement its supermarket sales and product market-share data. The generation of weekly rather than bimonthly reports for their clients is possible with these tapes.

Hot on the heels of Nielsen is a new entry into the marketing research industry. Information Resources, Inc. (IRI), is combining the capabilities of cable television, supermarket scanners, and computers to create a new standard in marketing research.

The IRI concept, BehaviorScan, was conceived in 1977 by John Malec, former part owner in a small market research firm, and Gerald Eskin, an econometrician and associate professor of marketing at the University of Iowa. Their basic premise was to use scanning registers to keep purchase diaries for homemakers.

The BehaviorScan concept adds a new twist to the collection of market data. IRI picked six small U.S. cities in which to conduct its studies, using a total of 15,000 women as the source of its data. It gave each woman an electronically encoded ID card to use when she grocery shops, equipped each woman's television with a microcomputer that monitors her viewing choices, and put electronic scanners in the supermarkets in each city. The cards, the scanners, and the television monitoring are supposed to establish patterns on each individual. Once these patterns are determined, IRI uses its facilities at local TV stations to replace commercials the participants would usually see with new test ads. It then measures the purchase response based on the data obtained from the scanner tapes.

The data indicates how successful an ad may be in altering purchase behavior. The combination of television viewing and purchase data tells advertisers what shows the buyers of different products watch. And all this information is readily available to the client within a week. IRI BehaviorScan has been described as coming "close to being a direct measurement of the advertising dollar."†

This is only the beginning. In the future IRI hopes to be able to define different demographic segments during a television show and to send demographically appropriate ads for the same product to each different segment. It would be like a huge direct-mail campaign for broadcasters!

There is some question concerning how much real benefit this sophisticated data provides. Nielsen, however, is not taking any chances. It is developing an IRI type program of its own.

With $6 billion spent each year on the advertising and promotion of consumer products, companies are willing to pay for information that helps them understand how they rate in comparison to the competition. The more accurate and quantitative the data, the more they are willing to pay. Market researchers like Nielsen and IRI face a continuing challenge to meet these information needs.

---

* Larry Marion, "Leader by Legacy," *Forbes*, May 25, 1981, pp. 110–12.
† Fern Schumer, "The New Magicians of Market Research," *Fortune*, July 25, 1983, pp. 72–74.

list of 11,000 (each name had an equal chance—1/11,000—of being chosen).

2. **Stratified random sample** (probability). The population is divided into categories, like age, and everyone in each category (stratum) is the same with respect to the criteria for division. A simple random sample is then taken from each stratum. Example: People are divided into the age groups of under 18, 19–25, 26–35, 36–45, 46–60, and over 60. A sample of 100 persons is chosen from each group. The total sample is 600 (6 strata × 100 people per stratum).

3. **Cluster sample** (probability). Certain geographic regions that are representative of the whole population are sampled. Typically, this approach is used to cut down on the travel costs involved in sampling a geographically disperse population. Example: It is found that Columbus, Ohio, is representative of consumers over the entire population. Therefore, a simple random sample of Columbus is selected.

4. **Convenience sample** (nonprobability). The researcher picks those members of the population who are most convenient to sample. Example: The researcher picks the members closest to his/her home.

5. **Judgment sample** (nonprobability). The researcher selects those whom he/she believes are representative respondents. Example: In conducting research in a grocery store for a baby food manufacturer, the researcher selects only adults carrying babies.

6. **Systematic sample** (nonprobability). The researcher selects each nth person. Example: In a grocery store the researcher conducts interviews with every fourth person that enters the checkout line.

7. **Quota sample** (nonprobability). The researcher selects members until he/she has obtained a certain number. Example: A researcher may want a sample of 50 males and 50 females. If part way through the study 50 males have responded, the researcher simply stops talking to males.

It should be clear from these examples that probability samples provide a great deal of realistic information but often are expensive and difficult to administer. Nonprobability samples provide less accurate information than probability samples but are less expensive and easier to conduct.

Research Methods   Once you have decided whom to use in your research, you must decide how to get needed information from them. The three major methods used in collecting primary data are the **experimental method, survey method,** and **observational method.**

Experimental Method   Experimental marketing research involves directly testing an item or an idea on target customers to determine whether it is suitable for a specific purpose or will bring about a desired result. In some cases the experimental method is used to determine a product's design, its package, price, potential market, or the suitability of various marketing strategies. For example, a company might test which of several proposed packages will sell best by using different packages in comparable retail outlets and measuring the sales in each store. Advertising campaigns are sometimes tested in local markets to determine which messages have the most effect on consumer purchases. Experimental studies are also frequently used to test new package sizes. A soft-drink manufacturer may test different bottle sizes in several regional markets over an extended period before introducing one or more new sizes nationally. Direct-mail advertisers use experimental marketing research to test which copy, colors, and mailing-piece sizes produce the best response.

Although experimental research is also used to test the acceptance of a new product before a decision is made to manufacture it in quantity, researchers frequently encounter difficulties in using the experimental method to conduct marketing research, because the experiment is difficult to control. The accuracy of experimental marketing research rarely, if ever, approaches the level of accuracy possible in a scientific laboratory. For example, in preparing a new campaign for a client, an advertising agency may set up dry runs of different advertising themes in several test markets throughout the United States. Because no two cities in the United States

have identical market characteristics, however, the findings will not be exactly comparable. Moreover, experimental research projects are often difficult to design and put into practice. As a rule, this type of research is also not only the most costly and time-consuming, but the exposure of a new product during the research period may give competitors an opportunity to come up with a competing product or strategy as well.

Survey Method The survey method consists of gathering information from respondents by directly communicating with them, either by mail, phone, or personal interview. The mail survey is the least expensive of the three options. The researcher prepares a questionnaire and mails it to members of the sample, usually enclosing a stamped return envelope and often some reward to facilitate returns. It is important to make certain the questionnaire is clear and, literally, self-explanatory. If any part is confusing, the potential respondent cannot ask the researcher for clarification. Misinterpreted questionnaires often are a problem, resulting in useless or incorrect responses. An additional problem is slow response or no response at all. It is not unusual for less than half of a sample to return a questionnaire.

With the use of wide area telephone service (WATS), telephone surveys have become a relatively inexpensive (though more costly than mail surveys) and fast method of surveying a sample. Without having to move from the office, a researcher can reach respondents anywhere in the nation. By asking questions from a prepared questionnaire (and filling in responses during the interview), much the same type of information obtained in a mail survey can be gathered over the phone. Because telephone surveys allow the respondent to ask for clarification of confusing parts of the questionnaire, however, much of the ambiguity inherent in mail surveys is avoided. Finally, because people seem less willing to hang up on a caller than to throw a questionnaire in the trash, response rates are typically better with telephone surveys.

The personal interview is the least ambiguous, yet most expensive, method of surveying. The expense results from the traveling the researchers must do in going to the respondents so the interview can be conducted face-to-face. The personal interaction allows more in-depth responses and all necessary clarification to take place. Although the amount of information gathered may be considerable, many researchers do not consider it worth the cost. One warning that should accompany personal interviews: In a face-to-face situation researchers often cannot resist the temptation to offer suggestions and hints to the respondents, thereby ruining the validity of the results.

The survey method has three primary advantages:

1. *It is adaptable to many situations for which facts or viewpoints cannot be determined by observation or experiment.* For example, it is often difficult for an airline to tell whether passengers have enjoyed the

inflight services provided. Some passengers are nervous or preoccupied about things other than inflight conditions, but have no complaints about the service. Because it is difficult to conduct experiments that will reveal the degree of passenger satisfaction, the best way to find out what customers think about an airline is to ask them. The survey method can be used, therefore, to gain information that would otherwise be inaccessible.

2. *It is fast.* For example, if a television station needs to develop a quick profile of its viewers, it can use a telephone survey to collect information in a matter of hours. Experimental or observational research would take much longer.

3. *It is relatively low in cost.* More information per dollar spent can usually be collected by the survey method than by any other research technique.

The survey approach does have some drawbacks. Four major disadvantages are:

1. *Many people are unwilling to cooperate with a telephone, mail, or personal survey.* People are often hesitant to give information about such highly personal matters as their income, sex, and drinking habits.

2. *Even when they are willing to do so, some respondents are unable to provide accurate information.* Often they cannot tell precisely why they chose a Chevrolet over a Ford or why they stop at one store instead of another. The motives behind a purchase may be subconscious or so mixed that they cannot be described accurately. Many people cannot supply information because their ability to recall is limited; for example, they cannot remember offhand all the magazines they subscribe to or even how many radios they have.

3. *Some respondents are reluctant to tell the truth.* If you ask young women in a status-conscious community where they buy most of their clothes, they are apt to tell you the names of shops that are more expensive than those they actually patronize.

4. *Often questionnaires are poorly designed, survey personnel are inadequately trained, and the people surveyed are not truly representative of the market.* Thus, even if the respondents are willing and able to supply correct information, implementation problems can cause inaccurate survey results.

What survey techniques are most popular with marketing research directors? Figure 3-5 lists responses gathered by Marketing Facts, Inc., and reported by *Advertising Age.* In one year the use of WATS line interviewing grew 43 percent, whereas personal, in-home interviewing declined 23 percent. Personal interviewing in shopping centers followed WATS line interviewing closely as the technique on which many marketing research directors chose to spend most of their budgets.

Figure 3-5				
Relative Importance of Data Collection Techniques				
	Received Most Money Last Year	**Growing in Use**	**Declining in Use**	**Net Difference**
Shopping mall intercept interviewing	35%	39%	11%	+28%
Personal, in-home interviewing	16	12	35	−23
Locally supervised telephone interviewing	11	10	27	−17
WATS line interviewing	38	48	5	+43
Focus group interviewing	13	26	12	+14
Controlled mail panel surveys	19	23	13	+10
Consumer panel purchase diaries	10	8	7	+ 1
Trade interview surveys	2	10	7	+ 3
Direct mail surveys	4	10	13	− 3

NOTE: Figures represent responses and opinions of marketing research directors.
SOURCE: *Advertising Age*, October 15, 1979.

(handwritten margin note: wide area telephone systems. sales is basic reason)

Observational Method　The observational form of marketing research involves viewing or taking note of some act or occurrence, often with the aid of such instruments as cameras or tape recorders. When this technique is used, people are not asked to describe what they buy, what magazines they read, or what television shows they watch. Instead, the researcher merely observes their behavior, often without their knowledge.

Observational research can be conducted either by trained observers or by various mechanical or electronic devices. For example, an **audimeter** is often used to record when television and radio sets are turned on and what stations they are tuned to. Many of the Nielsen television ratings are based on audimeter-gathered marketing research. Most observational research, however, is conducted in person.

The observational technique has two major advantages:

1. *It is more objective than surveys.*
2. *It produces more accurate results than surveys.*

These advantages come from the fact that an impartial observer is less biased and, therefore, will often more accurately describe behavior than the performer of an action.

The observational approach also has its disadvantages:

1. *It is more dependent on the observer's interpretation of what happened than other methods, and observers may misinterpret what they see.* Even though they are well trained, some of their observations may reflect their own prejudices.
2. *Many consumer actions are unobservable.* Most families do not conduct their debates about what kind of boat to buy or which motels to patronize in a public place. Nor are very personal situations and intimate activities likely to be open to observation. You cannot, for example, observe what kind of sleeping garments people wear.
3. *The cost of observational studies, though lower than that of experimental research, is generally higher than that of surveys.*

Primary Data Advantages   The key advantage of primary data is its *specificity*, that is, the fact that data are tailored to specific situations currently confronting a company. Each marketing situation differs to some extent from every other. Information that provides the most specific definition of possible solutions is naturally the most desirable.

A second advantage of primary data is its *practicality*. Because its collection involves contact with real situations, it helps make marketing research less of an ivory-tower activity. Although secondary sources may offer valuable background information, they do not have the same flavor of the marketplace as data generated by primary research.

A third advantage of primary data is its *confidentiality*. Only the firm authorizing the research has access to the findings.

Primary Data Disadvantages   Collecting first-hand information is almost always *costly*. Often the company's research budget simply doesn't cover much primary research.

A second problem is *time*. It usually takes a significant amount of time to construct a framework for primary research and more time to actually conduct a study.

A third important limitation of primary data is *duplication of effort*. Often primary research is a repetition of available secondary data that can answer many questions satisfactorily if the researcher knows where and how to look.

Analyze Data

Regardless of the method used to gather primary data, the researcher must code the completed information for it to be useful. **Coding** is the process of turning responses from the sample into an interpretable form. Typically, this entails assigning responses to categories and numbers to the categories so analysis can be performed.

Tabulation is a summary of the responses by the categories. These are often expressed as totals and percentages.

Finally, **analysis** involves the use of various statistical techniques to evaluate the responses with respect to the research problem. Because these statistical techniques are often quite complicated, analysis is normally performed with the aid of a computer (see this chapter's Marketing Milestone for a discussion of the value of computers to marketing researchers). Results of this analysis are interpreted to provide some insight toward solving the problem.

Recommendations

Given the problem under investigation and the interpretation of the research, the marketing manager must make recommendations to solve the problem. An example may help illustrate.

Seven-Up's "Feelin' 7-Up" campaign, with sports figures Tug McGraw and Sugar Ray Leonard, struck out. "Half the audience is young girls who don't care who Sugar Ray Leonard is," Charles W. Schmid, a Seven-Up vice president conceded. "We were not satisfied with our sales results from the old campaign."

The problem: What emphasis should new 7-Up advertisements have? Market research showed that half the consumers did not know 7-Up was caffeine free. Also, 66 percent of American males and 47 percent of teenagers were interested in buying a soda without caffeine.

The recommendation (based upon interpretation of the marketing research): Produce ads emphasizing the fact that 7-Up is caffeine free.[6]

Implementation and Feedback

Although we will discuss implementation throughout the book, note that it is part of a marketing researcher's responsibility to see that those responsible for implementation correctly understand the recommendations. Marketing researchers usually get their feedback through reports from the Internal Information System.

Characteristics of Good Marketing Research

The more carefully a research project is conducted, the more confidence marketing management can place in the findings. The quality of market research ranges from very crude to very sophisticated. Carelessly gathered data can provide a highly inaccurate picture of the market and may cost the company a great deal of money.

---

[6] Peter W. Bernstein, "Seven-Up's Sudden Taste for Cola," *Fortune*, May 17, 1982, pp. 101–103.

Because the primary goal of formal research is to design studies that will yield the most objective and reliable data possible, a good research project should have four basic characteristics—**rationality, objectivity, precision,** and **honest interpretation** of results.

Rationality   Rationality, as opposed to emotionalism, should be emphasized in all steps of the research process. Without such an approach a researcher will normally produce highly inaccurate and incorrectly interpreted results.

Objectivity   Researchers must try to free their research of personal prejudices or biases. They must take care that their own preferences do not affect either the design of the research project or their interpretation of the results. Neglecting to investigate pertinent areas when they suspect the findings will not be to their liking can be as harmful as stressing only those aspects of the research for which they feel a particular fondness. Research that is conducted to prove a point or to substantiate a prejudgment is obviously not objective.

Precision   An emphasis on precision is a third characteristic of good research. Are responses accurately interpreted and recorded? Is the information coded and analyzed accurately? Are the analysis techniques used correctly and the results stated correctly? All these questions should be answered with a strong "Yes."

Honest Interpretation   Judgment is always important in interpreting research information. For example, a research study by a department store indicating that consumer income in the area is above average does not necessarily mean that customers will buy above-average merchandise. Income is not the only determinant of consumer purchasing behavior. Sociological factors may also be involved. If consumers in the target area are primarily blue-collar workers, conclusions based solely on income may be grossly misleading.

Scope of Marketing Research

Any time a company tries to obtain information from or about its target customers, it is performing marketing research. A survey sponsored by the American Marketing Association found that 74 percent of the responding companies had formal marketing research departments.[7] This figure does not count the percentage that has no formal department but still conducts occasional research or hires professional research firms. Therefore, most firms recognize the importance of marketing research and utilize it in

---

[7] Dik Warren Twedt, ed., *1978 Survey of Marketing Research* (Chicago, Ill.: American Marketing Association, 1978), p. 11.

marketing decision making. Figure 3-6 summarizes the decision-making applications on which some companies spend marketing research dollars.

Research in the Social Sciences

Research is never as easy in a social science (such as marketing) as it is in a physical science. Directly or indirectly, human beings are usually the object of study in marketing research. Their behavior is infinitely more difficult to

Computers are now necessary components to the modern Marketing Information System, for although these systems can be informal in nature, it does not take a very large or sophisticated Marketing Information System to make the computer indispensable. Many Marketing Information Systems tap all the uncontrollable environments described in Chapter 2. Some mechanism must exist for compiling and analyzing this information and quickly passing it on to marketing management. Good environmental information will not help marketing managers do their jobs if it is out-of-date. Computers are essential components to the delivery of such timely information.

Computerized Marketing Information Systems allow marketing managers, through special computer programs, to test theories and assumptions, compare figures with last year's performance, and develop forecasts. A major portion of this effort is contingency analysis, or "what if" analysis. Marketing managers can take marketing strategies and test how their success would be affected if conditions changed. For example, a manager may ask, "What if we experience a recession?" or "What if our competition lowers its price?"

In many cases these computerized systems are so sophisticated that most company executives, including the president, have computer terminals in their offices, which leads to more informed marketing personnel. At Banco Internacional de Colombia the computerized system allowed marketing managers the most timely data, a fact which greatly impressed their clients.*

Whether used for analysis in marketing research or as the central component to the Marketing Information System, computers have greatly changed the way marketing managers do their jobs. Without them, much of the analysis and current information needed today to perform marketing activities would not be available. Marketing managers should always try to keep abreast of recent developments in computers. If the competition gets ahead, they will have a differential advantage in the potential to gather and analyze timely marketing information. The company with the most timely information stands the best chance of understanding and winning the favor of target customers.

* Mary Bralove, "Some Chief Executives Bypass, and Irk, Staffs In Getting Information," *Wall Street Journal*, January 12, 1983, pp. 1, 22.

analyze than that of white mice in a laboratory or chemical compounds under controlled conditions.

The environment in which marketing research is conducted is constantly changing. A study made five years ago using the most scientific of methods may be quite useless today. Why? Because people's opinions change. Just think how attitudes toward working women have changed in the last 30 years. In the 1950s women were still expected to stay home, raise a family, and be supportive of their working husbands. Today women not

Figure 3-6

Spending on Research Applications

	Size of Research Budget				
Area Receiving Most Spending	Under $1,000,000	Over $1,000,000	1979 Total	1978 Total	Net Change
Brand attitude and usage tracking	49%	30%	43%	33%	+10%
Consumer product testing	20	63	34	39	− 5
New product screening and evaluation	34	26	32	42	−10
Basic market strategy studies, such as image studies, trade-off or segmentation studies	34	26	31	22	+ 9
Advertising pre-testing and copy testing	24	41	29	29	—
Continuing advertising campaign evaluation and measurement	18	15	17	28	−11
Test marketing	18	11	16	25	− 9

SOURCE: *Advertising Age*, October 15, 1979.

only work but many also consider their role as a homemaker secondary to their outside careers. This attitude change cannot help but affect shopping behavior. For example, working women are much more prone to buy convenience foods, husbands are doing more of the shopping, and many grocery stores have changed their hours to accommodate dual career families.

It is difficult to set up experiments in which marketing problems can be studied exhaustively while all other variables are controlled. For instance, an experiment conducted in a supermarket to determine buyers' reactions to a new package may be affected by the time of day or week, the product's shelf position, competing products on the same shelf, the number of people in the store, and many other unnoted factors.

In addition, new statistical techniques for analyzing data are constantly being developed. Many techniques used regularly today did not even exist 10 years ago. The competent marketing researcher must always strive to remain informed of the newest statistical developments.

Limitations on the Use of Marketing Research

When making a decision, marketing managers would like to have as much relevant information as possible and an unlimited time frame for making it. But these conditions never exist. There is never enough money to pay for all the information marketing management could use, nor is there ever enough time to study every problem fully.

Cost–Benefit Analysis   Well-conducted marketing research is expensive, because it requires the talents of highly trained and experienced personnel—whether a company's own or that of a marketing research firm. In deciding whether or not to conduct a market research study, marketing management must weigh the costs of the project against the anticipated value of the derived information. Obviously, not all marketing decisions justify a formal, structured marketing research study. Some decisions must be based on the experience of marketing management. In general, however, the more important the decision is, the more it warrants an investment in marketing research.

Compared to large businesses, small businesses generally are at a distinct disadvantage, because they cannot afford to conduct formal marketing research studies and must rely on secondary sources of information.

The Time Factor   Some marketing research, especially if it is unsophisticated, can be conducted quickly. Through the use of surveys, for instance, marketers can measure preliminary consumer acceptance of a new movie or automobile model within a few days of its introduction. Most formal marketing research studies, however, require months to design, conduct, and interpret. Unfortunately, some marketing decisions will not wait that long. If a competitor makes a major change in promotional strategy or pricing, for example, a firm may find it necessary to modify its plans in a matter of days or weeks. Therefore, it may be necessary to take intelligent short cuts, such as asking key people for their ideas and suggestions, evaluating articles that may appear in the trade press about the matter, and reviewing past experience.

Industry Practice Restrictions   Often corporate rules restrict the way a marketing research project is conducted. For example, one large retail chain forbids its suppliers to interfere in any way with individual store operations. All suppliers must deal solely with the central office. This policy blocked the research design of a supplier that wanted to gather marketing information by conducting personal interviews of shoppers in the chain's stores. Marketing researchers must be aware that such restrictions do exist and try to develop a viable research design within the framework of these restrictions.

MARKETING INFORMATION SYSTEMS IN PERSPECTIVE

All three components of a Marketing Information System—internal information system, environmental monitoring system, and marketing re-

search—are important to marketing management. However, this information is simply a tool for marketing managers and is of little benefit, no matter how good, if used ineffectively or not at all. For example, Jack A. Madejchick, director of Chevrolet's marketing and information center, noted that marketing research showed consumers were impressed with import cars' price, fuel economy, and quality. He concedes, however, that although Chevrolet knew this, "we had one or two [of these factors] in our small cars but never all three" until 1981.[8] Clearly, marketing information is of little value if management does not act on it.

A Marketing Information System is an aid to thinking, not a substitute for it. Although it can provide information at incredible speeds, it cannot decide what action should be taken. It is true that you can program computers to make what appear, at first glance, to be decisions. For example, a computer can be instructed to direct the production department to increase, decrease, or terminate production of a certain product. But the computer programmer and the manager giving the programmer instructions—not the computer—actually make the decision.

Because designing a Marketing Information System is a highly technical activity, most marketing managers are not trained for it. Nevertheless, because they will make decisions based on the data the system provides,

---

[8] "Why Detroit is not Selling Cars," *Business Week*, August 30, 1982, pp. 63, 66.

they should communicate clearly what information they want, in what format they want it, and how often they need it. Unless properly advised, an overly zealous systems designer might develop a program that provides useless, irrelevant data in a form managers do not understand and at totally inappropriate time intervals. Communication, then, between marketing decision makers and information system experts is a must.

SALES FORECASTING

→ *The* **revenue** *or* **sales forecast** *is an estimate of how much money a firm will receive from sales of its product during a specified period.* Although the planning period is usually one year, estimates are normally broken down into monthly and quarterly predictions.

The sales forecast is the most important operational plan a business makes. All other financial plans are derived directly or indirectly from the sales forecast. For example, sales forecasts tell production managers how much to produce, personnel managers how many people to employ, and senior managers how much money may be available for expansion and modernization programs. Much of the information necessary for sales forecasts is derived from the Market Information System, and the forecasts are often the responsibility of the marketing manager.

HOW FORECASTS ARE MADE

Because revenue is at the crux of all business planning, revenue projections must be as accurate as possible. Some of the common methods used to make sales forecasts are trend extension, executive judgment, customer surveys, salespeople surveys, correlation analysis, time series analysis, and composites of all these methods.

Trend Extension

A simple yet widely used sales forecasting method, especially by small firms, is past sales. After reviewing sales for the past several years, a manager might reason that because sales have increased an average of 10 percent per year, the trend will probably continue, and he might therefore project a 10-percent gain for next year.

Although easy to apply, trend extension has a major limitation: It does not consider changes in product lines, competition, economic conditions, promotional strategies, and marketing management. Because it overlooks changes in both controllable and uncontrollable variables, trend extension is generally not a satisfactory method unless used in combination with other forecasting methods.

Executive Judgment

Using the pooled judgment of key personnel regarding the outlook for sales is also a common forecasting method. To prepare the forecast, each key marketing manager is asked for his or her opinion about future sales. For example, a national company organized into six geographic divisions may ask the divisional managers to predict sales for their particular divisions. Senior executives may then modify the composite estimate. An advantage of the executive judgment method is that it utilizes the combined expertise of the company's most experienced people. A limitation is that it relies on judgment, hunch, and intuition rather than the economic realities of the marketplace.

Customer Surveys

This approach to forecasting involves simply asking customers how much they expect to buy in the sales estimate planning period. Such surveys are often impractical, however, for although they may be feasible for industrial sellers with relatively few customers, they are too expensive and time-consuming to work for consumer goods companies.

One problem associated with customer surveys as a forecasting technique is the fickle nature of customers. Even if they know how much they plan to buy, they may decide to purchase from another supplier. In addition this forecasting device neither takes into account new business the firm may be trying to win, nor considers changes in the firm's controllable and uncontrollable environment.

Salespeople Surveys

A common forecasting method is asking sales representatives to estimate future sales for their territories and making a composite prediction from these estimates. An advantage of this approach is that salespeople know their customers' needs and the market conditions within their territories. A problem often arising is that their estimates may either be too optimistic, because salespeople are sometimes overly bullish about the future, or intentionally pessimistic so their quotas will be set low, making them look better and assuring them of larger commissions or bonuses.

Correlation Analysis

This method consists of finding a relationship between past sales and some other factor(s). For example, sales of steel relate closely (correlate) to overall economic activity, specifically to sales of automobiles and construction materials. When using correlation analysis to project sales, the forecaster makes estimates based on what is happening or likely to happen in another industry or in the overall economy. For instance, a firm specializing in marketing materials to home builders may project a sales decline if housing starts drop off. Correlation analysis is more sophisticated than the previously mentioned approaches, but often costs too much in time and money to be useful. For one thing, it is practically impossible to use correlation analysis without the aid of a computer.

Time Series Analysis

Often used for short-range forecasts (less than one month), time series analysis is actually a collection of different techniques that tries to analyze a past sales pattern and project it into the future. Its major advantage is that these techniques are relatively quick and inexpensive to use. The prime disadvantage is that it ignores all environmental elements: Only previous sales are analyzed.

Composite of Forecasting Methods

In practice a forecaster can use elements of each of these forecasting methods in predicting sales. In addition he or she should also consider changes in the company's marketing mix, that is, modifications in the product line, distribution system, promotional plans, or pricing structure. In the last analysis all forecasts are judgments, because no one knows what conditions will affect the future.

What Forecasting Methods Do Companies Actually Use?

It should come as no surprise that different forecasting methods are used for different forecast situations. We describe forecast situations by how far into the future we must make the forecast (one month versus two years, for example) and the corporate level of the forecast (individual-product forecasts versus company-sales forecasts).

A recent survey of the marketing managers responsible for forecasting in 160 U.S. companies found that they used time series methods most often for product forecasts of less than three months into the future.[9] As the level moved from product forecasts to corporate forecasts and time moved from three months up to two years, time series became less important whereas correlation analysis and executive judgment became more important. Thus, marketing managers rely on inexpensive time series methods for the many product-level, short-range forecasts, but they apparently feel more confident with their own judgment or with correlation analysis for the more important corporate, long-range forecasts.

---

[9] John T. Mentzer and James E. Cox, Jr., "Familiarity, Application, and Performance of Sales Forecasting Techniques," *Journal of Forecasting*, January–March 1984, pp. 27–36.

Surprisingly, the accuracy of forecasts in all companies was quite good. Accuracy—measured by the formula, Accuracy = $100 - |100 \times$ (Forecast − Sales)/Sales|—ranged from a high of 92 percent to a low of 74 percent. Thus, even the company with the poorest accuracy was only experiencing a 26-percent error rate in its forecasts.

WHAT IS THE FUTURE OF MIS/MARKETING RESEARCH?

In the years ahead sophisticated computer applications will have greater influence on developing information for marketing decisions. Thus, we can expect to see fewer marketing decisions based on guesswork and hunch as mathematical tools and computer science become used more frequently to obtain and process information relevant to marketing problems.

As research techniques improve, marketing managers will find it easier to implement the marketing concept. When more and better marketing information is processed quickly, marketing managers can select target customers more scientifically and make better use of the marketing controllable variables to fulfill consumer needs.

We will also find much more data converted from numbers into graphs and other pictorial displays, a process called **computer mapping** or **computer graphics.** Instead of reading numbers, data users can see what is happening to sales by geographic area, product lines, customers, retail outlets, and so on.

Increasingly, computers will display information in color, using different colors to indicate different conditions. For example, one company uses 5 colors to indicate sales volume for 16 different regions in the United States. Managers can tell at a glance how well the marketing program is going in each region. Colors indicating lower-than-projected results pinpoint where corrective action is needed. As one observer notes,

> Indeed, the marketing concept of gearing innovation and distribution to the wants and needs of customers and prospects will be made far more operational. In the past, manufacturing and financial managements have had "the numbers" and the powerful decision aids needed to reduce the areas for unaided judgment. Now, marketing management (and corporate management with a marketing orientation) will achieve as much or more risk-reduction and speedy reflexes for anticipating and managing dynamic competitive and environmental change.[10]

---

[10] Patrick J. Robinson, "'80s," *Marketing News,* November 16, 1979, p. 11.

The advent of personal computers can only enhance this process. Think of the potential for research and analysis when every executive has a computer terminal! One retail network (NAPA) can cost justify these personal computers in any store with over $25,000 in sales, so that even a small retail store manager has access to much marketing research information and analysis.[11]

SUMMARY

- Marketing Information Systems (MIS) are designed to provide immediate updates on critical information, such as inventory size and location and product sales. They are becoming more popular because of the increasing use of computers in business.
- MIS is composed of the Internal Information System, the environmental monitoring system, and marketing research.
- Marketing research is the systematic gathering, recording, and analyzing of data related to the marketing of goods and services.
- The marketing research process consists of: problem definition, examination of secondary data, problem refinement, primary data gathering, data analysis, recommendations, and implementation and feedback.
- Primary and secondary data are used in marketing research. Primary data comes from original research; secondary data consists of information already available from such sources as government publications and trade associations.
- The key advantages of primary data are that it (a) provides information tailored to specific situations and (b) is practical. The limitations of primary data are that it (a) is expensive, (b) is time-consuming, and (c) often provides information already available from secondary sources.
- The main advantages of secondary data are that it is (a) inexpensive, (b) is easy to obtain, and (c) requires little time to gather. The limitations of secondary data are (a) its limited applicability and (b) the possibility that the information may be out of date.
- Probability samples are more accurate representations of the research population than less expensive, more convenient nonprobability samples.
- Three basic methods are used in conducting marketing research: the experimental method, which involves testing an idea or a product on target customers; the survey method, which involves asking people ques-

[11] John T. Mentzer, "Technological Developments in Order Processing Systems," *International Journal of Physical Distribution and Materials Management*, No. 8, 1981, pp. 15–21.

tions about the problem being studied; and the observational method, which involves first-hand observation of consumer behavior.
- Good marketing research should be rational, objective, precise, and honestly interpreted.
- Marketing research is often constrained by costs, time, and industry practices.
- The sales or revenue forecast is an estimate of how much money a firm will receive from sales of its product during a specified period.
- Sales forecasts are made by (a) trend extension, (b) executive judgment, (c) customer surveys, (d) salespeople surveys, (e) correlation analysis, (f) time series analysis, and (g) composites of all these methods.
- Marketing managers typically use time series forecasting for short-range, product forecasts, but correlation analysis and executive judgment for long-range, corporate forecasts.

DISCUSSION QUESTIONS

1. How do marketing research and Marketing Information Systems differ in regard to the kinds of intelligence they provide marketing managers?
2. Explain the steps involved in a marketing research project.
3. What kinds of marketing problems are best solved by collecting primary data? Secondary data?
4. Why is it important to use secondary data to refine the problem before gathering primary data?
5. Select two types of probability and two nonprobability samples. Explain what makes them probability or nonprobability samples.
6. Under what circumstances is the experimental method the best marketing research method? Give four examples of marketing problems that might be solved through the experimental method.
7. What are the principal advantages and disadvantages of the survey method? How do you account for the extensive use of this research method?
8. What kinds of marketing problems might best be solved through observational research?
9. What do cost–benefit analysis, the time factor, and industry practice have to do with marketing research?
10. Discuss the pros and cons of each of the following forecasting techniques: trend extension, executive judgment, customer surveys, salespeople surveys, correlation analysis, and time series analysis. Why is a composite of all forecasting techniques a wise approach?

APPLICATION EXERCISES

1. A friend of yours wants to open a fast-food carry-out restaurant in your town. She plans to feature only one basic item—chili—and wants to call her restaurant The International House of Chili. Her plan calls for selling Japanese chili, German chili, Mexican chili, French chili, and so on, using recipes from those countries. Design a marketing research study to determine the potential for this restaurant. Who are the target customers? How would you gain information from them? What secondary data would you use? What research method? What type of sample?

2. A regional auto parts chain has hired you as a consultant. Through your observations you have concluded that one of the company's main problems is the lack of a formal Marketing Information System. Give a persuasive, thorough presentation to management to convince them that a Marketing Information System is vital to the company's future success. Use specific examples of the types and applications of readily available data and your proposed design for their MIS.

3. You are a college senior looking at career opportunities. How would you develop your personal Marketing Information System to explore your career possibilities? What sources of data could you use? What marketing research would you do?

CASE 3
Cars for Working Women[12]

In spite of large research budgets and huge corporate information systems, the U.S. auto industry always seems to be playing catch up with changes in consumer desires. This was certainly evident in the 1970's when Detroit product designers chose to ignore evidence that buyers wanted smaller, more fuel-efficient, quality cars and insisted instead on building the traditional large, more luxurious cars. The industry is still suffering from the resulting competitive inroads made by foreign imports.

A more recent example of the industry's failure to integrate research and marketing in a timely manner is its advertising approach to women. Research findings indicate that the percentage of working women has increased from 33 percent to 52 percent in the last 20 years. This dramatic increase has had an impact on their car-buying behavior. For instance, in 1982 women accounted for 40 percent of new-car

---

[12] Laurie Ashcraft, "Marketers Miss Their Target When They Eschew Research," *Marketing News,* January 7, 1983, pp. 10–11.

purchases—up from 21 percent in 1972—and actually influenced 80 percent of the remaining purchases. In addition women buy 60 percent of all service contracts.

For the most part U.S. car ads have failed to incorporate knowledge gained from these statistics. The typical ad continues to show women perched on the hood or otherwise admiring a car's appearance rather than behind the wheel. In short these ads have failed to evolve with the "car sense" of women drivers. As a result, according to a study sponsored by Conde Nast Publications, Inc., 47 percent of women feel that car ads do not effectively communicate to them.

To their credit some U.S. auto manufacturers are changing their mix to reflect the reality that "women do more than pick out the color of the upholstery." They are also training salespeople to effectively deal with women in showrooms, and advertising spots are attempting to appeal to women as serious and knowledgeable car buyers.

Detroit is, however, lagging behind other industries that have combined marketing and research teamwork to stay on top of trends. One example, the campaign for Enjoli fragrance, which pictures a woman as sassy, independent, and in control of her situation, has been on the leading edge of capturing the "new woman" trend. The number of women who said the Enjoli woman was like themselves has jumped from 30 percent to 56 percent in two years. Another example, the "take charge of your life" ads for Jean Nate fragrance, helped that declining brand (introduced in the 1930s!) double sales in three years.

Discussion Questions

1. If you were a marketing manager for Ford, how would you use this information on working women to market cars to them?
2. What other information on working women would you want before designing your marketing strategy?
3. Outline a marketing research project to gather this information.

CHAPTER 3 APPENDIX
Secondary Sources for Marketing Research

PRIVATE SOURCES

Business Periodicals Index (H.W. Wilson Co.; New York, New York)

This is the basic index to nearly 300 periodicals covering all areas of business. Sample headings include:

Business Forecasting
Forecasting
Earnings Forecasting
Sales Forecasting

Conference Board Statistical Bulletin (Conference Board; New York, New York)

Published monthly, the *CBSB* provides the status of leading economic indicators as to rising, level, or declining. Additional indicators include business executives' expectations, help-wanted advertising, and indexes of consumer confidence and buying plans.

Consumer Market Developments (Fairchild Publications; New York, New York)

Provides statement on current trends as well as statistics and trends in areas of population, household living arrangements, school enrollment, labor force, income, and personal consumption expenditures. Fairchild publishes about 20 other fact files in addition to this one. Most deal with various consumer products, such as clothing, appliances, housewares, furniture, and cosmetics.

Directory of Directories: An Annotated Guide to Business and Industrial Directories, Professional and Scientific Rosters, and Other Lists and Guides of All Kinds (Gale Research Company; Detroit, Michigan)

Detailed information on nearly 6,800 directories are included in this, as well as a title and subject index.

Directory of Industry Data Sources (Harfax; Cambridge, Massachusetts)

Over 10,000 sources that identify and describe published documents and research are listed. Among the contents are market research reports, investment banking studies, special issues of industry journals, and research data bases. Covers about 60 industries and includes a listing of forecasts available in volume 2.

Encyclopedia of Associations (Gale Research Company; Detroit, Michigan)

This is the basic guide to U.S. associations. Three major parts are included: (1) national organizations, (2) geographic and executive indexes, and (3) new associations and projects. This is very useful for consulting trade and manufacturers associations.

F and S Index: United States (Predicasts Inc., Cleveland, Ohio)

Over 1,000 business and trade journals are indexed by industries and products in major industry groups and alphabetically by company name.

Handbook of Basic Economic Statistics (Economic Statistics Bureau; Washington, D.C.)

Issued monthly, this is a compact compilation of more than 1,800 statistical series relating to all aspects of the national economy. The contents are selected and condensed from the data released by the federal government.

Million Dollar Directory (Dun and Bradstreet Corp.; Parsippany, New Jersey)

These three volumes list about 120,000 U.S. businesses with a net worth of at least $500,000. Companies are arranged alphabetically, geographically by state, and by standard industrial classification number. Information available includes address, telephone, sales, number of employees, major officers, and line of business by SIC.

Moody's Manuals (Moody's Investors Service; New York, New York)

Published yearly and updated weekly, Moody's covers seven basic areas: industrials, OTC industrials, transportation, banks and finance, public utilities, municipal and government, and international. Information included for each company consists of history, subsidiaries, principal operations, business and products, plus income accounts and balance sheets, major officers, number of employees, and address.

Sales and Marketing Management: Survey of Buying Power (Sales and Marketing Management; New York, New York)

This annual has two parts. Part I includes survey highlights and national, regional, state, county, and city data. Contains items regarding age breakdown of population, retail sales by store group, and percentage of households in effective buying income categories. Part II lists market projections to 1986 in areas of population, income, and retail sales. Also contains a survey on newspaper and TV markets.

Survey of Buying Power Data Service (Sales and Marketing Management; New York, New York)

This publication began several years ago and is very important to sales forecasting. It includes information on population, household income distribution, buying income, and retail sales. TV market data and metropolitan and county market projections for population, effective buying income, and retail sales.

Standard and Poor's Industry Surveys (Standard and Poor's Corporation; New York, New York)

Published in two volumes every quarter, this provides an in-depth analysis of 34 industries, extensive commentary and information containing nearly 1,500 companies, and includes future trends as well.

Statistics Sources: A Subject Guide to Data on Industrial, Business, Social, Educational, Financial, and other Topics for the United States and Internationally. (Gale Research Company; Detroit, Michigan)

Arranged alphabetically by subject. For each subject the publications in which statistics on that subject can be found are listed.

Statistical Reference Index (Congressional Information Service; Bethesda, Maryland)

This is a selective guide to American statistical publications from private organizations, state government sources, associations, business organizations, and trade journals. Sample headings include:

Business Outlook Surveys
Population Projections
Projections

Thomas Register of American Manufacturers (Thomas Publishing Company; New York, New York)

Over 115,000 U.S. companies are included. Volumes 1–9 list products and service; volumes 10–11 include company profiles—addresses, phone numbers, assets, sales offices, and distributors; and volumes 12–17 include company catalogs. Volume 12 also includes about 500 pages of trademark names.

Wall Street Journal Index (Dow Jones Company; New York, New York)

Comprehensive index to the *Wall Street Journal* consists of a company index and general index.

FEDERAL SOURCES

Periodicals

Business Conditions Digest (U.S. Department of Commerce, Bureau of Economic Analysis; Washington, D.C.)

This monthly publication provides a look at many of the economic time series found most useful by business analysts and forecasters. Includes cyclical indicators and other important economic measures such as gross national product, personal income, prices, wages, labor force, and unemployment.

Economic Indicators (Council of Economic Advisers; Washington, D.C.)

This gives retrospective information in a variety of areas, such as personal consumption expenditures, personal income, employment—unemployment, wages, business sales and inventories, prices, interest rates, and exports—imports.

Monthly Labor Review (U.S. Department of Labor, Bureau of Labor Statistics; Washington, D.C.)

Includes monthly data on employment and consumer price index changes, as well as statistics on wage and compensation data.

Survey of Current Business (U.S. Department of Commerce, Bureau of Economic Analysis; Washington, D.C.)

Includes articles on current business as well as statistics on a monthly basis. Also deals with production, inventories, retail trade, and foreign trade.

Other

American Statistics Index (Congressional Information Service; Washington, D.C.)

This monthly publication serves as a comprehensive guide and index to the statistical publications of the U.S. government. Consult index volume under heading of "Projections."

County Business Patterns (U.S. Department of Commerce, Bureau of the Census; Washington, D.C.)

Includes a county-by-county listing of various business establishments in terms of employees, payroll and number of establishments by employee size. Useful in analyzing market potentials, establishing sales quotas, and locating facilities.

Measuring Markets: A Guide to the Use of Federal and State Statistical Data (U.S. Department of Commerce, Industry and Trade Administration; Washington, D.C.)

This is an excellent publication that ties together various federal and state statistical publications in 12 hypothetical marketing and forecasting situations. It also includes information on the types of data useful for measuring markets published by federal and state governments. Statistics for population, income, employment, and sales are listed. Contains an excellent bibliography for additional references.

Statistical Abstract of the United States (U.S. Department of Commerce, Bureau of the Census; Washington, D.C.)

Published since 1878, the *Statistical Abstract* is the standard summary of statistics on the social, political, and economic organization of the United States. It is designed to serve as a convenient volume for statistical reference and as a guide to other statistical publications and sources. The last chapter includes "Recent Trends" in a number of selected categories.

U.S. Industrial Outlook for 200 Industries with Projections for 1986 (U.S. Department of Commerce; Washington, D.C.)

Includes over 50 major categories as well as an outlook for 1986 and long-term prospects. A list of additional references is also included at the end of each category.

CENSUS PUBLICATIONS

Census of Population and Housing

Includes general population characteristics, number of inhabitants, and summary characteristics for governmental units and SMSAs. Such facts as race, age, sex, household size, place of birth, years of school completed, marital history, place of work, travel time to work, occupation, and income are listed. Housing features include rooms, persons in unit, plumbing facilities, year structure was built, air conditioning, fuels for heating and cooking, mortgage status, and vehicles available. *Census Tracts* break down the above information into smaller divisions of SMSAs.

Census of Retail Trade

Arranged alphabetically by state, this publication includes retail sales of all establishments, percentage of change in sales of all establishments, percentage of change in sales and payroll from 1972 to 1977, number of particular retail establishments, sales, and kind of business groups by county.

Census of Service Industries

Includes data on such service industries as hotels, motels, personal and business services, automotive and miscellaneous repair, amusement and recreation services, dental and legal services, engineering, architectural, and surveying services, and establishments that are exempt from federal income tax under provisions of section 501 of the Internal Revenue Code. SMSA and county breakdowns are included.

Census of Wholesale Trade

Includes information on wholesale firms arranged by the U.S. as a whole, each state, each SMSA, each county, and each community over 2,500 population. Also includes number of establishments, sales, operating expenses, operating expenses as a percentage of sales, payroll, and number of employees.

Census of Manufacturers

Data are included on manufacturing firms by SIC number. Also, there are divisions by geographic area such as state, county, city, and SMSA.

Additional data from various censuses can be acquired in microfiche, prints from microfiche, and computer tapes. These are sold by the Customer Services Branch, Data Users Services Division, Bureau of the Census, Washington, D.C. 20233. Also, government documents can be consulted at various college, university, and larger public libraries. Department of Commerce International Trade Administration and Domestic Commerce Offices are located in Cleveland and Cincinnati. Small Business Administration offices can also provide assistance in using and consulting government publications.

TWO

Understanding
the Marketplace

CHAPTER

4 Demographic Analysis

STUDY OBJECTIVES

After studying this chapter, you should be able to

1. Discuss demographic data as it is used to segment markets.
2. Describe various demographic trends in our population.
3. Explain how those trends affect marketing.
4. Define such terms as Standard Metropolitan Statistical Area and Standard Consolidated Statistical Area.

I n Part One we discussed marketing and the importance of the consumer to the marketing concept. Marketing research and the Marketing Information System are key elements in studying consumers. But who are the consumers? Where do they live? How old are they? How much do they earn? Are they male or female? Are they married? Do they have children? How much education do they have? The answers to all these questions lie in something called demographics. **Demographics** *is the statistical study of populations with reference to their size, density, distribution, and vital statistics.*

It is important to understand demographics, because marketing managers use this information to break a population into homogenous segments (market segmentation) and eventually identify the segment (target market) to which the company wants to market its product.

For example, when Payless Cashways (a home improvement retailer) recently conducted a marketing research study to identify its target market, it found that its biggest customer segment was college-educated, white-collar males in their mid-30s with annual family incomes of more than $30,000.[1] This information was very helpful in identifying a marketing strategy to reach potential customers.

Using demographics, markets can be segmented in many ways, as Figure 4-1 shows. In our examination of demographics we will consider the entire U.S. population and its characteristics. Marketing managers are interested in broad population characteristics because they indicate:

- The size and characteristics of target markets
- The distribution of the population by geography and age
- Mobility trends of the population

In segmenting target markets marketing managers examine broad as well as highly specific changes in population characteristics. For example, when making store-location decisions, a marketing manager may need to be aware of changes in population size in different parts of a city. The Bureau of the Census, Department of Commerce, provides very detailed demographic information on a census-tract basis, including, among other items, information on the land area, population, birth rate, death rate, employment by type of industry, average weekly and hourly earnings, unemployment, adjusted gross income, crime rate, and median years of school completed by inhabitants in each metropolitan area, as well as various statistics pertaining to retail and wholesale trade. Here we will consider only general demographic factors.

---

[1] "Payless: Zeroing in on Suburbia," *Business Week,* September 7, 1981, pp. 104, 108.

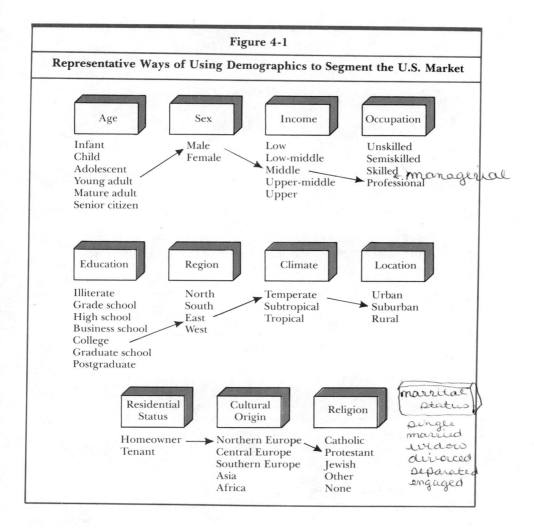

Figure 4-1

Representative Ways of Using Demographics to Segment the U.S. Market

Age	Sex	Income	Occupation
Infant	Male	Low	Unskilled
Child	Female	Low-middle	Semiskilled
Adolescent		Middle	Skilled & *managerial*
Young adult		Upper-middle	Professional
Mature adult		Upper	
Senior citizen			

Education	Region	Climate	Location
Illiterate	North	Temperate	Urban
Grade school	South	Subtropical	Suburban
High school	East	Tropical	Rural
Business school	West		
College			
Graduate school			
Postgraduate			

Residential Status	Cultural Origin	Religion	*marital status*
Homeowner	Northern Europe	Catholic	*single*
Tenant	Central Europe	Protestant	*married*
	Southern Europe	Jewish	*widow*
	Asia	Other	*divorced*
	Africa	None	*separated*
			engaged

POPULATION

In 1984 the population of the United States was estimated to be 233 million. Over the past three decades we have experienced continuous but uneven growth, as Figure 4-2 illustrates. The female percentage of the population, for instance, has remained relatively stable, but the median age for both sexes has increased slightly. Figure 4-3, which shows the birth and death rates for 1960–82, may help explain this aging of the population. Notice that while the death rate remained stable, the birth rate dropped from 24 to 16 births per 1,000 population due to factors such as a lower marriage rate, or increased acceptance of birth control, and a vast increase

Profile

George H. Gallup (1901–1984)

Since 1934 public opinion polls have provided valuable information for marketers, politicians, educators, and many others. Prior to that time, the accuracy of such polls was doubtful. Dr. George H. Gallup pioneered many of the techniques that today ensure credible results from the survey method of information gathering.

Journalism was George Gallup's first love. He created and published the *Daily Iowan* for his school, the University of Iowa, located in Gallup's home town of Jefferson. The town had no newspapers, and the *Daily Iowan* eventually was circulated to Jefferson residents in addition to university students.

After receiving his Ph.D., Gallup remained at the university for nine years, teaching journalism and psychology. He conducted surveys that focused primarily on readership of newspaper news articles, features, and advertisements.

In 1932 Gallup expanded his journalistic interests to include advertising. He became, in that year, director of research for Young and Rubicam, an advertising agency in New York City. He developed statistical methods for measuring consumer reaction to printed advertisements and other matters related to products advertised by the firm.

In 1933 Gallup expanded his quest for public opinion data to politics. He directed a campaign in which his mother-in-law, Ola Babcock Miller, became Iowa's first Democratic (and first woman) Secretary of State.

Gallup established the American Institute of Public Opinion in 1935. His objective was to measure the public's attitudes on social, political, and economic issues. He was the dominant influence behind several other organizations, including the International Association of Public Opinion Institutes, of which he was president, and Gallup and Robinson, organized to conduct advertising and marketing research, of which he was chairman emeritus.

Gallup based his techniques on a theory of "probable error due to size of sample," or, more simply, probability sampling. He once illustrated the theory by using 2,500 black and white beans. Gallup demonstrated that in only three out of every thousand samples would the proportion of black to white vary from the proportion found in the total 2,500.

For public response surveys the Gallup organization divides the country into descending tiers, according to population. The first tier is the size-of-community stratum, in which cities and rural areas are placed in one of seven categories. These categories range from cities with population of one million or more down to farm or open-country rural areas. Within each size-of-community division, the population is zoned into equal-sized groups of sampling units. Units are further subdivided into blocks or block clusters, where census data is available. Where statistics are not known, blocks or block clusters are drawn at random, each with an equal probability of being selected.

Interviewers are assigned particular housing units to visit and, typically, particular individuals to question. Gallup interviewers are relieved of responsibility in picking the people to be interviewed, Dr. Gallup said, because interviewers who choose their subjects tend to report responses only from the people who are easiest to get at and to question. The interviews are validated, again by sampling, through phone calls or letters to those who responded.

Dr. Gallup estimated the accuracy of this polling method, used since 1950, to be within 1 or 2 percent. It was not always so, however. Gallup's most famous error occurred in 1948, when he predicted that Thomas E. Dewey would take the vote from Harry S. Truman in their race for the presidency. Gallup later recognized that the error was caused by closing the poll too far in advance of election day and by disregarding the votes of those who were undecided when questioned.

His techniques have attained such a high degree of accuracy since then, however, that the U.S. Bureau of the Census and the Department of Agriculture use methods of gathering information that he developed.

Though he is best known for forecasting the outcome of presidential elections and sampling public opinion on other political issues, he was very active in marketing research. He founded Audience Research, Inc., in 1939 for the purpose of researching reactions to radio programs, book and movie titles, casts and stories.

"My chief advice to marketing students," Dr. Gallup told the author, "is to develop a marketing point of view."

> I mean by this that they should not think of marketing only in terms of dealing with the problems of A&P or General Electric or the other big corporations, but should apply what they have learned to the stores in their own towns and to the problems of products sold there. If they can begin to find answers at this level, they will find them at the top level also, because basically they are the same.

in the number of abortions. Thus, fewer young children and more older people combine to raise the average age for the population.

The decline in the overall birth rate has affected our economy in many ways. Industries that depend primarily on infant and very young consumers—such as the toy, infant and children's wear, and elementary-

Figure 4-2			
U.S. Population Information: 1960 to 1980			
	1960	**1970**	**1980**
Population	179,323,798	203,302,031	226,545,805
Percent change from previous decade	18.5	13.4	11.4
Percent Male	49.3	48.7	48.9
Percent Female	50.7	51.3	51.1
Median Age:			
Male	28.7	26.8	28.8
Female	30.3	29.3	31.3

SOURCE: Department of Commerce, Bureau of the Census, *Statistical Abstract of the United States, 1984*, pp. 9, 31.

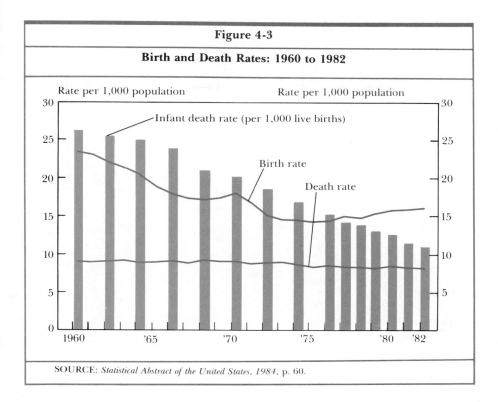

Figure 4-3

Birth and Death Rates: 1960 to 1982

Rate per 1,000 population   Rate per 1,000 population

Infant death rate (per 1,000 live births)

Birth rate

Death rate

SOURCE: *Statistical Abstract of the United States, 1984*, p. 60.

school construction industries—have experienced a reduction in demand. Fewer college students in the 1980s will prepare for careers in elementary education and related professions.

Barring some unforeseeable calamity, such as an uncontrollable epidemic, the death rate is highly predictable. Advances in medical and biological sciences in the years ahead may extend life expectancy by a decade or more, but these changes come slowly.

The future birth rate is more difficult to predict, because birth can be controlled. Casket manufacturers and morticians can predict the long-term demand for their products and services with much greater precision than manufacturers of diapers, baby bottles, and children's furniture.

Are we likely to see a return to the high birth rates of the 1950s and 1960s? One observer notes:

> the fact that the number of births has fishooked up somewhat in the past couple of years has led to speculation that we may be verging on another baby boom. Richard Easterlin, an economist at the University of Pennsylvania, supports that belief with his theory that birthrates are determined by the economic conditions that people of reproductive ages see around them. During

	Figure 4-4			
	Age Distribution: 1960 to 1982			
	Percentage of Total Population			**Percentage of Change**
Age	**1960**	**1970**	**1982**	**1960–82**
Under 5	11.3	8.5	7.5	−33.6
5–9	10.4	9.8	6.9	−33.7
10–14	9.4	10.2	7.8	−17.0
15–19	7.4	9.4	8.5	+14.9
20–24	5.9	8.1	9.4	+59.3
25–29	6.1	6.6	8.9	+45.9
30–34	6.7	5.6	8.1	+20.9
35–39	7.0	5.5	6.8	− 2.9
40–44	6.5	5.9	5.4	−16.9
45–49	6.0	6.0	4.8	−20.0
50–54	5.4	5.5	4.9	− 9.3
55–59	4.7	4.9	5.0	+ 6.4
60–64	4.0	4.2	4.6	+15.0
65 or over	9.2	9.8	11.6	+26.1

SOURCE: *Statistical Abstract of the United States, 1984*, p. 33.

the Depression, birthrates came down to historic lows. In recent years, people of childbearing age have had to scratch for an education and for jobs; they observed a cruel world, and down came the rates again. Now that there are going to be fewer of them, however, the new young people should find conditions better; with their growing sense of well-being, Easterlin thinks, will come earlier marriages and higher birthrates.[2]

Many demographers agree that the birth rate in the United States and in most industrialized nations will increase over the next decade, but few agree on how large the increase will be.[3]

The shift in population to older age groups has been equally as important to marketers as the change in birth rate. Figure 4-4 shows the percentage of U.S. population in common age categories. Clearly, the U.S. is getting older. As we said before, this has serious implications for marketers of children's toys (all groups up to age 15 are losing size), but creates considerable opportunities for companies marketing products to older

[2] Walter Guzzardi, "Demography's Good News for the Eighties," *Fortune*, November 5, 1979, p. 96.

[3] John J. Fialka, "Another Baby Boom Seems Near, but Experts Disagree on Its Size," *Wall Street Journal*, March 4, 1982, p. 31.

Americans. Categories experiencing large growth (55 years of age and over) have consumers with larger incomes, fewer children at home, and more leisure time. Marketing managers are already reacting to this opportunity by placing advertisements for such luxuries as premium liquors, plush hotels, and fine crystal in magazines aimed at the 55 and over consumer.[4]

Other marketers after the fast-growing 30–45 group have also reacted:

> Look at the latest gaggle of new products: Gillette is spending $17 million to launch Aapri, a mass-marketed facial scrub made of crushed apricot seeds. Privately owned Estee Lauder is plumping its Swiss Age-Controlling Skincare program. Sold through department stores, it is being heavily promoted. Revlon, meanwhile, is touting its recently introduced European Collagen Complex, which boasts a "new" natural skin softener. Avon is also launching a cream with collagen called Acolade. Early last year Elizabeth Arden gushingly introduced "cell renewal accelerating" Millenium. A full skin care regimen, it retails for $95.
>
> What's behind all this activity? Jim Waggoner, an analyst at Bear, Stearns, says, "Women and men aged 30 to 45 are the fastest-growing segment of the U.S. population. Those people wake up one day and say, 'That's not me in the mirror, is it?' So the cosmetics manufacturers are merely meeting the current product needs of their aging customers."[5]

As the last example illustrates, the needs, wants, and spending habits of consumers change in predictable ways as they grow older. Taken collectively, the people in any one age bracket will demand different products as they grow older. The study of age-related changes in demand is called **life-cycle analysis.**

Various ways have been developed to classify consumers into stages based on age. A model developed by Wells and Gubar follows:

1. The bachelor stage: young, single people
2. Newly married couples: young, no children
3. The full nest I: young married couples with youngest child under six
4. The full nest II: young married couples with youngest child six or over

---

[4] "Discovering the Over-50 Set," *Business Week,* November 19, 1979, pp. 194–95.

[5] Howard Rudnitsky and Janet Bamford, "Vanity, Thy Name is Profit," *Forbes,* May 25, 1981, pp. 47–48.

5. The full nest III: older married couples with dependent children
6. The empty nest I: older married couples, no children living with them, head in labor force
7. The empty nest II: older married couples, no children living with them, head retired
8. The solitary survivors: older single people
   a. In labor force
   b. Retired[6]

Figure 4-5, which is an overview of the life cycle described by the Wells and Gubar model, suggests how demand changes as people move from one stage to another. The chart assumes people marry and have a family. But demand changes with age even for people who never marry and for those couples who do not have children, although not necessarily as shown in the chart.

Finally, population growth has been quite uneven among the states. Between 1970 and 1982, 9 of the 50 states accounted for 64 percent of the 28,232,000 population growth—California with 4,753,000; Texas 4,082,000; Florida 3,624,000; Arizona 1,085,000; Georgia 1,051,000; North Carolina 934,000; Virginia 839,000; Colorado 835,000; and Washington 832,000.[7] This geographical shift in population helps marketing managers who are trying to establish their products in areas of the country with a high potential for population growth. For example, the shift of population to the Sun Belt recently led middle- to high-income Chicago retailer Marshall Field to change its marketing strategy. While trying to maintain its dominant position in the Chicago area, Marshall Field is also investing $45 million opening stores in Texas alone.[8] This is largely a recognition of the growing affluent population (Marshall Field's target market) moving to Texas.

URBAN CONCENTRATION OF POPULATION

Our population is becoming increasingly urban. In 1980, 75 percent of the population lived in ~~one of~~ the 318 **Standard Metropolitan Statistical Areas (SMSAs).** An SMSA is defined by the Bureau of the Census as:

1. One city with 50,000 or more inhabitants, or
2. A city with at least 25,000 inhabitants, which, together with contiguous places (incorporated or unincorporated) having population

---

[6] William D. Wells and George Gubar, "Life Cycle Concept in Marketing Research," *Journal of Marketing Research,* November 1966, pp. 355–63.

[7] *Statistical Abstract of the United States, 1984,* p. 14.

[8] "Marshall Field: Seeking New Markets in the South and West," *Business Week,* March 23, 1981, pp. 125, 129.

Figure 4-5

An Overview of the Life Cycle

Bachelor Stage: Young, Single People Not Living at Home	Newly Married Couples: Young, No Children	Full Nest I: Youngest Child Under Six	Full Nest II: Youngest Child Six or Over Six
Few financial burdens.	Better off financially than they will be in near future.	Home purchasing at peak.	Financial position better.
Fashion opinion leaders.	Highest purchase rate and highest average purchase of durables.	Liquid assets low.	Some wives work.
Recreation oriented.		Dissatisfied with financial position and amount of money saved.	Less influenced by advertising.
Buy: Basic kitchen equipment, basic furniture, cars, equipment for the mating game, vacations.	Buy: Cars, refrigerators, stoves, sensible and durable furniture, vacations.	Interested in new products.	Buy larger-sized packages, multiple-unit deals.
		Like advertised products.	Buy: Many foods, cleaning materials, bicycles, music lessons, pianos.
		Buy: Washers, driers, TV, baby food, chest rubs and cough medicine, vitamins, dolls, wagons, sleds, skates.	

SOURCE: William D. Wells and George Gubar, "Life Cycle Concept in Marketing Research," *Journal of Marketing Research*, November 1966, pp. 355–63.

---

densities of at least 1,000 persons per square mile, has a combined population of 50,000 and constitutes for general economic and social purposes a single community, provided that the county or counties in which the city and contiguous places are located has a total population of at least 100,000 (75,000 in New England).[9]

Figure 4-6 lists the populations of our 36 largest SMSAs. Collectively, they account for 40 percent of the total population. Some of these SMSAs are part of a new urban classification started by the Bureau of Census

[9] *Statistical Abstract of the United States, 1981,* p. 935.

Full Nest III: Older Married Couples with Dependent Children	Empty Nest I: Older Married Couples, No Children Living with Them, Head in Labor Force	Empty Nest II: Older Married Couples, No Children Living with Them, Head Retired	Solitary Survivor: In Labor Force	Solitary Survivor: Retired
Financial position still better. More wives work. Some children get jobs. Hard to influence with advertising. High average purchase of durables. Buy: New, more tasteful furniture, auto travel, nonnecessary appliances, boats, dental services, magazines.	Home ownership at peak. Most satisfied with financial position and money saved. Interested in travel, recreation, self-education. Make gifts and contributions. Not interested in new products. Buy: Vacations, luxuries, home improvements.	Drastic cut in income. Keep home. Buy: Medical appliances, medical care, products which aid health, sleep, and digestion.	Income still good but likely to sell home.	Same medical and product needs as other retired group; drastic cut in income. Special need for attention, affection, and security.

called **Standard Consolidated Statistical Areas (SCSAs).** Also termed a **megalopolis**, the SCSA is two or more contiguous SMSAs. Figure 4-7 lists the 16 SCSAs and their populations.[10]

---

[10] As of January 1983, the terms SMSA and SCSA were revised into three categories. Major urban areas (such as New York) are called Consolidated Metropolitan Statistical Areas—CMSAs. Major urban areas within CMSAs are called Primary Metropolitan Statistical Areas—PMSAs. Urban areas that stand alone (such as Roanoke, VA) are called Metropolitan Statistical Areas—MSAs. For a further description, see Eugene Carlson, "Soon MSA, PMSA, and CMSA will Replace Good Old SMSA," *Wall Street Journal,* October 12, 1981, p. 33; and "Census Data to Reflect More Precise Geographic Definitions," *Marketing News,* January 21, 1983, p. 20.

The U.S. Constitution provides for a census of the population every 10 years, primarily to establish a basis for apportioning members of the House of Representatives. From 1790, when the first census was conducted, to 1902, when the Bureau of the Census was established, an organization was assembled every 10 years to conduct the census. After 1902 the Bureau became a full-time government agency responsible for conducting the census and compiling statistics on various subjects. The most comprehensive source of these statistics is the *Statistical Abstract of the United States*, published annually by the Bureau of the Census.

Over the years the role of the census as a data-gathering vehicle of the federal government has expanded considerably. Since 1809 the Bureau has conducted a periodic Census of Manufacturers. Since 1929 it has also conducted a regular Census of Wholesale Trade, Census of Retail Trade, and Census of Service Industries. These have all been conducted on a regular basis every 5 years since 1967.

Information gathered by the various censuses includes geographic and demographic data on the population and on unit and dollar sales, geographic concentration, primary types of business operations, ways of conducting business, and industry type for various business groups. (Notice that much of

The continued growth of large urban masses has several implications for marketing. Most prominently, over 75 percent of the American population lives in less than 5 percent of its land area, so that a company can launch a near-national marketing campaign with a very limited geographic coverage. Further, studying the particular characteristics of specific SMSAs helps determine how to market a product in each. For example, will New Yorkers (many of whom do not drive) react to an effort to market a luxury car in the same way that Los Angeles residents (many of whom favor small cars) will react? Different combinations of the marketing controllable variables will probably be needed in each SMSA.

The concentration of population in metropolitan centers has had

the population demographics in this chapter and the corporate information in Chapter 6 come from census data published in the *Statistical Abstract*.)

Census data is invaluable to many marketing managers and, except for the most detailed data, is free. Even if a company wished to purchase every bit of available census data, it would only need $10,000, a small amount compared to the millions of dollars companies routinely invest in marketing products. Through the use of government sources in a public library, any marketing manager can gather all the demographic information presented in this chapter and much more. Very detailed demographic profiles of target customers can be compiled without the expense of conducting any marketing research. This information can then be broken down by geographic segments as small as zip code areas (city blocks in some cases), which is very helpful in planning product distribution and media campaigns. Furthermore, because more than 99 percent of all households were counted in the last census, the accuracy of census information is often quite good.*

Similar information can be gathered on corporate customers. Industrial marketers use census data, compiled by Standard Industrial Classification and geographic areas, to understand their customers better and to locate new prospects.

Without the census much of the information routinely used by marketers would not be available. Although created for another purpose, the census is a valuable resource for marketers and, as such, its development was truly a milestone in marketing.

* Peter K. Francese, "Bargain-Priced Census Data a Boon to Consumer, Market Researchers," *Marketing News*, May 25, 1981, p. 14.

some other effects on marketing, namely:

1. The appearance of more varied and specialized retail and service establishments, which can succeed only in heavily populated areas
2. Intensified competition for ultimate-consumer patronage, because consumers have more establishments from which to select
3. A longer shopping day in urban areas to accommodate residents who work different shifts
4. Easier and more frequent access to ultimate consumers for all forms of advertising media and easier physical distribution for some kinds of products.

Figure 4-6

The 36 Largest SMSAs in the United States

SMSA	Population (000)
New York, N.Y.–N.J.	9,120
Los Angeles–Long Beach, Calif.	7,478
Chicago, Ill.	7,102
Philadelphia, Pa.–N.J.	4,717
Detroit, Mich.	4,353
San Francisco–Oakland, Calif.	3,253
Washington, D.C.–Md.–Va.	3,060
Dallas–Ft. Worth, Tex.	2,975
Houston, Tex.	2,905
Boston, Mass.	2,763
Nassau–Suffolk, N.Y.	2,606
St. Louis, Mo.–Ill.	2,355
Pittsburgh, Pa.	2,264
Baltimore, Md.	2,174
Minneapolis–St. Paul, Minn.–Wis.	2,114
Atlanta, Ga.	2,030
Newark, N.J.	1,965
Anaheim–Santa Ana–Garden Grove, Calif.	1,932
Cleveland, Ohio	1,899
San Diego, Calif.	1,862
Miami, Fla.	1,626
Denver–Boulder, Colo.	1,620
Seattle–Everett, Wash.	1,607
Tampa–St. Petersburg, Fla.	1,569
Riverside–San Bernardino–Ontario, Calif.	1,557
Phoenix, Ariz.	1,508
Cincinnati, Ohio–Ky.–Ind.	1,401
Milwaukee, Wis.	1,397
Kansas City, Mo.–Kans.	1,327
San Jose, Calif.	1,295
Buffalo, N.Y.	1,243
Portland, Ore.–Wash.	1,242
New Orleans, La.	1,187
Indianapolis, Ind.	1,167
Columbus, Ohio	1,093
San Antonio, Tex.	1,073
Total	90,838

SOURCE: *Statistical Abstract of the United States, 1981,* pp. 920–25.

Figure 4-7

Standard Consolidated Statistical Areas (SCSAs)

SCSA	Population (000)
New York–Newark–Jersey City, N.Y.–N.J.–Conn.	16,120
Los Angeles–Long Beach–Anaheim, Calif.	11,496
Chicago–Gary–Kenosha, Ill.–Ind.–Wis.	7,868
Philadelphia–Wilmington–Trenton, Pa.–Del.–N.J.–Md.	5,549
San Francisco–Oakland–San Jose, Calif.	5,182
Detroit–Ann Arbor, Mich.	4,618
Boston–Lawrence–Lowell, Mass.–N.H.	3,448
Houston–Galveston, Tex.	3,101
Cleveland–Akron–Lorain, Ohio	2,834
Miami–Fort Lauderdale, Fla.	2,640
Seattle–Tacoma, Wash.	2,092
Cincinnati–Hamilton, Ohio–Ky.–Ind.	1,660
Milwaukee–Racine, Wis.	1,570
Indianapolis–Anderson, Ind.	1,306
Providence–Fall River, R.I.–Mass.	1,096
Dayton–Springfield, Ohio	1,014

SOURCE: *Statistical Abstract of the United States, 1981*, p. 926.

Figure 4-8		
Number of Households: 1960 to 1982		
Year	**Number of Households (in millions)**	**Percentage with Only One or Two Occupants**
1960	52.6	41
1970	63.4	46
1982	83.5	55
SOURCE: *Statistical Abstract of the United States, 1984,* p. 48.		

POPULATION BY HOUSEHOLD

As viewed by the Census, a household comprises all persons who occupy a housing unit such as a house, an apartment, a condominium, or other group of rooms that constitutes "separate living quarters." It includes related family members and all other unrelated persons who share the housing unit. A person living alone is also considered a household.

Demand for many products such as housing units, home appliances, automobiles, and utilities relates more closely to the number of households than to total population size. Figure 4-8 shows that the number of households increased a staggering 30.9 million between 1960 and 1982.

The rapid increase in the number of households during a period when population growth has been low can be attributed to a number of factors. One is the expanding number of people in the 20–34 age group (see Figure 4-4). Other factors include the decline in the birth rate, the decline in the marriage rate, and the increase in the divorce rate, all of which create more one- or two-person households. Figure 4-9 illustrates the fact that the number of marriages per 1,000 females has declined significantly since the early 1970s, whereas the divorce rate has climbed significantly.[11]

The percentage of the population that is 18 years and older and single (never married) is also growing. For women 18 and older the percentage that has never married increased from 12.3 in 1960 to 15.3 in 1982. For men the increase was from 15.4 in 1960 to 19.1 in 1982.[12]

An increase in the number of households is believed to positively affect total demand for certain product categories. When a couple divorces, for example, it often means that there will be two households instead of one. This increases the demand for housing units, appliances, home furnish-

---

[11] The divorce rate per 1,000 people increased from 2.5 in 1965 to 5.2 in 1980: *Statistical Abstract of the United States, 1984,* p. 84.
[12] *Statistical Abstract of the United States, 1984,* p. 43.

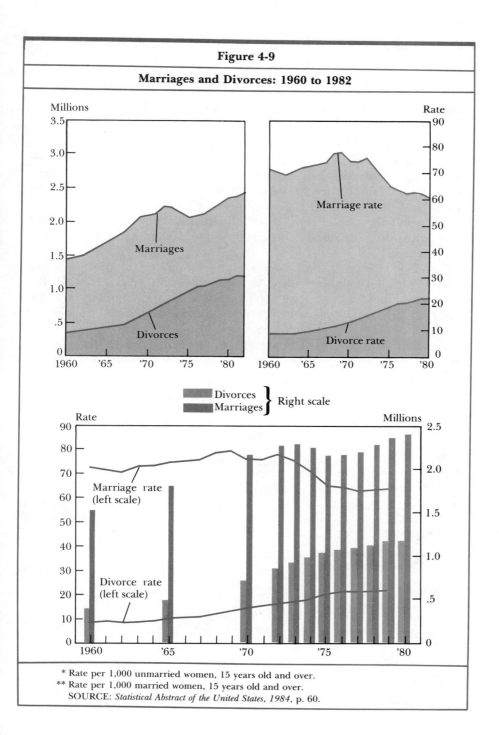

Figure 4-9

Marriages and Divorces: 1960 to 1982

* Rate per 1,000 unmarried women, 15 years old and over.
** Rate per 1,000 married women, 15 years old and over.
   SOURCE: *Statistical Abstract of the United States, 1984*, p. 60.

ings, and other shelter-related products. It also increases the demand for energy, which is less desirable.

POPULATION BY INCOME AND EXPENDITURES

Real income (expressed in 1982 dollars) for American families has increased considerably over the last 20 years (see Figure 4-10). As income level changes, consumption patterns typically change, too. For instance, more affluent families tend to spend less on such staples as food and clothing and more on luxury items. Figure 4-10 shows this effect. From 1960 to 1980 the percentage of household income spent on food and clothing dropped considerably, whereas the percentage spent on jewelry (a luxury) tripled.

Increases in income must always take inflation into account. (For this reason Figure 4-10 shows income in constant-dollar terms.) In 1970 the average household earned fewer dollars, but a single dollar bought more. That is, in 1970 $8,734 would purchase the same quality and quantity of goods that $21,711 would purchase in 1982.

The federal government monitors the purchasing power of the dollar through the **Consumer Price Index (CPI)**, which measures changes in

Figure 4-10			
Income and Expenditures: 1970 to 1982			
	1970	**1980**	**1982**
Median Family Income:			
Real dollars	$ 8,734	$17,710	$20,171
Constant (1979) dollars	$21,711	$20,745	$20,171
Expenditures (% of Total):			
Food, beverages, tobacco	24.1	21.9	21.2
Clothing	8.3	6.9	6.5
Jewelry	0.6	0.7	0.6
Gasoline and oil	3.6	5.1	4.6
Housing	15.1	16.0	16.8
Household operation	6.1	6.8	7.2
Transportation	3.5	3.7	3.4
Motor vehicles and parts	5.8	5.4	5.5
Furniture and household equipment	5.7	5.2	4.7
SOURCE: *Statistical Abstract of the United States, 1984*, pp. 452, 459.			

prices from a base year—presently 1967.[13] For example, suppose a certain group of products cost $100 in 1967, but $216 in 1984. The CPI would be ($216/$100) × 100, or 216.

The effect of rises in income and prices determines the real purchasing power of households. Over the last 20 years the money consumers could spend after taxes (called **disposable income**) and the money left over for such luxuries as vacations, dining out, and jewelry (called **discretionary income**) have increased considerably. This increase creates opportunities for marketing managers.

Demand for household aids such as microwave ovens, dishwashers, food processors, and trash compacters has increased significantly due in part to more discretionary income. The affluent spend up to five times more on kitchen appliances than the nonaffluent and nine times more on microwave ovens. In fact the average household earning over $40,000 per year spends $3,000 per year on home furnishings, $1,100 on home-improvement materials, and $1,147 on furniture. The average household earning less than $40,000 per year spends only $162 per year on furniture.[14]

Consumers spend more today on dining out, taking vacations, and enjoying a myriad of other services and luxuries than they did in 1960. One example of a store taking advantage of this discretionary-income market is Balducci's, a New York City gourmet shop. Such exotic items as quail eggs and stuffed baby eggplants appeal to their affluent target market. As one customer, young, affluent, and well-educated Dr. Heiliczer, put it, "I like to eat, and I might as well eat well."[15]

Note, however, that these increases in income are different for different regions of the country. To have a successful marketing strategy, marketing managers must be aware of the regional and national income trends and the effect on their products. It is up to them to use geographical breakdowns of income statistics to help make decisions about store locations, promotional budget allocations, billboard site locations, and so on.

POPULATION BY EDUCATION AND OCCUPATION

The population of the United States is steadily becoming a better-educated, white-collar group as more and more males and females obtain higher degrees of education and stay in school longer (see Figure 4-11). This

---

[13] Refer back to Figure 2-8 for a graph of the CPI.

[14] Fred L. Engelman, "Today's Affluent Younger, 'Poorer,' but Still Core Target for Marketers," *Marketing News*, May 15, 1981, p. 9.

[15] Janet Guyon, "Gourmet-Food Market Grows as Affluent Shoppers Indulge," *Wall Street Journal*, May 6, 1982, p. 31.

Figure 4-11			
Population by Education: 1960 to 1982			
	1960*	1970*	1982†
Completed High School:			
Percentage of males	23.1	30.1	34.1
Percentage of females	30.4	37.5	41.4
Completed College:			
Percentage of males	8.1	10.8	15.7
Percentage of females	8.1	9.7	14.9
Post-Graduate Studies:			
Percentage of males	10.1	14.1	21.9
Percentage of females	5.9	8.2	14.0
Median Years of Education:			
Male	10.7	12.2	12.6
Female	11.2	12.1	12.5

* Department of Commerce, Bureau of the Census, *Historical Statistics, Colonial Times to 1970*, pp. 602–17.
† *Statistical Abstract of the United States, 1984*, p. 146.

trend, which accounts for an increasingly well-educated and trained pool of labor, combined with the fact that in 1982 51.2 percent of all married women were employed, explains why a larger number of families are now in the upper-income brackets:

Fortune notes:

> Families with annual incomes of $25,000 or more already have a higher proportion of wives in the paid labor force—57 percent in 1977—than any other income class. Affluent members of the baby-boom generation seem to be especially aware of the difference a good woman can make. Some 2.1 million families headed by a person twenty-five to thirty-four made $25,000 a year or more in 1977. Two-thirds of the wives in this group worked.[16]

The trend toward the two-income family is likely to affect consumption in a number of ways—more meals eaten away from home, demand for

---

[16] Walter Keichel III, "Two-Income Families Will Reshape the Consumer Markets," *Fortune*, March 10, 1980, p. 112.

	Figure 4-12					
Population by Occupation: 1960 to 1982						
	1960*		1970*		1982†	
	(000)	**Percent-age**	**(000)**	**Percent-age**	**(000)**	**Percent-age**
White Collar	27,028	41.9	37,857	47.5	53,470	53.7
Professional and technical	7,090	11.0	11.561	14.5	16,951	17.0
Managers and administrators	5,708	8.9	6,463	8.1	11,493	11.5
Sales	4,799	7.4	5,625	7.1	6,580	6.6
Clerical	9,431	14.6	14,208	17.8	18,446	18.5
Blue Collar	25,475	39.5	29,168	36.6	29,597	29.7
Craftsmen	9,465	14.7	11,082	13.9	12,272	12.3
Operative	12,254	19.0	14,335	18.0	12,806	12.9
Nonfarm laborers	3,755	5.8	3,751	4.7	4,418	4.5
Service	7,902	12.2	10.251	12.8	13,736	13.8
Farm	4,132	6.4	2,448	3.1	2,723	2.7
Total	64,537	100.0	79,724	100.0	99,526	100.0

* Historical Statistics, Colonial Times to 1970, pp. 602–17.
† Statistical Abstract of the United States, 1984, p. 417.

higher quality and more efficient appliances, smaller housing units, purchase of more luxuries, and more vacations away from home.

Tied to education has been a growing shift in the labor force from blue collar and farm labor to white collar and service jobs (see Figure 4-12). With increased automation, education, and white-collar job complexity, we can expect this trend to continue.

The larger number of educated members in our labor force and the increasing number of dual career families hold important implications for marketing managers. An educated consuming public requires more honest, better substantiated advertising and marketing. Bradlee's, a discount department store, prospers by catering to these more informed consumers. As company president Av Goldberg put it, "A bargain would no longer be enough. These customers would be looking for quality goods at low prices."[17] In general dual career households require more convenience foods and products, want longer shopping hours from service companies and retail stores, need day care centers, and use mail-order catalogs more

---

[17] Peter Kadzis, "Up from Produce, on to Petticoats," *Forbes*, March 14, 1983, pp. 70–71.

Strategy

Gallo Versus Taylor

The average American wine drinker is between the ages of 25 and 54, well educated, enjoys an above-average income, and holds a semiprofessional or professional position. These demographic characteristics also describe the fastest growing segment of our population, a signal to wine makers that our generally low level of wine consumption is on the rise.

The potential wine sales this growing segment represents are being vigorously pursued by all wineries, both foreign and domestic. The two major domestic contenders are Gallo and Taylor.

The Gallo Winery is owned and operated by two brothers, Ernest and Julio. Since 1933, when they were able to raise the $5,900 they needed to start their Modesto, California, business, their sole mission has been to make and sell wine in a variety of different price and quality categories. It is this goal that has helped Gallo dominate the wine industry with a 25-percent market share.

Taylor Wines originated in the small Finger Lakes town of Hammondsport, New York, in 1880. For the next 97 years it functioned as a tightly owned family business producing mostly semisweet to sweet wines made from the native American grape. In 1977 the Coca-Cola Company bought Taylor, and it became the Wine Spectrum subsidary of Coke.

Since the takeover Taylor has emerged as the biggest threat to Gallo's dominance in the wine industry. The strategies each firm is using to capture a majority of the growing wine-sales dollar are evident from an examination of their marketing mixes.

Product. The majority of Gallo's sales have come from their lower-priced Carlo Rossi jug wines. However, the growth area in wine sales is the premium-priced wine, as well as the popular jug varieties. In response, Gallo is currently attempting to upgrade its image and achieve success in the premium-wine segment while protecting its overall market share.

Gallo has invested significant capital in research and development and a huge oak-cask aging cellar. The goal is to produce a higher-quality wine at a competitive price. The two brothers, Ernest and Julio, want to be known as "the greatest wine makers as well as the greatest wine marketers."*

Once Coke purchased the Taylor name, it immediately put all its efforts into producing a new California wine to compete with Gallo. Coke acquired the Monterey and Sterling Vineyards in California and began producing its California Cellars brand. Taylor also expanded into new types of wine almost immediately, developing a "light" low-calorie wine and wine in six-pack cans.

Coke wanted to position wine as an alternative to other beverages. To do so, it intended to build a family of products, from the California Cellars jug varieties, to take-along six packs, to the ultra-premium vintages produced by the Monterey and Sterling Vineyards.

Place. Gallo was the pioneer in wine-distribution techniques. For years it has assisted retailers in the display and promotion of its wines. It employed manuals like "How to Maximize Your Wine Profits" and training in shelf positioning long before others realized their impact on sales.

These practices were so successful that in 1977 other wineries complained to the Federal Trade Commission that Gallo had too much control over the distribution of wine to retail outlets. It was using its dominant position to restrain competition through "exclusionary marketing policies," they complained.

Taylor had developed extensive distribution channels over its 97-year history, which was one of the main reasons Coke considered acquiring it. Coke wanted a well-established name in the retail outlets. Next to Gallo the Taylor name was the best-known wine label in America. Taylor had an established sales force of 100 experienced wine agents and a distribution network that stretched from the East Coast to the Rocky Mountains. This was just the type of exposure Coke needed to push its Taylor California Cellars brand out into the marketplace as quickly as possible.

Promotion. Wine traditionally has been advertised in a low-keyed, subtle manner. Coke disregarded tradition in developing its ad campaign for the California Cellars brand, because it was convinced that the only way it could build brand identification for the new product was by using comparative ads. In the ads other brands were judged by wine "experts" to be inferior to the Taylor brand. The advantages of this style of advertising were twofold: The ads pulled consumers away from the other wines, but also created new users. For the first time consumers saw that you could compare wines on the basis of taste, just as you do soft drinks. The ads helped convince the potential wine consumer that no special knowledge was needed to choose and enjoy wines.

Coke spent tremendous amounts of money on such ad campaigns. Over $30 million was spent in 1980, about one-third of the amount spent by the entire wine industry. This extensive use of advertising challenged other wine marketers to take a more professional approach to wine marketing.

The fiercely competitive Gallos answered Coke's challenge with a new advertising theme geared to enhance their professional and quality image. Gone was the "folksy" advertising using the Gallo relatives to promote lower-

Continued

Continued

priced wines, like Sangria. The new sophisticated theme associated the Gallo name with quality wines and wines that win international awards. Unfortunately, Gallo's reputation as the leader in producing low-priced, average-quality wines made the image change very difficult.

Price. According to industry experts American wine drinkers often lack product knowledge about the wines they choose, so that "Americans are not brand loyal, but price sensitive" when choosing wines.† This fact puts Gallo at an advantage in the competition for the new wine consumer, because the vertical integration of the Gallo operation helps in keeping down production costs. Gallo owns the largest winery complex, its own glass bottle manufacturing plant, its own transportation fleet, plus 10 percent of the wholesaling operations it utilizes. The resulting economies of scale allow Gallo to sell its products far below the prices of comparable competitors' wines.

From a sales perspective Coke was successful in challenging Gallo's position as market leader. In just five years it moved the Taylor brand from fifth to second position in the wine industry. Despite this tremendous success Coke decided to sell the Wine Spectrum subsidiary (Taylor) to Jos. E. Seagram & Sons in October of 1983.

According to industry sources the reason why Coke sold out of the wine industry was unanticipated fierce and overwhelming competition from Gallo. Coke defended the move, saying the sale was "in line with our corporate strategy to concentrate our resources in the areas of our business where returns on assets are highest."‡

Now there are two different major competitors in the war for the ever-increasing wine sales dollar. It will be interesting to see how the strategies will change as these firms try to meet the needs of the emerging American wine market.

* "Creating a Mass Market for Wine," *Business Week*, March 15, 1982, pp. 108–18.
† "The Wine Wars Get Hotter," *Business Week*, April 11, 1983, pp. 61, 65.
‡ Ruth Stroud, "Seagram Zeros in on Gallo," *Advertising Age*, October 3, 1983, pp. 3, 85.

often than traditional households. Furthermore, dual career families make decisions differently than traditional families. According to one New York advertising executive, "Women are no longer finding their identity and self-esteem in brighter-than-bright dishes and glasses without spots." Two-income couples share decisions, want plenty of information, and respond to advertisements that are equally appealing to men and women.[18]

---

[18] Sue Shellenbarger, "As More Women Take Jobs, They Affect Ads, Politics, Family Life," *Wall Street Journal*, June 29, 1982, pp. 1, 25.

VALUE OF DEMOGRAPHIC DATA

We have only looked at some of the possible demographic data that can be gathered. Sex, race, religious preference, and number of children are a few more that marketers often find helpful. When using demographic data, it is important to first decide the types of data that are needed. In other words, what are the factors (age, income, and so on) that adequately describe the market segments? For example, many AM radio stations are shifting from a music to a talk-show format because of the growth in the 25–54-year-old group, which prefers the talk-show format.[19] Before they made any decisions, advertisers and radio stations identified age as the primary demographic characteristic to analyze in developing their marketing strategy.

Most advertising media gather demographic information so potential advertisers can match their demographic needs to those of the medium. Newspapers, radio, and television routinely gather data on the age, sex, income, location, occupation, and education of their markets.

DEMOGRAPHIC DATA LIMITATIONS

Although useful, demographic data is often too general. When a marketing manager needs specific county data on consumers, for instance, national data probably will be of little help. Data that is even more local is often too aggregated to totally answer marketing's questions.

Furthermore, demographic data is often out of date. Notice that much of the data in this chapter was two years old when it was compiled. National data is seldom more recent than two years, but market conditions can change dramatically in this time span. Therefore, marketers should not use such data without adjusting for conditions that have changed.

Finally, demographic data tells little about the psychological or sociological processes consumers experience, that is, it does not explain consumer behavior. Chapter 5 will be devoted to consumer behavior and consumption decision processes.

In summary marketing managers should use demographic data as a first step toward describing the market segments and their target market. Once the relevant demographic data has pinpointed the target market, marketing managers must use their understanding of consumer behavior

---

[19] "Why AM Radio Stations are Talking Up," *Business Week,* June 15, 1981, pp. 99–100.

to explain how the target market decides whether or not to purchase the product.

SUMMARY

- Demographic data is useful in determining market segments and selecting target markets.
- Three general population trends have been continuing for the last 30 years: continuous, but uneven, growth; a declining birth rate; and a stable death rate.
- The age of our population is shifting toward the 20–34 years old and 65 years old and over categories.
- Life-cycle analysis helps marketers understand buying patterns and select target markets by age category.
- Population growth has been particularly strong in the Sun Belt region of the U.S.
- Approximately 75 percent of our population lives in one of the 318 Standard Metropolitan Statistical Areas (SMSAs).
- In recent decades the number of households, especially one- and two-person households, has greatly increased.
- Our population is becoming increasingly affluent, educated, and white collar—facts that have affected spending patterns.
- Although demographic shifts are valuable in analyzing changes in consumption patterns, they should only serve as a starting point in the marketer's analysis of consumer behavior.

DISCUSSION QUESTIONS

1. Give several examples of industries or products that may benefit from the changes in age distribution in the United States. What other industries or products may be adversely affected?

2. Do you agree with predictions that the birth rate in the United States will remain relatively low? Why or why not?
3. How might data by Standard Metropolitan Statistical Area aid in developing a marketing strategy for cameras? A restaurant chain?
4. Critique the nine categories used for life-cycle analysis. Could additional categories be used? If so, describe them.
5. Does the increasing number of households in the United States have a negative impact on any products? If so, name them.
6. Explain how the increased income of consumers affects disposable and discretionary income. How will this affect consumption patterns?
7. Name some products that have benefited from the increase in dual career families. Name some that were hurt.
8. How does an increasingly more educated populace affect marketing strategy?
9. Describe the advantages and limitations of using demographic data.
10. How does demographic data help us to understand market segments and to select target markets?

APPLICATION EXERCISES

1. As marketing manager for a firm that makes microwave ovens, you must design a strategy to sell your product to dual career families. What product features would you emphasize? When would you run TV ads? How would you present the high price to target customers?
2. An important population trend is the rapid increase in the number of households. Consider this hypothetical situation: Mr. and Mrs. Walter Brown have two children, Jeff, aged 23, and Alice, aged 21. Both Jeff and Alice, who have been living at home while going to the local university, now decide to move out and rent unfurnished apartments. There are now three households instead of just one. What additional products (including services) are likely to be needed because of the move? In general does marketing management like to see the trend toward smaller households? Explain.
3. You are the marketing manager of a toy manufacturing company. Design a marketing strategy for both the next 5 years and the next 10 years based on your knowledge of the demographic variables for the present population of children 1 to 15 years old and the predicted child population for the future.

CASE 4

Demographic Problems for Jostens

One inevitable result of the passing of the post-war baby-boom has been the decline in student enrollment. High school enrollment peaked at 15 million in 1975, but is projected to decline to 12 million by 1990.[1]

One company concerned about this trend is Jostens, Inc., which holds some 40 percent of the market for class rings and yearbooks. While the company's specific marketing plans are not discussed publicly, it appears Jostens is attempting to ride out the demographic trends by placing greater emphasis on the company's traditional products—class rings and yearbooks for high school juniors and seniors. As evidence of this, the company has bailed out of its less than successful attempts to diversify into selling books and catalog cards to school libraries and wedding and engagement rings to retailers.

Much of Jostens' current approach revolves around attempts to redefine its traditional student market. For instance, the company is developing a small but growing market for mini-yearbooks among junior high and elementary school students. It is also putting greater emphasis on college students. In addition, it is wooing old, established alumni who regret leaving college without mementos of their undergraduate years.

Perhaps the company's greatest strength is its sales force, which expanded 15 percent to 1,000 members in the late 70's. That is larger than the combined size of its two nearest competitors, Balfour Company and Taylor Publishing. The majority of the force consists of former high school teachers and coaches who were dissatisfied with their income. They now take home an average income of $50,000 per year on 15 percent commissions.[2]

In addition to the demographic changes, Jostens has had to face another unfavorable trend in recent years—the decline in school spirit that has lingered on since the end of the Vietnam War era. Jostens has attempted to combat this trend by sponsoring "school spirit campaigns" which rely, in large part, on the enthusiasm and scholastic background of their salespeople. At these campaigns, Jostens' salespeople give administrators and student leaders advice on how to increase student spirit as well as free posters, pennants, and other paraphernalia. The aim is to rekindle the kind of student spirit that encourages the purchase of class rings and yearbooks.

---

[1] Bureau of the Census, U.S. Department of Commerce, *Statistical Abstract of the United States, 1984*, p. 140.

[2] "Jostens: A School Supplier Stays with Basics as Enrollment Declines," *Business Week*, April 24, 1980, pp. 124, 129.

Despite these strategies, however, some analysts doubt that Jostens can continue to grow simply by redefining their student market. What it all may boil down to is the fact that no amount of spirit-boosting fanfare will build high school enrollments again.

Discussion Questions

1. Evaluate the viability of Jostens' plan to expand school memento sales. Will demographic changes cause this market to "dry up"?
2. If Jostens were to diversify into other markets, which would you choose? Justify your decision with demographic information.
3. What strategy would you recommend?

5 Consumer Behavior

STUDY OBJECTIVES

After studying this chapter, you should be able to

1. Discuss the factors that influence the consumer decision-making process.
2. Explain the effect of culture, social class, family, reference groups, perception, motivation, learning, attitudes, and personality upon consumer behavior.
3. Describe the consumer decision-making process.
4. Explain how marketers use all this information to get consumers' attention and appeal to them.
5. List the factors that affect patronage.

As we saw in the last chapter, demographics can be helpful in identifying market segments and selecting target markets, but they do not tell the entire story. What makes individual consumers act the way they do? To answer this question, we must look at the area of consumer behavior.

When we study consumer behavior, we encounter the complex realm of human behavior. Here, "facts" are mostly theories, and even the most carefully researched marketing effort can fall flat because of some unpredicted (and perhaps unpredictable) aspect of consumer behavior.

Marketing management is intensely interested in questions involving consumer behavior. In a competitive society, as we have remarked before, marketers look at things this way: There are a certain number of people out there with a certain amount of money. How can we induce these people to buy our product, or to buy more of it? What can we do to make our competitors' customers switch to us? What advertising claims should we make? What sort of packaging and product characteristics (color, size, flavor, style, and so on) will win the most consumer favor?

In practice marketing managers function as applied psychologists, seeking various ways to direct purchasing behavior. The more marketing managers know about consumer behavior, the better equipped they are to influence it. Investigating consumer behavior helps them develop more effective marketing strategies.

Marketers must always realize that consumers bring a variety of purchasing motives to any buying decision, many of which even the consumer cannot identify. Figure 5-1 presents a model of the factors commonly thought to influence the consumer decision-making process. The observable influences are the demographic factors discussed in Chapter 4 and, hopefully, the marketing controllable variables discussed in Chapter 1. Equally important are such influences as culture, social setting, and psychology, all of which may not be observable. Before we discuss the actual consumer decision-making process and how marketers appeal to it, we must explore the cultural, social, and psychological influences upon this process.

CULTURAL INFLUENCES

Culture *is all of our environment that is created by people.* It consists of all tangible (products) and intangible (attitudes and laws) aspects. To some degree culture dictates our attitudes and behavior and, thus helps determine how we consume. For example, over the last 20 years our American

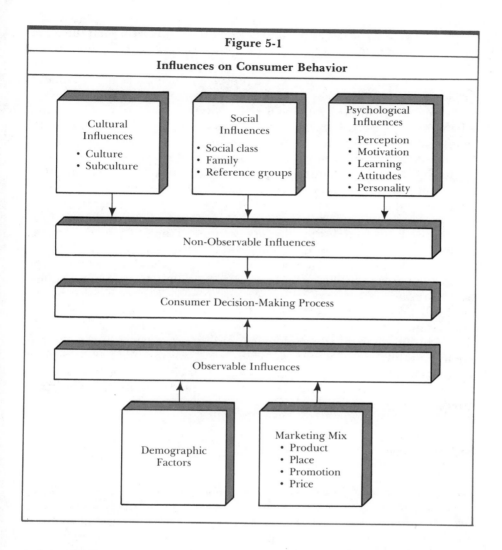

Figure 5-1

Influences on Consumer Behavior

Cultural Influences
• Culture
• Subculture

Social Influences
• Social class
• Family
• Reference groups

Psychological Influences
• Perception
• Motivation
• Learning
• Attitudes
• Personality

Non-Observable Influences

Consumer Decision-Making Process

Observable Influences

Demographic Factors

Marketing Mix
• Product
• Place
• Promotion
• Price

culture has been very youth oriented, especially for women. Because of this cultural orientation, women consume a great deal of cosmetics, all aimed at maintaining the appearance of youth. In a broader sense our culture influences what we eat and wear, how we relax, and where we live.

We become aware of cultural differences when we travel to other countries. Products we take for granted may be luxuries elsewhere, may require special adaptation for use abroad, or may simply be unavailable. In Spain, for example, an American would encounter many differences in consumer behavior. Such a visitor would probably first notice the differences in eating habits. Most Spaniards, for instance, view the American staple corn as a cereal best suited for use as pig and chicken feed. Americans, on the other hand, might be somewhat reluctant to enjoy such traditional Spanish foods as squid, octopus, and snails. Differences in apparel would seem less obvious to a visiting American, but it would probably be obvious that Spaniards in particular, and western Europeans in general, tend to dress more formally than we do in the United States. The first time our visitor tried to use a hair dryer or electric shaver he or she would discover that, because the type of voltage is different in Europe, one must have an electrical converter to use American appliances abroad. If our visitor stayed in Spain long enough to want a private telephone, it would probably come as a rather unpleasant surprise to learn that installation of a new phone may take as long as six months. As you can see, each culture has its own specific characteristics.

Cultural orientations do change over time. Think of how the acceptability of working women has changed our consumption habits. In 1960 women were still expected to marry, have children, and devote their efforts to creating a "happy home." Housewife consumption centered around home products, food, and personal items to make her more attractive to her husband and to appear the "good mother." Changing cultural orientation has made the working or career wife the norm rather than the exception. Consumption has turned more toward convenience items for the home and "dressing for success" in personal consumption. Before they attempt to develop a marketing strategy, marketers trying to reach the female market certainly must be aware of these cultural shifts and their effect upon consumer behavior.

Subcultures

A final aspect of culture that is of especial importance in our society is the concept of the **subculture,** which is *a group of persons of the same social or economic status, religion, and ethnic background that has its own values, interests, or goals but operates within a larger society.* The German-American subculture, Mexican-American subculture, and the teenage subculture are only a few examples. Because these subcultures often have unique consumption behaviors, it is important for marketers to investigate the influence of subcultures on a given marketing strategy. For example, marketers trying to reach the American Hispanic subculture should be aware that 12 million Hispanics watch Spanish-language programs on SIN National Spanish Television Network.[1] Such unique subculture consumer behavior patterns provide essential information for marketers.

---

[1] "Hispanic TV is Beaming in on The Big Time," *Business Week,* March 23, 1981, p. 122.

SOCIAL INFLUENCES

Social influences deal with behavior resulting from the interactions of people with each other. For our purposes, we can break these influences down into three main categories: social class, family, and reference groups.

Social Class

American society—as well as many other societies—is ranked into social positions of respect. *A* **social class** *is a group of people with similar ranking within a society.* In most modern societies this is not a formal caste system but rather an informal way to categorize people according to similarities of behavior, life-styles, and values. In the United States we have what are referred to as open social classes, that is, movement into and out of any particular class is possible.

A socioeconomic approach to marketing analysis can be very useful to an organization interested in modifying its image. Most successful businesses concentrate on serving patrons from certain social classes. What are the various classes? Social classes are typically defined by at least some combination of income, occupation, wealth, religion, and education. The well-known sociologist W. Lloyd Warner developed a sixfold classification of American society that is used widely to study and predict consumer behavior.[2] We present it here as an example of many such analyses:

1. *The upper upper class* includes probably less than 1 percent of the total population. It consists of socially prominent, wealthy families. The upper upper class is dedicated to upholding family traditions, living a very refined life, and rendering community and government service. Entry into this class, which includes such families as the Rockefellers and Vanderbilts, must generally be made through birth or marriage.
2. *The lower upper class* includes perhaps 2 percent of the families in our society and consists of people who are quite wealthy but have not been fully accepted into the highest echelon of the social structure. Senior executives and very successful professional people are typical of this class. Their value system is largely one of adapting themselves, insofar as they are able, to the style of living of the upper upper class.
3. *The upper middle class* includes successful professional people, owners of medium-sized organizations, managers, and junior execu-

---

[2] W. Lloyd Warner, "Classes Are Real," in Gerald W. Thielbar and Saul Feldman, eds., *Issues in Social Inequality* (Boston: Little, Brown, 1972), pp. 8–9.

tives. An estimated 10 percent of Americans belong to this class. Families in this group are usually very status minded and strive hard to achieve. Most people in this group are college educated and tend to cultivate a broad range of creative interests.

4. *The lower middle class* is the second largest of Warner's groups, comprising perhaps 30 to 35 percent of our population. Clerical workers, owners of small businesses, and the conventional white-collar worker belong to this category. Highly paid blue-collar workers are also part of this class. Members of this group are generally eager to be respected and devote much attention to maintaining a home, buying "good" clothes, saving for a college education, and living in a good neighborhood.

5. *The upper lower class,* perhaps more than any other group, fits the description of "average" or "ordinary" citizens. It is the largest class, accounting for about 40 percent of all families. Semiskilled workers and employees of small service establishments are representatives of this class. The upper lower class tends to place a premium on living as well as possible today, rather than saving for the future.

6. *The lower lower class* consists of unskilled workers and many of the unemployed—between 10 and 15 percent of our population. Its members are frequently apathetic and show little concern with self-betterment, keeping up with the Joneses, or creating a future. This class has relatively little motivation and is concerned mainly with its own day-to-day existence.

Income, of course, is not the only determinant of socioeconomic class. Warner also considered source of income, occupation, housing, and neighborhood in locating an individual's position on the social ladder. More recently sociologists have tended to replace questions about a person's neighborhood with questions about educational achievement. Occupation is now considered to be more important than income in determining a person's class. It sometimes happens, for example, that a family with all the other characteristics of the lower middle class earns as much as a family in the upper middle class. Because of its different educational level, attitudes, and general life-styles, however, its consumption patterns may differ greatly from those of upper middle class families.[3]

---

[3] The following articles delve further into the question of social class and its relationship to consumption patterns: Chester R. Watson, "Is It Time to Quit Thinking of Income Classes?" *Journal of Marketing,* April 1969, pp. 54–57; John W. Slocum, Jr., and H. Lee Mathews, "Social Class and Income as Indicators of Consumer Credit Behavior," *Journal of Marketing,* April 1970, pp. 69–74; James H. Myers, Roger R. Stanton, and Arne F. Haug, "Correlates of Buying Behavior: Social Class vs. Income," *Journal of Marketing,* October 1971, pp. 8–15;

	Figure 5-2	
	Social Class Characteristics	
Class	**General Characteristics**	**Consumption Behavior Patterns**
Upper-upper	Social elite, inherited wealth from socially prominent families.	Spend money as if it is unimportant.
Lower-upper	Very high income professional people who "earned" their position.	Nouveaux riches with many material symbols of their status. They buy largest homes in best suburbs, most expensive cars, swimming pools, and other symbols of conspicuous consumption.
Upper-middle	Career based on professional or graduate degrees.	Consumption in a conspicuous but careful manner. Shop "quality" outlets.
Lower-middle	"Typical" Americans with core of respectability, conscientious work habits, and culturally defined norms and standards.	Home important. Adopt standard home furnishings. Highly price sensitive. More shopping behavior.
Upper-lower	Blue collar, union members. Little social contact.	Brand loyal to national products.
Lower-lower	So called "disreputable" people. Little future orientation.	Impulse buyer, often pays too much for products, buys on credit.

SOURCE: Condensed from James F. Engel, Roger D. Blackwell, and David T. Kollat, *Consumer Behavior* (Hinsdale, Ill.: Dryden Press, 1978), pp. 126–28.

The various social classes typically exhibit different behavior patterns and, more importantly for marketers, different consumption patterns. For example, a member of the upper upper class often drives an expensive car such as a Rolls Royce or Mercedes Benz, a consumption behavior certainly not common to the lower lower class. Figure 5-2 illustrates a commonly used social-class categorization and some observable consumption patterns for each. Note that social class affects not only the type, quality, and quantity of goods consumed, but also the shopping patterns and stores patronized.

James H. Myers and John F. Mount, "More on Social Class vs. Income as Correlates of Buying Behavior," *Journal of Marketing,* April 1973, pp. 71–73; and R. Eugene Klipper and John F. Monoky, "A Potential Segmentation Variable for Marketers: Relative Occupational Class Income," *Journal of the Academy of Marketing Science,* Spring 1974, pp. 351–54.

Family

Throughout life we identify with various groups and hold certain positions (roles) within those groups. One group with a considerable influence on our lives is the family. Whether in youth when we fill the role of daughter/son or in later life as wife/husband, mother/father, these family ties influence us and our actions. Much of our consumption behavior is strongly influenced by what we feel the family expects of us. For example, many

bad breath. Due to its influence natural breath became unacceptable and a potential hazard to your health. The company had, in essence, helped create a consumer behavior—using mouthwash.

In 1965 Procter and Gamble entered the mouthwash market with Scope. It furthered the social unacceptability of bad breath by creating a new promotional device—"bad breath anonymous." Anyone could send the name and address of an offending person to the company, and the person would receive a 10-cent coupon toward the purchase of Scope.

Procter and Gamble's strategy with Scope was to convince consumers that using a mouthwash was not enough. It had to have a pleasant minty flavor and not one that left you with "medicine breath." Advertisements showed individuals being shunned by loved ones because their breath was not minty fresh. This campaign was successful in changing customers' perceptions. The market share of mediciney Listerine dropped.

In 1970 Listerine was delivered another blow. The Food and Drug Administration (FDA) ordered Warner–Lambert to stop making the claim that Listerine was effective in combating colds and sore throats. Despite the company's "test" results that supposedly proved Listerine's effectiveness, the Federal Trade Commission (FTC) also ordered Warner–Lambert to stop claiming Listerine could prevent colds. In 1975 the FTC went a step further and ordered Warner–Lambert to include this corrective statement in all ads: "Listerine will not prevent colds or sore throats or lessen their severity." In the consumer's eyes Listerine could no longer fulfill the basic need of good health. Market share dropped again.

In an attempt to recapture some lost ground, Warner–Lambert came out with Listermint in 1980, hoping to take advantage of Scope's influence on the market by introducing its own minty-flavored mouthwash.

The use of mouthwash is now an integral part of our behavior patterns. The makers of Listerine and Scope have accomplished this by significantly influencing our decision-making process. They both helped create an awareness in consumers of the need for better breath and provided the information necessary to make a choice by outlining the benefits of using mouthwash.

men today interpret their role in the family as more than just breadwinner. They also contribute to the maintenance of the family. A recent survey by New York ad agency Benton and Bowles, Inc., revealed that of 617 men[4]:

[4] Theodore Dunn, "Large Numbers of Husbands Buy Household Products, Do Housework," *Marketing News,* October 3, 1980, pp. 1, 2.

- 32% shop for food
- 74% take out the garbage
- 47% cook for the family
- 53% wash the dishes
- 29% do the laundry
- 28% clean the bathroom
- 39% vacuum the house
- 80% take care of the children

Thus, a man's attitude toward his role in the family affects not only his consumption patterns but also the family's as a whole. When more active participants help make many of the domestic shopping decisions, marketers of home products must appeal to both the wife and husband to effectively sell their products. More traditional husbands, in turn, leave the domestic shopping decisions to their wives. For these families marketers need only appeal to the woman.

Children also affect family purchase decisions. You only need to watch the effect a child has on a parent's shopping behavior in the toy section of a department store or the cereal aisle of a grocery store to realize this is true. It is not surprising, then, that cereal and toy manufacturers expend a great deal of effort marketing their products to children who in turn sway their parents to buy.

As this example illustrates, the family setting often creates a distinction between the consumer and the purchaser. The consumer actually uses the product, whereas the purchaser does the shopping and buying. They are not necessarily the same person. Consider, for example, the mother in a traditional family who buys groceries, clothing, and other goods to be consumed by all the members of the family. Marketers attempt to isolate the influences that make the mother buy what, when, and where she does and why she buys as often as she does. Certainly, her family's preferences in style, quality, color, and other factors influence her. Social and cultural factors of which she may not even be aware also influence her. For instance, without realizing it she may ask herself which product her own mother would have selected, then buy or reject the product depending on whether her relationship with her mother is positive or negative. The opinions, expressed or implied, of her friends or neighbors also often exert a subconscious influence on her purchases. The point is, as marketers we are more concerned with the purchaser's behavior than the actual consumer's behavior.

The role you play in the family and as a purchaser or consumer depends on your stage in the family life cycle. Figure 5-3 presents the family life-cycle stages and characteristics that marketers need to know. Clearly, how well a marketer interprets a certain consumer's family role largely determines the success of the strategy used to reach that consumer.

Reference Groups

Throughout our lives social groups to which we belong and to which we wish to belong have a great influence on us. These **reference groups** affect our attitudes, values, and consumption behavior. Figure 5-4, which provides examples of such groups, should make it clear that you belong to many reference groups throughout your life and usually several at any given time.

The reference group affects consumer behavior to the degree an individual identifies with that group. If you slightly identify with a particular social group, you may ask its opinion on certain products and, thus, use the reference group only as an information source. If belonging to a particular group is especially important, that group often dictates certain consumption patterns. For example, one sorority professes an affection for the color purple. To enhance the feeling of belonging, members buy a large number of purple items. Thus, this reference group strongly affects the consumption behavior of its members.

The success of many products depends on a favorable response from the right reference groups. Figure 5-5 presents some products and brands whose purchase is weakly or strongly influenced by reference groups. As diagramed, reference groups may exert a strong influence on the brand or product (upper-left cell) or may have no influence (lower-right cell). The reference-group influence on the product may be strong, but weak on the brand (lower left). Or it could be weak on the actual decision of whether or not the product is important, but strong on the brand selection once a decision is made to buy the product (upper right). Products in the upper-left cell are socially conspicuous, whereas products in the lower-right cell are judged more on their functional attributes. If marketers know whether reference groups are important to particular products and, if so, which reference groups affect the decision, they can then design a marketing strategy to sway these groups.

PSYCHOLOGICAL INFLUENCES

Although cultural and social influences help us understand consumers, we must also examine the individual. Much of our knowledge of consumer behavior comes from the study of psychology, that is, the study of how individuals behave. To help us understand individual consumer behavior, we should examine the psychological factors of perception, motivation, learning, attitudes, and personality. Although it is impossible to observe directly what is happening in consumers' minds, we can infer much of their thought processes by understanding these factors.

Figure 5-3

The Different Stages and Characteristics of the Family Life Cycle

Group	Age	Behavior	Products	Role in Buying Process	Sources of Information
Early Childhood	Birth–5	Total dependency on parents; ego centered; accompanies guardian shopping	Baby foods; cribs; clothes; toys; pediatric services; room vaporizers; breakfast cereals; candy; books	Limited influencer; consumer or user	Parents; television; friends
Later Childhood	6–12	Declining dependency on parents; development of thinking ability; peer competition; conscious of being evaluated by others; attends school	Food; toys; clothes; lessons; medical and dental care; movies; candy; uniforms; comic books	Influencer; limited decision maker; consumer or user	Parents; friends; school; television; comic books
Early Adolescence	13–15	Onset of puberty; shifting of reference group from family to peers; concern with personal appearance; desire for more independence	Junk food; comic books and magazines; movies; records; clothing; hobbies; grooming aids	Influencer; limited financer; decision maker; limited buyer; consumer or user	Family; peer group; school; television; radio; magazines
Late Adolescence	16–18	Transition to adulthood continues; obtains working papers and driver's license; concern with personal appearance increases; dating	Gasoline; auto parts; typewriters; cameras; jewelry and trinkets; cigarettes; books and magazines	Influencer; limited financer; decision maker; buyer; consumer or user	Family; peer group; school; television; radio; magazines
Pre-Marrieds		Enters labor market on a full-time basis; enters college; interest in personal appearance remains high; increased dating; varying degrees of independence	Auto; clothing; dances; travel; toiletries; quick and easy-to-prepare foods	Influencer; less limited financer; decision maker; buyer; consumer or user	Family; peer group; college; job; television; radio; newspaper; magazines

Young Marrieds	19–24	First marriage; transition to pair-centered behavior; financially optimistic; interest in personal appearance still high	Home renting; furniture; major appliances; second auto; food; entertainment; small household items	Influencer; financer; decision maker; buyer; consumer or user	Spouse; close friends; job; television; radio; newspaper; magazines
Young Parents	25–34	Transition to family-centered behavior; decline in social interests; companionship with spouse drops; leisure activities centered more at home	Houses; home-repair goods; health and nutrition foods; family games; health-care services	Influencer; financer; decision maker; buyer; consumer or user	Spouse; children; job; close friends; parents; television; newspaper; magazines
Middle Adulthood	35–44	Family size at its peak; children in school; security conscious; homemaker's time is impinged on; career advances	Durables are replaced; insurance; books; sporting equipment; yard furniture; gifts	Influencer; financer; decision maker; buyer; consumer or user	Spouse; children; job; extended family; television; newspaper; magazines
Later Adulthood	45–54	Children have left home; physical appearance changes; increased interest in appearance; community service; pair-centered	Clothing; vacations; leisure time services; food; gifts; personal health-care services	Influencer; financer; decision maker; buyer; consumer or user	Spouse; close friends; television; job; family; television; radio; magazines
Soon-to-be-retired	55–64	Physical appearance continues to decline; interest and activities continue to decline; pair-centered	Gifts; slenderizing treatments; manicures and massages; luxuries	Influencer; financer; decision maker; buyer; consumer or user	Spouse; close friends; television; job; family; newspaper; radio; magazines
Already Retired	65 and Older	Physical appearance continues its decline; mental abilities decline in sharpness; homebody behavior; ego-centered behavior; insomnia	Drugs; dietetic canned foods; laxatives; nursing-home care; denture products	Influencer; financer; decision maker; limited buyer; consumer or user	Extended family; television; surviving friends; radio; children

SOURCE: Adapted from Fred D. Reynolds and William D. Wells, *Consumer Behavior* (New York: McGraw-Hill, 1977).

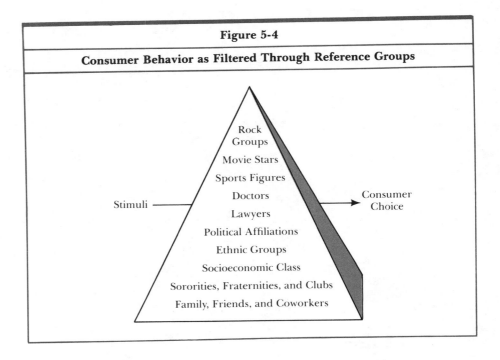

Figure 5-4

Consumer Behavior as Filtered Through Reference Groups

Rock Groups
Movie Stars
Sports Figures
Doctors
Lawyers
Political Affiliations
Ethnic Groups
Socioeconomic Class
Sororities, Fraternities, and Clubs
Family, Friends, and Coworkers

Stimuli ⟶ ⟶ Consumer Choice

Figure 5-5

Products and Brands Affected by Reference Groups

		Reference Group Influence on Product	
		STRONG	WEAK
Reference Group Influence on Brand	**STRONG**	Cars* Cigarettes* Beer (premium vs. regular)* Drugs*	Clothing Furniture Magazines Refrigerators (type) Toilet soap
	WEAK	Air conditioners* Instant coffee* TV (black and white)	Soap Canned peaches Laundry soap Refrigerators (brand) Radios

* Based on actual experimental evidence. Other products in this table are classified speculatively on the basis of generalizations derived from the sum of research in this area and confirmed by the judgment of seminar participants.

SOURCE: Adapted from Francis S. Bourne, "Group Influences in Marketing and Public Relations," in Rensis Likert and Samuel P. Hayes, Jr., eds., *Some Applications of Behavioral Research,* (Paris: UNESCO, 1957).

Perception

Through our five senses we see, hear, taste, smell, and feel our environment. **Perception** *is how we interpret our sensory input.* We like to think that we are aware of all the sights that enter our field of vision, the sounds that reach our ears, and so on. Actually, however, our senses are bombarded with so many stimuli that we consciously perceive only a small percentage of them. Research has shown that 13 percent of all advertisements are overlooked completely and 40 percent of the time the name of the product cannot be recalled.[5] This **selective perception**, which is the individual's mechanism for blocking out stimuli that are not thought to be important, keeps the number of conscious stimuli to a manageable number. However, we also perceive some stimuli subliminally.

Yesterday you were probably exposed to several hundred print, broadcast, telecast, and billboard messages. But how many of them can you describe today? Those you do not remember seeing or hearing, you may have perceived *subliminally,* that is, without being conscious of having perceived them. Often subliminal perceptions are accompanied by conscious perceptions. Such subliminal perceptions still influence behavior. For example, a billboard advertisement depicting a tired, hardhatted construction worker drinking a cold glass of milk consciously appeals to our perception of milk as refreshing and healthy. But its subliminal appeal may be that, beyond its basic association with childhood, milk is also a masculine, adult beverage. If this subliminal appeal is effective, it may boost sales of milk to male consumers who might otherwise have felt that milk is not an adult drink.

Perception is influenced by many factors. "We do not see things as *they* are, but as *we* are," say psychologists Willard and Marguerite Beecher.[6] We bring the knowledge and attitudes we have collected over our lifetimes to each input from our senses and interpret the input into a perception. A consumer may continue to buy a particular brand of coffee, even though tests show another brand is of higher quality, because the preferred brand is perceived to be more in keeping with the consumer's standards. This *perceptual defense* is the consumer's way of perceiving things in such a way that it protects his or her values.[7] In other words we perceive things in a way that lets our behavior seem (to us) logical and consistent.

---

[5] Bill Abrams, "Sponsor Recalls," *Wall Street Journal,* March 24, 1983, p. 35.

[6] Willard Beecher and Marguerite Beecher, *Beyond Success and Failure* (New York: The Julian Press, 1966), p. 46.

[7] E. McGinnies, "Emotionality and Perceptual Defense," *Psychological Review,* 56, 1949, pp. 244–51; and Leo J. Postman, Jerome S. Bruner, and E. McGinnies, "Personal Values as Selective Factors in Perception," *Journal of Abnormal and Social Psychology,* April 1948, pp. 142–54.

Sometimes our perceptions influence our behavior to an extreme degree. A study in color perception showed that people have especially strong associations with the color of food.[8] At a dinner party in England the steaks were whitish gray, the salads blue, and the coffee yellow. Celery was a gaudy pink, milk was the color of blood, and peas looked like black caviar. Most of the guests lost their appetites. Those who ate became ill. But the food was considered delicious by people who were blindfolded.

Other studies reveal that, in some instances, consumers perceive colors as determining strengths and weaknesses. Certainly, consumers feel that the color of the package has a great deal to do with the quality of the product inside. In one study, for example, housewives were given three samples of a detergent—one in a yellow box, one in a blue box, and one in a box that was both yellow and blue. The women said that the detergent in the yellow box was too strong—it even damaged their clothes. The product in the blue box was too weak—it left the clothes dirty. But the detergent in the yellow and blue box gave excellent results. Yet all three boxes contained exactly the same product!

Misperceptions also affect consumer behavior. The Campbell Taggart advertising agency attacked a problem it identified as consumer misperception about the nutritional value of enriched white bread by developing a campaign with the theme, "It isn't called the staff of life for nothin'."[9]

Motivation

Motivation can be defined as *desire for activity toward a certain goal.* When an individual recognizes an unfulfilled need (hunger, sex, prestige, and so on), tension is created. Motivation is our desire to take some action to relieve this tension. For example, when hungry, we may search for a restaurant. Several scholars have attempted to explain the motives that drive individuals.

Hierarchy of Human Needs   Psychologist Abraham Maslow structured a hierarchy of human needs or motives that shows the basic physiological needs must be satisfied before a person will devote any effort to other motives (see Figure 5-6).[10] Once the physical necessities are provided, the individual will strive for safety and security.

---

[8] Family Economics Bureau of Northwestern National Life Insurance Company, Minneapolis, Minnesota.

[9] "Campbell Taggart Fights Beard's Bum Rap," *Advertising Age*, March 3, 1980, p. 3.

[10] Abraham H. Maslow, "A Theory of Human Motivation," *Psychological Review*, Vol. 50, 1943, pp. 370–96; and Abraham H. Maslow, *Motivation and Personality* (New York: Harper and Row, 1954).

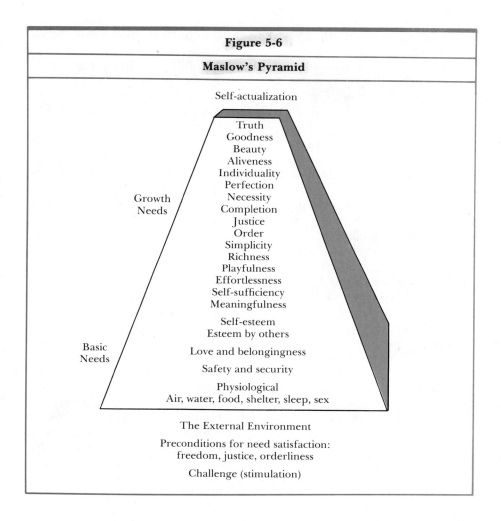

Figure 5-6

Maslow's Pyramid

Self-actualization

Growth Needs

Truth
Goodness
Beauty
Aliveness
Individuality
Perfection
Necessity
Completion
Justice
Order
Simplicity
Richness
Playfulness
Effortlessness
Self-sufficiency
Meaningfulness

Basic Needs

Self-esteem
Esteem by others

Love and belongingness

Safety and security

Physiological
Air, water, food, shelter, sleep, sex

The External Environment

Preconditions for need satisfaction:
freedom, justice, orderliness

Challenge (stimulation)

On the next higher level, the human strives to be loved and desired and to find a place in a group. If these needs are satisfied, needs for self-esteem and the respect of others will emerge. In marketing terms a consumer operating at this level of need will generally seek prestige and status by being the first to purchase new or higher-priced goods and services.

Growth needs then emerge that lead people to seek truth, goodness, beauty, order, justice, self-sufficiency, and meaningfulness. The ultimate goal of all human striving then becomes self-actualization, or becoming the person that individual believes he or she should be.

Theory of Self-Concept   To understand the complexity of individuals and their motives in a marketing context, we must also know something about the **ego**—that part of the personality concerned with the preservation of "the self."

According to Sigmund Freud, founder of the psychoanalytic school of psychology, human personality evolves from the interaction of the id, the ego, and the superego. Freud said that the **id** seeks to control personality by trying to obtain immediate satisfaction of basic drives and cravings. The **superego** seeks to control by denying the animalistic desires of the id. It tries, instead, to induce the individual to engage only in the most noble endeavors. It is our conscience. The ego, finally, arbitrates between the id and the superego. It resolves their conflicts and determines the behavior of "the self" that results.

Although modern psychologists have revised Freud's ideas somewhat, his theory of ego remains the basis for the theory of self-concept. "I" and "me" are words dear to all our hearts. The mental image we have of our "selves" is equivalent to the ego in a psychological sense. It is the human urge to preserve, protect, and enhance this *self-image,* or *self-concept,* that motivates almost all our behavior in the last analysis.

To marketers, the self-concept, or ego, is the supreme motivator of consumer behavior. Virtually all consumer purchasing decisions are related in some way to the conscious or subconscious question, "How will this help me or influence the way others see me?" Most of us, even those who act antisocially, need the approval of others to reinforce our self-image.

The Desire for a Better Self-Image   Students of consumer behavior generally agree that most people like to see themselves as better than they are. Most individuals, even if they never verbalize these emotions, would like to be somebody special, to get ahead, to have others envy them and their achievements. For this reason they like to own products that enhance their opinion of themselves and, hopefully, make other people realize how successful, important, and prosperous they are.

Human beings play many roles in their day-to-day encounters with others. Because few of us are successful in achieving all our goals, we often obtain ego satisfaction through fantasies. In the "game" of love, for example, we see ourselves pursuing or being pursued by the most attractive and desirable partners. In the game of business we see ourselves as the most effective workers or the highest earners. On the home front we imagine ourselves in a mansion staffed with servants. In college daydreams we visualize our grade reports as all A's—achieved with a minimum of intellectual input because of our great natural intelligence.

In brief we basically want to win whatever "game" we may be engaged in. Unmasked, we want to know the most important people, see our name in society columns, win applause, and be popular. Although few individuals will admit it, we want to be able to say to ourselves, "I am better than other people. I am a winner." These are the desires that have made for-

Winners always get roses.

You finally did it. Took on the meanest, nastiest mountain run you've ever seen.

And tamed it.

You beat the elements. Just like Suncloud Rose SunFilters. They cut haze. Slice through glare. Protect your eyes from harmful radiation. Like no ordinary sunglasses can. Which is why we call them SunFilters. Not sunglasses.

And their rose-colored lenses put you in the right frame of mind.

That's what it takes to be a winner.

Look for SunCloud Rose at winning stores and optical shops everywhere.

If there aren't any left, order yours from us: 2600 South Broadway, Los Angeles, CA 90007.

See you at the bottom of the mountain, champ.

SUNCLOUD ROSE ®*
SUNFILTERS™

tunes for those clever in advertising and product promotion. Jean Nidetch, founder of Weight Watchers, developed a multimillion-dollar empire on her understanding of the desire for a better self-image. She helped millions of people improve their appearance and health in the process, and later sold Weight Watchers to the H.J. Heinz Company.

The Law of Self-Interest Psychology teaches us that individuals are much more interested in their own welfare and that of their immediate families than in the welfare of others. Although we are often admonished to love our neighbors as ourselves, pragmatists know that we rarely do. Notice how often people passing a mirror or a window make adjustments in their hair, dress, or posture. Observe also the great difficulty most people have in listening to you tell them about your weekend—they would much rather bore you with every detail of what *they* did. Particularly when traffic is heavy, but even when it is not, many drivers are exceedingly reluctant to give another motorist the right of way. At airline boarding gates people often rush to enter the plane ahead of others, apparently to select a "choice" seat before someone else gets it. When they deplane, some passengers use all kinds of interesting tactics to get off first. These are just a few of countless examples of the law of self-interest in operation.

Because of the enormous strength of self-interest, advertisers and salespeople make many appeals to the ego. "You" and "your" are two of the most frequently used words in commercials. Some of the earliest words a child learns are "me," "mine," and "I"; and some of the earliest outbursts of anger are directed at those persons the child feels are tampering with his or her possessions and rights.

Learning

Learning *is how an individual's behavior is affected by previous experiences.* For example, the first time you buy a new automobile you may spend a large amount of time gathering information, because you have had no opportunity for prior learning. Say you buy a Ford Escort and are not happy with its performance. You have learned you do not like this particular model and maybe even Fords in general. Your next automobile purchase will be influenced by this learning experience. If the experience had been positive, you might have decided to buy a second Escort, a learned response. If a response continues to be positive (through repeat purchases), a repetitive response develops, which is called **habit**.

That people are creatures of habit is certainly true in the marketplace. Habit is a powerful force that determines to a very significant extent what retail and service establishments we patronize, which brands we buy, and how we make purchase decisions.

There are two main reasons for the enormous strength of habit. First, people develop habits to satisfy a need to feel secure, to eliminate fear of the unfamiliar. They feel uncomfortable in strange surroundings where, because of their ignorance, they may make an embarrassing mistake. Second, people tend to avoid doing anything that requires additional effort, especially if the activity is one that is often repeated, such as grocery shopping. "Just when I got to know where everything was in the supermarket, they changed things around," is a frequent consumer complaint. Habit, or routine, makes life easier, and in some cases more efficient. Thinking takes time and energy. Once a habit is established, people rarely give it a second thought. For this reason, habits are difficult to change.

Marketers spend a great deal of effort getting consumers in the habit of buying their products (called **brand loyalty**) or patronizing their stores (**store loyalty**). Once customers have become brand or store loyal (formed a habit), competitors will have considerable trouble drawing them away.

Attitudes

Attitudes may be defined as *a person's feeling toward a particular object or situation*. Attitudes may be positive or negative, are often formed over a lifetime, and are very resistant to change. Therefore, it is a very long and expensive process for marketers to change consumers' attitudes. For this reason marketers typically try to develop favorable attitudes in consumers for their products or modify a product to fit consumer attitudes.

Airwick followed the latter strategy in the home air-freshener market.[11] American attitudes are quite strong and positive toward pleasant fragrances in the home, but they like the freshener to be in an unobtrusive applicator. Therefore, Airwick shifted from their traditional green bottle with the pull-up wick to Stick-ups (an "invisible" air freshener that can be hidden in out-of-the-way places) and Carpet Fresh (a product to sprinkle on carpets and vacuum up the "damp musties"). These introductions were carefully tested against consumer attitudes. As Airwick's new products manager, Michael J. Sheet, put it, "We don't jump from the lab to the outside like other companies. We stop, check ideas out first, see what the consumers really want and the intensity of interest. Then we go back, really develop the product, and do more traditional research."

For marketers it is very important to address the correct attitude in developing a marketing strategy. For example, you may have a very positive attitude toward an IBM personal computer—think of the time savings in doing homework!—but the model you want costs over $2,000.

---

[11] "Airwick's Discovery of New Products Pays Off," *Business Week*, June 16, 1980, pp. 139–40.

Therefore, your attitude toward the computer may be positive, but your attitude toward *buying* one is negative. Marketers must concern themselves with consumer attitudes toward buying products.

Personality

Psychologists have not been able to agree on what personality is, even though we all have one. **Personality** *is the sum of our heredity, environment, and experience that gives us such traits as independence or submissiveness, extroversion or introversion, gregariousness or shyness, and so on.* Marketers have found little conclusive evidence of a tie between personality and consumption behavior.[12] However, marketing managers often use personality traits to market products. Independent, good-natured, and extroverted people are often portrayed consuming certain products. The implication is that in consuming the same product, you will exhibit the same positive personality traits. Whether such a marketing strategy is effective or not is not entirely known.

THE CONSUMER DECISION-MAKING PROCESS

All the influences previously discussed affect consumer behavior, but how does the consumer make an actual purchase decision? Although we cannot know the exact thought processes involved, we can learn about the general process a consumer goes through in making decisions, as Figure 5-7 illustrates.

Recognize a Need

First of all the consumer recognizes a **need**. The consumer must experience a feeling that he or she lacks something, or that some aspect of life would be improved by purchasing a particular type of product. Hunger pangs are an obvious example of need recognition. It is easy to know when something as basic as sustenance is lacking and to remedy matters by seeking food. Some needs are not so easily recognized. For example, young executives seeking prestige may search for products that enhance their self-image, but they may not be able to tell you why they purchased such products.

---

[12] Harold H. Kasarjian, "Personality and Consumer Behavior: A Review," *Journal of Marketing Research,* November 1971, pp. 409–19.

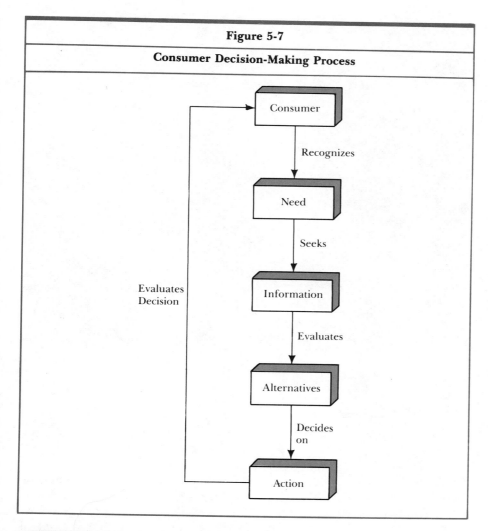

Figure 5-7

Consumer Decision-Making Process

Consumer

Recognizes

Need

Seeks

Information

Evaluates
Decision

Evaluates

Alternatives

Decides
on

Action

Search for Information

Whether the need is explainable or not, the consumer will search for information concerning how to satisfy the need. This information may come
from marketing sources, nonmarketing sources, or reference groups. In
the example of our young executive, he or she may decide to purchase a
new car to fulfill a prestige need, and may seek information on different
cars from dealerships, articles in papers and magazines, and the opinions
of peers. Such information may be casually and quickly gathered if the
decision is of little importance to the consumer or may be a long, careful,
studied process for important decisions.

Evaluate Alternatives

Given the information input, the consumer will attempt to reconcile the alternatives with his or her needs. Various factors of the marketing controllable variables (as perceived by the consumer) will be weighed for different products. Reference-group input will be considered (the executive may be swayed by the comment of a fellow executive who feels the Mercedes-Benz is "the ultimate executive prestige car"). Attitudes, motivation, personality, experience, reference-group consumption, and cultural influences will all come into play. Possibly the consumer will also consider the family's opinion. In fact all the factors and influences presented in Figure 5-1 will influence the evaluation of alternatives, and the consumer will use some internal scheme for weighting each of the influences in the evaluation process.

Decide on Action

The consumer must finally make the decision of whether or not to make a purchase and, if so, which particular alternative to select. The evaluation in the previous step will influence the decision, although the consumer often cannot describe the evaluation and decision process that occurred. Two consumers with very similar evaluations may make entirely different purchase decisions. The reason is locked somewhere in the consumers' minds.

For a number of reasons the consumer may be reluctant to buy the product, even after all the previous steps are completed. One reason may be a reluctance to part with any money. This conflict or **dissonance** is caused by the consumer wanting the product but not wanting to give up the money necessary to purchase it. Often, additional promotional messages are necessary at this stage to get consumers to part with their money. Even after the product is selected, purchase may be delayed until a retail outlet is selected.

Evaluate Decision

After taking an action, the consumer evaluates the wisdom of the decision. It is this learning experience that affects the consumer's future purchase decisions. Positive experiences may lead to routine repurchases (habit). Unpleasant experiences will probably lead to extensive information search and deliberation the next time. The unsatisfactory product may be "given a second chance," or it may not even be considered.

HOW MARKETERS APPEAL TO CONSUMERS

The goal of marketing management is to maximize consumer acceptance in the marketplace. Using their understanding of consumer behavior, marketers have created numerous successful appeals. In this section we will examine some of the ways marketers seek to attract consumers.

Appeals to Habit

Marketing management attempts to influence consumer habits in three broad ways in an effort to attract—and hold—a larger share of the market.

First, it tries to induce consumers to *break existing habits*. In order to get consumers to develop a new consumption habit, it is often necessary to get them to break a habit that now influences their behavior. This is rarely easy. Marketers must first induce consumers to question their current behavior, such as stopping by the same car rental desk in each airport they visit. Avis works hard at getting customers to break the Hertz habit, so that it has a better chance to attract their business.

Second, marketing management tries to induce consumers to *develop new habits.* Many promotional strategies are designed to induce us to shop in a new or different store or to buy a new or different brand. "A new breakthrough in shopping convenience" is only one of the many slogans used to urge people to form new buying habits.

Third, marketing management tries to *reinforce existing habits*. An intelligent marketer recognizes that other businesses are competing for existing consumer patronage. Constant effort is required to cement the firm's relationship with its clientele. Dissatisfaction with the quality of a store's service is probably the principal reason consumers break the habit of shopping in one place and move on to another. Similarly, dissatisfaction with some aspect of a product (its quality, utility, servicing, or price) often explains why we discontinue using one brand and adopt another.

Consequently, a wise marketer never takes consumer patronage for

analysis then reduced these items to 22 life-style dimensions. These dimensions were: price conscious, fashion conscious, child oriented, compulsive housekeeper, dislikes homekeeping, clothes maker, homebody, community minded, credit user, sports spectator, cook, self-confident, self-designated opinion leader, information seeker, new-brand tryer, satisfied with finances, canned-food user, dieter, financial optimist, wrapper, wide horizons, and art enthusiast. For example, new-brand tryers tended to all agree on such comments as "When I see a new brand on the shelf, I often buy it just to see what it's like," "I often try new brands before my friends and neighbors do," and "I like to try new and different things."

This information is very valuable in describing consumer behavior. For instance, users of eye makeup tended to be more fashion conscious than nonusers. Heavy users of shortening liked housekeeping, were child oriented, and were homebodies. Thus, a firm can define its target market more by how it consumes than by such indirect characteristics as age, income, and education.

Marketers typically use life-style characteristics to identify market segments and select target markets, position products, select distribution outlets, design advertising and media guidelines, and aid in pricing strategies. In short the development of psychographics and life-style analysis provides an additional important tool for marketers in understanding their markets, which, in turn, helps them in designing a more effective marketing mix.

---

* Fred D. Reynolds and William R. Darden, "An Operational Construction of Life Style," in M. Venkatesan, ed., *Proceedings of the Third Annual Conference of the Association for Consumer Research*, 1971, p. 482.

† Henry Asael, *Consumer Behavior and Marketing Action* (Boston: Kent Publishing, 1981), p. 232.

‡ William D. Wells and Douglas J. Tigert, "Activities, Interests and Opinions," *Journal of Advertising Research*, August 1971, pp. 27–35.

granted. Instead, the marketer continually searches for new ways to keep present customers satisfied. One retailer explained the policy of good service this way: "I treat each old customer the best way I can—like we were on a honeymoon. That dealer across the street is just waiting for me to louse up my relationship with my regulars. But I'm trying to hold my customers through better service."

Sensory Appeals

As noted earlier in the chapter, human beings have five physiological senses—smell, hearing, sight, touch, and taste. Our memories reinforce the use of these senses. We can remember what velvet feels like. We can remember the flavor of peanut butter and jelly sandwiches we ate as children. Many of us can recall the fragrance of a perfume or shaving lotion used by a loved one. In our mind's eye we can "see" images of the past.

Marketers use appeals to the senses extensively. As you listen to commercials or read print ads, notice how frequently five key sense-related words—TASTE, TOUCH, SEE, HEAR, and SMELL—are used to encourage you to try a product. Marketers appeal to the sense of smell by telling consumers, "Use a fragrance that stays with you all day," or, "Enjoy the wonderful aroma of freshly brewed coffee."

Marketers capitalize on the sense of hearing in many ways. Because its effects are often subliminal, music is used extensively to increase the effectiveness of advertising. Many stores use music to help customers relax and make parting with their money less painful for them. Music can also be used to modify our moods. Some music makes us want to march, whereas other music makes us want to make love, pray, or dance. The psychology of music is still a comparatively new field, but one that promises to attract more attention in the years ahead.[13]

Sight is the most important of all senses to marketers, who appeal to it primarily through the design and packaging of products and advertising illustrations. All other marketing variables being equal, an attractive package sells better. Sales are often affected by even minor modifications in a package. Appearance is also a major consideration in designing buildings and store environments that will attract customers. Safeway recently spent a great deal of time and money redesigning its traditional grocery store. Its new prototype store in Arlington, Texas, has such sight-appealing features as free-flow floor design, bright colors, live plants, and photomurals throughout the store. As project director Dennis Gerdeman put it,

> There's a little less merchandise per square foot than Safeway normally would get into a store, but we've made it more inviting for people to come into the store. You can see the little boulevard of shops in the center from the parking lot. You've got to spend a dollar to make a dollar, and this is so much more pleasant to shop.[14]

Appeals to the sense of touch are also common. Physical contact with a product is somehow reassuring. Makers of bathroom tissue have emphasized consumers' desire to touch products with TV commercials and ads that show the products being squeezed.

---

[13] "Mood Music Pays Off," *Chain Store Age,* January 1967, p. BM-3.
[14] Kevin Higgins, "Safeway Enters Quest for Supermarket of Future," *Marketing News,* January 7, 1983, pp. 1, 6.

Taste is appealed to extensively. A television food commercial done well can literally make your mouth water. So can an attractive print ad. Here the goal of the marketer is to make the product appeal to our taste buds, even though actual tasting is impossible. The food industry uses elaborate taste-testing techniques to give products such as cereals, soups, and coffees a flavor that will be popular with consumers.

The ideal promotional program appeals to all five basic senses. For example, a real-estate agent trying to sell a home site in a newly developed resort area might say, "Just *look* at the view from your front window. *Smell* the fresh scent of the pine trees that surround the property. *Feel* the soft breeze from the lake. *Listen* to the frogs and crickets. And can't you almost *taste* the charcoaled goodness of the steaks grilling on your patio?"

Naturally, as you know from your own experience, one sensory stimulation can enhance or detract from another: Unpleasant smells make us lose our appetites. The sight of a ripe strawberry or a melon in a magazine ad makes our mouths water. And, as you will recall from our previous example, strangely colored food often seems to have an unpleasant taste. Wise marketers use the psychological associations attached to our physiological senses to influence consumer behavior.

Appeals to Memory and Past Experience

Everything we have experienced or encountered becomes a part of us, whether or not we recognize it. Psychologists are very much aware of the effect our past experiences, even during infancy, have on our attitudes, beliefs, likes, and dislikes. The human brain is a fantastic data bank of past experiences. As such, it contains many clues to consumer behavior.

How often, for example, have we tried a product once, had an unpleasant experience with it, and sworn never to buy it again? At the same time we continue to buy other products that conjure up pleasant memories.

The fact that past experience often directs behavior in the marketplace is significant to marketing management in two ways.

First, it indicates that a firm should do everything possible to make its product, the environment in which it is purchased, and post-sale services as satisfying as possible. The degree to which consumers enjoy the *total* purchase experience, including after-sale satisfaction, often determines whether they will continue their patronage. In addition a well-satisfied consumer is likely to "pass the word" to friends.

Second, a firm should try to respond positively to any dissatisfaction consumers may have about buying or using its product, so that a bad experience does not leave a lasting impression. In some cases it may be necessary to replace or repair a product to prevent a bad experience from becoming entrenched in the customer's memory.

COMPETITION FOR CONSUMER ATTENTION

Motivating consumers is difficult, because there is so much competition for their attention. Approximately 1,500 commercial messages from various media bombard the average urban consumer each day. Due to selective perception, many, if not most, of the commercials we hear simply do not receive our conscious attention.

Degrees of Attention

Marketing managers need to recognize that the degree of attention we give such messages varies. We use the phrase "paying full attention" to mean that the listener or observer is free of all distractions and is concentrating entirely on what is being said or displayed. It is rare for anyone to devote full attention to anything—and then only for very brief periods.

Voluntary and Involuntary Attention

Attention is either voluntary or involuntary. When we go through the Yellow Pages to find a TV repair shop or read the classified ads to find a used car, our attention is said to be *voluntary*. We are deliberately surrendering our attention to commercial messages. For the most part, however, consumers give only *involuntary* attention to commercial messages. We do not often hear someone say, "I'm going to turn the TV on so I can watch some commercials."

Techniques for Attracting Attention

Because our environment contains a vast array of distractions, marketers focus much creative effort on ways to make products, business establishments, and advertisements "stand out," or attract consumer attention. Some of the more common devices used to "grab" the consumer's interest are:

1. *Size.* Bigness attracts. Unusually large signs, full-page ads, and oversized billboards attract more attention than their smaller counterparts.
2. *Motion.* We are more attracted to a shooting star than to one that appears to be motionless. So, too, we pay more attention to a moving sign than a stationary one. One of the most important advantages television has over other media is that the elements in a commercial move, thereby increasing its chances of attracting and holding attention.
3. *Isolation.* An individual is much more conspicuous when standing alone on a street corner than when in a group. Marketers have many ways of using isolation to attract attention—for example, by

putting a border around an advertisement or displaying only one product in a store window.

4. *Celebrities.* Marketers extensively use prominent actors, newscasters, athletes, and other well-known personalities, *because* they are prominent, to attract attention and to endorse products.

5. *The "right" voices.* All of us can say, "Now hear this!" Not all of us, however, will get the same response. Whether a message registers consciously at all depends to a great extent on how we say things, on our tone of voice. Some messages require a commanding, authoritative voice to attract attention. Other messages may provoke interest if the voice is feminine, soft, or sexy.

6. *Color.* As a rule color ads attract more attention than black and white ones. In addition, certain colors tend to produce a particular emotional response.

7. *Unusual sounds.* We grow so accustomed to certain sounds that they do not attract our attention. Accordingly, marketers often use special sound effects or loud noises to arouse our attention.

8. *Other attention-getting devices.* Marketers use many other means to make us see their products and listen to their messages. These include (a) pictures of pretty girls, handsome men, babies, and pets; (b) humor and humorous cartoons; (c) prominent positioning; (d) lighted signs; (e) eye-catching symbols; and (f) catchy, easy-to-learn jingles.

BELIEVABILITY MOTIVATES CONSUMERS

Although we are all somewhat gullible, we have also learned through experience not to believe everything we are told. Before making a purchase, many consumers want some assurance that they are not being exploited, fooled, or taken advantage of in some way. Marketers use various techniques to make promotional messages believable and prevent credibility gaps from developing.

Credible Promotional Messages

Credibility is achieved, in part, by making both the content of a commercial message and the manner of presentation seem honest, believable, and authentic. For example, makers of television commercials are careful to select actors who "come across" as both knowledgeable and trustworthy. To make a message for a health-care product appear believable, someone with the air of a medical authority may be chosen. We would not select someone who looked disreputable to do a bank advertisement. Care is also needed in deciding what to say in an advertisement. People often dismiss claims that are very bold.

credible - believable

Testimonials

A very common way to increase believability is to provide testimonials from satisfied users. Those giving the testimonial may be just "everyday folks" or prominent people, depending on the product and the type of ad. Using prominent individuals in an ad may give it prestige as well as credibility.

An Established Reputation

Another credibility-building technique is to make some reference to a company's past performance. Marketers often use phrases such as "Over 100,000,000 bottles sold!" "The oldest dealer in the city!" "Winner of this year's 'Progressive Engineering' Award!" and "Record-Breaking Consumer Acceptance!" to develop credibility by indirectly telling consumers that a firm or a product's reputation is excellent.

Quality Products and Services

The most important way to establish consumer credibility is to have a quality product, priced fairly, and backed up by satisfactory post-sale service. When consumers are satisfied, they are inclined to develop the habit of repeat purchases and also to tell their friends about the product. A wise marketer knows that, in the long run, even the most effective promotion and the largest budget cannot sell large quantities of an inferior product.

Other Ways to Establish Credibility

Marketers use a variety of other devices to convince consumers that product claims are true. One method is to point to a good's limitations as well as its strong points. A consumer may place more faith in what a salesperson says if told what the product *cannot* do. Product warranties, money-back guarantees, product demonstrations, free trials, and free samples also help establish credibility.

PATRONAGE MOTIVES: WHY PEOPLE BUY WHERE THEY DO

Why does one service station at a four-station intersection attract as much business as the other three combined? Why do some retailers in a shopping center flourish, whereas others barely break even? In preceding sections of this chapter we dealt with the reasons people buy *what* they do. Now we are ready to examine why they buy *where* they do.

Patronage motives explain why a consumer purchases a product from one dealer or store rather than another. This is a matter of great concern to marketing management. Firms constantly ask: What can we do to make

consumers shop in *our* store? How can we make *our* store the one consumers prefer to shop in? Obviously, patronage motives are exceedingly important to individual businesses. Retailers regard regular customers as bread-and-butter business, of course, and try to develop as large a loyal group of patrons as possible.

In a discussion of how market segmentation affects customer loyalty, Grazin and Miller suggest that retailers follow this sequence in their strategic planning:

> (1) Delineate the target market whose loyalty is sought; (2) determine the benefits sought by this loyalty segment; (3) find the personal characteristics of those seeking benefits the retailer feels can be provided; (4) formulate a strategy for providing these benefits.[15]

What "benefits" can retailers use to attract a loyal segment? Some factors that affect consumer reaction to particular establishments are price, location, quality, service, integrity, variety, and likeable and competent personnel.

---

[15] Kent L. Grazin and Kenneth E. Miller, "Simultaneous Loyalty and Benefit Segmentation of Retail Store Customers," *Journal of Retailing,* Spring 1979, p. 59.

Price

Price is perhaps the single most important reason a buyer regularly patronizes a particular outlet. The desire to buy is unlimited; but as we all know, the ability to buy (disposable income) is very much limited.

There is no simple formula for determining which price will prove most attractive for a given item. Some establishments, such as discount department stores, discount gasoline stations, and many supermarkets, however, make greater use of price appeals than others. They take large newspaper ads or plaster their windows with signs telling us an item is "priced right for quick sale!" or that they "will better any advertised price." Conversely, a product may be priced too low in some instances. David Carpenter, a California artist, has noted, "When I see that one of my paintings hasn't been sold, I usually tell the gallery owner to raise the price on it. Some people won't buy a painting for $500, but when they see the price going up, they'll think they've got a bargain at $800. Eventually, the prices of my paintings rise to meet my market."

Location

Very often much of a store's popularity is due to its location. People will frequently pay a little bit more for an item if they can buy it with less effort, as demonstrated by the convenience-food markets that have developed so rapidly in the past 15 years.

Location is especially important in merchandising gasoline, food, and other essential consumer goods. People are inclined to exert a minimum amount of effort in shopping for these products, and the closer a store is to large numbers of customers, the better its chances for success.[16] It is for this reason that chain stores will announce that they have "six conveniently located stores to serve you"; individual retailers will boast they are "located in the heart of the shopping district"; and Hertz will advertise, "Rent it here. Leave it there."

Quality

"Sure, it costs more, but I'm worth it." Such appeals to the ego are usually associated with personal items such as cosmetics and hair-care products. But they are also used to sell furniture, automobiles, and airline tickets. Some retailing establishments also make strong appeals based on the high quality of the merchandise they carry. They turn higher prices to advan-

---

[16] For a further discussion of the value of good location in attracting customers, see James A. Bruner and John L. Mason, "The Influence of Driving Time upon Shopping Center Preference," *Journal of Marketing*, April 1968, pp. 57–61, and Robert O. Herrmann and Leland L. Beik, "Shoppers' Movements Outside Their Local Retail Area," *Journal of Marketing*, October 1968, pp. 45–51.

tage by advertising that their merchandise is "priced higher because the quality is so much better." Such stores are often successful in attracting customers, because many consumers equate high prices with quality and dependability.

As consumers become more sophisticated, they tend to demand higher quality in the goods and services they buy. They respond more to such appeals as, "We guarantee every product we sell!" and "The quality goes in before the name goes on."

Service

Services, in this context, are intangible extras offered by a seller to encourage patronage. Credit, delivery, gift-wrapping, easy returns, guarantees, free installations, maintenance, and technical assistance are all services that help attract and hold a clientele.

Stores that are located within the same general area and that carry mostly the same products may seem so similar that consumers perceive no basic differences between them. Many retailers, therefore, emphasize the supplementary services they offer as a means of differentiating their store from others.

Consumers are drawn most often to those stores that offer the most complete "sales package." Appeals such as "All this at no extra cost," "We service what we sell," and "Free delivery within a 50-mile radius" reassure customers that they are getting a better deal.

Integrity

Consumers, especially those with considerable shopping experience, are influenced by a merchant's integrity, especially when the product is an intangible (such as insurance, security, or pest control) or when they are likely to need post-sale service (as in the case of automobiles).

The complexity of many of today's products and the attendant complicated warranties and service agreements are bewildering to the vast majority of consumers. Once they find a retail establishment they think can be trusted to fulfill advertising claims and post-sale service arrangements, they are likely to return there repeatedly.

Retailers who establish a record of honest dealing with consumers are several steps ahead of their competition. Advertising messages such as "member FDIC," "You're in good hands with Allstate," and "RCA—the most trusted name in electronics" appeal to consumers' desire for integrity in the marketers with whom they trade.

Variety

In many cases consumers tend to patronize stores that offer a wide variety of merchandise. The trend away from specialization that began with the supermarkets and department stores has been followed by discount stores—such as K Mart, Gemco, and Target—that offer such diverse products and services as garden supplies, automobile services, groceries, pharmaceutical products, pets, building materials, and eye-care services.

A wider variety of merchandise means more convenience for consumers, because they must make fewer stops for routine purchases. If a store also carries a variety of product lines, comparison shopping is simplified. Service establishments also benefit from offering customers variety. Note the emerging popularity of "mini" theaters, featuring different films shown in different sections of the same building, so that patrons can purchase tickets at one location and still have a choice of movies.

Customers respond positively to marketing appeals indicating variety, such as "Your choice of eight jets daily to Denver!" "We have the largest selection in town!" and "See our complete line of the latest fashions!"

Likeable and Competent Personnel

Marketing management has learned that, other things being approximately equal, customers will shop where the personnel are friendly and can provide professional advice.

A young woman trying to furnish her first home or apartment is apt to purchase more from a clerk who is well versed in interior decoration. Trying to replace poor-fitting curtains may be costly and frustrating. The store management that trains its personnel to offer competent advice gains a definite edge over its competitors.

Friendliness and courtesy motivate many consumers to make repeat purchases. Treating the customer politely is also a logical extension of the marketing concept. Many business people make extensive efforts to persuade customers of their employees' courtesy and knowledgeability. Advertisements often stress this theme by offering "trained experts" to assist shoppers, by reassuring potential buyers, "You're never a stranger when you shop with us," and by asserting that a particular store is "the friendliest place in town to shop!"

SUMMARY

- Consumers' cultural background, social conditions, and psychological factors influence their purchasing decisions.

- Cultural factors greatly affect consumer behavior. Marketers must consider possible differences in the cultural backgrounds of their target consumers when designing marketing programs.
- Cultural orientations change over time. Marketers must be aware of present and emerging cultural orientations.
- Different social classes exhibit observable differences in consumption and shopping behavior.
- Roles consumers play in their family affect the consumption behavior of themselves and other members of the family.
- The concept of the family life cycle helps explain the consumer behavior of family members.
- Reference groups are social groups with which we wish to be identified. These groups have varying degrees of effect on consumer behavior for different products and brands.
- How we perceive our environment through our five senses affects our consumer behavior.
- Much of motivation and consumer behavior can be explained by Maslow's hierarchy of human needs and the theory of self-concept, which holds that human beings are motivated to pursue, protect, and enhance their image of themselves. The law of self-interest, the desire for a better self-image, and the desire for status add to our understanding of the theory of self-concept.
- Learned behavior and habit in consumer behavior often lead to brand loyalty or store loyalty. Such habits, once formed, are difficult for marketers to change.
- A person's attitudes are formed over a lifetime of experiences and are very hard to change. Marketers must often change the marketing mix to meet these attitudes.
- Although no conclusive evidence exists that appeals to personality help sell products, many marketers try to influence consumer behavior by using personality traits to market products.
- To influence consumer behavior, marketing managers must understand the consumer decision-making process, the underlying reasons for it, the theories behind it, and the effect of culture, society, and psychology on it.
- Marketers appeal to consumers by developing new habits and breaking or reinforcing existing habits.
- Marketers try to appeal to the five senses, to memory, and to experience.
- Some techniques to make promotional messages credible are (a) using testimonials, (b) pointing to an established reputation, and (c) referring to high quality.
- Patronage motives explain why a consumer purchases products from one store rather than from another. Key patronage motives are price, location, quality, services, integrity, variety, and store personnel.

DISCUSSION QUESTIONS

1. What steps are involved in the consumer decision-making process? Why is understanding the process important to marketers?
2. What is a purchasing motive? Why should marketing people understand purchasing motives?
3. "Consumers may not be purchasers." Explain.
4. How may our purchasing decisions be affected by perception? Reference groups? Attitudes? Learning? Personality? Social Class? Family?
5. What is self-actualization?
6. Explain how each of the following relates to the theory of self-concept: the law of self-interest, the desire for a better self-image, the desire for status among one's peers.
7. Explain the hierarchy of human needs.
8. Define the term *patronage motive*. Explain how each of the following affects consumer behavior: price, location, quality, services, integrity, variety, likeable and competent personnel.
9. In what ways do marketers attempt to influence consumer habits?
10. Why do marketers make appeals to the senses?
11. What are some devices for attracting consumer attention? Explain the difference between voluntary and involuntary attention.
12. How can marketers make promotional claims believable?

APPLICATION EXERCISES

1. a. Examine your own shopping behavior by listing the names of the grocery store, restaurant, and service station you patronize most frequently. For each, in order of importance, list your patronage motives, that is, the reasons why you shop there.
   b. Give three examples of retailers you occasionally patronize for which convenience (location) is not an important consideration. Why do you return to these places?
   c. Give one example of a retail establishment you stopped patronizing in the past year for a reason other than its location. What reason did you have for making the change?
2. It is often difficult to prepare advertising messages consumers will believe. Pick a current magazine and select two advertisements—one you feel is highly believable and one you feel is not. Prepare a short report analyzing each ad and explaining why you believe one and not the other.

CASE 5

Can Egg Consumption Be Increased?

Three decades ago almost everyone in America ate an egg every day. Now breakfast habits have changed so much that many people hardly sit down to breakfast. They grab convenience foods such as cereals and "breakfast bars," instant coffee and sweet rolls, fruit juices, and milk.

One deeply felt influence on our changing breakfast habits was the 1961 report by the American Heart Association that advised the health-conscious American public, for its heart's sake, to limit its cholesterol intake. One egg alone, the public was informed, contains 85 percent of the recommended daily cholesterol allowance. Some heart specialists have since refuted the statement that a high cholesterol diet contributes to heart disease, but the public has not yet entirely relaxed its attitude toward eggs and other foods high in cholesterol.

What is more, a technological revolution, encompassing the 1971 discovery of a vaccine that prevents a killing virus in hens and better care and feeding through automation, has resulted in a larger supply of eggs than ever before. This larger supply comes at a time when people are eating fewer eggs. It is estimated that the nation's 270 million laying hens could be increased by 30 percent in 6 months if the demand were there.

Egg producers have banded together, under the name of the National Egg Board, to promote egg consumption for the entire industry. Major egg producers who belong to the National Egg Board have agreed to contribute a half-cent per dozen eggs produced for an advertising campaign. In its advertising the Board wants to stress the high protein value—the low caloric count—of eggs, that eggs carry a low price compared with other sources of protein such as meats, and that eggs have more staying power than other breakfast foods such as cereals.

Alex Barclay, an account executive for an advertising firm in New York, saw his father's operation of less than 100,000 hens eclipsed by the large corporate farms. In 1964 there were 1.2 million egg producers. In 1976 there were only 200,000, and 4,000 of these were responsible for 90 percent of the eggs produced.

The National Egg Board has just awarded an account to Barclay's firm, Reed, Sneade, and Jackson. Barclay's assignment is to develop the campaign to promote egg consumption in the United States. The National Egg Board wants its promotion to follow the line that eggs, like milk, are "a natural." The Board suggests both a practical and a glamorous approach toward the promotion—the rediscovery—of eggs.

Discussion Questions

1. Prior to designing the actual campaign to promote egg consumption, what cultural, social, and psychological factors should Barclay consider?
2. How can Barclay use the consumer decision-making process to explain consumer decisions about eggs?
3. If you were Barclay, how would you counteract the fear of cholesterol associated with eggs?

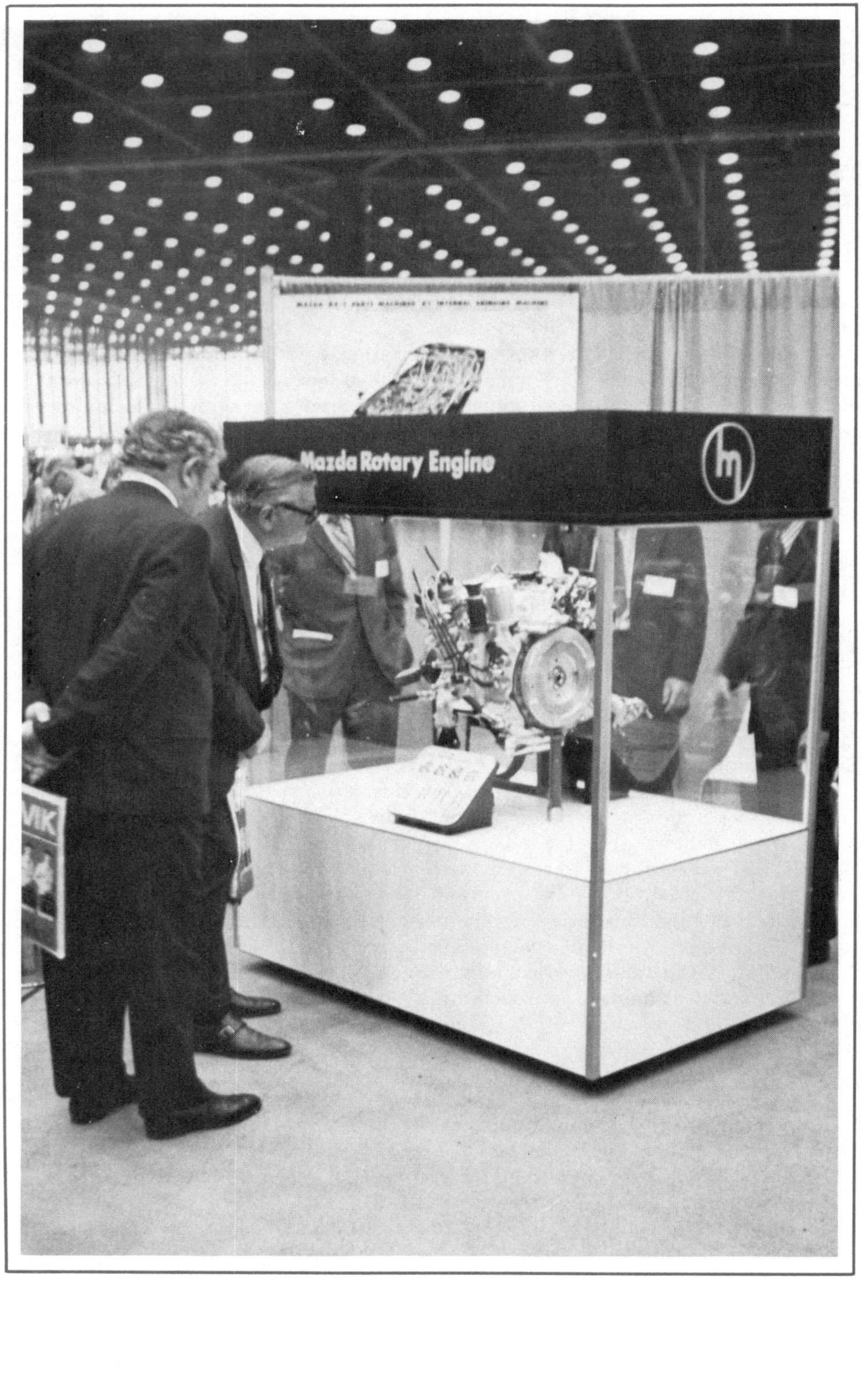
Mazda Rotary Engine

6 Organizational Buyers

STUDY OBJECTIVES

After studying this chapter, you should be able to:

1. Explain the differences between organizational consumers and ultimate consumers.
2. Describe how the marketing mix for organizational products differs from the marketing mix for ultimate-consumer products.
3. Classify industrial products according to their use.
4. Explain the demand characteristics of industrial marketing.
5. Discuss the decision criteria used by industrial consumers.
6. Describe factors that influence organizational buyers.
7. Discuss the role of leasing in organizational marketing.
8. Explain the role of marketing to the government.
9. Briefly outline federal procurement policies.
10. Discuss the advantages and disadvantages of marketing to the government.

I
n the preceding two chapters we examined the characteristics and behavior of ultimate consumers. Now we will direct our attention to organizational consumers, the behind-the-scenes market. Although there are similarities between the ultimate consumer and the organizational consumer, the differences are significant. As one observer noted, these two types of consumers "are as different as silicon chips and potato chips."[1]

WHO ARE ORGANIZATIONAL BUYERS?

Organizational buyers purchase products for one of three reasons. First, they purchase products that will become part of other goods. For example, a computer manufacturer purchases microchips because they are a necessary component of the product it sells—computers. Second, organizational buyers purchase products to use in conducting business. A manufacturer, for example, purchases machines, because the equipment will help it manufacture the products it sells. Third, organizations, including governments and noncommercial organizations such as churches and hospitals, buy products to use in providing some form of public benefit. The government, for example, buys tanks, planes, and ships to provide the public benefit of national defense.

In a nutshell organizational buyers purchase products (1) to make other goods, (2) to aid in conducting business or other economic activity, or (3) to provide a public benefit. In the broadest sense all profit-seeking and all nonprofit organizations are organizational buyers. For the purpose of this text we will call the first two types of organizational buyers **industrial buyers**.

Ultimate and Organizational Consumers Compared

The primary distinction between ultimate and organizational consumers is their motives for buying. Ultimate consumers purchase products to satisfy a personal or household need. Organizational consumers, on the other hand, buy products to make other products, operate a business, or provide some form of public service.

Figure 6-1 compares ultimate- and organizational-consumer behavior. The dissimilarities in terms of product, place, promotion, and price considerations are significant. Observe, for example, the differences in promo-

---

[1] James D. Hlavacek, "Business Schools Need More Industrial Marketing," *Marketing News,* April 4, 1980, p. 1.

tional requirement when selling to organizational consumers rather than ultimate consumers: Marketers must use more selective advertising media, must place more emphasis on rational appeals, must use personal selling more extensively, and must deal with the larger number of people normally involved in purchase decisions. Companies that sell both to ultimate and organizational markets usually maintain separate marketing departments to reach each target group.

Much of this chapter will deal with industrial buyers. We will discuss government buyers, as special organizational buyers, in the latter sections of this chapter.

Figure 6-1

Marketing Mixes for Ultimate Versus Organizational Consumers

	Ultimate Consumers	Organizational Consumers
I. Product Considerations		
Variety of products offered	Large	Virtually unlimited
Making of products to buyers' specifications	Uncommon	Very common
Number of product suppliers	Comparatively large	Comparatively small
Average size of purchase	Small	Very large
Nature of demand	Ultimate demand	Derived demand
II. Place Considerations		
Number of outlets	Very large	Limited numbers
Accessibility of location	Very important	Often not important
III. Promotional Considerations		
Advertising	Extensive use of mass media	More selective—little use of mass media
Personal selling	Limited	Very extensive
Use of trade shows and exhibits	Minor	Major
Purchasing skills of buyer	Limited	Sophisticated
Number of people involved in purchase decision	Seldom more than one or two	Often two or more
Reason for purchase	Personal or household needs	Satisfy business, institutional, or government needs
IV. Price Considerations		
Price policy	Usually one price to all	Often negotiated
Use of discounts	Moderate	Extensive

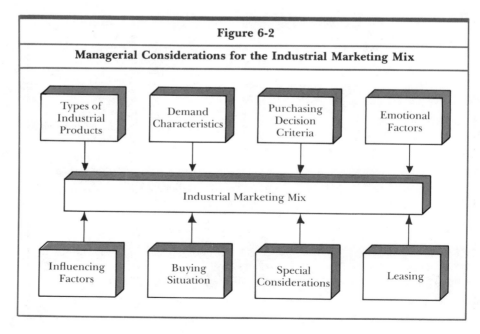

Figure 6-2

Managerial Considerations for the Industrial Marketing Mix

Types of Industrial Products

Demand Characteristics

Purchasing Decision Criteria

Emotional Factors

Industrial Marketing Mix

Influencing Factors

Buying Situation

Special Considerations

Leasing

THE INDUSTRIAL MARKETING MIX

Figure 6-2 provides an outline of the considerations involved in developing an industrial marketing mix. The major part of this chapter will consist of an examination of each of these considerations.

CLASSIFYING INDUSTRIAL PRODUCTS

There are hundreds of thousands of different industrial products. In fact the variety of industrial goods outstrips the variety of consumer products. When the ultimate consumer purchases a television set, he or she buys one product. In the long process of converting raw materials into a finished unit, industrial users buy, produce, and sell hundreds of different products. Because of the enormous number of products consumed by the industrial market, considerably more specialization in marketing strategies, as well as technical knowledge, is needed than in marketing to the ultimate consumer. In this field technical language is the rule, not the exception. Words such as "ektagraphic," "hydrocarbon," "shrink pack," and "palletization" are everyday terms to marketers of some industrial goods.

We usually classify industrial products into two broad categories: (1) products that are used in the production of other goods and become a physical part of another product and (2) products that are necessary to conduct business and do *not* become part of another product.

Products Used in the Production of Other Products

Four types of industrial products that become part of other goods are:

1. Raw materials
2. Semimanufactured goods
3. Components
4. Subcontracted production services

Raw Materials Raw materials are unprocessed physical inputs to the manufacturing process. Raw materials include a wide variety of both natural and "nurtured" resources. Those extracted from the earth include crude oil, coal, iron ore, and other mined minerals. Lumber and other forestry products are raw materials, as are agricultural products, livestock, poultry and dairy products, and the products of our fisheries.

Semimanufactured Goods These are products that, when purchased, have already undergone some processing but are "incomplete" in themselves, such as sheet steel that must still be pressed into the shape of a door before it can be installed on a car. Other examples of semimanufactured goods are castings, plate glass, and plastics.

Components A component is a complete product destined to become part of another, larger, more complicated product. Auto batteries, tires, headlights, and radios are examples of components that become part of another product, an automobile. Virtually all manufactured products are, in one sense, a combination of separately manufactured components.

Subcontracted Production Services Subcontracting, a process whereby one firm, called the prime contractor, contracts portions of a job to other firms, is a common practice in industrial marketing. Subcontracts are especially common in large-scale projects. The prime contractor for an apartment-house complex usually subcontracts the installation of electrical, heating, air-conditioning, and plumbing facilities to others. Prime contractors for shipbuilding and aircraft construction usually subcontract major portions of their work to other, more specialized firms. Businesses that function as subcontractors market their services to prime contractors rather than to the purchaser of the final product or installation.

Products Used to Conduct Business

Up to this point we have considered only those industrial products that become part of other products. There are many other industrial products that do not become a physical part of another product (or add value to it) but provide the environment in which productive activities are carried on. These products are classified as:

1. Capital investment goods
2. Operating supplies
3. Contracted industrial services
4. Contracted professional services
5. Utilities

Capital Investment Goods A capital investment good is a product or facility used to help in the production of other products. Manufacturing plants and installations, tools, machines, and trucks are common examples of capital items used by manufacturers. Capital goods used by retailers include store buildings, display counters, computers, and cash registers. Most capital investment goods are durable goods with a high unit value that last a considerable period of time and are normally purchased only after a careful evaluation of their quality.

Operating Supplies These are products that are used to keep a business operating normally, but that do not directly enter the production process. Literally tens of thousands of products—ranging from paper clips and cash register tapes to cleaning aids and lubricating oils—fall into this category. Operating supplies usually have a relatively low unit value, are consumed quickly, and do not require as much evaluation in purchasing as capital goods.

Contracted Industrial Services   This category includes such items as machine servicing and repair, cleaning, remodeling, waste disposal, and the operation of employee cafeterias. Contractors who supply these services generally can perform them more efficiently, at a lower cost, and with greater convenience than the business that hires them.

Contracted Professional Services   The industrial market requires a number of professional services that can be performed most efficiently on a contractual basis. Examples are printing, executive recruitment, advertising, legal work, professional accounting, data-processing work, and engineering studies. Suppliers of these services often specialize in serving one segment of the industrial market. Some advertising agencies, for example, handle clients in only one industry, such as machine tools or transportation.

Utilities   A fifth category of industrial products consists of energy, telephone communications, and water. The gas, electric, telephone, and water companies supply most of these needs, although some very large industries may generate some of their own power or maintain their own water supply. Although these same services are provided to ultimate consumers, they are normally made available to industrial users on different bases. For example, an electric company typically has an industrial rate structure for manufacturers; a commercial rate for retail stores, office buildings, and service establishments; and a residential rate for individual apartments and houses.

INDUSTRIAL DEMAND CHARACTERISTICS

Demand for industrial products is different from demand for consumer products in four ways: (1) Buyers are fewer, larger, and geographically concentrated, (2) the demand is derived, (3) demand is inelastic, and (4) demand fluctuates. Let us now explore each of these differences.

Few Large Geographically Concentrated Buyers

Most industries in the United States consist of only a few major competitors. In the automobile, refrigerator, home computer, and cosmetics industries, for example, you can count the major companies in each on both hands. These companies, in turn, have few locations where deliveries must be made, that is, to factories. These few locations, however, require large supply volumes to support their production processes.

An example should serve as an illustration. Essex Chemical is an industrial marketing company that supplies windshield sealant to auto assembly plants. Because there are less than 40 auto assembly plants in the United States, Essex only needs to market to 40 locations. To support production volume, however, Essex makes deliveries of sealant to each location by the traincar load. Compare this to the manufacturer of a consumer product such as lipstick. If nationally distributed, the lipstick will be marketed in literally thousands of locations, but at far lower volume than any one of Essex's locations would need of sealant.

American industry, and therefore the consumption of industrial goods, shows considerable regional concentration. Much of the demand for products marketed to the pulpwood and paper manufacturing industries is found in the South, where wood production is especially important.

Assistance Research Programs, Inc., has shown that most customers never register complaints with the company. Instead, they stop buying and begin bad-mouthing the product. With 800 numbers for complaints, 95 percent of all complaints that are quickly resolved result in repeat purchases. General Electric says its typical satisfied caller passes the word to 5 other people within 10 days.*

Therefore, telemarketing offers companies the potential of quick customer access for orders, information, or complaints. This access enhances the corporate image presented to target customers. As one complainer told Pillsbury, "Although I'm mad at the packaging, I think a company really cares about its customers if it puts an 800 number on the can."

The outgoing WATS line allows marketers to call customers and prospective customers at a lower rate than that charged for ordinary long-distance calls.

For WATS purposes the United States is divided into five zones. Customers may buy service within their own state, for the entire country, or for multistate regions in between. Instead of paying for each long-distance call they make, WATS users pay a flat rate for a certain number of hours per month under AT&T's "measured cost" plan. Calls made in excess of the hours purchased, called "cross-over hours," are billed quarterly.

Especially for industrial marketers, who often have fewer customers than consumer-product marketers, WATS lines provide the opportunity for a company to stay in constant contact with its customers. The WATS line allows salespeople not only to contact marginal customers, but also to stay closely in touch with more important customers between actual visits.

* Bill Abrams, "More Firms Use '800' Numbers to Keep Consumers Satisfied," *Wall Street Journal*, April 7, 1983, p. 31.

The aircraft industry is headquartered in only a few cities—Seattle, Washington; Burbank, California; Wichita, Kansas; and Marietta, Georgia. The Akron, Ohio, area is the primary target market for suppliers to the tire-making industry. Detroit, Michigan, is still the main center for auto production. Steel-making, shipbuilding, oil exploration, and coal mining are examples of other industries that are concentrated in only a few major production centers.

Derived Demand

The demand for industrial goods is *derived* from the demand for (1) consumer goods, (2) products needed by governmental agencies, and (3) goods used by nonbusiness, nongovernmental organizations. In a more immediate way other industries' needs also continually affect demand for the products of an industry.

Much of the demand for coal, for example, is derived from the demand for steel, which in turn is derived largely from the demand for automobiles and new buildings. The demand for wood pulp is derived from the demand for paper products consumed by both ultimate consumers and industrial users.

To illustrate the effect of a change in the buying behavior of one industry on another, assume that a home builder experiences a decline in demand. The decline may be due to *economic* forces (unemployment, high interest rates, or a decline in income), or it may be the result of *political* actions (zoning or other legislation that restricts the demand for homes). In either event the home builder will cut orders for materials and services. Suppliers of bathroom and kitchen appliances will immediately feel the impact. They in turn will cut back on *their* orders for steel and other ingredients of their products. Steel and other producers will also reduce their orders to *their* suppliers. The home builder will also decrease orders for items such as wallpaper and carpeting, which may lower economic activity in the paper and textile industries. Electrical and plumbing contractors and their suppliers will also feel the effects of the decline in home construction.

Economic activity in our society is highly interrelated—more so than most people realize. Any economic action that positively or negatively affects a major industry sooner or later affects markets in other industries, as well as the ultimate-consumer market.

Clearly, the demand for industrial products is derived mainly from the demand for consumer products. In general, when demand in the ultimate-consumer market is strong, demand in the industrial-consumer market is also strong, because industry invests in expanding production and inventories. The converse is also true. When demand in the ultimate-consumer market declines, the demand for industrial products falls.

Inelastic Demand

This derived nature of industrial demand creates a price inelastic demand situation. Price inelastic demand suggests that changes in price do not greatly affect the demand for industrial goods, because individual industrial goods normally constitute a small percentage of the price of a finished good. Because demand is derived, a price change in a small component of the final product will have little effect on the final product's price.

Let us look at an example. Suppose a refrigerator (the manufacturer sells 1,000 units per year for $890 each) has a component part the manufacturer purchases for $5. One component is needed per refrigerator—1,000 per year. Now suppose the cost of the component to the manufacturer doubles from $5 to $10, then the effect on the refrigerator is to raise its price from $890 to $895—a price rise the consumer may not even notice. Because one component is still required in each refrigerator and refrigerator sales were not affected, the derived demand for the component part stays the same at 1,000. A price increase of 100 percent had no effect on demand! This is certainly a price inelastic product. Most industrial goods exhibit similar small demand changes based on price changes. Only when the price rises sufficiently for the buyer to switch suppliers is demand significantly affected.

Fluctuations in Demand

Again as a function of the derived demand for industrial goods, demand for industrial products, in general, tends to fluctuate more widely than demand for ultimate-consumer goods. During periods of economic contraction, for example, new plant expansion may be cut drastically or postponed indefinitely. As a result, suppliers of capital goods such as major equipment may be forced to limit their production. At the other extreme, during boom periods demand for industrial products may run far ahead of the norm, leading first to shortages and then, often, to unwanted surpluses.

A key reason for the comparatively wide fluctuation in demand for certain industrial products is government policy, particularly as it relates to changes in defense spending. Over a three-to-five-year period firms can never accurately predict what the government will decide to do about building aircraft, missile systems, submarines, and other costly products. Changes in state and local government spending also create significant fluctuations in demand for industrial products.

PURCHASING DECISION CRITERIA

As ultimate consumers we make many of our purchase decisions because of emotional considerations. Our buying often lacks rationality. Industrial-consumer buying behavior, on the other hand, tends to be more rational and economical.

The principal rational factors that motivate industrial users are:

1. Product quality
2. Cost
3. Post-sale service
4. Efficiency
5. Seller reliability
6. Terms of sale
7. Ease and speed of delivery
8. Variety

Product Quality

Quality is important to the industrial user. It is a relative term, and in the absence of some descriptive adjective it is difficult to determine what degree of quality is meant. Generally, the industrial user knows in advance what quality will meet production requirements. In industries that have grading procedures, quality descriptions may be very specific. Industrial marketers frequently stress quality in their promotional programs. "We invite comparison," "The quality goes in before the name goes on," and "quality components throughout" are pet phrases.

Cost

Industrial users tend to purchase in large quantities. Furthermore, they know that the price they pay will have a bearing on the prices they must charge for *their* products. Therefore, industrial users evaluate cost much more carefully than ultimate consumers do. After an industrial buyer has determined the desired quality, buying the product at the right price is a paramount consideration. A savings of only 1 or 2 percent per unit can make a significant difference. To be sure of getting the lowest possible cost, industrial buyers often use competitive bidding and do extensive checking. Marketers attempting to compete on a price basis may advertise "an ingenious plan to cut costs," "larger allowances," or "low-cost maintenance."

Post-Sale Service

Many products intended for the industrial user are highly technical and require considerable post-sale servicing. Utilities, for example, purchase a great deal of electrical equipment that the seller's technicians must service. The machine-tool industry purchases many types of products such as large stamp presses, that may require years of servicing. In industrial marketing, program engineers, technicians, and other specialists are frequently involved in both designing and servicing products. Some appeals that stress continuing service are "We take complete service responsibility," "Repair personnel on call at all times," and "We guarantee maintenance."

Efficiency

Industrial users are very concerned with efficiency. Questions such as "How can we cut costs?" "How can we reduce the labor input on this project?" and "What can we do to reduce waste?" are foremost in the minds of industrial users. Industrial marketers attempt to answer those questions with product appeals such as "reduces set-up time 40 percent," "fast, efficient—saves labor," and "cuts reproduction costs by as much as 35 percent."

Seller Reliability

The cheapest product can turn out to be the most costly if the seller cannot deliver it on schedule or if the quality is not what was promised. Industrial users, therefore, will frequently pay a premium to a supplier they feel is totally reliable. The sophisticated industrial buyer asks many questions before making a commitment to a supplier—for example: "Is the supplier likely to have a strike in the near future that would disrupt the production schedule and delay delivery?" "Does the supplier have the physical capability and the technological know-how to manufacture parts according to our specifications?" Industrial users often keep data on sellers to make sure they eliminate from future consideration those that prove unsatisfactory.

Reliability has other dimensions as well. Industrial users want to know the level of competence and experience of the seller's engineers, technicians, service, and other personnel. "What is their track record?" is a question typically asked by industrial users. In purchasing components buyers want to know what will happen if the seller's product later causes a malfunction in the finished product. Will the supplier assume some or all of the liability?

Terms of Sale

Negotiations over the terms of sale are important in marketing to industrial users. Many questions, such as "Does the seller extend credit and on what terms?" "What about guarantees?" "Can we get the same delivered price at all our locations?" and "What allowance will the seller give us on our old equipment?" are asked before a purchase agreement is reached. Firms often advertise flexibility in the terms of sale—"Let us help you finance your purchase," "We sell or lease—you decide," "Terms to suit you," and so on.

Delivery

In industrial marketing delivery schedules are often agreed on far in advance. Orders may be placed for delivery six months later. Often, too, it is imperative that products arrive precisely on time. If they are late, production down-time may result. If products arrive before the scheduled delivery date, limited warehouse space may make it impossible to accept them. Industrial marketers stress the delivery factor in their promotional programs by claiming "We defy our competitors to top our delivery capability," "Regional warehouses located to serve you quickly," or "Emergency deliveries on a 24-hour basis."

Variety

Many industrial users prefer to buy as many products as possible from one supplier, so that in addition to cutting down on the total number of suppliers, they may also obtain price concessions. Furthermore, because orders for everything but the most routine items may involve extensive negotiations, dealing with a small number of suppliers who maintain extensive inventories of a wide range of goods may save the buyer time. Industrial marketers stress variety by such slogans as "complete systems engineering," "over 7,000 standard assemblies," and "unmatched variety in colors and texture."

EMOTIONAL FACTORS

On the whole industrial buyers tend to be more cautious and logical than ultimate consumers. They generally make a conscious and deliberate attempt to "think rationally" and "do what is best for the company." Figure 6-3 illustrates how industrial and final consumers might view the same products differently. Industrial buyers are not totally rational in their buying behavior, however. Industrial users are, after all, ultimate consumers when not at work. Even when they try not to be, they are influenced to some extent by their emotions.

In marketing such varied products as office furniture and aircraft for business use, appeals are made to status as well as to efficiency. To a considerable extent firms in major industries, including banks and insurance companies, erect impressive office buildings to help them project a progressive image to the public and, in part at least, to strengthen the egos of executive personnel. In other words sellers to industrial users often support their rational claims with appeals, frequently very subtle, to the buyer's emotions.

Let us examine the various emotional and rational factors influencing the industrial buyer's decision and the type of buying situation.

Factors That Influence Buyer Behavior

Both rational and emotional factors influence industrial buyers. When several suppliers offer similar products at similar prices, little basis exists for a rational purchase. Therefore, personal factors influence the decision. When products differ substantially, however, buyers will adopt a more rational approach to evaluate the characteristics and functionality of each.

Webster and Wind classified four factors influencing organizational

Figure 6-3

Industrial Users and Ultimate Consumers Evaluate the Same Products

Product	Questions Asked by Typical Industrial Users	Questions Asked by Typical Ultimate Consumers
Typewriter	Will it increase office efficiency?	Will it help my son prepare better school reports?
	What is its capital investment value?	Will it improve my correspondence?
	Does it have special features that will help improve our company image?	Is a portable electric machine worth the extra cost?
Automobile	How efficient is the vehicle to operate?	How does it enhance my status?
	Would it be more economical to lease or purchase it?	What is its potential trade-in value?
	What is the expected working life span of the car?	Will I get reasonable gas mileage?
Telephone	Will expanded service lower the cost of communicating with our customers?	How long will it take to have one installed?
	Should our intercom system be separate from or connected to the telephone system?	Can I get three jacks and two telephones?
		What colors and styles are available?

(including industrial) buyers: environmental, organizational, interpersonal, and individual.[2]

Environmental Factors   Organizational buyers are influenced by all the environments we discussed in Chapter 2. Buyers often change their purchases based on their feelings about the economy. When a recession seems to be developing, organizational buyers usually cut back on purchase of capital investment goods and try to lower inventories of raw materials, semimanufactured goods, and components. When the economy is strong, the reverse process occurs.

The government environment also affects organizational buyer behavior. For instance, the deregulation of the trucking industry—an industrial marketing service—caused considerable change in the behavior of organi-

---

[2] Frederick E. Webster, Jr., and Yoram Wind, *Organizational Buying Behavior* (Englewood Cliffs, N.J.: Prentice-Hall, 1972), p. 2.

zational buyers of trucking service. Many companies, for example, bought their own trucks so they would not have to deal with the uncertain environment of contracting for trucking service.[3] Organizational buyers are similarly affected by their perceptions of the technological, competitive, and social environments.

Organizational Factors As discussed in Chapter 2, every organization has its directions, objectives, and strategies. The organizational buyer must be aware of these organizational factors in making purchasing decisions. For example, if one objective of a corporation is to market only the highest quality products, buyers for that company may spend little effort searching for the lower cost supplier. Rather, they will try to find the highest quality suppliers, then obtain the best price possible from them. Marketers must be aware of organizational directions, objectives, and strategies in appealing to the organization's buyers.

Interpersonal Factors When making a purchasing decision, the organizational buyer often has to interact with production managers, engineering staff, product planners, accountants, and a myriad of other corporate members. Each of these members has a different level of status, authority, and persuasiveness in the eyes of the buyer. Which people the buyer interacts with, the value of their input, and the strength of their opinions all influence the buyer's final decision.

Individual Factors Each organizational buyer has individual motivations, attitudes, perceptions, personality, and experiences. Just as in consumer behavior, these factors will influence the final purchase decision. Organizational marketers, in the final analysis, must try to know their customers and adopt strategies aimed at specific environmental, organizational, interpersonal, and individual buyer characteristics.

Buying Situation

The type of decision required also affects the decision process through which an organizational buyer passes. We can classify these types of decisions, or buying situations, as straight rebuys, modified rebuys, and new tasks.[4]

Straight Rebuy A straight rebuy refers to a purchase made so many times in the past that the buyer gives little or no thought to the new purchase. Supplier selection is based largely on how satisfied the organization

---

[3] Robert E. Krapfel and John T. Mentzer, "Shippers' Transportation Choice Processes Under Deregulation," *Industrial Marketing Management*, 11, 1982, pp. 117–24.

[4] Patrick J. Robinson, Charles W. Faris, and Yoram Wind, *Industrial Buying and Creative Marketing* (Boston: Allyn & Bacon, 1967).

has been with past suppliers. No effort is made to find new suppliers. Paper clips, stationery, and other office supplies are good examples of straight rebuy purchases. Established suppliers try to maintain "automatic" repurchases, whereas outside suppliers try to get purchasers to rethink their decisions.

Modified Rebuy   A modified rebuy occurs when the specifications for a previously purchased product are changed or a new supplier is sought for the same product. For example, a company may decide to switch from carbon-paper to carbonless billing forms.

In a modified rebuy some search for new suppliers will occur. To keep the account, past suppliers will try to emphasize the superiority of previous experience, whereas new suppliers will try to highlight the superiority of their product/service offering.

New Task   A new task exists when an organization must make a purchase for the first time. The greater the risk to the organization, the more participants will be involved in the decision and the more time will be devoted to information gathering. In the new-task situation organizational marketers must try to identify and appeal to the environmental, organizational, interpersonal, and individual factors influencing all decision makers involved. Both rational and emotional appeals may be necessary.

SPECIAL CONSIDERATIONS IN MARKETING TO ORGANIZATIONAL USERS

As we have discussed, the purchasing behavior of organizational users differs from that of ultimate consumers in numerous ways. Besides those differences already discussed, buyers of organizational products are usually trained specialists, and several of them may be involved in one purchasing decision. That decision may require extensive deliberation leading to complex negotiations concerning the terms of sale. In addition the final product may be custom-made to the organizational user's specifications.

Trained, Specialized Buyers

Organizational buyers tend to be well trained and much better informed about the products they buy than ultimate consumers. Many of us, even if we do read the ingredient list on a package, often do not understand what many of the terms mean. The transportation specialist told to purchase a fleet of automobiles for a company's sales force will probably make an exhaustive analysis of depreciation, per-mile operating costs, trade-in values, and other factors prior to making a commitment. An ultimate consumer may consider such things when buying an automobile for personal use, but usually only superficially.

Strategy

John Deere Versus International Harvester

When even the manufacturers of competing products admit that there isn't much difference between their offerings, what makes one far more successful than the other?

In the battle for supremacy in agricultural machinery and heavy construction equipment John Deere is the undisputed leader, whereas International Harvester is on the verge of bankruptcy. At present John Deere holds 50 percent of the market share for all types of farm equipment.*

Both firms were begun in the same decade (the 1930s) and in the same state (Illinois) by men who invented successful farm implements. Blacksmith John Deere produced a steel plow that would break up the brick-hard sod of the middle west. Cyrus McCormick designed a mechanical reaper. The company he founded to manufacture it was first called the McCormick Harvesting Machine Company. Later it merged with the Deering Harvester Company and several other small farm-equipment makers to become the International Harvester Company we know today.

Each company has its loyal customers, of course. Throughout the Midwest fields are dotted with the red tractors, threshers, combines, seeding machinery, and binders made by International Harvester. Neighboring farms, meanwhile, proudly display the green plowers, cultivators, and corn and cotton planters that demonstrate John Deere's admonition to anticipate the farmers' needs and fill them.

Deere, however, consistently gains in sales and profits. International Harvester does not. Deere's emphasis on quality undoubtedly plays a large role in its continuing success. For example, in order to maintain complete quality control, it manufactures many components used in its products. Whereas Harvester has recently almost eliminated its research department in a cost cutting move, Deere regularly spends over 5 percent of sales on research and development. Deere then uses the results of its research as a marketing tool. As Deere's engineers improve a part, the company sends it out to dealers for distribution to customers—free of charge! It's a terrific way to build customer loyalty.

In direct response to its customers' needs, Deere has always geared product research and development toward increasing machine efficiency. Deere's customer base consists primarily of the huge thousand-acre farmers who have hundreds of thousands of dollars tied up in perishable field crops and who are willing to pay more for a Deere tractor if it helps them get those crops in on time.

Deere is able to supply the farmer with all this quality and efficiency at a relatively low cost partly because it has used its huge research and development budget for improving its own manufacturing facilities. The automation of its plants has lowered costs as much as 43 percent in some areas. The Deere facilities have been described as "some of the most up-to-date manufacturing facilities in the world, in any industry."†

Deere points with the greatest pride, however, to its dealer network. Over 5,000 independent dealers in 100 countries sell and service the Deere products that are made so carefully in the United States, Canada, Mexico, Argentina, and Turkey. Deere is careful to make its dealers feel that they are team players working for a common objective. The company supports its dealers through regional marketing units that provide training in sales, service, business management, inventory control, and promotion. Deere also assists its dealers in making sales by offering help in creative financing, like interest waivers and extended payments, an important consideration to the recession-weary agricultural customer.

International Harvester, on the other hand, has been slow to integrate marketing into its product-oriented organization. In 1973 it appointed its first corporate marketing manager. At the same time it started decentralizing its decision-making processes. Each of the nine branches had its own marketing planning manager with the authority to make changes in marketing strategy as needed. With this arrangement Harvester hoped it could be innovative rather than reactive to competition.

In recent years Harvester has tried to improve relationships with its dealers and customers. About a fourth of its 2,000 dealers quickly increased their sales under the company's marketing-assistance program, which offered customers a free computer analysis of the types of machinery that would most efficiently serve their particular purposes.

Harvester has also been cutting costs in order to avoid bankruptcy and to become more competitive. It has streamlined its significantly over-staffed management force and cut unprofitable product lines. Harvester sold its construction-equipment division in 1982 for about $70 million.‡ Because Harvester's production of component parts is too costly to keep the price of the finished product competitive, outside suppliers are now providing many of the parts traditionally made in-house. The current emphasis throughout the company is on profitability, not just volume.

Deere has been meeting the needs of the industrial consumer right along by providing a high quality, efficient product at a fair price. Post-sale service is exemplified by its distribution of new product improvements to its customers. The company also is constantly adapting sales terms to meet the economic environment. Harvester has made some attempt to meet the industrial consumer's needs. Unfortunately, it may have started too late.

---

* Jill Bettner, "Planning Deep and Wide at John Deere," *Forbes*, March 14, 1983, pp. 119–26.
† Ibid., p. 120.
‡ "Can Don Lennox Save Harvester," *Business Week*, August 15, 1983, pp. 80–84.

Purchasing Decisions Involving Several Individuals

Ultimate consumers usually make purchasing decisions alone or in consultation with members of their families. Purchasing decisions made by organizational users, on the other hand, may involve many individuals, especially when the products are not routine purchases. A contractor trying to land the job of building a new factory may find it necessary to talk to department heads, accountants, engineers, designers, and various other specialists in order to land the deal. Senior executives often participate in nonroutine purchasing decisions. For example, the president of an airline is intimately involved in the purchase of new aircraft. Understandably, the more individuals whose preferences, viewpoints, and requirements must be considered, the more complicated the transaction becomes.

Negotiated Terms of Sale

The terms of sale to ultimate consumers are usually simple and well defined, and they involve little negotiation. In marketing to organizational users much more involved discussions may take place over a wide variety of matters, such as the length of the contract, penalty clauses if delivery is not made as agreed, post-sale engineering services to be provided by the seller, and warranties. Prices for organizational goods are often more difficult to determine, especially in the case of products or installations designed for one specific customer, because the costs to the seller can only be estimated.

Delayed Completion of a Sale

Unless buying a home, an automobile, a boat, or some other costly item, the ultimate consumer usually makes a very rapid decision to buy or not to buy. When buying something as costly and complex as a computer, an automated production system, or a pollution-control device, however, an organizational buyer may take up to several months or even a year to make the purchase decision. Furthermore, the product or installation may not be delivered for months or years after a purchasing agreement is reached.

Custom-Made Products

Occasionally, ultimate consumers purchase goods such as clothing, draperies, or jewelry that are designed especially for them. Some well-to-do ultimate consumers may have homes built according to their architect's specifications. Generally, however, most ultimate-consumer purchases are from "open stock." Organizational users, however, frequently demand one-of-a-kind products, such as special conveyor systems, blast furnaces, or computer programs. A mass-transit authority may require considerable modifications in the appointments or other features of vehicles before accepting delivery.

Stress on the Seller's Ability to Perform as Agreed

Ultimate consumers usually ask few questions about the seller's ability to meet his part of the bargain. They inspect the product, make the decision to buy, and the purchase is completed. Organizational buyers frequently place orders with contractors and suppliers for delivery far in the future. The failure of the seller to perform as agreed can be very costly. A manufacturer of television sets, for example, wants assurance that suppliers of components will deliver them as agreed so that production will not be held up. Organizational users, therefore, often carefully check out a seller's production capability and financial stability prior to making a purchase.

Significant numbers of ultimate-consumer purchases are made on the basis of convenience rather than economy. To organizational users few purchases are "unimportant." Very minor differences in per-unit price can cost them thousands of dollars if the order is large. Organizational buyers, therefore, tend to shop around much more than ultimate consumers and frequently maintain a resource file of suppliers to contact for specific goods.

LEASING AND THE ORGANIZATIONAL MARKET

Leasing is an arrangement whereby one party, the lessor, agrees with another party, the lessee, to "rent" a product for a certain period of time. Leasing is becoming increasingly important in industrial marketing. As Anderson notes:

> It is estimated that the original cost value of industrial equipment on lease in the U.S. is now about $150 billion. Leases account for the acquisition of 20% of all capital goods in the U.S. Domestic growth rates for leasing range between 10% and 15%.[5]

A wide variety of products are marketed on a lease basis, including transportation equipment (trucks, railroad cars), high technology products (computers, medical diagnostic equipment), and farm products (tractors, irrigation equipment). Anderson notes that a lessee derives six traditional benefits from leasing:

1. 100-percent financing.
2. Working capital is freed.
3. Credit capacity is maintained.
4. No equipment need ever be disposed of.

---

[5] Paul F. Anderson, "Industrial Equipmental Leasing Offers Economic and Competitive Edge," *Marketing News*, April 4, 1980, p. 20.

5. Equipment may be acquired when other financing sources are not available.
6. Equipment obsolescence is never a risk.

In addition to these benefits Anderson points out several other advantages of leasing: 100 percent of costs may be deducted for tax purposes, ownership of property is not diluted, and the after-tax cost of leasing is less than the after-tax cost of owning the product. One important disadvantage of leasing as opposed to buying is that the lessee does not acquire ownership of the leased product.

To the lessor the principal advantage of leasing is an opportunity to increase revenues. Some organizational customers cannot afford or prefer not to make outright purchases. The principal disadvantage to the lessor is reduced cash flow. One way or another, the lessor must be able to finance the leased product, usually for several years.

THE GOVERNMENT MARKET

During our discussion of organizational buyers we have concentrated mainly on industrial organizations. However, government organizations represent sizeable opportunities for marketers and, therefore, deserve special mention. The largest single identifiable market or customer in the world is the United States government. State and local governments are also very large markets for goods and services.

Government Purchases

The government buys thousands of different products ranging from paper clips to computers. The general needs of the government may be outlined as follows:

1. *Standard products,* such as office machines, cars, furniture, and computers.
2. *Office supplies* and general housekeeping products.
3. *Specialized products and services,* such as arms, research studies, and biological research equipment.

In the remaining sections of this chapter we will examine the government as a customer, paying special attention to its procurement policies and purchasing organizations. We will also discuss the role of the government as a vendor of surplus. Finally, we will take a brief look at the advantages and disadvantages of marketing to the government. Unless otherwise noted, we will discuss only marketing to the federal government, both

because of its size and because state and local governments have increasingly patterned their purchasing policies on those of the federal government.

GOVERNMENT PROCUREMENT VERSUS INDUSTRIAL BUYING

Government purchases differ in three essential respects from purchases by private business. First, the government buys goods mainly for use, not for resale. Second, government purchases are not motivated by a desire for profit. Third, government purchasing is subject to many legal and budgetary restrictions intended to safeguard the expenditure of public funds. Traditionally, it is the policy of the government not to compete with private industry in manufacturing goods or in rendering services.

Almost all of the tangible goods purchased by the government are bought from private industry. Although the federal government owns some manufacturing plants and equipment, such property is leased to private business for the production of defense-related products. The government uses its own personnel to provide many services to the public (veterans' insurance, social security, advice to farmers, education, and similar activities), but many other services (such as garbage collection, engineering studies, medical care, and research) may be performed by private businesses on a contract basis.

FEDERAL PROCUREMENT POLICIES

Three basic principles guide government procurement. First, all known responsible suppliers must be given an equal opportunity to compete for government contracts through bids or negotiations. Second, all goods and services purchased must meet predetermined specifications and standards. Third, all supplies, equipment, and commodities offered by a supplier must be inspected and approved by the government before the vendor is paid.

Procurement Through Competitive Bids

Whenever possible, the federal government encourages competitive bidding for contracts. Advertisements in various media and direct-mail announcements to suppliers are used to interest the maximum number of businesses in various contracts. A deadline is set for bids, and the lowest responsible bidder whose proposal fully meets the specifications receives the job.

Procurement Through Negotiated Contracts

In some cases it is either impractical or uneconomical for the government to use competitive bidding. The most important conditions under which government purchases are negotiated rather than based on competitive bidding are: (1) There is only one supplier, (2) the contract is for service provided by an educational institution, (3) products needed are for experimental or research purposes, (4) secrecy is required, and (5) the purchase is under $10,000.

When the government negotiates a purchase, it still attempts to encourage competition, typically by directly contacting several responsible suppliers and inviting them to make proposals. In this case, however, the government is not obligated to grant the contract to the lowest bidder, because other factors, such as expertise, experience, and engineering talent, may be more important than price.

What Constitutes a "Responsible" Supplier?

Although government contracting officers must make contract awards on the basis of the lowest quoted price, it is not always easy to determine whether a supplier is "responsible." Many factors may be involved. For example, the supplier may be a new firm with no track record, or it may be an established firm with no previous experience as a government contractor. In the case of developmental work there may be no firm that has ever made a similar product.

Generally, in attempting to determine whether the bidding company is responsible, the contracting officer will investigate its plant, production capabilities, testing facilities, quality-control procedures, financial status, and so on. The officer will also consider the bidder's reputation for honesty and dependability.

Notifying Prospective Suppliers of Government Needs

Because its policy is to encourage the largest possible number of responsible businesses to bid or negotiate for contracts, the government uses a variety of publications to advise prospective suppliers of its needs. One of the most valuable is the *U.S. Government Purchasing and Sales Directory*. Published by the Small Business Administration, it contains a detailed list of products purchased by both civilian and military government agencies, the locations of government purchasing offices, and procedural information useful to suppliers, contractors, and subcontractors dealing with the government. The *Commerce Business Daily*, published each workday by the Department of Commerce, runs a list of proposed federal procurement and subcontracting leads, contract awards, sales of surplus property, and foreign business opportunities.

In addition many federal agencies publish brochures that outline specific procurement needs and the procedures suppliers should follow—for example, "Selling to the Military" (Department of Defense), "How to do Business with the DSA" (Defense Supply Agency), "Selling to the U.S.D.A." (Department of Agriculture), "How to Sell to the U.S. Department of Commerce," and "Selling to NASA" (National Aeronautics and Space Administration).

Specifications and Standards

In virtually all government procurement extensive use is made of specifications and standards. **Specifications** provide an accurate description of the product or service needed and the quality that will be acceptable. **Stan-**

dards reduce to an acceptable minimum the number of qualities, colors, sizes, varieties, and types of materials and commodities purchased. The characteristics of those items that will satisfy the bulk of government requirements with due regard for commercial availability, adequate quality, and related considerations are adopted as standards. Standards are used for hundreds of products purchased by the government, from batteries to file cabinets.

When purchasing high-performance military equipment, the government encourages competitors, so that it can determine which suppliers most nearly meet specifications. A recent case in point is the $4-billion contract to build the cruise missile. Boeing and General Dynamics were the competitors. Systems designed by the two companies were flight tested for eight months before the government decided that the Boeing design was preferable. In awarding the contract to Boeing, then Air Force Secretary, Hans Mark, said, "Both contractors turned in good products. The differences between the two designs were small, but they were significant enough to make a good firm decision. Boeing's system is better."[6]

Inspection of Goods Prior to Payment to the Vendor

As a matter of policy government agencies must inspect all goods and make certain they meet the technical requirements and specifications outlined prior to making payment. The "inspection" may entail chemical, engineering, and functional tests. If items are rejected, the supplier's invoice will not be paid. A file is also kept on the performance of all suppliers for consideration in awarding future contracts.

In the case of very costly products—such as aircraft or submarines—the government assigns contracting officers to the project. These inspectors maintain offices on the supplier's premises to make certain that specifications are followed. Government auditors are also used on major projects. Part of their responsibility is to audit transactions between prime contractors and subcontractors.

Promotional Efforts Aimed at Government Buyers

Considerable personal selling, advertising, and sales promotion are directed at individuals who help influence and make purchasing decisions. This is especially true in the marketing of military equipment, which accounts for the largest part of government purchasing.

---

[6] "Master of the Air," *Time*, April 7, 1980, p. 52.

Companies such as Teledyne and Fairchild heavily promote their military hardware to key members of Congress and the Pentagon. At the annual Air Force Association Convention, for instance, Congressmen and generals view films, attend presentations, inspect mock-ups, and participate in such activities as the "Salute to Congress" night.[7] All are marketing promotional activities aimed at selling the companies' products to the government.

MARKETING GOVERNMENT SURPLUS

Normally we think of the government as a buyer of goods and services, but it is also a seller of products and real estate no longer deemed essential to the national welfare.

Marketing Goods

Among the myriad items sold periodically by the government are automobiles and other ground vehicles, aircraft, hardware, plumbing and heating equipment, office supplies, apparel, and industrial equipment. Property offered for sale may be new or used. It may be usable if repaired or have value only as scrap.

The Department of Defense and the General Services Administration (GSA) are the main outlets for surplus property. Interested potential buyers are notified through catalogs, mailings, announcements in the news media, notices posted in public buildings, and announcements in the *Consumer Business Daily*. Most property is sold to the highest bidder. Bids may be sealed, or a public auction held.

Marketing Real Estate

The GSA is responsible for the disposal of real estate no longer needed by the government. It offers all types of real estate—residences, factories, warehouses, and office buildings, as well as unimproved vacant land—for sale from time to time.

Interested potential buyers are notified of the availability of government-owned real estate in the same way they are notified of sales of other property. Again, sealed bids may be invited, or the property may be sold at

---

[7] Joseph Kane, "Armaments Arcade," *Time*, September 29, 1975, pp. 74–75.

a public auction. In the case of complex industrial facilities and special-purpose properties, the GSA may use real-estate brokers.

THE GOVERNMENT MARKET IN PERSPECTIVE

We often hear businesses that deal with the government complain of excessive red tape, "run-arounds," "waste," and "inefficiency." Yet some of our largest companies sell well over half their total production to the government. Obviously, the government market is critical to these firms. In addition tens of thousands of medium-sized and small producers depend on government procurements for their livelihood. Because businesses cannot be forced to market to the government, we can assume that it constitutes a profitable outlet for many firms.

Advantages

Although government business may not be profitable for all firms, profit is the major goal in seeking government contracts. The following are some profit-related benefits associated with marketing to the government: lower per-unit production costs, increased expertise, and fewer layoffs.

Lower Per-Unit Production Costs   Some firms seek government contracts as a way of lowering their per-unit production costs on nongovernment production runs and increasing their use of production facilities. For example, suppose a company has fixed costs of $100,000, sells 1,000 units, and has no government business. Its fixed cost per unit is $100. If it can obtain a government contract for 1,000 units, its average fixed costs on all units will decline to $50 ($100,000/2,000 units). Government contracts may also help the business make fuller use of its equipment, space, or raw materials, so that it achieves a higher level of productivity and can make more profit on units sold to nongovernment buyers.

Increased Expertise   Research and development contracts in particular may help a business widen and deepen the skills of its employees. The company may then later apply these improved skills to the production of new products for nongovernment markets. Aircraft manufacturers, for instance, often use expertise gained from military contracts to improve the design of their commercial aircraft.

Fewer Layoffs   When layoffs occur in a company, even for short periods, some workers (usually the best qualified) find other employment and may not return when business revives. Thus, some businesses find government contracts a useful means of preventing widespread employee layoffs.

Disadvantages

The following are generally considered the major disadvantages of marketing to the government: low profit margins, the uncertainty of future business, and the complexity of dealing with the government.

Low Profit Margins Businesses frequently complain that profit margins on government contracts are less than those on comparable contracts with private businesses. Competitive bidding causes some companies to make unrealistically low cost estimates to obtain a contract, only to discover later that their profits at the bid price are very low or nonexistent.

The Uncertainty of Future Business In recent decades many government contracts have been for aerospace and military projects. Such programs can be cut back drastically with relatively little advance notice as national priorities shift. Firms that depend heavily on such business may face severe marketing problems when cutbacks occur.

Businesses that sell a significant share of their total output to the government have learned from experience that it is never wise to have "too many eggs in one basket." Administration planners, Congress, and various executive departments make frequent policy changes that affect the government's demand for various goods and services. Wise government marketers try to maintain several projects in different areas so one cutback will not threaten the company's survival.

Complexity Doing business with private firms or the general public generally involves less red tape than doing business with the government. In some cases sellers have trouble even finding out which government agencies are potential customers for their products. Other commonly heard complaints are that the government takes too long to reach purchasing decisions and that too many different officials are involved in such decisions.

SUMMARY

- Organizational users purchase products to use in making other goods, to conduct business, and to provide a public benefit. Ultimate consumers purchase products to satisfy a personal or household need.

- Organizational users fall into three categories: industrial, noncommercial, and government.
- Industrial products can be classified as either products that become part of other goods or products used to conduct business.
- Most industrial purchasers are subject to emotional factors and the rational motives of product quality, cost, post-sale service, efficiency, seller reliability, terms of sale, ease and speed of delivery, and variety in deciding their purchases.
- Organizational buyers are affected by environmental, organizational, interpersonal, and individual factors and buying situations.
- Organizational buyers are usually trained specialists. Often, several individuals are involved in the purchase decision. Extensive negotiations are often necessary, and considerable time may be required to negotiate an organizational sale. Many organizational products are custom-made.
- Leasing is becoming increasingly important in organizational marketing. For the lessee, 100-percent financing is available, working capital is freed, credit capacity is maintained, equipment is easily disposed of, equipment may be acquired when other financing is not available, and equipment obsolescence is not a risk.
- The U.S. government is the world's largest identifiable market. The variety of products it buys is almost unlimited.
- When possible, the federal government purchases through competitive bidding. It procures through negotiated contracts when (1) there is only one supplier, (2) the contract is for service provided by an educational institution, (3) products needed are for experimental or research purposes, (4) secrecy is required, or (5) the purchase is under $10,000.
- As a matter of policy government agencies are required to inspect all goods and to make certain they meet specifications prior to making payment.
- The government is an important marketer of surplus products and real estate no longer considered essential to the national welfare.

DISCUSSION QUESTIONS

1. How might the marketing mix differ in marketing automobiles to ultimate consumers and industrial consumers?
2. List five examples each of (a) products that are used in the production of other products and (b) products that are necessary to conduct business, but do not become part of other products.

3. What does derived demand have to do with industrial marketing?
4. "Demand for industrial products, in general, tends to fluctuate more widely than demand for ultimate-consumer goods." Why are wide fluctuations in demand of significance to the industrial marketer?
5. Explain how each of the following may influence the decision of an industrial-products buyer:
   (a) product quality
   (b) cost
   (c) post-sale service
   (d) efficiency
   (e) seller reliability
   (f) terms of sale
   (g) ease and speed of delivery
   (h) variety
6. Explain how environmental, organizational, interpersonal, and individual factors and the type of buying situation may affect the decisions of organizational buyers.
7. Contrast the purchasing behavior of organizational users with that of ultimate consumers in terms of
   (a) specialized knowledge of the buyer
   (b) number of decision makers involved
   (c) terms of sale
   (d) time lag involved in making the sale
   (e) desire for custom-made products.
8. Explain how leasing works. Why is leasing becoming increasingly important in organizational markets?
9. How does government procurement differ from industrial buying?
10. In bidding on government contracts, what constitutes a responsible supplier?
11. What are the main advantages and disadvantages of marketing to the government?

APPLICATION EXERCISES

1. From a recent issue of *Fortune, Forbes, Dun's Review,* or *Business Week,* select five advertisements for analysis. For each, determine (a) which of the purchasing criteria of industrial users mentioned in the text were appealed to, (b) what emotional appeals, if any, were made, and (c) what appeals, if any, were made to environmental, organizational, interpersonal, or individual influences.
2. Assume that the government has decided to shift $10 billion from defense spending to rebuilding the nation's highways. Explain (a) the probable changes in the demand for different product categories as a result of this decision and (b) which type of expenditure, for defense or highways, generates the most purchasing power among consumers.

CASE 6
Problems for General Motors' Steel Suppliers[8]

General Motors set the steel industry on its ear in 1982 by announcing that it would no longer buy steel at list from its traditional suppliers. Instead, the auto giant is borrowing a page from its Japanese counterparts and requiring steel companies to submit bids for future business. The message is clear: GM intends to pursue its future with the steel makers as partners working on cutting costs.

Price is not all GM is evaluating, however. In addition it is considering production quality, past delivery performance, plant locations (with the most desirable being close to GM plants), manufacturing efficiency, and commitment to the steel business. GM is applying these tests to the more than 5,000 products it buys from at least 20 steel mills.

Several reasons are behind this drastic policy shift. First, GM feels that fewer suppliers making more products will invariably result in economies of scale that will save GM money. Next, GM executives claim that they wish to reward efficient producers. Says one executive, "Paying list prices is unhealthy . . . it ignores the fact that some producers are more efficient than others." Finally, the trend toward smaller cars and the long recession have drastically cut the amount of steel GM buys from each supplier.

Whatever the reasons, the steel industry is less than enthusiastic about the new plan. Steel executives are arguing that GM's six-point evaluation program could mean sudden death for an industry already in the throes of severe recession. They point to the financial infeasibility of locating new plants near GM production facilities and gearing their own operations to those of GM.

Some steel executives doubt that GM will stick to the new approach for long, because it is such a drastic shift from the past. The attitude that "you just can't cut off your historic suppliers" is prevalent.

In any case the old cliche that time will tell whether GM sticks to this new way of doing business certainly applies. In the meantime, however, steel executives are worried. Says one, "GM didn't get the idea from us."

---

[8] Amal Nag, "G.M.'s Changes in Buying Steel Upset Industry," *Wall Street Journal*, May 6, 1982, p. 31; and Steven Flax, "How Detroit is Reforming the Steelmakers," *Fortune*, May 16, 1983, pp. 126–29.

Discussion Questions

1. What classification of products is GM buying from steel suppliers?
2. Suppose you worked for a small steel manufacturer in Youngstown, Ohio, that sells 70 percent of its output to GM. What factors would you emphasize in convincing GM to buy your steel?
3. How would the changes in GM's buying policy affect your marketing strategy? Make specific product, place, promotion, and price suggestions for your company.

7 Market Segmentation and Target Marketing

STUDY OBJECTIVES

After studying this chapter, you should be able to

1. Explain the relationship between markets, market segments, and target markets and the importance of each to marketing.
2. Discuss the various ways in which markets are segmented and the variables used in each.
3. Describe undifferentiated, differentiated, and concentrated target-market strategies and the advantages and disadvantages of each.
4. Explain why measurement of market potential is important in target marketing and how measurement is accomplished.
5. Describe how demographics, consumer behavior, marketing research, and the Marketing Information System are important in target marketing.
6. Discuss the importance of target marketing in determining the mix of the marketing controllable variables.

Throughout Part Two of this book we have discussed purchasers. In Chapters 4 and 5 we talked about how to identify purchasers and how they act. In Chapter 6 we examined the special case of organizational purchasers. Now we will turn our attention to identifying market segments and selecting target markets from these purchasers.

Market segmentation and target marketing are crucial to everything we do in marketing and affect all the product, place, promotion, and price decisions we will discuss throughout the remainder of this book. Two different target markets may want very different combinations of the marketing controllable variables. Thus, marketers will have to develop different marketing mixes for each target.

Demographics, psychographics, and consumer behavior are all necessary inputs to target marketing. Selection of target markets is necessary before any marketing strategy can be developed. How can we do marketing research if we do not know who and where the consumers are? How can we design an effective mix of the marketing controllable variables if, again, we do not know who our target customers are? As a first step toward examining market segmentation and target marketing, we will look at the concept of a market.

WHAT IS A MARKET?

The term "market" has many meanings. For our purpose *a* **market** *is the total number of people or organizations that have a need for a product as well as the desire and purchasing power to buy it.*

In marketing discussions the word "market" is often preceded by such adjectives as "rural," "youth," "low-income," "high-prestige," "urban," "ghetto," "geriatric," or "juvenile," which tell us something about the consumer group under investigation. Various adjectives also describe industrial markets. There is a "professional" market, a "government" market, an "OEM" (original-equipment manufacturer) market, an "educational" market, an "institutional" market, a "commercial" market, a "real-estate" market, an "investment" market, and so on.

For analytical purposes—as well as for the development of marketing strategy—merely placing a descriptive adjective in front of the word "market" is not adequate. More precision is needed to ensure that marketers spend their dollars in the most effective manner possible.

Total Market, Market Segments, and Target Markets

The **total market** *for a product consists of all people who want to purchase it during a given period of time.* The total market for new automobiles, for example,

Figure 7-1		
Target Market Effect on the Marketing Controllable Variables		
Variable	**Luxury Hotel**	**Budget Motel**
Product	Emphasis on high quality service, good furnishings, room service.	Emphasis on essentials, no frills or room service, low-cost functional furniture.
Place	In choice downtown, suburban, or waterfront locations.	In less central locations, such as near major highways or on the outskirts of the city.
Promotion	Stress service, dining facilities, location.	Stress accessibility, low cost.
Price	High to very high. Price not emphasized in promotion.	Low to medium. Emphasized in promotion.

includes all the people who are considering purchasing one this year. The total market for shoes includes all the people who buy shoes.

However, marketers do not always try to market to the total market. They may select a segment or segments of the total market. The selected segment becomes the target market. A **market segment** *consists of a reasonably homogeneous group of people who want or have a need for a similar kind of product and who have the money to buy it.* A **target market** *is the specific market segment the marketer decides to pursue with a mix of the marketing controllable variables.* Figure 7-1 illustrates how the marketing controllable variables would change for two different target markets in the same total market.

MARKET SEGMENTATION

It is usually impractical to try to satisfy an entire market with one product. Assume, for example, that you want to go into the restaurant business in a large city. Your goal is to appeal to everyone who eats in restaurants. To be successful, you would need an enormously varied menu, an extremely wide variety of prices, and a location everyone likes. Rather than trying to appeal to the total restaurant market, you would select a segment of it—perhaps people who prefer French, Italian, or Chinese food, or people who are budget conscious. Thus, market segmentation has the benefit of practicality.

Market segmentation also provides a more precise description of the target customers. As the restaurant example illustrated, targeting restaurant diners in general is not enough. We must specify the type of diners. This helps us determine when and where our target customers dine, the atmosphere they prefer, and the prices and services expected.

A precise description helps guide the development of the marketing

controllable variables. As Figure 7-1 illustrated, marketers can much more effectively design product, place, promotion, and price if a good description has been developed for the market segment they are after.

Finally, market segmentation allows for a more accurate assessment of the company and its competition. Rather than analyzing the relative success of the company against its competition on an overall basis, marketing management can conduct a segment-by-segment analysis. This appraisal helps the company determine where it is strong and where it may have trouble with the competition.

Criteria for Effectiveness

These benefits clearly make market segmentation a valuable step in designing a marketing strategy. However, for market segmentation to be useful to marketers, each segment must (1) be of sufficient size, (2) have sufficient purchasing power, (3) be accessible, (4) have measurable differences from other segments, and (5) have members that are similar in what marketing mix they find appealing.

Size A segment must be large enough to generate a profitable sales level. The size constitutes not only the number of customers, but also how much and how often each will purchase. For instance, a manufacturer of soft drinks needs segments with millions of customers, each of whom spends less than a dollar on each purchase. Boeing Aircraft, however, needs a segment with only several customers buying 10 to 20 planes (each at a cost of tens of millions of dollars).

Although customers in a segment may want a product and be able to purchase it, there may not be enough of them to meet the size criteria. For instance, even though there are many very tall people willing to pay a premium to fly in airplanes with extra leg room, not enough of them exist for Boeing to produce such planes at a profit. Therefore, it is a segment that Boeing has ignored because of its insufficient size.

Purchasing Power   People who want a product do not necessarily constitute a viable market segment. They must have purchasing power to qualify as consumers. Many of us would like to own a Mercedes or spend a month at a first-class hotel on an exotic island. Such elements of the good life may be denied us, however, because we have insufficient purchasing power.

In the final analysis our purchasing power determines how much we as individuals, as families, or as a nation can consume. Market potential corresponds closely to the level of purchasing power within the market. As purchasing power increases, market potential expands. Conversely, when purchasing power declines, market potential declines.

Purchasing power has three principal components: income, wealth, and credit. That is, we have three ways to finance purchases. We may (1) pay for goods out of our current income, (2) draw on our savings accounts or convert other forms of wealth into cash, or (3) arrange to pay later by using credit.

Not only is purchasing power a prerequisite for a market segment, but different market segments also can be partially defined by the purchasing power of their members. Figure 7-2 illustrates how the residential real-estate market is segmented by the income component of purchasing power. Clearly, the amount of down payment (wealth) and the ability to obtain a mortgage (credit) will also affect the segmentation of this market.

Accessibility   A market segment may have the size and purchasing power necessary, but not be accessible to promotion or distribution. For example, a market segment for quality blue jeans may exist among gold prospectors in Northern Canada, but a manufacturer may disregard this segment because it is too difficult to communicate with and deliver the product to the target customers. However, a manufacturer of sports equipment may market a tennis racquet to the amateur tennis enthusiast because this segment may be efficiently reached by traditional means of promotion (*Tennis* magazine, among others) and distribution (tennis pro shops).

Measurable Differences   In order for marketing research to identify them and find out what they want, market segments must have some measurable differences from other segments. We will examine ways of identifying market segments later in the chapter.

Purchasing power
① fiscal policies
② monetary policies
③ minimum wages

public sector spending programs
① social security
② veterans programs
③ public housing
④ educational programs

state
① workmen's compensation insurance
② unemployment insurance
③ medical programs
④ educational program

—>

These segments must also have some differences with respect to the marketing controllable variables. The whole point of identifying market segments and selecting target markets is to design unique mixes of the marketing controllable variables for each. If each segment responds to the same marketing mix, there is no point in identifying individual segments. If, for example, all customers had the same attitudes toward the quality and price of refrigerators, there would be no need for different models. We could all buy the same type of refrigerator.

Similar Marketing Mix   The other side of the discussion just presented is the fact that members *within* the same market segment should be fairly similar with respect to the marketing mix they find appealing. If some homogeneity did not exist within segments, marketers would have to develop a separate marketing mix for each customer. In such a situation the marketer and each customer would negotiate a specific mix of product, place, promotion, and price. This mix would differ for the next customer. Although quite a common practice in organizational marketing, tailor-making most consumer products would be almost impossible. To achieve any efficiency, marketing managers have to group consumers into segments that want or need something similar, then design a marketing mix to fit those wants and needs.

		Figure 7-2		
		Housing Market Segmented by Purchasing Power		
Target Market	**Product**	**Place**	**Promotion**	**Price**
Low Income	Prefabricated materials, low-priced appliances, small lot ¼ to ½ acres, standardized design, under 1,800 square feet.	Subdivision on low-cost land close to industrial or commercial district.	Stresses low price; extensive use of newspaper, TV, and radio promotion; much appeal to young people who are just starting out.	Low
Middle Income	Some prefabricated materials, medium-priced appliances, ½ to one acre lot, 1,800–3,500 square feet, partially standardized design.	Subdivision on medium-priced land, not adjacent to industrial or commercial districts.	Price emphasized; newspapers used extensively, but not TV and radio; strong appeal to people on their way up the success ladder.	Medium
High Income	Little use of prefabricated materials, best-quality appliances, one to five acre lot, 3,500–12,000 square feet, many extras (pool, tennis), designed by architect.	Not in subdivision, nor necessarily easily accessible to freeways, considerable distance from industrial, commercial districts and airports.	Moderate newspaper advertising, but no TV or radio; heavy appeal to executives and professional people who have "made it."	High

How Consumer Markets Are Segmented

We can identify market segments by any number of variables. Which and how many variables to use is the decision of the marketing manager. Typically, market segmentation variables can be grouped into geographic, demographic, usage, and psychological variables. Figure 7-3 presents a list of some variables in each group.

Geographic Variables   Geographic variables are the basic characteristics of regions, states, cities, counties, and towns. Marketers are concerned with differences in subculture, climate, population, and density in geographic areas. Subcultural differences may indicate unique consumption behavior to which the company can market a product. Dr. Pepper recognizes regional differences in marketing its soft drink. Although distributed, and lightly consumed, nationally, certain areas of the Southwest are Dr. Pepper

---

Figure 7-3

Variables Used to Segment Markets

Geographic	Demographic
• Region • Urban, suburban, rural • City size • County size • State • Subculture • Climate • Population • Density	• Age • Occupation • Sex • Marital status • Education • Family size • Income • Family life cycle • Mobility • Religion • Nationality or race • Social class
Psychological	**Usage**
• Motivation • Attitudes • Learning • Personality • Perception • Life style	• Volume usage • End use • Brand loyalty • Benefits desired • Price sensitivity

---

strongholds. In many small towns in Texas, Oklahoma, and Kansas annual average consumption approaches 300 bottles per person![1] Although the company spends money to market the product nationwide, it spends most in the geographic regions where Dr. Pepper is strong in order to encourage already loyal drinkers to consume more.

Climate often indicates broad purchasing pattern differences. Consider, for example, the different usage levels of air conditioners, furnaces, water and winter sports equipment, and clothing in Minneapolis and New

---

[1] Richard B. Schmitt, "Dr. Pepper Co. Prods Peppers to Drink More," *Wall Street Journal,* January 13, 1983, p. 33.

Orleans. The general patterns of cold/warm, rainy/dry, and windy/calm weather conditions affect much of our consumption and, therefore, create different segments for marketers.

Population is a general indicator of the market size a geographic region represents. Clearly, a geographic segment with a million people holds more potential as a segment than one with 100 people.

Market density, which is a measure of how concentrated the population is, helps marketers decide how easy it will be to reach consumers. Usually measured in terms of people per some land area, such as a square mile, a dense population represents a more accessible market segment. Compare, for example, the relative ease of reaching the 437,000 people that live within 10 miles of Tacoma, Washington, as opposed to reaching the 400,000 people living in the 586,400 square miles of Alaska. A dense market requires less retail outlets, fewer advertising media, and fewer salespeople to reach the same number of people.

As we indicated in Chapter 4, parts of the U.S. market are quite dense. In fact more than 75 percent of our population lives in 5 percent of the land area. By selecting dense market segments, a marketer can reach most of the population while distributing to a small land area.

Differences in density often indicate different shopping behavior. Persons in denser areas tend to have faster-paced lives with more stress and crime. Products emphasizing security and convenience often sell better in dense population areas than in sparsely populated areas. The same is true for tension-relieving products and such stress-reducing services as spas or vacations.

Demographic Variables   In Chapter 4 we discussed the importance of demographics to marketers. For many products market segments are readily identifiable from some combination of the demographic variables listed in Figure 7-3. Waldenbooks took advantage of demographic shifts to identify market segments and choose its target market. Recognizing that better educated, more affluent Americans would find increased reading and possession of books attractive, Waldenbooks has 750 outlets in shopping centers where this market segment shops and plans to open an additional 80 to 90 outlets per year for the next several years. Waldenbooks' strategy is based on the fact that this market segment buys books not just to read, but to be owned, looked at, and given as presents. These consumers may or may not spend more time reading, but they are spending more money buying books.[2]

Many companies use other demographic variables to identify market segments. Again, the important consideration is whether the consumers in the different segments defined by the demographic variables have measur-

---

[2] Jeff Blyskal, "Dalton, Walden and the Amazing Money Machine," *Forbes,* January 18, 1982, pp. 47–48.

able differences in demographics and different preferred marketing mixes.

Usage Variables   The amount and manner in which a product is used is a valuable way of defining market segments. The *amount,* or usage rate, identifies segments by such descriptions as heavy, medium, and light users. Different strategies are developed for each. Heavy users are encouraged to become brand loyal, medium users to buy more often, and light users to at least try the product.

value of this breakdown, other government agencies have also adopted the zip code system to organize data. The Internal Revenue Service, for example, now compiles consumer-income information for all 35,000 areas. Since 1970 the Census Bureau has provided statistics on the sex, age, marital status, race, parentage, education, employment status, and occupation of inhabitants of each code area, as well as other information of interest to marketers.

Consumers who live within a given zip code area manifest homogeneous buying habits, even though the households in the area may differ from each other. For example, a family making $20,000 who lives in an area where $30,000 is the income norm tends to purchase goods as the $30,000 families do. The converse is also true.

Further delineation of potential target market segments is provided by the nine-digit zip code system installed in 1981. The expanded code identifies a mailing piece's designation specifically by block or building, giving marketers much more detailed target-market information.

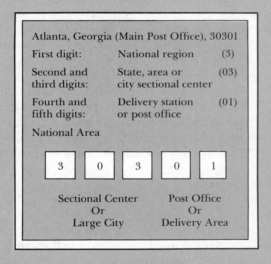

Atlanta, Georgia (Main Post Office), 30301

First digit: National region   (3)

Second and   State, area or   (03)
third digits: city sectional center

Fourth and   Delivery station   (01)
fifth digits: or post office

National Area

| 3 | 0 | 3 | 0 | 1 |

Sectional Center   Post Office
Or   Or
Large City   Delivery Area

The *manner* of usage is the use for which the product was purchased. Two consumers buying the same product for different uses may have very different consumer behavior and, thus, respond to different marketing mixes. A final consumer may purchase a power drill for occasional use around the house and may want a low-priced product. An industrial user may be interested in the same drill for use on the production line and, therefore, is more interested in durability. Two customers buying the same product for different reasons will find different marketing controllable variables appealing to them.

Benefit segmentation is a variation of usage segmentation in which customers are grouped according to the needs a product can satisfy. Thus, consumers may be divided according to their need for such things as value, convenience, prestige, and so on.

Spaghetti Pot restaurants used benefit segmentation to find its target market in the fast-food restaurant business. Recognizing that consumers did not want another fast hamburger chain, Spaghetti Pot identified its target market as working women who wanted take-home food that looked home-made. A meal consisting of spaghetti, meat sauce, meatballs, salad, cheese, and garlic bread provided the benefits of convenience and quality. Because research showed that 75 to 80 percent of this market segment would purchase this meal for dinner (after 4 P.M.), Spaghetti Pot restaurants are only open from 4 to 9 P.M.[3]

Psychological Variables   Sometimes markets are segmented by the psychological variables of personality or life-style. Marketers of such products as cosmetics, clothing, and perfumes develop marketing strategies based on the psychological reasons a consumer buys their products. Marketers try to select positive personality traits such as independence, intelligence, or sensuality to identify with their products. The difficulty with personality traits is that they are almost impossible to measure.

As the Marketing Milestone in Chapter 5 suggested, life-style analysis is based on how people live—their attitudes, interests, and opinions. Life-style segmentation divides the market according to how people spend their time, the importance they place on various things in their lives, their feelings about themselves and issues, and demographic variables such as income and education.[4] Clearly, the way people live affects their consumption behavior. For example, life-style analysis of food consumption revealed four life-style segments.[5]

1. *The Hedonists* want the good life, foods that taste good, are convenient, and not expensive. They are regular consumers of soft drinks, beer, margarine, presweetened cereal, candy, and gum.
2. *The Don't Wants* are the mirror image of the Hedonists, avoid all the "no-no" ingredients, and will sacrifice taste and convenience and pay more to avoid sugar, artificial ingredients, cholesterol, and fat. They are major consumers of decaffeinated coffee, fruit juice, unsalted butter, corn oil margarine, yogurt, and sugar-free foods and beverages.

---

[3] Kevin Higgins, "Ambitious Spaghetti Pot Network Targets Working Woman Segment of Fast Food Market," *Marketing News,* January 8, 1982, pp. 1–2.

[4] Joseph T. Plummer, "The Concept and Application of Life Style Segmentation," *Journal of Marketing,* January 1974, p. 33.

[5] Edward M. Tauber, "Research on Food Consumption Values Identifies Four Market Segments; Finds 'Good Taste' Still Tops," *Marketing News,* May 15, 1981, p. 17.

3. *The Weight Conscious* are primarily concerned with calories and fat, are not particularly nutrition or taste conscious, but want to avoid sugar, cholesterol, and salt. They are large consumers of iced tea, diet soft drinks, diet margarine, and sugar-free candy and gum.
4. *The Moderates* are average in everything and balance all the above tradeoffs. They exhibit average consumption in all food categories.

A food marketer could use these descriptions to decide which segment would be most interested in its product and what mix of the marketing controllable variables would be most appealing. You need only watch commercials for Diet Pepsi and hear the refrain "Diet Pepsi won't go to your waist" to realize this product was designed and marketed to appeal to the Weight Conscious market segment.

Although psychological segmentation can be useful, its application has been limited primarily because it is difficult to use compared to other methods. Information on consumers' income, age, education, and so forth is much easier to obtain than information on their personalities, attitudes, interests, and opinions. Second, the relationship between psychological variables and buying behavior is often difficult to determine. Finally, psychological segments may not be accessible without further definition. Our life-style segment of the Hedonists, for example, tells us little about where they live and shop or what media they watch.

Organizational Market Segments

Although many of the ways of identifying consumer market segments also apply to organizational market segments, some differences do exist. As with consumer segments, organizational market segments are identified by geographic, size, and usage variables, and the segmentation is quite similar to what we discussed earlier. However, industrial users are also identified by industry.

Industry   Instead of segmenting industrial buyers by demographics, marketers use a similar type of variable termed the **Standard Industrial Classification System (SIC)**. SIC codes place industrial buyers in numbered categories based on their economic activity or the business they are in. The U.S. economy is divided into 11 divisions, which are then divided into major industry groups. Figure 7-4 lists the SIC divisions and an example of several industry groups for one division.

The two-digit industry groups are then divided into specific three-digit subgroups and four-digit numbered industries. For example, wholesalers of automobiles are in Division F, Group 50, and Subgroup 501. Their SIC code is a combination of these codes or F5012.[6]

Much information on products purchased, sales, and expenditures by each industry is published by SIC codes, and virtually every company in every U.S. industry is included in them. Once a marketing manager knows the SIC code for a particular market segment, a wealth of information on that segment is available from the U.S. Department of Commerce. Therefore, much like demographics for consumer markets, SIC codes are a readily available method of segmenting industrial markets and obtaining information on those segments. This information can be quite valuable in selecting the target market and designing an appropriate mix of the marketing controllable variables.

SELECTING TARGET MARKETS

Dividing a market into segments helps a company identify the opportunities available to it. Once segmentation is finished, the firm must decide which segments to pursue. To determine this, marketing must measure the potential of each segment, then decide how many segments should be

---

[6] U.S Department of Commerce, Office of Federal Statistical Policy and Standards, *Standard Industrial Classification Manual, 1972* and *1977 Supplement to the Standard Industrial Classification Manual.*

Figure 7-4

Standard Industrial Classifications

Division Letter	Division	Major Group Number	Major Groups (Division F)
A	Agriculture, forestry, fishing		
B	Mining		
C	Construction		
D	Manufacturing		
E	Transportation	50	Wholesale trade—durable goods
F	Wholesale trade		
G	Retail trade	51	Wholesale trade—nondurable goods
H	Finance, insurance, and real estate		
I	Services		
J	Public administration		
K	Nonclassifiable establishments		

targets. We will leave the issue of market potential until later in the chapter and, for now, discuss alternative target market strategies.

Target Market Strategies

Companies commonly use one of three alternative target marketing strategies.[7] First of all a company can choose to ignore differences in market segments and offer only one marketing mix to its total market (**undifferentiated strategy**). Or it can choose numerous segments, with a different marketing-mix offering to each (**differentiated strategy**). Finally, the firm can choose one segment on which to concentrate all its marketing effort (**concentrated strategy**). Figure 7-5 illustrates each strategy.

Undifferentiated Strategy   An undifferentiated strategy assumes that all segments of the total market are similar with respect to wants and needs for the company's product. Under this strategy a company would design and market its product to appeal to the broadest number of consumers.

Companies use an undifferentiated strategy when marketing products that are uniform in nature. Salt and gasoline are two examples. Because it is difficult if not impossible to develop product variations and because the place, promotion, and price variables offer little basis by which to segment the offering, one marketing mix is used for the entire market. Until the

---

[7] See Wendell R. Smith, "Product Differentiation and Market Segmentation as Alternative Marketing Strategies," *Journal of Marketing*, July 1956, pp. 3–8; and Alan A. Roberts, "Applying the Strategy of Market Segmentation," *Business Horizons*, Fall 1961, pp. 65–72.

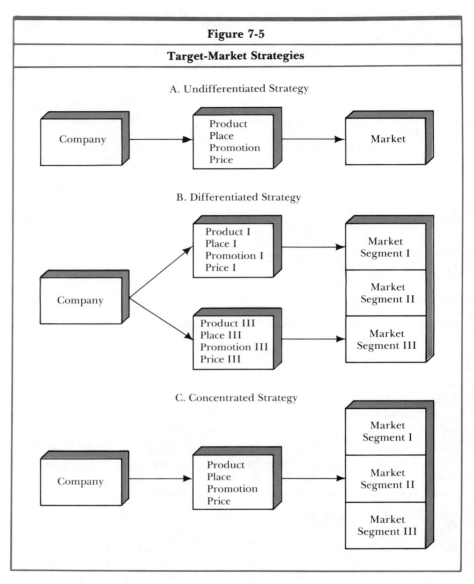

Figure 7-5

Target-Market Strategies

A. Undifferentiated Strategy

Company → Product / Place / Promotion / Price → Market

B. Differentiated Strategy

Company → Product I / Place I / Promotion I / Price I → Market Segment I

Market Segment II

Company → Product III / Place III / Promotion III / Price III → Market Segment III

C. Concentrated Strategy

Market Segment I

Company → Product / Place / Promotion / Price → Market Segment II

Market Segment III

mid-1970s Volkswagen took an undifferentiated approach in trying to sell its one offering, the Beetle, to everyone. Advertisements emphasized how all consumers in the automobile market should consider buying a Beetle.

A company often adopts an undifferentiated strategy to gain cost economies. A uniform product means that production does not have to build different models, thus lowering its costs. The narrow product line also keeps transportation, inventory, and order-processing costs down. Because only one advertising campaign is needed, advertising costs are lower. Finally, the company can avoid the cost of researching and planning strategies for different segments.

However, inherent dangers exist in using an undifferentiated strategy. There are few markets in which everyone finds the same marketing mix equally appealing. If the competition develops specific mixes for each segment of a market, a company using an undifferentiated approach may find that each segment has a more appealing offering designed specifically for them by the competition. Thus, an undifferentiated marketing strategy may capture little or none of the market. Volkswagen's recognition that other manufacturers had segmented offerings led to the phasing out of the Beetle and the introduction of Volkswagen's present differentiated strategy.

Differentiated Strategy   When a firm identifies market segments, singles out several as targets, and develops specific marketing offerings for each, it is following a differentiated strategy. Unique combinations of product, place, promotion, and price are developed for each target market. The company in Figure 7-5B has chosen segments I and III and developed specific marketing mixes for each. This company has also decided not to market directly to segment II.

Even with basic products that are uniform in nature (again, gasoline is an example), a company may use place, promotion, and price to segment its offerings. This attempt to establish consumer preference for one company's product (although it is physically similar to the competition's product) is called **product differentiation**. Through superior distribution, promotion, and pricing, the company tries to differentiate its product from all others. The success of the company's product differentiation is largely determined by the quality of its place, promotion, and price strategies and whether any of the product features it used to differentiate the offering are important and credible to its customers.

With Michelob, Michelob Light, Budweiser, Busch, Bud Light, LA and others, Anheuser–Busch has long followed a product differentiation strategy. Although little variation exists in the brewing process, huge expenditures on advertising, promotion, and pricing practices have helped create different target markets for each Anheuser–Busch product. You need only watch a Busch advertisement (outdoors theme) and a Michelob ad (affluent urbanite theme) to realize each is aimed at a different target market. Is this beer giant going after any more segments? As Dennis P. Long, president of Anheuser–Busch's beer division put it, "If you segment this country geographically, demographically, and by competitors, it gives you great confidence that there is still considerable room for us to grow."[8]

Whether all four marketing controllable variables or just the three nonproduct ones are varied for each segment, a differentiated strategy typically creates more overall sales for a company than an undifferentiated

[8] "The King of Beers Still Rules," *Business Week,* July 12, 1982, pp. 50–54.

strategy. However, the costs are also higher. Because a different product variation is offered to each target, product development and production costs are higher. Marketers must not only aim advertising and promotion at smaller groups of people, but also must vary them for each group. Therefore, these costs are higher. The same is true for distribution costs. More specialized outlets are used, resulting in higher inventory and transportation costs.

Because a differentiated strategy creates higher sales and costs than an undifferentiated strategy, it is hard to say which strategy is superior. In the final analysis the best strategy will depend on the specific cost, product, and customer characteristics of each situation.

Concentrated Strategy Many companies cannot market to an entire market or even to several segments of a market simply because they lack the resources for such large undertakings. Instead of ending up with a small share of large markets, companies practicing a concentrated strategy try to capture a large share of one profitable segment.

The maker of 35-mm Leica cameras, for instance, simply does not have the resources to compete with such giants as Minolta, Canon, Kodak, or Polaroid. These four camera makers spend millions of dollars advertising their many models of cameras. Leica, however, makes only two models, both selling for around $1,600. Considered by consumers and promoted by the company as the "Rolls-Royce" of 35-mm cameras, Leica has targeted its market segment as the advanced amateurs who take many pictures but still depend on the camera for picture quality. Therefore, they buy only what they perceive to be the "best" camera. Worldwide this market segment purchases 30,000 Leicas a year.[9]

This example shows that a small company can compete with much larger companies by concentrating on one target market. Although the large company spends more on marketing overall, the concentrator may spend more in its one market segment. If it chooses a profitable segment, it can find this strategy quite lucrative.

However, a concentrated strategy holds considerable risk. Such a company's marketing consists of "putting all its eggs in one basket." If the mix developed to reach the target market fails, if the size of the market is insufficient to support profitable sales levels, or if another larger company also concentrates in that segment, the marketing strategy (and the company) may fail. At least in a differentiated strategy other segments may make up for the failure of one segment.

Because of these risks a concentrated strategy is usually chosen when the company's resources are simply too limited to allow a differentiated or undifferentiated strategy.

---

[9] Ann Hughey, "Leica Cameras Sell Well at $1600 Apiece, Filling the 'Rolls-Royce' Niche in the Market," *Wall Street Journal,* June 22, 1982, p. 37.

Strategy

Perrier and Bollini

The success or failure of a product depends largely on whether or not the marketers can use target marketing strategies to their best advantage. The marketing history of Perrier exemplifies how closely product success is correlated with sound market segmentation and target decisions.

Perrier, pronounced "Perry A," is a naturally carbonated spring water bottled in France. It was first commercially bottled in 1858, but achieved little success. In 1903 a French physician named Perrier convinced wealthy Englishman Sir John Harmsworth to buy the spring and develop it into a successful venture.

Harmsworth decided to promote Perrier as the "champagne of bottled water." By emphasizing quality, he hoped to attract the rich and affluent segment of the European market.

In 1946 the Harmsworth family sold the spring to Gustav Levin for $2,000. Levin sought to broaden the market for Perrier by appealing to both the rich and the general public. This approach helped to make Perrier a popular drink in many of Europe's exclusive restaurants, as well as throughout the average population. In Europe Perrier outsells Coke and Pepsi by wide margins.

In the 1970s it became apparent that Perrier had saturated the Western European market. For years Levin had been told there was not a large market for Perrier in the United States, because Americans were not accustomed to drinking mineral water. Sugar-saturated soft drinks were too entrenched, and costs would be too high. Levin was advised to continue selling Perrier in the United States only in fashionable bars where it was a substitute for alcoholic beverages. Even though the market studies were negative, however, Levin was convinced that there was a large market for Perrier in the United States.

Levin decided to market Perrier in the United States as a noncaloric, fashionable alternative to soft drinks and alcoholic beverages, thereby capitalizing on the concern for good health. Marketing Perrier through supermarkets would be tricky if Levin wanted to maintain Perrier's aristocratic image.

MEASURING MARKET POTENTIAL

In selecting target markets marketers must first measure the potential for sales in the segment. **Market sales potential** *is the company's best estimate of*

In 1976 the company hired Bruce Nevins to direct marketing operations in the United States. Nevins' marketing plan called for retaining the snob appeal of Perrier, yet attracting the average middle-class supermarket customers as well. Two major marketing changes were made. First, the retail price for a 23-ounce bottle was dropped from a dollar to 69 cents. Second, by deciding to use soft-drink and beer wholesalers instead of Perrier distributors to deliver the product, Nevins opened up more outlets for the product.

Perrier was still priced about 50 percent higher than the average soft drink, so promotion was directed exclusively at the adult market. The distribution system was changed from expensive bars and government shops to supermarkets and convenience stores.

Perrier's promotion began in 1977 with a $2-million ad campaign. This amount was upped to $11 million in 1979. Orson Wells appeared in many of the TV commercials, explaining that Perrier comes from a spring in Southern France and is naturally carbonated. Print ads also stressed Perrier's lack of calories, artificial coloring, or other additives.

The marketing plan succeeded. Sales jumped from $1 million in 1976 to $30 million in 1978 and $120 million in 1979.

Nevins is now attempting to duplicate his Perrier success in the wine industry. His new entry into the wine market is the Bollini brand.

Marketing research revealed there is a growing market segment among wine drinkers. These are the drinkers who have graduated from the 3- or 4-dollar jug wine, but have not yet reached the 8- to 15-dollar bottle level. This is Nevins' target market.

Nevins is using an indirect approach to reach this market. He will target his marketing efforts at the wine critics who, although a very small proportion of the population, hopefully will act as opinion leaders and influence those in the target market to try the Bollini brand. Nevins anticipates that this trickle-down effect will bring him his next 10 percent of the wine market.

To enhance his highly targeted strategy, Nevins is avoiding the "wine saturated" TV media.* Instead he has devoted most of the ad budget to four-color Sunday supplements and ads in urban magazines.

Nevins' work with Perrier and the Bollini wines illustrates that market segmentation and targeting strategies must be based on a good understanding of the product, the competition, and the marketplace. Each strategy has its place, and it is up to the marketer to decide what is appropriate for a product. Nevins picked the right strategy for Perrier, but has he picked the right strategy for Bollini wines? Only future sales results will tell us.

* Pamela Sherrid, "Encore?," *Forbes*, December 20, 1982, pp. 119–21.

total sales in a specified period of time for a market segment given a specific level of marketing activity. Because marketing is largely responsible for identifying, creating, and stimulating demand, the level of marketing activity is a necessary prerequisite for estimating sales potential. This estimate includes an assumption not only about the company's level of marketing activity, but also about all competitors' marketing activities.

The amount of sales that one company can achieve in a market segment in a specified period of time is the **company sales potential**. The overall size of the market potential greatly influences company sales potential. No company can achieve sales greater than the total possible. In addition company marketing activity in relation to competitor marketing activity affects how large a share of the market sales potential the company will achieve.

Company sales potential is usually estimated by either the breakdown or the buildup approach. In the **breakdown approach** the marketing manager utilizes economic forecasts to achieve an overall estimate of the market sales potential. Company sales potential is then "broken down" from this estimate by analyzing the company's and the competition's marketing activities and the effect on market share.

In the **buildup approach** the marketing manager obtains estimates of potential purchases of the company's product either directly from customers or by sales territory from salespeople. These individual estimates are then added together or "built up" to the total company sales potential.

How does marketing gather and analyze the information necessary for these two approaches? Much of the economic and salespeople information comes from the environmental monitoring and internal information components of the Marketing Information System. Marketing research gathers customer intentions. This information is analyzed and developed into estimates of sales potential by using the sales forecasting techniques discussed in Chapter 3.

Regardless of the approach taken, measurement of market potential is essential in selecting target markets. Marketing cannot afford to spend money developing a marketing mix aimed specifically at the target market if that target will not generate enough sales to cover the costs. Without measuring market potential, marketing managers have no idea which market segments might generate profitable sales for the company.

TARGET MARKETS IN PERSPECTIVE

The next four parts of this book deal, respectively, with the product, place, promotion, and price variables of the marketing strategy. All aspects of decision making for each variable are guided by its target market.

Target markets are the core of any marketing strategy. The Marketing Information System attempts to gain information on environments affecting the target. Marketing research gathers information about members of the target market. Demographics, psychological factors, and consumer behavior are used to describe and understand the target market. Marketers use all these tools, in turn, to design product, place, promotion, and price strategies that most effectively reach the target market.

In discussing Parts Three, Four, Five, and Six of this book we should never forget that the wants and needs of the target market guide all these activities. In the same sense marketing managers should never forget this all-important facet of the Marketing Concept.

SUMMARY

- A market consists of all people who want to purchase and have the purchasing power to buy a product during a given time period.
- A market segment is part of a market that wants a similar marketing mix, is measurably different from other segments, is accessible, and is of sufficient size and has purchasing power to buy the product.
- A target market is the market segment to which marketing decides to offer some combination of the marketing controllable variables.
- Markets are segmented on the basis of geographic, demographic, usage, or psychological variables.
- SIC codes provide useful information to industrial marketers, much like the information demographics provide to consumer marketers.
- In selecting target markets a firm can follow an undifferentiated, differentiated, or concentrated strategy.
- Undifferentiated strategies offer one marketing mix to the entire market. Although it is cost efficient, this strategy runs the risk of not appealing strongly to any segment.
- In a differentiated strategy marketing selects certain target markets and designs a unique combination of the marketing controllable variables for each. It is a more costly approach, but is more directly aimed at what each target customer wants.
- A concentrated strategy offers one marketing mix to only one target market. A risky strategy, it should be followed only when resources are limited.
- Measurement of market potential is essential in deciding whether or not a market segment should be a target market.
- Every decision made on products, place, promotion, and price should be influenced by the target markets.

DISCUSSION QUESTIONS

1. Why is market segmentation desirable for such products as soft drinks or beer?
2. Select three products you purchased recently. Describe the total market and the market segment in which your purchase fits.

3. Take one of the markets you selected in Question 2. Describe each segment of this market in terms of size, purchasing power, accessibility, measurable differences, and similarities in preferences.
4. Describe a market that could be segmented by geographic variables. Demographic variables. Usage variables. Psychological variables.
5. Give an example of an advertisement you have seen which is targeted toward Hedonist food purchasers. Don't Wants. Weight Conscious. Moderates.
6. Pick a company from an advertisement on television. Go to the library and find the SIC code for this company.
7. Explain the differences, advantages, and disadvantages of undifferentiated, differentiated, and concentrated target market strategies. For each, give an example of a company following that strategy.
8. What are the differences between the buildup and breakdown approaches to measuring market potential?
9. Explain how information gathered from marketing research and the Marketing Information System could be used with the sales forecasting techniques discussed in Chapter 3 to estimate market potential.
10. Discuss the importance of target marketing to planning the marketing controllable variables.

APPLICATION EXERCISES

1. Analyze five television commercials, and answer these questions:
   a. What segments of the total U.S. market do you feel the advertisers are attempting to reach? Describe these segments in terms of any geographic, demographic, usage, or psychological variables you think are appropriate.
   b. Are all appeals made on network commercials national in scope, or do some of them cater to regional preferences?
   c. How do local commercial messages differ from those shown on network television?
2. You and a friend are planning to open a stationary and office supply store near campus. Explain what your total market, market segments, and target market(s) would be. What information would you like to gather on your target markets and the environment? How would you go about estimating the potential of this target?

CASE 7

Copeland's Considers Moving Back to the Cities

The idea for Copeland's Cafeterias came in Birmingham, Alabama, in 1920, when a country boy, gone to work in town, longed for a place to eat that set a table like his mother did back home—that is, a table laden with a variety of hearty, tasty choices. J.R. Copeland is still the titular head of Copeland's, but his grandson, Robert Andrews, is the general manager of the chain, which now has 75 Copeland Cafeterias in 60 cities.

Copeland's still operates under the same policies with which the cafeterias were begun and became successful. The present problem is competition from the quick service, family-oriented restaurants, such as steak houses and seafood places that have sprung up and flourished during the past two decades.

All Copeland Cafeterias are housed in free-standing buildings or in 10,000 to 15,000 square feet of leased space in shopping centers. Total investment per unit for all equipment averages $30,000. No two cafeterias are furnished, arranged, or decorated alike.

Marketing research shows that 53 percent of Copeland's customers are married, have children over 18, are college-educated and churchgoing. No alcoholic beverages are sold at Copeland's.

Copeland's began in urban areas, but as the inner cities began to erode, Copeland's became concerned about its future success. By the end of 1975 it had moved all but eight of its cafeterias to the high-traffic suburban areas that showed the highest potential for population and economic growth.

Competition is extremely severe in most suburban areas where Copeland's cafeterias are located. Time and again Copeland's has learned that the better the location in terms of traffic and spending power, the more competition there is. Also, even though it is a cafeteria, many consumers apparently think the hamburger, chicken, steak, and fish outlets provide faster service. Another consideration is that many people no longer want to choose from the wide variety offered by cafeterias. They prefer to buy food from the short menus offered by the fast-food outlets.

Robert Andrews thinks maybe the time has come to return to the central cities. He reasons that (1) many middle-aged and older people, who are good cafeteria patrons, are returning to the central cities, (2) the downtown and near-downtown areas have a large working population that must eat lunch someplace, and (3) major rebuilding and modernization programs are under way in many downtown areas.

Discussion Questions

1. Assume you are a marketing consultant hired by Andrews to help decide whether to leave the suburbs and relocate his cafeterias in the cities. Describe his market, market segments, and target markets.
2. What information would you gather on his target markets? How would you gather it?
3. How would you measure the potential for his targets? How would the answers to all these questions affect your recommendations?

PART

THREE
Product Decisions

8 Product Strategy

STUDY OBJECTIVES

After studying this chapter, you should be able to

1. Give a comprehensive definition of the term product.
2. Describe the differences between convenience products, shopping products, and specialty products.
3. Explain the product-mix concepts of width and depth and how they are related to target-market strategies.
4. Describe product positioning, different positioning strategies, and the use of positioning maps.
5. Define branding, brand name, brand mark, and trademark and explain the advantages of branding.
6. Differentiate between family and individual brand names.
7. Discuss manufacturer, retailer, and generic brands and the "battle of the brands."
8. Explain what a package is and why packaging is important.
9. Explain how packaging serves as a marketing tool, list the primary packaging functions, and outline the characteristics of an effective package.
10. Discuss the role of labeling in packaging.

T throughout the next four parts of this book we will discuss each of the four marketing controllable variables. Possibly the most visible of these variables, from the customer's point of view, is the product.

WHAT IS A PRODUCT?

All organizations market something. In the study of marketing we call that something the product. Satisfying customers with products is the basis for all marketing effort. To a customer in a television store the product may be a new Sony Watchman; to the federal government it may be some new defense system; to a manufacturer it may be a new machine for the production line.

Because a **product** is defined as *something an organization markets,* intangibles are also products. The product marketed by a theater is entertainment. A commercial bank markets loans, safe-deposit boxes, and various banking services. The product of a consulting firm is the skill, knowledge,

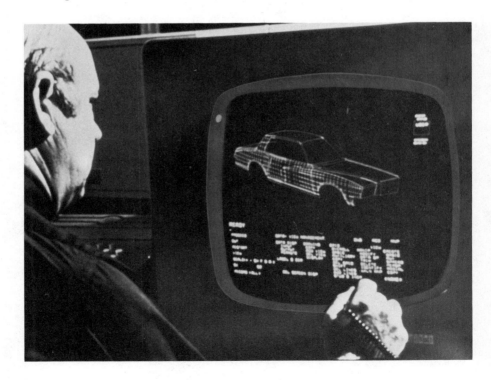

and experience of its partners and employees. Motels market a place to sleep. Airlines market transportation. A television station markets time to show commercials. A telephone company markets communication. An electric utility markets power.

A product may sell for as little as one cent (candy) or for several billion dollars (an aircraft carrier). It can be a totally unprocessed raw material, such as fill dirt used to lay the bed for a new highway, or it can be a highly engineered product, such as a computer.

Some products are extremely perishable. A newspaper, for example, is sought out one day and becomes a wrapper for garbage the next. Other products, such as houses, are designed to last for decades. A product may be essential to life (food) or totally unessential (a tour of the Bahamas).

A product, in other words, is something an organization markets that will satisfy a personal want or fill a business or commercial need. It may be tangible or intangible, sought or not sought, inexpensive or costly, essential or nonessential to human life, simple or complex, perishable or durable. It may satisfy physical needs (clothing) or purely psychological desires (makeup).

This definition of a product does not necessarily describe all the benefits received by the purchaser. For example, buying lipstick to keep lips from cracking ignores the myriad reasons lipstick satisfies customer psychological needs. An expanded definition of the "product" includes the actual product and all the peripheral factors that contribute to a consumer's satisfaction. For example, a person who purchases a television set "buys" more than a tangible object to provide entertainment. The consumer also buys the engineering reputation of the manufacturer, the warranty, credit and delivery terms, the brand name, the courtesy of sales and service personnel, and the prestige of owning the product. All these things are part of the "product."

The "product" marketed by an airline can be defined narrowly as physical movement between two places. If we take an expanded view of the product, however, air travel includes a number of definable but intangible factors such as the courtesy, competency, efficiency, and understanding of the people who sell tickets, check baggage, greet you at the gate, serve you aboard the plane, say goodbye as you deplane, and deliver your baggage in the terminal. The whole experience provided the traveler constitutes the product—the something sold—by an airline.

There are two principal advantages to the expanded definition of a product. First, it makes it clear that in some situations a company can modify a product without changing it physically. Redesigning a company's image is often more helpful than redesigning a particular product. Second, the expanded interpretation of a product provides management with more opportunities to increase consumer satisfaction—and thereby consumer acceptance. It makes the total company a marketing-oriented organization.

Diane Von Furstenberg
(b. 1946)

Princess by marriage, queen of the American fashion industry by virtue of creativity and determination: This capsule description only begins to tell the fabulous story of Diane Von Furstenberg, the designer who put American's pantsuited women back into dresses.

Born to an upper-middle-class Jewish couple, Diane Halfin was educated in Europe's best finishing schools. A bachelor's degree from the University of Geneva completed her formal education and introduced her to Egon Von Furstenberg.

Diane and Egon traveled to the United States early in the 1960s. Getting to know American women struck a creative spark in Diane. She perceived that no longer would the intelligent, energetic women of America follow the dictates of New York or Paris designers. She was convinced there was a market for attractive, practical, moderately priced dresses.

Several years were to pass before she could put her theory to the test, however. She and Egon married in 1969. The ensuing rejection by Egon's father, a German prince of the traditional Prussian school of thought, drove the couple to other lands and heightened Diane's ambition to be her own person.

She spent three months learning textile printing techniques from Angelo Ferreti, an Italian manufacturer. In 1970 the young Von Furstenberg family (son Alexandre made them a threesome) moved to New York.

CLASSIFYING PRODUCTS

If we are to follow the philosophy of the Marketing Concept, we must start with the customer in order to classify products. The target markets chosen for the company, the type of products those targets buy, and how those targets buy them determine the type of product and how it is marketed. We will classify products based on their end use and how customers go about selecting them.

The first classification we can make based on end use is consumer

With three dresses she had made from Ferreti fabrics on her arm, Von Furstenberg made the rounds of Seventh Avenue, the garment district, chief center of apparel manufacturing in the United States. Totally lacking knowledge of the industry, unable to present her designs at their best, she met consistent rejection from manufacturers who were still promoting pantsuits for women.

Eventually, encouraged by Diana Vreeland, chief editor at *Vogue* magazine Von Furstenberg held a "showing" in a New York hotel room. She urged customers to "feel like women—wear a dress."* The simplicity of her now-famous wrap dress and the soft cling fabrics she chose for her designs made her an instant success.

Showing her mettle, Von Furstenberg handled the entire business, including bookkeeping, alone for two years. Then it outgrew her. In 1972, with a loan of $30,000 from her father, she opened a showroom on Seventh Avenue. Sales exceeded a million dollars that year. Four years later retailers around the world bought $64 million worth of Von Furstenberg dresses.

Immediately afterward, the fashion world did one of its characteristic about-faces. It had clearly tired of Diane's clingy wrap dresses. Sales plummeted. Undaunted, Von Furstenberg spent two years reorganizing her company, then came back bigger than before.

Diversification, licensing, and promotions have been her tools. She designs a wide range of consumer products, including clothes, cosmetics, fragrances, and furniture. Licensees manufacture her designs, paying handsome royalties to use her name. Promoting her designs must be one of her favorite occupations, judging by the great amount of time she spends doing it. She is no stranger to the department-store counter where women come to exchange their money for products bearing the famous Von Furstenberg signature. Not without reason did she tell the press, "I am my own best advertisement."†

* "Diane Von Furstenberg," *The Executive Female*, January–February 1980, p. 18.
† Miriam Bassman, "Von Furstenberg Says She's Her Own Best Ad," *Advertising Age*, November 28, 1977, p. 1.

[handwritten margin note: Classification / Convenience / shopping / speciality]

products versus industrial products. **Consumer products** are purchased for ultimate consumption in the satisfaction of personal or family needs. **Industrial products** are consumed in the production of other goods and services. The same product can be classified differently, depending on the customer for which it is marketed. A hand calculator, for example, could be marketed as a consumer product if it is distributed in retail stores, advertised on television for personal use, and priced for consumers. The same calculator could be marketed as an industrial good if it is sold through industrial supply houses, promoted in trade journals as a valuable executive aid, and priced for company volume purchases. Clearly, the same product can be classified in either category depending on the other marketing controllable variables that help create the extended product.

Industrial products are often subcategorized by their end use, as we discussed in Chapter 6. Consumer products are usually grouped by the way in which consumers shop for them, and fall into three main categories—convenience products, shopping products, or specialty products.

Convenience Products

As the name implies, consumers are not willing to devote much time or effort obtaining convenience products. These products are frequently purchased, relatively inexpensive items for which the consumer has little or no brand loyalty. Thus, the first brand encountered will probably be purchased. Consumers have a good deal of prior knowledge about convenience products and need not spend much time shopping to obtain information.

Examples of convenience products are soft drinks, bread, milk, and gasoline. Ask yourself: When was the last time you shopped all over town to decide what brand of milk to buy? Probably, the low relative cost, quick consumption time, and lack of perceived difference in quality led you to buy at the first grocery store you visited.

The essential marketing strategy for convenience products is to have them readily available to consumers in many convenient outlets. Just look at the number of Coca-Cola and Pepsi machines available. When potential consumers want a soft drink, they need expend little effort to obtain one.

Because retailers often carry several competing brands, they devote little promotional effort to convenience products. Most promotion comes from manufacturers. Packaging is an important part of the product and the manufacturer's promotional effort. Because most convenience items are available on a self-service basis at the retail level, the package often must sell the product. Again, look at the elaborate machines Coca-Cola uses to attract and sell Coke to convenience shoppers. As a point-of-purchase promotion so the product can "sell itself," some new machines even play the "Coke is it" theme everytime a purchase is made.

A special case of convenience products is **impulse products**. These items are convenience products that are purchased on a whim. Deciding at the last minute to buy a candy bar while standing in a check-out line is an example of an impulse purchase. Impulse goods are marketed much like other convenience goods, but are typically placed near the place of final payment. Grocery stores, for example, place many impulse goods by check-out counters where the customer is waiting in line (may be bored and more prone to whim purchases) and will pay soon after picking up the impulse product. Although convenience, packaging, and manufacturer promotion are important, in many cases the key to impulse-product marketing is to place the product near the point of payment so customers pay before changing their minds.

Shopping Products

Products for which the consumer is willing to expend a considerable amount of effort searching for information and making a decision are called shopping products. The consumer usually has very little information about the product initially. Because the purchase is relatively expensive and is made infrequently, however, the consumer considers it important enough to warrant shopping around to obtain information. Comparisons based on quality, style, price, service, and warranties are made before a decision is reached. Little brand loyalty exists, and a consumer may buy one brand on one occasion and a different brand the next time.

Examples of shopping products include stereos, appliances, furniture, and clothing. A family may spend weeks or even months gathering information and weighing alternatives in purchasing a dishwasher. In the process they may visit many different outlets and examine many brands. Such behavior is normal for shopping products.

Fewer retail outlets are required to market shopping products, primarily because consumers are willing to seek out outlets. Retail location should be chosen so that the consumer will be exposed to the product at least once if several locations are visited. Promotion is a necessary part of the marketing strategy to inform customers about the product features, quality, and price. Because they carry fewer competing brands, retailers contribute more to the promotional effort. Price is a very important variable, because consumers will search for a lower price or better quality at the same price. Promotional messages should emphasize price relative to quality.

Specialty Products

Specialty products are items for which no substitute exists and consumers are willing to expend a considerable amount of effort to obtain. Because consumers are very brand loyal, that is, because they will consider no other brand as a substitute, they are willing to pay a higher price to get what they want. Examples of specialty products include designer clothes, certain types of automobiles, and popular products for which exclusive patents are held.

Usually, only a limited number of outlets carry specialty goods, because consumers are willing to expend the extra effort to get them. In fact, many products are treated as specialty products simply because they are exclusively available. Some retailers argue that designer clothes by Bill Blass, Pierre Cardin, and Halston are losing their specialty-product status because customers can purchase them not only in Saks Fifth Avenue, Neiman–Marcus, and Bloomingdale's, but also in discount stores. Says Alvin Summers, general merchandise manager at I. Magnin & Co. in San Francisco, "We've gone from having no designer names to everyone having them. If everyone has the same thing, why should the customer come into my store?"[1] To maintain exclusive distribution, many high-fashion retailers are developing their own private-label specialty products.

Promotion of specialty products is aimed at telling customers where the products are available and at maintaining their "specialty" status. Price is high to maintain a quality image and to recoup the cost of limited distribution. Because consumers will consider no substitutes, prices are often quite high. In fact many retailers market designer items at 115 percent above their own cost![2]

PRODUCT-MIX DECISIONS

Few companies today market only one product. Many, in fact, offer thousands of products to customers. To coordinate product strategy, marketers must understand the relationship between the various products marketed by the corporation. When a company produces two or more products that are similar in the need they satisfy, in the way they are used, in the customers who buy them, or in the outlets in which they are marketed, these products are said to be part of the same **product line**. For example, S.C. Johnson makes numerous products for consumer markets, but we could say its myriad RAID products are part of its insect-control product line and its Johnson Wax products are part of its floor-care product line. Retailers also have product lines. K Mart has a men's clothing line, a paint line, a hardware line, and many others.

The total of all products offered by a company, called its **product mix**, includes all product lines and all products within each line. Product mix is usually described by its *width* and *depth*. A company with a wide product mix has a number of different product lines. A company with a large number of products in each line has a deep product mix. Because General Electric makes light bulbs, small appliances, large appliances, industrial electrical machinery, and many other product lines, we could say it has a wide product mix. Because GE also makes many products within each line, it also has a deep product mix.

Wide product mixes reflect a firm's attempts to be in many markets. A company may identify numerous markets in which it can compete and plan

---

[1] "Why Designer Labels Are Fading," *Business Week,* February 21, 1983, pp. 70, 75.
[2] Ibid.

product offerings in each as a way to expand corporate sales level. General Electric, for example, may have decided to enter the large-appliance market when it felt it could no longer expand sales in the small-appliance market.

A deep product mix reflects a firm's attempts to reach numerous target markets within the overall product line's market. Therefore, when a corporation adopts a differentiated strategy in a particular market, a deep product mix will develop for that product line. Figure 8-1 illustrates the relationship between product-mix depth and width and target-marketing strategies.

In Figure 8-1A the company is pursuing an undifferentiated strategy (one product for the entire market) and, therefore, has a product mix that is narrow and shallow. The company in Figure 8-1B is pursuing two markets, giving it a wider product mix. Within each market the company is using a differentiated strategy, thus giving it a deeper product mix. Obviously, different combinations of undifferentiated, differentiated, and concentrated strategies for numerous markets could be developed. For instance, a company could offer one product in a certain product line for a given market and numerous products in another line for specific target markets in that market. To plan the product mix, marketing must first

Figure 8-1

Product Strategy and Target-Market Strategies

A. Undifferentiated Strategy—Narrow, Shallow Mix

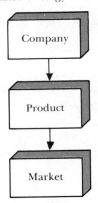

B. Two Markets, Both Differentiated Strategy—Wider, Deeper Mix

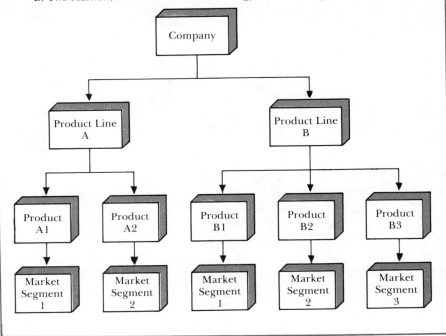

decide what markets to enter and what target-market strategies to follow in each market. Product strategy then follows from these decisions.

PRODUCT POSITIONING

An important aspect of product strategy is the development of product position. **Product position** is the consumers' perception of the product relative to other product offerings. These other product offerings can be competitive products as well as the company's other products. For example, Coca-Cola's Diet Coke was a brand introduced to fit a certain position relative to Pepsi products and Coke's other product offerings.

Products can be positioned by *product features, benefits offered,* or *comparison to other products.* Some product features are quality, options, and price. For example, RC100, a no calorie, no caffeine soft drink, was introduced in order to fill a certain need in the diet-cola market for specific product features. The product was positioned both by the features it offered (cola taste) and by the features it removed (caffeine).

Positioning a product by the benefits it offers emphasizes not so much the product, but what it will do for the consumer. When Jergens' marketing research showed that customers wanted a therapeutic hand lotion, Jergens Aloe & Lanolin lotion was positioned to fill this need. Interestingly, this new product took few sales away from Jergens' traditional Jergens Lotion, which was positioned as a cosmetic hand lotion.[3] Both products offered benefits that appealed to certain target markets.

Marketers position many products by comparison to other products. Seven-Up has positioned its product as the "Uncola," or as an alternative to colas. Avis Rent-A-Car has positioned itself against Hertz as "trying harder." To successfully use this positioning strategy, marketing must emphasize some identifiable benefit, so that its product looks better for the comparison.

The basis used for product positioning depends on the specific characteristics of the company, the product, the competition, and the target market. Companies often use a **positioning map** to compare certain characteristics of their products to competitors'. Figure 8-2 illustrates a product-positioning map for automobiles that was prepared by Chrysler. The characteristics may vary for different product types, but in this case consumers were most concerned about sportiness/conservative and practicality/class. Numerous existing products are shown where consumers perceive them on the map. Plymouth, for instance, is seen as a practical, somewhat conservative car.

---

[3] "'Thoroughly' Researched Aloe & Lanolin Stirs Competition in Hand Care Market," *Marketing News,* December 25, 1981, p. 4.

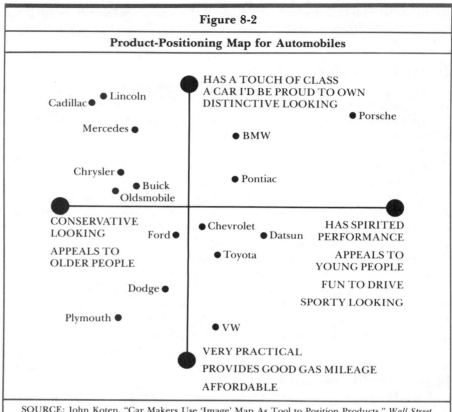

Figure 8-2

Product-Positioning Map for Automobiles

HAS A TOUCH OF CLASS
A CAR I'D BE PROUD TO OWN
DISTINCTIVE LOOKING

Cadillac ● Lincoln

Porsche ●

Mercedes ●

BMW ●

Chrysler ●

Pontiac ●

● Buick
Oldsmobile

CONSERVATIVE
LOOKING   Ford ●

HAS SPIRITED
PERFORMANCE

● Chevrolet
● Datsun

APPEALS TO
OLDER PEOPLE

● Toyota

APPEALS TO
YOUNG PEOPLE

FUN TO DRIVE

Dodge ●

SPORTY LOOKING

Plymouth ●

● VW

VERY PRACTICAL

PROVIDES GOOD GAS MILEAGE

AFFORDABLE

SOURCE: John Koten, "Car Makers Use 'Image' Map As Tool to Position Products," *Wall Street Journal*, March 22, 1984, p. 33.

Marketers use these maps to determine where their products are in relation to others and where opportunities for new products exist. From Figure 8-2 you can see that little competition exists in the sporty/practical segment. However, before Chrysler positions a new car in that segment, it should conduct marketing research to determine the sales potential for such a market and what characteristics the new product should possess, so that consumers will perceive it as sporty, yet practical.

Thus, the positioning map can be very helpful in determining the position of a product and in identifying opportunities, but marketing should investigate such opportunities further to determine their size and their potential for profitability.

BRANDING

Branding, *the practice of identifying a product or line of products by a special name or symbol,* goes back at least to the Middle Ages. It may be done by producers or middlemen, and it has both advantages and disadvantages.

Early in the development of the guild system, individual craftsmen used special marks to identify their goods, so purchasers could trace the maker of what they bought. Another advantage of the marks, or brands, was that the guilds could use them to balance the supply and quality of goods. A craftsman who was overproducing could be discouraged from further production until supply and demand were brought back into balance. This system also gave the guilds a degree of control over the marketing of inferior goods.

These two goals of branding, *identification* and *control,* are still important today. Before discussing them further, however, we need to clarify some of the terminology related to branding.

Branding Terms

A **brand** *is the name, term, symbol, design, or combination of these that identifies a product.* A **brand name** *is a letter, word, or group of words that can be spoken.* Panasonic, Whirlpool, and Atari are all brand names.

A **brand mark** *or* **logo** *is a symbol using letters, pictures, or both to distinguish a product.* McDonald's golden arches is an example of a brand mark. So, too, is the GM Mark of Excellence or Apple Computer's apple with a bite out of it.

A **trademark** *is a brand name or logo that is given legal protection.* The term Xerox is a trademark that legally can only be used by Xerox Corporation or with its permission.

Trademarks are not legally protected in the usual sense, because ownership is acquired only through use. A trademark may be registered with the U.S. Trademark Office if the firm can prove that it is the first to use it, but the firm itself must see to it that no one else uses it.

To protect a trademark from usage by other companies, firms often must resort to filing suits in civil courts. Some trademarks are so commonly used that they pass into the language as a new word. "Cellophane" is an outstanding example of a trademark that lost its exclusivity because consumers began to use it to describe all brands of transparent tape. Other examples of brand names that were once the property of one firm but are now in the public domain are zipper, thermos, and aspirin. Some firms that market products of this nature attempt to protect their trademarks by educating the public to recognize their legal right to the name. Figure 8-3 shows an advertisement published by the Xerox Corporation to remind

Strategy

Ralston Purina Versus Allen Products

Ralston Purina and Allen Products are the nation's largest dog-food companies. They illustrate the importance of basing product-mix and product-line decisions on the target-market strategies of the company. Although both companies make both dry and canned dog food, they have made their reputations and major sales by specializing in one or the other.

Ralston Purina and Allen Products dominate two separate categories of dog-food products. Ralston Purina leads in sales of dry. Allen Products, maker of Alpo, is the leader in moist (canned) dog foods, though it also markets a dry version under the same name.

As the moisture content of their major products differs, so does their product positioning. Ralston Purina projects a folksy image with its red and white checked bags. William H. Danforth, the company's founder, based this package design on the red and white gingham fabric he saw used by the neighboring farm women. Ralston Purina's down-home image assists them in marketing to a broad segment of the American dog-owning public, which is a major company objective. In contrast, Allen Products decided in 1959 to target those households that could afford to buy a premium-priced product.

From its famous Checkerboard Square corporate headquarters in St. Louis, Missouri, Ralston Purina directs 15 plants that manufacture foods for a variety of farm animals and pets. Dry nugget foods are called "chows," the name employed by the doughboys of World War I to describe their field rations. "Where Purity is Paramount" was a slogan of the company's early years. From it came the word Purina.

Allentown, Pennsylvania, is the home of the nation's second largest marketer of dog food, Allen Products. Alpo leads the canned dog-food market, which follows dry foods as the second largest category of pet foods in sales. (Semimoist foods form the third category of pet foods). It was the creation of Robert F. Hunsicker, who began his Al-Po Dog Food Company in a rented garage with an investment of $200. America's foremost canned dog food survived the shortage of cans occasioned by World War II. Hunsicker himself cooked, froze, and packed the food in cardboard containers.

Direct marketing to supermarkets and other retail food outlets characterizes Ralston Purina's distribution system. Salespeople working from regional sales offices keep the firm's products prominently displayed on grocery store shelves while soliciting new accounts. In contrast the considerably smaller Allen Products markets through brokers, taking advantage of the economies offered by intermediaries who stock shelves, secure new accounts, and devise promotional campaigns as well.

Presently, product demonstration dominates the advertising of Alpo, with pictures of cuddly canines gobbling the beef chunks offered by celebrities such as Lorne Greene and various hosts of NBC's Today and Tonight shows. Ralston Purina's approach appeals to the imagination of pet owners. One successful series of commercials featured a miniature chuckwagon (with a red and white checked canvas top, of course) drawn by tiny horses disappearing into a kitchen cupboard as a mystified pooch looks on.

The two companies have directly challenged each other from time to time, both in their ads and by appeals to the National Advertising Review Board (NARB) to excoriate the competitor's claims. Both companies have also been challenged by the NARB or government agencies. Allen changed its claim that Alpo was "100% meat" to "complete and balanced" when the Federal Trade Commission and the Food and Drug Administration complained. NARB was instrumental in persuading Ralston Purina to drop the phrase "tender, juicy chunks" from advertising picturing a reddish-colored product made from soybeans.

In their efforts to meet and beat competition, Allen Products and Ralston Purina have expanded their product lines. Alpo had considerably greater success in marketing its dry dog food than the abortive attempt Ralston Purina made to market a canned dog food in the 1950s. However, Ralston Purina came back with another dog food, Fit & Trim, when the low-calorie pet-food concept was successfully established by General Foods' series of Cycle foods for dogs of various ages and degrees of activity.

As America's birth rate has declined, the number of pets has increased. One out of every four households included a dog in 1983, giving a potentially lucrative and profitable market to pet-food marketers. Although Ralston Purina and Allen Products cater to the same general market, differences in their product line, product mix, and product positioning illustrate that the market and target market must be the basis of these decisions. To ensure the success of their efforts, marketers must properly integrate differences in promotion strategies and distribution systems with product decisions.

Figure 8-3

Protecting a Registered Trademark

What the world needed.
An ad written by lawyers.

Ahem.
We hate to be stuffy; but legally speaking,
please remember that Xerox is a registered trademark.
It identifies our products. It should never be
used for anything anybody else makes.
You remember that, and we won't write
any more ads.

consumers that Xerox is a registered trademark, not a generic term for photocopies or photocopying machines.

The Lanham Act, passed in 1946, established the procedures for registering brand names and trademarks of goods involved in interstate or foreign commerce. Registration is not compulsory but is advisable, especially for companies marketing their goods abroad. The date of a trademark registration will also have a bearing on court decisions should a dispute over ownership arise. In addition the law treats two years of nonuse of a trademark as a signal that the trademark has been abandoned.

One author has set down several rules companies should follow in protecting their trademarks[4]:

1. A trademark must be distinguished from other words in print, even if only by capitalization. HERCULON olefin fiber is correct, but herculon olefin fiber is not.
2. If possible, a trademark notice ® should follow the mark.
3. The trademark should be used with the generic name. "Vaseline petroleum jelly is good for burns," is correct, but "Vaseline is good for burns," is not.
4. Trademarks should never be used in the possessive form. "Xerox's superior quality," is wrong, but "Xerox copiers' superior quality," is correct.
5. Trademarks should always be used in the singular. They are not nouns so they cannot be plural. "Casio brand calculators are best," is correct, "Casios are best," is not.
6. The best way to avoid two common pitfalls is to think of a trademark as a proper adjective. Never use a trademark as a verb or a common adjective. "Buy a Dacron shirt," is an example of a common adjective. "Buy a shirt made of Dacron polyester fibers" is correct.
7. Companies should always identify their ownership of a trademark. For example, "Plexiglas is a registered trademark of Rohm & Haas."

In a recent change in the legal environment of trademarks, a federal-court decision ruled that Parker Brothers no longer has a trademark on Monopoly. In the past marketers have defended their trademark by conducting consumer surveys that identify the name as a trade name. For instance, DuPont successfully defended Teflon in this manner. The makers of a game called Anti-Monopoly, however, conducted a survey that showed consumers would buy the game Monopoly from any manufac-

---

[4] Ellen M. Kleinberg, "Trademarks: The Care and Feeding of Brand Name Identities," *Industrial Marketing*, October 1980, pp. 56, 58, 62, 63.

turer. The Parker Brothers name did not affect the consumers' decision, because they were buying the game, not Parker Brothers' reputation. The court ruled in favor of Anti-Monopoly.[5] Many feel this decision will make trademarks harder to defend. In the future companies may have to promote their trademarks in connection with the company name to keep them from becoming "generic."

Advantages of Branding

There are several advantages to effective branding. Primarily, it helps create confidence in the firm's products. Because producers who elect to brand products put their reputations on the line, they tend to build consistent quality into them. The fact that the consumer can rely on the product encourages repeat purchases, or customer loyalty. A brand name or trademark also helps a consumer identify the product easily and quickly. Many consumers are quite willing to pay a slightly higher price (most nationally branded products cost a little more) for consistency and dependability.

Control is another important advantage of branding. A producer who markets branded products has more control over pricing, advertising, and other promotional activities, as does a middleman who contracts with producers to manufacture goods appearing under a particular brand. Branding frequently has great promotional value. A producer who manufactures washing machines for Sears retailed under the brand name Kenmore cannot advertise that fact. Sears receives the customer's loyalty in this case. However, a producer of washing machines marketed under its own name may advertise and otherwise promote the product in ways that will ensure customer loyalty to the brand regardless of the reputation of the retailers who carry it. General Electric and Westinghouse have been very successful with this approach.

Warranties and service facilities must also be evaluated before deciding whether to brand a product. General Electric, Westinghouse, Sears, and other marketers of major brands make a point of incorporating effective performance guarantees and repair or return privileges into their branding policies. A company that does not wish to or cannot take on this responsibility is probably better off not branding its goods.

Another important consideration is the firm's marketing capability. Branded products must be marketed in the full meaning of the term. A producer which has no sales staff of any kind and no research or advertising department, whose financial position is questionable, or which has had little success in establishing effective channels of distribution would be well

---

[5] "No Monopoly on Monopoly," *Business Week*, March 7, 1983, p. 36.

advised to manufacture to others' specifications. Conversely, a producer which is financially sound, well staffed, and highly regarded by the community could obtain greater independence, flexibility, and control by marketing at least some products under its own brand name.

Selecting an Effective Brand Name

In recent years it has become popular to create brand names by using a computer to coin hundreds or thousands of new words, then selecting the most desirable. Exxon and Citgo are examples of brand names "invented" in this fashion. The increasing popularity of this practice points up a growing difficulty in brand-name creation: the tremendous number of brand names already in use or registered with intent to use (approximately 500,000) makes it extremely difficult to come up with a fresh, original name.

Branders are also putting computer technology to work in another way. Because personally checking each possible brand name to make sure it is not already in use or not yet registered is a laborious and time-consuming task, computer reference services have sprung up that can research existing terms quickly.

What are the characteristics of a good brand name? The most effective brand names seem to be those that are easy to pronounce but sound distinctive (Brillo), are easy to recall (Kool), have a meaning or spelling closely associated with the product (L'eggs), are easily translatable into foreign languages for international marketing (Kodak), and are appropriate to the target market and product (Barbie Doll). Preferably, the term selected should meet all these criteria.

Appropriateness to the target market and product can be very important. One line of sportswear, for example, is designed especially for young women who want their clothes to reflect their free-swinging life-style. The brand name, Luv, is particularly appropriate. Brand names should also convey the quality of the product in some manner. Consumers are quite willing to buy goods of different quality for different purposes (such as less expensive olives for salads and more expensive ones for hors d'oeuvre trays), but they do not respond well to seeing the same brand on both varieties.

Family and Individual Brand Names

Marketers of numerous products who want to brand must eventually decide whether to identify a complete product line by the same brand or use different brand names for each item. Both strategies have been highly successful.

In the food and home-products fields Kellogg and Procter & Gamble are frequently cited for their successful handling of these decisions. Procter & Gamble (P & G) uses the *individual brand-name approach*. Although the firm markets several detergents, their brand names (Tide, Duz, Salvo) are quite different, and you can find the company's name only in the small print on the package label. One reason P & G follows this strategy is that it has designed these products for virtually the same purpose and target market: homemakers who require high-powered detergents for their automatic washing machines. By not identifying these products with the company name, P & G eliminates the risk that a consumer dissatisfied with one will refuse to buy another in the series.

Kellogg, on the other hand, uses names known as a *family of brands*. The "family" is identified by the prominent placement of a common name on each of the company's products. Kellogg's strategy is to use the reputation of the family brand to enhance the reputation of each product.

However, because brand names imply a high degree of consistency in quality, all products bearing a single brand name should be comparable. If significant differences in product quality exist, the company must inform consumers. For many years Sears marketed some of its home fixtures under the Homart brand. However, it labeled and advertised products meeting varying standards of quality as "good," "better," and "best." A & P supermarkets take another approach to the problem, using different family brands to identify varying grades of products. Ann Page is a higher quality brand of bakery, canned, and frozen foods than Sultana, a companion line of less expensive products.

Manufacturer, Retailer, or Generic Brands

It is not always the manufacturer who establishes the brand. Sears' Kenmore line has been a very successful retailer brand. However, **manufacturer brands** represent the majority of sales for most product categories. Consumers often trust these brands under the assumption that the manufacturer will control quality. Manufacturers spend large sums of money promoting their brands and distribute them through many retail outlets. Thus, prices are usually higher on manufacturer brands.

To build a loyal customer following, many retailers have developed their own brands, referred to as **retailer brands** or **private brands**. Although sales volume differs, some retailers like Sears generate the majority of their revenue through private brands. Private brands are generally lower in price, less heavily advertised, and often perceived by consumers to be lower in quality. Obviously, a retailer brand is distributed only in those retail outlets and, thus, receives less intensive distribution than manufacturer brands.

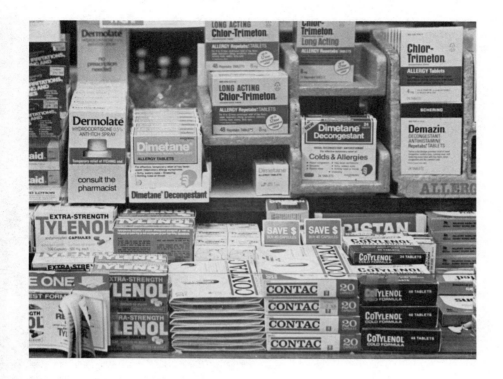

A recent development is that of **generic brands**, products with no identification other than their contents. The French supermarket chain of Carrefour originated generic brands as *produits libres* (free products).[6] Marketed on the premise that the product quality is just as good but the products are free of any promotional or packaging expenses, they are aimed at economy-minded target markets. Generic brands have been moderately successful in the United States (1.5 percent of grocery sales), especially taking sales away from retailer brands.[7] In many cases retailers have introduced their own line of retailer generics (such as Kroger's Cost Cutter Brands) to combat the inroads made by generics.

Because retail stores have limited shelf space for products, manufacturer, retailer, and generic brands frequently compete with each other for

---

[6] For a more detailed history of generic brands, see Charles Burke, "Plain Labels Challenge the Supermarket Establishment," *Fortune,* March 26, 1979, pp. 70–76; and "No-Frills Food: New Power for the Supermarkets," *Business Week,* March 23, 1981, pp. 70–80.

[7] Ibid., "No-Frills Food."

MARKETING

Milestone

Product Warranties

A **warranty** is an assurance to consumers that a product will meet certain performance standards. An **express warranty** is an explicit statement to the consumer about some product standard; a hundred hours of burn life for a light bulb is an example. An **implied warranty** does not have to be stated to be in effect, but promises a product is fit for use, packaged properly, and makes no misleading promises on the label. In its simplest terms, whether implied or expressed, a warranty is the same thing as a guarantee, and both are regulated by the same laws. However, the term guarantee is used more frequently in promotional messages.

As we might expect, the first laws regarding product warranties concerned the dangers in bad-food marketing practices. In 1266 English law made it a criminal offense to sell "corrupt" food for immediate consumption.* Protection against the purchase of clothing that did not meet the seller's claims was added to the English legal code in 1607.

For many centuries it was very difficult for a consumer to sue a manufacturer of a faulty or dangerous product. These difficulties were intensified by the 1842 decision in the case of Winterbottom vs. Wright. The court held that although unsafe coaches built by Wright caused injury to the driver (Winterbottom), Winterbottom could not sue Wright. The court said the warranty was between Wright and Winterbottom's employer, who leased the coaches. Winterbottom, therefore, could not recover damages from a warranty to which he was not privy.

The growth of technology and increased social consciousness combined to

the same shelf space. Manufacturers and retailers particularly want to obtain customer loyalty and profitability through their brands. This competition for shelf space is often called the *battle of the brands.* Many manufacturers have been accused of introducing a large number of similar brands in an attempt to monopolize shelf space and force out other manufacturers' brands, retailer brands, and generics, a strategy called **brand proliferation**. Retailers may also counter by introducing several brands and giving preferred shelf location to them. This brand proliferation forces many marginal brands out of the market and often confuses the customer. In a

improve the consumer's position after the turn of the century. The advent of complicated machinery such as automobiles, farming equipment, and assembly-line machines resulted in decisions that placed greater responsibility on the makers of the machines for their safety in operation. Scandals in the food industry led to broadened powers for the Food and Drug Administration in regulating the wholesomeness and safety of these products.

Today consumers are protected by a number of laws and government agencies charged to look out for their welfare. One of these laws, the Magnuson–Moss Warranty Act, provides, in part, for the following:

1. Warranties must be written in language laypeople can understand.
2. Warranties, when offered, must be labeled "full" or "limited." For the latter, limitations must be spelled out clearly. A manufacturer offering a full warranty must specify the length of time during which it is to be considered a full warranty; any part or product found to be defective must be repaired or replaced during that time, or the consumer is to be given a full refund.

Although at first glance warranties appear to be a way to protect consumers from marketers, they are actually an aid in marketing. Warranties ensure the maintenance of product quality and safety, or the manufacturer will be held responsible. The continuing tradition of strong product warranties allows consumers to develop confidence that the products they buy are either what they purport to be or the manufacturer will make them so. This atmosphere of responsibility encourages marketers to be honest in their claims for products, and the attitude of confidence lends credibility to these claims. Both make the job of selling quality products that much easier.

* Reed Dickerson, *Products Liability and the Food Consumer* (Boston: Little, Brown, 1951), p. 20.

recent survey by the New York advertising agency of Batten, Barton, Durstine & Osborn, 40 percent of respondents felt the number of competing brands made shopping difficult. In addition the majority of respondents felt there were too many brands of cigarettes, dry cereal, alcoholic beverages, cough remedies, bar soaps, beer, cars, and soft drinks.[8]

[8] Bill Abrams, "Shoppers are Often Confused by All the Competing Brands," *Wall Street Journal*, April 22, 1982, p. 31.

PACKAGING

The **package** contains, protects, and identifies the basic product. The firm markets the package as much, if not more, than it does the product. Packages range from the very simple to the very complex. For example, the narrow paper band that holds a small bunch of bananas together is a very simple package. It may or may not be imprinted with the producer's name or brand. At the other extreme are the elaborate containers designed to package expensive perfumes.

Packaging is most important in the case of consumer convenience goods. Automobiles or major appliances—durable goods in general—are not packaged in the conventional sense. These products rely on design, not on packages, to help induce demand. Most industrial goods are either not packaged at all, or, if they are, the package is intended primarily to protect the product during shipment and storage. Raw materials such as mineral products, lumber, and grain are not packaged.

In our highly sophisticated distribution system, an enormous number of goods are **prepackaged**. For the system to work there must be both a sense of integrity on the part of the producer and a corresponding degree of trust on the part of the consumer. The simple act of purchasing breakfast cereal illustrates the trust the consumer must place in the company responsible for the package. Buyers cannot actually see the cereal. Nor can they be absolutely certain that the package contains corn flakes, bran buds, or whatever else it says on the box. They cannot even be certain that the weight printed on the package is correct or that the cereal is fresh. Deliberate misrepresentation, of course, is a short-sighted marketing policy, because few consumers will make repeat purchases if they feel they have been cheated. It is also illegal, and a producer knows that complaints from individual customers or consumer-watchdog groups may lead to government investigation as well as declining sales.

These conditions—producer integrity, consumer trust, and government controls—do not exist in many underdeveloped countries. In many parts of Asia, for example, consumers will not buy prepackaged goods due to the many opportunities this system gives the producer to tamper with the contents.

Packaging as a Marketing Tool

In our study of packaging we should note the importance of a systems approach to marketing. A maximally effective marketing program is unlikely if a company views packaging as an independent activity, product design as another independent activity, sales and promotion as a third, transportation and storage as a fourth, and pricing as a fifth. Each of these marketing functions plays a vital part in company profits, but it is their coordination into a harmonious whole that greatly increases the potential for success of the entire marketing program. Each, in turn, plays a part in packaging decisions.

Packaging is much more than frosting on the cake. When there are many products that have the same or highly similar functions, packaging may well make the difference between success and failure, because it often is the only factor differentiating the products.

Packaging assumes great significance when the consumer cannot see or examine the product itself at the point of purchase. You cannot, for example, physically inspect milk, orange juice, baked beans, and a host of other food products in a supermarket. The package label must explain the pertinent facts about the product, and it is the package design rather than the appearance of the product that must stimulate consumer desire.

Marketing management is very much aware that the product's package is a sales tool. The large number of competing products, especially in the ultimate-consumer field, coupled with the decline in personal selling (in discount stores and supermarkets, for example) make attractive, attention-getting packaging imperative. Often, products must sell themselves, supported only by media and point-of-purchase advertising.

Primary Packaging Functions

Developing the most effective packages is not an easy task, as suggested by the checklist of packaging considerations in Figure 8-4. The list, comprehensive as it is, could be expanded to several times its present length for a large number of products. Basically, a package fulfills the three functions

---

Figure 8-4
Evaluating a Package's Point-of-Sale Effectiveness

The package, in many cases, is the producer's last chance to communicate the product's message to the consumer. After all the advertising and public relations work has been done, the package must frequently stand on its own in a face-to-face confrontation with customers in the marketplace. Positive answers to all the questions below will help to ensure a successful package.

- Does the label tell customers what they want and need to know?
- Does it instantly identify the type of product the package contains?
- Is the package distinctive?
- Is it compatible with the firm's advertising image?
- Does its size make it competitive with similar products?
- Do its size and shape aid in distribution?
- Does it direct attention to its contents rather than monopolize the consumer's attention?
- Does it attract attention from the greatest possible distance?
- If cost is an important consideration, does the package design allow for a prominent display of the price?

included in our definition of the term. It contains, protects, and identifies the basic product.

Containment   A package defines, in some manner, the space in which a product is contained. The package contents may be premeasured, pre-weighed, presorted, preassembled (or left unassembled), then placed in a specially designed wrapper, box, carton, crate, can, bottle, jar, tube, barrel, drum, or pallet for convenient distribution. In some cases containment may be the only function of a package. For example, if you purchase apples at a roadside stand, the "package" provided may consist simply of a plain brown paper bag in which to carry the fruit. A supermarket, on the other hand, may precount six apples, place them in a cardboard tray, and surround them with a cover of plastic film. Either way, the requirement of containment is fulfilled.

Protection   A second function of a package is to protect the product, so that it will survive the distribution system and reach its ultimate destination in sound condition. In many cases the package also lengthens the good's shelf life and protects it for a reasonable length of use time. Proper packaging helps prevent breakage, retard spoilage, and avoid contamination. A new development in packaging, the aseptic package, allows such perishables as milk and fruit juices to be stored unrefrigerated for six months without loss of flavor or nutritional value. Already, half of all milk sold in Europe is packaged this way.[9]

Identification   In fulfilling this function, packaging and labeling are virtually inseparable and closely related to branding. Most packages bear, at the very least, the name of the product, its maker, and (in the case of food or drugs) its ingredients. The vast majority of packages carry extensive additional information. Data may also be imprinted on the product itself (serial and model numbers, for example).

Today marketing managers almost take for granted that the package will contain and protect the product. From a marketing viewpoint *identification of the product* is the most important aspect of packaging. The package becomes a point-of-sale form of advertising. A recent survey of 150 consumers found that 60 percent said packaging influenced their purchase decisions.[10] This helps explain why companies are extremely slow to change the basic design of a package that sells well. Figure 8-5 shows four products whose packages have undergone only very minor changes in appearance for a number of decades.

---

[9] Robert Ball, "Warm Milk Wakes Up the Packaging Industry," *Fortune*, August 9, 1982, pp. 78–82.

[10] Stuart M. Berni, "Consumers Want Food Packaging That Can Be Easily Resealed: Survey," *Marketing News*, May 28, 1982, p. 9.

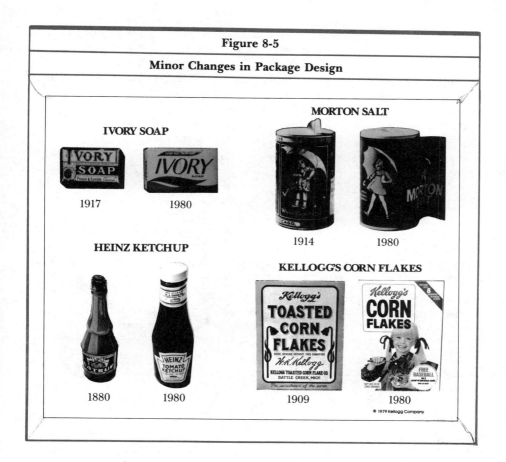

Figure 8-5

Minor Changes in Package Design

IVORY SOAP

1917   1980

MORTON SALT

1914   1980

HEINZ KETCHUP

1880   1980

KELLOGG'S CORN FLAKES

1909   1980

© 1979 Kellogg Company

Additional Packaging Goals

In order to enhance product sales, a package should (1) be convenient, (2) be attractive, (3) have promotional appeal, and (4) be economical. As you read the following discussion, remember that a company must consider the needs of middlemen, as well as those of ultimate users, in making a packaging decision. Although wholesalers and retailers are not as likely as consumers to accept or reject a product on the basis of its package, they tend to spend more effort promoting those that best fulfill the following criteria.

Convenience   Convenience should be viewed primarily from the standpoint of the user. Packages for consumer goods should be light enough to be hand carried, even if this requires charging the customer more money. A hundred-pound sack of flour may be economical, but most consumers find one- to five-pound boxes or bags easier to carry and store. Aspirin bottles containing 100 pills are more economical than small tins containing twelve, but a bottle is too cumbersome to carry in a purse or pocket.

Soft-drink manufacturers have long been deeply concerned with convenience in packaging. For many years manufacturers packaged soft drinks in glass bottles with lift-off caps that required a bottle opener. In the 1950s aluminum cans appeared on the market. They were lightweight, unbreakable and nonreturnable, but opening them still required a special tool. In the 1960s the self-opening can gained widespread use. Invention of the pop-top can meant that soft drinks could be opened anywhere. Soft-drink producers who failed to adopt this new package found themselves with a declining market share.

The dimensions of a package also play an important role in convenience. Cereal eaters may remember, a few years ago, concerted complaints that many cereal boxes were too tall to be stored upright in standard kitchen cabinets. Most cereal-package designers, recognizing the importance of convenient home storage, soon modified their boxes to fit a normal shelf.

Another aspect of convenience, as far as ultimate consumers are concerned, is whether they can easily reclose the package securely once they have opened it. Bottles or jars with caps that screw back on are important for many products, especially in recessionary times. As Package Designers Council President Stuart M. Berni put it, "Consumers caught in the current economic squeeze want packaging which can be resealed to prolong the freshness of unused food portions." In a PDC survey of 150 consumers three of the four most important packaging characteristics were storage life (including leftover storage), ease of resealing, and ease of storing at home.[11]

Convenience for retailers is another packaging consideration. Even a casual stroll through a supermarket or other self-service store reveals that competition for shelf space is intense. Because there is usually little or no vacant shelf space, a retailer will usually make no special effort to arrange a display of oddly shaped packages that cannot easily be stacked.

Attractiveness A primary objective of packaging is to enhance the appearance of the product. Some products are actually more readily identified by the shape of their packages than by any other visual element. The contents of a carton of eggs, for example, are usually identified long before the shopper reads the information printed on the package.

Color can have a dramatic effect on our reactions. Often it can be used to improve the appearance and appeal of a product. Certain colors may be repeated throughout a product line to emphasize its distinctiveness and to ensure easy product identification. This practice is quite common among

---

[11] Ibid.

The president of Braxton, Braxton & Whipple, Inc. should never write a friend as president of Braxton, Braxton & Whipple, Inc.

In today's society, with its hectic pace, a personal note is particularly appreciated.

For, in addition to what is written, it says something more—that you've taken time out of your busy schedule to express your friendship.

However, that warm gesture is not compatibly conveyed on a business letterhead.

The answer, of course, is stationery of your own.

And the paper that's best for your personal stationery is the paper that the best companies value for theirs: Crane.

Crane papers are made of the finest fiber known for stationery: 100% cotton.

Resulting in the most handsome papers upon which your thoughts can be expressed.

At the finest stores you know. Crane & Co., Inc. Dalton, Massachusetts. 01226.

Crane

We've been taking your words seriously for 181 years.

cosmetics manufacturers, who may package an entire line in a particular shade of lemon yellow or soft pink, using coordinated labeling that lets the consumer recognize the maker of the various products in the line immediately. Nature Valley uses this approach by having similar package designs on all brands of Nature Valley Granola Bars but using a different, distinctive color package for each flavor. Thus, consumers come to identify the color with the flavor they prefer.[12]

Promotional Appeal　Closely allied to package attractiveness, but broader in scope, is promotional appeal. As we have seen, due to modern self-service retailing, products frequently must sell themselves. The more attractive and eye-appealing the package is, the faster the product is likely to sell. For products retailed in self-service stores or vending machines, the package is a vital point-of-purchase sales tool. Therefore its promotional appeal is especially important. Even the best quality product priced at the lowest level possible may go unnoticed unless it stands out from competitive products in the same display.

Several factors contribute to a package's promotional appeal, some of which are closely related to labeling and branding. Its color and shape, the typeface used, the trademark or other illustrations it contains, the information given on it, and its price all play a part in determining its promotional appeal.

Economy　It has been estimated that packaging costs account for approximately four cents of every dollar spent on consumer products. Some authorities estimate that more money is spent on packaging than on advertising. Certainly, then, the desirability of selecting both an effective and an economical package is apparent.

Overpackaging, however, is expensive and should be avoided. For example, it would be foolish to package plastic hairbrushes in hinged-top plastic boxes when cardboard boxes would serve as well. On the other hand, a manufacturer of more expensive, natural-bristle brushes who wished to court a prestige-conscious market might find the more expensive package justified by factors other than its functional value. The economics of using various packaging materials should be constantly reevaluated as new ones come on the market.

LABELING

The most obvious and necessary function of a package label is to identify the product. In the PDC survey mentioned earlier consumers rated ease of

---

[12] "Packaging Design Seen as Cost-Effective Marketing Strategy," *Marketing News,* February 20, 1981, pp. 1, 6.

Figure 8-6

Product Label with Specified Nutritional Contents

recognition as the second most important characteristic of a package.[13] A complete label also identifies

- Who made the product
- Where it was made
- Its ingredients
- How it should be used

[handwritten margin notes] F.T.C. State of products identity state of name + place of business State of net per package

Today few products are permitted to go to the market without some form of identification. Even fresh produce often displays a gummed label identifying its origin.

Although some goods may be adequately identified by giving the name of the product and the seller, most require a somewhat more extensive description of their nature and use. The law requires that processed foods, patent drugs, some cosmetics, textiles, and numerous other goods carry a fairly complete list of ingredients (see Figure 8-6). Labels on other products, such as furs, may be required to provide information on their place of origin.

Many products must furnish instructions for their use. Commercial plant foods, for example, must explain the amount to be used and the recommended frequency of feedings. Many producers who do not have to furnish instructions for using their products do so anyway as a way of

---

[13] Berni, "Consumers Want Food Packaging That Can Be Easily Resealed."

increasing sales. Manufacturers of many food items provide recipes and serving suggestions on the package. Clothing manufacturers provide laundering instructions on their labels. Most labels are designed to help sell the product. A company chooses the arrangement of type, the illustrations, and the color to attract the consumer's eye, make the package distinctive, and encourage recognition by the consumer, who often views it in the midst of many other products.

We noted earlier that many packages constitute a form of point-of-purchase advertising. Label design is an integral part of this type of on-the-shelf promotion. Distinctive package labels can also be used to advantage in advertising the product through visual media.

SUMMARY

- A product is anything a firm markets and includes the actual product and all accompanying factors that satisfy the customer's needs.
- Products can be classified as consumer or industrial products. Consumer products are further categorized as convenience, shopping, or specialty products.
- Consumers are not willing to devote much time or effort to finding convenience goods. Therefore, marketing strategy for these products concentrates on availability.
- Because consumers spend considerable effort deciding on shopping goods, marketing emphasizes promotional messages of information and persuasion.
- The loyalty of consumers to specialty products allows for more exclusive distribution and higher prices.
- Marketing managers must make product-mix and product-line decisions based on the company's chosen markets and target-market strategies.
- Positioning a product with respect to competitive products and the company's other products is important in defining the target customers for which the product was designed.
- Branding is the practice of identifying a product or line of products by a special name or symbol. Its goals are identification and control.
- Selecting the "right" brand name is important. Good brand names are easy to pronounce, easy to recall, have a meaning closely associated with the product, are easily translatable into foreign languages, and are appropriate to the target market.
- A package contains, protects, and identifies a product. In some cases firms do more to market the package than the product.
- Packaging is a basic marketing tool. Often the package makes the difference between success and failure, especially when consumers cannot see or examine the product.

- The primary marketing functions of packaging are to contain, protect, and identify the product. From a marketing viewpoint identification is the most important aspect of packaging.
- A good package is convenient to handle, transport, and display. It is also attractive, has promotional appeal, and is economical.
- A package label identifies who made the product, where it was made, its ingredients, and how it should be used.

DISCUSSION QUESTIONS

1. Define the term product. What is the product of an airline? A book publisher? An insurance company? A motion-picture producer?
2. Give an example of a convenience product, a shopping product, and a specialty product. What characteristics of each make them fit in these categories?
3. Define the terms *product mix* and *product line*. Explain the difference between product width and depth.
4. Describe the various ways in which products may be positioned.
5. What is a brand name? How does it differ from a trademark? How does a trademark differ from a logo?
6. Name several advantages of branding. Under what circumstances is it advisable to brand a product?
7. List several characteristics of a good brand name. What is the difference between an individual brand and a family brand?
8. "In a real sense the package is the product." Explain.
9. What role does consumer trust play in packaging procedures? Does it influence the producer's integrity in setting packaging policies?
10. Identify and explain the three packaging functions.
11. Many highly successful products, such as Tide, Coke, and Bufferin, have had their packages changed little or not at all for decades. How can you account for this?
12. Why should a package be convenient to use? Attractive? Have promotional appeal? Be economical to produce?
13. Why are labels important in marketing a product?

APPLICATION EXERCISES

1. Select a company and describe its product mix. Name the product lines and the products within each line. Does its mix have width, depth, both, or neither? What target marketing strategy is the company following?

2. Select a product category and develop a positioning map for all products in that category based on the two characteristics you think are most important. Are there any opportunities for positioning new products? How would you decide if this opportunity has potential?

3. (a) What do you think is the most effective consumer product package available today? Give five specific reasons to support your choice.
   (b) What do you think is the least effective consumer product package available today? Give five specific reasons to support your choice.

4. Assume you are going to market a new line of jeans for women and men. Select a brand name and then explain why you think your selection is a good one.

CASE 8
Gillette Enters the Shampoo Brand Battle[14]

While sales of most consumer products buckled under the recessionary pressures of the early 1980s, sales in the $2-billion shampoo industry displayed a surprising 10-percent annual growth rate. Lured by this growth potential, manufacturers are feverishly working to enter the battle for shelf space in supermarkets and drugstores, and are expected to spend about $110 million in advertising their products and at least as much in promotional support to retailers.

In addition to the size and growth potential of the market, manufacturers are attracted by the relatively small investment in equipment needed to make the product. Thus, marketing and advertising techniques are pivotal ingredients for success. Perhaps the key ingredient, however, is the ability to capitalize on the ever-changing consumer tastes that have made the shampoo industry one of the most difficult in which to succeed.

Along with the accompanying competitive pressures, the changing nature of consumer tastes has spurred the pace of new brand introduction. Such major personal care product manufacturers as Gillette, Helene Curtis, Lever Brothers, and Noxell all introduced or test marketed new brands in 1981. The industry leader, Procter & Gamble, test marketed Ivory, its first nonpremium-priced shampoo, which was positioned to compete with Helene Curtis' Suave and Revlon's Flex. Procter & Gamble's three flagship brands—Prell, Head & Shoulders, and Pert—hold a combined 17-percent market share.

Gillette, one of the more aggressive marketers, introduced two new brands. The first, Silkience, cost about $40 million to introduce and was one of the most successful of the new products. The cost of introduction included heavy advertising, free samples for 27 million households, and price promotions. Silkience grabbed an almost immediate 3.5-percent market share. Gillette's second major entry, For Oily

---

[14] "A Free-For-All on the Shampoo Shelf," *Business Week*, September 28, 1981, pp. 32–33; and "Gillette Targets Largest Segment of Hair-Care Market with $22.9 million New Product Launch," *Marketing News*, May 28, 1982, p. 16.

Hair Only (FOHO), was prompted by research that showed oily-haired people constitute the largest segment of the hair-care market. Despite that segment's size, however, no one had marketed a product exclusively designed for its use.

A key result of brand proliferation in the industry is the move by retailers to be more selective in allocating their limited shelf space. Mary E. Burton, merchandise manager for Jewel Company's OSCO Drug Unit, says, "With this pickup in introductions, [retail] buyers are forced to show more discipline in determining which brands to carry or discard." Ms. Burton contends that the key yardsticks for retailers are "the sales numbers and the amount of money the manufacturer will put behind the brand."

Discussion Questions

1. If you were the shampoo brand manager for Gillette, how would you convince retail buyers to carry your products? Why is it important for Gillette to have all its brands on a retailer's shelf?
2. Visit your local drugstore and prepare a description of all the shampoo brands carried on the shelf. Develop a positioning map of these products based on the two shampoo characteristics you think consumers find most important.
3. Based on the map developed in Question 2, where should Gillette position its next shampoo product? What research should Gillette conduct before introducing this product?

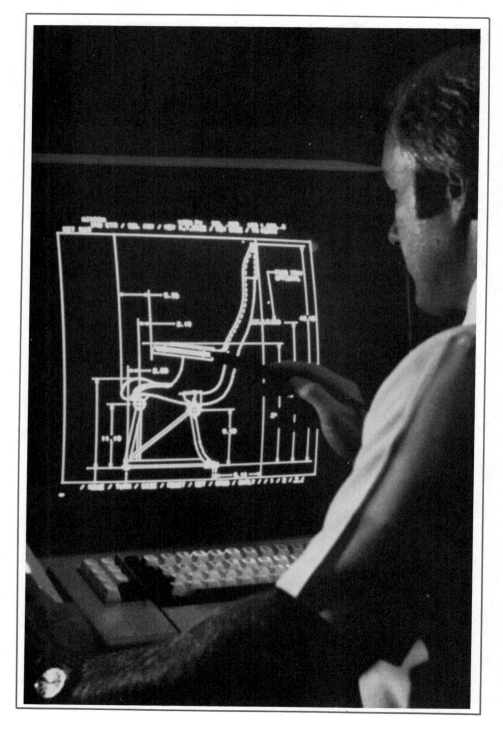

9 Product Management

STUDY OBJECTIVES

After studying this chapter, you should be able to

1. Discuss the stages of the new product development process.
2. Explain why new products succeed or fail.
3. Describe the adoption process and its importance to marketers.
4. Discuss the diffusion process and its relationship to the product life cycle.
5. List the characteristics and strategies of each stage of the product life cycle.
6. Discuss the value of the product life cycle to marketers.
7. Explain why marketers should be concerned about product perishability.
8. Discuss reasons for product modification and ways in which modification can be accomplished.
9. Discuss the importance of product deletion decisions.

Getting consumers to buy products is a basic goal of marketing. Products are important in all facets of marketing. Most of the promotional budget is spent to tell people about the product's merits; most marketing research is done to determine how to sell more of the product; engineering and production have but one ultimate purpose—to make the product; physical distribution is concerned exclusively with storing and moving the product; and in a typical sales meeting more time is devoted to informing sales personnel about how to sell the product than anything else.

Marketing managers, because they are closest to the customer, are best informed about customer needs, desires, and willingness to buy. This makes them a primary source of information about what products and product characteristics are desirable. This is true in the case of both consumer and industrial products. In industrial marketing salespeople and various intermediaries meet customers personally and learn their preferences and needs. This intelligence is then passed on to the research, design, engineering, and production departments for further consideration and implementation.

In this chapter we will deal with managing the product throughout its life—from its inception as an idea to its removal from the market. To begin this analysis, we will look at the organizational methods companies use to manage the new product development process.

ORGANIZATION FOR NEW PRODUCT MANAGEMENT

The process of turning information into new products must be managed. Several different approaches are used to organize new product management. Some companies set up new product committees or separate departments, whereas others may use venture teams or product managers in developing new product ideas.

New Product Committee

The new product committee, or product plans board, as it is sometimes called, is the most widely used organizational structure to make decisions about new products. Top experts from key functional areas—production, engineering, finance, research, and marketing—usually make up the committee. The main function of a new product committee is to review (reject or approve) ideas and concepts for new products; normally, generation of new product ideas is not a major part of the committee's activity.

An advantage of this form of organization is that it is composed primarily of powerful individuals from within the corporation. Thus, the authority exists to move new product ideas to introduction. The primary disadvantage is that all members of the committee have other responsibilities, which usually take precedence. Therefore, committee members are often not committed to their new product responsibilities and tend to let new product development take a backseat to the day-to-day running of the company. As a result, many new product ideas are never fully developed.

New Product Department

Management in some firms believes that the conception, development, and ultimate marketing of new products is so essential that a separate department should be assigned responsibility for these functions. That is, the primary responsibility of individuals in this department is the development of new products. Typically, such departments evaluate new product ideas, supervise production of pilot models, and conduct market acceptance tests.

The principal advantage of a new product department is that the responsibility for new product development is *specifically assigned* to particular individuals, and others can turn over ideas and recommendations to them for consideration. This forces dedication to the new product development process. The disadvantage is that a new product department has less authority to accomplish its goals than a new product committee has. Its budget also may not be large enough to implement all of its desired projects.

Venture Team

Under the venture team concept for new product development, a company assembles a group of specialists to work on the entire development of a new product. Key members of the venture team typically include such specialists as engineers; marketing, production, and distribution personnel; and financial analysts. Each can make a specific contribution to the total effort.

As the venture team makes progress, it may receive additional personnel. Because the team usually has easy access to top management, its recommendations can be acted on quickly. The venture team is *ad hoc* in nature and is disbanded when it completes its specific mission—which may extend over months or years.

Product Managers

Many organizations have product or brand managers, especially those that make similar products, such as detergents and cereals. A product manager usually has an input, sometimes major, sometimes minor, in proposing and evaluating new product ideas. However, the main job of a product manager is to "take over" once the company has decided to market a product. The advantage is that the new product has a champion. The disadvantage is that the product manager may be so busy managing an existing product that he or she has no time for new product development.

Typically, product managers work under the marketing manager. They usually have no line authority over the field sales force or over the advertising agency. Nevertheless, their jobs are important and involve selecting target markets, developing sales promotional materials, and making recommendations on how to sell the product. They also approve (within constraints) advertising budgets and materials, pricing policies, and sales goals.

Companies that use product managers evaluate them on the basis of results. Often product managers within an organization are expected to compete just as vigorously with one another as with other companies.

NEW PRODUCT DEVELOPMENT

Companies that wish to remain successful should always be developing new products. As we shall see later in this chapter, the life expectancy of a product is limited. New technology and new forms of products are constantly making existing products obsolete. You need only look at the personal computer market to see the potential for obsolescence in new products. In 1970 the first affordable hand-held calculators came onto the market. Products that did simple math functions cost around 100 dollars. Today, less expensive hand-held computers that perform a myriad of functions have made these calculators obsolete. It is safe to say that in five years better products will also make these computers obsolete. To avoid an obsolete product mix, marketers should always be developing new products.

It is best to approach new product development as an organized, step-by-step process in which the feasibility of the new product idea is evaluated at each step. This steplike process lessens the likelihood of introducing a product that will fail. Figure 9-1 presents the new product development process used by many companies. We will examine each step individually.

Idea Generation

Idea generation *is the ongoing process of systematically developing new product ideas that are consistent with the company's objectives.* It is particularly important to develop product ideas that are consistent with corporate objectives, because otherwise time and effort will be wasted developing products the company has no intention of introducing. Idea generation should be systematic in that various sources are accessed on a regular, established basis. Without this systematic orientation idea generation is a rather haphazard affair which may overlook many opportunities.

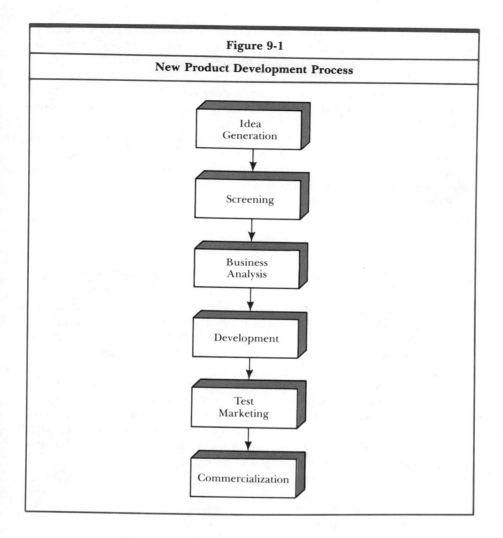

Figure 9-1

New Product Development Process

Idea
Generation

Screening

Business
Analysis

Development

Test
Marketing

Commercialization

The corporation itself is an excellent place to start searching for new product ideas. Many companies encourage employee suggestion programs, have formal research and development groups, and organize regular brainstorming sessions. **Brainstorming** consists of bringing together a small group of employees and encouraging them to come up with as many ideas as possible. Any idea, no matter how outlandish, is acceptable. The purpose is to produce many ideas for later evaluation.[1]

---

[1] Alexander F. Osborn of the advertising agency Batten, Barton, Durstine, & Osborn developed the technique of brainstorming. For further details on this procedure see Alexander F. Osborn, *Applied Imagination: Principles and Procedures of Creative Thinking* (New York: Scribner, 1957).

Customers are often valuable sources of new product ideas. Customer suggestions and complaints may lead to revision of existing products or to entirely new products. Other channel members also may be able to suggest new product ideas. Retailers are in an especially good position to let the company know what products their customers are interested in. Company salespeople can also be very valuable in gathering customers' new product ideas.

By watching the products and advertisements of competitors, a company can often gather many new product ideas. Finally, many companies and universities specialize in new product development, and a firm can utilize them to develop products in areas it wishes to pursue. To identify opportunities for new product ideas, marketers should not ignore any of these sources.

Screening

Screening *is the process of determining which ideas generated in the previous step merit more study.* This step is important because the steps that follow it— business analysis, development, testing, and introduction—are quite expensive. The elimination of bad ideas at this stage can mean the saving of a great deal of corporate funds. Thus, idea generation is developing as many ideas as possible, whereas screening is narrowing those ideas down to a few good ideas.

The screening process tries to guard against two types of mistakes: (1) further development of bad ideas and (2) discarding good ideas. To minimize the likelihood of both these mistakes, many companies have a two-step screening process. In the first step a committee is charged with the initial screening. In the second step a member of upper management hears out any manager who feels the committee made a mistake in rejecting a particular idea. If this member of upper management overrules the screening committee, further development can continue. Thus, a second opinion is obtained to reduce the chance of missing good opportunities. Texas Instruments' Speak and Spell learning aids for children initially was rejected by its screening group, but continued in development because of this two-step screening process. Thus, an eventually successful product was saved from early rejection.

Screening committees have numerous criteria to consider in evaluating an idea. The appropriateness of the idea to the firm's objectives is one. For example, brainstormers at IBM might come up with an idea for a new breakfast food but because IBM has no experience in making or marketing food products, the screening committee would probably discard the idea. New products must also fit corporate productive capabilities, salespeople expertise, distribution channels, and organizational abilities.

Product criteria are also important. Is the product technically feasible?

Can the company actually produce it? Will its features be believable? Is it a sufficient improvement over existing products? Are the raw materials to produce it available? Only products that receive yes answers to all these questions should survive the screening step.

Market criteria should also influence screening decisions. Is the product consistent with the company's quality image? Does it fit the product mix, or will it cannibalize (take sales away from) other products in the mix? Is the market of sufficient size and spending power? Will sales be cyclical or seasonal?

A popular approach to screening the better ideas that are generated is **concept testing**. In concept testing a prototype of a new product is shown to groups of potential consumers for their reactions. The prototype consists of a picture or model of the product with proposed promotional literature. The purpose is to determine how consumers will react to the product. Is the product easy to understand? Are its features believable? Are benefits over existing products clearly identifiable? What wants or needs does it satisfy?

Concept tests help marketers answer these questions and determine who would buy the product, how much and how often it would be bought, and what products it would replace. In addition consumer comments may indicate ways to improve the product idea and continue development.

Because concept tests usually involve a limited number of customers, they allow marketers to determine rather cheaply if an idea has the potential necessary to justify further development.

Business Analysis

Ideas that survive the screening step are subjected to **business analysis**. Many of the questions asked in screening are the same in this step, but more detailed analysis is involved. Basically, this step tries to determine whether the company can profitably market the idea. First, marketing estimates market potential by trying to determine the level of initial and long-range demand for the product at various price levels and how long the product will sell before it becomes obsolete. How many competitors, the strength of those competitors, and what share of demand they will capture is also analyzed. When Apple Computer considers a new idea, the fact that IBM will immediately introduce a competitive product may discourage introduction. IBM is a very powerful marketing corporation. Only if Apple believes its product can profitably compete with IBM in the market would development continue.

The marketability of the product and its compatibility with the company also affect demand. Marketability is determined by the believability of the product, how easy it is to convey messages about the product in promotion, and the ability to offer product variations for different target markets. Compatibility is the fit of the new product with present salespeople and distribution expertise, product mix, present price levels, and production capabilities. The final estimate of demand at various price levels gives the company an idea of the revenues it can expect from the new product.

Costs are also analyzed. Can existing production and distribution systems be used? If not, what are the costs of developing new systems? How much will it cost to promote the product? The more complex the product or the more competition expected, the higher promotion costs will be. How expensive are the raw materials and the production processes? How expensive will the product be to transport and store? All these questions make up the cost components of the new product. The company must analyze costs and revenue projections to determine the potential profit from the product. Pro forma profit and loss statements are generated at this stage. If an acceptable profit flow cannot be realized within a given period of time, the product idea will probably be dropped.

Development

Up to this point the product has existed only as an idea, description, drawing, or maybe a model. Ideas that survive to the development step are given

to engineering or research and development (R&D), which will attempt to develop a product that safely embodies the attributes of the product idea and that the company can produce and distribute at a reasonable price. This may represent quite a challenge, sometimes requiring the invention of new technology to fulfill the product idea's attributes.

Patents are reviewed to determine whether the new product incorporates aspects that the company should patent. Also, if patents already exist, the company must obtain permission to use the patented items in the new product.

Any safety hazards of the product are reviewed and, hopefully, removed. It is the aim of development to produce a marketable product that will not hurt anyone.

Various package designs are considered to determine which best fits the product attributes. The package that best promotes, identifies, contains, and protects the product at a reasonable package cost will be selected.

Finally, development should be a closely coordinated effort between R&D and marketing. Only R&D can design a product with the technical capabilities to perform the desired attributes safely. However, R&D personnel often become so involved in product and engineering design that they lose sight of the fact that the product must be marketable. Technically delightful features are of little value if the target market does not want or

care about those features. It is marketing's responsibility to see that the product is technically feasible and, most importantly, meets the needs of the target market as defined in the product idea. Some companies are instilling a marketing orientation in their engineers by arranging regular meetings between them and customers. As Jacques Robinson, vice president and general manager of General Electric's Video Products Division, put it, "Engineers working at the drawing board are getting their directions from customers. The whole business is oriented toward bringing the technology and the customer demand together."[2] Finally, marketing must develop the other three marketing controllable variables that will accompany the product to introduction.

Once the product is developed, it goes through extensive functional and consumer tests. **Functional tests** *are experiments designed to determine how fast the product wears out, whether it does what it should, and whether it is safe.* Many home products are tested extensively on laboratory animals to determine whether they will adversely affect the health of customers.

Consumer tests *are actual use experiments of the product to determine whether the attributes of the product idea are discernible to the consumer.* Whirlpool, for example, has volunteer employees take new appliances home for periods up to a year to determine whether the product has desirable attributes and if any problems arise in actual use.

Development is very expensive, often more expensive than all previous steps combined. The auto industry, for instance, regularly spends billions of dollars on the development step for new car lines. For General Motors' "X-body" series (Skylark, Citation, Phoenix, and Omega) the cost was almost $3 billion! This cost illustrates that only very good product ideas should survive the screening and business analysis steps and pass into development.

Test Marketing

Test marketing involves the limited introduction of a new product in selected markets. The purpose of test marketing is to try out the product and the rest of the proposed marketing strategy in the marketplace and to correct any defects in the strategy prior to large-scale introduction. Many companies use test marketing to minimize the risk of a major product failure.

Test markets are usually cities that marketing management believes will be representative of the overall national consumer reaction to the product. Due to the high cost of test marketing usually only two or three test cities are chosen.

---

[2] "Listening to the Voice of the Marketplace," *Business Week,* February 21, 1983, pp. 90, 94, 95.

Testing time may vary from two months to two years, depending on the company's lead over competition, the repurchase rate of the product, and the desire for secrecy. Test marketing's goal is to gather information on the sales of the product; its repurchase rate; the characteristics of consumers; where the product is bought; competitive reactions; the effect on sales of the company's other products; and the strengths and weaknesses of distribution, promotion, and price.

Test marketing, however, has many risks. First, it is very expensive. A single test market may cost over $250,000 and still result in the conclusion that the product should not be introduced.

Test marketing also gives the competition a chance to study the new product and gain time copying it. If the product is successful, the competition has saved the cost of test marketing. They merely observe the company's test markets and improve on its strategy. Further, competition often tries to sabotage test markets by changing their prices, advertising, and promotion to confuse the results.

Even if competition does not interfere, test markets are not totally reliable predictors of national results. Differences between test markets and the national market will exist. Channel members and salespeople also may act differently toward the product when it is new than when it is established.

For all these reasons many firms question the value of test marketing, and some skip this step altogether. For example, when Coca-Cola introduced its caffeine-free versions of Coke, Tab, and Diet Coke, it skipped test marketing. Its reasons for the move included the company's marketing strength, the popularity of caffeine-free products, and the fact that Pepsi and Royal Crown were already in the market. Brian G. Dyson, president of Coca-Cola's soft drink unit, summed up this attitude: "We've taken the time to do our homework right. The public perceives a need for these drinks, and we're ready to give them to them." To company executives the risks of waiting outweighed the risks of not test marketing.[3]

Commercialization

Whether the company runs test markets or not, at some point it either drops the product or goes into full-scale introduction. The **commercialization** step involves developing manufacturing and distribution systems to deliver the product to all intended markets. Pricing policies are set, and promotional messages are sent to all markets. Any changes found necessary in the test markets are made, and the product's complete marketing strategy is implemented.

---

[3] "Coke Plunges into No-Caffeine Cola," *Business Week*, May 9, 1983, p. 35.

Commercialization is extremely expensive. The company commits capital expenditures to manufacturing and distribution systems, and begins advertising and promoting the product on a massive scale. In many cases the cost of carrying inventory at all retail locations and at distribution points will run into millions of dollars.

This step involves great risk for the company. If the product fails, the company could lose millions of dollars. For this reason many companies use a **roll-out strategy** when commercializing. Under this strategy a new product is introduced in several markets with a minimum of initial investment. If the product is successful, additional markets are developed, with the profits from the first markets financing introduction in the new markets. Eventually the product reaches complete introduction, all with less financial risk to the company. The danger of such a strategy is that complete introduction may take years. This gives the competition a chance to copy the product and perhaps even beat the company to complete introduction.

It should be pointed out that the product development process involves the initial development of as many ideas as possible. From that point on marketing is refining or eliminating ideas continually to come up with winning products. Hopefully, losers are dropped before the company in-

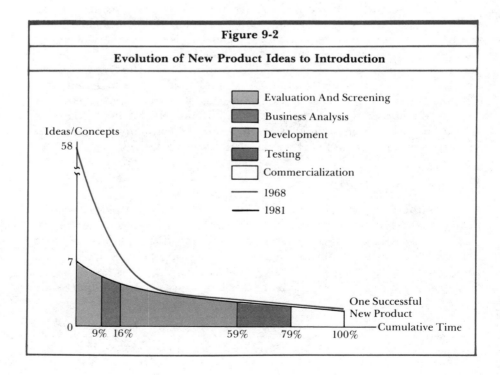

Figure 9-2

Evolution of New Product Ideas to Introduction

Evaluation And Screening
Business Analysis
Development
Testing
Commercialization
1968
1981

Ideas/Concepts
58
7
0

9% 16%   59%   79%   100%

One Successful
New Product
Cumulative Time

vests too much money. According to a survey in 1968 it took 58 ideas to yield a single successful new product.[4] When the survey was repeated for 700 companies in 1981, it found that it took only seven ideas to yield one successful new product.[5] Figure 9-2 illustrates the results of these two studies. Booz, Allen & Hamilton, which conducted both surveys, concluded that the increasingly sophisticated way companies develop new products was responsible for this dramatic improvement. Companies are doing a much better job of eliminating bad ideas at early stages before they commit too many resources. In spite of this increasing sophistication, however, many new products still fail in the commercialization step.

WHY NEW PRODUCTS FAIL OR SUCCEED

Although many products do not succeed, researchers have identified several factors that help determine whether a product will succeed or fail.[6] First, does the product exhibit a unique superiority over competitive offerings? If the product does not stand apart as a superior product, its chances of survival are lessened. Was the product thoroughly planned? Was the target market identified and researched and the product designed from that research? If the answer is no, the likelihood that the product will not appeal to the target market is increased.

Was the product introduced at the proper time and at the proper rate? Many times luxury products are introduced during recessions. Such faulty timing hurts the chances of success. Proper rate implies a compromise between a fast introduction to limit competitive reaction and a slow introduction to reduce financial risk and allow for greater product analysis. The product and the competition largely determine the proper rate of introduction.

How technical is the product? The more technical the product, the more "bugs" might be found in the introduction. Too many defects could lead to customer disenchantment. Technical products are also harder to explain to customers, making their acceptance less likely.

How easy is it for customers to try the product? One of the reasons

---

[4] Booz, Allen & Hamilton, *Management of New Products*, 1968, p. 9.

[5] Carl Bochman, "New Product Management for the 1980's," *Product Development and Management Association Conference,* October 1981.

[6] R.C. Cooper, "The Dimensions of Industrial New Product Success and Failure," *Journal of Marketing*, Summer 1979, pp. 93–103; R.C. Cooper, "Why New Industrial Products Fail," *Industrial Marketing Management,* January 1975, pp. 315–26; C. Merle Crawford, "Marketing Research and the New Product Failure Rate," *Journal of Marketing*, April 1977, pp. 51–61; J. Hugh Davidson, "Why Most New Consumer Brands Fail," *Harvard Business Review*, March–April 1976, pp. 117–22; and David Hopkins, *New Product Winners and Losers* (New York: The Conference Board, 1980).

The process of developing new products can be very expensive. Getting from idea generation to commercialization often costs the developer millions of dollars; in some cases even billions! However, once the product is developed, what is to prevent a competitor from introducing an identical copy of it? Thus, the developer incurs all the expense of developing the product, and someone else merely copies it and reaps the profits.

Product patents came about as a means to protect developers of totally new products from such unfair copying by competitors. A **patent** gives the inventor of a product exclusive rights to sell it for 17 years. In the United States any novel product can be patented through the U.S. Patent Office if it is useful and a working model can be provided. The owner of a patent can either sell the product or license others to sell it. Other firms are prohibited from selling products that are "illegally similar" to the patented product.

In 1953 drug manufacturer Schering–Plough was granted a patent on the antibiotic Garamycin. Although the patent ran out in May of 1980 and the company cut the price of Garamycin to meet competition from generic brands, Schering–Plough has enjoyed the exclusive right to sell the product for 17 years. Sales were often over $80 million a year in the U.S. alone, and profits from worldwide sales of this one product were in excess of $100 million in 1979.* With the promise of other successful products, and patents to protect them, Schering–Plough continues to invest in the development of

microwave ovens caught on so slowly was that customers could not buy (try) one initially for less than several hundred dollars. Because free samples of consumer nondurable products can be given away, customer trial is easier and success is more likely.

Do consumers perceive much risk in the purchase? As with microwave ovens, the price affects the consumer's perceived risk. However, the product's social importance is also a factor. If the product is socially visible, consumers may be afraid to buy a product their reference groups will see as a mistake. Promotional messages conveying the social acceptability of the product may lessen the perceived social risk and increase the product's chances of success. Bearden and Shimp also found that an improved prod-

new products, as do many other companies, regardless of the development costs.

A company can invest its money in developing a totally new product, secure in the knowledge that if the product is successful, it will receive all profits from sales for 17 years. Without such a protection as patents, little incentive would exist for developing new products. Why spend all that money on development? It would be much easier to wait until someone else introduced a new product and merely copy it. Obviously, if all companies took this approach, no new products would be introduced.

Many new product developments are not patentable, however. Only *totally* new (novel) products are patentable. Most new product developments are really variations of other products. The development of a power drill with a new grip, for example, is a variation of a power drill and probably not patentable. The Black & Decker Workmate, however, was a totally new concept in portable work tables and was granted a patent.

Although any new product development is expensive, totally new products are the most expensive and risky. A company must spend much money to develop and test the new technology. Because it is totally new, the developer has no idea before introduction whether anyone will buy it. This added expense and risk makes the protection of a patent necessary. Without it, companies would play it safe and only develop less expensive, safer variations of existing products. Patents are the government's way of encouraging new inventions. In effect, the patent guarantees an inventor a monopoly and all the profits from the invention for 17 years. Clearly, the offer of patent protection acts as an incentive for the invention, development, and introduction of new products.

* "Schering–Plough: What Happens After a Key Patent is Lost," *Business Week*, August 18, 1980, pp. 115, 118.

uct warranty may offset the perceived risk from a high price.[7] Thus, expensive products with superior warranties stand a better chance of succeeding than expensive products with normal warranties.

ADOPTION PROCESS

Once a product is introduced, consumers are exposed to it and make a decision whether or not to try it. The process consumers go through in

[7] William O. Bearden and Terrence A. Shimp, "The Use of Extrinsic Cues to Facilitate Product Adoption," *Journal of Marketing Research*, May 1983, pp. 229–39.

making this decision is called the **adoption process**. First, consumers become *aware* of the product's existence. Second, they develop *interest* in the product and gather more information about it. Third, consumers go through an *evaluation* of the information they obtained in order to decide whether or not to try it. If consumers do decide to try the product, they enter the fourth stage of *trial*. Based on their experiences from trying the product, consumers either *adopt* the product and continue to use it or *reject* the product and do not purchase it again.

The adoption process has several implications for product managers. When they introduce new products, they should aim advertising at creating product awareness and interest in as many target customers as possible. Later, advertising can provide information that the customer can use to evaluate the product. If consumers are in the evaluation stage, but do not seem willing to move on to trial, sometimes free samples or demonstrations can help move the adoption process along.

Furthermore, because different people become aware, interested, evaluate, try, and adopt products at different rates, there is a tendency for products to gain total market acceptance gradually. *This process of products going from introduction to total acceptance is called the* **diffusion process**.

DIFFUSION PROCESS

The diffusion process categorizes the different adopters of a product by how quickly they move through the adoption process. **Innovators** are the first group to adopt a product and are, on the average, 2.5 percent of the target market.[8] They are typically young, affluent people who pride themselves on trying new products and owning "state-of-the-art" products. Marketing to this group emphasizes a product's newness and its technical superiority.

The next group to adopt a product is the **early adopters**, who constitute approximately 13.5 percent of the target market. They are affluent individuals who enjoy the status of owning new products. More importantly, they are often opinion leaders who affect the decisions of other members of their reference groups. Therefore, it is important to get this group to adopt the product.

The **early majority** represents about 34 percent of the target market. Average in economic status and above average in social class, this is the first part of the mass market to buy the product. This mass-market orientation requires marketing to put more emphasis on advertising than for previous groups.

---

[8] Target market percentages for the five diffusion process categories are drawn from Everett M. Rogers, *Diffusion of Innovation,* (New York: Free Press, 1962), 81–86.

The second part of the mass market is the **late majority**, 34 percent of the target market. Lower in social and economic status, these consumers are more tradition-bound and slower to adopt new products. The product is a socially accepted item before this group tries it.

Finally, the **laggards** represent 16 percent of the target market. Low in income and social status, tradition-bound, and conservative, this group is very suspicious of new items. Many companies choose to ignore laggards as too hard to win over.

As the percentages indicate, a product will probably start selling slowly after introduction, sell at an increasing rate through the early majority, and increase in sales at a decreasing rate as the late majority adopts it. For products such as frisbees, this entire process may take weeks; for products such as microwave ovens, it may take years.

As this discussion implies, the way the adoption and diffusion processes affect sales often follows predictable patterns. Competition, profitability, and marketing strategies also often follow predictable patterns over the life of a product. The analysis of these patterns is called the **product life cycle.**

PRODUCT LIFE CYCLE

Although not all products follow predictable product life cycles, many follow predictable patterns of sales and profits (see Figure 9-3). There are four stages in the product life cycle—introduction, growth, maturity, and decline—each with characteristic marketing strategies. Figure 9-4 summarizes these stages.

Introduction

The **introduction stage** is the same as the commercialization step in the new product development process. In this stage the product is new, customers (mostly innovators) are still learning about its features, and few firms offer the product. Promotional expenditures are aimed at establishing acceptance for the general product category, not necessarily one company's product. This creation of **generic demand** is accomplished through messages that inform the target markets about product features. Unit costs are high because of low production output. Due to large promotional expenditures and high production costs, it is the least profitable stage of the product life cycle. Introducing color television, for example, cost RCA $130 million in research, development, and legal clearances. The product was on the market for seven years before RCA made any profits.[9]

---

[9] David Sarnoff, "How Color TV Was Born," *Nation's Business*, February 1969, pp. 70–73.

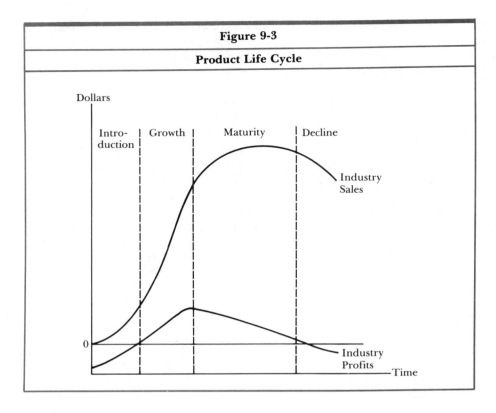

Figure 9-3

Product Life Cycle

Dollars

| Intro-duction | Growth | Maturity | Decline |

Industry Sales

0

Industry Profits

Time

Growth

In the **growth stage** the early adopters and early majority are buying the product, so sales go up at an increasing rate and profits are realized from the product sales. Many competitors start to enter the market, and promotion switches to creating **selective demand**, that is, demand for the specific company's product. Superiority of the company's product over the competition is emphasized. Production reaches sufficient volume to create economies of scale and reduce unit costs. Companies try to increase the number of distribution outlets to make their product more convenient to buy. Personal computers, now in the growth stage, are sold in a number of retail outlets. These include specialty stores, department stores, direct sales forces, office-equipment dealers, mail order, and third-party systems retailers.[10] Prices drop to reflect lower unit costs and increased competition.

---

[10] "The Coming Shakeout in Personal Computers," *Business Week,* November 22, 1982, pp. 72–75, 78, 83.

During the growth stage for hand calculators, for instance, the cost of Texas Instruments' basic calculator dropped from its introductory price of $149.95 to $79.95. This lower cost was possible through production efficiencies and was necessary because Casio, Bowmar, Hewlett-Packard, and a host of others had competing products.

Maturity

In the **maturity stage** the product has become an accepted item and the late majority begins to purchase it. Sales increase at a slower rate, level off, and eventually decline slightly. The lack of growth in industry sales creates a profit squeeze, forcing the marginal companies to drop out of the market. Companies that stay in the market try to lower costs to remain competitive and invest heavily in promotion to maintain their market shares. They expand the number of outlets to reach more people and offer a full product line to appeal to as many profitable target markets as possible. It is predicted that the more than 150 companies now producing personal computers will decline to about 12 by 1986. The key to those that survive will be the implementation of lower costs and an extensive distribution system.[11]

Decline

In the **decline stage** product obsolescence is setting in, probably because a new product has been introduced to replace the present one. Sales decline at an increasing rate. Improvements in the product cease, and promotion is minimized to reduce costs. The number of outlets decreases, less expensive methods of distribution are sought, and the product is priced to support profitability until it is discontinued. IBM, for example, typically sells typewriters through its own sales force, an expensive method. Now that its Selectric II models have been made obsolete by its new Selectric III models, they are sold only through less-expensive wholesale distributions, thus lowering distribution costs and maintaining profitability until IBM discontinues the line.[12]

At this point the company must decide whether to drop the product or develop a **product extension strategy**. In product extension new uses are found for old products, thus extending their useful life and saving them from obsolescence. Arm & Hammer baking soda provides an excellent example of a product extension strategy. Sales of this product were declining, because fewer people were baking from scratch. Cake mixes were

---

[11] Ibid.

[12] "IBM to Begin Using Outside Dealers to Sell 3 Typewriter Models," *Wall Street Journal*, February 22, 1983, p. 38.

Figure 9-4

How Changes in Product Life Cycle Affect the Marketing Mix

Factor	Introduction	Growth	Maturity	Decline and Possible Abandonment
Competition and industry factors	Only one or a few firms enter market; little competition; moderate financial investment.	Strong product acceptance; many competitors enter the market; large financial resources needed; numerous failures.	Stable acceptance; number of firms begins to decline; strenuous competition.	Decline in market acceptance; few firms still producing.
Product and technological factors	Emphasis on research and development; experimentation with numerous models; product unsophisticated.	Continued technological development as more firms compete for market share; mass production; wide variety of similar products.	No major modification or innovatons; long production runs.	Research and development ceases; technology used to develop other products; product begins to phase out.
Place	Few outlets; limited availability.	Increasing number of outlets and increased availability.	Many outlets; easy availability.	Number of outlets begins to decrease.

making baking soda obsolete. Arm & Hammer revived sales by promoting its baking soda as an excellent means of controlling odors in the refrigerator, freezer, sink, and toilet. Not only did the strategy save this dying product, but it also spawned a whole line of baking-soda-based cleaning products.

Many products in the decline stage may be candidates for product extension. Cadwell Davis Savage advertising agency has identified 12 possibilities for product extension[13]:

---

[13] List compiled from "Ten Ways to Restore Vitality to Old, Worn-Out Products," *Wall Street Journal,* February 18, 1982, p. 31; and "Marketers Should Consider Restaging Old Brands Before Launching New Ones," *Marketing News,* December 10, 1982, p. 5.

Factor	Introduction	Growth	Maturity	Decline and Possible Abandonment
Promotion	Considerable investment to develop product acceptance; wide variations in selling and advertising techniques employed by competing firms.	Great emphasis on promotion; numerous promotional approaches used as firms compete for the market.	Industry leaders continue to invest heavily in promotion to retain their share of the market; much similarity in promotional appeals.	Decrease in promotional effort by most firms; little if any effort to develop new users of the product.
Pricing	Pricing tends to be experimental; wide variations exist.	Price differences of competing products are significant, but begin to follow the established leaders.	Price differences are minor for established products.	Price competition becomes strong as remaining firms fight for product survival.
Profits	Early firms usually sustain losses because of low demand and high development and promotional expenses.	Innovators make substantial profits; peak profitability for most firms.	Profits begin to decline for established firms.	Profits low or nonexistent; some firms beginning to lose money.

1. *Does the product have new or extended uses?* Arm and Hammer Baking Soda sales increased markedly after the product was promoted as an air freshener.
2. *Is the product a generic item that can be branded?* Frank Perdue put his name on chickens, and Sunkist did the same with oranges and lemons.
3. *Can the product form or package be changed?* Bold detergent's life was extended with the technological breakthrough of a fabric-softening ingredient, creating a new segment of price-conscious users of softeners.
4. *Can disadvantages be turned into advantages?* J.M. Smucker used its funny-sounding name for a slogan for its jams and jellies: "With a name like Smucker's, it has to be good."

5. *Can you market unused byproducts?* Several lumber companies are in the kitty litter business.
6. *Is there a broader target market?* Procter & Gamble reversed Ivory Soap's declining sales in 1971 by promoting it for adults, not just babies.
7. *Can you sell it in a more compelling way?* Procter & Gamble's Pampers sales took off when the company switched from emphasizing convenience for mothers to emphasizing keeping babies dry and happy.
8. *Is the category under or unadvertised?* When advertising for feminine protection increased from $10 million in 1975 to $50 million in 1977, sales exploded, with the heavy advertisers benefiting.
9. *Can you expand distribution channels?* Consolidated Foods' Hanes unit did so when it marketed L'eggs pantyhose in supermarkets.
10. *Can you cut price and build volume and profit?* Johnson & Johnson made a success of Tylenol by reducing its price to match Bristol-Myers' Datril.
11. *Can the price be increased and a franchise built with more advertising?* Chivas Regal was a moderately priced party Scotch until the price was raised to the top of the line. Extra profits were used to increase advertising.
12. *Is there a marketplace or social trend to exploit?* Dannon yogurt sales skyrocketed after the product was linked to consumer interest in health foods.

All these opportunities should be considered for declining products before the decision is made to drop them from the corporate product mix. Although the risk of failure may be high, product extension can sometimes be less expensive and more profitable than new product introduction.

Value of the Product Life Cycle

As we said, not all products follow a predictable product life cycle. Even among those that do, the length of each stage can vary widely. A new video game, such as Space Invaders, has a product life cycle that is usually shorter than one year, but the life cycle of Kellogg's Corn Flakes is now over one hundred years old and still not in decline. In addition it is difficult to actually tell when one stage ends and another starts. For instance, could you say when video cassette recorders moved from the introduction to the growth stage?

In spite of these problems the product life cycle is valuable to product management. First, it reminds marketers that all products have a limited life. The wise marketing firm is always developing new products to generate new sales and profits when mature products begin to decline. Many

companies manage their products through a **product portfolio**. Under this approach marketers always try to have a combination of developing, introduced, growing, and mature products. Mature and growing products help finance the developing and introduced products which, in turn, eventually replace the declining products. In this way companies are never caught without profitable products in their mix.

The product life cycle also gives marketers an indication of what to expect in the future for their products. The competition, sales, and profitability may not be perfectly predictable, but in each stage marketers have a general idea of what to expect (rapid growth and new competition in the growth stage, for example) and can plan accordingly.

PRODUCT PERISHABILITY

In the long run virtually all products disappear or perish. This happens for three reasons. First, many products, such as fresh fruits, meats, and vegetables, will start to deteriorate quickly unless they are frozen or canned. Although this is an extreme example, a totally indestructible product probably does not exist. Given enough time, even the most durable good will deteriorate.

Second, products perish because of advances in technology. The DC-3 was the workhorse of the airlines for many years. Today DC-3s are scarce, yet not all these planes wore out. Some still fly very well and with

MARKETING

Strategy

Betamax Versus SelectaVision

Nowhere has the battle between two consumer-electronics giants been more dramatic than in the introductory and acceptance stages of home video tape recorders. Not since color television appeared in millions of American homes has a home entertainment product stirred so much desire among potential owners.

Home video tape recorder (VTR) machines record programs from a television receiver for later replay. The development of this product took almost two decades. In 1950 Ampex of America produced a VTR that cost $100,000. The price restricted its appeal to only the television industry, which was freed from the high cost and limitations of live broadcasts.

David Sarnoff, then president of Radio Corporation of America (RCA), saw the potential for a VTR that could be used anywhere by virtually anyone. In 1951 he directed research toward this aim.

Sony also began research and development of the VTR in 1951. Instead of starting from scratch, Sony's chairman, Aiko Morita, negotiated with Ampex for the right to use the process it originally developed and used in its machines. In just a few months Sony produced a VTR that sold for $10,000. It was an immediate success. The National Football League used it for player training. Small television stations began taping their newscasts, thereby saving up to 80 percent of the cost of film. Airlines used VTRs to train pilots and convey information to passengers. Sony established a subsidiary called Video-Flight to show motion pictures on airplanes.

Meanwhile, RCA was struggling to develop a video disc unit, but was unable to bring it to market. Basic to the problem was a series of disappointing personnel appointments by Sarnoff, as well as financial setbacks caused by the recession of 1973 and losses of $490 million on a line of computers.

At last, in 1976, Ed Griffiths took control of RCA. As he reorganized the company and reordered its product priorities, the video disc system Sarnoff had envisioned was set aside. Adopted in its place was the VTR system developed by Matsushita, which RCA marketed under its own label and the tradename SelectaVision. By the end of 1976 RCA had sold 50,000 units, basically due to the longer length (up to four hours) of its tape.

Sony introduced its Betamax line of VTRs in 1975. It had a one-hour recording capacity. Sony met RCA's challenge of a longer recording time by featuring a two-hour tape by the end of the year. Shortly afterward, Sony developed the Betamax four-hour cassette changer, from which the term VCR (video cassette recording system) was coined.

While length of tape provided the battleline for challenge between RCA and Betamax, pricing gave another. Both products project a luxury electronics "gadget" image, but when prices approached $1,000, the market for VCRs expanded substantially. In fact, by the end of the 1970s demand for the machines exceeded supplies, and waiting periods of several months for delivery to retailers were not uncommon.

The demand for VCRs was enhanced by the efforts of Sony and RCA. They both engaged in massive advertising campaigns (guarding their expenditures closely from public knowledge), concentrating on the Christmas season. Direct-mail and point-of-purchase displays supplemented these campaigns. Their advertising messages stressed the idea that with a VCR you can tape a favorite program while asleep, away from home, or while watching a program on another channel. It was Sony's original thought that Betamax is a time-shift machine that can make any time "prime time."

In 1980 RCA resurrected the video disc system idea. The steep price of the VCRs ($600–$2,000) and the prerecorded cassettes ($50–$70) had given them only a 3-percent market penetration. RCA saw an opportunity for its video disc. Its strategy was to position the video disc player as a pure entertainment machine, differentiated from the VCR by its low price and ease of use. The disc player was to have a broader appeal. RCA anticipated the sales of video disc systems would exceed 300,000 units in 1983.* By expanding its product line, RCA generated over $200,000,000 from sales of the video disc players while maintaining its VCR market share of 22 percent in 1983.†

Sony, which holds 22.7 percent of the VCR market, is battling RCA's video disc through advertisements pointing out that the system is incapable of recording.‡ It simply plays back. By making this distinction clear, Sony hopes that future video disc sales will not be made to potential VCR buyers.

Both RCA and Sony are constantly adding new features and capabilities to their video systems in an effort to gain more of the video entertainment market. With RCA having two distinct products in the competition, it might have a better chance of winning.

* *Mart Magazine*, February 1983, p. 24.
† *Economic World*, May 1983, p. 26.
‡ *Standard and Poor's Corporate Descriptions*, March 1983, p. 7397.

proper maintenance could last for several decades. The demise of the DC-3 can be traced not to physical failures, but to changes in aircraft construction. Someday the 747 may seem as antiquated as the DC-3. Technical advances are responsible for much product perishability in fields such as electrical appliances, automobiles, transportation, communication, and other areas in which products are highly engineered.

Third, products pass away as people's life-styles and tastes change. A consumer's education, type of work, habits, economic status, and social customs are reflected in the kinds of products bought. Sometimes, if the good is a nonessential item, people may simply become bored with it and stop purchasing it. Fads and fashions may change. All this affects the perishability of a wide range of products.

The Terminology of Product Perishability

Several terms are used in marketing literature to define different degrees of perishability. *The word* **fad** *is used to describe a product that enjoys an intense but short-lived popularity.* Fads are found in a host of products, such as records, toys (the hula-hoop is a classic example of a fad), books, and home video games.

The word **fashion** *is used to describe the prevailing or accepted style or group of styles in dress or personal appearance.* A fad may last only one season or part of a season, but a fashion may last several years before being replaced. However, as fashions change, products based on the old fashion become obsolete.

The word **styling** *is often used to indicate the design characteristics that give distinctiveness to automobiles, appliances, and various other manufactured products.*

The term **new model** *implies that a product has been changed sufficiently, either technically or in style, to make its predecessors more or less obsolete.*

Dealing with Product Perishability

All products are perishable. Therefore, marketing management must plan for and adjust to the demise of what it sells. In the especially dynamic field of fashion apparel, retailers guard against being overstocked on certain lines in case the prevailing fashion changes. Apparel producers also do not want to be caught with large inventories of a certain style when the fashion dies.

Producers of technical products must concern themselves with what is likely to be in demand several years from now. Automobile manufacturers require a lead-time of about three years to plan and build a new model. Aircraft producers require even more time, up to 10 years, to get a product from the drawing board to their customers. If projections of consumer desires are off target, the consequences for the firm can be very serious.

PRODUCT MODIFICATION

Marketing managers deal directly with the question of what modifications to make in products to increase their attractiveness to customers and extend their life cycle. Some modifications are simply changes. They make a product look, taste, feel, smell, or sound different. Other modifications are improvements. They improve the product in a functional or engineering sense.

Reasons for Product Modifications

In a broad sense firms make product modifications to hold and hopefully enlarge their share of the market. There are also more specific reasons for involving marketing managers in product modification considerations.

First, marketing managers want to *satisfy the customer better*. Products are modified principally to make customers like them even better than they already do and to win new customers. Customer loyalty is very unstable. To keep it and at the same time to win more customers, marketing managers continually look for ways to make the goods they sell more appealing.

Second, they want to *combat changes made by competitors*. In an economy characterized by widespread competition, firms respond to changes made in competitive products by making changes (hopefully for the better) in their own line. Should one auto producer introduce a successful new brake system, its competitors would hurry to follow suit to reduce the risk of losing customers.

Third, they want to *differentiate their product from competitive offerings*. Many products, such as aspirin, health tonics, bread, salt, and laundry bleach, are very similar. Those responsible for marketing such items seek ways to differentiate their products and to establish a consumer preference. Often the differences between brands appear minor. One may have a package with more eye appeal, the backing of a particular authority in the field, or an extra bit of glamour in its advertisements.

Fourth, they are required to *meet government standards or follow government directions*. One result of rising consumerism has been a greatly increased government effort to require producers to make safer products or to at least warn consumers of possible dangers associated with their use. Processed-food producers using cyclamates were required on very short notice to remove that ingredient from all products that contained it. Auto manufacturers are required by law to make major modifications in exhaust systems. Cigarette makers are required to include on their packages the message, "Warning: The Surgeon General Has Determined That Cigarette Smoking Is Dangerous to Your Health." Furthermore, we can expect more—not less—government influence on product modifications in the future.

DANSKIN 🤸 NOT JUST FOR DANCING.™

THE LEOTARD – IN DISGUISE

THE WAY IT FITS, THE WAY IT FEELS — THAT'S PURE LEOTARD, PURE DANSKIN® BUT THE WAY IT LOOKS IS BRAND NEW AND FUN AND A DELIGHTFUL CHANGE. OUR SPIRITED HUNTER'S CHECK IN RED OR BLUE WITH BLACK. DANCE IN IT. STRETCH IN IT. TUCK IT UNDER A FAVORITE SHIRT. BRAVO.

DANSKIN.

Figure 9-5
Opportunities for Product Modification

Physical Changes	Nonphysical Changes
Size	Warranties
Weight	Service facilities
Shape or design	Brand names
Accessories	Trademarks *financing*
Taste	Price
Quality *Color*	Advertising claims or media *rebate*
Texture	Retail outlets
Materials *odor*	Shelf space
Additives	Promotional coupons
Ingredients	Store personnel
Durability	Packaging

How Can a Product Be Modified?

If we accept the definition of a product as "what a firm markets," then only our imagination limits the ways in which a product can be modified. Figure 9-5 illustrates some of the many ways common products can be changed. Of course, whether a specific modification is "right" depends on a host of marketing and engineering considerations. However, the opportunities for making changes are many, and the range of options is great.

Companies marketing intangible products can modify what they sell in many ways. An airline can modify its product (travel) by changing the uniforms of its flight attendants, offering faster baggage service, different seat configurations, different meals, easy pay plans, and different schedules. Similarly, a commercial bank can modify its product (various financial services) by establishing new, more convenient branches, offering free checking accounts, engaging in community activities, and providing space for civic-group meetings.

Sources for Product Modification Ideas

In our dynamic, marketing-oriented economy a product that remains the same for a long period risks declining acceptance. Management must be constantly on the lookout for ideas involving product modifications, even minor ones. Ideas for product modifications come from many sources.

Unsolicited Customer Suggestions   Product users like to give advice, much of it in the form of letters saying, "You ought to change the product in such and such a way," or "What we need is a product that does this or that." Providing 800 numbers so customers can call with their ideas or complaints is one way of encouraging such customer involvement.

Middlemen's Recommendations   Wholesale and retail merchants are excellent sources of product modification suggestions. Because they see products compete for consumer patronage, middlemen can often recommend changes in an item that will increase its sales.

Competitors' Innovations   An alert firm closely monitors the changes its competitors make in product styling, design, packaging, construction, and so on. Even a casual observer of our marketing system can spot a great deal of "followship" or "copyitis" among competitors. Certainly, competitors quickly imitate product changes that result in an increased market share for a producer.

Technical and Engineering Research   Though the amount and quality of product research vary greatly from firm to firm, some companies invest heavily in this activity on the assumption that the firm which develops the most advanced products will enjoy a dominant or at least strong market position.

Marketing Research   Marketing research is used extensively, especially by consumer goods companies, to gather ideas for product modifications and to evaluate proposed changes. For example, producers of prepared cake mixes, beverages, detergents, and toothpastes typically test customers' reactions to proposed product changes prior to making a decision.

Advertising Agencies   The people who prepare advertising campaigns are directly and intimately involved with the question, "What will help sell more of the product?" Thus, they can be an excellent source of product modification ideas.

Other Sources   Clever marketing managers remain alert to useful product ideas from any source. Some companies have regular *employee-suggestion programs*. Trade shows are another source of ideas, as is the business or trade press.

PLANNED OBSOLESCENCE

Although all products have a limited life span until they become obsolete, many critics of the new product development process feel obsolescence is deliberately speeded up. We usually associate the term **planned obsolescence** with *products intentionally produced to wear out, break down, or go out of fashion in a relatively short period of time in order to ensure a large replacement market*. Both the practice itself and the extent to which it exists are highly controversial topics.

Quality Versus Quantity

Many products on the market today that are called consumer durables actually have a relatively short life cycle. For this reason those who manufacture them are sometimes charged with having selfish motives (that is, with wanting to create a large replacement market in order to increase their profits). Producers, in turn, argue that it is impossible to increase the quality of products without increasing their costs and that some trade-off between durability and costs must be made in order to make goods available at a price large numbers of people can afford. Although there is undoubtedly a great deal of truth to this argument, consumers suspect that it is not always true—that it would not cost very much more to make, say, washing machines that would last indefinitely—and that a higher price would not be too high if it were offset by a decrease in the frequency of replacement.

Style Changes

Style changes are another controversial aspect of planned obsolescence. Critics of the auto industry, for example, feel that too much emphasis has been placed on product appearance and not enough on improved functional efficiency. To many people the frequent changes in body styles, grill designs, interior trim, and so on are a waste of human, material, and capital resources. Few, if any, industrial leaders would admit to changing the appearance of their products simply to make last year's version seem outmoded. They are much more likely to argue that they have added some important engineering changes as well.

Despite such disclaimers, in the past several decades many changes in washing machines, automobiles, and numerous other products have been principally changes in appearance, not advances in engineering. When confronted with statements to this effect, producers are likely to reply that consumers demand style changes.

Advertising copywriters know that the word "new" is one of the strongest attention-getting words in our language. Many people actively seek change, and most people welcome at least some change. Proponents of style changes argue that the consumer should be the final judge of whether frequent modifications in product design are desirable and that new models sell better than old ones. Those opposed to frequent style changes charge that advertising brainwashes consumers into believing that newer versions of everything, from cars to eyeshadow, are essential to their happiness. Critics of planned changes also charge that many of the "new discoveries," "secret ingredients," and "revolutionary developments" claimed by producers of such products as soap, toothpaste, headache remedies, and gasoline are unnecessary and that ads using these terms are misleading.

PRODUCT DELETION

Marketing management tends to devote much attention to developing and adding new products than to deleting products that are no longer profitable. This is a serious mistake. One observer has noted:

> Every weak-selling product that is permitted to linger in the line creates a burden of hidden costs, which may not always be reflected in financial accounting reports. Weak products tend to consume a disproportionate share of a manager's time, tie up production on short runs, and generally require more attention than healthy products. Devotion to weak products may delay the aggressive search for replacements and threaten the company's future profitability.[14]

Why is Product Deletion De-emphasized?

Managers invest more time in new product planning than in assessing the profitability of existing products for various reasons. First, managers may feel that a product that has turned sour may rebound in the future. Second, the marketing promotional program—not the product—may be to blame for disappointing sales. Third, sentiment or some emotionally based reason may keep the product in the line. It may be, for example, that one of the principal owners of the business likes the product. Fourth, management may retain a poorly selling product because it believes the firm's customers would be disappointed if it deleted the product, which might adversely affect sales of other products. Fifth, and probably most importantly, management lacks full information about what it costs the firm to retain the weak product. Many firms still do not have cost accounting procedures that measure all direct and indirect costs associated with manufacturing and marketing a product.

Needed: Better Information and Decisive Action

A number of models have been developed to show managers how to determine which products show little chance of becoming profit contributors.[15]

---

[14] Robert W. Eckles "Product Line Deletion and Simplification," *Business Horizons,* October 1971, p. 71.

[15] For an example of one such model see John T. O'Meara, "Selecting Profitable Products," in Bursk Chapman, ed., *New Decision Making Tools for Management* (Cambridge, Mass.: Harvard University Press, 1963).

These models generally include data about sales volume trends, gross margins, price level trends, projected market growth, customer loyalty, share-of-market trends, attitudes of the sales force and the middleman structure, and probable competitive response. However, marketing managers are becoming aware that deciding which products to drop is just as important as deciding which products to add.

Why Certain Products Are Dropped

The decision whether to discontinue a product is often based on how fast it sells. Companies using computers that report inventory data weekly or daily know exactly how specific products are selling. If sales are consistently below projected levels, it is time to start thinking about discontinuing the product. Prior to making a final decision to drop an item, however, executives may try to find answers to several questions, such as: Are the disappointing sales due to the product or to other factors such as adverse economic conditions? Can we make some changes in the product to give it more appeal? Should we try more promotional support or a different advertising theme before we give up on the item?

It is again appropriate to note that virtually all products in one way or another are perishable and sooner or later are deleted from the vendor's product line. How many products on display in retail stores 25 years ago are still sold today?

SUMMARY

- Successful companies are always involved in developing new products.
- Managing new product development is a steplike process.
- The purpose of idea generation is to develop ideas for new products that are consistent with company objectives. Ideas can be obtained from company personnel, customers, channel members, competition, and new product specialists.
- Screening involves narrowing ideas down to those that are feasible and fit corporate objectives. It guards against developing bad ideas and discarding good ideas.
- Concept tests are inexpensive ways to screen promising ideas.
- During the business-analysis step projected sales and costs are analyzed to determine whether the company can market the product profitably.
- Development consists of designing the actual product to safely fulfill the

attributes of the product idea, and conducting functional and consumer tests.

- Test marketing involves the limited introduction of the product in selected markets to test the marketing strategy and gauge customer reactions. Although often providing valuable information, test marketing is expensive, allows competitors to look at the product, and can produce inaccurate results.
- Full-scale introduction of the product is commercialization. To minimize risk, many companies use a roll-out strategy rather than a full-scale introduction.
- Many ideas must be generated to develop one successful product. Products which are superior, were thoroughly researched and planned, were timed right, are easily understood, and minimize consumer perceived risk are more likely to be successful.
- The adoption process helps us understand the steps a consumer goes through in deciding to try a product. The diffusion process categorizes people by how quickly the adoption process is completed.
- Many products exhibit a life cycle consisting of four stages: introduction, growth, maturity, and decline.
- The introduction stage is characterized by little competition, few product variations or distribution outlets, large promotional expenditures, and low or negative profits.
- The growth stage is characterized by many competitors, product improvement, emphasis on promotion to secure market share, more outlets, and rapidly increasing profits.
- Maturity witnesses level or falling sales, attempts to hold market share through promotion and distribution, and marginal competitors leaving the market.
- Decline involves either the decision of when to drop the product or how to extend its life.
- The product life cycle has limitations but reminds us that all products are perishable and the successful firm will have new products ready to replace the declining ones.
- Product modifications are changes in a product to make it more satisfying to customers, to combat changes by competitors, to differentiate the product from competitive offerings, and/or to meet government standards.
- Products can be modified in many ways. Sources of product modification ideas include customers, middlemen, competitors, innovations, technical and engineering research, marketing research, and advertising agencies.
- Although more emphasis is placed on product development, product deletion is an important marketing responsibility that should not be ignored.

DISCUSSION
QUESTIONS

1. Explain the new product development process. What is the purpose of each step in this process?
2. Pick two recent product introductions, one that has succeeded and one that failed. Explain what factors about each caused its success or failure.
3. Explain how the adoption process, diffusion process, and product life cycle are related.
4. Define the term product life cycle. How are the marketing controllable variables different in each stage?
5. What are the shortcomings of the product life cycle to marketers? What is its value?
6. Some products (such as certain brands of soft drinks, candy, chewing gum, and breakfast cereals) have changed very little over a period of decades. Does this fact refute the product life cycle concept? Explain.
7. What is a fad? Give several examples of fads in clothing, entertainment, and food or drink.
8. For at least five years home video games have enjoyed growing popularity. Why? At what stage in the product life cycle does this product fall?
9. Why is product modification an ongoing concern to marketing managers? Differentiate between physical and nonphysical product changes.
10. Explain why product deletion is not emphasized in marketing. Should it be and why?

APPLICATION
EXERCISES

1. Select five products on the market today. What stage of the product life cycle is each in? What characteristics place each in that particular stage?
2. Choose one product (an automobile, a kitchen appliance, or a pair of shoes, for example). Then list five physical and five nonphysical changes that could be made to hopefully increase sales.
3. Doing research if necessary, make a list of five products not mentioned in this chapter that were widely used ten years ago but have now virtually disappeared. In each case point out the main reasons for the product's demise. Next, develop a list of five products marketed extensively today that you feel will have virtually disappeared ten years from now. Explain why you think these products are on their way out. How could one of these products be changed to extend its life?

CASE 9
Hot Times for Kero-Sun[16]

William Litwin, president, founder, and principal owner of Kero-Sun, Inc., and a former Pan Am pilot, first saw a Japanese kerosene heater on a cousin's boat in California in 1975. He was impressed and bought one for his own house. Then "a series of reactions went off in my mind." The time was right after the oil crisis of 1973–74, and Litwin knew that most Americans were looking for a way to save on energy. Litwin imported 50 of the kerosene heaters from a Japanese manufacturer and sold them all. He then went to Japan to talk with the manufacturer about representing the company exclusively in the U.S. Litwin had to go deeply into debt to purchase his first large batch of heaters, but business began to grow by leaps and bounds, and Litwin's debt was soon turned to profit.

Kero-Sun has always spent freely on advertising. In the early years Kero-Sun spent a great deal attempting to convince skeptical consumers that kerosene heaters are safe. By 1978 Kero-Sun was growing at such an astounding rate that Litwin left his job as a pilot in order to devote more time to his rapidly growing company. In each of the five years from 1976 to 1981 Kero-Sun achieved sales gains of at least 100 percent. In 1981 Kero-Sun enjoyed approximately 35 percent of the kerosene-heater market, which was estimated at 3 million units. In 1982, however, growth slowed to about 25 percent more than the previous year, and a number of competitors entered the market.

The market for kerosene heaters was expected to continue growing, but at a slower rate. Predictions for 1983 sales were substantially below original expectations. "This industry can't be expected to grow at the dazzling rate of the past," said Litwin, calling 1983 a "shakeout year." Kero-Sun was beginning to feel the pressure of facing more than 70 competitors. Many big companies entered the market, including Sears and Japan's Matsushita, which planned to introduce kerosene heaters under its Panasonic label. With such intense competition in the kerosene-heater market, many retailers were being forced to offer discounts. Kero-Sun changed its advertising emphasis from product safety and use to brand name and high quality. Mr. Litwin insisted Kero-Sun "profits are healthy, but not remarkable." Nevertheless, Kero-Sun was taking steps to stave off the competition and increase its market. It introduced a new product line, a large stationary kerosene heater called the Monitor, and Litwin was toying with the idea of starting a special chain of retail stores to be called Energy America. Kero-Sun appeared to recognize that industry growth was slowing and competition was becoming increasingly intense. However, the company was not content to rest on past performance.

---

[16] Ann M. Morrison, "Hotter Competition for the Heater Leader," *Fortune*, March 8, 1982, pp. 93–95; and Maria Shao, "Kero-Sun, The Pioneer in Kerosene Heaters, Struggles as Growth Slows, Rivals Emerge," *Wall Street Journal*, December 17, 1982, p. 29.

Discussion Questions

1. In what stage of the product life cycle was the kerosene-heater industry in 1983? What facts support your answer?
2. If you were Mr. Litwin, what steps would you take to ensure corporate survival? Why?
3. Is the Energy America chain a good strategy? Why?

10 Marketing Services and Nonprofit Products

STUDY OBJECTIVES

After studying this chapter, you should be able to

1. Explain the variety and importance of service products in our economy and the reasons for their increasing popularity.
2. Outline the bases for competition in the marketing of services.
3. Discuss the special considerations that govern the marketing of services.
4. Outline the special product, place, promotional, and price considerations that are involved in marketing nonprofit products.
5. Discuss the ethical considerations related to the marketing of nonprofit products.
6. Discuss the probable future of social marketing.

Throughout Part Three we have examined products. Although we usually think of a product as something tangible, in many cases it is a service. In addition products or services are often sold by organizations with goals other than making a profit. These services and nonprofit products represent special cases of the product variable, and we will examine them in this chapter.

SERVICES

One of the most dramatic changes in our economy in recent decades has been the increasing share of income spent for services. In 1984 Americans spent approximately 48 percent of their incomes for products that could not be touched, smelled, or tasted—and in some instances could not even be seen or heard. About half the labor force works in service industries, and more than one-third of all commercial enterprises are service establishments.

Consider for a moment just some of the purchases made by the typical American family. On a given day various members of the family may visit a doctor, have their teeth examined, see a movie, have a car repaired, play golf, take ballet lessons, fly to another city to visit a relative, have their hair styled, retain an accountant to compute their taxes, purchase some form of insurance, negotiate a bank loan, seek a lawyer's advice, or ask an architect to design a new home for them. In each of these activities they are spending money for services rather than tangible goods. When we board a pet, buy a ticket to a hockey game, consult with a physician, put money in a video-game machine, sleep in a motel, contract with someone to remove snow, or take tennis lessons, we are buying services, not tangible products.

Industrial users also spend a significant portion of their resources on services. Businesses purchase an array of services from accounting, legal, research, engineering, and other firms that specialize in providing various forms of technical assistance. They also purchase transportation, insurance, financial advice, advertising, and so on.

A **service** is any act or work performed for another in exchange for something of value. Because it is an act, services are *intangible*—they cannot be sorted, transported, or saved for future use. They occur when the act is performed. In addition services are *inseparable* from the performer. The performer must be present to perform the service, unlike a product that can be removed from the manufacturer and still perform its function.

In many respects services are marketed in the same way as physical products. However, because of the intangibility and inseparability of services, they sometimes require special handling.

Types of Services

Leading commercial-service industries include the providers of:

1. *Personal services,* such as laundries, health spas, hair salons, and photography studios.
2. *Lodging,* such as hotels, motels, and camper parks.
3. *Amusement,* such as movie theaters, video arcades, and bowling alleys.
4. *Repairs* for items such as wristwatches, televisions, and automobiles.
5. *Transportation,* such as airlines, railroads, truck lines, and cab companies.
6. *Communications,* such as telephone and broadcasting companies.
7. *Financial help,* such as commercial banks and loan companies.
8. *Brokerage services,* such as firms that buy and sell stocks, bonds, and commodities for their clients.
9. *Real-estate services,* such as firms that sell, rent, or manage property.
10. *Insurance,* such as firms that sell and service insurance policies to cover a wide variety of risks.
11. *Business services,* such as advertising agencies, news syndicates, market researchers, and telephone-answering services.

Classifying Services   Services can be classified by whether they are primarily consumer or organization oriented; human or machine centered; professional or nonprofessional; profit or nonprofit; regulated or nonregulated; large, medium, or small; and very intangible or somewhat intangible.[1] Haircuts, personal life insurance, and dental work are exclusively consumer-oriented services. Business consulting, machinery repair, and plant maintenance are exclusively nonconsumer services. However, many services such as air travel, legal services, and accounting may be both consumer and nonconsumer oriented.

Human- or machine-centered services refer to the method by which the service is performed, that is, how many people, as opposed to machines, are needed to perform the service. Haircuts are human-centered services, as are accounting services and ski instruction. Electric utilities, transportation, and communications are machine-centered services.

Professional services are provided by individuals with highly developed, and often hard to obtain, skills. Doctors, lawyers, and consultants are all examples of professionals who perform services for their clients. Indi-

---

[1] Some of these classification criteria were drawn from John M. Rathmell, *Marketing in the Service Sector* (Cambridge, Mass.: Winthrop Publishers, 1974).

Electronic Funds Transfer Systems

As we shake our heads with wonder that people ever made the awkward, bulky barter system work, so may future generations wonder how we endured the inconvenience of paper money, coins, and checks.

The technology exists to free us from the necessity of carrying cash or writing checks, addressing envelopes and affixing stamps to pay bills. Gaining widespread acceptance of Electronic Funds Transfer Systems, or EFTS, is one of marketing's biggest challenges. When it happens, it will be a milestone comparable in importance to the development of money.

Commercial use of EFTS is much greater than private use. Electronic technology is used to transfer funds between banks participating in the Federal Reserve System through a network called the Fed Wire. A second network, called the Bank Wire, provides the same service between commercial banks. A third network exists for the communication of transactions made with national bank credit cards.

The average person in the street has been reluctant to let go of the traditional tangible qualities of cash and checks. Yet evolution to EFTS may be inevitable merely because of cost. In 1980 banks processed nearly 32 billion checks at an average cost of 13 cents each.

The movement toward adoption of Electronic Funds Transfer Systems for ultimate consumers began in the early 1970s. Presently, it provides services at several different levels, some of which are available in only a few cities.

viduals with less-developed skills perform nonprofessional services, such as janitorial maintenance, taxi rides, or shoe shines.

Nonprofit services are often undertaken by the government or a private organization to serve some public need. Universities, churches, and museums are examples of both government and private nonprofit services.

Although not run by the government, many services are government regulated. Some, mostly nonprofit, organizations are nonregulated (churches). However, most services are either specifically regulated by the government (utilities, transportation companies, and banks), regulate themselves (doctors and lawyers), or are subject to general regulation applying to all companies. Some service activities such as lawn care or house

Most widely used is the Automatic Teller Machine (ATM), the 24-hour 7-day per week electronic banking device. ATMs dispense cash, accept deposits, reveal account balances, and perform various other services—but only for individuals with properly coded plastic cards. The most successful early ATM was pioneered in Atlanta, Georgia. Because consumers were wary of dealing with a cold, impersonal machine, First National Bank developed a humanized personality for the device and named it Tillie the Teller. Tillie and her 27 twin sisters were processing about 4 million transactions a year by their third birthday. Less widely available is pay-by-phone. This EFTS service allows subscribers with touchtone phones to gain direct access to a computer that will handle automatic payment of certain prearranged bills and deduct the amount from the subscribers' checking accounts. No checks are involved.

Point-of-sale (POS) Terminals are used in many cities. Sales clerks may "talk to" the customer's bank through an on-the-spot terminal. The amount of the purchase is automatically deducted from the customer's account. No checks or cash are involved.

Chief among the objections most consumers register to the concept of EFTS are that

- Account information might be made available to unauthorized people, thereby invading the privacy of the account holder.
- Record-keeping problems might be increased.
- The account holder would not be able to "stop payment" after reconsideration of a transaction.
- EFTS' instantaneous transfer eliminates the safety margin or "float" many check writers depend on for timely payment of their bills.

Despite these and other objections, it seems that the EFTS will probably be used extensively.

Successes such as that of Tillie the Teller demonstrate how sensitive marketing can help consumers adapt to the new technology.

painting are not regulated because of the small size of individual operations.

Size of the service performers can vary greatly. Utilities are normally multibillion-dollar operations that serve millions of people. Lawn-care performers, however, may measure income in dollars and serve only a few clients.

Finally, the degree of a service's intangibility can be helpful in classifying it. Primarily, services are either very intangible and consumed immediately, or last over a short period of time. Most services fit in the first category. However, some services such as equipment rental are not instantaneous and last as long as the rental continues. Although the benefit from a service may last an undetermined length of time, the performance of the actual service is often short in duration. For example, a visit to the dentist for teeth-cleaning may take only half an hour, but the perceived benefit of brighter teeth may last for months.

Reasons for the Growth of Services

The phenomenal growth in the demand for services in recent years can be attributed to four factors:

1. The introduction of new products
2. Greater prosperity
3. The increasing number of dual-career families
4. The growing complexity of our private and business lives

New Products   New products have been responsible for the evolution of many service industries. The development of the automobile early in this century gave birth to nearly 200,000 service establishments that provide repairs for motor vehicles.

Decades later the emergence of television was followed by a burgeoning colony of repair shops, educational services, consulting firms, and other businesses required or made possible by the new broadcast medium. More recently, the rapid growth in computer sales has been accompanied by a corresponding growth in computer services such as programming, repairing, and time-sharing. It is easy to predict that the proliferation of personal computers will also give birth to similar services for consumers. Clearly, whenever new tangible products emerge, we can expect new services to follow.

Greater Prosperity   Many services can either be performed by the family unit, hired out, or postponed indefinitely. Amusement and travel services, for example, are not essential to human existence. However, as spendable income increases, we find that consumption of such services also increases. Each new generation appears to expect more of the good things in life (many of which are services) than the previous generation. So, to the extent that real income rises over time, we can expect the demand for services to increase faster than the demand for tangible products.

Dual-Career Families   The increase in the number of dual-career families has caused a corresponding increase in the demand for certain services. Day care for small children, laundry and dry-cleaning services, housecleaning services, restaurants, and prepared-food operations have all benefited from increased demand as more and more wives become full-time workers. As dual-career families become even more prevalent, it is easy to envision the development of a wider array of services to make home care and child rearing easier for both working spouses.

Complexity of Private and Business Life The growing complexity of living and doing business in our modern, ever-changing environment is an important reason for the increase in service firms. A generation ago many consumers could repair their own radios, automobiles, and other products. Today even very common products, such as microwave ovens or home video games, are so complex that the owner often has no alternative but to have them repaired by experts.

Similarly, advertising, financial investment, real-estate management, and a host of other business functions have become so complex that a firm must either employ specialists or retain independent service establishments to perform the work. Income-tax regulations have become so complex that even the general public has turned to accounting firms for help. Our need for expert assistance, in both our private and business lives, is likely to increase even more in the future. This means, then, that services will become even more important.

Bases for Competition in the Marketing of Services

Three factors are particularly important in the marketing of services: the reputation of the seller, the skill of the person who does the work, and the value added by auxiliary services.

Reputation of the Seller A good reputation is generally even more important to the vendor of services than to the firm selling tangible products. Although physical products may be inspected in advance of purchase to evaluate their styling, functional efficiency, and durability, the arrangements for the purchase of a service must generally be made prior to experiencing it. A man who brings his suit to a dry-cleaner, his car to a shop, or himself to a reducing salon cannot inspect the service he will receive until it has been performed. Accordingly, the reputation of whoever performs the service is exceedingly important. It is often this reputation that convinces the consumer to purchase the untried service.

Vendors of identical goods are also often judged on the basis of the services they offer. To consumers who need loans, money is money. In deciding where to get it, they will consider, in addition to the interest rate, such things as the speed and convenience with which the loan can be negotiated and the attitude of the lender's personnel. Because they cannot learn about these things firsthand without actually applying for the loan, they must depend on hearsay or advertising claims. The purchaser of an airline ticket may consider, in addition to promises of tasty dinners and pleasant flight attendants, the airline's reputation for safety and reliability.

Reputation is exceptionally important in marketing medical, legal, accounting, architectural, and other professional services that are not extensively advertised or "sold." One of the first things a new resident of a community asks neighbors or associates is to recommend a dentist or a doctor. Vendors of professional services in particular and of all services in general rely on word-of-mouth advertising to a greater extent than vendors of tangible products. This is also true in the business world. When a company decides to hire a new advertising agency, it bases its selection more on the reputation, or track record, of the firm than on anything else. Business buyers are even more exacting than consumers in their requirements and must rely on the reputation of the service firm's ability to perform. Because a service company cannot demonstrate a product, its reputation for dependability, skill, and creativity becomes its chief promotional aid.

Not only is a service usually completed before the buyer is able to evaluate its quality, but defective or unsatisfactory service also cannot be returned. Marketers of services such as auto repair may guarantee their workmanship, but in a literal sense the service is not returned. In many instances the consumer has no recourse but to try another vendor next time.

Skill of the Performer Tangible products are produced, but services are performed. Due to quality-control procedures, each product in a mass-produced line of tangible goods such as appliances or hardware is virtually identical to every other product in the line. This is not true of most services. The quality of an auto mechanic's work may vary somewhat from day to day depending, for example, on whether he feels particularly challenged by a puzzling mechanical problem.

The skill, technique, and approach of the individuals providing services cannot be standardized to the same degree as the machines that produce tangible products. For this reason the overall performance of a service vendor is highly important. Consumers frequently make tangible purchases from vendors who know little about the product and have no particular skill. They rely on the skill of the producer in making a good product. The purchaser of a service such as hairstyling, on the other hand, is more concerned with the stylist's ability than with anything else. Stylists can be certain that if they fail to satisfy the customer, their services will not be sought again. If they fail to satisfy most of their customers, they will be out of a job. Similarly, music lovers purchase tickets to a concert mostly on the basis of the performer's known skill in providing enjoyable entertainment. If the performance is poor, the turnout for future concerts may be poor, too.

Value Added by Auxiliary Services Many services are accompanied by auxiliary services. Quite often these companion services differentiate the

"Nonstop to Australia. Qantas, you're pushing it." Nonstop Qantas 747s from Los Angeles to Sydney. One-stop to Melbourne. Koalas Against Qantas. (The Australian Airline.)

product from similar intangibles marketed by other firms. Consider two passenger airlines, both of which fly Boeing 747s. Because the equipment (the plane) and the basic service (transportation) are identical, related services, such as the frequency of departures, the degree of pampering received in flight, the ease with which reservations can be made, and the swiftness with which baggage can be reclaimed, are likely to influence the consumer's choice. All these services are auxiliary to the airline's primary service, transportation.

Banks often compete on the basis of the companion services they offer. For example, two banks in the same city may be "full-service" banks, which means they provide checking and savings accounts, loans, safe-deposit boxes, and similar services. However, as an extra service one bank may offer a "loan" automatically credited to the customer's checking account whenever he or she overdraws, whereas the other stamps the check "insufficient funds" or charges a substantial fee for honoring it.

Many marketers of tangible products also add value to what they sell by providing auxiliary services. Some apparel retailers, for example, offer free alterations. Drapery shops usually provide installation services. Many restaurants feature entertainers in their lounges.

MARKETING
Strategy

VISA Versus MasterCard

The use of plastic money is widespread in this country and becoming increasingly popular in the international market. The proliferation of the cashless purchase is mainly due to the two major bank credit cards, VISA and MasterCard.

More than 55 percent of all Americans hold all-purpose credit cards issued by various financial institutions.* Such cards are the newcomers to consumer credit, having had their beginnings in the 1950s. VISA, originally called BankAmericard, was the first to be issued. It was sponsored by San Francisco's Bank of America and was intended for use only in California. Some years later, in 1966, the bank set up a subsidiary to license banks in the United States to issue BankAmericard. It also arranged with Barclays Bank, Ltd., to issue "Barclaycard" throughout the United Kingdom.

In 1970, with the card system having grown rapidly, National BankAmericard Incorporated (NBI) was established as an independent membership corporation. A departure from the former licensing system, NBI was owned by its members (issuing banks or other organizations) and governed in proportion to their cardholder sales volume. VISA U.S.A., Inc., as NBI was renamed in 1977, has the same structure.

This "equity ownership" is the chief distinguishing feature between VISA and MasterCard. MasterCharge was set up in 1967 to compete with BankAmericard. The name was changed to MasterCard in 1980. MasterCard itself is a trademark held by InterBank Card Association (ICA), a nonprofit organization. ICA licenses banks to issue MasterCards. Beyond that, it acts as a national trade association to service member institutions and their affiliates.

Aside from the differences in their internal structure, the two cards have much in common. Witness these similarities:

Target market. People interested in the installment method of payment traditionally defined the largest target market for VISA and MasterCard. Most of these individuals are gainfully employed and at the low end of the economic scale. Both companies are beginning to realize that their segmentation strategy should not be based on those who are interested in credit, but rather on the convenience of paying with plastic. This target market is larger and offers greater revenue potential for VISA and MasterCard.

* "A New Marketing Blitz in the War of the Plastic Cards," *Business Week*, July 23, 1984, pp. 126, 128.

Product. The ability to precisely define its business gives VISA an advantage over MasterCard today and in the future. VISA sees itself in the "transfer of value" business.† This broad definition facilitates the family-of-products concept it has adopted. Its family consists of (1) debit cards that transfer money from a bank account almost immediately after the time of purchase, (2) traveler's checks that carry the VISA logo and the name of the issuer (Barclays Bank has stopped issuing its own traveler's checks and now deals only with VISA checks), and (3) the traditional credit card.

ICA realized its need to change basic philosophies and in 1980 began revamping its organization. Part of the change was to adopt the family-of-products idea. After finally resolving some legal barriers, ICA is in the traveler's-check market and expects to issue a debit card soon.

VISA has beaten ICA consistently in terms of the efficiency of its product. Its better authorization and interchange systems increased the acceptance of the VISA card by retailers and consumers.

Place. Both cards are international. Reports in the 1980s placed MasterCard holders at 75,000,000 worldwide and 59,000,000 within the United States. VISA held a slight but growing edge, with 84,000,000 cardholders internationally and 63,000,000 domestic customers.

To increase its visibility, VISA no longer restricts its cards to financial institutions. In association with an affiliated financial institution, a company such as the American Automobile Club or Hertz Rent-a-Car can have its own name imprinted on the blue band across the top. Many large companies welcome the opportunity, VISA believes, to provide an additional service tailored especially for their members and customers. Billing is handled by a local cooperating bank.

VISA is continually pushing to have its product accepted at more locations. J.C. Penney has agreed to accept the VISA card in its stores. The agreement ties Penney's computers directly into VISA's network, bypassing the merchant bank and eliminating its percentage on each sale. This agreement is another step toward a complete electronic transfer of funds system and is the direction VISA hopes to take the "transfer of funds" industry. ICA is not interested in such contracts.

Promotion. The renaming of BankAmericard to VISA consolidated and enhanced the card's image. Previously, it had been issued under 22 different names. The name VISA has the connotation of glamour and travel, and it does not suggest a single financial service, like credit. Furthermore, the name is pronounced virtually the same all over the world and is recognized readily everywhere. ICA has not been so lucky with MasterCard. It is still struggling to convince the market that the name change from MasterCharge implies a use for the card beyond credit. Internationally, the MasterCard logo and name share promotional space with other cards because of joint venture

† Walter Kiechel, III, "Explosion in the Bank Card Cafeteria," *Fortune*, September 8, 1980, pp. 70–82.

Continued

Continued

agreements with foreign cards. Consequently, MasterCard is suffering from a fragmented identity abroad.

Price. Both companies charge a percentage of billings to the merchants and other subscribing organizations. Cardholders may pay the entire amount due within one month, which about 50 percent of them do. Or they may use the cards as installment credit by paying about 1.6 percent per month (19 percent per year) on the unpaid balance.

In 1980 both companies saw the need for a change in pricing. The number of people paying off their balance within one month was almost half of all users. Insufficient interest revenues combined with the increasing cost of financing credit-card receivables forced the firms to introduce annual usage fees in many states. The $10- to $15-per-year payment met with little resistance, and there has been no significant drop in accounts since its initiation.

VISA is number one in the "transfer of value" business, partly because of the greater efficiency of its operations and its better customer awareness. The rest is based on its willingness to accept a broad definition of its industry and to use it to advantage. To stay competitive, ICA must follow suit. As we move closer to a cashless, checkless society, the opportunities for both firms will increase as the desire for the conveniences they offer grows.

Special Considerations in Marketing Services

Six special considerations in the marketing of services should be noted:

- Ownership is not transferred.
- Appeals to the imagination are needed.
- Promotion may be free.
- Tangible products are assets, whereas services are considered expenses.
- Most services cannot be stored.
- Production and consumption are simultaneous.

Ownership is not Transferred   When a tangible product such as a motorcycle is purchased, the buyer takes ownership and control. However, when the motorcycle owner has the bike serviced, there is no transfer of ownership of the adjustments made by the mechanic. In the purchase of services the buyer is always dependent on the seller until the service has been consumed. Afterwards the benefits of the service may continue, but the service itself ends and the potential to perform the service again still belongs to the original performer. No ownership has been transferred.

Appeals to the Imagination Needed   Because a service cannot be experienced in advance, the seller must appeal to the consumer's imagination in describing its benefits. A firm marketing a motorcycle or a television set can ask the prospective consumer to handle it, look it over, and perhaps try it out. A firm selling a service must appeal to the prospect's ability to visualize the benefits from the service.

In marketing life insurance, for example, the seller may try to create an image in the prospect's mind of the happiness economic security provides or the financial difficulties the family may encounter should the consumer die with inadequate coverage. In selling a tour to some faraway place, a travel agent helps clients visualize the romance, fun, and excitement of a trip to the exotic land. In marketing educational services such as courses in television repair or computer programming, the seller stresses future benefits such as a "good job," "high pay," and "job security." All these appeals are designed to help people see not what is, but what can be if they purchase the services.

Promotion May Be Free   Some of the best-known service organizations spend very little on advertising and sales promotion. Professional football teams, golf tournaments, horse races, and other sporting events are well known to the public primarily because the various media consider such happenings newsworthy and give them extensive free publicity. Movies, plays, operas, and similar theatrical products, although advertised to some extent, are also promoted through unpaid publicity provided by print and broadcast media. The free promotion given some forms of services may prove to be negative, however, because publicity is not always positive. When a movie gets a bad review or a professional basketball team is criticized by the media, ticket sales are likely to be below expectations.

Services Are Considered Expenses   Most services lose much if not all of their economic value at the time of purchase. On the other hand, most tangible products retain some economic value for months, years, or even decades. Consumer products such as automobiles, appliances, and furniture as well as industrial products such as equipment and machinery have some resale value long after the initial purchase is made.

Services, in short, usually depreciate fully upon purchase, whereas tangible products depreciate more slowly. Moreover, there is no market for used services. One cannot resell a movie seen yesterday or a plane trip taken last summer. In accounting, tangible products are listed as assets, but services are considered expenses.

Most Services Cannot Be Stored   Merchants who market tangible products can put them in storage until they are needed, but there is no way to stockpile services in the conventional sense. On any given flight an airline has a certain number of seats available. If a plane takes off from New York for Los Angeles with only 60 percent of those seats occupied, 40 percent of the available capacity is lost forever. There is no way to store empty seats for a future flight. Nor is it possible for an architect, a surgeon, a consultant, or a shoe repairman to store, in a literal sense, the service he or she provides.

In many instances a service is created when it is needed. Although it is true that entertainment can be stored and enjoyed repeatedly by means of recordings and cassettes (which are tangible products), a live musical performance is a unique experience, and never again, even at repeat performances, can it be duplicated.

Closely related to their inability to be stored is the perishability of services. To a far greater extent than any tangible product, services are perishable. Unless consumed when offered, a service may perish totally. Individuals who want to attend a movie or sporting event, but arrive too late to view it, find the product they wanted to buy gone. Even if the individual does reach the movie or sporting event on time, it (the product) is consumed in the space of a few hours, and nothing remains of it except the memory.

Simultaneous Production and Consumption   In the case of tangible products, production and consumption are clearly distinct activities. For example, bread is baked and then consumed later. In the case of services, however, production and consumption take place at the same time. We "consume" a football game, a telephone call, or a college education as these services are "produced." Benefits from the consumption of services, however, may extend over a period of time. The services provided by a surgeon may extend a life, and the enjoyment from a vacation trip may last for months.

Marketing by Service Organizations

Service companies have traditionally lagged behind manufacturing firms in developing and using marketing. One study of 400 service and marketing firms found service companies less likely to have marketing departments, to use sales plans and training, and to make use of marketing professionals (consultants, marketing research firms, or advertising agencies).[2] A later study found that although service firms were using less marketing, the frequency of its use was increasing.[3] It is likely that as competition between

---

[2] Richard M. Bessom and Donald W. Jackson, Jr., "Service Retailing: A Strategic Marketing Approach," *Journal of Retailing*, Summer 1975, pp. 75–84.

[3] Philip Kotler and Richard A. Connor, Jr., "Marketing Professional Services," *Journal of Marketing*, January 1977, p. 71.

service companies increases, the use of marketing will also increase. Certainly the increased competition in the banking industry has led to greater use of marketing strategies by banks.

Traditionally, laws and professional codes of ethics have prohibited medical, legal, dental, and accounting professionals from using advertising and other marketing tools. In order to build or expand their practices, they relied on their reputations, community contacts, referrals by other professionals from related fields, and recommendations from existing clients and patients.

This nonpromotion tradition is changing. The Supreme Court has made several positive rulings concerning the legality of advertising by professionals, and professional codes of ethics prohibiting promotion are gradually being modified.

One key reason some professionals want to advertise is that competition for clients and patients is increasing. Between 1972 and 1982 there was only a small increase in the total population, but the number of accountants increased from 720,000 to 1,193,000, the number of lawyers from 322,000 to 630,000, and the number of physicians from 332,000 to 486,000.[4]

Advertising by professionals is a controversial issue. Those endorsing it argue that it is justified because (1) a professional invests a great deal of money and time to earn the right to practice; (2) advertising may result in more income to the professional, enabling her or him to reduce fees; and (3) patients and clients benefit from knowing more about what the professional has to offer. Those opposed to promotion by professionals argue that (1) advertising is unprofessional; (2) it leads to price competition, which is not a good basis for building a professional practice because it may lead to a lower quality of service; and (3) professionals, more than any other group, should put service ahead of profit.

NONPROFIT MARKETING

Nonprofit marketing is conducted by organizations that seek to serve some aspect of the public interest rather than seek financial profits. Figure 10-1 lists examples of nonprofit organizations. Marketing nonprofit products, often called **nonbusiness marketing** or **social marketing**, is a special challenge to marketers. Nonbusiness organizations (except the government) depend on donations and contributions from private citizens, and many are experiencing rising costs. As Kotler noted, more than 170 private colleges have closed since 1965 (unable to attract money or students); hospital

---

[4] U.S. Department of Commerce, Bureau of the Census, *Statistical Abstract of the United States, 1984,* p. 419.

Figure 10-1
Nonprofit Organizations
Federal, state, and local governments
Labor unions
Religious bodies
Foundations
Political parties and candidates
Social movements (such as Planned Parenthood)
Charitable organizations (Red Cross, United Appeal)
Civic organizations (Lions, Kiwanis, Rotary)
Private colleges
Boy Scouts and Girl Scouts
Trade associations
Many hospitals
College alumni associations
Social causes, such as antismoking, antilitter, and anti-nuclear energy campaigns

costs are soaring, with predictions that over 1,400 hospitals will close in the next 10 years; the Catholic Church has experienced declines in weekly attendance of those under 30 years old (from 55 percent attendance in 1966 to 39 percent in 1975); many performance groups cannot attract audiences and even when they do, still lose money; and many organizations, such as the YMCA, Salvation Army, and Girl Scouts, are re-examining their mission in an effort to halt membership declines.[5]

Nonprofit marketers often serve target markets that profit-seeking firms rejected as uneconomical. The Red Cross, for example, offers emergency aid at no cost to the victims. Clearly, this cannot be a profit-generating venture. Because of this tendency to serve nonprofitable segments, nonprofit organizations often serve one market segment but draw their funding from others. The Muscular Dystrophy Association tries to serve those stricken by muscular dystrophy, but runs a telethon every year to solicit funds from the general public. Thus, the public at large may, for humanitarian reasons, pay for nonprofit products that only a small portion of the population will ever use.

---

[5] Philip Kotler, "Strategies for Introducing Marketing Into Nonprofit Organizations," *Journal of Marketing,* January 1979, p. 37.

More people have survived cancer than now live in the City of Los Angeles.
                              We are winning.

        Please support the

AMERICAN CANCER SOCIETY®

Nonprofit Marketing Controllable Variables

As with profit marketing, nonprofit marketing controllable variables are the product, place, promotion, and price decisions made for each specific target market.

Target Markets   Selecting target markets for nonprofit products may be simple or complex. For a labor union, identification of target customers is fairly simple. The target market consists of all employees in a specific industry who are eligible to join the union. It is also easy to identify target markets for trade associations (all businesses in the industry served by the association) and for professional associations (all members of the profession).

Identifying target customers is moderately complicated for a church. The target market might be defined as "all former members, nonchurch members, and members of other churches who are unhappy with their current affiliation." Selecting target customers for civic clubs and lodges is also moderately difficult.

In the case of social and charitable organizations identification of target customers is quite difficult. Theoretically, everyone is a prospective contributor to an antilitter campaign or to the Salvation Army, but it is very difficult to market even such generalized services to everyone.

Product Considerations   Because nonbusiness products are services or intangibles, they are more difficult to define than commercial products. For example, a tour of duty in the U.S. Army might be marketed as a nonbusiness product with the following description:

> a complex bundle of intangible attributes which combines as one family of brands in the generic product class of "multiyear experiences." The benefits are intangibles such as personal growth, education, skill training, excitement, adventure, travel, and opportunity to help one's country.[6]

The product of Planned Parenthood is advice in planning births for the ultimate benefit of both parents and children. The 55-mile-per-hour speed limit is difficult to describe as a product, but translates into "energy conservation, safety, lower fuel costs, and patriotism."

Meanwhile, the product of a labor union can be defined much more concretely as "shorter hours, better pay, improved working conditions, and more benefits."

---

[6] Michael L. Rothschild, "Marketing Communications in Nonbusiness Situations or Why It's So Hard to Sell Brotherhood Like Soap," *Journal of Marketing*, Spring 1979, p. 15.

Place Considerations   Place is often difficult to describe in marketing nonprofit products. Where, for example, is the best place to market a political candidate or contributions to charity? Political candidates do maintain headquarters and branch offices, but the place where the nonprofit product is "purchased" may be a post-office box. Military recruiters maintain offices in many cities, but they also travel to schools and universities to place their product directly with prospects. Sometimes the place is a busy intersection where motorists waiting for a green light are asked to contribute to some cause. The place may be a person's home where he or she is visited by a canvasser or telephoned by someone seeking a contribution or a pledge to vote for a political candidate.

Promotional Considerations   Promotion of social products involves all elements in the promotional mix. Personal selling is used extensively in marketing memberships in unions, trade associations, civic clubs, and churches. Members invite other people to join such groups.

Advertising is used extensively to promote charitable contributions, gifts to alumni associations, blood bank drives, anticrime campaigns, and military enlistments. Much advertising time and space in the form of public service announcements are donated by the media (see Figure 10-2).

Sales promotion tools are also used. Bumper stickers, badges, and plaques are given to members and contributors (purchasers of nonprofit products) to encourage others to join and/or contribute.

Public relations in marketing social products assumes various forms (such as seeking free publicity in print and broadcast media). Invitations to the White House for social occasions are extended to people who make large campaign contributions or aid in a campaign in some special way. Lobbying for legislation is another form of public-relations effort used in marketing nonprofit products.

One key promotional problem in marketing many nonprofit products is the difficulty of convincing target consumers that they will personally benefit. The law of self-interest sometimes stands in the way. People often reason, "Why should I donate to the United Appeal? None of what I give will come back to me." "Why should I put my trash in a waste container? A lot of other people don't." Rothschild notes:

> In the private sector, the purchaser of the product is generally also the consumer or a member of the consuming unit (e.g., the family). In nonbusiness cases, the product often provides little direct measurable benefit to the purchaser. For example, a person who considers purchasing the concept of driving more slowly pays (in time lost) for a product which primarily benefits society (with greater energy reserves). Since the purchaser may not immediately perceive the personal benefit, it must be

---
Figure 10-2

Public Service Announcement

Richard Brown thought he was too young to have a stroke. He wasn't.

Because having a family, a good job and a bright future doesn't protect anyone from a stroke. In fact, nearly one million Americans — many with those assets — die of heart disease and stroke each year. And 200,000 of them die "too young."

The American Heart Association is fighting to reduce early death and disability from heart disease and stroke with research, professional and public education, and community service programs.

But more needs to be done. You can help us support research and education by sending your dollars today to your local Heart Association, listed in your telephone directory.

Put your money where your Heart is.

American Heart Association

WE'RE FIGHTING FOR YOUR LIFE

---

pointed out more clearly. Many social issue promoters and charities experience this difficulty.[7]

However, purchase of many nonprofit products (church tithes, political contributions, donations to the March of Dimes) is tax-deductible. Promoters of such service-oriented organizations often stress this point to prospective contributors.

Price Considerations   The purchase of social products may or may not involve money. Labor unions, trade associations, and civic clubs usually charge membership dues. Religious organizations may assess members or may let them contribute as much as they feel they can or want. Charitable

---

[7] Ibid., p. 12.

organizations rely on donations and may urge target customers to "let your conscience be your guide." Often the purchase does not involve money, but is the donation of time (community beautification projects), products no longer needed or wanted (Salvation Army), blood (Red Cross), or talent (fund raising for political candidates).

Ethical Considerations In Nonprofit Marketing

Some people feel it is unethical to market education, religion, politicians, and social causes in a manner similar to marketing detergents, automobiles, and vacations. Of course, less subtle questions arise in the marketing of social products and services. Consider, for example, the following account of a purely imaginary—but thoroughly possible—charity campaign:

Angels Unlimited was formed as a nonprofit business offering fund-raising services that would benefit such diverse groups as the Red Cross, the Salvation Army, a children's hospital, and the local cultural arts council. During the first year of operation the nonprofit business spent only $15,000 to market its "product" on television, billboards, and in the local newspaper, but donations throughout the city totaled over $200,000. After Angels Unlimited announced the final figure, the various charities that were to receive the funds expected sizeable donations. However, each of the 20 charities received less than $3,000. After some inquiries were made, the chairperson of the cultural arts council was told that only $60,000 of the $200,000 had actually found its way to the various charities. Angels Unlimited had used the remaining $140,000 to pay the upkeep on its offices (only $1,200 for rent and $500 for janitorial services), advertising expenses ($15,000), and the salaries of its six full-time employees ($123,000). "In other words," the chairperson said, "you've spent $140,000 to raise $60,000." "You could put it that way," said the president of Angels Unlimited. "But if we hadn't spent that much, we wouldn't have raised the $60,000."

Laczniak, Lusch, and Murphy conducted a study to determine some of the ethical dimensions of social marketing. They raise a number of important questions to people involved in social marketing.[8]

- Is the increased involvement of marketing specialists in the promotion of ideas, personalities, and organizations a beneficial development from the standpoint of U.S. society?
- What specific segments of the public benefit the most? Who loses? How can such social costs and benefits be operationally defined?

[8] Gene R. Laczniak, Robert F. Lusch, and Patrick E. Murphy, "Social Marketing: Its Ethical Dimensions," *Journal of Marketing*, Spring 1979, p. 35.

- To what social causes or ideas might social marketing offer the most immediate societal benefits?
- What are some of the specific ethical questions facing social marketers today?
- What constitutes a "good" (or bad) product or idea? What constitutes a "good" (or bad) marketing practice? What is the responsibility of the firm to consider such issues?
- Does individual responsibility sometimes exceed the responsibility vested in the firm?
- What is "different" conceptually and practically about social as opposed to traditional marketing?
- Do social critics primarily "object" to certain marketing techniques, or is it the idea/organization/person being marketed that is the source of objection?
- Can social marketers avoid making distinct value statements and still conduct effective campaigns?
- Can members of the general public distinguish between ethical marketing practices as opposed to the ethical implications of the social product being marketed?
- How can possible abuse of social marketing be prevented or controlled?

The Future of Nonprofit Marketing

Managers of nonprofit organizations will probably place greater emphasis on marketing in the future. Educational institutions, hospitals, associations, and other nonbusiness organizations are becoming increasingly aware that they, like business organizations, must compete for the consumer dollar. To not compete is to invite extinction. In addition the marketers served by nonprofit organizations are demanding products better suited to their needs. For example, college administrators are beginning to recognize that the courses they want to offer may not be the same courses students demand. Finally, the stigma long associated with marketing nonprofit products is beginning to diminish. More managers of nonprofit seeking organizations are beginning to accept the idea that it is not wrong to develop products, make them available at convenient locations, promote them to target consumers, and set prices for them. Nonprofit organizations may not adopt marketing job titles such as marketing director, manager of marketing research, and salesperson soon, but nonprofit organizations will probably make increasing use of marketing tools and techniques in the future.

SUMMARY

- A service is any act or work performed for another in exchange for something of value.
- Services are intangible and inseparable from the performer.
- Almost half our income is spent for service products. Service industries employ nearly 50 percent of the labor force and account for over one-third of all commercial enterprises.
- The main kinds of services are personal services; lodging; amusement; repairs; transportation; communications; and financial, brokerage, real-estate, insurance, and business services.
- Services can be classified as consumer or organization oriented; human or machine centered; professional or nonprofessional; profit or non-profit; regulated or nonregulated; small, medium, or large; and very intangible or somewhat intangible.
- The growth of the service industries can be attributed to new products, increasing prosperity, and the growing complexity of private and business life.
- The main bases for competition in marketing services are the reputation of the seller, the skill of the performer, and the value added by auxiliary services.
- Special considerations in marketing services are that (a) ownership is not transferred, (b) appeals to the imagination are needed, (c) promotion may be free, (d) service products are expenses rather than assets, (e) services cannot be stored, and (f) production and consumption are simultaneous.
- Marketing of services is becoming an increasingly common and acceptable practice.
- Increasing emphasis is being placed on marketing nonprofit products. This activity is often called social marketing.
- Nonprofit marketers often serve a particular target market, but gather money from the general population.
- Just like profit organizations, nonprofit organizations must identify target markets and make product, place, promotion, and price decisions to satisfy these targets.
- Despite ethical considerations, it is probable that more attention will be given to social marketing in the future.

DISCUSSION QUESTIONS

1. "We live in an age in which intangible products are becoming increasingly important." Explain. Is the trend toward spending more of our incomes for services likely to continue? Why or why not?
2. Why is the reputation of the seller more important in marketing services than in marketing tangible products?
3. What role does the skill of the performer play in marketing services?
4. Explain how each of the following affects marketing of services:
   (a) Ownership is not transferred.
   (b) Appeals to the imagination are needed.
   (c) Promotion may be free.
   (d) Service products are expenses.
   (e) Most services cannot be stored.
   (f) Production and consumption are simultaneous.
5. Many consumers and some government officials feel that physicians should advertise. From the standpoint of the consumer what do you perceive as possible advantages and disadvantages of promotion by physicians? From the standpoint of the physicians?
6. What is a nonprofit product? Why is more attention being given to marketing nonprofit products?
7. Define the target markets for a private college, Planned Parenthood, and the Girl Scouts.
8. What product, place, promotional, and price considerations are involved in marketing membership in a college alumni association? A person running for the Senate? A religious crusade?
9. Prepare both sides, pro and con, on the topic "Social Marketing Is Ethical." Then explain how you feel on the issue.
10. In your view what is the future of social marketing likely to be?

APPLICATION EXCERCISES

1. You are now president of your school's alumni association. There are about 41,000 living graduates of the school, but only 8,200 belong to the alumni association. The executive committee of the association has set two major goals for you. First, increase membership from the present level to 20,000. Second, increase alumni-contribution revenue from $250,000 to $750,000. Explain what marketing steps you would take to accomplish these goals.

2. A local lawyer has recently hired you to develop a marketing strategy for his services. Because he is the newest lawyer in the area, your client wants to develop a large clientele but is concerned that people will not trust a lawyer who advertises. Develop a marketing strategy that will accomplish his goal while addressing his concerns.

CASE 10
Houston Grand Opera[9]

Despite the fact that spending on services has increased dramatically in recent decades, many U.S. opera companies are struggling financially. However, the Houston Grand Opera, directed by former opera singer David Gockley, is flourishing. In a decade the annual budget increased from $420,000 to $7 million, the total number of performances rose from 27 to more than 400, and season subscriptions jumped from 4,113 to 13,500.

Unlike many traditional opera companies, the Houston Grand Opera places as much emphasis on earnings, new product development, and marketing as on the performance itself. Mr. Gockley says, "The company must perform well on the stage and on the balance sheet." With government subsidies reduced, production costs rising, and competition increasing, the Houston Grand Opera plans to use marketing techniques to maintain its financial stability in a field in which marketing has rarely been used.

Traditionally, opera has been a form of entertainment enjoyed by the affluent members of high society. Most opera companies perform only the traditional European classics and are reluctant to change. Mr. Gockley is trying to change opera's high-society image and market it to a mass audience. The Houston Grand Opera is advertised on T-shirts and television commercials and has diversified its program. While still performing the traditional European classics, it also has expanded its program to include light operas that are sung in English, contemporary rock musicals, and a few controversial operas featuring nudity on stage. The Opera has also gone on the road and established the country's only free, outdoor opera. Other areas of diversification include a junior touring company (sort of a "farm team" for young singers), and the Houston Opera Studio, which trains fledgling artists. Mr. Gockley believes the future of his company depends on its ability to aggressively market a wide range of products to an increasing number of people. He sees growth and diversification as keys to the long-term survival of the Houston Grand Opera.

---

[9] George Getschow, "Houston's 'P.T. Barnum of Opera' Thrives by Emphasizing Marketing, Bottom Line," *Wall Street Journal,* March 9, 1982, pp. 33, 39.

As well as being quite conscious of production costs, the company is aggressively seeking to boost income. By producing an opera that appeals to the masses, Mr. Gockley has been successful in capturing local and national corporate support for the organization. The Houston Grand Opera has been called the "P.T. Barnum of Opera," because it will do whatever it takes to attract people.

Discussion Questions

1. What is the Houston Grand Opera's target market?
2. Mr. Gockley has just hired you to design a marketing strategy for the Opera. Define your product, place, promotion, and price variables.
3. Given your answer to Question 2, how would you "promote" contributions from the community and from corporations?

FOUR
Place Decisions

11

Marketing Channels

STUDY OBJECTIVES

After studying this chapter, you should be able to

1. Define marketing channels and explain the importance of marketing channels in moving products from producers to consumers.
2. Discuss the functions performed by channels of distribution.
3. Describe the various types of channel structures and where each is often used.
4. Define contractual and administered channels and discuss the five sources of power used in administered channels.
5. Discuss vertical and horizontal channel integration and define Vertical Marketing Systems, franchises, and cooperatives.
6. Discuss the various factors affecting channel selection.
7. Define intensive, selective, and exclusive distribution and why a company would choose each.
8. Discuss channel conflict and cooperation.

I n Part Four of the book we will examine the place marketing controllable variable. This chapter will cover marketing channels (also called channels of distribution), the area of channel management, and channel management's role in marketing strategy. Chapters 12 and 13 will deal with the channel members called wholesalers and retailers, respectively. Chapter 14 will discuss the very important marketing strategy aspect of physical distribution—delivering the product to the point of sale.

CHANNELS OF DISTRIBUTION

A **channel of distribution** *is the path a product takes as it moves from the producer to the user.* That path includes all intermediaries (called **middlemen**) who facilitate the movement of the product to the user. *The objective of* **channel management** *is to select the most effective, efficient, and profitable path.* Economic success is not guaranteed simply because a producer makes a "good" product for which there is a need. Unless the producer can move the "good" product to the consumer at the time and place the consumer wants it and at a price that makes it reasonably competitive with other products, it will not find a market.

Our economy contains a multitude of manufacturers, processors, fabricators, and other producers who make an almost infinite variety of products. It also contains over 230 million ultimate consumers and hundreds of thousands of industrial users. Between producers and consumers or users, a large structure of wholesale and retail middlemen perform the services needed to move products from one to the other.

We can classify channel members as either merchants or agents. **Merchants** *take title to merchandise and resell it.* **Agents** *never take ownership, but receive a commission or fee for expediting exchanges.*

Regardless of the channel members involved, all channels have certain characteristics in common. The overriding goal for all members of a channel is the delivery of the product to the user. If the user does not or cannot purchase the product, all members of the channel suffer. If a retailer does not make a sale, no replacement product is ordered from the wholesaler or manufacturer.

IMPORTANCE OF CHANNELS

Marketing channels members are often criticized as unnecessary to the efficient distribution of goods. For example, wholesalers are said to add extra costs and steps to product distribution. However, channel members actually perform vital roles in efficiently distributing products.

First, channels *minimize the total number of transactions* necessary to market products. Figure 11-1 illustrates a simplified version of this process. For three consumers to purchase the products of three manufacturers, a total of nine transactions must occur. However, if all three manufacturers sell their output to a single channel member, who in turn sells to all three consumers, the total number of transactions is six. Imagine how compli-

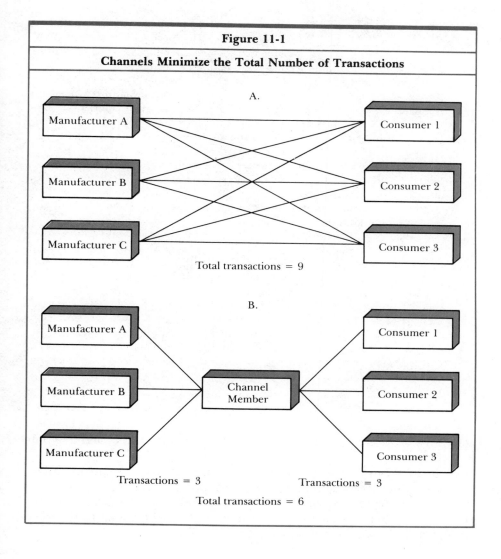

Figure 11-1

Channels Minimize the Total Number of Transactions

A.

Manufacturer A

Manufacturer B

Manufacturer C

Consumer 1

Consumer 2

Consumer 3

Total transactions = 9

B.

Manufacturer A

Manufacturer B

Manufacturer C

Channel Member

Consumer 1

Consumer 2

Consumer 3

Transactions = 3   Transactions = 3

Total transactions = 6

MARKETING
Profile

Stanley Marcus
(b. 1905)

Stanley Marcus is a second-generation retailer, born to the business established by his father, aunt, and uncle. The business has expanded under his marketing leadership, in which he carries on his family's tradition of quality and customer satisfaction.

Herbert Marcus, his sister Carrie, and her husband Al Neiman established Neiman–Marcus in 1907. Ladies' ready-to-wear was a new industry then, and Neiman–Marcus merchandised it well. By stressing quality and value, the store soon became the leading fine clothing store for the city of Dallas. As its reputation for high quality and unusual merchandise spread, Neiman–Marcus became the second most popular tourist attraction in Texas.

Marcus believed that for every piece of merchandise there is a right customer and that it is the merchant's job to bring the two together. Consequently, Marcus employees paid a great deal of attention to making sure their customers left the store satisfied or at least without having bought the "wrong" merchandise.

A series of disagreements in 1928 led to a corporate and family split. Herbert Marcus bought Al Neiman's interest in the store for $250,000, and Carrie and Al divorced. Carrie remained with the store, and Stanley was brought in to fill Neiman's job as head of merchandising for the better apparel department. Though new to that particular job, Stanley Marcus had grown up with the store. He had worked in the alterations, fur, and shoe departments and as a floorwalker.

Stanley immediately began to experiment with new ideas as he learned the executive side of the business. During the 1930s Neiman–Marcus introduced both personalized gift-wrapping to retailing in general and the luncheon fashion show to the retailing of apparel.

cated this process could be with thousands of manufacturers and 230 million consumers!

The next time you go to the grocery store notice how many manufacturers' products are represented in your shopping cart. Imagine how cumbersome the channel system would be if you had to contact each manufacturer directly to purchase each product! As a channel member the grocery store drastically minimizes your total transactions.

When his father died in 1950, Stanley became president and chief executive officer. He continued to uphold his father's high standards and added a few of his own. For example, when he learned that most retailers sought to persuade manufacturers to reduce the price of a garment, Stanley offered to pay more. A better quality garment was the result. He was always available to help a salesperson close a sale, whether for a $50,000 fur coat or a $10 sweater. Such personal attention from the president of the store generally satisfied customers.

Neiman–Marcus regarded the prospect of expansion as a dilemma. Expansion would mean that contacts with customers and staff would be less frequent and personal. Obtaining financial backing sufficient to maintain the high quality of merchandise that was Neiman–Marcus' trademark would be difficult as well.

Stanley plunged in, though, to complete a new store in a Dallas suburb that his father had begun before his death. It was successful, but further expansion was impossible due to lack of capital. It was very important to the Marcus family that its retailing expertise and philosophy should prevail. Stanley looked for, and found, additional financial backing from a partner who would not attempt to influence the operation of the business. New stores in major cities across the United States soon followed.

"We have one inviolable rule in our organization—that the customer comes first—and any staff meeting can be interrupted to meet the call of a customer," Stanley Marcus says in describing the store's dedication to service.* In reference to quality, "I firmly believe that quality is remembered long after price is forgotten."†

"If I were a marketing student," Marcus told the author, "I would make every effort to supplement my classroom education by actual experience in the field of selling to the consumer. I would not be particular about what I sold or in which field, whether it be behind the counter of a department store or as a door-to-door salesperson. You can't know the real secrets of marketing until you've made a sale."

* Stanley H. Marcus, *Minding the Store* (New York: Little, Brown, 1974), p. 18.
† Ibid., p. 372.

Second, channel members are exchange experts. As such, they make the same transactions over and over again. This *routinization of transactions* makes them more efficient at distributing products.

The first time you buy a home you will know little of the necessary legal actions that accompany such a transaction. However, your real-estate agent (who has performed this transaction many times) has a routine established to help you through the process more efficiently. This is true of almost all marketing channels. Routinized transactions make the flow of products from producer to consumer more efficient.

Third, businesses try to create four forms of utility for the consumer: form, time, place, and possession. Form utility, which is presenting a product in the form the consumer wishes to purchase, is created through product design. However, *time, place,* and *possession utility* are all created by marketing channels. Time and place utility refer to having the product available for sale at the time and place the consumer wants. Without channels of distribution a consumer would have to order a product from the manufacturer, wait until it was produced, and then go to the plant to pick it up. Possession utility allows the consumer to take ownership of the product. Not only the product, but also the title to the product must move through the channel so that when the product is physically available, ownership can also be transferred.

Finally, without channel intermediaries many manufacturers could not or would not distribute their goods. Many manufacturers lack the *financial resources* to develop channels for their products. The cost of maintaining numerous warehouses and thousands of retail locations is often too great for even the largest companies. Even when mighty IBM introduced its personal computer, it could not afford to open a chain of retail stores. Instead, it turned to Sears and Computerland as channel members to help bear the expense of distributing its product.

In many cases consumers want to shop for a variety of products at one location. Thus, to distribute its own products, a manufacturer would have to carry complementary products it does not make. For instance, if Campbell's Soup distributed its own product, it would have to carry a whole grocery line just to complement its products. This is a cost few manufacturers are willing to bear.

Furthermore, manufacturers are typically experts at making products, not distributing them. Therefore, they can profit more by making the product and leaving the distribution to distribution experts—channel intermediaries. Thus, even if a manufacturer could afford to distribute its own product, it usually can make more money concentrating on production and leaving distribution to others.

FUNCTIONS CHANNELS PERFORM

Regardless of the number or type of channel members, all channels perform certain functions. A primary function of marketing channels is what Alderson called the **sorting process**.[1] The sorting process is based on the

---

[1] Wroe Alderson, "Factors Governing the Development of Marketing Channels," in R. M. Clewett, ed., *Marketing Channels for Manufactured Products* (Homewood, Ill.: Richard D. Irwin, 1954), pp. 5–22.

idea that products exist in nature in heterogeneous supply, that is, in different qualities. Consumers, in turn, demand heterogeneous products—many different items. The sorting process, which all channels perform, takes this heterogeneous natural supply and turns it into the type of heterogeneous supply consumers want.

The first step in this process is **sorting out,** or breaking heterogeneous *four processes of sorting process* supplies down into homogeneous groups of equal quality. A farmer dividing his eggs into different grades is sorting out.

Accumulation consists of taking these homogeneous groups and bringing them together at one supply point. When Kroger buys grade A eggs from numerous farmers and brings them all to one warehouse, it is accumulating.

When Kroger takes these eggs and sends them to various regional warehouses, based on forecasts of regional demand, it is performing the **allocation** step. This is also called "breaking bulk."

Finally, the consumer does not want to go to Kroger for just eggs, but rather for a variety of grocery products. Kroger, therefore, sends eggs and numerous other products to each store, so consumers can satisfy their heterogeneous demands. This creation of variety is called **assortment**. Whether the channel is owned entirely by one company or is a cooperative effort of independent suppliers, manufacturers, wholesalers, and retailers, all channels perform the functions of sorting out, accumulating, allocating, and assorting.

In addition, to accomplish the goal of moving products to the consumer (accomplishing time, place, and possession utility), channels must also perform the functions of marketing research, buying and selling, negotiation, physical distribution, promotion, product and price planning, customer service, financing, and risk taking. *Marketing research* includes an analysis of other channel members as well as customers. For example, when a manufacturer considers a change in the price structure of its product line, research is necessary to determine how not only consumers will react, but also the retailers who carry the products. In addition, retailers often have a better grasp of the market (they are closer to it) and are, therefore, in a better position to conduct marketing research. It is a narrow-minded manufacturer that ignores the marketing research or market information passed to it by its retailers.

In order to pass the title of a product to the consumer, ownership must pass through the channel. Thus, channel members are constantly involved in the *buying* and *selling* of products. This process requires *negotiation* among channel members, not only on the terms of sales, but also on many other channel issues, which we will address later in the chapter.

It does the consumer little good to be able to purchase the product (take ownership) if the product is somewhere else (lack of time and place utility). Therefore, the vital marketing function of *physical distribution*, that is, physically delivering the product to its point of sale, must be performed by the marketing channel. Physical distribution is sufficiently important that we will devote all of Chapter 14 to it.

Promotion is a subject Part Five will deal with in detail. However, we should mention here that all channel members are involved in the function of promotion. Manufacturers often run national advertisements, retailers run local ads, and wholesalers (and all other channel members) are active in personal selling.

Because all channel members are involved in marketing the product, their input is often considered, even sought after, in *product* and *price planning*. Channel members may have valuable information on product changes or new product ideas, and the manufacturer really has no control over price after selling a product to the next intermediary in the channel (See this chapter's Marketing Milestone).

Customer service, the activities involved in keeping customers satisfied, is the concern of all channel members. Retailers may try to present pleasant shopping conditions, helpful and cheerful salespeople, and a reasonable return policy. The wholesaler may try to provide overnight delivery so the retailer is not out of stock. The manufacturer may provide an 800 number for customer complaints and convenient repair facilities. Because all channel members depend on customer satisfaction to keep products flowing through the channel, each is ultimately responsible for customer service.

Financing and *risk taking* in a channel of distribution go hand-in-hand. If you stop and think about it, the last thing that occurs in a marketing channel is a sale to the user. Therefore, all other marketing-channel functions occur before the consumer gives the channel any money. These functions cost money. Therefore, someone has to finance the marketing research, the promotion, the sorting process, and the holding of inventory. All of this involves risk. From General Motors that invests $2 billion in developing a new car line it thinks will sell, to the individual dealer with $250,000 in an inventory of cars he or she thinks customers will like, all channel members are taking risks.

TYPES OF CHANNELS

A distribution channel is a *system,* each part of which performs necessary economic services and, to some extent, cooperates with other channel members. The profit of each link in the distribution system depends largely on how well other channel members do their job. Teamwork is important. A producer may make a good product and advertise it extensively to stimulate ultimate consumer demand, but if retailers do not give it enough shelf space or if wholesalers fail to keep retailers stocked, all the channel members will suffer. To understand this system, we must first understand the prevalent structures of marketing channels.

Figure 11-2
Channel Structures
Consumer Channels

Consumer Channels

Producer → consumer

Producer → retailer → consumer

Producer → wholesaler → retailer → consumer

Producer → agent middleman → wholesaler → retailer → consumer

Industrial Channels

Producer → industrial user

Producer → agent → industrial user

Producer → wholesaler → industrial user

Producer → agent → wholesaler → industrial user

Channel Structure

Distribution systems range from very simple to quite complex. However, most consumer products follow one of the channel types illustrated in Figure 11-2. Most industrial products are distributed through one of the channel types in Figure 11-2.

Producer–Consumer   The direct producer-to-consumer channel is used mostly by industrial marketers, but it is also used to move some consumer goods. Products sold directly to the ultimate consumer by the producer include magazine subscriptions, aluminum siding, custom-tailored clothing, and some farm products. However, in terms of total volume the direct-to-the-ultimate-consumer channel, despite its conspicuousness to most people, is not very important.

Industrial goods, such as major technical installations and building materials, often are sold directly, as are products intended for government use.

Producer–Retailer–Consumer   This channel is used for an almost infinite variety of consumer goods—clothing, appliances, automobiles, petroleum products, and a wide variety of products with a relatively high unit value. Amway, for example, built a billion-dollar business selling to its retailers (called distributors) who sell to ultimate consumers. Large-scale retailers in particular figure significantly in this channel system. Much of the merchandise sold by large retailers is made to their own specifications, often under their own brand names or labels.

The producer–retailer–consumer channel is feasible if quantities are large or the unit value of a good is high enough to absorb the costs of direct selling. It would hardly be profitable for a soap manufacturer to sell directly to small grocers, but IBM can sell personal computers directly to Sears and Computerland.

Producer–Wholesaler–Retailer–Consumer   A longer channel of distribution is customary for convenience goods that require wide distribution, such as many food products, and some types of apparel, drug, and hardware. Products that are marketed in this manner to a broad segment of consumers generally have a low unit value. Many producers cannot maintain sales forces large enough to canvass all the potential consumers of their products. It is generally the manufacturers of these product lines that need

Willfully and knowingly advertising, offering for sale or selling any commodity at less than the price stipulated in any contract entered into pursuant to the provision of Section 1 of the Act, whether the person so advertising, offering for sale or selling is or is not a party to such contract, is unfair competition and is actionable at the suit of any person damaged thereby.

Other states rushed to enact similar laws. Yet, until 1937 such arrangements were not permitted in interstate commerce. Public pressure forced Congress to pass enabling legislation that allowed the states to enforce nonsigner's clauses. The Miller–Tydings Act, passed as a rider to a District of Columbia bill over the strenuous objections of President Roosevelt, removed resale price control of trademarked products under state fair trade laws from the prohibitions of the Sherman Antitrust Act and declared that making such contracts would not be an unfair method of competition under the Federal Trade Commission Act.

Just as the economic climate fostered the birth and growth of fair trade laws, a shift in that climate brought about their demise. The seller's market of the 1940s gave way to surpluses in the peacetime economy of the 1950s. Consumers began to view resale price maintenance as a way to block price competition and to keep prices rising faster than their incomes. Discount retailers moved in to meet the demands of consumers for lower-priced goods, thereby ushering in a new phase in retailing. Manufacturers could not avoid using discounters to maximize their markets.

By 1952 fair trade laws were basically unenforceable. They continued to linger in some states, however, until consumer advocates succeeded in nullifying them with the Consumer Goods Pricing Act of 1976, which made it illegal to use resale price maintenance in interstate commerce.

the services of wholesalers and retailers most, because for them it is often the only efficient and affordable channel from producer to consumer.

Producer–Middleman–Wholesaler–Retailer–Consumer Primarily, products with a wide geographic distribution that are carried by many small retailers are distributed through this channel. The need to distribute the product over a wide area to many end points makes the use of an extra channel member desirable. In the food field, for example, producers often use brokers to attain wider distribution of their products. The brokers in turn use wholesalers, who are better equipped to deal directly with small grocery retailers.

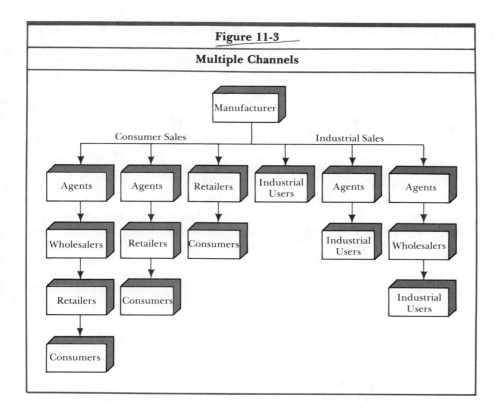

Figure 11-3

Multiple Channels

Manufacturer

Consumer Sales

Industrial Sales

Agents — Agents — Retailers — Industrial Users — Agents — Agents

Wholesalers — Retailers — Consumers — Industrial Users — Wholesalers

Retailers — Consumers — Industrial Users

Consumers

Single Versus Multiple Channels   Some products, such as proprietary drugs, may reach customers by more than one route, termed **multiple channels**. Aspirin may be purchased through a drugstore, in which case the probable channel is producer–wholesaler–retailer; or it may be given to a patient in a hospital, in which case the channel is probably producer–institutional buyer–consumer. Figure 11-3 illustrates possible multiple channels for a manufacturer of hand tools.

Many consumer products are marketed in a variety of outlets. The trend toward **scrambled merchandising** has vastly increased the number of potential retail outlets for convenience goods such as cigarettes, candy, and magazines. Numerous cosmetic items and even some lower-priced lines of apparel have also become part of this new trend. Retailers' efforts to make every inch of floor space as profitable as possible, by stocking as many fast-moving items as possible, have created multiple channels for many of these products. Hairspray is a prime candidate for marketing through multiple channels. A producer of hairspray may distribute the product through beauty salons, department stores, drugstores, discount houses, supermarkets, and convenience stores, using different intermediate buyers in all or several cases.

Although an aggressive producer may want to use every means of distribution available, it must recognize that multiple channels are a potential source of conflict. The drugstore that agrees to stock a well-known toiletry item may be extremely dissatisfied to find this item also for sale in supermarkets. If the producer uses the services of both a drug wholesaler and a food broker to attain this end, it again increases the chances of conflict within the channel. Conversely, the wholesaler or retailer who stocks many very similar competing items may eventually find itself cut off from a source of supply.

Easco, the second largest manufacturer of hand tools in the United States, utilizes a multiple-channel strategy. Long a supplier of tools for Sears (47 percent of Easco's sales), Easco is now branching out and selling its tools through all K Mart stores (manufacturer–retailer channel), 6,000 True Value Hardware Stores (manufacturer–wholesaler–cooperative retailer channel), and to 500 hardware and home-center stores (manufacturer–wholesaler–independent retailer channel). To alleviate some of the conflict this multiple-channel strategy has created with Sears, Easco is using much of its new marketing knowledge to help Sears sell its products. Explains Easco President Richard P. Sullivan, "We want to build those other channels, and we want to build Sears as fast as it can be built." Sullivan predicts Sears will account for 55 percent of Easco sales by 1989.[2] Thus, a multiple-channel strategy often requires efforts to reduce conflict among channel members.

Contractual Versus Administered Channels

Because channels often contain several independent members, some method is necessary for assigning the responsibilities of each member and setting the overall goals of the channel. In many channels contracts or agreements between channel members determine these responsibilities and goals. In a **contractual channel** *a contract spells out all the distribution functions mentioned earlier, price, and any other factors particular to that channel.* Thus, a contract would specify such responsibilities as who carries inventory, who pays for advertising, delivery dates, and quantity discounts. For example, automobile dealerships have contracts with the manufacturer specifying the responsibilities of the producer and the dealer. The factory handles new car advertising and product design, and dealers cannot refuse to accept a car line, even if they are certain customers will not buy it. As

---

[2] "Easco: Turning to New Customers While Helping Sears Promote Tools," *Business Week,* October 6, 1980, pp. 62, 66; and "Easco: Using Profits from Aluminum to Repair Its Tool Business," *Business Week,* July 2, 1984, p. 90.

Buffalo Chevrolet dealer Donald F. Lake put it, "Dealers participate in a market the factory is supposed to create. If the market isn't there, or it has shrunk 30% to 40%, there's nothing we can do."[3]

In an **administered channel** *the dominant company would set the goals for the channel and divide the responsibilities among the channel members.* Depending on their relative strength, the manufacturer, wholesaler, or retailer could be the channel leader. The channel leader in an administered channel usually controls other channel members with one of five sources of power: coercive, reward, legitimate, referent, or expert.[4]

Coercive power *is the ability of the channel member to take something of value away from another channel member.* For example, if Sears threatened to stop buying from Easco, the hand-tool manufacturer mentioned earlier, Easco would lose 47 percent of its sales and probably go out of business. Such coercive power gives Sears the ability to exert a great deal of control over Easco.

Reward power *is the ability to give something of value, primarily profitability, to another channel member.* If Sears tells Easco that if Easco complies with Sears' wishes, Sears will pay it more money, Sears is using reward power.

Legitimate power *is the belief by other channel members that the leader has the "right" to control the channel.* Industry tradition often determines this "right."

Referent power *is the consumer goodwill attached to the leader's name.* For example, many independent, fast-food restaurateurs would be willing to let McDonald's lead them if they could become McDonald's franchisees. Being associated with McDonald's would enhance the reputation of their restaurants. Also, many small retailers may make concessions to a large manufacturer, so that the manufacturer will allow them to carry its nationally known products. The retailer is giving in to referent power (to be associated with these well-known products).

Expert power *is held by a leader that has exclusive knowledge or abilities.* An especially efficient method of managing inventory is an example of expert power. To benefit from the leader's expertise, other channel members must allow the leader to control the channel.

Channel Integration

As the last section implied, not all channels are made up of independent companies. Some channels have members that are controlled by contracts or agreements. Other channels have various members who are all owned

---

[3] "Auto Dealers Try to Hang On," *Business Week,* May 4, 1981, pp. 128, 130.

[4] For a complete review of the literature dealing with the use of power in channels, see John T. Mentzer and Kenneth A. Hunt, "A Conceptual Reexamination of Channel Power and Control," in Paul F. Anderson and Michael J. Ryan, eds., *Scientific Method in Marketing* (Chicago: American Marketing Association, 1984), pp. 106–09.

by the same company. *The degree to which a channel is controlled by one company is termed* **channel integration**.

Vertical Integration   Combining two or more levels of a channel of distribution under the management of one company is called **vertical integration**. K Mart, for example, is a retailer that also owns and manages its own wholesaling operations. Thus, it is a retailer that has vertically integrated the wholesaling level of its channel. Kroger is another example of a vertically integrated retailer (supermarket), but in Kroger's case it has vertically integrated not only the wholesaling, but also much of the manufacturing operations in its channel. Total vertical integration would include all functions performed by the channel under one company. Exxon Oil Company is an example of such a company. Exxon owns oil wells, refineries, transportation, terminals, and gas stations. The advantage of vertical integration is that one channel member can coordinate all the activities, assets, and functions of the channel. Therefore, vertically integrated channels are often more efficient. However, such integration may be prohibitively expensive.

A **Vertical Marketing System (VMS)** *is what we call a channel that is totally vertically integrated—everything from production to retailing is owned by one company.* Although a company distributing its goods in this way must make a considerable investment, it is ensured that all members of the channel share the same goals and that all activities can be coordinated. McCammon characterized conventional channels as "highly fragmented networks in which loosely aligned manufacturers, wholesalers, and retailers have bargained with each other at arm's length, negotiated aggressively over terms of sale, and otherwise behaved autonomously."[5] VMSes, on the other hand, act as a unified system. Sherwin–Williams paints, Sears, and Holiday Inns are all examples of Vertical Marketing Systems.[6]

Although the coordinating aspects of VMSes are desirable, the cost of these systems is often prohibitive. Therefore, franchising has arisen as a method of achieving much of the coordination of VMSes without incurring the costs. **Franchising** *is a form of marketing and distribution in which a parent company grants an individual or other company the right to do business in a prescribed manner over a specified period of time in a given location.*[7] The parent company granting the franchise is the **franchisor**. Although rights vary by franchise, it may include the right to sell the franchisor's product, use its name or logo, be privy to secret ingredients or formulas, use a special store layout and system of operation, and attend special training programs.

---

[5] Bert C. McCammon, Jr., "Perspectives for Distribution Programming," in Louis P. Bucklin, ed., *Vertical Marketing Systems* (Glenview, Ill.: Scott Foresman, 1970), pp. 32–51.
[6] Ibid., p. 45.
[7] Charles G. Burch, "Franchising's Troubled Dream World," *Fortune*, March 1977, p. 117.

Starting with Coca-Cola in 1900 and Rexall Drug in 1902,[8] franchise channels today exist in every type of business. McDonald's, Burger King, and Wendy's are three franchises with which any fast-food lover is familiar. Franchises can exist between any two channel members. Ford, Chrysler, and General Motors are examples of manufacturer–retailer franchises. Coca-Cola is a manufacturer–wholesaler franchise. Eckerd Drug is an example of a wholesaler–retailer franchise. Baskin–Robbins is an example of a franchisor that has franchisee factories produce its ice cream and franchisee retailers sell it. Retail franchisees pay $120,000 for store design, construction and equipment costs, and a 10-year right to use the name. Each retail franchisee also pays Baskin–Robbins a royalty on ice-cream sales.[9]

As was mentioned earlier, the franchisor establishes franchises to reap the benefits of controlling the channel without incurring the expense for owning all channel members. The franchisee typically joins the franchise to benefit from the franchisor's name and national advertising (referent power) and from the franchisor's experience in marketing and distributing products (expert power).

Horizontal Integration   Often, *channel members on the same level in a channel join together*. This **horizontal integration** may be under one company or may be a cooperative effort among independents. K Mart is an example of the former type of horizontal integration. By owning many retail outlets, K Mart can realize savings from buying in mass quantities and distributing to its individual stores. Also, it can use a standardized type of store and store management. Thus, customers anywhere in the United States will recognize a K Mart store, and all stores have the advantage of uniform management practices. Finally, advertising and market research on a national scale can benefit all stores.

The disadvantage of corporate horizontal integration is that companies such as K Mart lose much of their flexibility. With thousands of stores, it is difficult to quickly react to target-market changes. Also, huge sums of money must be available to integrate horizontally through ownership.

To achieve the advantages of horizontal integration without the disadvantages of capital investment and inflexibility, many channel members form cooperatives. A **cooperative** is "an organization of independent channel members joined together contractually to act as one company, even though each member remains independent." Spartan Grocery Stores in Michigan is an example of a retail cooperative. Although each store is independently owned, they all bear the Spartan name and logo and all buy through the central Spartan operation. Thus, each store benefits from quantity purchases, uni-

---

[8] Robert M. Rosenberg and Madelon Redell, *Profits from Franchising* (New York: McGraw-Hill, 1969), p. 41.
[9] "The Scoop on Ice Cream Sales," *Business Week,* September 20, 1982, p. 72.

MARKETING

Strategy

Red Carpet Versus Century 21

Real estate is one of the most important products marketed in our economy. Over 100,000 firms are involved in marketing real estate, the great majority of which employ an average of only four people.

Traditionally, real-estate marketing firms (brokers) have been highly localized and known only in one community. To be successful, a real-estate broker needed only to develop marketing skills to the best of his or her ability, a wide circle of influential friends, and public respect.

But times have changed. The increasing mobility of the population has meant that many people move into communities in which they do not know a "good" real-estate company. This has set the stage for real-estate franchising. Americans have become used to brand names for almost everything they buy, from fried chicken to motels. So, why not a brand name for real-estate firms?

Real-estate franchising organizations are founded on the premise that the collective strength of thousands of independent brokers enables each to better serve clients and thereby make more money.

Red Carpet was a pioneer real-estate franchisor beginning in 1966 with three offices. Founded by Anthony Yniquez, Red Carpet had more than 1,200 franchised affiliates in 1980. The first franchises sold for $500. By 1980 the average cost was over $8,000.

Century 21, founded in 1970 by Arther Bartlett and Marshal Fisher, is the largest real-estate franchisor with more than 8,000 franchises. Originally, a Century 21 franchise sold for $500. By 1980 the typical price was over $10,000. Century 21 offers a package of services similar to those of Red Carpet.

Both Red Carpet and Century 21 have two target markets: "Start Ups" (people who are just entering the real-estate business) and established real-estate brokers. In the first category are people who have had two or three years of experience in real-estate sales and are in the process of obtaining a broker's license.

The second category consists of people who already operate a successful real-estate business, but who want to take advantage of a nationally known name, proven selling and management ideas, and a referral system.

In exchange for the franchise fee both Red Carpet and Century 21 provide:

1. A positive image based on a common brand name
2. Consumer acceptance through television and other forms of mass advertising

3. Improved performance through sophisticated selling and listing techniques
4. Publicity and public relations support
5. Help in recruiting and training salespeople
6. A national referral service
7. Management counseling

Under the real-estate franchise system the umbrella firm does not exert strict control. The franchisee remains independent, but acquires the advantages of the franchisor's name, mass advertising, management services, and other expertise. In addition to the franchise fee the franchisor charges the franchisees a percentage of gross sales to use for mass advertising.

One important difference in the approach to franchising by the two firms is that Century 21 sells "Master Franchises," whereas Red Carpet does not. Using the master franchise approach, Century 21 sells regional franchises in which the investor buys the rights to sell franchises to local real-estate brokers in a specific geographical region. The master franchises sell for $85,000 to $150,000.

The master franchise approach provided needed cash flow when Century 21 was young and enabled it to expand more rapidly than Red Carpet, which did not adopt the concept. Red Carpet feels that the master franchise makes it more difficult to manage the franchisees.

The organizational structures of the two firms differ significantly, with Century 21 more highly centralized than Red Carpet. Century 21 is divided into 34 regions, each of which is responsible for recruiting new brokers, providing training, and implementing marketing programs. Franchisees in each region belong to area councils. The councils determine how advertising revenues paid by the franchisees are to be used in their area.

Red Carpet is highly innovative. It invented the wall-to-wall protection plan, a form of warranty for home buyers, which other real-estate franchisors, including Century 21, have adopted.

Both Red Carpet and Century 21 are highly successful and are experiencing rapid growth. Even though Century 21 entered the market four years after Red Carpet, it is much larger. It charges more for a franchise than Red Carpet and charges a higher percentage of the franchisee's gross volume for its advertising fund, enabling it to spend much more for advertising and other forms of promotion.

Despite the success of these two companies real-estate franchising has its critics. Some real-estate brokers are hesitant to subordinate their own identity to that of a national organization. Some also feel that the educational and training services are not worth the cost, because they can obtain such information through readily available books.

Nevertheless, real-estate franchising is a growing phenomenon. Almost half of all U.S. real-estate brokers are now affiliated with a franchisor. The percentage is almost certain to increase in the future.

form advertising, and standardized management practices. Flexibility is maintained because each store can react to its particular local market. Costs of starting the organization are also minimized, because no one company had to raise the money to build all the stores. The cost was spread over many independent members.

Horizontal integration does not exist exclusively on the retail level. Such large companies as IBM, General Motors, and Exxon are all examples of manufacturers horizontally integrated through ownership. Cotter and Company is an example of a wholesale cooperative, whose organization includes 7,000 True Value Hardware Store members.[10]

CHANNEL SELECTION

Many factors affect a corporation's decision about what distribution channel to use for its products. The four most important factors it must consider are:

1. The target customers
2. The product
3. The producer's status and objectives
4. The middleman's status and objectives

Target Customers

The first question that management should answer when selecting a channel is, "Who are the ultimate users of our products?" Once management has determined this, it is easier to decide what route to use to reach the final users. Although the answer may seem obvious, more often than not it is rather complex. Consider the target markets for one simple product, paper towels. The "in the home" market for this item is a large one, but substantial amounts of paper towels are used also by educational institutions, restaurants, military bases, office buildings, industrial plants, hospitals, and airports. An executive who markets paper towels may find that a lot of work is needed to determine what channels to use to reach all potential customers.

The marketer of electronic components such as transistors may also find it is not so easy to identify all possible users. Some users may be original-equipment manufacturers. Others may handle repairs and replacement parts. International customers may constitute still another target group. The same product, whether intended for the ultimate consumer or the industrial user, is often purchased under widely differing circum-

---

[10] Jeff Blyskal, "Screws, Bolts and Tighter Competition," *Forbes*, May 24, 1982, pp. 146, 148, 149.

stances and sometimes for differing purposes. This complicates channel selection.

Most producers make a number of different (although perhaps similar) products. In our highly specialized marketing system this often means that a firm must use several different channels to reach all the target consumers for the various items in its line. For example, consider the possible channels of distribution for a large drug manufacturer with an extensive line of both prescription medicines and nonprescription health aids such as aspirin, cough medicines, and vitamins. Prescription drugs reach the ultimate user by a path different from that of nonprescription health aids. Prescription drugs are marketed through physicians, drugstores, hospitals, clinics, the military, and veterinarians. Health aids, on the other hand, reach ultimate consumers through food stores, discount houses, department stores, vending machines, drugstores, government commissaries, and numerous other outlets.

Product Considerations

Product considerations include the type of product, its perishability, bulk, price, post-sales services, whether it is a custom design, and the product mix.

Product Type Aspinwall identified five market characteristics for products: replacement rate, gross margin, accompanying services, consumption period, and search time to secure the product.[11] Products with high replacement rates, low gross margins and services, short consumption periods, and low search times tend to be convenience goods and need outlets without much assistance from store personnel. Products with low replacement rates, high gross margins and services, long consumption periods, and long search times tend to be shopping or specialty products and require outlets with more store support.

Generally, channels of distribution tend to be long for convenience goods, because they are retailed through many outlets and little contact is needed with the manufacturer for accompanying services. Manufacturers of chewing gum, for example, require distribution in tens of thousands of stores and vending machines. If they wanted to deal directly with retailers, they would need such a large army of salespeople to contact each store that the costs would be prohibitive. Wholesalers, however, because they represent a number of manufacturers, can profitably handle a combination of small orders for different brands. As a result, producers of convenience goods frequently use wholesalers to move what they manufacture to retailers.

---

[11] Leo Aspinwall, *Four Marketing Theories* (Boulder: University of Colorado, 1961).

Shopping and specialty goods, on the other hand, are sold in fewer outlets and usually have a much higher gross margin than convenience goods. Because fewer outlets are involved and the high gross margin justifies a greater sales effort on the part of the producer, shopping and specialty goods are often sold through short channels. For example, it is common for the producers of furniture and office machines to sell their products directly to retailers.

Perishability Highly perishable food products such as fresh fruit, vegetables, and milk tend to have short channels because of the time factor. Some nonfood items such as "fad" fashions are also considered perishable because of the danger that they will quickly go out of style. Thus, they too require short channels.

Bulk Bulk is another factor that affects channel selection. Products that are costly to load, transport, and unload—such as coal, petroleum, lumber, and stone—tend to have short channels. Thus, the number of times the product must be moved is kept to a minimum.

Price Generally, the higher the unit value of a product, the shorter the channel. Conversely, the lower the unit value of a product, the longer the distribution channel. Producers of costly industrial equipment, aircraft, and computers, for example, usually sell directly to the user or through their controlled sales branches. At the other extreme, low-priced goods, such as hardware items and candy bars, have much longer channels of distribution.

Post-Sales Services Purchasers of complicated industrial equipment, such as plant installations and automated equipment, require considerable post-sale technical service. Post-sales service is also important for many consumer durables such as washing machines. When post-sale service is important, the distribution channel is usually short, involving only the producer and the industrial user or the producer and the retailer.

Custom Design A large share of sales to industrial customers are of products that must be made to the user's specifications. Western Electric, the primary producer of telephone equipment purchased by the Bell System, for example, designs equipment to meet its customers' needs. Other tailor-made or custom-designed products sold directly by the producer to the user are electrical generators and railroad equipment. Commercial aircraft, although not necessarily engineered to meet the needs of a specific airline, are nevertheless almost always outfitted to suit the purchaser's requirements. Most federal government purchases of military equipment are tailor-made to specifications of the appropriate government agency. Custom-designed products are usually sold directly to the user by the maker.

Although tailoring the products to suit the user's needs is more important in the case of industrial goods, some consumer products, such as draperies, designer fashions, some furniture, and kitchen cabinets, are also custom-made. In such cases the channel of distribution is short. Usually the producer sells directly to the ultimate consumer.

Product Mix   A producer of a number of related products is more apt to use a shorter channel than a producer of a single product. Consider the case of a manufacturer of drug sundries. If only one item is manufactured, the cost of calling directly on retailers is almost certain to be prohibitive. However, if the manufacturer produces a dozen or more related drug sundries, all of which it can sell to the same customer, sales to retailers rather than wholesalers may be feasible.

Producer's Status and Objectives

In some situations the company's economic capabilities play a significant part in determining the channel used. For example, other things being equal, a financially strong company that can afford to recruit, train, manage, and maintain a sales organization is more likely to go directly to retailers, industrial users, and distributors than a financially weaker producer. Young companies frequently use agent middlemen and wholesalers. For example, when Ricoh originally entered the U.S. market for copiers 10 years ago, it could not afford to market its own product and, therefore, sold copiers indirectly through several intermediate companies. Now, as the largest unit seller of copiers in the world, it can afford a channel directly from Ricoh to its exclusive dealers.[12] Its economic status allows this strategy, and its corporate objective of $300 million in annual sales revenues in the U.S. requires it.

Middleman's Status and Objectives

Basically, the middleman structure exists to provide services that many manufacturing organizations cannot perform economically. In establishing a distribution channel, the marketing manager will scrutinize a potential middleman's ability to provide auxiliary services the firm cannot perform for itself. These may include, among other things, financing, storage, personal selling, and widespread product exposure.

From the producer's point of view, each potential middleman's position and goals should be compatible with its own. Or, if the producer's is the weaker position, the middleman should be strong in those areas in which the producer is lacking. Before committing itself to a distributor, a firm will want to know whether the middleman is stable, whether its financial position is sound, whether it has a good reputation among customers, and whether its cost of doing business would greatly raise the final price of the product.

---

[12] John E. Stuart, "Copier Firm Seeks Top Spot by Developing Dealer Network," *Marketing News*, October 1, 1982, pp. 1, 13.

Another important question for channel management is whether the distributor's purchasing power is so great that it may wind up dictating the firm's product policies. To a very significant extent, large-scale retailers such as Sears, J.C. Penney, Kroger, and Safeway are able to purchase goods in very large quantities and, therefore, buy most of what they retail directly from the producer. In addition, retailers of this size often decide the specific product characteristics, including the brand name, of the products they handle. In this sense their products are tailor-made to their specifications, a fact that could mean extensive changes in the producer's marketing goals.

INTENSITY OF MARKET COVERAGE

Market coverage *is the number and type of outlets in which a product is sold.* **Intensive distribution** *is a form of market coverage in which every available outlet is allowed to stock the product.* **Selective distribution** *utilizes only specific outlets, each of which meets certain corporate criteria.* **Exclusive distribution** *allows only one outlet in any one geographic area.*

Intensive Distribution

A company with a policy of intensive distribution uses the maximum possible number of retailers to distribute its product. Producers of convenience goods generally follow this policy, because they want to achieve the widest market coverage possible. They will also incur large distribution costs and loss of channel control in order to maximize sales. Although the unit gross margin is low, total profitability (if sales volume is achieved) will be high. The quality, location, or capability of the retailer is secondary, because the important aspect is maximum exposure of the product to the maximum number of consumers. Sugar, salt, beer, and candy are just some of the many consumer convenience goods for which intensive distribution is desirable.

 *Convience goods*

Selective Distribution

A company with a policy of selective distribution is, as the term states, selective in choosing outlets. The retailer must meet certain standards established by the producer in order to handle the products, which are generally shopping goods. A producer with a policy of selective distribution will decline to sell to some potential retailers, perhaps because of the quality of the retailer's operation (the condition of the store, its location, and reputation) or because of the amount of volume the retailer can generate. The purpose is to maintain a quality image around the product.

 *Shopping + speciality goods*

Exclusive Distribution

In exclusive distribution a producer intentionally limits the number of retailers in any geographic area. Typically used for specialty goods, exclusive distribution maintains an image of superiority for the product (it can only be found in the "best" stores). Products distributed in this manner normally have high gross margins. The goal is to maintain channel control and the price, not to maximize sales volume. Many brands of designer clothes are distributed in this manner.

speciality goods

Limits on Channel Member Selection

A producer is free to select the channel it wants for its products. It does not, however, have complete power to choose the specific businesses within the channel that will handle its products.

For many businesses, the selection of specific channel members must often be a compromise between whom they would like to handle their products and who can be persuaded to stock the goods. Many clothing manufacturers, for example, would like to have the most prominent department stores in each city stock their lines. In practice, most garment makers must settle for less prestigious outlets.

Ultimate consumers have considerable freedom to spend their money for what they want where they want. The same is true of businesses. Middlemen cannot be forced to buy from certain producers. Retailers cannot be forced to buy from certain middlemen.

Powerful manufacturers of highly advertised, widely accepted branded products such as General Electric can almost pick the dealers they want and get them on their terms. Most manufacturers are not so big and powerful, and their products do not even come close to selling themselves in the stores. In many cases a manufacturer will need to exercise considerable persuasion to induce middlemen to carry its products. Furthermore, extensive negotiations over price, delivery, credit, service, and other terms of sale may be required before the wholesaler or retailer accepts an item.

No retailer can handle more than a small fraction of the products vendors offer it. On the other hand, few manufacturers can supply merchandise to more than a small percentage of the businesses that would like to carry their products. Large, financially strong businesses, whether middlemen, producers, or service establishments, tend to be very selective in choosing their suppliers. So, in the real world, the producer often has limited power to induce big customers to "do business."

CHANNEL CONFLICT AND COOPERATION

The normal attitude in a marketing channel is one of cooperation. After all, channel members all have the same general goals of profitability, access to supply sources, efficient and effective distribution, and customer loyalty. These goals are accomplished by cooperating with other channel members to efficiently move the product from its supply source to the final consumer. In the ideal sense each channel member should cooperate fully with every other channel member, and each should earn a profit commensurate with its contribution to the total effort. We must remember, however, that channel members are motivated by the law of self-interest. In practice it is very common for one channel member to try to gain at the expense of other channel members.[13]

One important area of conflict between channel members concerns price. Typically, the channel member that is selling wants to obtain as high a price as is possible. Meanwhile, the channel member that is buying wants to pay as little as possible.

Price, however, is only one and sometimes not even the most important conflict between channel members. The channel member that is selling generally wants the channel member that is buying to "cooperate" in such

---

[13] For more on cooperation and conflict, see John T. Mentzer and Kenneth A. Hunt, "The Use of Power: A Process Model of the Marketing Channel Behavioral Dimensions," *Working Paper* (Blacksburg: Virginia Polytechnic Institute, 1983).

ways as buying in large quantities, paying cash, promoting the product aggressively to its customers, and giving the product good display space. Meanwhile, the channel member that is buying wants the channel member that is selling to make concessions such as selling in relatively small quantities, making frequent deliveries, providing easy credit, and paying for advertising to help resell the product.

An additional source of conflict among channel members is a lack of agreement as to the *role* each channel member should play. All channel members expect each other member to perform certain activities (that member's role). Manufacturers are expected to maintain quality control. Wholesalers should provide a mix of products and enhance communication. Retailers should merchandise products effectively. However, when a disagreement develops over the role a member should perform, conflict will result.

For example, when Seven-Up started aggressively advertising its soft drink as caffeine-free and deriding Coke and Pepsi, conflict developed among its distributors. Many Seven-Up bottlers also represent Coke and Pepsi. Seven-Up, which saw its role as promoting its product, ran into problems when its bottlers received pressure from Coke and Pepsi not to support the campaign. The bottlers saw their role as Coke or Pepsi bottlers first and Seven-Up bottlers second.[14] Thus, Seven-Up's channel did not support its campaign as enthusiastically as it expected.

Figure 11-4 illustrates some specific examples of conflict between channel members based on role disagreement. Note that each channel member has a somewhat different orientation and set of immediate business goals. We can make four generalizations concerning conflicts between members of a channel of distribution.

First, *the stronger the channel member is in terms of product acceptance, financial resources, and size, the greater is its leverage in imposing its terms on other channel members.* For example, a manufacturer with a product that is in strong demand can generally get other channel members to make more concessions than a producer whose product is in lesser demand. In similar fashion a large and financially strong retailer can usually negotiate more favorable terms than a weaker competitor.

Second, *there is normally much negotiation between channel members to arrive at price, terms of sale, and servicing arrangements.* A wholesale salesperson, for example, tries to convince the retail buyer to buy in large quantities, whereas the buyer may negotiate for small shipments until the level of demand has been established. Except for the ultimate consumer, all channel members are experienced in the art of negotiation.

Third, *compromise between channel members is necessary.* Whether buying or selling, each channel member tries to negotiate the best possible terms.

---

[14] "Seven-Up Uncaps a Coke—and an Industry Feud," *Business Week*, March 22, 1982, pp. 98–100.

Figure 11-4

What Producers and Retailers Want from Each Other

PRODUCERS WANT RETAILERS TO:

- Order in large quantities.
- Promote their merchandise aggressively.
- Give the best display space to their products.
- Sell goods at low prices to increase sales.
- Offer inducements such as low-cost credit delivery and gift-wrapping to move merchandise.
- Not handle products that are directly competitive with their own.

RETAILERS WANT PRODUCERS TO:

- Sell in small quantities.
- Sell at low prices so their gross margin will be large.
- Advertise extensively to ultimate consumers to stimulate demand.
- Deliver orders when it is convenient for the retailer.
- Take back faulty merchandise and goods that will not sell easily.

What Producers and Wholesalers Want from Each Other

PRODUCERS WANT WHOLESALERS TO:

- Serve a large, successful group of retailers of the type the manufacturer wants to handle its products.
- Maintain an intelligent, well-trained, effective sales organization to call on retail accounts.
- Have adequate—and if necessary special—warehouse facilities to store the manufacturer's products in economical quantities.
- Make regular deliveries to retailers.
- Be financially stable and either pay cash for merchandise or meet bills promptly.
- Promote the manufacturer's products rather than competing merchandise.
- Pass on ideas and suggestions relative to customer needs, prices, sales promotion, and merchandising strategies.

WHOLESALERS WANT PRODUCERS TO:

- Advertise creatively and extensively to the ultimate consumer to increase retail sales.
- Give them special price concessions that will increase their profits.
- Deliver promptly and in relatively small quantities if the wholesaler so desires.
- Provide liberal and flexible credit terms.
- Give them exclusive rights to sell fast-moving, highly profitable items.
- Accept goods proved to be defective which the wholesaler accepted from the retailer as returned merchandise.

What Wholesalers and Retailers Want from Each Other

WHOLESALERS WANT
RETAILERS TO:

- Sell the product at the lowest possible price to move more of it.
- Pay promptly.
- Order in big quantities and at regular intervals.
- Give their products the best possible display space.
- Advertise their products extensively to boost sales.
- Carry their line exclusively.

RETAILERS WANT
WHOLESALERS TO:

- Give them a good price that will increase their gross margin.
- Have a liberal returned-goods policy—take back merchandise that is even slightly damaged or will not sell after a reasonable time.
- Deliver frequently and accept small orders.
- Not insist on prime shelf or counter space for their products.
- Provide effective display materials that require little space or care.
- Not object to their carrying their own brands or competing products.

What Producers and Agent Middlemen Want from Each Other

PRODUCERS WANT AGENT
MIDDLEMEN TO:

- Give the major portion of their time and energy to developing the demand for the manufacturer's products rather than the other lines they carry.
- Have a strong clientele of retailers, wholesalers, or users that will purchase the manufacturer's products in large quantities and at a price it sets.
- Not insist on "too high" a commission schedule or on a drawing account.
- Not object if the manufacturer rejects certain orders submitted by the agent because of the customer's credit, size, location, or other factors.
- Not harbor ill will toward the manufacturer if it decides to replace the agent with another agent or with its own sales representatives.

AGENT MIDDLEMEN WANT
PRODUCERS TO:

- Give the agents ample time to develop a market for the product.
- Advertise extensively in media that will reach the product's users to make the agents' selling job easier.
- Price the line below competitive products to make it simpler to induce customers to buy.
- Pay unusually high commissions and permit them to draw against future earnings.
- Have a lenient credit policy that enables most accounts solicited by the agents to "pay later."
- Agree not to make certain customers "house accounts," so that the agents will be paid commissions on all business from their territory.

However, the terms negotiated are rarely all one-sided. For example, a manufacturer may succeed in inducing a retailer to pay what appears to be a premium price, but, in turn, the retailer may succeed in convincing the manufacturer to advertise the product more aggressively than it had intended. One channel member may get an extra large order from another channel member on the condition that extra favorable credit terms be extended. Even Coca-Cola must compromise with its distributors. Bottlers were disgruntled by the company's practice of running one commercial nationwide, even though both the franchisees and the company pay equally for the TV spots. In an effort to compromise, Coca-Cola's 500 independent U.S. bottlers now will select the commercials they feel are best suited to air in their locales (the ad cost will still be split). As Harvey E. Anderson, president of Rochester (N.Y.) Coca-Cola Bottling Company, said, "In wintertime we were forced to buy water skiing in Hawaii (TV commercials) even if we were sitting in the middle of a blizzard. I know they're working on skiing in the Adirondacks, which is appropriate for this part of the country.[15]

Fourth, *conflicts between channel members should be resolved to facilitate the most efficient distribution system.* To the extent that this goal is not achieved, all members of the channel ultimately suffer. A car maker, for example, catering to the law of self-interest, may decide to lower the gross margin its dealers can charge. However, the net results may be less promotional effort on the part of the dealers, fewer sales, and lower profits for both the auto maker and the dealers. In the well-developed channel structure the performance of each member affects the performance of each other member.

Programmed Merchandising to Solve Conflicts

Ernst advocates programmed merchandising to secure better cooperation between channel members. Under a programmed system all channel members intentionally cooperate in planning, communication of intentions, and coordination of effort. Figure 11-5 gives a comparison of a programmed channel to a conventional channel. Ernst notes the advantages of a programmed system for retailers as[16]:

- Adequate and timely availability of merchandise
- Preferential consideration from key sources
- Assortment planning and merchandise control assistance
- Clearly specified inventory investment requirements

---

[15] "Coke's New Program to Placate Bottlers," *Business Week,* October 12, 1981, p. 48.
[16] Reprinted from Ronald L. Ernst, "Distribution Channel Detente Benefits Suppliers, Retailers, and Consumers," *Marketing News,* March 7, 1980, p. 19, published by the American Marketing Association.

Figure 11-5

Relationships in a Conventional Channel Versus a Programmed System

Characteristics	Conventional Channel	Programmed System
Nature of contacts	Negotiation on an individual order basis	Advanced joint planning for an extended time period
Information considered	Supplier sales presentation data	Retailer's merchandising data
Supplier participants	Supplier's territorial salesperson	Salesperson and major regional or headquarters executive
Retailer participants	Buyer	Various executives, perhaps top management
Retailer's goals	Sales gain and percentage markup	Programmed total profitability
Supplier's goal	Big order on each call	Continuing profitable relationship
Nature of performance	Event centered; primarily related to sales volume and other short-term performance criteria	Specific performance criteria written into the program

SOURCE: Ronald L. Ernst, "Distribution Channel Detente Benefits Suppliers, Retailers and Consumers," *Marketing News*, March 7, 1980, p. 19.

- High levels of vendor service with regard to product quality and general account maintenance
- Economy and efficiency through shifting functions, such as ordering, to the supplier

For suppliers the advantages include:

- The development of maximum sales and profit potential without competing for it on a day-to-day basis
- Continuity of promotion and sales for more economical scheduling of production and distribution activities
- Improved sales forecasting ability for manufacturing and distribution planning
- Achievement of maximum product exposure through retail outlets
- Achievement of a totally coordinated, planned, and controlled marketing approach to reach the consumer
- Clearly specified retailer inventory requirements, thus allowing inventory management and control efficiencies

The central idea behind programmed management of a distribution channel is that all members should view themselves as a team with specific roles to play. Properly implemented, a programmed system should result in greater efficiency for all members of a channel.

CHANNEL LEADER

In the distribution of many products a channel leader emerges. A **channel leader** determines the composition of the channel and, to a considerable extent, what marketing activities other channel members will perform.[17]

Channel leaders may be either producers, wholesalers, or retailers. Auto makers are an example of a producer channel leader. The auto company selects its dealers or retailers. It supplies them with promotional aids, sets service policies, establishes maximum prices for the cars, and in other ways defines the marketing role of the retailer.

Independent Grocers' Alliance (IGA), True Value, and Super Valu are three examples of channels in which the wholesaler is the channel leader. The wholesaler decides what products will be carried, negotiates with the producers, and dictates much of the merchandising practices to the retailers.

Examples of retailers serving as channel leaders are large chains such as K Mart, J.C. Penney, and Sears. These retailers have many products made to their specifications, have them branded, and in other ways dictate to the producer what marketing activities it will perform.

The most obvious channel leaders are found in franchise organizations. Although a franchisee is an independent business, the franchisor is the channel leader and determines the product mix, plans advertising and promotion, sets prices within limits, and determines the marketing mix. The contractual relationships between franchisors and franchisees spell out, usually quite specifically, the marketing role of each party.

SUMMARY

- A marketing channel is the path a product takes as it moves from producer to user.
- Merchant and agent middlemen perform the services needed to move products from producers to users.
- Marketing channels minimize the total number of transactions necessary from producer to user; routinize these transactions; create time, place,

---

[17] Robert W. Little, "The Marketing Channel: Who Should Lead this Extracorporate Organization?" *Journal of Marketing,* January 1970, pp. 31–38.

and possession utility; and distribute products when producers will not or cannot do it.

- All channels perform the functions of sorting out, accumulation, allocation, assortment, marketing research, buying and selling, negotiation, physical distribution, promotion, product and price planning, customer service, financing, and risk taking.
- Many alternate channel structures exist. When a company sells the same product through several structures, it is using multiple channels.
- Contractual channels are controlled by a contract. Administered channels are controlled by the use of coercive, reward, legitimate, referent, or expert power.
- Vertical integration occurs when one company controls other levels within its channel.
- A Vertical Marketing System is a company that controls the entire channel.
- Franchising is a method of achieving VMS coordination without the costs of ownership. In franchising the franchisor grants its franchisees the right to do business in a prescribed manner over a specified period of time in a given location.
- Horizontal integration is achieved when several companies on the same level in a channel are controlled and act as one company. This can be accomplished through ownership or cooperatives.
- Channel selection is affected by target customers, the product, the producer's status and objectives, and the middleman's status and objectives.
- Intensive distribution is used to achieve the maximum possible market coverage for a product.
- Selective distribution is used when retailers must meet certain criteria to be an outlet for a product.
- Exclusive distribution attempts to limit distribution to one outlet in any given geographic area.
- Although cooperation is the normal condition in marketing channels, conflict may arise over numerous issues.
- Programmed merchandising has been suggested as a way to reduce conflict and enhance cooperation.
- Channel leaders often emerge in a marketing channel. These leaders can be manufacturers, wholesalers, or retailers.

DISCUSSION QUESTIONS

1. "Economic success is not guaranteed simply because a producer makes a good product for which there is a need." How does this fact relate to channel management?

2. Explain how marketing channels minimize total transactions; routinize transactions; and create time, place, and possession utility.
3. Explain the functions of the sorting process.
4. What are some of the conditions under which a producer would be likely to sell directly to ultimate consumers? Directly to retailers? Directly to wholesalers?
5. Compare single versus multiple channels. Why are multiple channels sometimes used to distribute the same product?
6. Discuss the five sources of power used to control administered channels.
7. Explain vertical versus horizontal integration. What are Vertical Marketing Systems? Franchises? Cooperatives?
8. How does channel choice depend on target consumers? Product factors? Producer's status and objectives? Middlemen's status and objectives?
9. Under what conditions would a firm want intensive distribution? Exclusive distribution? Selective distribution?
10. Ideally, each channel member should cooperate fully with every other member. In practice, why don't they?
11. What specific conflicts may arise between wholesalers and retailers? Between producers and wholesalers?
12. What is "programmed merchandising"? What are its advantages for retailers? For wholesalers?

APPLICATION EXERCISES

1. You are a national wholesaler of parts for foreign and domestically produced motorcycles. Big Muff is a producer of a new type of muffler that is selling well. Big Muff markets directly to motorcycle repair shops and to retailers that sell parts to motorcycle owners. You want to carry the Big Muff line. Prepare at least six arguments you would use to convince Big Muff management that it should sell through you and in effect allow you to take over much of its marketing effort.
2. Find three examples of products (not mentioned in the chapter) that are distributed through multiple channels. Also find specific examples of the use of coercive, reward, legitimate, referent, and expert power to control administered channels.

CASE 11

Procter and Gamble Tries to Change Its Image

Procter and Gamble (P & G) has often been viewed as a necessary evil by many retailers. With an annual advertising budget of $670 million,[1] P & G pulls con-

---

[1] "100 Leading National Advertisers," *Advertising Age,* September 9, 1982, p. 1.

sumers into stores. The company, however, has been criticized as being rigid and arrogant in its policies. The most frequent complaints from retailers include P & G's intense scrutiny of stores' performances and P & G's stingy trade-allowance policies (discounts given to retailers as a sales promotion tool).

However, since 1982 P & G has been trying to improve its image among retailers. With the recession in the early 80's, P & G experienced little growth or declining unit volume in its major products. Plus, the company was feeling resistance in the trade to support its brands properly. In order to reverse those negative trends and maintain an average 7.5 percent annual growth rate,[2] P & G began changing in several areas, including trade allowances.

In the past, P & G closely monitored newspapers in its marketing areas to check on local advertising of its brands. Merchandise displays were constantly checked by sales reps, who would re-assemble shelves themselves, if it was necessary to obtain their agreed-upon shelf space. In spite of all the strict monitoring, which annoyed retailers, P & G was not matching competitors' discounts.

To begin P & G's image improvement, the consumer-products power-house changed its billing policy. Some trade allowance changes included more localized cooperative advertising and advertising coverage requirements were loosened. The company also began listening to its customers' needs. Rules affecting qualification for trade allowances were relaxed. Customers were given reduced prices when they picked up certain products in their own trucks. Shortly after the changes were instituted, a 17 percent increase in earnings from operations and a 5 percent sales increase were experienced.[3]

However, some retailers are not convinced that P & G has abandoned its desire to control every facet of the business. P & G's off-invoice allowance policy permits it to bill any customer who does not perform the stipulated promotions. Moreover, P & G can cut off credit to those who do not return allowances given for unperformed services. The company is also trying to eliminate the widespread practice of warehouse stores and retailers purchasing only discounted goods and bargain merchandise. No other manufacturer carries such strict policies.

Warehouse chains have continued to fight P & G, but larger customers such as Kroger have been delighted with the new policies and view P & G as a more cooperative channel member. Competitors, however, see the changes as threatening.

Discussion Questions

1. What sources of power make P & G the leader in its channels? Why?
2. Is P & G following an intensive distribution, selective distribution, or exclusive distribution strategy. Explain.
3. If you worked for a small local retail chain, what would be your strategy for dealing with P & G?

---

[2] *The Procter & Gamble Company 1982 Annual Report*, pp. 30–31.
[3] "Why P & G Wants a Mellower Image," *Business Week*, June 7, 1982, pp. 60, 64.

12 Wholesaling and Wholesale Institutions

STUDY OBJECTIVES

After studying this chapter, you should be able to

1. Discuss the role played by wholesalers in product distribution.
2. Explain the difference between wholesale and retail transactions.
3. List the functions performed by wholesalers.
4. Explain how wholesale middlemen are classified and list the specific functions performed in each category.
5. Outline the role of merchant wholesalers.
6. Distinguish between merchant wholesalers and agent middlemen.
7. Outline the conditions under which the various kinds of agent middlemen are used.
8. Discuss trade shows, merchandise marts, and public warehouses and explain how they relate to wholesaling.
9. Explain why wholesalers are important to our economic system.

W e may see or visit many types of retailers each day, but we seldom see wholesalers. The enormous activity that goes on behind the scenes to supply retail stores and industrial users with products is invisible to most of us. Yet wholesalers play a key role in the place marketing controllable variable. They occupy the middle position in the channel of distribution for many products.

WHOLESALING TERMS

The best guide to wholesale activity is the data published by the Bureau of the Census. We will use that agency's definitions and classifications throughout this chapter.

A **wholesale transaction** can be defined as *any nonretail sale*. The following are representative wholesale transactions:

1. Sales by farmers to processors
2. Sales of petroleum products to refineries
3. Sales by manufacturers to retail stores
4. Sales by manufacturers to wholesalers
5. Sales to governmental agencies
6. Sales to foreign buyers
7. Sales by manufacturers to industrial users

One way to understand the nature of wholesaling is to analyze the differences between a wholesale and a retail transaction. First, *wholesale transactions are usually much larger than retail transactions.* The word "wholesale" correctly suggests "bulk" or a large quantity. Although it is true that a retail druggist may order only one item from a wholesale drug company or an auto repair shop may buy only one hubcap from a parts wholesaler, in most cases individual wholesale transactions involve a much larger volume than single retail transactions.

Second, *the wholesale price of a given item is usually less than the retail price.* To meet expenses and earn a profit, retailers must mark up merchandise when they resell it. In some cases a retailer may actually sell a specific product for less than was paid for it in order to bring people into the store (where, hopefully, they will also make other purchases). Such an item is called a **loss leader.** Or a retailer may make an unwise purchase decision on occasion and be forced to mark merchandise down to below cost. This is unusual, however, and does not constitute a wholesale offering. Retailers who advertise "we sell at wholesale" are not really selling at wholesale. They are still selling at retail, but use such phrases merely to appeal to the consumer's love of a bargain.

Third, *the purchaser's motive for buying at wholesale differs greatly from the retail customer's motive.* Very simply, the wholesale buyer is motivated to earn a profit on the resale or use of the product; an ultimate consumer is motivated to satisfy some personal or family want or need.[1] Thus, a wholesale drug house might say, "Earn a whopping $2 profit per dozen on our aspirin," in appealing to a retailer. In reselling the same aspirin to an ultimate consumer, the retailer's appeal might be, "Say goodbye to your headache fast with our aspirin."

A retail transaction occasionally may be larger than a wholesale sale. Sometimes the retail price may be less than the wholesale price for the same item. *In the final analysis it is the motive of the purchaser that distinguishes a wholesale transaction from a retail sale.*

Wholesaling

Wholesaling includes the functions of assembling merchandise, breaking bulk, storage, selling, and delivery, as well as other functions that will be discussed later in the chapter. Regardless of whether they are performed by a manufacturer, a wholesaler, or a retailer, these functions are all part of wholesaling.

A **wholesaler** is a business that specializes in performing some or all of the wholesale functions previously noted. The wholesaler may also engage in retailing or processing, but only insofar as these activities are incidental to the performance of wholesaling functions. As we will see, there are widely different types of wholesalers.

The services performed by the various types of wholesalers differ considerably. Figure 12-1 shows what kinds of services each major classification provides.

Wholesale Transaction Volume

Because retailers mark up the price of goods purchased from wholesalers, you might assume that total retail dollar volume exceeds total wholesale dollar volume. Such is not the case. Total wholesale volume was about two times as great as total retail volume in 1982, because (1) the same product may be sold two or more times at wholesale, but only once at retail; (2) sales to industrial users are always considered wholesale transactions; (3) sales to

---

[1] An important exception is the government, which is not motivated to earn a profit.

Figure 12-1

Functions Performed by Wholesalers

MERCHANT OR TITLE-TAKING WHOLESALERS

Services Performed for Customers	Full-Function Wholesalers	Cash and Carry Wholesalers	Drop-Shippers	Rack Jobbers
Anticipates customer needs	yes	yes	no	no
Carries inventory	yes	yes	no	yes
Assembles and divides	yes	yes	no	yes
Delivers	yes	no	no	yes
Provides credit	yes	no	yes	sometimes
Assumes risk of ownership	yes	yes	yes	yes
Provides information and advice	yes	no	yes	yes
Services Performed for Producers				
Sells producers product	yes	yes	yes	yes
Carries inventory	yes	yes	yes	yes
Helps finance by owning inventory	yes	yes	yes	yes
Reduces credit risks	yes	yes	yes	yes
Provides advice and information	yes	yes	yes	sometimes

foreign customers are labeled wholesale, not retail; and (4) sales to the government are considered wholesale transactions.[2]

CLASSIFYING WHOLESALERS

Any description that includes the full array of wholesalers and wholesaling activities looks complicated at first glance. Wholesalers, like retailers, may be classified in several ways, depending on whether you wish to determine the breadth of their product line, whether or not they are independently owned, and the services they offer.

---

[2] U.S. Department of Commerce, Bureau of the Census, *Statistical Abstract of the United States, 1984,* p. 797.

NONTITLE-TAKING AGENT MIDDLEMEN

Manufac-turer's Agents	Selling Agents	Merchan-dise Agents	Commission Merchants	Import-Export Agents	Auction Companies	Resident Buyers
yes	yes	yes	yes	yes	no	yes
rarely	no	no	yes	no	no	no
no	no	no	yes	no	yes	no
no	no	no	yes	yes	no	no
no	no	no	sometimes	no	no	no
no	no	no	no	no	no	no
yes	yes	yes	yes	no	no	no
yes	yes	yes	yes	yes	yes	no
rarely	no	no	yes	no	yes	no
no	no	no	no	no	no	no
no	no	no	no	no	no	no
yes	yes	yes	yes	no	no	no

Breadth of Product Line

Wholesalers vary considerably in regard to the extent, or breadth, of merchandise they carry. Some commonly accepted terms for classifying wholesalers on this basis are explained below.

General Merchandise Wholesalers General merchandise wholesalers *carry a broad assortment of unrelated or loosely related products such as hardware, drug sundries, food products, and electrical supplies.* This type of firm was important when the general store flourished in the United States. With the advent of urbanization, retailer specialization, and improved transportation, however, general merchandise wholesalers have declined greatly in importance. ⌐take own of the gds.

General-Line Wholesalers General-line wholesalers *carry a complete supply of items in one line.* They are very important in such product categories as

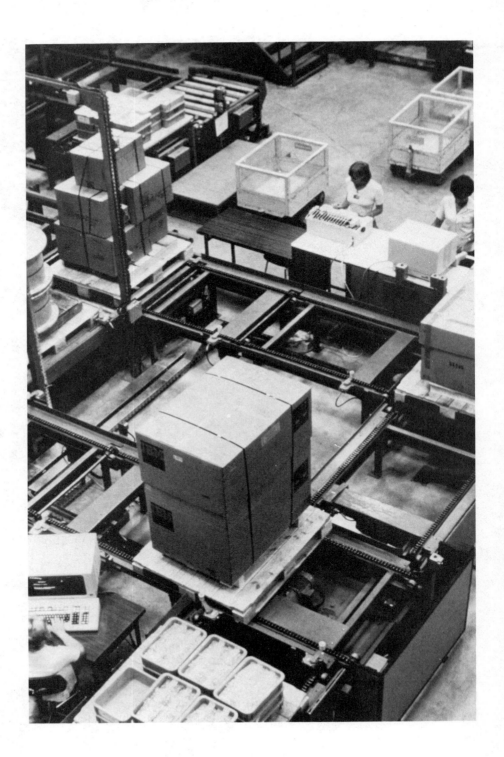

drugs, hardware, groceries, and major appliances, and are the most important wholesaler category in terms of sales. American Hospital Supply is an example of a general line wholesaler. This wholesaler can supply 60 percent of everything a hospital uses, from bandages to bed linens to blood oxygenators.[3] However, it only stocks items related to hospital needs. Thus, the general line category.

Specialty Wholesalers   **Specialty wholesalers** *handle only a segment of a broad line.* They are becoming increasingly important in many industries. Because they are specialized, they can offer better service to their retail accounts, and they have fewer inventory problems. Beer distributors are an example of such wholesalers. Although many brands and types of refreshment drinks exist, beer distributors typically carry only beer and represent only one company.

Independence and Service

As mentioned earlier, wholesalers can be classified by whether or not they are independently owned and by the services they offer. Figure 12-2 illustrates this classification and Figure 12-3 illustrates the importance of each class in terms of number of establishments and sales.

COMPANY-OWNED WHOLESALERS

Some wholesaling establishments are owned and operated by manufacturers, although they have little to do with the actual manufacturing operations. These are typically referred to as **manufacturer's sales branches and offices**. The essential difference between a *sales branch* and a *sales office* is that the branch operation maintains an inventory, whereas the sales office does not. Manufacturer's sales branches and offices are especially important in the marketing of automobiles and other motor vehicles.

Automobile manufacturers typically have sales branches or offices in major metropolitan centers. Auto retailers place their orders with the branches or offices rather than with the manufacturing plant. This type of wholesaler establishment is also very important in the marketing of chemicals, electrical equipment, and industrial machinery. By operating their own sales branches or offices, manufacturers keep greater control over the marketing of their products.

---

[3] Anne B. Pillsbury, "The Hard Selling Supplier to the Sick," *Fortune*, July 26, 1982, pp. 56–61.

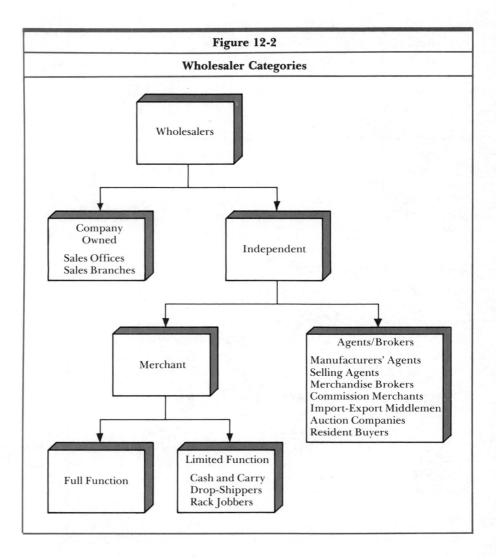

Figure 12-2

Wholesaler Categories

Wholesalers

Company Owned

Sales Offices
Sales Branches

Independent

Merchant

Agents/Brokers

Manufacturers' Agents
Selling Agents
Merchandise Brokers
Commission Merchants
Import-Export Middlemen
Auction Companies
Resident Buyers

Full Function

Limited Function

Cash and Carry
Drop-Shippers
Rack Jobbers

Most gasoline, oil, and other petroleum products are marketed through **bulk tank stations or terminals**. These wholesalers specialize in reselling petroleum products to petroleum retailers and industrial users. Major petroleum companies such as Texaco, Shell, and Fina own and operate many of these facilities. Like manufacturers' sales offices or branches, these bulk tank stations and terminals give the parent company greater control over the marketing of its products to ultimate consumers and industrial users. Some stations and terminals however, are independently owned and specialize in marketing to small petroleum retailers.

Figure 12-3

**Number of Establishments and Sales Volume by
Type of Wholesaler: 1972 and 1977**

	Number of Establishments		Percentage of Total Establishments	
	1972	1977	1972	1977
Merchant Wholesalers	289,974	307,264	78.4	80.2
Manufacturers Sales Branches and Offices	47,197	40,521	12.8	10.6
Agents, Brokers and Commission Merchants	32,620	35,052	8.8	9.2
Total Wholesale Trade	369,791	382,837	100.0	100.0

	Sales (thousands)		Percentage of Total Wholesale Sales	
	1972	1977	1972	1977
Merchant Wholesalers	353,918,969	676,057,580	50.6	53.7
Manufacturers Sales Branches and Offices	355,678,995	451,854,912	36.9	35.9
Agents, Brokers and Commission Merchants	85,625,680	130,487,776	12.5	10.4
Total Wholesale Trade	695,223,644	1,258,400,268	100.0	100.0

SOURCE: U.S. Department of Commerce, Bureau of the Census, *1977 Census of Business, Wholesale Trade—Geographic Area Series* 52–19.

INDEPENDENT WHOLESALERS

Independent wholesalers are classified by whether or not they take title to the merchandise they distribute. **Merchant wholesalers** take title, whereas **agents** and **brokers** do not.

Merchant Wholesalers

Merchant wholesalers purchase the goods they intend to resell. Figure 12-3 shows that such wholesalers account for more than 50 percent of the total sales volume of all wholesale middlemen. They have more establishments, more sales, and more employees than any other type of wholesaler.

Merchant wholesalers deal in both consumer and industrial products. Those that handle consumer products are commonly called *service wholesalers, regular wholesalers, jobbers, or full-function wholesalers.* Those that deal in industrial products are generally referred to as *industrial distributors.*

Merchant wholesalers are active to varying degrees in almost all product lines. In the consumer-goods field they are especially important in the grocery, drug, and hardware trades. Merchant wholesalers marketing to industrial users handle a significant volume of automotive parts, chemicals, piece goods, electrical equipment and supplies, and industrial equipment.

Depending on the services offered, merchant wholesalers are either full-function wholesalers or limited-function wholesalers.

Full-Function Wholesalers   Even in this age of bigness the majority of manufacturers and retailers are small. The **full-function** or **service wholesaler** is particularly important in serving small and medium-sized manufacturers, retailers, and industrial users. This type of middleman can perform services for both its suppliers and its customers more economically and effectively than they can. For example, Avnet Corporation is a full-function merchant wholesaler of electronic semiconductors. Avnet has 30 manufacturers providing it with the 300,000 different parts it stocks for its 80,000 customers. Avnet fills 10,000 orders a day, averaging $375 per order. Therefore, it serves as a link between the large electronics manufacturers and the thousands of little semiconductor users, none of which could afford to carry so many different parts.[4]

The services offered by full-function wholesalers include buying for customers, assembling and dividing merchandise, delivering merchandise, warehousing, extending credit, assuming risk, and providing information and advice. While reading the following descriptions of these services, try to imagine how Avnet performs each for its customers and its suppliers.

Buying for Customers   Service wholesalers make it their business to know the merchandise needs of their customers. By serving many customers in the same type of business, they develop an appreciation of what is selling at retail or what industrial users require. Because they are contacted by many manufacturers that attempt to sell them merchandise for resale, they are able to evaluate what merchandise is available. Thus, wholesalers reduce to some degree the buying expertise required of small retailers and

---

[4] Nick Galluccio, "Peddling the Chips," *Forbes,* February 16, 1981, pp. 99–101.

industrial users, and in a sense, act as purchasing agents for their customers.

In performing the buying function, the wholesaler saves its accounts a vast amount of effort. For example, even a small drugstore carries several thousand different items. Imagine, for a moment, how many employees it would need just to contact the manufacturers of all these products. Imagine, also, how time-consuming and economically impractical it would be for the manager of such a store to listen to hundreds of presentations by manufacturers' sales representatives, accept hundreds of deliveries, write hundreds of checks, and do the attendant bookkeeping each month. It would be much easier for the drugstore to deal with one wholesaler for all its supply needs.

Because the wholesaler buys in volume for many customers, it can also obtain merchandise at a much lower price than individual retailers would pay if they purchased relatively small quantities of products directly from manufacturers.

Selling for Suppliers The service wholesaler performs an important selling function for many producers. The manufacturers of products needed by the small drugstore in the previous example would find it very costly to hire, train, and manage a sales organization to call on tens of

Strategy

American Hospital Supply

The hospital supply distribution business has been described as a "no-technology business—basically a lot of warehouse shelves and a truck."* American Hospital Supply is changing that image. The company has brought the industry into the 20th century with its aggressive high-tech marketing efforts.

The metamorphosis is the result of the efforts of one man, Karl Bays, chairman and chief executive officer of American. When he took over in 1970, the company was number six in the industry and in desperate need of new blood. Most of the management had been around since the 30s. They were not interested in changing American's operations to match the changes taking place in the health-care industry.

Bays was different. He saw that the hospital industry was changing. Public policy had made health care a right, not a privilege. Technological advancements had increased the variety of treatable ailments. Despite the increased use of their facilities, hospitals were in financial trouble, with double-digit inflation making their operating costs skyrocket. Prodded by the federal government, hospitals began to look for a way to cut costs.

Bays realized that in order to stay in business, American would have to help hospitals do the cutting. American would have to change from a simple warehouse operation to a full-function wholesaler.

The first step for American was to computerize all of its internal finances, inventory control, and record keeping with a system called ASAP (analytical systems automated purchasing). The way American extended the use of ASAP to the customer put it out in front of other suppliers. American supplied over 3,000 hospitals with terminals connected directly to ASAP and to one of its 152 distribution centers, thus allowing hospital purchasing agents to order directly from it at any time. Purchasing agents type their order in and almost immediately receive printed confirmation, giving the price of the items ordered and their delivery date. ASAP eliminates the paper shuffling of ordering thousands of needed supplies. American claims that ASAP will cut the cost of a purchase by 20 percent.†

American not only helps smooth out order processing, but also helps hospitals reduce the cost of having those supplies available by teaching them how to operate with lower inventory levels. Because American can deliver supplies within 24 hours 90 percent of the time, there is no reason for hospitals to carry the traditional 88-day inventory. By turning inventory faster, hospitals can free up scarce capital.

American also benefits from ASAP. Because American was, until recently, the only supplier with the computerized advantage, it had captive customers. It was so easy to order from American that hospitals ignored other distributors. As a result the average ASAP order contains 5.8 items compared to an industry average of 1.7, and customers spend three times as much money with American as they did before the company instituted ASAP.

Another key to American's success is its wide range of product offerings, many of which are manufactured and exclusively offered by the company. American can sell a hospital up to 60 percent of all the supplies it needs.

American's constant monitoring of the health-care market proved to be beneficial again in 1977. Many nonprofit hospitals were forming cooperatives in an effort to cut costs by taking advantage of volume discounts. American realized that it was not organized to take advantage of the cooperative practice. Each division at American had its own marketing department, which signed separate agreements with the hospitals. To capitalize on the sales potential of the new hospital groups, American developed a company-wide marketing department whose sole purpose was to develop a marketing strategy for these groups. With a centralized marketing department one salesperson represents all of American's products and the hospitals sign only one purchase agreement. American offers price ceilings and rebates to these groups to make the company's wide purchase agreements more attractive.

American has run into an antitrust suit because marketing strategies like this one have been described as exclusionary. American insists that its efforts were to set up a consultant type of relationship with hospitals and hospital groups. It feels it is being punished for being bigger and better than its competitors.

The legal action has not deterred American in its campaign to change hospital supply distribution. It has invested $225 million in the research and development of new products, and intends to enhance its logistics network, especially the distribution facilities and computer communications, to accommodate the expected growth in sales from the overseas market. It will also begin building a position outside the hospital market. Health care is being directed out of the hospital, and American wants to be well established in all areas of the health-care market.

The ability to listen for changes in the marketplace and to adapt to them has been the key to American's success. Through this marketing orientation American has transformed itself and others in the hospital supply distribution industry from simple warehouse operations to full-function wholesalers. However, American's goals are set beyond this point. It sees itself as a hospital consultant that just happens to be able to sell you all the supplies you need.

* Anne B. Pillsbury, "The Hard-Selling Supplier to the Sick," *Fortune*, July 26, 1982, pp. 56–61.
† "Systems that Slash Hospital Costs," *Business Week*, September 8, 1980, pp. 76A–76C.

thousands of stores, each of which would purchase only a small quantity of goods.

It is more economical for many firms to sell in relatively large quantities to service wholesalers than to call on thousands of small retailers or industrial users. The wholesaler's sales representatives normally will sell the products of a number of manufacturers, thereby lowering the per-unit selling expense.

Service wholesalers are frequently criticized because they do little creative selling. They stock many competitive items and do little to promote the products of any one manufacturer. The typical wholesaler's sales representative is more of an order taker and less of a demand creator than manufacturers would like. Nevertheless, one of the biggest sales objectives of many manufacturers is to persuade wholesalers to stock their products, because no wholesaler can stock everything. As we will see in later chapters, manufacturers that sell through wholesalers frequently invest large sums in advertising and sales promotion, thereby minimizing the need for creative selling by wholesalers' sales representatives.

Assembly and Division　Two related wholesaler functions, assembling merchandise in large quantities from many manufacturers and then dividing it into small quantities (*breaking bulk*), benefit both the manufacturer and the retailer. Being able to sell in truckload or carload lots reduces the manufacturer's per-unit transportation and handling costs. Small shipments cost much more per unit than large shipments. The retailer benefits by being able to purchase goods in relatively small quantities, thereby avoiding overbuying and inventory problems. However, because the wholesaler represents many producers, the retailer can also order a variety of items from the same wholesaler and receive them all in one shipment.

Delivery　Most service wholesalers make deliveries on a regular basis and, if need be, many will make special deliveries to their accounts. Usually, the service wholesaler can make deliveries more quickly and much more economically than a manufacturer. In practice this means that a retailer or an industrial user need not keep as large an inventory as would be required if manufacturers made direct deliveries. This, in turn, means that less capital is tied up in inventory, and greatly reduces the risks of a product deteriorating or becoming obsolete before sale.

Warehousing　Wholesalers are specialists in storage and can often perform this function much more efficiently than either manufacturers or retailers. When wholesalers perform the storage function, both the manufacturers' and the wholesalers' customers benefit. The manufacturers need less warehouse space and personnel, and the typical small retailer can devote a larger portion of its total physical space to displaying the items it carries.

Credit Extension　Service wholesalers commonly grant credit to their accounts. Typically, retail customers are offered a discount if they buy on a cash basis or pay within a certain period of time. However, it is often to the retailer's advantage not to pay cash, especially when buying seasonal goods that may not sell for several weeks or months.

The wholesaler is often in a much better position than a manufacturer to extend credit to retail accounts. The bookkeeping costs alone would make credit extension prohibitively expensive for many manufacturers selling in small quantities to thousands of retail outlets. Furthermore, the wholesaler has a much more intimate knowledge of its retail customers' financial capabilities than a distant manufacturer would.

Assumption of Risk Because the service wholesaler takes both title to and physical possession of the merchandise, it helps reduce the risk for manufacturers. Obviously, once the wholesaler has taken possession of and paid for the merchandise, the manufacturer need no longer worry that it will become obsolete or deteriorate physically before it is sold. The wholesaler also assumes the risk that the retailer or industrial user may not pay for merchandise sold on credit.

Information and Advice Because the wholesaler services hundreds, sometimes thousands of retail or industrial accounts, it learns a great deal about what its accounts require to succeed in business. Accordingly, wholesalers are often able to give advice on sales and merchandise trends, display techniques, inventory management, accounting, and financial control. Some wholesalers sponsor seminars for their customers to advise them of up-to-date marketing procedures and tactics.

Manufacturers often pay a heavy price for ignoring information and advice from their wholesalers. Coors Beer, once considered the up-and-coming brewer, had a loyal following of wholesalers. In the 1970s over two-thirds of all Coors distributors sold nothing but Coors products. However, many Coors distributors feel that company officials ignore their recommendations. In 1980 Coors replaced its elected distributor advisory committee with a company-picked committee. By 1982 Coors had dropped from fifth to sixth in industry sales and more than half of its wholesalers sold competing beers or wines along with Coors.[5] Company officials give various reasons for this decline, but ignoring wholesaler advice and information certainly did not help.

Limited-Function Wholesalers Merchant wholesalers are called **limited-function wholesalers** when they do not perform all the functions normally associated with the full-function, or service, wholesaler. Although relatively few distributors fall into this category and their sales as a group are relatively small, their methods of operation are interesting as examples of the many adaptations wholesalers make to serve their customers.

Three types of limited-function wholesalers are cash-and-carry wholesalers, drop-shippers, and rack jobbers.

---

[5] Brenton R. Schlender, "Heady Days are Over for Coors Wholesalers as Sales Pace Drops," *Wall Street Journal*, October 6, 1982, pp. 1, 27.

Cash-and-Carry Wholesalers As their name implies, **cash-and-carry wholesalers** *do not extend credit or deliver merchandise to their retail or industrial accounts.* Most of them specialize in staple products such as tobacco and dry groceries, and much of their business is done with "high-risk" small retailers that do not have satisfactory credit ratings and whose business is therefore not solicited by service wholesalers. Because they provide fewer services, cash-and-carry wholesalers have lower operating expenses than service wholesalers.

Drop-Shippers Very simply, a **drop-shipper** *sells merchandise to a customer and then arranges for the producer or manufacturer to deliver it directly (drop ship) to the buyer.* Drop-shippers do not perform the functions of storage and delivery, nor do they physically handle the merchandise they deal in. They do, however, take title to the goods and assume any risks that are involved in doing so. They do most of their business in coal, coke, lumber, stone, and various other building materials.

Drop-shippers are useful to their suppliers, because they have first-hand knowledge of who needs to buy what. Furthermore, because they take title to the merchandise and also handle the billing, they relieve the supplier of financial risk and accounting inconveniences. Drop-shippers are useful to their customers, because they are knowledgeable about sources of supply and can arrange all the details of obtaining and delivering the goods.

Rack Jobbers **Rack jobbers** *perform the selling and delivery functions at the same time.* They are most common in the field of perishable groceries, where they relieve the retailer of a substantial burden of risk. Rack jobbers maintain a rolling inventory in their trucks and fill orders immediately. Most of their orders are quite small. They are one of the least important types of wholesalers in terms of total sales. Because their operating expenses are much higher than those of a regular wholesaler dealing in the same goods, their potential for growth is small. truck distributors

Agents and Brokers

Up to this point we have discussed only title-taking merchant wholesalers. However, there are many middlemen that do not take title to the goods they handle but instead act as agents for sellers and, in some instances, buyers. middleman   don't take title

Merchandise agents and **brokers** differ from merchant wholesalers in two ways: They do not take title to the products they handle, and they usually perform fewer functions. Most of their activity involves negotiating transfers of title, not such functions as storage and delivery.

Approximately half of all agents and brokers are sole proprietorships. Principally because they perform fewer functions and take less risk, the operating expenses of merchandise agents and brokers are considerably lower than those of merchant wholesalers or manufacturers' sales branches and offices. This type of wholesaler, commonly called an **agent middle-**

man, is active in many product lines, especially in the marketing of food, livestock, and industrial machinery.

Agent middlemen fall into seven categories: manufacturers' agents, selling agents, merchandise brokers, commission merchants, import and export agents, auction companies, and purchasing agents or resident buyers.

Manufacturer's Agents A **manufacturer's agent**, *often called a* **manufacturer's representative** *or "rep," is authorized by a principal (a producer) to sell all or part of the principal's line in a clearly defined territory.* The manufacturer's representative has considerably more freedom than an employee such as a sales representative would have. For example, a manufacturer's agent normally (1) uses sales techniques of his or her own design, (2) selects the accounts to be cultivated within the territory, (3) works when he or she chooses, (4) personally maps out an itinerary, (5) may employ sales representatives who do not have direct contact with the manufacturer, and (6) may, unless the agreement with the principal clearly prohibits it, represent related but noncompeting lines. In exchange for this freedom the manufacturer's agent works on a commission basis and pays his or her own travel and other business expenses.

The manufacturer or principal maintains a certain amount of control over the situation, however. Under the typical arrangement, the territory in which the agent can sell is clearly spelled out. It may consist of several states or only part of one state, depending on the size of the potential market and the location of customers. Furthermore, it is the manufacturer, not the agent, that controls the price and terms of sale. In practice a manufacturer's agent often recommends changes in price, delivery dates, credit arrangements, and product design to the principal, but cannot modify the terms of sale without express authority.

Usually, the manufacturer's agent represents the principal on a continuous basis or until one party decides to terminate the agreement. He or she also frequently negotiates sales with the same customers over an extended period. Manufacturer's agents are used extensively whenever one or a combination of the following conditions prevail:

When a small manufacturer has a geographically widespread market Retaining manufacturer's agents is often an ideal way for a small firm with a widely dispersed market to handle distribution. For example, a small dress manufacturer with a nationwide market has basically two distribution alternatives: It can recruit, train, manage, and pay its own sales organization, or it can divide its market into logical territories and use manufacturer's agents to cultivate potential accounts. If it chooses the second alternative, its sales expenses will be variable, because it only needs to pay commissions on actual sales. It therefore avoids the many fixed costs involved in establishing an employee sales force. Using manufacturer's agents gives the manufacturer more capital and time to devote to production.

When experienced and knowledgeable representation is needed   Even when a firm can afford its own sales force, it may still opt to use manufacturer's agents in order to secure the best possible sales talent. Because manufacturer's agents are independent business people, they have, broadly speaking, a greater incentive to succeed than employee sales personnel. Furthermore, as specialists in a narrow product range, manufacturer's agents have an extensive knowledge of the products they sell. In addition they work at developing trade contacts and generally have a comprehensive understanding of their customers and their requirements.

When a product is new and demand is uncertain   Partly to conserve capital for other purposes, partly because of inexperience, and partly because of the high risk involved, many firms use manufacturer's agents in the initial stages of marketing a new product. If the product catches on and a large market develops, the manufacturer may elect to reduce the size of the agent's territory to permit more intensive distribution, or it may decide to hire its own sales force. If the product fails, the manufacturer merely discontinues its relationship with the manufacturer's agent and the cost of distributing the product disappears.

When product sales are seasonal   The entire yearly production of some products sells in a relatively short period of time (sometimes only a month or two). For these products it is economically infeasible to maintain a sales force throughout the year. Manufacturers of such products may use manufacturer's agents only during the selling season, so the sales expense drops to zero in the off season. The manufacturer's agent, in turn, will try to find other products that sell well in the off season.

When the market is too thin to justify a company sales force   The demand for some products is too small in any given geographic area to justify a company sales organization. Yet, because they typically carry several lines, manufacturer's agents may be able to represent the product.

When it is convenient for managerial and administrative reasons   Operating any business is a complex undertaking, and some firms may choose to use manufacturer's agents because doing so relieves them of a variety of time-consuming problems. For example, because it eliminates or reduces the need for a company sales force, it simplifies the sales-management function for the firm.

Selling Agents   **Selling agents** are similar to manufacturers' agents in that both are independent business people and both specialize in negotiating sales for principals. Operationally, however, there are several differences between them.

First, a manufacturer's agent handles only a portion of the principal's output, whereas a selling agent handles all of it and is not restricted to a territory.

Second, unlike the manufacturer's agent, the selling agent has considerable authority from the principal to negotiate prices, delivery dates, and other terms of sale. Selling agents often have their headquarters in major metropolitan areas hundreds or thousands of miles from their principals. Checking every detail of every contract with them would be difficult, if not impossible.

Third, in some instances, especially in the textiles field, the selling agent may supply financial assistance to the principal.

Like manufacturer's agents, selling agents are respected for their knowledge of the market, sales skills, and overall marketing know-how. They are found mainly in the marketing of textiles and, to some extent, coal, lumber, metal products, and canned food. The typical selling agent handles much larger transactions than the manufacturer's agent and has fewer accounts. It is not unusual, for example, for a selling agent to sell the principal's entire output to one customer.

We have seen how the use of manufacturer's agents greatly simplifies a manufacturer's sales-management task. Retaining selling agents simplifies the sales-management function for a principal even further. The selling agent, who normally employs sales representatives, actually functions as the producer's marketing department.

Merchandise Brokers   *A limited-function middleman who buys or sells for a* ⟵ don't take *principal on a sporadic or one-time basis is called a* **merchandise broker**. Such a ⟶ title broker is usually retained by a seller to locate purchasers for a specific product, line, or production run. He or she is given little or no control over prices or terms of purchase, and is rarely authorized to conclude a sale. Generally, the broker is expected to have an extensive knowledge of supply, demand, and prospective customers within a given field and to negotiate the most favorable terms obtainable for the principal. Afterward, the broker retires from the scene, and the principal makes the decision to accept or reject the arrangement. For their services brokers charge approximately 2 percent of the net sale price.

In some fields, such as groceries, middlemen who have gradually begun to perform much wider functions on a more or less continuing basis are still referred to as brokers. Actually, food "brokers" more closely resemble manufacturer's agents. Brokers are especially valuable to buyers and sellers of highly specialized goods and seasonal products that do not require constant distribution.

Commission Merchants   **Commission merchants** *supply storage space and act as contacts between the producer and buyer.* Although they sometimes work as brokers, they are generally empowered to conclude a sale, whereas a broker usually is not.

Commission merchants are most important in the fields of agricultural commodities and textiles. A producer may ship goods to a centrally located marketplace and "consign" them to a commission merchant to obtain the best price. Commission merchants do handle the disposition of goods on arrival, although they do not take title to them. They are compensated, as their title implies, by a percentage of the sale price.

Import-Export Middlemen   Import-export agents, brokers, and commission houses operate in a manner similar to other nontitle-taking middlemen but specialize in international marketing. In many instances their greatest economic contribution lies in arranging the financing of purchases, which can be a particularly difficult area in international exchanges. Their help can prove quite beneficial to both the buyer and the seller.

Auction Companies   Although few in number, auction houses provide low-cost, convenient sites for transactions between buyers and sellers of products whose prices are strictly a function of supply and demand. They are particularly important to agricultural firms and livestock producers, used-car dealers, antique and art dealers, and fur and tobacco merchants.

Prices of goods sold at auction are not established in advance, but develop on the spot as purchasers make known what they are willing to pay. If an offer is acceptable to the seller, the transaction is completed.

Auction companies charge a commission for providing a location for bidding, auctioneers, and temporary storage. Their overhead is generally low, because their facilities are quite functional. They are usually located close to transportation facilities and can reship goods rapidly.

Resident Buyers   *A middleman who functions much like an independent agent in industries noted for highly centralized production is sometimes called a* **resident buyer**. In the distribution of apparel, for example, small clothing retailers throughout the country may retain independent "buyers" residing in New York City or other major production centers to purchase portions or all of the stock for the outlets. The resident buyer views merchandise from a number of apparel manufacturers, selects those items or lines most likely to fit the needs of a retailer's clientele, and arranges for their purchase and shipment to the store. In some cases a resident buyer may purchase identical items for stores in widely separated geographic areas, thereby qualifying the retailers for quantity discounts they could not otherwise obtain.

OTHER WHOLESALE ACTIVITIES AND INSTITUTIONS

Certain economic activities and facilities peculiar to wholesaling—namely, trade shows and exhibitions, merchandise marts, and public warehouses—are responsible for a growing portion of wholesale transactions.

Trade Shows and Exhibitions

Although the terms are often used interchangeably in marketing, there is a difference between trade shows and exhibitions. Technically, **trade shows** involve a major sales effort, an actual attempt to induce buyers to place orders on the spot. **Exhibitions** are primarily a presale activity. They are intended to expose merchandise to potential customers who, hopefully, will buy later. Both are distinguished from other distribution activities by one particularly interesting aspect: Competing producers or their sales representatives temporarily combine their promotional efforts to induce the maximum number of retail or industrial buyers to visit the show or exhibition. Shows and exhibits are used in the marketing of many different product lines, especially consumer goods such as apparel, furniture, toys, shoes, books, and giftware.

Trade shows are very popular in the wholesaling of women's and children's apparel. More than 60 groups of sales representatives in the United States hold more than 300 shows annually in major cities, with each group conducting perhaps three or more shows per year. The shows are held in hotels, auditoriums, civic centers, or merchandise marts. The exhibitors include more than 9,000 wholesale apparel sales representatives. Manufacturer's agents may also participate in these shows. As an aid to attending retailers, many groups produce fashion shows that give apparel buyers an opportunity to spot trends in styles, fabrics, and colors very early in the season. Many trade shows also provide clinics, show films, and conduct seminars to bring buyers up to date on industry events.

Exhibitions are commonly held in conjunction with trade-association conventions. Such meetings attract people, such as contractors, engineers, or physicians, who have common business or professional interests. Manufacturers that market products used by such groups often display merchandise at—and have their sales representatives attend—conventions in order to develop prospects and create goodwill. In most cases no actual sales are made, because the purpose of the exhibit is merely to increase the effectiveness of the sales representatives in follow-up calls.

Still another type of exhibition, in this case one open to the public, is the **model exhibit,** which is conducted to promote the products of an industry among ultimate consumers. For example, in many localities there are annual boat, auto, and mobile home shows open to the public. Here again, the emphasis is on attracting the prospective customer's interest rather than on actual selling.

Merchandise Marts

The **merchandise mart,** often described as "a shopping center for retailers," provides concentrated display space for manufacturers and exhibitors of many different types of merchandise. They are usually closed to ultimate consumers, and retail buyers must be registered to be admitted.

In cities such as Atlanta, Chicago, Dallas, Denver, Los Angeles, and Miami, merchandise marts have become a favorite place for trade shows and exhibits, as well as year-round displays. Many "regional" marts have

MARKETING
Milestone
Merchandise Marts

Merchandise marts are changing the scheme of distribution in the United States. Since the early 1960s the number of marts has grown steadily. Today even promoters in smaller towns have or are planning marts—from Clark, New Jersey, to Salt Lake City and Seattle. The new furnishings complex in the District of Columbia, the Washington Design Center, cost over $23 million to purchase and renovate and includes space for displays by 120 manufacturers. The Design Center attracts buyers from an area stretching from Philadelphia to Norfolk, an area with 5.5 million middle- and upper-class customers.*

The largest mart complex is in Dallas. It includes The Trade Mart, Home-furnishings Mart, Market Hall, Decorative Center, World Trade Center, and the Apparel Mart. Together they cover 9 million square feet.

The major items displayed in merchandise marts are furniture, apparel, gifts and decorative accessories, toys, and other ultimate-consumer products. In recent years, however, producers of machine tools, electronic devices, printing equipment, and other industrial products have demonstrated an interest in mart displays. This interest is likely to increase in the future. Marts

developed recently in such cities as Washington and Philadelphia.[6] In addition to the space devoted to permanent showrooms, which are leased for one to five years, mart managers customarily reserve transient space for temporary exhibits. Promotional activities are similar to those of planned shopping centers in that the "image" of the mart is publicized to interest buyers in all the tenants.

Public Warehouses

Public warehouses—businesses that provide storage facilities and perform related wholesaling functions—are used by manufacturers and wholesalers that for one reason or another do not want to own or operate their own warehouse facilities. Public warehouses provide four kinds of storage space: regular "floor" storage, refrigerated storage space, bulk-liquid storage space, and frozen-food lockers. The management, when notified by the storer, fills orders and in many cases makes deliveries.

[6] "Merchandise Marts are Getting Contagious," *Business Week,* September 28, 1981, pp. 31–32.

are generally planned as regional centers that will serve a multistate area. Due to the speed and economy of modern jet travel, some even attract buyers from distances of several thousand miles. New York's merchandise marts, for example, still draw buyers from all over the country.

Merchandise marts represent a further evolutionary step in the way certain products are wholesaled. A merchandise mart brings buyers and sellers together in a way convenient for both. The mart environment is functional, but in keeping with modern decorative trends and technological advances. It provides effective conditions for transacting business, whether the objective is to actually make a sale, to introduce a new line, or to contact potential buyers. Therefore, a merchandise mart has a better image than many of the other facilities, such as old hotels or auditoriums, formerly used for trade shows or exhibits.

Visiting a mart helps retailers to determine trends and lets them compare prices and lines in a fraction of the time it would take to do so on their own premises. The search for new suppliers is also simplified by the publication of buyers' guides, which serve as directories of mart tenants and temporary exhibitors.

The proliferation of lines in nearly all categories of consumer goods contributes to the growth of marts. With the escalating cost of travel both retailers and buyers benefit from being able to view and compare many different lines under one roof. It is a distinct advantage that helps assure the continuing growth of merchandise marts as a marketing milestone.

* "Merchandise Marts are Getting Contagious."

Another function of public warehouses is to keep a record of the storer's inventory. The storer can then use this record, in the form of a warehouse receipt, as collateral for a bank loan.

ARE WHOLESALERS REALLY NECESSARY?

One of the oldest and most persistent criticisms of marketing is that "there are too many middlemen." Those who take this position reason that a reduction in the number of middlemen would mean lower prices for consumers. Five observations seem to be in order.

First, *it is possible to eliminate a wholesale middleman, but not the functions he or she performs.* A drug manufacturer, for example, may elect to bypass wholesalers and sell directly to retailers. However, in order to do so, it must assume the work, or functions, of the wholesalers. That is, it must assemble, warehouse, sell, and deliver the product; provide credit; and otherwise service retail customers. Manufacturers that sell most or all of their output to one or several giant retail chains may find it practical to assume these functions. In some instances the retailer may elect to fulfill some wholesale functions, such as warehousing. These functions must be performed, and producers of products with a low unit cost usually find it uneconomical to maintain sufficient storage facilities, sales staff, and delivery capability to reach the maximum number of retailers.

Second, in our competitive business environment *businesses that do not perform needed economic services eventually disappear.* A wholesaler whose services are not helpful to manufacturers, retailers, or industrial users will find itself bypassed. Patterns of wholesale distribution are dynamic. Certainly, manufacturers will bypass wholesalers when it is to their advantage to do so, and retailers will buy directly from manufacturers if it increases their profits. In our intensely competitive economy businesses seek to increase revenue and decrease costs by whatever means they can. If wholesalers could be eliminated, they would be.

Third, wholesalers add little cost to products. Critics of wholesaling argue that wholesalers add unnecessary costs to the distribution of products. However, in its Annual Report on American Industry, *Forbes* magazine reported that the median net profit margin for wholesalers was 1.3 percent of sales.[7] It could easily be argued that wholesalers create efficiencies far in excess of 1.3 percent. Therefore, wholesalers add less cost than they save in product distribution. *Wholesalers actually lower the cost of product distribution.* As Ace Hardware dealer Roy Nyberg, put it, "[The wholesalers] reduced cost of goods by 16 percent. We gave the consumer 10 percent in lower prices and got an extra 6 percent profit."[8]

Fourth, *wholesalers help small businesses to survive.* Many large manufacturers and retailers can do their own wholesaling, but the vast majority of manufacturers and retailers are too small to afford the expenses of performing wholesale functions. Even large manufacturers often use wholesalers for efficiency and reinvest the money saved in the company. Semiconductor manufacturers, for example, distribute directly to large buyers, but wholesalers serve their smaller customers. The money saved is used for research and development (typically 10 to 20 percent of sales in that industry).[9] Thus, the manufacturer and its wholesalers efficiently serve two different target markets.

Finally, *wholesale middlemen help to simplify distribution by reducing the number of transactions.* For example, if a small independent hardware store stocked 1,000 different products produced by 100 manufacturers, most of the retailer's time would be spent checking invoices and writing checks. The 100 manufacturers would find their volume per transaction so small

---

[7] Richard Greene, "Thirty-Sixth Annual Report on American Industry—Wholesalers," *Forbes,* January 2, 1984, pp. 226–28.

[8] Jeff Blyskal, "Screw, Bolts and Tighter Competition," *Forbes,* May 24, 1982, pp. 146, 148, 149.

[9] Galluccio, "Peddling the Chips."

that it would not be profitable. It is far more efficient for the retailer to use the services of two or three wholesalers, rather than to buy directly from 100 or more manufacturers.

SUMMARY

- A wholesale transaction is any nonretail sale.
- Wholesale transactions differ from retail transactions in three ways: Transactions usually involve more items, price per unit is usually less, and transactions are motivated by profit rather than personal satisfaction.
- Services performed by wholesalers for their customers include anticipating their needs, assembling merchandise, maintaining inventories, delivery, granting credit, giving advice and information, and taking title to merchandise.
- Wholesalers can be classified by the breadth of their product line, whether or not they are independently owned, and the services they offer.
- Merchant or title-taking wholesalers can be divided into full-function (service) wholesalers or limited-function wholesalers.
- Services performed by full-function wholesalers include: buying for customers, selling for suppliers, assembly and division, delivery, warehousing, credit extension, assumption of risk, and providing information and advice.
- Limited-function wholesalers take title to merchandise, but do not perform all the functions of service wholesalers.
- Wholesalers that do not take title to the products they handle are also called agent middlemen. The main categories are manufacturer's agents, selling agents, merchandise brokers, commission merchants, import and export agents, auction companies, and resident buyers.
- Trade shows and exhibitions, merchandise marts, and public warehouses aid wholesalers in performing their functions.
- Although wholesalers can be eliminated, the wholesaling function cannot.

DISCUSSION QUESTIONS

1. "The purchaser's motive for buying at wholesale differs greatly from the retail customer's motive." Explain
2. Define the term *wholesaler*. What are the principal wholesaling functions?

3. Why does the total volume of wholesale transactions greatly exceed the volume of retail transactions?
4. What is the key distinguishing feature of merchant wholesalers? What types of merchant wholesalers are there, and how do they operate?
5. "Some wholesaling establishments are owned and operated by manufacturers." Explain.
6. What are the typical functions performed by service wholesalers?
7. Define *limited-function wholesaler*. What are the three main categories and how does each operate?
8. What is a nontitle-taking middleman? Into what seven categories can nontitle-taking middlemen be divided?
9. What are the differences between trade shows and exhibitions?
10. How do merchandise marts function? How do they serve sellers? Buyers?
11. "Wholesalers provide a necessary service in the distribution of products." Explain.

APPLICATION EXERCISES

1. In a recent issue of the *Survey of Current Business* find the wholesale price index. Make a list of the 10 products whose prices increased the most over a year and a second list of the 10 products whose prices increased the least or declined. What factors can you suggest to explain why some wholesale prices increased more than others? In general how do wholesale-price fluctuations compare with retail-price fluctuations?
2. "Full-service wholesalers will be relatively less important 20 years from now." Prepare a report evaluating this proposition, giving consideration to such factors as anticipated changes in retailing, marketing by manufacturers, spending for services as opposed to spending for tangible products, and population shifts.

CASE 12
Super Valu Stores[10]

Super Valu Stores, Inc., is the nation's largest grocery wholesaler. Net earnings for the fiscal year ending in February 1983 were $68 million from total sales of $5.2 billion. Super Valu's wholesle food sales, which account for more than 85 percent of the company's sales and earnings, doubled in real terms from 1977 to 1983.

---

[10] Bill Saporito, "Super Valu Does Two Things Well," *Fortune*, April 18, 1983, pp. 114–17.

Part of Super Valu's success stems from its ability to help its independent retailers achieve economies of scale without having to bear the burden of a large corporation's overhead. The retailers receive advantages that only chains normally have, such as low prices from suppliers, up-to-date stores, good locations, and sophisticated operations systems. The independent Super Valu retailer can usually earn $1\frac{1}{2}$ to 3 percent net profit after taxes, significantly above the industry average of less than 1 percent.

Super Valu is very proficient in helping retailers run supermarkets. "Super Valu can find the site, design the store, finance the equipment, set the shelves, train the butchers and clerks, plan the promotions, write the advertising, count the money, and insure the whole works, bologna to bagboy." Gene Hoffman, former president of Kroger Co., is the Super Valu executive in charge of links with the food retailers. Hoffman is convinced that "the leading wholesalers are beginning to drive the retail market, rather than merely supplying it, because they've made their retailers better merchandisers."

Super Valu also provides retailers with resources they could not afford on their own. Planmark, Super Valu's architecture and engineering division, uses a computer-aided design system, which enables architects to call up over 100 different store plans. Retailers select a general format and may have details altered to meet special needs. SLASH (Site Location Analysis Strategy Heuristic) is the company's development team. After finding promising store sites, the team does a total market evaluation. "They know more about our community than we did," commented one retailer about its work. Super Valu also provides retail counselors, who visit the stores to offer advice and detect problem areas.

Super Valu is also very efficient in the operation of its 16 grocery warehouses. John Morrissey, Super Valu's senior vice-president for distribution, has made a science of the distribution process by carefully studying a product's path from the processor to the retailer, looking for competitive advantages along the path.

A key to the efficient operation of the warehouses is the minimization of time and travel distance required to find and retrieve merchandise, and the concurrent maximization of storage density. This is particularly difficult in grocery warehouses, which on the average turn inventory $1\frac{1}{2}$ times a month. Also, delivery schedules are of extreme importance; orders must be timely.

In spite of these difficulties Super Valu, through the use of advanced computer modeling and old-fashioned industrial engineering, has been able to raise its storage density substantially. A computer simulator, which analyzes various warehouse arrangements, assists engineers in these areas by determining if a "reset" would cut costs and improve efficiency. Super Valu usually does 6 to 10 resets a year with the idea of cutting costs to achieve a competitive advantage.

Discussion Questions

1. What classification of wholesalers would you call Super Valu?
2. Is Super Valu an example of why wholesalers should exist or why they should be eliminated? Why?
3. Suppose you work for Super Valu in store relations. How would you convince an independent retailer to join Super Valu? Give specific reasons from the case and this chapter.

13 Retailing

STUDY OBJECTIVES

After studying this chapter, you should be able to

1. Explain the importance of retailing.
2. Classify retailers by size, ownership, product-line breadth, level of service, and whether or not a store is maintained.
3. Describe franchising, franchise agreements, and criticisms of franchising.
4. Define wholesaler-sponsored and retailer-sponsored cooperatives.
5. Discuss the various types of planned and unplanned shopping areas and the advantages and disadvantages of planned shopping centers.
6. Explain the importance of store image, atmosphere, and merchandising to retail strategy.
7. Discuss the wheel of retailing, scrambled merchandising, vertically integrated retailers, leased retailing departments, retailing of services, and in-home retailing.

R etailing is the most visible marketing institution. Consumers see and patronize retailers daily. Imagine how empty a town or city would be if there were no gasoline stations, drugstores, supermarkets, or other retailers.

Retailing is all the activities involved in selling goods and services to final consumers for private or family use. Regardless of the company performing these activities—manufacturer, wholesaler, or retailers—if it is to the final consumer, it is retailing. Companies whose primary activities are retailing are called **retailers**. Most retailing takes place in stores, but it also occurs through the mail, in vending machines, and by door-to-door canvassing.

Retailing is our most varied marketing institution for several reasons. At one extreme are sales proprietors who have no employees. At the other extreme giants such as Sears (the nation's largest retailer) employ approximately half a million people. Some retailers carry only one product; others carry 100,000 or more. Retailers also vary greatly as to the kind of clientele to whom they appeal, the quality and price of the products they stock, and how they promote their products.

RETAILING IMPORTANCE

We need retailing for three main reasons: its economic importance, the importance of the functions it performs, and its importance to other channel members.

Economic Importance

Retailing has a significant impact on our economy. According to the government's 1977 census of retailing there were about 1.9 million retail stores and approximately 32,800 nonstore retailers in the United States.[1] In 1982 these retailers accounted for the employment of 13.8 million people, or 12.5 percent of our labor force.[2] This does not even include workers employed in retail services.

Total retail sales equalled $1,038.8 billion in 1981.[3] However, this massive dollar volume occurred in small, individual sales. In 1979 the average size of a retail sale for department stores was $14.52, for specialty stores it

---

[1] U.S. Department of Commerce, Bureau of the Census, *Statistical Abstract of the United States, 1984*, p. 803.

[2] Ibid., pp. 407, 798.

[3] Ibid., p. 802.

was $28.77,[4] for convenience stores (7-Eleven, for example) it was under $2.00,[5] and for medium-sized supermarkets it was $10.07.[6]

Clearly, retailing represents a substantial portion of our economy and of marketing in particular. Additionally, because so many retail institutions are small, retailing provides a wide variety of opportunities for people who want to enter business on their own.

Retailing Functions

Retailing helps add value to products by creating place, time, and possession utilities. Food retailers, for example, add place utility to products by making them available at convenient locations; time utility is created by storing food until consumers want it; and possession utility is added when the product is exchanged for money.

In addition, retailers perform the assortment function of the sorting process (see Chapter 11). By stocking the products of many manufacturers, retailers provide consumers with an assortment of goods from which to choose, relieving manufacturers of the task and expense of operating outlets solely for their products.

Importance to Other Channel Members

In Chapter 11 we noted that members of a marketing channel are interdependent. Because retailers are specialists in selling to ultimate consumers, they perform an important marketing function that most manufacturers either choose not to perform or cannot, for economic reasons, perform efficiently. Manufacturers, therefore, have a vital interest in the effectiveness of the retailing system. More effective retailing tends to create more demand for manufactured products, and manufacturers of consumer goods tie their production to retail sales. Our retailing system does much to facilitate mass distribution, which paves the way for mass production.

Wholesale intermediaries have a similar interest in the performance of retailers. Over time, a wholesaler cannot sell more consumer goods than its retail customers can buy.

RETAILER CLASSIFICATIONS

Many types of retailers exist. To understand each of them, we will classify retailers by their size, their type of ownership, the breadth of their product line, their level of service, and whether or not they maintain an actual store.

---

[4] "The Good and Not-So-Good News FOR," *Stores,* October 1980, p. 21.
[5] Pamela G. Hollie, "Food is Pumping Up Net at Arco," *New York Times,* March 3, 1980, p. D5.
[6] "Grocery Industry Report for 1979," *Progressive Grocer,* April 1980, p. 130.

Figure 13-1		
Retailers Classified by Size		
Paid Employees	**Percentage of Retail Stores**	**Percentage of Retail Sales**
0–2	57	11
3–9	28	21
10–19	8	15
20 or more	7	53

SOURCE: U.S. Department of Commerce, Bureau of the Census, *Statistical Abstract of the United States, 1980*, p. 843.

Retailer Size

Most retailers are small. Figure 13-1 shows that retailers with 20 or more employees account for only 7 percent of all retail establishments, yet do 53 percent of total retail volume. At the other extreme retailers with less than 3 employees account for 57 percent of the establishments, but only 11 percent of total sales.

Small Retailers Lack Economies of Scale   Small retailers buy in smaller quantities than their large counterparts. As a result merchandise often costs them more per unit, because they cannot take advantage of quantity discounts. Often, small retailers cannot afford the high rent in major shopping centers and must settle for less desirable locations. Small retailers cannot afford to employ advertising, display, and other merchandising experts. Their big competitors can. Furthermore, small retailers do not receive as much advertising support from manufacturers as do their large competitors. Few small stores, for example, can afford to participate in cooperative advertising.

Retail Margins   Retailers generally have higher markups than manufacturers or wholesalers. Figure 13-2 lists average markups for several different types of retail establishments. The general population's awareness of the high markups in retailing produces two interesting results. First, many people are enticed into establishing a store, because they believe they will make a lot of money. Second, many consumers become critical of retailers, because they feel prices are too high. After all, these consumers argue, retailers do not change the form of the products they sell.

However, the high failure rate in retailing suggests that retailer markups in general are not inordinately high. Retailing is an intensely competitive activity. Small retail businesses often fail. In recent years even very large retailers such as W.T. Grant and Arlans have been forced to terminate operations. Actual bankruptcies that cause a loss to creditors are only part

Figure 13-2

Average Gross Margin for Selected Stores: 1978

Type of Store	Gross Margin as a Percentage of Sales
Restaurants	61.2
Home furnishings stores	41.6
Clothing stores	41.0
Department stores	39.6
Office supply stores	37.3
Hardware stores	34.7
Pharmacies	34.2
Appliance stores	27.2
Lumber and Building materials	26.8
Lodging industry	26.5
Supermarkets	22.0

SOURCE: "Expenses in Retail Business," a publication of NCR Corporation.

of the failure problem. Many retailers that cease operations do so voluntarily, simply because profits are extremely low or nonexistent. Even large retailers like Woolco may voluntarily close operations.

Retailers incur a number of costs that critics often overlook. For example, many products (food and clothing, for example) are perishable, promotion is costly, employee productivity is often low, thefts by employees and customers reduce profits, and favorable locations are costly. When you examine the net margin of retailers—gross margin minus the costs of operations—retailing presents a much different picture. Figure 13-3 shows

Figure 13-3

Net Profit Margin by Selected Retail Type

Retail Type	Median Net Profit Margin
Supermarkets	1.3%
Department stores	3.5
Discount and variety stores	2.3
Drug chains	2.8
Fast-food chains	4.2
Specialty stores	3.5

SOURCE: "Thirty-Sixth Annual Report on American Industry," *Forbes,* January 2, 1984, pp. 229–34.

these figures for large types of retailers. Clearly, retailing is not as profitable as many believe.

Type of Ownership

Four types of ownership can be distinguished in retailing: independents, corporate chains, franchises, and cooperatives. **Independent retailers**—that is, *retailers falling into the single store, independent category*—compose about 90 percent of retail institutions.[7] *A* **corporate chain** *is a group of two or more stores that is centrally owned and managed and carries the same lines of merchandise in all stores.* Although the number of corporations is smaller than the number of independents, corporations account for 79.8 percent of the sales of all retailers.[8] **Franchises** and **cooperatives** were mentioned in Chapter 11. However, these two forms of retail ownership are so prevalent, we will discuss them in greater detail later in this chapter.

Breadth of Product Line

Retailers may carry as few as one product (candy machines) or over 100,000 products. The more products a retailer carries, the wider its **product breadth**. Retailers can be categorized by breadth of product line into single-line retailers, limited-line retailers, or general-line retailers.

Single-Line Retailers   **Single-line retailers** *specialize in one product line.* Appliance stores, bakeries, automobile dealers, and certain computer stores are all examples of single-line retailers. Although they may be affiliated with one particular manufacturer, single-line retailers are usually operated as independent businesses.

Limited-Line Retailers   *Stores that carry considerable depth, but only in a few product lines, are called* **limited-line retailers**. Typically named for the product lines they carry, limited-line retailers include furniture, jewelry, clothing, and hardware stores. In the apparel field many boutiques have gained popular acceptance by offering extensive merchandise carefully selected to suit the desires of particular target markets. "Queen size," maternity, "size 9 and under," and lingerie shops are but a few examples.

Lane Bryant and Roaman's stores, both owned by the retail chain The Limited, are limited-line retailers catering to the "special size" woman. Although The Limited aims its stores at young, style-conscious college age

---

[7] Morris L. Mayer and Barry J. Mason, "Discount Department Stores Will Prosper in the '80's Despite Intense Competition," *Marketing News*, March 7, 1980, p. 6.

[8] U.S. Department of Commerce, Bureau of the Census, *Statistical Abstract of the United States, 1984*, p. 798.

and working women, it purchased Lane Bryant and Roaman's to appeal to women who are overweight but still have an eye for quality and style.[9]

General-Line Retailers   **General-line retailers** *carry many different product lines in varying depths.* They are descended from the old general stores, which still operate in some rural areas. The principal types of general-line retailers are supermarkets, department stores, discount stores, convenience stores, and catalog showrooms.

Supermarkets   A **supermarket** *is principally a food store, although it sells fast-moving nonfood items as well.* It is departmentalized and carries a full line of food products, including fresh meats, produce, dairy products, dry groceries, and such household items as paper towels, cleaning aids, and drug sundries. Supermarkets are primarily self-service stores.

The first generation of supermarkets was born during the Depression of the 1930s. Until then, small neighborhood stores did all food retailing. Due to their small volume, their general inefficiency, and the practice of selling on credit, their marketing costs were high and their gross margins

---

[9] "Limited Inc.: Expanding Its Position to Serve the Rubenesque Woman," *Business Week,* November 22, 1982, pp. 56, 58.

exceeded 30 percent. Because consumer income was exceedingly low during the Depression, the promoters of early supermarkets used price appeals to win consumer patronage. The first supermarkets were located in low-rent districts, had very inexpensive fixtures, and provided little personal service compared to the small stores. They emphasized self-service, free parking, and low prices. Most of the original supermarkets operated as independent stores. However, as the success of this form of merchandising became apparent, large food chains such as A & P and Kroger turned to supermarkets as their principal method of reaching the public.

The second generation of supermarkets dominated food marketing during the 1940s and 1950s. The earlier barnlike facilities gave way to larger stores in better locations that provided a more pleasant shopping environment. In the late 1960s a third generation of supermarkets emerged. These new stores sought out the best locations in major shopping centers. They become larger and more elaborate. The current generation of supermarket managers places increasing emphasis on quality merchandise, an attractive store environment, and courteous personnel. Price competition remains strong, and specials are heavily advertised.

Kroger, the second largest supermarket chain with 1,199 food stores in 19 states, epitomizes the new generation of supermarkets. The company surveys 250,000 consumers a year to find out what they want. There are cheese shops and delis for gourmets, beauty aids and cosmetics for the fashion-conscious, and even auto parts, pharmaceuticals, and banking services for one-stop shopping. Some test stores even have restaurants and beauty salons attached.[10] Many new supermarkets are becoming truly service-oriented retailers.

Department Stores **Department stores** *carry an unusually wide variety of merchandise*—ready-to-wear clothing, piece goods, home furnishings, appliances, housewares, and a host of other items. Most department stores provide more customer services than other retailers.

Department stores emphasize fashion goods and usually are the fashion leaders in the community. They locate in central business districts and in major shopping centers, where they occupy the anchor position.

As a rule department stores cater to a very broad segment of the total population in a community and carry merchandise for just about every pocketbook. Because of the expensive services they provide, these stores generally have a significantly higher gross margin on merchandise than most other retailing institutions.

Some department stores function strictly as independents, with no formal relationship to other retailing institutions. Others are operated by major retailing chains such as Sears, Montgomery Ward, and J.C. Penney.

---

[10] Bill Saporito, "Kroger, the New King of Supermarketing," *Fortune,* February 21, 1983, pp. 74–76, 78, 80.

Discount Stores **Discount stores**, sometimes called **mass merchandisers** because they carry a wide variety of products, are one of the most important forms of contemporary retailing. Mayer and Mason note that discount stores have five specific appeals compared to conventional department stores.[11]

1. The lowest-priced lines and the lowest prices within the market area.
2. Wide breadth and depth of consumables, such as health and beauty aids and housewares.
3. Aggregate convenience including location, parking, hours, and ease of purchase. The latter features supermarketlike front ends, total merchandise display, wide aisles, easy-to-see-and-locate merchandise groupings, shopping carts, and usually a single display floor.
4. Advertising leverage in brand names.
5. Important leverage in a changing international environment, because they buy in greater depth than the traditional department store.

Many large conventional department stores such as Dayton Hudson, Rich's, and J.C. Penney have entered the discount field. K Mart is the largest discount store chain. Central management of discount stores maintains tight inventory control over branch stores and requires branch managers to follow highly standardized policies.

Variety Stores **Variety stores** *usually sell a wide variety of low-priced, convenience products.* These stores typically carry such items as sewing paraphernalia, stationery, toys, and housewares. S.S. Kresge and F.W. Woolworth are both variety stores.

Convenience Stores Retailing is characterized by its adaptability to consumer needs. The growth of suburban communities, the ever-pressing demands on consumers' time, and the resulting need for a convenient place to "pick up just a few items" gave birth, in the 1950s, to retailing institutions called **convenience stores**.

The increasing consumer demand for fast service has been the most important factor in the rapid growth of convenience stores. During busy hours shopping in a supermarket takes more time than many consumers have to spend. Lines are usually very short in a convenience store, and many consumers do not mind paying 20 to 30 percent more for most products if they need only a handful of items. In recent years many convenience stores have added self-service gasoline to their product lines.

---

[11] Mayer and Mason, "Discount Department Stores Will Prosper in the '80's."

Catalog Showrooms Many consumers are reluctant to purchase from catalogs because they cannot inspect the products. In addition many retailers cannot afford the showroom space to carry a wide variety of products. These two facts have led to the development of the catalog showroom, which is actually a warehouse with a small showroom for customers. Shoppers come to the showroom and order from catalogs. The product is then brought forward for the customer to inspect and pay for. Because the limited showroom cost allows the retailer to carry a vast assortment of products and keep prices low, this is one of the fastest growing types of retailers.

Level of Service

Retailers are also classified by the level of service offered to their customers. **Self-service stores** display merchandise for shoppers to examine, but make no effort to sell the products or even to assist store patrons. **Full-service stores**, on the other hand, offer considerable assistance from store personnel in finding merchandise, offering information, selling the product, and even allowing limited trial of the product.

Because full service is more expensive in terms of training and the number of store personnel necessary, it is used for higher-priced products and stores. Department stores and many limited- or single-line retailers selling higher-priced or higher-margin products such as cosmetics are full-service operations.

Self-service is used to lower store operating costs and prices. Discount stores, variety stores, and supermarkets emphasize self-service.

Some stores offer a combination of both. Certain department stores have little service available in their "bargain basements," but offer considerable assistance in cosmetics or their apparel boutiques. These varying levels of service occur all in the same building.

Shiseido Cosmetics, for example, spends $600,000 a year training "consultants" to work in department stores, demonstrating and describing the use of its products. The purpose is to offer full service and information in selecting cosmetics to Shiseido customers. As Shiseido Executive Vice President Andrew E. Philip said, "A consumer is looking for service when she walks into a department or specialty store, and that's what we're going to give her."[12]

Nonstore Retailing

All the retail forms we have discussed so far offer a location where customers may come to shop. Many retailers, however, maintain no such facility. The Bureau of the Census classifies mail order houses, vending machine operators, and direct-sales firms as **nonstore retailers**. Most nonstore retailers are quite small. In 1977 nonstore retailers averaged only fourteen paid employees.[13] Nevertheless, they are interesting examples of the diverse approaches to retailing.

Mail Order Houses   **Mail order retailing** was made famous by Sears and Montgomery Ward. Although these two retailing giants still do a large volume of business by mail, they are no longer classified as mail order houses because the greater part of their sales is through stores.

Many other large retailers (especially department stores) do some catalog business, but they are not classified as mail order houses because the major part of their business also comes from direct, over-the-counter sales. Among the more numerous mail order retailers are sellers of novelties, fruits, meats, plants, organic foods, and various specialty goods.

Superficially, mail order retailing is simple. You obtain some merchandise, print a catalog or a few pages of descriptive material, acquire a mailing list, mail the promotional piece, and then, hopefully, receive orders from consumers. In practice, however, success is indeed limited. The 11,000 mail order houses in the United States in 1977 accounted for less than 1 percent of total retail sales.

---

[12] "Shiseido's New Face in the U.S.," *Business Week,* May 11, 1981, pp. 100, 105.

[13] All statistics on nonstore retailers are drawn from the *Statistical Abstract of the United States, 1984,* p. 803.

Direct-to-the-Consumer Retailing   Although **house-to-house retailing** accounts for less than 1 percent of all retail sales, its high visibility makes it a familiar form of retailing. Organizations engaged in direct selling use three general approaches to reach buyers. First, they may literally go from door to door in a neighborhood, canvassing each home. Second, they may use the "plan a party" method in which a consumer, usually a homemaker (who receives a gift or other consideration for services), gives a party for friends and neighbors at which the salesperson makes a presentation. Third, they may attempt to contact prospects over the telephone or by mail and then make calls on those from whom they get a promising response.

Many door-to-door salespeople are merchants in that they have purchased the goods they have to sell. The Fuller Brush salesperson, for example, buys merchandise from the company and then sells it to consumers. This is also the method used by Avon and many other direct-selling organizations.

In specific situations the door-to-door method has met with great success. For example, the Southwestern Company in Nashville, Tennessee, which specializes in marketing Bibles, dictionaries, and encyclopedias door-to-door, is a highly successful organization. It uses only college students as salespeople and operates only during the summer. Many people also cite the advantages of door-to-door selling as a method of training individuals in sales techniques.

Vending Machine Operators   **Vending machine operators**, also called **automatic merchandisers**, account for less than 1 percent of all retailers and less than 1 percent of total retail sales. Yet this form of nonstore retailing has become increasingly important in the marketing of such consumer goods as sandwiches, cigarettes, candy bars, and soft drinks.

In the last twenty years vending machine operators have also entered the hot food market, with such items as hamburgers and miniature casseroles. Machines offering a selection of hot meals are found in manufacturing plants, college dormitories, and other areas where large numbers of people want fast, convenient food service.

FRANCHISING

Although we discussed franchising in Chapter 11, its importance to retailing warrants expansion here. Many small retailers fail or achieve only mediocre results due to ineffective management. This and lack of knowledge hurt the small retailer more than lack of incentive. Franchising seeks to overcome this problem by combining the advantages of chain-store operations with those of a relatively small, independent business.

Definitions and Background

A **franchise** *is a right or license to do business. A* **franchisor** *is a business or an organization that grants this right. A* **franchisee** *is a business or an individual that buys or obtains this right.*

Although franchising has become a household word since the 1950s, it has been a popular way of doing business for much longer. The automotive industry was one of the first to make widespread use of franchising. Virtually all automobile dealers are franchised. Most gasoline service stations are owned by franchisees, not by the petroleum producers. What is new about franchising is its application to the distribution of an extremely wide variety of products in different industries. Fast foods, income-tax advisory services, motels, computer schools, and clothing stores are just a few of the hundreds of types of businesses that are franchised. In 1983 there were a total of 465,000 franchised establishments totaling 39.9 percent of all retail sales.[14]

Fast-food companies such as those specializing in fried chicken, roast beef, fish and chips, hamburgers, and pizza are among the most popular franchise systems, yet the fast-food industry accounts for only about 2 percent of total sales by franchise concerns. What is often overlooked in totaling up franchise sales is the enormous volume of business done by service stations, motel chains such as Holiday Inn, and automobile dealerships.

Setting Up a Franchise Operation

The *modus operandi* for setting up a franchise system is generally as follows:

1. The franchisor comes up with an idea for doing business that can be duplicated easily in many outlets. These ideas range from new ways to make and serve hamburgers to new ways to operate a hotel.
2. Pilot projects are established to test the system and identify and solve technical and promotional problems. If the result is a marketing formula that has a good chance of success, the franchisor goes ahead with its plans.
3. Once it is convinced that the system will work, the franchisor begins to sell franchises to franchisees.
4. The franchisor concentrates on helping its franchisees succeed and on selling additional franchises.

---

[14] Ibid., p. 806.

The Franchise Agreement

Although arrangements vary, the most common form of agreement between franchisor and franchisee is as follows:

1. The franchisor charges the franchisee a flat fee for the right to buy and operate the franchise. The amount of this fee partly depends on the profits to be made and the popularity of the franchisor.
2. The usual agreement requires the franchisee to pay the franchisor a percentage of the gross income from the operation of the franchise.
3. The franchisee agrees to purchase all or a major portion of its supplies and merchandise from the franchisor.
4. The franchisee is frequently required to pay either a flat fee or a percentage of gross receipts into an advertising fund, which is used to promote the system.

In addition the franchisee usually must agree to follow closely the merchandising and other operational guidelines set by the franchisor.

Franchisors generally promise the franchisee assistance in finding a location, a proven formula for doing business, help with advertising, the use of a nationally or regionally known name, architectural blueprints for the outlet, and identification materials such as store signs and placemats.

Most successful franchising systems have a set formula for doing business and permit few, if any, deviations from this standardized approach. Some organizations in the fast-food field require franchisees to attend schools in which every detail of the business is explained. Inspectors employed by the franchisors visit the franchisees regularly to be sure that they are applying the merchandising formula agreed on.

Controlled "Independence" and Franchising

One of the major attractions of franchising for many franchisees is the promise, expressed or implied, that they will be in business for themselves, enjoy the freedom of being independent businesspeople, and at the same time have the advantages of a corporate chain. How accurate is this picture? Al Lapin, Jr., founder of the International House of Pancakes Restaurants, had this to say: "That independent businessman idea is misunderstood. Maybe in Samoa you can find one. A man becomes a franchisee because he wants to belong. If he tells me he doesn't like to take orders . . . I won't sign him up."[15]

---

[15] Charles G. Burck, "Franchising's Troubled Dream World," *Fortune*, March 1970, pp. 116–121, 148, 150, 152.

Experience indicates that franchising systems that require close adherence to proven policies do much better than those that permit franchisees to establish their own policies.

Criticisms of Franchising

Some estimates show that as many as 93 percent of all franchise outlets that were in the United States in 1975 were started after 1954. Any business system that grows so fast is apt to produce a large number of failures as well as certain business practices that are unethical, illegal, or unfair.

Most criticisms of franchising are directed toward franchisors. They have been accused of making overly large promises and, on occasion, of exploiting franchisees. In some instances franchisors have made money selling franchises on the basis of "enormous" business potential, but then failed to help franchisees convert the promise into revenue.

The following specific franchisor practices have come under criticism:

1. Canceling franchise agreements for minor contract infringements.
2. Limiting the right of the franchisee to transfer ownership of the franchise.
3. Charging franchisees excessive fees and demanding royalty payments out of proportion to sales.
4. Requiring franchisees to buy merchandise, supplies, and equipment from franchisors at prices above what the franchisees would have to pay elsewhere.
5. Demanding control of the selling price regardless of local conditions.
6. Putting intense pressure on franchisees to expand.

Critics of franchising argue, probably with considerable validity, that most franchise agreements are one-sided and favor the franchisor. Nevertheless, it is likely that franchising will continue to be an important method for establishing retail outlets in the future. In many cases the advantages received by the franchisees sufficiently outweigh their loss of control. As long as this is true, franchising will continue to grow.

COOPERATIVES

The rapid growth of chain stores in the 1920s forced many independent merchants to close their doors. The chains, with their superior buying power, better management, and strong consumer identification, had competitive advantages that made many small retailers and wholesalers wonder how they could fight back.

One result of this competitive struggle was the evolution of **cooperatives**, sometimes called **voluntary chains**, a form of retailing that combines a central organization and independent but closely allied retailers. These groups behave to some extent like chain operations and, to the general public, may appear to be chains. In reality, they are not.

Cooperatives came into being when independent stores recognized the disadvantages of competing with corporate chains. They could not buy merchandise in large enough quantities to get the most favorable prices and terms, they could not afford big advertising budgets, they could not apply professional management techniques, and their brands were not as well known. They needed a system whereby they could combine their purchasing power to give them a price advantage, promote the same brands, share management know-how, and engage in joint advertising.

Types of Cooperatives

Two main types of voluntary groups emerged: **wholesaler-sponsored groups** and **retailer-sponsored groups**. In the first case a wholesaler takes the initiative in establishing the group, recognizing that its survival and profitability depend on the success of the retail outlets that buy from it. The wholesaler, typically, invites retail customers to enter into an agreement whereby they promise to buy most (if not all) of their merchandise from it, use a common name, promote common brands, contribute to a joint advertising fund, and standardize their operations.

The retailer-sponsored voluntary group results when a group of retailers, recognizing their common problems, elect to set up their own warehouse facilities, engage in joint buying, and adopt a common name and other identifying symbols. Members of the group frequently use joint advertising and exchange ideas on policies and promotions.

Wholesaler-sponsored groups such as IGA and Super Valu are far more important numerically and in terms of sales than retailer-sponsored groups. Most cooperatives are in the food field, although they are common in the drug and hardware industries, also. In the food field the total sales of the cooperatives exceed the total sales of the corporate chains.

RETAIL LOCATION PATTERNS

Because most retailers deal with consumers face to face, store location is of primary importance. Retailers may, within the limits prescribed by various zoning boards, choose where their outlets will go. Tradition and evolution play a part in location decisions, as does the degree of sophistication attained by the retail store owner or corporate leadership.

Location can make or break retailers, especially those who sell convenience goods such as food, gasoline, groceries, and carry-out items. It is only slightly less important to retailers of shopping and specialty goods. In some cases location—being in the right place—is as important as good service, appropriate merchandise, and effective merchandising techniques.

Because the value of a location may change over time, even established retailers must reevaluate their positions periodically. Factors beyond the merchant's control may affect the value of a location. Population shifts from the central city to suburbia, new highways, changes in the type of resident in the neighborhood, and changes in the types of commercial establishments in the immediate area all influence the continuing appropriateness of a location.

Most retailers have a choice of locating in one or two major types of shopping areas. Every community of any size includes both "unplanned" and "planned" shopping districts. We will examine both types to see what factors marketing management must consider in making a location decision.

Unplanned Shopping Areas

Unplanned shopping areas are concentrations of stores that grew as a result of independent decisions by individual store owners. They reflect no coordinated effort to allocate space, optimize the number of stores handling various types of merchandise, provide parking facilities, or unify the architectural design. Most downtown shopping districts, so-called secondary shopping areas, and street or roadside stores fall in this category.

Downtown Shopping Districts Downtown shopping districts that began near the original center of the community are common to almost every town and city. Because they grew with the community, new merchants located as near the center as possible, and little or nothing was done to determine the optimum number of stores carrying each kind of merchandise, to lay out streets and design traffic patterns convenient for shoppers, or to standardize the architecture of the various buildings in the district.

Traffic congestion, the population shift to suburbia, and the failure of some downtown merchants to keep up the appearance of their stores has led, in many cases, to a general exodus of major retailers. The result has been a decrease in the importance of a downtown store location. Many cities, such as San Diego and Detroit, are taking steps to upgrade the appearance of older shopping districts, provide additional parking, and ease traffic congestion, in an effort to keep existing merchants in the area and to lure new merchants into the downtown area.

Secondary Shopping Districts Most American neighborhoods surround a collection of retail establishments that grew up as a result of the rezoning of residential areas to permit commercial activity. It was advantageous for retailers to be near other stores because of the increased incentive for consumers to shop in the area. These secondary shopping districts are generally characterized by a haphazard arrangement of stores and on-street parking. There is more emphasis on convenience goods than in downtown shopping districts, although clothing stores, florists, shoe and shoe-repair stores, launderers, and dry cleaners are common. Since the advent of planned shopping centers, secondary shopping districts have decreased in importance.

Street or Roadside Stores   Small groups of retail establishments located in a row, usually along one side of a street, constitute a third type of unplanned shopping district. Composed perhaps of a sandwich shop or small restaurant, a service station, a small grocery store, and one to five additional stores, these districts are on the increase in many cities due to burgeoning apartment complexes, which create high population density in a small area. Again, all arrangements for the location, architecture, and concentration of store types are made by individual proprietors, whether independent owners or chains.

Planned Shopping Centers

Historically, merchants locating in unplanned shopping districts could do little about parking, the number of other similar stores, and other factors that affect the value of location. It was not until the 1950s and '60s that planned shopping centers, which took these problems into consideration, became a significant trend.

The derivation of the term "planned shopping center" is obvious: The site, the number, type, and architecture of the stores, and many other aspects of the center are *planned*. Usually, a real-estate development company takes the initiative in building and managing a center. It then leases space to appropriate retail establishments.

Three types of planned shopping centers can be identified: (1) small neighborhood shopping centers, (2) medium-sized community shopping centers, and (3) large regional shopping centers.

Neighborhood Shopping Centers   Shopping centers are usually classified according to their size or the number of consumers they can serve. Small neighborhood centers have 30,000 to 100,000 square feet of selling space and are usually designed to serve a market of 7,000 to 20,000 people. Often, the leading tenant is a supermarket or drugstore.

Community Shopping Centers   Middle-sized planned shopping centers have between 100,000 and 300,000 square feet of selling space and are designed to serve populations of 20,000 to 100,000 consumers. A variety store or a small department store is usually the leading tenant, and there is more emphasis on shopping goods than in the neighborhood center.

Regional Shopping Centers   Regional shopping centers are designed to serve a large number of consumers, up to a million. They range in size from 300,000 to 1,500,000 square feet and provide a wide variety of convenience, shopping, and specialty goods. The primary attraction is generally a branch of one or more of the community's leading department stores.

Advantages of Planned Shopping Centers

The center concept has a number of key advantages. Among other things a planned shopping center provides (1) a mix of stores that will attract the maximum number of shoppers to the center; (2) free off-street parking; (3) controlled architecture; (4) standard promotional policies and store hours; and (5) a location convenient for large numbers of consumers.

Controlled Competition   Only a certain number of stores, often only one offering each type of merchandise, may locate in a planned shopping center. The aim of the developer is to have the right combination of stores to attract the maximum number of customers. In unplanned shopping districts it is common to find either too many competitors or too little variety.

Free Parking   Traffic congestion has reached such proportions in many cities that on-street parking is not allowed in some areas. Simultaneously, land values have increased to such an extent that it is often too expensive to devote large areas to parking. A major advantage of planned shopping centers is their ability to provide adequate free parking for customers.

Attractive Architectural Plan   Although the term "attractive" is relative, most planned shopping centers reflect a carefully considered, architecturally sound building plan. Because all the stores in the center are usually constructed simultaneously or within a period of a few years, there is no danger that one store's image will suffer because a store nearby is old and deteriorating.

Centralized Control   All tenants in the center, which is managed by the developer, are subject to certain rules regarding fair competition and the maintenance of the center's image. Policing of promotional procedures (an activity often engaged in cooperatively by center occupants) and specific arrangements for the upkeep of the premises free individual retailers of these important responsibilities.

Concentration of Consumer Traffic   The primary goal of every planned center is to attract a maximum number of shoppers. A side benefit is that all traffic within the center is ostensibly there for the purpose of buying. This is not so in downtown areas, where much of the traffic consists of people going to or from work.

Disadvantages of Planned Shopping Centers

Despite the many advantages of planned shopping centers, we should also consider some of their negative aspects.

Poor Planning   Although well-planned shopping centers are a definite spur to the progressive development of retailing in an area, others are often poorly planned, designed, maintained, and managed. Some are either too large or too small for the market area they hoped to serve. Occa-

Shopping centers proliferated after World War II. By 1955 there were 300. Two decades later an estimated 18,500 had been constructed. Forty percent of them were less than five years old. Today shopping centers comprise approximately 7 percent of all commercial construction.

Centers are classified as neighborhood (the smallest), community, or regional (the largest), depending on the size of the center and the trade area served. Regional centers, which compete most actively with downtown shopping districts, feature at least one major department store and a full complement of shopping and specialty goods outlets. Consumers may drive from 20 to 40 miles to shop there. By contrast, a neighborhood center is usually located within 10 minutes of the consumer and offers convenience goods of a fairly routine nature.

Reilly's Law of Retail Gravitation demonstrates that consumers will drive to the nearest big place (town, store, shopping center) for their shopping.[*] Thus, convenience often supersedes price and selection when the consumer decides where to shop. Downtown areas find it increasingly difficult to compensate the consumer for the hassles of crowding and too few parking spaces with their advantages of variety, quality, and lower prices.

Shopping center innovations have not ceased, however. Not content with a market share ranging from 35 to 65 percent, some shopping centers are revising their tenant mix by making such additions as offices for doctors and other professionals as well as branch libraries, giving consumers even more reason to patronize the centers. In a move to bring shoppers back to downtown areas, many cities, such as Baltimore and Chicago, are even building inner-city malls.[†]

Another innovation is the vertical shopping center. In downtown Chicago, for example, WaterTower Place is a multistory, multitenant shopping center. The success of this innovation will no doubt be seen more in the future in other cities where costs of a sprawling shopping center are prohibitive.

[*] William J. Reilly, "Method for the Study of Retail Relationships," *Research Monograph*, 4, Bulletin No. 2944; (Austin, Texas: University of Texas Press, 1929).

[†] "The Shopping Mall Goes Urban," *Business Week,* December 13, 1982, pp. 50, 52; and Frederick C. Klein, "Downtown Chicago's State Street Mall Fails to Revive Area's Stores, Disappointing Many," *Wall Street Journal,* May 9, 1983, pp. 33, 39.

sionally, two centers may be located so close together that neither can achieve adequate sales. In other cases a center is built prematurely, before there is sufficient population in the area and, thus, goes out of business before sales can develop.

Limited Opportunities for Unproven Retailers   To protect their financial investment, shopping center developers usually lease to tenants who are proven magnets for consumer traffic. Thus, the small or new merchant whose financial rating is less secure may lose out to the retailer who is widely known.

High Rents Because shopping centers are generally located on prime real estate and allocate a large portion of the total land area to nonrevenue-producing parking facilities, developers seek to recover their investment by charging high rents. The cost of space is usually based on a minimum guaranteed rental plus a percentage of sales, a cost too high for many retailers.

Despite these disadvantages the trend toward planned shopping centers is not likely to stop. The continuing growth of the suburbs, our increasing dependence on automobiles, and the relatively higher incomes of suburban residents compared to many inner-city inhabitants all prompt merchants to welcome the opportunity to locate in a planned shopping center.

RETAIL STRATEGY

Like any other company, retailers must plan their marketing strategy based on their target markets. The place variable is determined by location. Promotion decisions are much like those of any other company. However, much of the marketing strategy for retailing is determined by store *image, atmosphere,* and *merchandising.*

Store Image

To develop a store image, both shopper and store characteristics must be understood. Shopper characteristics include demographics, psychographics, life style, behavior, and perceptions, whereas store characteristics include clientele, location, promotional emphasis, integrity, convenience, and economy.[16]

To develop a store image strategy, a retailer must determine the desired characteristics of its target markets and match its image to those characteristics. K Mart has long been successful as a retailer catering to the price-conscious target market. Its advertisements ("the savings place"), store design, and limited-service orientation have all enhanced an image of a low-priced, economical place to shop. In an effort to capture more middle- and high-income customers, however, K Mart is introducing new stores that not only carry the company's traditional staples, but also carry de-

---

[16] Edgar R. Pessemier, "Store Image and Positioning," *Journal of Retailing,* Spring 1980, pp. 96–97.

signer clothes, feature wider counters, and sport a more expensive look.[17] The strategy is to keep the "savings place" image, but at the same time project a "quality" image in order to expand its target markets.

Store Atmosphere

A more specific part of store image is its atmosphere. Kotler defines atmosphere, or atmospherics, as the conscious designing of a store's space to create emotional effects that enhance the probability consumers will buy.[18] An obvious example of atmosphere occurs in mass merchandise retail stores with bakeries whose exhaust vents are located above the front door. The first thing a customer smells on entering the store is fresh-baked goods. Many stores use the distinct odors of prepared food or perfume to enhance sales.[19]

Many stores try to keep noise levels low and minimize the sense of crowding. A noisy, crowded store encourages shoppers to finish shopping quickly and leave. Quiet, expansive stores encourage browsing.[20]

As with image, stores should try to match their atmosphere to the characteristics desired by their target market. In the earlier K Mart example, the company was looking for ways to encourage shoppers to browse longer, something its economy-minded shoppers were not doing. Therefore, the new stores have round clothing racks to encourage inspection, jewelry displays rather than vending machines at the entrance, wider counters, and more attractive shelfing—all to give a less crowded, casual atmosphere. K Mart Chairman Bernard M. Fauber crisply summed up the new atmosphere strategy: K Mart wants to "get the customer to stay longer and buy more."[21]

Store Merchandising

Merchandising involves carrying the right mixture of products in the retail store. The "right mixture" includes the products consumers want and expect in the store and that generate an acceptable profit for the retailer. Again, the image the retailer wishes to project influences merchandising. If a high-quality image is desired, the retailer will carry only the finest quality

---

[17] Jeremy Main, "K Mart's Plan to be Born Again, Again," *Fortune,* September 21, 1981, pp. 74–85; and Charles W. Stevens, "K-Mart, Beset by Steady Drop in Earnings, Tries to Attract Higher-Income Shoppers," *Wall Street Journal,* August 10, 1982, p. 29.

[18] Philip Kotler, "Atmospherics as a Marketing Tool," *Journal of Retailing,* Winter 1973–74, p. 50.

[19] Edward M. Tuber, "Why Do People Shop?" *Journal of Marketing,* October 1972, p. 47.

[20] Gilbert D. Harrell and Michael D. Hutt, "Crowding in Retail Stores," *MSU Business Topics,* Winter 1976, p. 34.

[21] Main, "K Mart's Plan."

and brand names in each line. If an economical image is desired, the retailer will stock good-quality, but low-priced products.

Continuing the K Mart example to the area of merchandising, note that the company's efforts to upgrade its image have prompted it to merchandise not only good quality off-brand items, but also such prestige brands as Izod sports shirts, Puma running shoes, Seiko watches, Minolta and Pentax cameras, and Chanel and Givenchy perfumes.[22] As this example has illustrated, retail image, atmosphere, and merchandising must all be coordinated to meet the wants and desires of the target markets.

RETAILING IN THE FUTURE

Retailing has changed a great deal in this century. Many of these changes still continue today. In addition several characteristics of our society are responsible for the creation of additional changes in retailing, as we will discuss below.

---

[22] Main, "K Mart's Plan."

The Wheel of Retailing

The term *wheel of retailing* refers to what happens when retailing is entered by innovators whose primary appeal is low price. The wheel is said to turn, because the innovators usually tend afterward to upgrade their stores, add more services, and place less emphasis on price as the main attraction. In other words as a form of retailing matures, its practices become more traditional, more service-oriented, and less price oriented.[23]

Numerous examples of the wheel of retailing can be cited. The first supermarkets had simple, inexpensive fixtures, were located in low-rent areas, and provided no frills. Over time, as the wheel turned, they added various services, sought prime locations and their costs of doing business increased. The history of discount stores followed a similar pattern. Early stores emphasized price above all else, and services were very limited. As this form of retailing evolved, however, discounters gradually moved away from almost total emphasis on price toward an ever-increasing variety of services, which, of course, increased prices. As each retail form moves toward more service, invariably another retail competitor enters the scene offering low prices and, thus, starts through the wheel again.

Scrambled Merchandising

The trend toward **scrambled merchandising**, *a policy of carrying many unrelated items in one store,* often on a nondepartmentalized basis, began in the 1950s and shows no signs of reversing. Today the *food store* is usually a misnomer, for we expect to find drug sundries, hardware items, magazines, school supplies, records, garden supplies, and even clothing in many such stores. A large *drugstore* may be a combination stationery shop, restaurant, small-hardware outlet, music store, patent medicine shop, and toy store. A recent survey of drug and discount stores (supposedly nonfood stores) found that 97 percent carried beverages, 95 percent had snacks, and 70 percent stocked food items.[24] Clearly, the trend is toward carrying whatever sells.

Vertically Integrated Retailers

Many corporate and cooperative retailers operate so many stores that they can realize considerable quantity discounts if they place orders for all stores at one time and have them delivered to one location. For this reason many large retailers such as K Mart, Sears, J.C. Penney, and Kroger run their

---

[23] Stanley C. Hollander, "The Wheel of Retailing," *Journal of Marketing*, July 1960, p. 37.

[24] "Survey Finds Most Nonfood Outlets Stock Food Products," *Marketing News*, May 28, 1982, p. 9.

L'eggs Versus No Nonsense Panty Hose

The marketing battle between L'eggs and No Nonsense is one of the most interesting of the second half of this century.

In the late 1960s, Hanes, an old line company in the hosiery field, became aware of a sizeable market for hosiery in food, drug, and discount stores. Thus, it decided to develop a line of hosiery for this market.

Hanes undertook an intensive research program to get a focus on its target market. Market research indicated that (1) the market was fragmented with over 600 brands; (2) price was featured in promotion, not quality or location; and (3) the retailers' return was less than for most food and drug products. Research conducted among consumers indicated that (1) hosiery sold in supermarkets and drug stores was low quality; (2) there was little brand allegiance; and (3) many women returned to department stores and clothing shops to buy hosiery.

Hanes decided to enter the convenience store market. The package designer came up with the idea of an egg-shaped package. The color of the package designated the style and color of the hose.

Next, Hanes commissioned the design of a display, which had to use minimal floor space. The result was the L'eggs Boutique, which measured 2 feet in diameter and 6 feet in height and could display 24 dozen pairs of pantyhose.

Hanes decided to stress quality rather than price in its introductory program. L'eggs entered the market at $1.39, or about 30¢ more than most of the competition.

It is always difficult to get retailers to stock a new product, because it requires display space and ties up capital. The display unit created by Hanes overcame the space problem. To overcome the money-tied-up-in-inventory problem, Hanes elected to sell on consignment. Under the consignment arrangement, the retailer did not have to invest in inventory or fixtures. Hanes did everything except ring up the sale at the cash register. A 24-dozen Boutique saved the retailer $350 in inventory cost and was estimated to produce $1,350 in profit per year.

Hanes spent $10 million in its introductory promotion campaign, which was about double the amount spent on advertising by the entire hosiery industry. Furthermore, Hanes spent additional millions on introductory coupons and other forms of sales promotion.

Hanes also had a new idea for product distribution. L'eggs sales personnel delivered L'eggs to the stores, making certain that a full range of products was in stock and that the display was attractive and clean.

L'eggs had an excellent turnover and produced revenue per square foot seven times greater than the average for all products in retail stores.

In the meantime the hosiery industry had been watching Hanes' operations. Kayser Roth entered the market in 1973 with No Nonsense and became the major competitor against L'eggs.

Kayser Roth adopted similar marketing tactics to Hanes, but to differentiate their strategy from Hanes, Kayser Roth developed a more durable product by using 7 filaments of flat knit yarn compared with L'eggs construction of 4 filaments.

To combat the shape of the egg, Kayser Roth developed the resealable pouch that could have a second use as a container for buttons, screws, or other purposes. To combat the L'eggs Boutique display, Kayser Roth developed a similar but larger display stand of $77\frac{1}{2}$ inches, capable of holding 440 pairs of pantyhose.

To combat L'eggs' price, Kayser Roth opted to charge the consumer less and give retailers a higher gross margin (45 percent versus L'eggs 35 percent). To combat L'eggs' promotion, which subtly stressed "L'eggs will make you sexually more appealing," Kayser Roth stressed a more rational appeal—"No Nonsense fit, No Nonsense comfort, No Nonsense price."

To drive these points home, Kayser Roth developed an aggressive advertising campaign comparing No Nonsense with L'eggs. No Nonsense commercials and print ads emphasized that No Nonsense was a better constructed product and cost less than L'eggs.

In 1975 Hanes sued Kayser Roth for "deceptive advertising." It asked for a permanent injunction and $20,000,000 in damages because of the Kayser Roth campaign. Kayser Roth did not feel Hanes had a good case, but at the time the company wanted to merge with Gulf and Western and did not want a lot of negative publicity. Accordingly, Kayser Roth agreed not to mention L'eggs in any future advertising. The law suit was dropped.

Both companies have expanded their product line. Hanes introduced L'eggs Sheer Energy and Sheer Elegance brands to attract the department store hosiery shopper to the boutique. Kayser Roth recently brought out its Ultra Sense brand to compete with the L'eggs counterpart.

As of 1985 L'eggs and No Nonsense were still the main brands of pantyhose sold in supermarkets, drug stores, and other convenience stores, respectively accounting for about 17 and 12 percent of the hosiery market. What future strategies they will follow is in question, but certainly each will try to expand its share of the market at the other's expense.

own wholesale operations, as do cooperatives such as Super Valu, True Value, and IGA.

In many cases this vertical integration has given the retailer enough buying clout to become the channel leader. In the case of vertically integrated Sears, the negotiating power of the number-one retailer in the country is obviously much greater than that of a one-store independent retailer. The cost savings and negotiating power that accompany vertical integration will probably encourage retailers to continue this trend in the future.

Leased Retailing Departments

A long-term but increasingly important retailing trend is **leased retailing** operations. Retailing is both a highly specialized and an intensely competitive activity. To compete effectively, many retailers, especially department stores and mass merchandisers, elect to lease departments to specialists, who presumably can operate them more efficiently. Drug departments, beauty salons, and restaurants are frequently leased operations. More and more, department stores are also leasing such traditionally independent departments as dental, financial, and legal offices.

Under the usual lease arrangement the retailer (the lessor) leases a department to a specialist (the lessee) who agrees to operate it and pay the lessor either a percentage of gross receipts or a flat sum at regular intervals. The lessor typically agrees to provide the usual store services, such as credit and delivery, to customers of the leased department. Usually the leased department is so well integrated with the overall store operation that the consumer does not even know it is leased.

Both parties stand to benefit from the arrangement, directly and indirectly. The lessor-retailer receives compensation from the lessee and also benefits financially from additional sales resulting from the increased store traffic attracted by the leased department. Furthermore, the lessor-retailer achieves these benefits without committing store personnel and capital to the department or incurring the risks associated with operating it.

The lessee-retailer benefits from the store traffic generated by the lessor-retailer's other operations, the regular services provided by the lessor-retailer; and the use of the space and physical facilities supplied by the lessor-retailer.

Retailing Services

Increasingly, retail stores are going into direct competition with service establishments by marketing intangibles. Examples include insurance, such as Allstate by Sears; repair services, such as those for jewelry, appliances, and shoes; beauty salons, health spas, and cosmetic clinics; interior decorating and rug cleaning; tool rentals; and custom-made clothing. Even dental-service franchise chains are increasing dramatically. Such chains as Dental Health, United Dental Network, and Omnidentix Systems use standard layouts, management practices, and advertising just like any other retail franchise organization.[25]

In-Home Retailing

A combination of factors—traffic congestion in major cities, crowded stores, more demands on consumers' time, more dual career families, and more consumers working different shifts—has helped increase the importance of in-home retailing. It is simply easier in many cases to examine a catalog, find the desired item, telephone the store (which often accepts phone orders 24 hours a day, 7 days a week), and either have the product delivered or pick it up at a nearby distribution outlet.

General merchandise retailers such as Sears and J.C. Penney have led the development of catalog retailing, although department stores and mass merchandisers also use it extensively. Telephone catalog selling offers many advantages to retailers. They can keep the store "open" 24 hours a day, they do not need sales personnel, can process orders around the clock, need not display merchandise, can deliver products in their original cartons, and can store goods in warehouses, where space costs less than in stores. Some of the larger retailing institutions use computers and automated conveyor systems to handle such orders, reducing costs and speeding delivery.

However, consumers are unable to physically inspect the goods prior to the purchase, which results in a returned-goods problem of considerable proportions. To overcome this problem, retailers are placing increased emphasis on clear, precise descriptions of products in their catalogs.

In a more recent development some cities utilize their cable television system to let consumers shop from home, using two-way televisions linked to the cable system.[26] Called *videotex*, product and price lists can be accessed for member stores and orders placed from the comfort of the consumer's home. Large retailers and manufacturers such as Sears, J.C. Penney, Grand Union, General Mills, Johnson & Johnson, ITT, Federated Department Stores, and Dayton–Hudson are all experimenting with videotex systems, which give consumers access to computer and TV hookups with text and cartoonlike graphics. Services include banking, shopping, and travel and entertainment reservations.[27]

---

[25] Myron Magnet, "Here Comes McDentists," *Fortune*, February 21, 1983, pp. 135, 136, 138, 139.

[26] Larry J. Rosenberg and Elizabeth C. Hirschman, "Retailing Without Stores," *Harvard Business Review*, July–August, 1980, pp. 103–12.

[27] Bill Abrams, "Electronic Shopping Awaiting Consumer, Corporate Support," *Wall Street Journal*, June 16, 1983, p. 33.

Although such systems are becoming more prevalent, it is doubtful whether in-home shopping will ever eliminate retail stores. A survey of 2,163 households revealed that only 10 percent were interested in having a two-way television system for in-home retailing, because most consumers like to see the product before they buy.[28]

Shopping is still largely a social function. People like to see the product, touch it, and even observe others in the process of shopping. Says William Boehm, director of economic research for Kroger, "We are social creatures. We do things in part because we enjoy social interaction."[29] Given the sociological phenomenon of shopping, in-home shopping will not bring about the demise of the more traditional retail stores and shopping centers in the foreseeable future. However, it will provide a new aspect to the already varied retailing scene.

SUMMARY

- Retailing is a major source of employment. It creates the economic utilities of time, place, and possession, provides the sorting process function of assortment, and provides the valuable customer contact for manufacturers and wholesalers.
- We can classify retailers by their size, type of ownership, breadth of product line, level of service, and whether or not they maintain a store.
- Although most retailers are independents, the majority of sales occur through corporate chains.
- Single-line retailers specialize in retailing one basic product. Limited-line retailers carry only a part of a broader merchandise line. General-line retailers carry many different products and lines.
- A supermarket is principally a departmentalized food store and operates on a self-service basis.
- Department stores carry an unusually broad variety of merchandise and provide more services than other types of retailers.
- Discount stores, or mass merchandisers, feature low prices as their basic appeal and operate on a self-service basis.
- Variety stores sell a wide variety of low-priced convenience products.
- Convenience stores provide fast service and charge significantly higher prices than supermarkets.

---

[28] "Only 10% of Consumers Interested in Shopping at Home via 2-Way TV," *Marketing News,* May 29, 1981, pp. 1,3.

[29] Bill Abrams, "Electronic Shopping is Called Imminent, but Doubts Persist," *Wall Street Journal,* June 23, 1983, p. 33.

- Catalog showrooms offer a wide selection while keeping show-room costs low.
- The major types of nonstore retailing are mail order houses, direct-to-the-consumer retailers, and vending machine operators.
- Franchising attempts to combine the advantages of chain store operations with those of small independent business.
- Voluntary groups conduct a form of retailing that combines a central organization and several independent retailers. Some are sponsored by wholesalers and some by retailers.
- Unplanned shopping centers are concentrations of stores that grew as a result of independent decisions by individual store owners. Most downtown shopping districts, secondary shopping districts, and street or roadside stores are unplanned shopping centers.
- Planned shopping centers are planned in the sense that the site, number of stores, architecture, and other aspects of the center are predetermined.
- Retailing strategies include store image, atmosphere, and merchandising.
- Current trends in retailing include scrambled merchandising, vertically integrated retailing, leased retailing departments, retailing services, and in-home retailing.

DISCUSSION QUESTIONS

1. Why is retailing important?
2. Why do people criticize the "high" gross margins of retailers? What is wrong with these criticisms?
3. What are some distinguishing characteristics of single-line retailers? Limited-line retailers? General-line retailers? Supermarkets? Department stores? Discount stores? Convenience stores? Catalog showrooms?
4. Is direct-to-the-consumer retailing likely to be more or less important a decade from now?
5. What does a franchise agreement typically require of the franchisee and the franchisor?
6. How do cooperatives work?
7. Are unplanned shopping centers likely to exist after another 20 years? Why?
8. Can a planned shopping center become too large? Why or why not?
9. What new retailing trends and innovations do you feel are emerging in the late twentieth century?
10. Explain the wheel of retailing.

APPLICATION EXERCISES

1. Some observers believe that cable television, together with home computers, will greatly increase shopping at home. Consumers will simply punch certain numbers, view selected products on the TV screen, and make their purchase decisions. In a brief report evaluate the potential of this form of retailing.
2. Review three recent editions of the *Wall Street Journal*, looking for advertisements for franchise opportunities. What types of franchise are for sale? After reading the ads, what do you feel are the five most important questions a prospective franchisee should ask before purchasing a franchise?

CASE 13

J.C. Penney Creates an Affluent Atmosphere[30]

J.C. Penney, long the place to shop for paint, hardware, and lawn and garden supplies, is changing its image. Over a five-year span Penney will spend $1 billion refurbishing and redesigning its 450 largest stores. It is replacing linoleum with parquet floors and chocolate-colored carpeting, nearly doubling aisle widths, and adding partitions to suggest each department is a separate boutique. Glass display cases now show off jewelry where paint used to be. Penney brand name towels are arranged by colors to give a rainbow impression. Live plants decorate the escalators, mirrors cover each column, and accents have been added to brighten everything. All is designed to appeal to a more up-scale clientele.

The massive refurbishing is an ongoing reaction by Penney to the profit squeeze it is experiencing from competition. Department stores were taking the high end of its business, whereas mass discounters were capturing the low end. Penney decided to go after the more profitable high end. Penney's shoppers today will find Harris Tweed coats, labels such as Jordache, Levi Strauss, and Adolpho, and a Halston apparel line in the women's section.

However, it is not a strategy without danger. As a New York retailer observed, "I think they're going to try to compete with department stores, but their biggest problem is their Penney name. It's going to be a tough one (to overcome)." Says the chief executive of a large retail chain, "They're making a wise move in strengthening their apparel, but if they're thinking of going 'upscale,' that is infinitely more difficult. The worst sin a merchant can commit is to try to be all things to all people."

---

[30] Claudia Ricci, "J.C. Penney Goes After Affluent Shoppers, But Store's New Image May Be Hard to Sell," *Wall Street Journal*, February 15, 1983, p. 35.

The new strategy has disgruntled some previous customers. "I was going to buy a garbage can," said one shopper at the Atlanta Perimeter Mall Penney store. "They used to be in the garden shop over there," she said, pointing to the new children's apparel shop. Also surprised that the fabric shop is being phased out, she concluded with, "I guess I'm going to be shopping here less."

Even some of the new target customers are not easily won over. As one affluent shopper put it, "I like the wood, I like the parquet, I like the plants, but they still don't have quite enough merchandise to have a good selection."

Atlanta store personnel, however, have noticed an increase in affluent customers frequenting Penney's. Especially pleasing is the fact that upscale department store personnel are beginning to "shop" Penney to check prices and selection. Sales gains at all of the remodeled stores are prompting Penney to speed up its overhaul.

Is performance better than expected? "Obviously," says Penney's chairman Donald V. Seibert, " or we wouldn't be moving the way we are with the rest of our stores."

Discussion Questions

1. Identify the key elements in Penney's new image, atmosphere, and merchandising. How would you characterize its old image, atmosphere, and merchandising?
2. Do you think Penney should make such a drastic shift in its target markets or merely upgrade its merchandise?
3. What questions would you want to ask target customers before answering Question 2?

14 Physical Distribution

STUDY OBJECTIVES

After studying this chapter, you should be able to

1. Define physical distribution and physical distribution service.
2. Explain the importance of physical distribution to companies and to the economy.
3. Discuss the objectives of physical distribution.
4. Describe order processing and why it is important.
5. Discuss the importance of transportation and describe each mode of transportation and its advantages and disadvantages.
6. Explain why inventory is necessary, the costs of inventory, and how inventory management balances inventory costs and physical distribution service.
7. Explain the goal of warehousing and the advantages and disadvantages of private and public warehouses.
8. Describe the objectives of materials handling.

Satisfying the customer is a marketer's overriding concern. If the customer is not satisfied, the organization cannot accomplish its goals—whether they are profit or nonprofit goals. Part of customer satisfaction is having available for sale in undamaged condition the product the customer wants, when and where the customer wants it. *Providing the right product at the right place at the right time is called* **physical distribution service (PDS).** PDS is accomplished through the marketing activity of physical distribution.

The National Council of Physical Distribution Management defines physical distribution as:

> the term describing the integration of two or more activities for the purpose of planning, implementing and controlling the efficient flow of raw materials, in-process inventory and finished goods from point of origin to point of consumption. These activities may include, but are not limited to, customer service, demand forecasting, distribution communications, inventory control, materials handling, order processing, parts and service support, plant and warehouse site selection, procurement, packaging, return goods handling, salvage and scrap disposal, traffic and transportation, and warehousing and storage.
>
> Note that this definition includes inbound, outbound, internal and external movements.[1]

For our purposes we will define **physical distribution** as *all the activities required to physically move the product from the manufacturer to the final customer.* Those activities include order processing, transportation, inventory control, warehousing, and materials handling.

IMPORTANCE OF PHYSICAL DISTRIBUTION

Physical distribution is possibly the most underappreciated marketing function, yet it is especially important both to individual businesses and the total economy. Although few consumers realize it, physical distribution is a large part of every dollar they spend. Physical distribution costs account for

---

[1] *NCPDM: What It's All About* (Chicago: National Council of Physical Distribution Management), pp. 1–2.

Figure 14-1
Physical Distribution Cost-Saving Potential

Price	$1.00
Manufacturing Costs per Unit	0.30
Other Marketing Costs per Unit	0.25
Physical Distribution Costs per Unit	0.25
Profit per Unit	$0.20

Sales = 1,000,000 units per year

Profit = $0.20 × 1,000,000 = $200,000

Increase physical distribution efficiency by 20 percent (physical distribution costs drop to $0.20 per unit), then profitability rises to $0.25 per unit or $250,000 per year.

over half of all marketing costs.[2] It is approximately 14 percent of sales for manufacturing companies and 26 percent for other channel members.[3] Thus, physical distribution represents such a huge cost center for a corporation that small increases in efficiency often represent large dollar savings to it.

Figure 14-1 illustrates this potential through the simple example of a company in which 25 percent of sales goes toward physical-distribution costs, with a 20-percent lowering of physical distribution costs increasing profitability by 25 percent. To achieve the same profitability with the old unit profit margin of $0.20, marketing would have to increase sales to 1,250,000 units (up 25 percent) *without spending any more money on marketing!* The fact that physical distribution represents such a large share of marketing costs makes it a prime candidate for enhancing the corporate profitability of many companies.

Physical distribution also represents a potential profit-generating area, as does any other marketing function. If a company can deliver products faster and more consistently than its competitors, it will have a differential advantage. Similarly, a company whose product is always on the retail shelf when the consumer wants it will be at an advantage over a company whose product is often out of stock. Superior physical distribution service can generate increased sales in the same sense that a superior advertising campaign or a superior product can.

---

[2] Stephen B. Oresman and Charles D. Scudder, "A Remedy for Maldistribution," *Business Horizons*, June 1974, p. 61.

[3] Bernard J. LaLonde and Paul H. Zinszer, *Customer Service: Meaning and Measurement*, (Chicago: National Council of Physical Distribution Management, 1976).

The cost of not achieving adequate physical distribution service can be severe. The inability of IBM to initially supply its Personal Computers quickly to its retailers made both IBM and its retailers lose many sales. Due to underestimated demand IBM could only supply one personal computer for every seven ordered. "We're starved for product," said Rich Inatome, president of Computer Mart, a computer retailer losing $300,000 a month because of the shortage. Warned Anthony P. Morris, president of another retailer, "We'll see dealers going belly up because of this." For IBM this shortage meant many customers were buying competitive brands rather than waiting for an IBM. As Computer Works President Seymour Merris put it, "Thank God for Compaq. My lost IBM sales in May were $750,000. If I hadn't had Compaqs to sell, I'd have lost about $160,000, bottom line.[4]

Physical distribution also plays an important role in our economy. On a national level physical distribution creates time and place utility. It does shoppers in Columbus who want oranges little good to know they are available in Florida. Neither does it help a manufacturer in Seattle to know his steel is ready but in Pittsburgh. Some means must exist to physically move these products from where they are produced to the time and place where they are desired. Physical distribution provides these means.

Efficient physical distribution makes it possible for geographic regions to specialize in producing products that best fit the natural resources, climate, and other local characteristics of that region. The orange-growing industry can concentrate in Florida and California, secure in the knowledge that our physical distribution system provides the means for delivering fresh oranges anywhere in the country. Without an efficient physical distribution system each region could consume only what it produced and no product could be marketed on a national basis.

Finally, physical distribution is important to our economy because so much of our national wealth is tied up in physical distribution facilities. If we were to total our national investment in highways, railroads, airports, pipelines, waterways, inventory, and warehouses, it would certainly run into trillions of dollars!

PHYSICAL DISTRIBUTION OBJECTIVES

The broad objective of a physical distribution system is to move products to other channel members and to consumers in the most efficient way possible that is consistent with the level of service that customers require. Efficiency and satisfactory service are key goals of physical distribution, but they may

---

[4] Richard A. Shaffer, "IBM Shortage," *Wall Street Journal*, June 3, 1983, p. 23.

conflict with each other. It may be more efficient in terms of cost, for example, to ship products by rail. However, in terms of service the customer may demand extra fast delivery, which may dictate the use of air freight. In practice managers must make frequent trade-offs between efficiency and service to achieve the best end result—profitable sales and a satisfied customer. To achieve this end result, physical distribution managers must try to accomplish three goals: cost efficiency, better physical distribution service, and increased profitability.

Cost Efficiency

Effective management of physical distribution provides many opportunities for cost reduction. Determining the optimum number and location of warehouses, improving materials handling to speed movement of products inside warehouses, increasing stock turnover through better inventory management, and using sealed containers to ship products are examples of ways intelligent management of physical distribution can reduce costs.

However, many physical distribution costs are interrelated. For example, one company tried to reduce its inventory cost by carrying less inventory at each location. It succeeded: Inventory costs dropped by $100,000 per year. However, to keep customers happy, it had to use faster modes of transportation to compensate for lower inventory levels, and annual transportation costs rose by $135,000. The result? Total physical distribution costs rose by $35,000 per year.

To avoid such mistakes, physical distribution managers usually utilize the **total cost concept** to analyze physical distribution cost efficiency. Stated simply, the total cost concept dictates that before making a final decision a physical distribution manager must analyze all costs affected by alternative decisions and the interrelationships of those costs. The decision that creates the lowest total cost and still meets corporate objectives is the most desirable.

Figure 14-2 illustrates one example of total cost concept analysis in physical distribution. In the decision to add more warehouse locations, research has revealed that, for most physical distribution systems, transportation costs decrease to a point and then increase and inventory costs rise at a decreasing rate as additional warehouses are added. Thus, the combination of these factors determines the place of lowest total cost for the warehouse decision.

Returning to our original example, the total cost concept would dictate that the physical distribution manager should only have reduced inventory as long as the savings in inventory cost was greater than the increased transportation cost.

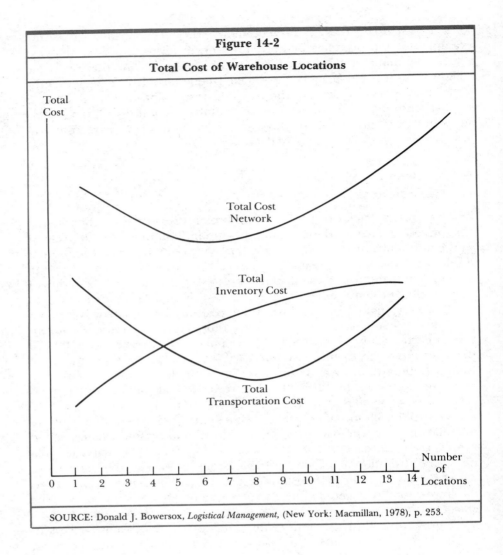

Figure 14-2

Total Cost of Warehouse Locations

Total Cost

Total Cost Network

Total Inventory Cost

Total Transportation Cost

Number of Locations

0 1 2 3 4 5 6 7 8 9 10 11 12 13 14

SOURCE: Donald J. Bowersox, *Logistical Management*, (New York: Macmillan, 1978), p. 253.

Physical Distribution Service

Buyers often base purchasing decisions on which supplier provides the "best" physical distribution service. When other marketing controllable variables are equal, buyers will normally buy from the supplier who can consistently deliver undamaged products the fastest. Consumers are also more likely to develop brand loyalty for products that are consistently available in retail stores than for products that are often out of stock. For example, in a survey by Walter and LaLonde, 64 percent of the shoppers switched brands and 14 percent switched stores when faced with a stockout (the product desired was not on the shelf).[5] Clearly, manufacturers and retailers have much to lose if physical distribution service is not adequate.

What exactly is physical distribution service? Mentzer and Krapfel describe three aspects of PDS: availability, timeliness, and quality.[6] The goal of the physical distribution system is to provide these aspects in the amount desired by target customers.

Availability means literally having the right product in the right place at the right time. Is the product available when the consumer wants it? Availability is often measured as the percentage of times a product is out of stock.

Timeliness implies the ability to fill orders as quickly as the consumer desires them. Take your own experience with mail order purchases. If you expected your purchase within two weeks after placing an order but it took two months, you would not be satisfied with the company's physical distribution service. You may even stop buying from them. In that case lack of timeliness would lose the company a customer.

Quality means delivering the product in the condition desired. Quality of PDS is lost if the product is damaged, is the wrong size or color, or is the wrong product. When you see a retailer selling damaged merchandise at low prices, the retailer is suffering (in lost profit) from inferior PDS quality.

To properly support the other marketing controllable variables, physical distribution must deliver available, timely, quality physical distribution service. It does a company little good to design a good product and promote and price it correctly if physical distribution delivers it late or damaged.

Increased Profitability

You may have noticed that the first two objectives are somewhat at odds with each other. How can physical distribution keep products on the shelf (which requires money tied up in inventory), make timely deliveries (which requires faster, more expensive transportation and order processing), and keep the product undamaged, but still hold costs down? The answer lies in a compromise between the best physical distribution service possible for the costs incurred. To find that point, we need to look at the *total costs* of the physical distribution service decision.

Every time a customer tries to buy a product that is not available and buys a competitor's product, the company has lost a sale. The cost of that lost sale is the profit the company would have made. Therefore, the worse a company's physical distribution service, the more sales will be lost, and the

---

[5] Clyde K. Walter and Bernard J. LaLonde, "Development and Test of Two Stockout Cost Models," *International Journal of Physical Distribution*, Vol. 5, No. 3, 1975.

[6] John T. Mentzer and Robert E. Krapfel, Jr., "Physical Distribution Service: A Fundamental Marketing Concept?" *Working Paper*, (Blacksburg, VA: Virginia Polytechnic Institute, 1984).

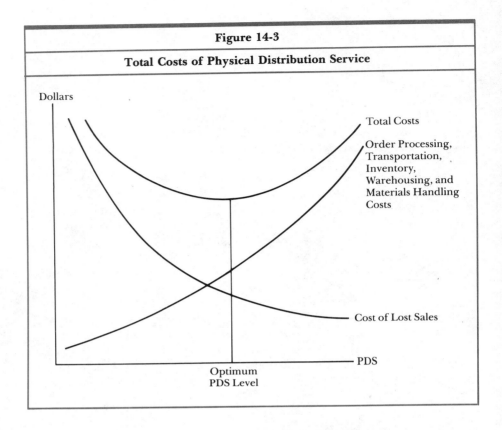

Figure 14-3

Total Costs of Physical Distribution Service

Dollars

Total Costs

Order Processing,
Transportation,
Inventory,
Warehousing, and
Materials Handling
Costs

Cost of Lost Sales

PDS

Optimum
PDS Level

higher the total cost of lost sales. By improving PDS the company can lower this cost but it will have to spend more on order processing, transportation, inventory, warehousing, and materials handling. Figure 14-3 illustrates this situation. The physical distribution manager is constantly striving for the right compromise between maximizing physical distribution service and minimizing the costs of obtaining that service. That compromise exists where the total costs are minimized.

How physical distribution minimizes costs and maximizes services through the activities of order processing, transportation, inventory control, warehousing, and materials handling will occupy our attention for much of the rest of this chapter.

ORDER PROCESSING

A two-way flow exists in physical distribution systems. Products flow from the manufacturer through channel members to customers. Orders for products flow in the other direction. For example, when a grocery store

runs low on corn flakes, the store places an order for more cereal with the wholesaler, which eventually also places an order with the manufacturer.

The objective of order processing is rapidly processed, accurate orders. To maintain the timeliness aspect of physical distribution service, orders must be processed quickly. To maintain quality, accuracy must be preserved. Often, correcting order processing mistakes takes much more time and costs more than initiating the order in the first place.

Order processing systems are often quite simplistic and inexpensive. Manual systems in which a clerk checks items for ordering, fills out an order form, and mails it to the supplier are the simplest. The supplier, in turn, manually processes the order. However, these systems are quite slow and subject to much inaccuracy.

Many companies use computerized systems in which a computer-monitored inventory system determines the order and transmits it by telephone lines to another computer, which fills the order. Such systems have the potential to process orders virtually instantaneously, but are very expensive.

Many computerized systems are initiated by **electronic point of sale (EPOS) terminals**. Resembling cash registers, these terminals are connected directly to a retail store's computer so that whenever a particular item is purchased, the terminal records the sale on the order processing

Figure 14-4
Universal Product Code (UPC)

system. When inventory falls too low, the computer automatically sends an order to the supplier.[7] Again, these are very rapid, accurate systems, but quite expensive.

The recent development of the **universal product code (UPC)** has greatly enhanced order processing efficiency. Because each store item has its own UPC code (see Figure 14-4 for an example), the clerk operating an EPOS terminal merely "reads" the code into the computer with a laser scanner. The sale, its price, and if necessary an order to a supplier are then automatically processed. Use of UPC codes greatly reduces errors made by check-out clerks entering the wrong product numbers during a sale.

In all these order processing systems more accuracy and speed is gained by using a more sophisticated, more expensive system. Thus, the

---

[7] John T. Mentzer, "Technological Developments in Order Processing Systems," *International Journal of Physical Distribution and Materials Management*, Vol. 11, No. 8, 1981, pp. 15–21.

Figure 14-5				
Intercity Freight Movement by Mode of Transportation				
	1970		**1982**	
	Billions of Ton-Miles	**Percent**	**Billions of Ton-Miles**	**Percent**
Railways	771.0	39.83	812.0	36.06
Motor vehicles	412.0	21.28	502.0	22.29
Inland waterways	319.0	16.46	375.0	16.65
Pipelines	431.0	22.26	588.0	24.78
Air	3.3	0.17	4.9	.22

SOURCE: U.S. Department of Commerce, Bureau of the Census, *Statistical Abstract of the United States, 1984*, p. 607.

Figure 14-6					
Comparison of Transportation Modes*					
	Railroads	**Trucks**	**Pipelines**	**Water**	**Air**
Availability	2	1	5	4	3
Timeliness	3	2	5	4	1
Quality:					
Dependability	3	2	1	4	5
Safety	4	2	1	5	3
Cost	3	4	1	2	5
* 1 = highest rank; 5 = lowest rank.					

physical distribution manager must still make the compromise between timeliness and quality of physical distribution service and system cost.

TRANSPORTATION

Transportation, to a marketer, means the movement of raw materials, semifinished products, or parts from the point where they are produced to the point where they are processed or assembled and the movement of finished products to the point of purchase. It is necessary because the vast majority of products are not consumed where they are produced. By far the largest share of the transportation effort consists of moving industrial goods such as raw materials, components, and semifinished products

Figure 14-7				
Typical Modes of Transportation for Various Products				
Railroads	**Trucks**	**Waterways**	**Pipelines**	**Air**
Grain	Food	Iron ore	Petroleum	Apparel
Coal	Apparel	Forest products	Gaseous products	Computers
Lumber	Textiles	Petroleum	Chemicals	Scientific instruments
Cement	Raw materials	Grain	Water	Emergency parts
Stone	Appliances	Coal		Highly perishable foods
Iron ore	Petroleum	Chemicals		Mail
Chemicals	Mail			
Automobiles				

rather than ultimate-consumer products. Again, marketing's concern with transportation centers around timely and quality movement of products at an affordable price.

Products arrive at their destination by one or a combination of five transportation modes: railway, motor carriers (trucks), pipelines, watercraft, and aircraft. Figure 14-5 shows the relative importance of these modes, each of which has particular characteristics of availability, timeliness, quality, and cost. Figure 14-6 compares each mode on these aspects of physical distribution service, and Figure 14-7 shows typical products carried by each mode.

Railroads

Railroads are a low-cost form of transportation oriented toward hauling large-volume shipments—one train can carry many times the volume of a truck. It is particularly suitable for movement of bulk goods whose unit value is low, such as grain, coal, lumber, cement, iron ore, and stone. In many cases it is more convenient than water transport.

On the other hand railroads are not as readily available as trucks and cannot offer "door-to-door" service. Rail companies have sought to alleviate this problem by offering a coordinated service, called **piggyback**, in which flat cars are used to haul preloaded trucks. Thus, the long-haul cost savings of trains are combined with the pick-up and delivery capability of trucks.

However, trains are also quite slow compared to trucks and not as safe. Due to the rough ride of train cars on the tracks and during coupling operations, delicate products are easily damaged. When physical distribution service demands faster, safe delivery, rail cannot effectively compete with truck transportation.

Furthermore, for much of this century leading up to the 1970s, railroads made very little money. Therefore, they could not invest in equipment and tracks, which fell into disrepair. However, numerous federal laws in the 1970s, designed to revitalize railroads, gave billions of dollars to the railroads for capital improvements. These acts culminated with the *Staggers Rail Act of 1980,* which gave railroads considerable freedom from Interstate Commerce Commission (ICC) control. In addition, the ICC has taken a more liberal view of railroad mergers.[8] The result has been more efficient, viable railroads, which offer improved service at a low cost for physical distribution of large shipments.

---

[8] James Cook, "Here Come the Megamergers," *Forbes,* June 9, 1980, pp. 39–40; "A Big Rail Merger Takes it Slow," *Business Week,* September 29, 1980, pp. 77, 80; and John D. Williams and John A. Prestbo, "Chessie, Seaboard Get ICC Green Light to Merge Via Swap of Stock Valued at About $1.7 Billion," *Wall Street Journal,* September 25, 1980, p. 6.

Motor Carriers

Our second mode of transportation, the trucking system, is a product of this century. The advent of motor vehicles in the early 1900s ushered in an era of road building that is still going on.

Whereas railroads have been forced to discontinue service to many population centers, trucks can provide speedy service to an increasing number of points. The Interstate Highway System contributes significantly to the ease of shipment by truck.

The importance of trucking is not fully indicated in Figure 14-5, which shows only intercity freight, not intracity freight. Trucks carry a vast quantity of goods between points within major metropolitan centers.

Trucks have several advantages over other forms of transportation. First, they are convenient. They provide shippers with door-to-door service. Second, they are fast. It is much quicker to move goods by truck than by inland waterways. Usually, trucks can provide quicker service than the railroads, too, especially over short distances and when they are not limited by set schedules. Third, motor carriers are a very flexible form of transport. Trains, ships, pipelines, and even aircraft are limited to some extent by what it is physically or economically feasible for them to handle. Motor carriers, because they range in size from very small trucks to tractor-trailer rigs and because they can (more readily than other forms of transport) be specially designed to carry specific types of products, can handle a wide variety of shipment sizes and goods. Fourth, thanks to our highly developed road system, trucks can reach even remote areas. Fifth, trucks can travel over a public highway system, whereas trains must use privately constructed and maintained track systems that are more expensive to operate. Finally, products are fairly safe in trucks and usually arrive in an undamaged condition.

Like other forms of transport, motor carriers also have disadvantages. First, there is the high cost of loading and unloading small less-than-truck-load shipments. Second, because of their comparatively small size, trucks are less desirable than trains or ships for transporting bulk goods such as grain and coal. Third, the need for drivers to make frequent rest stops on long hauls and the traffic congestion encountered in cities make shipping by truck slower than it would otherwise be. Fourth, although trucks may be fully loaded one way, they often must make the return trip partially loaded or empty (called an *"empty backhaul"* or *"deadheading"*). Although unprofitable return trips are also a problem for other means of transport, they are more serious in the trucking industry. All these factors combine to make motor carriers generally a more expensive mode than railroads.

Since 1978, however, the government has deregulated motor carriers considerably. Many changes in ICC regulations and the passage of the *Motor Carrier Act of 1980* have given trucking companies much more freedom in pricing and other marketing strategies.[9] It also has made the industry much more competitive, thus helping companies that use trucks to move their products. As a direct result of motor carrier deregulation, American Greetings Corporation has saved $1 million annually in distribution costs, whereas Lever Bros. Company saved $5 million in 1981 and $2 million in 1982. It also has improved the physical distribution service companies can offer. As Harry D. Gobrecht, Vice President of Transportation at U.S. Gypsum Company, expressed it, "We put a premium on service, and we have been absolutely able to get better service with the Motor Carrier Act."[10]

---

[9] For a more detailed discussion of motor carrier deregulation, see John T. Mentzer and Robert Krapfel, "Reactions of Shippers to Deregulation of the Motor Carrier Industry," *Journal of Business Logistics,* Vol. 2, No. 2, 1981, pp. 32–47; and John T. Mentzer and Robert E. Krapfel, "Reactions of Private Motor Carriers to TOTO and Compensated Intercorporate Hauling Rights," *Transportation Journal,* Spring 1981, pp. 66–72.

[10] "Shippers are in the Driver's Seat," *Business Week,* October 18, 1982, pp. 182, 184, 186.

Pipelines

Unobtrusive and silent, pipelines are used principally to transport petroleum and gaseous products from the points where they are produced to consumption centers. They are essentially a twentieth-century development, and their growth has largely paralleled that of the automobile, the principal user of petroleum products.

Pipelines are the most dependable and one of the safest modes of transport, because they are largely unaffected by weather, traffic, and the other problems of an above-surface environment. In addition, upkeep is low. Once a pipeline is in place, it requires comparatively little maintenance. Finally, pipeline operation requires relatively few employees.

Pipelines have several limitations. First, a pipeline is an incomplete transportation system. Other methods must be used to deliver the product from terminals and bulk tank stations to petroleum retailers and industrial users. Second, the high cost of installing a pipeline limits the areas that can be served directly. Third, pipelines are efficient carriers of only certain products, such as petroleum.

Waterways

Shippers of bulk goods such as iron ore, petroleum, steel, grain, and coal route a large amount of traffic through the Great Lakes and the rivers and canals that make up our inland waterway system. The extremely low cost of water transport makes it very attractive to shippers of products with a low value per pound.

The first man-made addition to our natural inland waterway system was the Erie Canal, completed in 1825. The St. Lawrence Seaway, finished in 1959, is a very important facility, because it opens our upper-Midwest industrial centers to the Atlantic, providing an impetus to both domestic and international shipping. The Mississippi River system and the Great Lakes together account for the bulk of our inland shipping.

The main advantage of water transportation is its low cost. A second advantage is that a large quantity of bulky commodities can be shipped at one time. However, water transportation suffers from several disadvantages. First, it is very slow and rough and, therefore, limited to products with low perishability that are not easily damaged. Second, much of our inland-waterway system is unusable several months of the year because of ice. Finally, other modes of transportation are often needed to carry the product to its ultimate destination.

Air Transportation

In 1978, air transport accounted for only 1.7 percent of the total tonnage moved domestically. It is used principally for the shipment of items of high value and low bulk and goods that are needed very quickly because of some emergency. Industrial products, for example, may be shipped by air if they are needed to keep a factory operating. According to the Air Transport Association the most important items shipped by air are apparel, computers, calculating and accounting machines, tool and die equipment, scientific instruments, parts for automobiles and aircraft, and food.

The principal advantages of air transportation are speed and safety. The principal disadvantages are its high cost and dependence on some other form of transport to move the goods to their final destination. The importance of air transport in general is likely to continue growing as a new generation of large aircraft and new, more efficient airports and ground handling equipment make this mode feasible for more shippers. However,

struction plans, each state must make certain that its proposed highways meet the Bureau's standards. This means they must be:

- Four lanes, each of which is 12 feet wide, with opposing lanes divided by a median, shoulders at least 10 feet wide and bridge clearances of 13 to 15 feet.
- Free of intersections, traffic lights, stop signs, and blind hills.
- Gently graded on inclines, and "far sighted" around curves.

The numbering system used for Interstate Highways was devised by the American Association of State Highway Officials. The association also stipulates the color of signs along Interstate Highways. Green and white are reserved for directional signs, whereas blue and white signs designate rest areas and off-highway service establishments such as restaurants and service stations. The highway numbers appear on shields in colors of the American flag.

The Interstate Highway System, now essentially complete, is considered a well-conceived and executed plan. Movement of people and goods on the system has an estimated use benefit ratio of $2.90 for every dollar invested in its construction. It is also estimated that the system saves 8,000 lives and millions of dollars of property damage each year.

From a physical distribution perspective, the system provides a way for companies to quickly and inexpensively ship their products anywhere in the United States. Because trucking companies help pay for the system through fuel taxes (although the system is largely subsidized by the taxes automobile owners pay), it keeps their costs low and mostly variable and helps them stay cost competitive with other modes of transportation. Clearly, the system contributes greatly to the economic development and well-being of the United States.

the high cost of fuel will remain a limiting factor for growth of this mode of transportation in the foreseeable future.

Legal Classification of Carriers

Because transportation is so vital to our nation, transportation companies are subject to government regulation. The ICC regulates interstate commerce by railroads and motor carriers. The Federal Energy Regulatory Commission regulates pipelines, whereas the Civil Aeronautics Board regulates air carriers, and the Federal Maritime Commission regulates water carriers. By law, transportation companies are classified as common carriers, contract carriers, private carriers, or exempt carriers.

Common Carriers A **common carrier** is a transportation company that offers to haul certain products for *anyone* on certain routes. Federal and state governments closely regulate common carriers. Their routes, prices, products hauled, and even financial decisions are subject to regulatory scrutiny. Although deregulation has given common carriers much more freedom than they previously had, they are still closely regulated.

Contract Carriers As their name implies, **contract carriers** are engaged by the shipper on a contractual basis. They agree in advance to make a specific number of shipments to specific destinations for a specific price. Contract carriers are regulated, but not as rigidly as common carriers.

Private Carriers Many shippers, especially many trucking fleets, are classified as **private carriers**. To earn this classification (and thus avoid much regulation by state and federal agencies), (1) the carrier must own the commodities being shipped, (2) the commodities must be related to the company's principal business, (3) the company must employ the drivers, and (4) the company must own or lease the equipment being used. However, changes in ICC regulation have confused the distinction between private carriers and common or contract carriers. Under certain conditions a private carrier can also be a common and/or contract carrier.[11]

---

[11] Mentzer and Krapfel, "Reactions of Private Motor Carriers."

Exempt Carriers   Based on the products carried (primarily agricultural), some carriers are granted the privilege of being exempt from government regulation. Exempt carriers need only meet federal and state safety regulations.

Auxiliary Freight Services

Various auxiliary freight services considerably broaden the range of facilities available to shippers. Working within the framework of the five modes of transportation, they provide additional services that are particularly appreciated by many shippers of small packages.

The U.S. Postal Service   The U.S. Postal Service is an important medium for moving large quantities of relatively small packages. Retailers make extensive use of **parcel post** to mail merchandise to customers, and manufacturers use it to ship small parts. The chief advantages of this service are its convenience, its dependability, and its relatively low cost. If a business ships a great deal by parcel post, the Postal Service may establish a branch station on the premises.

The development of the zip-code system has greatly facilitated the movement of products by parcel post. For example, a nursery shipping plants to customers in many parts of the United States formerly would have had a problem arranging for its shipments to arrive at specific planting times. Now, using zip codes to identify different climatic areas greatly simplifies the problem of shipping to meet a specific arrival time. **Air parcel post** has the same advantages as regular parcel post and, in addition, is much faster (although considerably more costly).

Express Package Service   The United Parcel Service (UPS), a privately owned "Parcel" service, operates in most states and many cities, and was one of the first express package companies. UPS offers customers an advantage over parcel post, because it makes pickups for a small charge and guarantees delivery within three days. Difficulties encountered by the U.S. Postal Service in recent years have led to a significant growth in companies of this type. Increasingly, shippers want faster service than the Postal Service provides. Companies such as Federal Express, Purolator, and Emery Freight are meeting this market need by offering the same pickup and delivery as UPS, but guaranteeing overnight delivery.

Freight Forwarders   Operating in a sense as transportation middlemen, freight forwarders assemble small shipments from a number of customers in a specific city or geographic area. An individual shipping only a small quantity would have to pay an expensive less-than-carload or less-than-truckload rate. The freight forwarder, by combining many small shipments, pays the cheaper carload or truckload rate. Some of these savings are passed on to the shipper.

Strategy

Federal Express Versus Airborne

The contest for leadership in the air freight business has been likened to a war movie featuring pilots flying predawn missions to deliver multimillion-dollar payloads. Federal Express is a young firm, founded in 1973. Until then, Airborne and Emery Air Freight had most of the air freight business.

Federal Express had a new approach. First, it did not use commercial airlines, but its own air fleet. Second, Federal Express concentrated on the huge small-package market. This segment had been neglected by other companies, which left it to the Post Office, United Parcel, and the now-defunct Railway Express.* Yet the market for delivery of small packages (under 70 pounds) is very large—an estimated 25 million packages annually.†

The company now controls approximately 33 percent of the small-package air freight business.‡ Interestingly, Frederick W. Smith, its founder, developed the essentials of his idea in an economics term paper at Yale. He received a C, but his grade did not deter him from his goal.

Federal Express began in 1973 with fourteen DASSAULT Falcons and 389 employees. It served 25 cities. The company funneled all packages, regardless of destination, through one central sorting system at their Memphis "hub" and then put them on planes to their final destination.

Federal's unique advantage has been the ownership of all of its facilities. Federal owns its own jets and delivery vans, which all are staffed by Federal's own employees. This across-the-board ownership and the unique Memphis "hub" result in delivery control so tight that Federal can advertise overnight deliveries with 99-percent accuracy.§

A great deal of Federal's success is also due to the mass marketing techniques used in its advertising. Rather than advertise to upper or middle management through trade and business publications, it aims its television, radio, and newspaper ads at the individuals responsible for getting the packages delivered—the secretaries and mailroom personnel of the world.

Shippers' Cooperatives A shippers' cooperative functions in much the same way as a freight forwarder, but it is owned by a group of shippers that move similar items. Its method of operation is simple. The group establishes an office, arranges for pickups from members, and coordinates ship-

After a shaky start, Federal Express has emerged as the leader in the overnight package delivery service. As of 1982, Federal had 12,000 employees and shipped 140,000 packages each night to 93 cities. Its air fleet consists of 65 aircraft, with 24 additional planes on order from Boeing.[**]

In order to remain on top, Federal Express keeps expanding its service. In June of 1981 it introduced its Overnight Letter, which is guaranteed delivery by 10:30 AM the next day. Federal is planning to expand into the overseas market and is presently positioning its electronic capabilities so it will be able to handle electronic document transfer of overnight letters.

Federal's success transformed the air freight industry so radically that Airborne adopted many of its techniques. Traditionally, Airborne was a freight forwarder. It concentrated on gathering and consolidating fairly heavy shipments, moving them by commercial airlines, then delivering packages to their final destinations on trucks.

In 1976 Airborne jumped into the express small package service by leasing and later, in 1980, buying its own fleet of planes. It also has its own "hub" in Ohio, which is capable of sorting 75,000 packages a night. Unlike Federal, Airborne continues to service the large package (over 70 pounds) market. This provides a few advantages. Airborne can ship later in the day than Federal, and it routinely ships items internationally.[††]

Airborne has always been a direct-sales-oriented company. A sales force of 180 and an extensive direct-mail program are the crux of its marketing effort. Consequently, when Airborne entered the express mail business, it was not as well known as expected. Airborne is now copying Federal's mass marketing approach by using television exposure to create customer awareness.[‡‡]

Federal Express, only an idea a decade ago, is now the industry leader with sales of $800 million in 1982,[§§] compared with Airborne's $295 million.[***] It will be interesting to watch how the marketing strategies of these firms evolve in the future.

* Lynn Languary and Connie Leslie, "Dog Fights in the Air Freight War," *Newsweek*, September 3, 1979, p. 55.
† "All Aboard the Bandwagon," *Forbes*, November 26, 1979, p. 60.
‡ Philip Maher, "Marketing Against Federal Express," *Industrial Marketing*, December 1981, pp. 94–100.
§ Tom Oliver, "The Memphis Connection," *Marketing and Media Decisions*, May 17, 1982, pp. 62–63, 128–29.
** Ibid.
†† John R. Dorfmann, "Sincerest Flattery," *Forbes*, January 31, 1983, p. 50.
‡‡ Maher, "Marketing Against Federal Express," p. 96.
§§ *Standard & Poor's Corporate Records*, November 1982, p. 6048.
*** Ibid., July 1983, p. 3972.

ments to each destination. Each shipper pays on a prorated basis according to the percentage weight of its shipment.

Bus Lines   Although the main purpose of intercity bus lines is to move people, they also offer convenient and fast transportation to customers shipping products of relatively high value and low bulk. Fresh flowers and photographic materials are two of the items shipped frequently by bus. Transportation by bus has the advantages of simplicity and reliability. The shipper delivers the parcels to the bus terminal, where they are loaded directly on the carriers. They are then dropped off at the bus terminal in the city of destination. The chief disadvantage of bus lines is that they normally do not provide pickup and delivery service.

Coordinated Shipments   Usually offered by transportation companies, coordinated shipments offer the shipper the advantages of several modes of transportation. Railroads, as previously mentioned, offer the coordinated service of piggyback, which combines the pickup and delivery service of motor carriers with the long haul cost savings of trains.

Many coordinated services center around **containerized shipping.** Containers are large (often tractor-trailer size) metal boxes that can be filled and shipped as one unit. Containers are filled at the shipper's location, loaded onto trucks, taken to the railroad, loaded onto railcars or even ships, transported, and unloaded all as one unit. This significantly lowers the transportation cost for the shipper and the inconvenience for the transportation company. It also shortens delivery time and, by reducing the handling, improves quality.

Selecting the Transportation Mix

In designing the company's transportation mix marketing management must make three basic decisions: (1) which mode or combination of modes it should use, (2) which specific carriers within the mode or modes it should select, and (3) whether it should own or lease some or all of the transportation facilities needed. Normally, management will consider the following factors:

1. The acceptable amount of time for the goods to move from the pickup point to the point of delivery.
2. The cost of alternate methods of transportation.
3. The convenience of alternate loading and unloading arrangements.
4. The reliability and safety of each mode.

If time is a critical factor—as, for example, when the product has a very high value relative to its bulk or size and it is important to keep inventory levels low (so less money is tied up in inventory)—then management will select the fastest transportation mode or combination of modes (usually air coupled with motor carriers). If time is of secondary importance, as in the case of most raw materials, management is likely to use slower and cheaper forms of transportation (water, pipeline, or rail).

Figure 14-8		
Costs of Shipping Products by Air Versus Truck or Rail		
Cost Factor	**Air**	**Truck or Rail**
Transportation charges	Much higher	Much lower
Cost of capital tied up in inventory	Much lower	Much higher
Purchasing expenses	Lower	Higher
Warehousing expenses	Lower	Higher
Insurance	Lower	Higher
Product obsolescence and perishability	Lower	Higher
Theft	Lower	Higher
Inventory taxes	Lower	Higher
Handling costs	Lower	Higher
Product depreciation	Lower	Higher
PDS	Higher	Lower

The second major consideration is cost. Physical distribution expenses account for a sizable share of total marketing costs. Like other marketing costs, they are reflected in the selling price of a product. The more expensive the transportation mode, the more expensive the product will be to the final customer.

Convenience is especially important to small shippers, which find it uneconomical to maintain a traffic department or their own transportation facilities. However, convenience is related directly to cost. Normally, the more services and conveniences a shipping service provides, the higher the cost to the customer. Pickup and delivery are never "free."

Reliability (consistently getting the goods to their destination on time) and safety (delivering the goods undamaged) are very important for certain types of products. IBM, for example, has long used household movers to transport computers from its manufacturing plants to customers, principally because of the high degree of reliability and safety of this type of carrier compared with other transportation services.

As with all other decisions in physical distribution, selecting the transportation mix is a compromise between physical distribution service and cost. Timeliness and availability can be enhanced by using faster transportation modes, and quality can be improved by using safer, more dependable modes, but this all costs more money. Also, the transportation decision affects the total cost of other physical distribution activities. Figure 14-8 shows how selecting air transport over truck or rail usually affects physical distribution costs and service. Although air transportation costs considerably more, it lowers many other physical distribution costs and raises PDS. Therefore, the physical distribution manager has to look at the total cost and PDS effect of any transportation decision.

INVENTORY CONTROL

Imagine the inconvenience you would endure if your car broke down and the mechanic told you that no parts were available, that you would have to wait for the manufacturer's next production run to have it repaired. Or imagine the nutritional state of our citizenry if bread were available only during the harvest season for wheat and other grains.

Inventory is an important, costly, and often complicated marketing function that is performed in varying degrees by virtually all producers and most middlemen. The ingredients that become bread are stored in inventory numerous times before being combined in the finished product. Wheat, the basic raw material of bread, may be stored in a farm granary for several months before being transferred to a larger grain elevator. Later, after a further period of storage, it may be sold to a processor, which, after still another period of storage, converts it into flour. The flour, after additional storage, is finally used to make bread. At each of those storage points the owner is said to be carrying inventory. **Inventory** *is a supply of raw materials, work-in-process, or finished goods being held for further processing or sale.*

Why ~~Inventory~~ *storage* is Necessary

~~Inventory~~ *storage* is essential to:

1. *Balance seasonal production and year-round consumption.* Many products, particularly agricultural goods such as grains and fruit, are produced seasonally but consumed all year long. Thus, part of the harvest must be stored to meet future demand.
2. *Balance year-round production and seasonal consumption.* The demand for some products, such as boats, snow tires, clothing, butane gas, and lawn mowers, is seasonal. Producers of such goods may find it advantageous to operate manufacturing plants on a year-round basis and store the products until the consumption season.
3. *Age or season the product.* Some products require time to reach a peak of flavor, ripeness, or taste. Bananas, tobacco, coffee, brewed and distilled beverages, and some meat products may be stored for weeks, months, or even years before they are ready to be consumed. Other products such as hides, furs, and lumber may have to be stored for a period before they can be used.
4. *Meet normal demand.* An obvious reason for inventory is to have products available when customers want them. Manufacturers, wholesalers, and retailers do not want to lose sales because a product is out of stock (the availability aspect of PDS). To avoid this, they maintain an inventory from which orders can be filled. Keep-

ing goods in inventory is one of the principal costs of doing business.

5. *Take advantage of special purchase opportunities.* Occasionally, a business may have an opportunity to buy a large quantity of goods at a favorable price because the seller is going out of business or discontinuing production of an item or a line. Companies also buy in large quantities to protect themselves from anticipated price increases. If the price savings will exceed the storage costs, the purchase is worthwhile.

Storage

Inventory Costs

As with all other physical distribution activities, inventory can provide physical distribution service benefits to the overall marketing effort, but at a cost. For many companies this cost is considerable. It is estimated that General Motors spends $3 billion annually to maintain its $9 billion worldwide inventory.[12] We must consider three components when computing storage costs: cost of capital invested in inventory, warehousing costs, and risk.

Cost of capital investment considers the cost of having money tied up in inventory. If a company has borrowed money to purchase inventory, the cost is the interest paid on the borrowed capital. If a company uses its own funds to finance inventory, the cost is the income lost from not investing the money elsewhere (called *opportunity cost*). The more inventory carried, the larger the amount of money invested in inventory and, thus, the higher the cost of capital investment.

Warehousing costs include the costs of providing a location where the inventory can be stored, materials handling and transfer costs, warehouse administration costs, and the other direct and indirect expenses of operating a physical facility. Because much of the cost is fixed, the more inventory that passes through a particular warehouse in a given time period, the lower the warehousing cost per unit (the fixed cost is spread over more units). For this reason one performance measure watched by inventory managers is inventory turns, or turnover rate. **Turnover rate** is calculated as:

$$\text{Turnover rate} = \frac{\text{Units sold per year}}{\text{Average inventory}}$$

The turnover rate shows how many times the inventory was completely turned over and is, therefore, a measure of the warehouse throughput. For

---

[12] John Koten, "Auto Makers Have Trouble with 'Kanban'" *Wall Street Journal,* April 7, 1982, pp. 35, 42.

example, if 100,000 units of one product are sold and the average inventory is 20,000, the turnover rate is 5. The higher the turns for a given sales level, the lower the average inventory and the more efficiently the inventory is being managed.

Risk costs are those expenses related to loss of inventory. Whether through theft, damage, shrinkage, lost items, or obsolescence, a certain amount of inventory cannot be sold at the price desired or even sold at all. The cost of insurance also is included in this category. Higher inventory levels create more opportunity for loss and, thus, a higher risk cost.

Obviously, inventory costs money, but the company also runs a financial risk by not carrying inventory or carrying a limited amount. These risks are:

1. *Lost sales.* Because many ultimate consumers and industrial users cannot or will not wait for a product until the seller orders it from a supplier, the firm may lose sales by not having goods in stock.
2. *Lost quantity discounts.* Many sellers grant substantial discounts for quantity orders. The buyer must compare the costs of storage with the savings to be had by buying in quantity.
3. *Lost goodwill.* Obviously, a business runs the risk of losing goodwill and patronage if it is out of stock too often on fairly routine items.
4. *Uneconomic order sizes and handling expenses.* When a firm buys in very small quantities, the per-unit costs of handling and order processing obviously go up. The paperwork needed to purchase one unit is often as great as that needed to purchase 1,000 units.

Inventory management *is the control of inventory to balance the costs of capital investment, warehousing, and risk with the physical distribution service and cost implications of not carrying inventory.*

Inventory Management

Inventory management involves the delicate practice of having an adequate but not excessive amount of product assortments in stock. If an excessive inventory is accumulated, the amount of storage space required, product deterioration, obsolescence, and capital employed combine to make costs rise. If an inadequate inventory level is maintained, some physical distribution service (and, consequently, sales and customers) will be lost. This, too, costs a firm money.

At its simplest level inventory management is the decision when to order—called the reorder point—and how much to order—called the order quantity.

Reorder Point   The **reorder point (ROP)** *is the amount of inventory on-hand when a new order is placed.* It is a function of the lead time, the usage rate of inventory, and the safety stock. **Lead time**, which is *the number of days that pass between the placement of an order and its arrival,* is affected by the ordering system, the distance from the supplier, and the transportation mode used. The **usage rate of inventory** *is how fast inventory sells.* Suppose, for example, lead time is normally 10 days and the usage rate is 6 units per day. The reorder point should be 10 × 6, or 60 units.

However, this calculation ignores uncertainty. Sales are not the same every day, and orders do not always arrive in the same number of days. Trucks break down, rail cars are temporarily misplaced, and suppliers may be out of stock. All these events may make lead times longer, but they cannot be predicted. Sales also may be unusually high in a given lead time. To prevent stockouts caused by such occurrences, most companies carry safety stock. **Safety stock** *is inventory in excess of what is expected to sell during the lead time.* It is carried as insurance against uncertainty. Therefore, the inventory reorder point equals:

ROP = (lead-time days × expected sales per day) + safety stock

How much safety stock to carry? That depends on the physical distribution service level the company wants to maintain. In our earlier example, the ROP was 60 units without safety stock. Now let us suppose management decides that we should run out of stock no more than 10 percent of the time. Past records reveal that 90 percent of the time we sell less than 84 units in any given order lead time. Therefore, safety stock of 24 units is added to the 60 units, giving a reorder point of 84 units. With this ROP we expect that 90 percent of the time demand during the order lead time will be less than the 84 units we had on hand when we placed the order. The other 10 percent of the time we will stock out.

Why not carry more safety stock? Probably because it is too expensive. The determination of the ROP is always a compromise between the desire for 100 percent physical distribution service and the cost of carrying the inventory to obtain it. Few if any companies can afford the costs of maintaining 100 percent PDS.

Order Quantity   Once we decide to place an order, how many units should we request? The answer to this question is a function of the costs of placing the order, the costs of carrying the inventory, and the cost of stocking out between orders. Figure 14-9 provides a graph of the relationship between the size of an order and these costs.

Every time an order is placed, some costs are incurred. The cost of preparing the order, sending it, and processing it are all **order processing costs**. As Figure 14-9 demonstrates, order processing costs go down with increased order size, because large orders necessitate fewer orders in a given time period. Thus, the cost of processing an order occurs less often. Suppose, for example, order processing costs are $10 per order and we sell

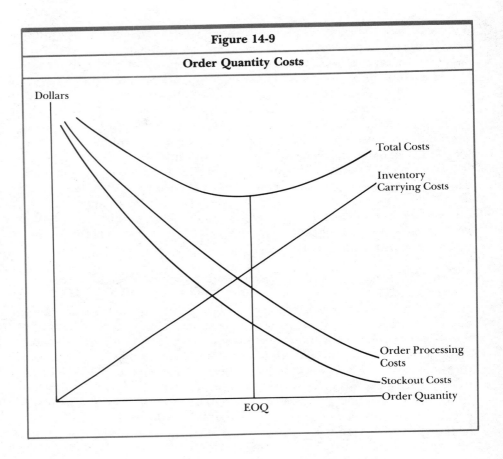

Figure 14-9

Order Quantity Costs

Dollars

Total Costs

Inventory Carrying Costs

Order Processing Costs

Stockout Costs

Order Quantity

EOQ

1,000 units each year. If our order quantity is 200 units, we will place 5 orders each year, for a total order processing cost of 5 × $10, or $50. If we order 500 units each time, we only order twice, and order processing costs for the year will equal $20.

However, the more units we order at any given time, the more inventory we will carry. A measure of inventory carried is the **average inventory** which equals:

$$AI = (OQ/2) + SS$$

where AI = average inventory, OQ = order quantity, and SS = safety stock.

In our previous example, suppose we carried no safety stock. Our average inventory in the first case was half the order quantity of 200 units, or 100 units in inventory on the average. In the second case average inventory was half of 500 units, or 250 units.

The cost of keeping this inventory is called **inventory carrying costs** and, as Figure 14-9 illustrates, it increases as inventory goes up. In the example, when the order size went up 150 percent (200 to 500), the average inventory increased by the same percent (100 to 250). Because the cost for carrying each unit in inventory is constant, the inventory carrying cost would also increase by 150 percent.

This is a normal inventory management problem: Increasing order quantity lowers ordering costs but increases inventory carrying cost. The opposite is also true: Lower order quantity decreases inventory carrying cost, but increases ordering cost.

The third component of the order quantity relationship is the cost of stocking out between orders. Every time we place an order, there is a chance we will run out of inventory before that order arrives. This **expected stockout cost** is the probability of stocking out times the cost to the company of losing the sales. Therefore, each time an order is placed, an expected stockout cost occurs. The less often we order (that is, if we order larger quantities), the less opportunity there is to stock out. Figure 14-9 shows this relationship of decreasing stockout costs to increasing order size.

Regardless of the order size, if we carry more safety stock, the probability of stocking out and the expected stockout cost will be lower. Thus, the stockout cost line in Figure 14-9 is for a given safety stock level. If we raise safety stock (higher PDS), the entire expected stockout cost line would shift down (stockouts less likely) and the entire inventory carrying cost line would shift up (carrying more inventory in safety stock).

For any given safety stock level the optimum order quantity is the lowest total of order processing cost, inventory carrying cost, and stockout costs. This is called the **economic order quantity** and marked as EOQ in Figure 14-9.

To find the EOQ mathematically,

$$EOQ = \sqrt{\frac{2(D)(O)(S)}{(I)(C)}}$$

where EOQ = economic order quantity, D = annual demand, O = ordering cost, S = expected stockout cost, I = inventory carrying cost, and C = dollar value of a unit of inventory.

Suppose, for example, one unit of a given product was worth $100, annual demand was 1,000 units, ordering costs were $25, inventory carrying costs were 0.25 of unit value per year, and a physical distribution service level of 95 percent (a stockout rate of only 5 percent) was chosen, which led to an expected stockout cost per order cycle of $106. The economic order quantity would be:

$$EOQ = \sqrt{\frac{2(1000)(25)(106)}{(0.25)(100)}} = 460 \text{ units}$$

or a little over two orders per year.

The combination of the reorder point and economic order quantity are the way in which inventory management balances costs and physical distribution service. The goal is to provide as much PDS as possible at the lowest possible cost. Inventory managers first determine the ROP based on the lead time, demand, and desired PDS level. Given the safety stock determined in the ROP decision, they then select the EOQ by balancing order processing costs, inventory carrying costs, and expected stockout costs.

WAREHOUSING

Inventory must be stored in some facility. Whether it is an open field for storing coal or a refrigerated building for frozen foods, most products spend some time in a warehouse before reaching the final customer. Figure 14-10 lists the major types of warehouses and the products for which they are used.

The goal of warehousing is to provide storage facilities that are convenient for inbound shipments and located to offer physical distribution

Figure 14-10
Types of Storage Facilities

Yard or Ground Storage Facilities Used for lumber, coal, automobiles, stone, building materials, bricks, metal ores, airplanes.	**Cold Storage Warehouses** Used for meats, frozen foods, ice, flowers, eggs, certain types of drugs, butter, some medical supplies, cadavers.
Special Commodity Warehouses Used for grains (grain elevators), fruits, computers, defense systems, cotton, leather, medical supplies, pharmaceuticals.	**Tank Storage Facilities** Used for petroleum products, gases, water, milk, vegetable oil, chemicals.
Bonded Warehouses Used for liquor, imported goods, tobacco, furs, perfume (products subject to federal tax).	**General Merchandise Warehouses** Used for furniture, appliances, clothing, paper, batteries, tires, books.

service to customers. The more warehouses a company has, the better its physical distribution service. However, warehouses are expensive to build and maintain, so a company must decide how many to have and where to locate them to maximize PDS while holding warehousing costs down.

A company must also make the decision between using public or private warehouses. *Private warehouses* are storage facilities owned and operated by the company. Because these warehouses may cost millions of dollars to construct and maintain, they are a high fixed-cost way of storing products. Due to this high fixed cost the company must keep a large volume of products moving through the facility, and therefore uses private warehouses only when it is certain of a large, constant volume of sales. One major advantage of using private warehouses is that it gives a company more control over its products. It also allows greater physical distribution service.

Public warehouses are storage facilities owned and leased out by other companies. Space is leased on a square-foot basis and may be leased month-to-month. Using public warehouses turns a company's warehousing cost into a variable cost: The greater the sales volume, the more space needed, the higher the warehousing costs. Thus, a company often uses public warehouses when its sales volume is too low to warrant a private warehouse.

In addition public warehouses offer more flexibility—a company can have storage facilities in certain areas only at certain times. Many companies use public warehouses for seasonal products, which are stored in certain areas only when demand exists in those areas.

Public warehouses are also used for new-product introductions. If the product fails, the company can discontinue warehousing space. If the product succeeds, the company can add a private warehouse later. Certainly, the company does not wish to commit millions of dollars to a private warehouse before the success of its product is assured.

Public warehouses do offer less control over inventory than private warehouses. Thus, when physical distribution service is especially important, marketing management may not be willing to turn control of the company's inventory over to a public warehouse.

The increasing emphasis on physical distribution service as an integral part of the marketing strategy, combined with the widespread use of computer systems, has led to a new concept in storage: the **distribution center**. No longer merely a warehouse, the distribution center is designed to rapidly process orders and ship products. Oriented more toward moving inventory through the center than simply storing it, distribution centers often lower inventory levels (and costs), eliminate the need for several other conventional warehouses, and improve physical distribution service. Many experts in distribution feel the distribution center personifies the effort to maximize physical distribution service while controlling costs.

MATERIALS HANDLING

Materials handling *is the activity of moving products into storage areas and then moving them out as orders are filled.* Much of modern materials handling is automated. In some storage facilities, especially distribution centers, orders are filled by computer. In one company's distribution center, for example, orders come in over telephone lines from over 100 grocery stores and are entered directly into the computer. The computer, in turn, schedules the release of products from storage bins directly onto conveyors that deliver the products to the shipping area.

The key objectives of materials handling management are to (1) have the right assortment and quantity of products in storage, (2) fill orders quickly, accurately, and efficiently, using as little labor as possible, (3) minimize theft, and (4) minimize damage to products. Although it is perhaps not as exciting as some other aspects of marketing, materials handling accounts for a considerable part of the marketing dollar for many firms and is quite important in maintaining physical distribution service.

PHYSICAL DISTRIBUTION IN MARKETING STRATEGY

Marketing managers should be aware of the potential losses that can result from ineffective performance of physical distribution.

1. *Order processing.* Ineffective order processing can result in orders (a) taking too long to fill, (b) being shipped to the wrong customers, (c) being inaccurately filled, and (d) not being billed properly.
2. *Transportation.* Malperformance of transportation can produce a variety of losses, such as (a) shipment of products to the wrong location, (b) selection of less efficient modes or combination of modes, (c) excessive time used to deliver products, and (d) damage to products in transit.
3. *Inventory.* Ineffective inventory management results in losses such as (a) inaccurate records of what products are available in what location, quantity, and condition and (b) too much or too little merchandise being available in relation to demand. Goods kept in inventory too long incur unnecessary costs. The longer merchandise is kept in storage, the greater the cost in (a) obsolescence and deterioration, (b) taxes, (c) lost opportunity, (d) theft, (e) insurance, and (f) space.
4. *Warehousing.* Warehouses unsuited to the product; inappropriate locations; and the use of public warehouses when private ware-

houses would have been better, or vice versa, all lead to unnecessarily high warehousing costs and lower physical distribution service.

5. *Materials handling.* Improper materials handling results in such costly problems as damaged merchandise, "losing" products by placing them in the wrong location in the warehouse, and excessive product damage.

As you can see, a well-designed product, promotion, and price strategy will not succeed without support from physical distribution.

SUMMARY

- The main elements of physical distribution are order processing, transportation, inventory control, warehousing, and materials handling.
- Physical distribution is important to companies because it represents such a large cost area, and physical distribution service is an important marketing competitive variable.
- Physical distribution is important to our economy because it creates time and place utility, allows national distribution of products, and constitutes much of our national investment.
- The goals of physical distribution are primarily cost efficiency, physical distribution service, and increased profitability.
- The total cost concept advocates analyzing all costs affected by a decision and choosing the alternative that yields the lowest total cost.
- Physical distribution service includes the aspects of availability, timeliness, and quality.
- Most decisions in physical distribution are a compromise between minimizing costs and maximizing physical distribution service.
- Order processing tries to achieve rapidly processed, accurate orders within cost constraints.
- Transportation involves the selection of a mode of transportation, carriers within that mode, and auxiliary services.
- Railroads, motor carriers, pipelines, waterways, and air are typical modes of transportation. All have unique advantages and disadvantages that make each suitable for certain types of products.
- Legal classifications of carriers are common, contract, private, and exempt carriers.
- Although inventory is necessary, its costs include capital investment, warehousing, and risk. Lost sales, lost quantity discounts, lost goodwill, and uneconomic order sizes are all costs of not carrying inventory.

- Inventory management involves the decisions of when to order (reorder point) and how much to order (order quantity).
- The economic order quantity (EOQ) is an attempt to minimize the total cost of inventory carrying costs, order processing costs, and costs of lost sales.
- Warehousing decisions concern how many warehouses to have, where to locate them, and whether they should be public or private.
- Materials handling objectives are to have the right products in the right storage location, fill orders efficiently and quickly, and minimize theft and damage.

DISCUSSION QUESTIONS

1. Why is physical distribution important to the individual firm? To our economy?
2. What are the goals of physical distribution?
3. Explain the total cost concept. Physical distribution service. How do the two conflict?
4. What kinds of products are likely to be transported by rail? Truck? Water? Pipelines? Air? Why?
5. Define common carrier, contract carrier, private carrier, and exempt carrier.
6. What are the costs of carrying inventory? Of *not* carrying inventory?
7. What is a distribution center? How does it differ from a warehouse?
8. What are the advantages and disadvantages of private warehouses? Public warehouses?
9. What are the objectives of materials handling?
10. What are the potential effects on marketing strategy of ineffective physical distribution?

APPLICATION EXERCISES

1. Go to the grocery store and identify two products that are out of stock. For each, make specific suggestions about how the company that markets these products could improve physical distribution service by changes in order processing, transportation, inventory, warehousing, and/or materials handling.
2. For a product you manage, the reorder point is 100 units, 30 units of which are safety stock. The order processing cost is $15 per order, the company sells 375 units per year, the product is worth $65, inventory carrying cost is 0.27 of unit

value per year, and expected stockout cost per order is $70. What is the EOQ? What is the average inventory? What is the turnover rate?

3. Most people agree that the Interstate Highway System is a tremendous economic asset. Some people feel that an interstate railway system financed jointly by the government and the railroads should be designed and implemented. Prepare pro and con arguments concerning the possible development of an Interstate Railway System. Then explain how you personally feel about the idea.

CASE 14
Lawson Products[13]

Founded as a parts distribution company by Sidney L. Port in 1952, Lawson Products operated out of a 3,000-square-foot warehouse in Chicago until 1956. By 1981 the corporate headquarters were located at their 123,600-square-foot facility in Des Plaines, and four regional warehouses offered an additional 200,000 square feet of storage space.

Lawson occupies a unique niche in the over $29 billion industrial distribution industry, which is comprised of more than 6,500 companies. Lawson has concentrated solely on the distribution of maintenance and repair parts for capital equipment. This field has the advantage of being virtually recession free: When a company needs a repair part, it cannot wait for better economic times to buy it.

However, the disadvantage of this field is that repair parts are very sensitive to physical distribution service. When a major piece of equipment breaks down, replacement parts are needed *now*. Any company that cannot guarantee 24-hour delivery times need not even compete.

Lawson management recognizes how important physical distribution service is to the accomplishment of corporate marketing goals. As Chester D. Lynn, Chairman of the Board, states it, "Our constant objective is to provide the right parts—the right quality parts—at the right place and time and in the right quantity to do the job." Since 1976 the corporation has filled over 98.5 percent of all orders within 24 hours. In 1981 it was 99 percent.

Lawson has accomplished this impressive physical distribution service record by automating much of its distribution system. It receives orders on a seven-day-a-week, round-the-clock basis through an 800 number telephone ordering system (telemarketing). Thus, order communication takes two minutes rather than the several days it would take if the company used the postal service. Because the computerized order processing system allows instantaneous inventory checks, credit reference, and automatic invoice and shipping bill printing, Lawson can fill and deliver the order to the customer in less time than it used to take simply to deliver the order by mail to the company.

---

[13] Chester D. Lynn and Daniel J. Meyo, "Lawson Products: Learned Distribution," *Handling & Shipping Magazine*, Vol. 22, No. 10, pp. 6–20.

Lawson management remains committed to integrating physical distribution into overall marketing plans. After all, in the maintenance and repair parts channel, salesmen cannot sell if the company has a poor physical distribution service reputation. Chairman Lynn says, "The distribution operation will continue to make a significant contribution to the sales and marketing objectives of Lawson's management, and will support the company's progression toward orderly and uninterrupted increases in sales and profits in the future."

As sales volume passes the $100 million level, however, Lawson management recognizes the need to revamp and refine the distribution system to maintain physical distribution service at such high sales levels.

Discussion Questions

1. Do you think Lawson's policy of maintaining a 99-percent physical distribution service level is too high? Why?
2. Could the service level be allowed to drop as sales volume increases? What steps would you recommend to keep service high?
3. What questions would you ask customers about physical distribution service before answering Questions 1 and 2?

PART

FIVE
Promotion Decisions

15 Promotion

STUDY OBJECTIVES

After studying this chapter, you should be able to

1. Define promotion, advertising, publicity, personal selling, sales promotion, and packaging.
2. Discuss the importance of promotion.
3. Describe the communication process, uncontrolled communication, and their impact on promotion.
4. Explain how AIDA and the hierarchy of effects, company resources and policies, and target-market characteristics affect promotion planning.
5. List the major characteristics of advertising, publicity, personal selling, sales promotion, and packaging.
6. Describe the factors that affect the promotional mix.
7. Discuss the major techniques for setting the promotion budget.

I n this part of the book we will discuss the manner in which companies communicate with target customers and the environment. *Promotion is the communication aspect of marketing.*

Perhaps there was a time when, with no urging needed and guided only by neighbors' recommendations or travelers' tales, the world beat a path to the doors of those who built the best mousetraps. If John Brown over in the county seat made a good plow, word got around. Those days ended, however, if they ever existed, as our economy shifted from one of relative scarcity to one of comparative abundance—as both the number of consumers and the number of mousetrap-makers grew. As competition for consumer dollars intensified, a need emerged for planned, controlled promotion.

Over the years, transmitting product information to potential buyers in a manner designed to prompt positive action has grown increasingly sophisticated. We have developed new ways to communicate. We have learned to identify and segment markets. We have made intensive studies of motivation and buyer psychology. We have come to rely increasingly on marketing research rather than hunches. We have come to depend on planned communications to stimulate demand. Today, few firms operate on the principle that all you need is a good product. Marketing managers know that even the best product will not sell itself.

WHAT IS PROMOTION?

As we said, promotion is communication. Specifically, **promotion** *is all communication activities undertaken by a company to inform people about its products, services, corporate image, or social intent.* The company's promotional mix includes the use of five elements: advertising, publicity, personal selling, sales promotion, and, to some degree, packaging.

Advertising *is any paid form of impersonal presentation of products or ideas of commercial significance to prospective buyers.* Because using media such as TV, newspapers, radio, and magazines is impersonal and one ad reaches numerous people, the cost of reaching one prospective buyer is far less than the cost of reaching a potential buyer through personal selling.

Publicity *is any nonpaid impersonal communication about a company or its products appearing in the media as news.* Publicity is free in the sense that the media make no charge for communicating the information. A firm, however, may have people on its payroll who prepare news releases for the media. Of the five elements in the promotional mix, however, publicity is not under the direct control of the firm or message sender. As a result, if negative news about a company or its products appears in the media, the company can only try to release news statements to counter or explain it.

Personal selling *is the personal presentation of products or ideas of commercial significance to prospective buyers.* Note that this promotional method uses personal communication to reach one or several individuals. As such, it is more expensive per person than advertising, but usually more persuasive.

Sales promotion *consists of activities other than personal selling, advertising, and publicity that stimulate consumer purchasing and dealer effectiveness.* Companies usually use sales promotion activities such as displays, trade shows, exhibitions, and demonstrations to augment other promotional activities.

Packaging, discussed in Chapter 8, is part of many companies' promotional mix. A well-designed, attractive, and appealing package is critically important in achieving sales for some products.

The combination of these elements constitutes a company's promotional effort. How well this is accomplished determines how much consumers and the public know about the company and its products. Promotional failure often means product or even corporate failure.

IMPORTANCE OF PROMOTION

A company may have the best designed product, the most effective distribution system, and the fairest price, but the company's offering will not sell if the customers are not aware of it. Therefore, promotion is a critical element in any marketing strategy. Where the target customers are, what they read, what they watch, and what messages will appeal to them are crucial decisions in reaching and communicating with customers. Without proper promotion the other marketing controllable variables will not succeed.

Promotion also represents a significant portion of our economy. In 1983 alone, 25 companies in the United States spent $1.2 billion advertising just on television.[1] Personal selling permeates our entire economy. A survey by the Sales Manpower Foundation revealed that the selling efforts of the average manufacturer's salesperson "provide a livelihood for approximately 36 other workers, 18 within his own company, plus the others indirectly affected by his sales in related industries such as transportation, banking, advertising, wholesaling and retailing."[2] When we also consider the money and personnel involved in publicity, sales promotion, and packaging, it becomes very apparent that promotion represents a large portion of our economic activity.

---

[1] John Koten, "Creativity, Not Budget Size, Is Vital to TV-Ad Popularity," *Wall Street Journal,* March 1, 1984, p. 31.

[2] *Cost of Selling Survey,* (New York: Sales Manpower Foundation, 1968), p. 1.

Promotion can also be of crucial importance to the success of an individual company. In October of 1982 the announcement of seven deaths caused by cyanide-laced Tylenol capsules sent sales of the Johnson & Johnson product plummeting. However, positive publicity from Johnson & Johnson's full disclosure of facts (it eventually came to light that Johnson & Johnson was not at fault), intensive efforts to recall and test all capsules on the market (at a cost to the company of $100 million), aggressive advertising and personal selling by the company after the incident was over, and promotion of a new, safer product package helped Tylenol eventually to regain its 35-percent share in the pain reliever market.[3] Without this extensive promotional effort Johnson & Johnson would probably have been forced to withdraw Tylenol from the market.

---

[3] Thomas Moore, "The Fight to Save Tylenol," *Fortune,* November 29, 1982, pp. 44–49.

and supplying spokespersons for films and programs that reach more than 200 channels and stations.

Fox has enjoyed success in other endeavors as well. She is an ardent feminist. With Betty Friedan, author of *The Feminine Mystique,* she founded the National Organization for Women in 1966. NOW is dedicated to achieving full equality for women and is supported by male members as well as female. Fox's husband, Dr. Shepard Aronson, supports the goals of feminism and has served as board chairman of NOW's New York chapter.

She is also a past president of The Women's Forum, an association of prominent women who meet to discuss those problems peculiar to the handful of women who achieve high executive status. Fox helped to organize the First Women's Bank and Trust. She was the first woman to be named Business Leader of the Year by the Americans for Democratic Action (in 1979).

Muriel Fox is a familiar presence in corporate boardrooms. She is a director of the Harleysville Insurance Company; of the United Way of New York, Connecticut, and New Jersey; and of the International Rescue Committee. She also finds the time to serve as president of Mediacom, where she helps train business executives to put their best image forward in public situations.

Fox feels it is important for business and media to communicate. She says, "There is nothing mysterious or nefarious in business influence on the media. Society benefits in the long run from getting a chance to hear a variety of competing voices loud and clear—including the voices of industries that provide our jobs and our quality of life and our national and personal security."[†]

* "100 Top Corporate Women," *Business Week,* June 21, 1976, p. 65.
† Helen C. Smith, "Muriel Fox Is Not a Queen Bee," *Atlanta Constitution,* September 13, 1977, p. 3B.

PROMOTION AND THE COMMUNICATION PROCESS

The broad goal of promotion is to explain the merits of a product so effectively to target customers that they will purchase it. The goals of specific promotion programs are varied and may include selling more of the product to existing customers, selling the product during off seasons, increasing sales by promoting new uses for the product, and so on. Although some firms have more money to spend for promotion than others, no firm has unlimited resources. Therefore, each company must determine for itself which of these goals is most important and how much the company can afford to spend to reach it.

The term **systems approach** refers to the perception of, and working with, interrelated factors in order to solve a problem or achieve a goal in the most efficient and economical way. When marketing managers view

communications as a system, the entire communications process can be perceived. Bottlenecks and duplication of effort can be reduced and overall effectiveness improved. A systems approach promotes a more balanced promotional effort.

In any marketing communications system there are seven elements: (1) the message source, (2) the coded message, (3) message delivery vehicles, (4) the message receiver, (5) the decoded message, (6) intelligence feedback, and (7) noise (see Figure 15-1).

The Message Source

The communications process is initiated by the **message source**. It is the source who stands to gain or lose from the effectiveness or lack of effectiveness of the communication. It is also the source who (1) establishes the communications budget, (2) selects the target market, (3) designs or arranges for the preparation of the message, (4) selects or approves the message delivery vehicles, (5) arranges for intelligence feedback, and (6) tries to reduce noise.

The source ordinarily uses a spokesperson. These spokespeople can be company representatives, celebrities, customers, or actors. Many compa-

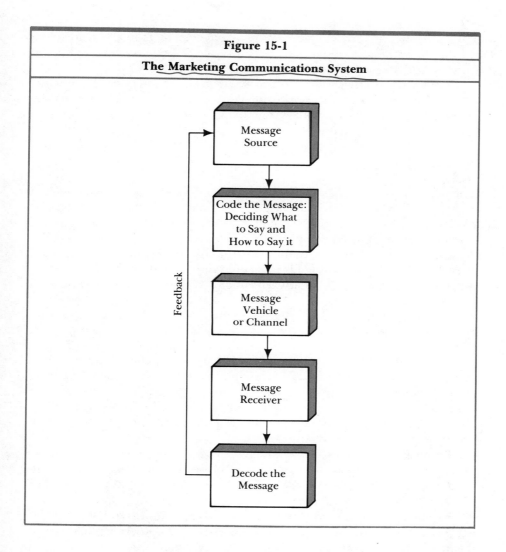

Figure 15-1

The Marketing Communications System

Message Source

Code the Message: Deciding What to Say and How to Say it

Message Vehicle or Channel

Message Receiver

Decode the Message

Feedback

nies use company representatives—Lee Iaccoca for Chrysler, Frank Borman for Eastern Airlines, and assembly workers for Ford, for example—in an attempt to add an element of experience and sincerity to the source. In personal selling the representative is the salesperson.

To draw attention to the message and improve product awareness, many companies use celebrities as spokespeople, such as Bill Cosby for Jell-O, James Garner for Polaroid, and various athletes for Miller Lite. American Express has been quite successful with a variation of this approach—that is, using celebrities whose names are more famous than their faces.

Sometimes advertisements feature actual customers in an effort to get the target customer to identify with the product. Blind taste tests or hidden cameras are often used to increase credibility.

Finally, many advertisements use actors to obtain attention and portray the product's attributes in a professional manner. Because the actor may be an unknown to the target market, much repetition may be necessary to communicate the message.

The Coded Message

The **message** *is the complete package that explains why the message source feels it is advantageous for the target customer to buy the product.* Although an unlimited number of different messages can be prepared for any product, most will contain information about the company and the product's name, the product's image, why it is better than competing products, and its benefits and attributes. When the message is presented impersonally through advertising, it is a **commercial** or an **advertisement**. When it is presented personally, it is a **presentation**.

The message may contain words, language, pictures, or symbolism. Such words as "new," "improved," or "fast acting" are often used to catch the target audience's attention and reinforce the message.

Language is the printed or verbal discussion of the product and its attributes. A **one-sided message** presents only the product's benefits. **Two-sided messages**, which present both the product's benefits and some of its shortcomings, are sometimes used in an attempt to improve credibility. However, the danger exists that the message may convince the target audience not to buy the product.

Pictures are often used to communicate the appearance of the product or to create an image. When an ad for Coca-Cola shows Coke being consumed by young people at a picnic, the image is that Coke should be part of fun activities.

Symbolism tries to draw on human needs and desires to sell the product. Prudential Insurance's theme "Get a piece of the Rock" and its logo of the Rock of Gibraltar are symbols of lasting stability, and appeal to an insurance customer's desire for security. Miller Lite commercials have effectively used the human desire for humor to sell beer. In addition many companies use fear to sell their products.[4] Fear of bad breath helps sell mouthwash. Fear of not providing for loved ones helps sell life insurance.

---

[4] For further discussion see John T. Burnett and Richard L. Oliver, "Fear Appeal Effects in the Field: A Segmentation Approach," *Journal of Marketing Research,* May 1979, pp. 181–90; B. Sternthal and C. Craig, "Fear Appeals: Revisited and Revised," *Journal of Consumer Research,* December 1974, pp. 22–34; and Homer E. Spence and Reza Moinpour, "Fear Appeals in Marketing—A Social Perspective," *Journal of Marketing,* July 1972, pp. 39–43.

Even fear of "ring around the collar" is successful. Although critics claim that Wisk commercials have insulted women and damaged the product's credibility, the ads have helped sell $200 million of the product every year. As the author of the "ring" theme, James Jordan says, "It would be fair to call that commercial a screeching commercial, an abrasive commercial, an intrusive commercial, but the one thing you can't call it is a bad commercial because the purpose of a commercial is to do a commercial job."[5] Others have not been so lucky. Any time symbolism—especially fear—is used, the danger exists that target customers will interpret the message differently than intended and that sales may even be hurt.

The Message Delivery Vehicles

Once the message is ready, it must be delivered. Marketing uses five vehicles to transmit the message: advertising, publicity, personal selling, promotion, and packaging. The choice of the delivery vehicle or vehicles depends on the product, the target customers, and the message. In the case of many consumer goods, all five delivery vehicles may be used to communicate the message to prospective buyers.

The Message Receiver

The person who receives the message is the target customer. The type of prospective buyer selected has an important bearing on other elements in the system. It will determine, for example, whether the message itself is technical or nontechnical and emotional or rational. It will also affect the message delivery vehicle. Personal sales representatives and advertisements in technical publications will reach a different market from ads in fashion magazines or on radio and television.

The Decoded Message

When the receiver translates the message into meaning, it is decoded. A successful message will be decoded in essentially the same way that it was encoded. However, it is quite difficult for a message source to send a message and have it received exactly as intended. Noise and the fact that people perceive the same thing in different ways often distort messages. The promotion manager's primary concern is that a message is decoded with the essential points still intact.

---

[5] Bill Abrams, "Ring Around the Collar Ads Irritate Many Yet Get Results," *Wall Street Journal,* November 4, 1982, p. 33.

Feedback

Feedback *is the reaction to the message.* Marketers hope consumers will react favorably to an advertisement by purchasing the intended product. If they do not, then the feedback is negative, indicating something went wrong in the communications process.

Feedback to a message presented in person by a salesperson can be evaluated immediately and adjustments in the message can be made. Negative feedback made by the message receiver—such as "Your terms of sale don't meet our requirements"—tells the salesperson to communicate how, in fact, the terms are favorable. With advertising, feedback is less direct and in many cases sales are lost, because the message cannot be adjusted to feedback.

Noise

Noise *means interference in any stage of the communications system.* Consider the distractions you may experience while a commercial is being broadcast over your car radio: Other people may be talking to you; your attention must remain on the road; and you may be thinking about your job.

Noise can occur at any stage in the system and usually results in a distorted or partly obscured message. The more noise that exists in a communications system, the less likely the receiver will decode the message as the source intended.

Uncontrollable Communication

Although the goal of promotion is to send controlled communication about the company to the target markets, much of the communication we receive about companies is uncontrolled. Rumors and public announcements are communications that a company generally cannot control. For example, when public announcements of the relationship between Rely tampons and toxic shock syndrome were made, the news coverage seriously affected product sales. Certainly, the makers of these products did not desire or control this communication.

Rumors, or more generally, word-of-mouth communication, occurs when consumers talk to other consumers about products. If you have ever said to a friend, "I tried Product A, and it tasted terrible!", you have participated in word-of-mouth communication. Although uncontrolled by a company, this type of communication can be very influential.[6] In fact one study found word-of-mouth communication to be twice as influential as

---

[6] Johann Arndt, *Word of Mouth Advertising: A Review of the Literature,* (New York: Advertising Research Foundation, 1967).

television ads and four times as influential as store displays in new food product adoptions.[7]

A marketing manager should never underestimate the power of word of mouth and public announcements as influential events. Even though companies cannot entirely control this form of communication, they should nonetheless be aware of its potential.

PROMOTION PLANNING

To effectively accomplish the communications system, a company must plan its promotional efforts by setting objectives, developing strategies, and determining the budget.

Promotional Objectives

The primary objective of promotion is to achieve the desired response through communication. To better understand responses to communication, models of possible responses have been developed, of which the two most popular are the AIDA and the hierarchy of effects models.

AIDA and Hierarchy of Effects   AIDA is an acronym for the steps a consumer is thought to follow in purchasing a product. These stages are:

1. Awareness
2. Interest
3. Desire
4. Action

In other words a consumer must first be made *aware* of the product, have an *interest* in it aroused, and, finally, *desire* to possess it before purchase (*action*) will occur. Promotional messages may be aimed at any or all of the AIDA steps. For instance when ITT ran ads to enhance its image after marketing research revealed that 60 percent of the public confused ITT with AT & T, the company was trying to create awareness.[8] When American Home Products uses Catherine Deneuve as spokesperson for its new facial moisturizer, Youth Garde, the company is trying to create awareness of the new product, interest in its attributes, desire to possess the youthful appearance it purports to give, and action in the form of purchase.[9]

[7] *Progressive Grocer,* October 1967, p. 71.

[8] Bill Abrams, "How ITT Shells Out $10 Million or So a Year to Polish Reputation," *Wall Street Journal,* April 2, 1982, pp. 1, 16.

[9] Susan Fraker, "American Home Products Battles the Doubters," *Fortune,* July 25, 1983, pp. 59–64.

The **hierarchy of effects** model is merely an expanded version of AIDA.[10] The steps in the hierarchy of effects are:

1. Awareness
2. Knowledge
3. Liking
4. Preference
5. Conviction
6. Purchase

Awareness is the consumer's ability to remember the brand name. *Knowledge* is some grasp of the features and attributes of the product. *Liking* is a positive attitude toward the product. *Preference* is the desire to have the product over alternative products. Although preference may exist, the consumer may not buy the product due to money constraints or social pressure. *Conviction* is the intention to actually buy the product, and *purchase* is the act of buying.

We can better understand the steps in the hierarchy of effects model by considering the psychological concepts of cognitive, affective, and behavioral responses. **Cognitive response** refers to an awareness or knowledge and thus describes the first two steps of the hierarchy. **Affective response** implies a liking or preference. **Behavioral response** is an outflow from the process and therefore refers to the purchase decision.

Promotional objectives must be based on which step in the process the target market appears to be in. The company can then design promotion to move the target market to the next step and eventually to get it to purchase. For example, a new product needs communication that initially creates awareness and knowledge. Therefore, general product attributes can be emphasized. When the target market is in the early steps of the hierarchy of effects, the objective is to create primary demand. **Primary demand** *is an awareness, knowledge, and liking for the general category of products.*

If the target market has knowledge of the product and a liking for it, the company should aim promotion at creating a preference for its particular brand. *Promotion aimed at creating specific brand preference, conviction, and purchase is trying to create* **selective demand**.

Company Resources and Policies   The resources and policies of a company also influence its promotional objectives. Resources concern how much money, time, and personnel the company is willing to devote to the promotional effort. Various promotional vehicles cost different amounts of money and require different degrees of personnel commitment. The com-

---

[10] Robert J. Lavidge and Gary A. Steiner, "A Model for Predictive Measurements of Advertising Effectiveness," *Journal of Marketing*, October 1961, p. 61.

"Take a close look.
I want the best for my skin.
I use Youth Garde."
Catherine Deneuve

Youth Garde is a creamy, rich formula
that goes beyond moisturizing. It helps
keep your skin from aging too soon.
So you can face the world with
smoother, firmer, younger-looking skin.
No woman can face the world—or
the close-up camera—more
beautifully than Catherine Deneuve.
Why does she choose Youth Garde?
"My skin has been through a lot.
Makeup changes, hot lights and sun,
tension, and those little ravages of time.
"Youth Garde gives it all the moisture
and protection it needs to keep it
glowing. And to keep it from aging
before the rest of me."
Discover what Youth Garde
can do for you.

Guard your youth with new Youth Garde.
At drug and food stores everywhere.

pany will require more resources, for example, if it mounts a national personal selling and television program than if it chooses a regional newspaper plan. National coverage costs a great deal in training and maintaining personal salespeople, and national television ads can be extremely expensive. One 30-second commercial on the final episode of M*A*S*H cost $450,000! Many companies simply do not have the resources for such promotional expenditures.

Corporate policy refers to the manner in which the company approaches promotion. Two popular promotion approaches are the push and pull policies. A company is following a **push policy** to promote its products when it concentrates promotion at the next level of distribution. (See Figure 15-2.) For example, a producer of bicycles is using a push policy when most of its promotional effort is aimed at wholesalers who in turn promote the product to retailers. Retailers then are expected to promote the product aggressively to ultimate consumers. When a push policy is followed, much emphasis is placed on personal selling. Relatively minor emphasis is placed on advertising and sales promotion.

The basic idea behind a **pull policy** is for the producer to stimulate ultimate consumer interest so extensively that consumers will "demand" that retailers stock it. Retailers then will "demand" that wholesalers carry the product. A pull policy places great emphasis on advertising and some emphasis on sales promotion, but less on personal selling. Implemented

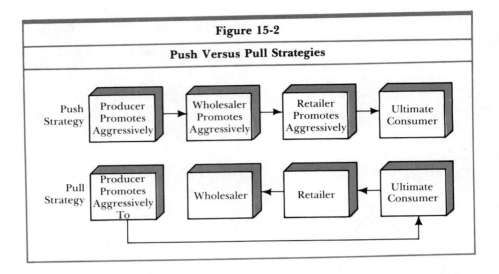

Figure 15-2

Push Versus Pull Strategies

Push Strategy: Producer Promotes Aggressively → Wholesaler Promotes Aggressively → Retailer Promotes Aggressively → Ultimate Consumer

Pull Strategy: Producer Promotes Aggressively To → Wholesaler ← Retailer ← Ultimate Consumer

effectively, a pull policy results in the product being "pulled" through the channel. In reality most companies use some combination of push and pull policies.

Target Market Characteristics   The target market a company is pursuing will partially determine the promotional objectives. How large is the target market? Is it regional or national? What are its demographic and psychographic characteristics? The answers to these questions will all affect corporate promotional objectives.

If the target market is small and geographically concentrated, the company can probably emphasize personal selling. Large, national markets will most likely require objectives that emphasize advertising.

Demographics and psychographics may tell a company the type of promotional vehicles to use in reaching its target market. Personal selling, for example, will be much more effective than magazine ads in communicating with illiterate people. Although this example is rather obvious, many more subtle promotional objectives can be determined by an awareness of the target market's sex, age, income, and life style.

Promotional Strategies

The promotional strategy takes the objectives and makes decisions on the proper combination of advertising, publicity, personal selling, sales promotion, and packaging to accomplish these objectives. Every marketing manager should understand the specifics of each of these five areas of promotion. We will discuss advertising and publicity in depth in Chapter 16, and will address personal selling and sales promotion in Chapter 17. Packaging was discussed in Chapter 8. However, to understand the promotional mix, we will give an overview of each here.

Advertising **Advertising** *is any paid method of nonpersonal communication about an organization and its products transmitted through a mass medium.* The most common mass media are television, radio, newspapers, magazines, outdoor advertising, and direct mail. Advertising offers the flexibility of reaching an extremely large audience (often measured in tens of millions) or small, precisely defined groups.

Besides flexibility, advertising offers several other advantages. First, it can be very cost efficient. Because it can reach an extremely large number of individuals, the cost per person is often low. For example, although a one-page ad in *Time* can cost $60,525, it is likely to reach 4,609,708 people, so that the cost per one thousand people reached is only $13.13.[11] Advertising also often lends prestige to a company. The visibility that the Chevrolet division of General Motors gains from sponsoring numerous television shows, for example, enhances its public image. Finally, advertising allows the message to be repeated numerous times, thus reinforcing the strength of the message.

The disadvantages of advertising rise from its impersonal nature. Because advertisements reach many people who are not part of the target market, the advertiser has spent money reaching people who have no intention of buying. A misplaced advertisement may reach millions of people, but few who will actually buy. Have you ever seen an advertisement for the purchase of a corporate jet? A man may see an ad for lipstick, or a woman may view an ad for a new type of men's shoes. All are examples of an advertisement reaching people who are not part of the target market.

Even if the advertisements reach the right people, the cost may be prohibitive. The cost for a 30-second commercial on the ABC television network during the 1984 Olympics was over $250,000.[12] Many companies simply cannot afford the cost of an extensive advertising campaign.

Because of its impersonal nature, it is also very difficult to measure advertising's effect on sales. Which sales occurred after one ad, many ads, or no exposure to ads at all? Additionally, it is hard to determine if advertisements are even helping (maybe hurting) sales.

Finally, the two-way communication offered by personal selling is usually a more persuasive method of promotion than the one-way communication afforded by advertising.

Publicity **Publicity** *is any nonpaid form of nonpersonal communication.* Usually viewed as largely independent of the company's control, publicity nor-

---

[11] *Consumer Magazine and Farm Publication Rates and Data,* July 27, 1983, pp. 410–15.
[12] Bill Abrams, "Advertisers Growing Restless Over Rising Cost of TV Time," *Wall Street Journal,* January 27, 1983, p. 29.

For over 30 years advertisers had to choose among six basic media: television, radio, magazines, newspaper, direct mail, and outdoor. Many would argue that a new advertising medium, cable television, has developed in the last 10 years. Whereas regular television is beamed over the airwaves from local television stations to anyone with an antenna, cable television can only be received by households with cable wiring. Certain cable stations can only be watched if the subscriber pays for a "descrambler." The potential for cable is great. As of January 1982, 45.3 million households (55.2 percent) in the United States had cable available, and 23.3 million (28.4 percent) were actually subscribers to basic cable services.

Although viewed on a conventional television set, cable offers the advertiser considerably greater control over the programming that surrounds its advertisements and the audience that views them. Different cable networks are very specific in the programs carried and, therefore, are attractive to narrowly defined target markets. A cable advertiser can avoid much of the waste associated with conventional television by reaching only members of its target market.

A few examples show just how specific cable can get. The ARTS network broadcasts mostly cultural fare and as of 1982 reached 6,300 households (7.7 percent). Black Entertainment TV (BET) reaches 8,803 households (10.8 percent) and features programs and advertisements aimed at the black community. The Continental Broadcast Network has particular times devoted to Christian programs, which reach 14,700 homes (18.0 percent). Cable Health Network (CHN) has round-the-clock health and science programming for its 4,000 subscribers. Cable News Network (11,072 homes) has all news, and the

mally takes the form of a news story concerning the company and/or its products. Although publicity is a nonpaid form of communication, it certainly is not always free. The costs of preparing news releases and encouraging the news media to use them can be considerable. Companies that use publicity effectively usually have public relations representatives or hire a public relations agency, neither of which is an inexpensive alternative.

Because the general public views publicity as independent of the com-

Weather Channel (3,000 homes) has all weather. ESPN (14,138 homes) broadcasts all sports, whereas Daytime (5,000 homes) is devoted exclusively to women's programming, and MTV (3,000 homes) shows only music videos. Other cable networks exclusively broadcast movies and ethnic programming in Spanish, French, and other languages.

Although pay cable subscriptions (purchasers of these specific channels) were only 15.1 million households in 1982, it is estimated that this number will swell to over 40 million by the end of the decade. More important than the total numbers is the target market specificity. An advertiser wishing to reach the Spanish-American target market can advertise on the National Spanish TV Network and reach 2,773 Spanish households. Conventional television cannot provide such specific demographic information.

The potential for greater demographic breakdown of cable audiences also exists. To date cable operators have done little marketing research concerning their subscribers. As Geers Gross Advertising stated in its report, *Cable TV Update*, "The absence of acceptable audience research is the greatest stumbling block of advertisers in cable."

However, cable's direct electronic link between the operator and the subscriber provides unprecedented research potential. For example, it is feasible to determine *exactly* which homes are watching which channel at any given time. It is only a matter of time before more specific analysis of cable audiences will exist, analysis more detailed than any other advertising medium provides.

Thus, the development of cable TV constitutes an entirely new medium of advertising and a new aspect for marketing managers to consider in developing the promotional mix. As such, it is a major and still evolving milestone in marketing.

* "Cable Programming Catches Up with Demand," *Business Week*, February 22, 1982, pp. 130–32; "Only Use Cable to Reach Narrow Audience, Experiment, or Improve Coverage," *Marketing News*, May 28, 1982, p. 1; and Craig Reiss, "Advertisers Guide to Cable Programs," *Marketing and Media Decisions*, November 1982, pp. 127–49.

pany, it may have a more positive effect on corporate image and product sales than advertising. The public views it as more "believable" because it came from an unbiased source. Publicity can be negative, however. News of product recalls or corporate fraud can seriously damage a company's marketing viability. Therefore, the company should try to manage publicity so that it presents an image which is positive and consistent with the rest of the company's marketing strategy.

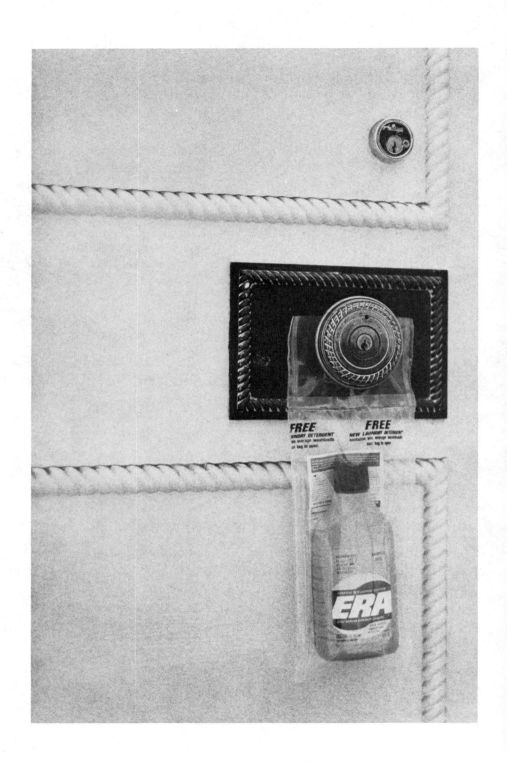

Personal Selling **Personal selling** *is a form of personal communication designed to inform and persuade target customers.* It includes industrial salespeople calling on companies, clerks in retail stores, door-to-door salespeople, and telephone sales calls to homes or companies. The primary advantage of personal selling is its immediacy. The salesperson is in personal contact with the target customer, which leads to numerous advantages. First, personal selling offers a greater communicative and persuasive impact than any other form of promotion. Because personal selling allows immediate feedback, the salesperson can adjust the promotional messages as the meeting progresses. Questions from the target customer can be dealt with immediately. The salesperson can also monitor verbal exchanges, body language, and facial expressions to guide the communication process (except in the case of telephone sales, of course).

Because personal contact must be made to conduct personal selling, it can be a very expensive method of promotion, considerably more expensive than advertising on a per-person basis. However, its persuasive potential makes it more than worth the cost for a large number of companies.

Sales Promotion **Sales promotion** *is an attempt to augment other promotional efforts.* It includes free samples, sweepstakes and contests, coupons, demonstrations, and trade shows. Sales promotion and promotion should not be confused. Promotion is the company's *overall* communication and persuasive effort, whereas sales promotion includes those activities used to *augment* advertising, publicity, personal selling, and packaging. When Eastern Air Lines was experiencing stiff competition on its New York to Boston and New York to Washington shuttle flights, it turned to sales promotion for a differential advantage. During July of 1981 Eastern gave away 250,000 coupons to passengers on those two routes that offered $50 off any transcontinental flight. Clearly, this sales promotion was intended to augment, not replace, Eastern's other advertising, publicity, and personal selling efforts. Were they successful? As David B. Kunstler, Eastern's Vice President of Sales and Advertising, put it, "There's no question as to their effectiveness where you distribute them."[13]

Sales promotions generally fall into two groups. **Consumer sales promotions** *are aimed at the final consumer and are designed to "pull" products through the channel.* When you receive a free sample of a new laundry soap in the mail, you are the recipient of a consumer sales promotion. **Trade sales promotions** *are aimed at salespeople, wholesalers, and retailers, who are encouraged to aggressively market products or "push" them through the channel.* When a manufacturer offers a two-week vacation in the Bahamas to the salesperson who sells the most merchandise, the company is using trade sales promotions.

---

[13] "Coupons Ride the Eastern Shuttle Again," *Business Week*, July 27, 1981, p. 27.

Packaging   Although we extensively discussed packaging in Chapter 8, it bears repeating that a product's package serves not only a functional role, but a promotional one as well. Especially for products sold in self-service outlets, the product must virtually "sell itself." Companies invest considerable time and money in developing packages that identify the product, communicate its attributes, and persuade the consumer to purchase it over competing items. In a sense the package must augment and complete the AIDA process. It must create awareness of its existence on the shelf, interest in it, and desire for it over competing brands.

The Promotional Mix   *How much emphasis a company places on the various promotional vehicles is called the* **promotional mix**. Because publicity, sales promotion, and packaging mostly augment the other two vehicles, the promotional mix is largely a decision of how much emphasis to place on advertising versus personal selling. Although most companies use both, typically either advertising or personal selling is emphasized. The relative emphasis is determined by the characteristics of the product and the target market, the stage of the product life cycle, and the promotional budget.

Figure 15-3 lists some of the *product characteristics* that help determine whether a product should be promoted primarily by advertising or personal selling. To illustrate, let us compare selling computers to selling hand soap. Because computers have a high unit value, potential buyers will be giving up a great deal of money in the purchase and will need to be persuaded. Thus, the more persuasive vehicle of personal selling is needed. Furthermore, a computer is sophisticated and difficult to understand, so a demonstration of its attributes may be necessary. This can best be accomplished by personal selling. Because customers do not buy computers often, we have lost the customer if we miss the sale, which gives us all the more reason to communicate personally with the customer to arrange any product variation desired and a trade-in allowance if necessary.

Because hand soap has a low unit value and is repurchased often, the

---

Figure 15-3

Promotional Mix Product Characteristics

Personal Selling Emphasized When the Product:	Advertising Emphasized When the Product:
Has a high unit value	Has a low unit value
Is highly sophisticated	Is simple
Needs demonstration	Needs no demonstration
Has a low replacement rate	Is purchased often
Is made to customer-specific requirements	Is a standard product
Involves trade-ins	Involves no trade-ins

company is less concerned over losing a sale and the consumer is more willing to try the product. Thus, less persuasion is needed. Further, the use of hand soap is easily understood and requires little demonstration. Finally, no special product variation or trade-ins are required, so the feedback of personal selling is less important. Therefore, a soap manufacturer should emphasize advertising in its promotional efforts.

We can continue this example to examine the target market's effect on the promotional mix. Specifically, the *target market's size and geographic location* influence the use of personal selling versus advertising. Because customers for large computers are few (maybe several thousand) and are located in industrial or commercial centers, it is much more practical to have salespeople call on each potential customer.

However, the target market for hand soap numbers over 200 million people in the United States alone. It is impractical to have salespeople call on all these potential customers when they can be reached through the mass media of advertising.

Therefore, companies with products whose target markets are small and geographically concentrated tend to promote primarily by personal selling. This does not mean that they do not advertise. However, their primary method of promoting their products is personal selling. Advertising, publicity, sales promotion, and packaging merely augment the primary promotional vehicle.

The *media viewing habits of the target market* also influence the promotional mix. For example, a company's target market for certain types of agricultural products may be farmers in remote areas. If the company finds that this target market pays little attention to advertising, then it must emphasize personal selling. This is especially important in international marketing. When promoting products in certain underdeveloped countries, the company may find that no advertising media exist and that cultural tradition dictates that sales can only be made on a face-to-face basis. In such situations the promotional mix definitely must emphasize personal selling.

The *stage of the product life cycle* can also influence the promotional vehicle emphasized. Figure 15-4 provides some guidelines for the five promotional vehicles in each product life cycle stage. In the development stage a general awareness of the product is created through publicity and general product advertising. Video cassette recorders (VCRs) are an example. Long before their availability on the market, articles in magazines and items on news shows were discussing the potential of these new products (publicity). Additionally, companies like Sony were advertising the main product features to create primary demand.

As introduction occurs, publicity and primary advertising continue, but personal selling and sales promotion are added to gain dealer support. Personal selling emphasizes product features and demonstrations.

In the growth stage advertising switches to creating selective demand.

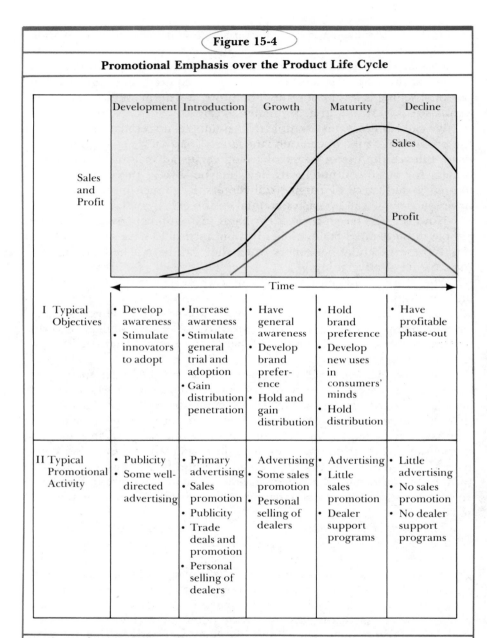

Figure 15-4

Promotional Emphasis over the Product Life Cycle

	Development	Introduction	Growth	Maturity	Decline
Sales and Profit					
I Typical Objectives	• Develop awareness • Stimulate innovators to adopt	• Increase awareness • Stimulate general trial and adoption • Gain distribution penetration	• Have general awareness • Develop brand preference • Hold and gain distribution	• Hold brand preference • Develop new uses in consumers' minds • Hold distribution	• Have profitable phase-out
II Typical Promotional Activity	• Publicity • Some well-directed advertising	• Primary advertising • Sales promotion • Publicity • Trade deals and promotion • Personal selling of dealers	• Advertising • Some sales promotion • Personal selling of dealers	• Advertising • Little sales promotion • Dealer support programs	• Little advertising • No sales promotion • No dealer support programs

SOURCE: James F. Engel, Martin R. Warshaw, and Thomas C. Kinnear, *Promotional Strategy*, 4th ed. (Homewood, Ill.: Richard D. Irwin, 1979), p. 649.

"Now that you know about VCRs, here's why you should buy Brand X" is a common theme. Personal selling to dealers also continues.

The wide acceptance in the maturity stage makes personal selling less feasible, so increasing emphasis is placed on advertising (mass promotion). In the decline stage little promotional activity occurs because the product phaseout decreases the need for any promotion.

Therefore, the promotional mix is largely affected by the product, the target market, and the product life cycle stage, which, combined with the marketing manager's knowledge of the advantages and disadvantages of advertising, publicity, personal selling, sales promotion, and packaging, is crucial in determining the promotional strategy. The final input to the promotional strategy is the budget.

The Promotional Budget

The goal of promotion is for an organization to communicate with its target markets and persuade target customers to purchase its products, services, or ideas. Part of the promotion planning process is deciding how much money the organization is willing to invest in this communication and persuasion. This is called the **promotional budget**.

Theoretically, setting the promotional budget should be approached from an economic perspective, that is, we should spend money on promotion till we reach the point at which *marginal revenue equals marginal cost.* In theory every additional dollar we spend on promotion (the marginal cost) should have some positive effect on sales (marginal revenue). As long as sales increase more than total costs, we are better off by promoting more. However, when costs start increasing more than sales, we should spend no more on promotion.

In actuality the theoretical approach is virtually impossible to use. The exact effect promotional expenditures will have on sales is hard to determine, and the total costs associated with the new sales level may be equally difficult to estimate. Additionally, competitive reactions are not directly considered. In setting the promotional budget, most companies use one of five techniques: percentage of sales, competitive parity, all you can afford, return on investment, or objective and task.

Percentage of Sales   A simplistic and, unfortunately, widely used promotional budgeting technique is the percentage of sales. Companies using this technique set the yearly promotional budget at a constant percentage of sales. Besides being easy, this technique is also conservative because it ties expenditures to sales.

However, this technique has no relationship to corporate promotional objectives, and it ignores competitive actions. *Promotion is viewed as a result of sales instead of the other way around.* Thus, the company lowers promotion expenditures in slow sales periods (exactly when it should increase promo-

Strategy

Coca-Cola Versus Dad's*

Coca-Cola and its main product Coke have been the major force in the $25 billion soft-drink industry for almost a hundred years. The key to the company's promotional strategy is advertising. Although it also spends millions every year on such sales promotions as contests, coupons, and dealer incentives, the lion's share of its promotional budget goes for advertising (well over $150 million in 1982).

Television, radio, magazines, and newspapers constantly bombard the target market with the "Coke is it!" theme. The strategy has certainly been successful. In 1982, Coca-Cola had sales of $6.2 billion and held a 34.5-percent share of the U.S. soft-drink market. In fact the soft-drink industry is largely oligopolistic, with the five top companies controlling over 78 percent of the total sales (PepsiCo 25.1 percent; Dr. Pepper, 8.2 percent; Seven-Up, 6.3 percent; and Royal Crown, 4.1 percent). These large competitors all follow Coca-Cola with massive advertising expenditures. In 1982 Coca-Cola and PepsiCo alone spent over $300 million just on television advertising.

How does a small player compete in a market of such giants? Dad's Root Beer, a Chicago-based subsidiary of IC Industries, provides a good example, and the key is local advertising and sales promotions. As corporate spokesman Harry D. Clark put it, "With the heavy competitive situation right now in the soft drink industry . . . Dad's likes to spend its promotional dollars on merchandising efforts other than advertising." About 35 percent of the company's promotion expenditures goes for advertising; the other 65 percent goes to sales promotions, which are many and quite creative.

Dad's tries to run promotions that tie in with particular holidays or seasons—Father's Day, of course, is called Dad's Day. In 1982 Dad's sponsored the Great Dad's Steak Out around Father's Day. Local bottlers offered dollar-off coupons for the purchase of any meat, any brand of charcoal, and Dad's. Ads were run in newspapers featuring the coupon, designed to accommodate the store's logo and the charcoal brand.

A summer promotion tied to the local radio station invited listeners to "Float with Dad's Root Beer and WLOL-FM [Minneapolis] down the Apple River." For every empty 12-pack of Dad's brought to any of eight tube rental agencies on the Apple River, consumers received a $2 discount on the rental. WLOL matched the number of spot ads purchased by Dad's. Outdoor ads, in-store displays, and signs at the tube rental centers also promoted the event. Thus, through a cooperative strategy Dad's offered a promotional package with sales promotion incentives and only paid for half of its advertising time.

Halloween is a big sales promotional time for Dad's. The Real Monster Halloween Sweepstakes was an example. Newspaper ads, cents-off coupons, and radio and TV spot ads helped promote the sweepstakes in which the grand prize was a trip for two to the British Isles—including a visit to Loch Ness and, hopefully, the Monster. Proof of a Dad's purchase was necessary to enter the Sweepstakes. In an interesting trade sales promotion twist to the same sweepstakes, sales representatives could win Kodak instant cameras by photographing the in-store displays. The most interesting pictures won the cameras. Other trade sales promotions have included a week for two on the Riviera for all bottlers that increased their January to July sales over the previous year, and cash and prizes for route salespeople who exceed their sales quotas.

Another consumer trade promotion strategy has been to tie sales of Dad's to snack foods. In 1981 Dad's hung four-ounce samplers of Orville Redenbacher's Gourmet Popping Corn and a supply of his Buttery Flavor Popping Oil on the necks of regular and diet Dad's. Point of purchase material and displays were placed in the soft-drink and popcorn sections of stores. The results were dramatic. The Cincinnati bottler reported a 459-percent sales increase. Green Bay, Wisconsin, sales shot up 860 percent.

In the area of publicity Dad's sponsors local ball teams and cohosts a fishing derby for the handicapped. Frequent public service announcements by local radio stations and extensive newspaper coverage create local goodwill for the company.

Certainly, these strategies will not knock Coca-Cola out of the leader's spot, but they help a small contender survive in a tightly defined target market of the overall soft-drink industry. This concentrated strategy does not try to take on Coke on a national basis, but sticks to a product Coca-Cola does not market, root beer, and puts all its promotional efforts into geographic markets where Dad's is strong. Efficiency in promotional expenditures is emphasized. Although their resources, objectives, and strategies are quite different, Coca-Cola versus Dad's offers a good insight into the different forms the promotional mix can take.

* Peter W. Bernstein, "Seven-Up's Sudden Taste for Cola," *Fortune,* May 17, 1982, pp. 101–03; "Coke's New Program to Placate Bottlers," *Business Week,* October 12, 1981, p. 48; "Coke Plunges into No-Caffeine Cola," *Business Week,* May 9, 1983, p. 35; "In '82, Big Advertisers Spent More on TV," *Wall Street Journal,* March 31, 1983, p. 31; "It's Coke vs. Pepsi—Again," *Business Week,* August 2, 1981, pp. 64–65; Barbara Rudolf, "Bottle Scars," *Forbes,* February 15, 1982, pp. 76–77; and "Soft Drink Maker Makes Liberal Use of Promotions in Marketing Program," *Marketing News,* February 16, 1982, pp. 10–11.

tion) and raises them in high sales periods (when it could lower promotion). The percentage of sales technique also puts marketing managers in the uncomfortable position of trying to forecast future sales levels without knowing the promotional budget! Although widely used, it is hardly a realistic approach to promotional budgeting.

Competitive Parity Under the competitive parity technique, a company spends an absolute dollar amount, or a ratio of promotion costs to sales, equal to that of a competitor or an industry average. The rationale for such a technique is to remain in a constant position (parity) relative to the competition. Competitive parity is an improvement over percentage of sales in that competition is considered, but it still has serious disadvantages.

It assumes that both companies are very similar and that the competitors know what they are doing. Hoover, which sells vacuum cleaners primarily by advertising, clearly should not use competitive parity and set its promotion budget based on what is spent by Electrolux, which depends primarily on personal selling. The cost differences between these two approaches would make budget comparisons meaningless. Additionally, differences in corporate image, goals, and distribution systems make competitive parity a less viable promotion budgeting technique. It should be used only for very similar companies.

All You Can Afford Companies with limited resources often adopt a promotion budget based on what they can afford. Usually, the money budgeted is far less than what corporate management would like to spend, but allocating more would endanger the company's liquidity.

The problem with this technique is that the budget and the promotional objectives are unrelated. A company can easily miss profitable promotional opportunities under the excuse, "We cannot afford it."

Return on Investment The rationale for this technique is that promotion should be viewed not as an expense, but rather as an investment in future corporate sales.[14] Using this technique, companies estimate the profit-generating potential of promotional expenditures and compute the return on investment from these expenditures. They then approve promotional costs that meet some corporate criteria for an acceptable return on investment. The advantage to this technique is that it relates promotional expenditures to corporate profit goals. Additionally, it approves only the best promotions, thus forcing the development of more effective promotional strategies.

The failing of this technique is the inability of management to accurately estimate the effect of promotional expenditures on sales and profit-

---

[14] Joel Dean, "Does Advertising Belong in the Capital Budget?" *Journal of Marketing,* October 1966, pp. 15–21.

ability. Although a reasonable approach to promotional budgeting, this failing has limited the use of the return on investment technique to comparatively few companies.

Objective and Task   With the objective and task technique, the company clearly outlines the promotional objectives it wishes to accomplish, then determines the promotional budget necessary to reach these objectives. The advantage of this technique is that it clearly ties promotional expenditures to stated objectives, emphasizes marketing research to determine how to promote, and examines the costs associated with objective attainment. One disadvantage is the difficulty in estimating costs of obtaining the promotional goals. Another is that measurement of performance against goals can be difficult. Still, it is by far the most realistic promotional budget technique.

The Budget and the Promotional Mix

The promotional budget greatly influences the promotional strategy and mix. Limited budgets necessitate less personal selling and little if any national advertising. In addition, the less expensive advertising media (newspapers, for example) will be used more extensively.

Although publicity may be important to the corporate promotion strategy, a limited budget may force a company to take a more passive role in publicity and not incur the cost of creating positive publicity. More liberal budgets allow the use of a promotional mix that will best achieve promotional objectives.

SUMMARY

- Promotion is the communication aspect of marketing.
- The promotional mix entails the use of advertising, publicity, personal selling, sales promotion, and packaging.
- Promotion represents a significant segment of our economy and a crucial aspect of the corporate marketing strategy.
- The seven elements of the marketing communications process are the message source, the coded message, the message delivery vehicles, the message receiver, the decoded message, feedback, and noise.
- Message sources take the form of company representatives, celebrities, customers, or actors.
- The message typically contains information on the company and product name(s); the product image, benefits, and attributes; and may contain words, language, pictures, or symbolism.

- The greater the noise in a communications system, the less likely the message will be received as intended.
- Uncontrolled communication can be more influential than the company's promotion efforts.
- Promotion planning involves setting objectives, developing strategies, and determining the budget.
- The AIDA and hierarchy of effects models of communication response help guide the development of promotional objectives.
- Primary demand is an awareness, knowledge, and liking for a general category of products. Selective demand is the preference, conviction, and purchase of a specific brand.
- Promotional objectives are influenced by corporate resources and policies.
- A push promotion policy attempts to promote the product to the next level in the marketing channel. A pull policy promotes the product to the final consumer.
- Promotional objectives are affected by the size, location, and characteristics of the target market.
- Advertising is cost efficient on a per-person basis, often adds prestige to the company image, and allows for message repetition. However, advertising may reach many people not in the target market, it can be expensive, results are hard to measure, and personal selling is often more persuasive.
- Publicity can be a very positive promotional vehicle, but because it is uncontrolled, it can also be negative.
- Personal selling can be more effective and offer more feedback than any other promotional vehicle. However, it is very expensive on a per-contact basis.
- Sales promotion involves activities designed to augment a company's advertising, publicity, personal selling, and packaging strategy.
- Consumer sales promotions are designed to "pull" the product through the channel. Trade sales promotions are designed to "push" the product through the channel.
- How much emphasis a company places on each of the promotional vehicles is called the promotional mix. It is largely influenced by the product and target market characteristics, the stage of the product life cycle, and the promotional budget.
- In setting the promotional budget, most companies use either the percentage of sales, competitive parity, all you can afford, return on investment, or objective and task technique.
- The problem with the percentage of sales technique is that it views promotion as a result of sales instead of the other way around.
- Competitive parity is more realistic than percentage of sales, but assumes the company is similar to competitors.

- Even though the all you can afford technique does not relate the budget to promotional objectives, many companies with limited resources can afford no other budgeting technique.
- Although the return on investment technique is more reasonable than the previous three, its use is limited by the difficulty in developing reliable estimates of the effect of promotional expenditures on sales and profitability.
- The advantage of the objective and task technique is that it clearly ties promotional expenditures to promotional objectives and emphasizes marketing research to determine promotional strategy.

DISCUSSION QUESTIONS

1. Explain why promotion is important to a company's marketing strategy.
2. Define the elements of the marketing communications system. How is this helpful in making promotion decisions?
3. Give three examples of symbolism in advertising.
4. Explain the AIDA and the hierarchy of effects models and how they aid in promotion planning.
5. Define selective and primary demand.
6. What is the difference between a push policy and a pull policy?
7. How are promotional objectives affected by target markets?
8. Define and list the characteristics of:
   (a) advertising
   (b) publicity
   (c) personal selling
   (d) sales promotion
9. What is the difference between consumer sales promotions and trade sales promotions?
10. How is the promotional mix affected by the product? The target market? The product life cycle? The promotional budget?
11. Describe each of the following promotion budgeting techniques:
    (a) percentage of sales
    (b) competitive parity
    (c) all you can afford
    (d) return on investment
    (e) objective and task

APPLICATION
EXERCISES

1. Select three advertisements and explain which step(s) of the hierarchy of effects they are addressing. How would you improve on their approach?
2. Pick a business in your town and design a promotional mix for its primary product or service. Justify your selection of promotion vehicles. Describe how you would set the promotional budget for the company.

CASE 15
Promotions Make United's Skies Less Friendly[15]

For many years the U.S. airline industry was tightly regulated. The federal government tightly controlled prices, finances, routes, and marketing. With the deregulation of the industry in 1978, airlines had much more leeway in marketing strategies. In the summer of 1979, United Airlines surprised its rivals by offering coupons for half-price fares on future flights. The success of its coupon promotion was summed up by United's Advertising Vice President Fred W. Heckel, "Some people thought our half-fare coupons would not help last summer . . . the fact is that they were a big success, filling our planes in just 11 days after a long strike. That's something that was never done before."

This success led United to announce its "Take-Off" contest in April of 1980. Passengers were given a card with nine spots to be rubbed with a coin. If three spots in a row showed an airplane, the cardholder won a free round-trip flight. The response to the promotion was overwhelming for United and frightening for rivals.

Predictably, the rivals followed suit. Pan American gave international fliers souvenir plates, American and TWA started contests of their own, and all airlines started cutting prices. United spent $3.5 million advertising its contest, and rivals matched its strategy with similar expenditures.

Much of the airlines' promotional strategy is aimed at the frequent flier. For some airlines 20 percent of their passengers purchase 70 percent of their seats. To capture this target market, Eastern offered its Frequent Traveler Bonus Program of credits toward free air fare when Hertz cars were rented. Continental offered a similar credit system with National Car Rental and Hilton Hotels, and Western Airline has one with Avis.

Use of Marketing Information Systems to identify key fliers has helped promotional efficiency. As American Airlines' Marketing Vice President Thomas G.

---

[15] Now the Battling Airlines Try Mass Marketing," *Business Week*, April 28, 1980, p. 104; and "The Sky's the Limit in Luring the Frequent Flier," *Business Week*, October 18, 1982, pp. 152–53.

Plaskett stated, "The side benefits of being able to identify your market are astounding. I can take $1 million out of media, where it's like a teaspoon of water in the ocean, and put it in direct mail and get tremendous efficiency." American periodically mails promotional offers to inactive AAdvantage (the American frequent fliers club) members and usually gets a 10-percent response.

Is all this promotional activity helpful, or has the competition merely added expense to United's way of doing business and brought it no new customers? Industry analysts disagree on the results. One analyst feels, "It's one thing to ask people to 'Fly the Friendly Skies of United.' It's something else to ask them to 'Fly the Lucky Skies,' and I'm not at all certain that the contest approach won't be harmful in the long run."

Discussion Questions

1. What specific airline promotional strategies can you identify?
2. Do you think United's promotional efforts will generate more total flying or merely steal fliers from rivals? Will United's promotions have any effect if rivals simply match them?
3. What promotional strategy would you recommend to United?

16

Advertising and Publicity

STUDY OBJECTIVES

After studying this chapter, you should be able to

1. Explain the role of advertising in the overall selling effort.
2. Discuss the objectives of advertising.
3. Define the terms pioneering and competitive as they apply to advertising.
4. Explain how nonbusiness institutions use advertising.
5. Describe the classifications of advertising as national, local, or cooperative.
6. Characterize trade, industrial, farm, and professional advertising.
7. List several examples of advertising costs and discuss the different ways various advertising media communicate a product's message to target customers.
8. Explain the importance of timing and creativity in advertising.
9. Explain how an advertising agency differs from an in-house advertising department.
10. Identify the major objections to advertising.
11. Explain how publicity affects a company's image.
12. List the specific goals of public relations.

Advertising and publicity are the mass media aspects of the promotional effort. Both appeal to large groups of people. The main difference between the two is that advertising is paid for and controlled by the company, whereas publicity is not. We will begin our discussion with advertising and conclude the chapter with publicity.

ADVERTISING

Advertising permeates almost all facets of modern life. Whenever we scan a newspaper, look at a magazine, listen to radio, watch a TV program, open our mail, or walk down a city street, the chances are that we will be exposed to commercial messages. It is virutally impossible for anyone to escape contact with some form of advertising.

The range of advice furnished us by advertisers is almost unlimited. Consider for a moment the ways in which advertisers tell people how to live. Commercial messages tell us:

1. *What to eat*—"the bread that's better for you because it's eight hours fresher!"
2. *What to wear*—"easy-care fabrics that need no ironing!"
3. *How to care for our bodies*—"with the deodorant (soap, toothpaste, foot powder, mouthwash, shaving lotion) that keeps you fresh all day!"
4. *Where to shop*—"at the shopping center that's fun for the whole family!"
5. *What to drive*—"the automobile with style!"
6. *Where to take our vacations*—"in a fun-filled paradise for the whole family!"
7. *And how to get there*—"on the airline that's ready when you are!"
8. *Where to put our money*—"at the bank that cares about you."
9. *How to protect our loved ones*—"with life insurance from someone who knows your insurance needs!"
10. *How to provide for our retirement*—"with the savings plan that lets you retire at age 55."
11. *And even where to be buried*—"where perpetual care is guaranteed."

Advertising is very important to society. It pays for a large part of our recreation and entertainment, lowers the cost of our newspapers and magazines, enables us to view free television shows, and probably encourages most of us to work harder to buy things we didn't know we needed until they were advertised. Advertising is also controversial. As we will see later, it is criticized extensively.

Advertising is also important to the communication goals of a company. As the old saying goes, "Doing business without advertising is like winking at someone in the dark. You know what you are doing, but nobody else does." However, in the marketing of most products advertising does not constitute the entire promotional program, but is simply part of the overall effort to sell the product. It is important, then, for marketing management to decide the specific role advertising should play.

For example, although companies advertise large computers and related equipment extensively, the advertisements alone cannot be expected to make the sale. For one thing, a substantial amount of money is involved. For another, there are a host of technical and financial matters that must be resolved to the prospect's satisfaction before an order will be placed. In this example, advertising is expected to make a prospect aware of his or her needs and to make the prospective customer receptive to a visit by the manufacturer's sales representative. In other words a company often uses advertising to make buyers aware of a product and receptive to a detailed face-to-face presentation of it.

Advertising is also only part of the total promotional mix in selling to ultimate consumers, especially in marketing shopping goods. Automakers advertise extensively, but personal selling by the auto dealer's staff is still needed. Even in the case of many convenience goods, advertising must be supplemented by point of sale displays and other sales promotion devices.

Advertising Expenditures

In 1982 the total advertising volume in the United States was $66.58 billion.[1] Figure 16-1 gives the dollar amounts spent in each advertising medium. Newspapers represented 26.6 percent of the total revenues, magazines 5.6 percent, television 21.5 percent, radio 7.0 percent, direct mail 15.5 percent, and outdoor 1.1 percent. Other media, which include business and farm publications and the Yellow Pages accounted for 22.7 percent of total expenditures.[2] These expenditures have remained a fairly constant percentage of the U.S. Gross National Product, approximately 2 percent.[3]

Advertising expenditures continue to grow. Robert Coen predicts that U.S. advertising expenditures will exceed $320 billion by the year 2000, whereas worldwide expenditures will pass $460 billion. Advertising ex-

---

[1] "Banner Year Forecast for Ad Industry," *Marketing News*, September 2, 1983, pp. 1, 16.

[2] Robert J. Coen, "Ad Industry Topped Others in Recession," *Advertising Age*, May 30, 1983, pp. 3, 42.

[3] U.S. Department of Commerce, Bureau of the Census, *Statistical Abstract of the United States, 1982–83*, p. 418.

Medium	Millions of Dollars Spent	Percentage of Total Spent
Figure 16-1		
Advertising Expenditures for 1982		
Newspapers		
National	2,452	3.7
Local	15,242	22.9
Total	17,694	26.6
Magazines		
Weeklies	1,659	2.5
Women's	904	1.4
Monthlies	1,147	1.7
Total	3,710	5.6
Farm publications	148	0.2
Television		
Network	6,210	9.3
Spot	4,360	6.6
Local	3,759	5.6
Total	14,329	21.5
Radio		
Network	255	0.4
Spot	923	1.4
Local	3,492	5.2
Total	4,670	7.0
Direct mail	10,319	15.5
Business papers	1,876	2.8
Outdoor		
National	465	0.7
Local	256	0.4
Total	721	1.1
Miscellaneous		
National	7,067	10.6
Local	6,046	9.1
Total	13,113	19.7
Total		
National	37,785	56.8
Local	28,795	43.2
Grand total	66,580	100.0

SOURCE: Robert J. Coen, "Ad Industry Topped Others in Recession, *Advertising Age,* May 30, 1983, pp. 3, 42.

penditures will have risen 1,000 times in the twentieth century.[4] In addition this century has seen the invention of two major advertising media (radio and television). Clearly, advertising is a dynamic and expanding industry.

The Big Advertisers

A large share of advertising expenditures comes from relatively few advertisers. In 1982 the 100 leading advertisers spent $17.1 billion on advertising in major media, 25.7 percent of all advertising expenditures that year.[5] Figure 16-2 lists these top 100 national advertisers and their advertising expenditures, whereas Figure 16-3 gives the advertising-to-sales ratio of the 10 leading advertisers.

Advertising Objectives

Advertising's primary objective is to help increase sales. However, a firm's specific advertising objectives may include one or a combination of the following: (1) to increase the number of units purchased, (2) to introduce new products, (3) to counteract competition, (4) to increase the number of product uses, (5) to increase sales in an off season, (6) to remind consumers about a product and reinforce promotional messages, (7) to maintain brand loyalty, (8) to build a positive business image, (9) to obtain dealer support, and (10) to secure leads for and lend assistance to salespeople.

Increase Sales   Much advertising, especially for consumer convenience goods, is intended to encourage the consumer to buy more of the product. Many companies extensively advertise brand names to enhance sales. In addition producers' groups advertise numerous general products, such as orange juice, avocados, eggs, raisins, beef, and coffee, to increase sales of the general product category. Orange juice growers advertise to convince consumers, "It isn't just for breakfast anymore." Avocado advertising increased consumption from 5 percent of U.S. households to 50 percent. Beef producers tell us, "Somehow, nothing satisfies like beef."[6] All such ads have as their objective an increase in sales.

---

[4] Robert J. Coen, "Vast U.S. and Worldwide Ad Expenditures Expected," in *The Shape of Things to Come: The Next 20 Years in Advertising and Marketing*, (Chicago: Crain Publications, November 13, 1980), pp. 10–16.

[5] Marion L. Elmquist, "100 Leaders Parry Recession With Heavy Spending," *Advertising Age*, September 8, 1983, pp. 1, 168.

[6] Kathleen A. Hughes, "Coffee Makers Hope New Ads Will Reverse Declining Sales," *Wall Street Journal*, September 1, 1983, p. 27; and Terri Minsky, "Beef Industry Turning to Ads to Change Meat's Reputation," *Wall Street Journal*, April 1, 1982, p. 29.

Introduce New Products   Many advertising campaigns stress distinctly new products as well as new models and modifications of old models. Advertising is the quickest and most effective way to acquaint a mass market with a new product or a new version of an old product. Kodak introduced its new pocket-sized camera, essentially a new version of an old product, with intensive national advertising in magazines, on radio, and on television. Lady Schick, maker of a warming device for cleansing creams and moisturizers, also used a saturation campaign to tell consumers about its brand new product.

Counteract Competition   The main purpose of many advertising campaigns is to combat inroads made by a competitor's advertising into the firm's market share. Although much advertising is designed to attract new consumers (people who have never tried a specific product before), a great deal of advertising simply tries to induce consumers to switch from one brand to another. When one competitor—say, a major soft-drink com-

The link becomes more important each year as advertising expenditures increase for radio and the newer broadcast medium, television. Radio and TV stations and networks sell time, and the prices charged differ according to the time of day, week, or year; the size of the audience; the total amount of time purchased; and many other variables. In 1983 network television prices for units of 30 seconds ranged from over $200,000 for commercial time on a prime-time special down to $2,500 for a Saturday morning program. Local TV station prices were expectedly much lower, hovering in the hundreds rather than thousands of dollars.

Television advertising, in particular, must deal with restrictions that result from the medium's extraordinary power to influence its audience. Partly as a result, advertising expenditures for TV trailed newspaper advertising by over 5 percent, with revenues totaling several billion dollars less. In this regard the Television Advertising Board reported that for 1978 "after deducting $3.9 billion for classified advertising for which TV can have no counterpart under FCC rules, $240 million for cigarette advertising that is legally off limits to TV and $60 million for hard-liquor advertising that television doesn't accept, newspapers' total revenue from common-category advertisers was $480 million less than TV's revenues from the same classification."†

Continued growth in advertising revenues is predicted for both broadcast media. Certainly Americans are seldom far from a radio or television set—a ready-made audience for the advertisers who would woo them through the use of broadcast commercials.

* Robert J. Coen, "Ad Industry Topped Others in Recession," *Advertising Age*, May 30, 1983, pp. 3, 42.
† "Ten Years to Overtake Newspapers, Says TVB," *Broadcasting*, March 5, 1979, p. 114.

pany—launches a new advertising campaign that appears to be taking consumers away from a rival, we can expect the adversely affected firm to counterattack with a new or more aggressive campaign of its own.

A special type of competitive advertising called **comparative advertising** tries to present the company's product favorably by comparing it to the competition. For example, Vanish advertisements insinuate that other toilet bowl cleaners might ruin your plumbing, the makers of Totino's pizza say that other frozen pizzas "taste like cardboard," and Scope says Listerine gives users "Medicine Breath." The guiding principle is: "Don't tell customers why they should buy your product. Try to persuade them *not* to buy your competitors."[7]

Probably the hottest comparative advertising battle today is between

[7] Bill Abrams, "Comparative Ads Are Getting More Popular, Harder Hitting," *Wall Street Journal*, March 11, 1982, p. 29.

Figure 16-2

Top 100 Advertisers in 1982 (Millions of Dollars)

Rank	Company	Advertising Expenditures	Rank	Company	Advertising Expenditures
1	Procter & Gamble	$726.1	28	Mattel Inc.	217.9
2	Sears, Roebuck & Co.	631.2	29	U.S. Government	205.5
3	General Motors Corp.	549.0	30	Bristol–Myers Co.	205.0
4	R.J. Reynolds Industries	530.3	31	Dart & Kraft	199.2
5	Philip Morris Inc.	501.7	32	Esmark Inc.	197.8
6	General Foods Corp.	429.1	33	Norton Simon Inc.	191.2
7	AT & T Co.	373.6	34	Consolidated Foods Corp.	178.0
8	K Mart Corp.	365.3	35	Chrysler Corp.	173.0
9	Nabisco Brands	335.2	36	Pillsbury Co.	170.4
10	American Home Products Corp.	325.4	37	Gillette Co.	163.0
11	Mobil Corp.	320.0	38	RCA Corp.	160.1
12	Ford Motor Co.	313.5	39	ITT Corp.	159.1
13	PepsiCo Inc.	305.0	40	General Electric Co.	159.0
14	Unilever U.S.	304.6	41	CBS Inc.	159.0
15	Warner–Lambert Co.	294.7	42	Gulf & Western Industries	155.0
16	Beatrice Foods Co.	271.0	43	Kellogg Co.	154.2
17	Johnson & Johnson	270.0	44	Seagram Co. Ltd.	153.0
18	Colgate-Palmolive	268.0	45	Eastman–Kodak Co.	142.8
19	McDonald's Corp.	265.5	46	Sterling Drug	140.2
20	Coca-Cola Co.	255.3	47	American Cyanamid Co.	133.0
21	General Mills	244.4	48	Chesebrough–Pond's	131.0
22	Anheuser–Busch Cos.	243.4	49	Time Inc.	130.1
23	H.J. Heinz Corp.	235.7	50	Richardson–Vicks	129.3
24	Batus Inc.	235.0	51	Schering–Plough Corp.	123.9
25	Warner Communications	232.2	52	Campbell Soup Co.	121.0
26	J.C. Penney Co.	230.0	53	Beecham Group Ltd.	120.7
27	Ralston Purina Co.	220.0	54	Mars Inc.	120.0

Rank	Company	Advertising Expenditures	Rank	Company	Advertising Expenditures
55	Nissan Motors Corp., U.S.A.	117.6	78	American Brands	72.3
56	Revlon Inc.	113.0	79	American Motors Corp.	72.0
57	Nestle Enterprises	112.5	80	Pan American World Airways	72.0
58	Toyota Motor Sales	111.3	81	UAL Inc.	70.6
59	Quaker Oats Co.	106.1	82	Mazda Motors of America	70.5
60	Loews Corp.	103.3	83	Kimberly–Clark Corp.	69.3
61	Volkswagen of America	98.0	84	Wm. Wrigley Jr. Co.	67.0
62	CPC International	96.7	85	Pfizer Inc.	65.7
63	American Express Co.	95.5	86	20th Century-Fox Film Corp.	65.0
64	American Honda Motor Corp.	94.9	87	AMR Corp.	61.6
65	E.I. du Pont de Nemours & Co.	92.9	88	Hershey Foods Corp.	60.0
66	Trans World Corp.	91.6	89	Eastern Air Lines	57.4
67	North American Philips Corp.	90.6	90	Stroh Brewery Co.	55.5
68	SmithKline Beckman Co.	89.5	91	GrandMet USA	54.0
69	Union Carbide Corp.	83.7	92	Royal Crown Cos.	50.3
70	MCA Inc.	80.1	93	Noxell Corp.	49.6
71	Xerox Corp.	80.0	94	Delta Air Lines	49.3
72	Clorox Co.	76.3	95	Polaroid Corp.	47.8
73	Greyhound Corp.	75.2	96	Canon U.S.A.	47.0
74	IBM Corp.	75.0	97	Wendy's International	44.9
75	S.C. Johnson & Son	74.6	98	Hiram Walker Resources Ltd.	44.4
76	Brown–Forman Distillers Corp.	74.0	99	E & J Gallo Winery	42.9
77	Miles Laboratories	72.3	100	American Broadcasting Cos.	42.8

SOURCE: Marion L. Elmquist, "100 Leaders Parry Recession with Heavy Spending," *Advertising Age*, September 8, 1983, pp. 1, 168.

Figure 16-3		
Advertising-to-Sales Ratio of Top 10 Advertisers		
Company	**Expenditures (Millions)**	**Expenditures as a Percentage of Sales**
Procter & Gamble	$726.1	5.8
Sears, Roebuck & Co.	631.2	2.1
General Motors	549.0	0.9
R.J. Reynolds	530.3	4.1
Philip Morris	501.7	4.3
General Foods	429.1	0.9
AT & T	373.6	0.6
K Mart	365.3	2.2
Nabisco Brands	335.2	5.7
American Home Products	325.4	7.1

SOURCE: Marion L. Elmquist, "100 Leaders Parry Recession with Heavy Spending," *Advertising Age*, September 8, 1983, pp. 1, 168.

McDonald's, Burger King, and Wendy's.[8] In 1982 Burger King started advertising that its Whopper tasted better than McDonald's Big Mac or Wendy's single hamburger, because Burger King broils and the other two fry. Wendy's countered by challenging Burger King to a national taste test, contending its meat was fresher. Wendy's advertisements described the other two restaurants' burgers as "frozen stiff" and emphasized the inconveniences of special orders. In 1983 Burger King took aim at McDonald's by featuring a family named McDonald who switched to Burger King and emphasizing that millions of others have also switched. Has the campaign worked? In January of 1983 Burger King sales were up 16 percent from the previous year, but both Wendy's and McDonald's were seeking legal action for what was termed "misleading advertising." Finally in 1984, Wendy's coined the phrase, "Where's the Beef!" in comparing the others' hamburgers.

Increase the Number of Product Uses   Some advertising campaigns try to induce consumers to use the product for more purposes, thereby increasing their total consumption. Campbell's Soup, a major manufacturer, features recipes for a variety of nonsoup dishes in which soup is one of the principal ingredients. This approach is a very popular one with producers

---

[8] "Battle of the Burgers: Wendy's, Burger King, McDonald's to Mix It," *Wall Street Journal*, September 27, 1982, p. 17; "Burger King's Ads Cook Up a Storm," *Business Week*, October 11, 1982, p. 39; Bill Abrams, "Some New Ads May Rekindle Burger Battle," *Wall Street Journal*, March 4, 1983, pp. 24, 30; and "Burger King Beefs Up Its Jabs and Jokes," *Business Week*, September 26, 1983, pp. 42–43.

THE WENDY'S NATIONAL ADVERTISING PROGRAM, INC.

TITLE: "FLUFFY BUN"

LENGTH: 30 SECONDS
COMM'L NO.: WOFH-3386

CUST. #1: It certainly is a big bun.
CUST. #2: It's a very big bun.

CUST. #1: A big fluffy bun.

CUST. #2: It's a very...big...fluffy... bun.

CUST. #3: Where's the beef?
ANNCR: Some hamburger places give you a lot less beef on a lot of bun.

CUST. #3: Where's the beef?

ANNCR: At Wendy's, we serve a hamburger we modestly call a "Single"— and Wendy's Single has more beef than the Whopper or Big Mac. At Wendy's, you get more beef and less bun.

CUST. #3: Hey, where's the beef? I don't think there's anybody back there!

ANNCR: You want something better, you're Wendy's Kind of People.

of a great variety of food products. Producers of aluminum foil, plastic wrap, and similar goods also suggest multiple uses for their products. Arm and Hammer Baking Soda turned around its declining sales by convincing customers the baking ingredient could also be used as an air, drain, and refrigerator freshener.

Increase Sales in Off Seasons Most products, from road machinery and automobiles to soft drinks, have a seasonal purchase or natural usage period. To offset this fact, many advertising campaigns are designed to stimulate sales year-around. To even out sales over a 12-month period, an ice-

Strategy

Goodrich Versus Goodyear

For many years Goodrich faced the difficult problem of consumer identification with Goodyear, its long-standing competitor. Because the names Goodrich and Goodyear are so similar and because Goodyear is much larger and advertises more extensively (Goodyear had a 1981 market share of 30 percent and spent $25 million on TV advertising—nearly half of the total tire industry's TV dollars spent), many consumers thought that Goodrich was really Goodyear.*

The Goodyear Tire and Rubber Company was founded in 1898, Goodrich in 1912. Both companies are best known for making tires, but each company also manufactures chemicals and other products for the industrial market. Both companies have about 50 subsidiaries throughout the world, and both are headquartered in Akron, Ohio.

Goodyear has long been well known for its blimps. Every year millions of tire customers see the Goodyear blimp on isolated cameras while watching football games. Goodyear was a pioneer in the lighter-than-air craft industry and built the first engine-powered airship. In addition Goodyear is the oldest and largest tire manufacturer in the world.

Because of Goodyear's size and pervasive presence in the tire industry and because of the similarity of the companies' names, Goodrich ads simply reinforced Goodyear's promotion. For example, although Goodrich was the first American tire company to introduce a radial tire, most consumers thought Goodyear was the innovator. In fact a study showed that most consumers gave Goodyear credit for being the largest producer of radial tires when it had not made one.† As one observer notes, Goodrich could "reinvent the wheel and Goodyear would get most of the credit."‡ It was almost as if Goodyear had two promotional budgets, its own and Goodrich's.

Goodrich knew that it was the American leader in the production of radial tires. In 1972, when demand for radials began to take off and the company realized it must establish an identity separate from Goodyear, Goodrich selected a new advertising firm, Grey Advertising, to help solve the identification problem. The Grey agency recommended two alternatives: Change the name of the company or eliminate the name confusion through comparative advertising. Changing the company name was rejected because it would be too expensive, would require too much time, and because the name Goodrich had achieved extensive identification in the industrial market.

Comparative advertising was selected as the alternative. Goodrich and Goodyear had been fierce, but friendly competitors for over half a century. There was no intent to slight Goodyear. The goal was to help consumers realize that Goodrich was not the same as Goodyear. Goodrich wanted to clear up the name confusion and increase consumers' awareness of its leadership in radial tires.

A comparative advertising campaign was developed, primarily focused on the Goodyear blimp. Passing references such as the following were made: "And if you still get our names confused, just look up in the sky. If you see an enormous blimp with somebody's name on it, we're the other guys." (Interestingly, both Goodyear and Goodrich produce blimps for the Navy). Advertising people began to refer to Goodrich's promotion as the "Non-Blimp Campaign."

Goodrich aggressively drove home its theme lines "Goodrich not Goodyear" and "We're the other guys" through print and television advertising. The strategy worked. Consumer recall of these slogans jumped from 10 to 50 percent. Awareness of the Goodrich brand increased 222 percent.§

Goodrich executives felt that the "We're the other guys" campaign was one of the most successful in history. The campaign was updated over the years, and "the other guys" line is still featured in much of Goodrich promotion.

As part of its new strategy, Goodrich also decided to make its advertisements more credible by not conveying the impression that its tires are indestructible. It avoided direct comparison of its tires with Goodyear's products, because even unbiased experts cannot reach a firm conclusion as to which is better.

Meanwhile, Goodyear, still the undisputed leader in tire production, fought back. One strategy was to cut prices. Because it has a much larger volume than Goodrich, it could spread its costs over more units.

The company has also changed its advertising theme to capitalize on the success of the blimp. Themes such as "Come up to Goodyear" and "The Blimp is Behind You" are used to unify Goodyear's advertising.**

Although competition between the two companies is still keen, more people now identify Goodrich as an entity apart from Goodyear. This is largely due to its advertising strategy.

---

* "Goodyear: Will Staying No. 1 in Tires Pump Up Profits?" *Business Week*, July 12, 1982, pp. 85, 88.
† "Goodrich Out to Dispel 'Misuse' of Its Own Name," *Advertising Age*, December 4, 1972, p. 2.
‡ Jack Trout and Al Ries, "Positioning Cuts Through Chaos in Market Place," *Advertising Age*, May 1, 1972, pp. 51–54.
§ Patrick C. Ross, "Goodrich, Not Goodyear, Works at Telling It Straight," *Advertising Age*, October 7, 1974, pp. 2, 8.
** Jay McCormick, "Goodyear's Unity Bid Inflates Blimp," *Advertising Age*, February 22, 1982, p. 72.

cream manufacturer may elect to advertise its product aggressively during the winter months. Manufacturers of air-conditioning systems encourage consumers to buy during the fall and winter and "save money." Swimming-pool makers advertise preseason sales that "save you up to 30 percent." By increasing sales during slack seasons, producers can utilize production facilities and labor more fully and reduce storage costs.

Remind and Reinforce   As the name suggests, **reminder advertising** lets consumers know that an established brand is still available and what its attributes are. Popular soft drinks, chewing gum, and motel chains such as Holiday Inn make considerable use of reminder advertising. **Reinforcement advertising** is used to convince current consumers they have made the right purchase and should buy the product again. These advertisements often emphasize ways to get more satisfaction from the products. Because many consumers may have second thoughts after purchasing consumer durables such as cars or kitchen appliances, manufacturers of such products often use reinforcement advertising.

Maintain Brand Loyalty   Many businesses work very hard over a period of years to develop brand allegiance. Once a brand is established, it is certain to attract imitators. Accordingly, many advertising campaigns are directed at winning or retaining the consumer's loyalty. Much of the strategy of Coca-Cola advertising is designed to maintain brand loyalty. Many soft-drink producers have attempted to imitate Coke over the years, and its "Coke is it" theme is one way the company fights back. "You can be sure if it's Westinghouse" is another slogan designed in part to maintain the loyalty of present consumers.

Advertising is said to be **pioneering** when it is used to acquaint the customer with a distinctly new product. Because it is used when a product is in the introductory phase of the product life cycle, there is little competition. Therefore, no effort is made to identify or compare brands. Pioneering advertising endeavors to create **primary demand**, demand for the general product category. Early advertising by airlines, for example, sold the concept of flying rather than the services of individual airlines.

Competitive advertising occurs during the growth and maturity phases of the product life cycle. The goal is to create **selective demand**, demand for that company's particular brand, or brand loyalty. As such, most competitive advertising is built around the idea of persuading customers that "our product is the best buy." With commerical airlines now an accepted mode of travel, advertisements have become more competitive to create brand loyalty. Says the president of People Express Airlines, "Airlines used to have lots of clouds in their ads. Now they give fare costs, conditions of ticket purchase and flight times."[9]

---

[9] John D. Williams, "Airlines Give Up 'Image' Ads to Promote Cut-Rate Prices," *Wall Street Journal*, April 15, 1982, p. 29.

Build a Positive Business Image Much advertising is of an *institutional* nature. The immediate objective is not to sell products, but to impress either the consuming business public that the firm is patriotic, progressive, imaginative, possessed of a public conscience, or exceptionally concerned with quality. Public utilities make extensive use of this type of advertising. Many well-known slogans, such as "progress is our most important product" (General Electric), "quality is job 1" (Ford), and "your safety is our business" (Firestone), have an institutional objective.

Obtain Dealer Support Typically, manufacturers' salespeople who call on wholesalers and retailers have advance notice of their company's upcoming advertising campaigns so that they can play up the campaign to middlemen—saying, in effect, "Look, our tremendous ad campaign will bring customers into your store asking for the product. It'll be presold." A retailer is much more inclined to stock a product if an advertising campaign is being planned that will bring customers into the store to buy it.

Assist Salespeople Some advertising is designed to produce leads that can be followed up by personal sales calls. Coupons to be filled out by interested individuals are an example of advertising that attempts to achieve this objective. Many invitations to "register here to win a free prize" are primarily intended to provide lists of prospects for the firm's sales force. Advertising designed to secure leads is especially common in the area of industrial goods, and a high percentage of ads for these products carry a coupon for inquiries.

In addition much advertising is aimed at "preselling" a product before the salesperson makes contact. It is much easier for a salesperson to conclude a sale if the target customer already knows something about the product and the company.

The Effect of the Target Market on Advertising

Different organizations have different target markets. Consequently, advertising objectives and strategies vary according to the nature of the target market. We can get a sense of these differences when we examine advertising by nonbusiness organizations, consumer-oriented advertising, and advertising to business buyers.

Advertising by Nonbusiness Organizations   Most nonbusiness organizations today have accepted the fact that advertising can be a very effective way to change or modify public opinion and behavior. Religious organizations use many media to stimulate church attendance and interest. The federal government has advertising campaigns to achieve many different objectives, such as increasing enlistment in the armed forces, encouraging citizens to stop smoking, and educating taxpayers in how to prepare tax forms. Labor unions sometimes use advertising to publicize their side of a contested issue or to attract members. Nonprofit organizations such as the March of Dimes, the United Fund, the Salvation Army, and the Red Cross use advertising to win public support and contributions.

Most American businesses belong to one or more trade associations. A broad goal of many of these associations is to increase consumer demand for what their members sell. The Florida Citrus Commission, for example, sponsors advertising campaigns designed to make Americans more conscious of the advantages of orange juice produced in the state of Florida. In similar fashion the American Dairy Association promotes milk and other dairy products, the Wool Institute encourages consumption of wool products, and the Cotton Council urges that more cotton be used in the manufacture of consumer products.

Consumer-Oriented Advertising   Advertising aimed at consumers may be national or local. The key aspect of **national advertising** is that it is manufacturer-sponsored. Because a campaign does not need to be conducted nationwide to be considered national, the name is somewhat misleading. Actually, the geographic area covered is irrelevant as long as the broad purpose of the advertising is to encourage consumers to buy a particular product wherever it is found.

Whereas national advertising urges people to buy a certain product, **local** or **retail advertising** persuades them to buy it in a certain store. Local advertising promotes the store more than it promotes specific products and usually features several items.

National advertising typically goes into detail about the product, how it is made, and its benefits to the consumer. Local advertising, on the other hand, usually assumes that the consumer knows the benefits of the product and stresses instead the advantages of buying from a particular retailer. For example, national advertising for an automobile may tell consumers, "This car is styled for the future, carefully engineered, has six basic improvements over last year's model, and goes through 311 individual inspections before it comes to you." Meanwhile, local advertising for the same car may feature a certain dealer that claims to have the lowest prices in town, the finest service facilities anywhere, a convenient location, and friendly, courteous salespeople.

Most producers encourage a combination of national and retail advertising. In **cooperative advertising**, which is one way of accomplishing such a combination, manufacturers "cooperate" with retailers by co-sponsoring or contributing to the cost of local retailer advertisements. Manufacturers do so mainly for two reasons. First, retailers can obtain lower rates in local media than national advertisers and therefore get more product exposure for a given amount of money. Second, financial contributions to retailers' ad budgets encourage retailers to promote the manufacturer's product more aggressively.

Traditionally, cooperative advertising calls for a 50–50 split in advertising costs between retailer and manufacturer. However, many producers now insist on paying only for the number of lines used to advertise their own products. Many manufacturers will not participate in cooperative advertising because of problems in preparing ads for insertion in local media.

Legal problems are also involved. Under the Robinson–Patman Act, producers must distribute promotional aid to buyers on a proportional basis. Therefore, if a manufacturer contributes heavily to a large-volume retailer's advertising campaign, it must be prepared to supply a proportionate amount to smaller retailers.

Interestingly enough, much of the cooperative advertising available to retailers goes unused. In 1983 manufacturers made over $7 billion dollars in cooperative advertising available to retailers, but $3 billion of it went unclaimed primarily because many retailers simply do not keep track of the cooperative advertising available to them.[10]

Advertising to Business Buyers Advertising directed at businesses is classified in four ways: *trade advertising, industrial advertising, farm advertising,* or *advertising to professional buyers.*

Trade Advertising Trade advertising is directed at buyers for resale. Its primary objective is to encourage wholesalers and retailers to purchase and promote the manufacturer's product. Consequently, profitability is the major theme. Media aimed directly at channel members, such as trade journals and direct mail, are the primary vehicles for trade advertising.

Industrial Advertising Whereas trade advertising sells finished products to buyers for resale, industrial advertising promotes goods that will be used in the operation of a business or will become part of another product, and emphasizes qualities such as economy, efficiency, strength, reliability, durability, and convenience. This advertising often is placed in specific trade journals such as *Iron Age* (steel manufacturers) or *Modern Materials Handling* (purchasers of physical distribution products).

Farm Advertising There are over 280 farm publications in the United States. Farmers, as industrial users, are important buyers of machinery, chemicals, insecticides, and other agriculture-related products. Ad messages directed to those engaged in agriculture stress efficiency, low cost, profitability, durability, and similar product attributes.

A recent survey of midwestern farmers reported that 74.2 percent planned to spend over $2,000 to purchase a microcomputer in the near future. Primary uses would be cash flow analysis, analyzing selling opportunities, and financial planning—tasks any industrial purchaser would require of a microcomputer.[11] Thus, the farm market can often be treated as a special category of industrial advertising.

Professional Advertising In recent decades professions such as medicine, dentistry, law, education, engineering, and architecture have greatly expanded. Although professional people may not always use or resell a

---

[10] "Integrate Coop With Other Ad Programs for Best Results," *Marketing News,* May 27, 1983, p. 6.

[11] Douglass G. Norvell and Stephen A. Straub, "The Time is Now to Actively Promote Microcomputers to the Farmer Market," *Marketing News,* July 22, 1983, p. 5.

product themselves, they often influence others to do so. For example, an architect may recommend certain kinds of flooring and roofing materials, exterior finishes, and window glass to clients. Drug advertisements are aimed at physicians, not as users or resellers, but as "recommenders" to their patients. Advertising to professional people is highly important for certain products, but accounts for only a minor portion of total advertising expenditures.

The Media Plan

An **advertising medium** *is the vehicle used to carry the advertising message from the sender to the intended receiver.* There are six major media available to advertisers today: radio and television (which are commonly called **broadcast media**), newspapers and magazines (which are called **print media**), direct mail, and outdoor media (billboards, signs, posters). *The **media plan** is the company's chosen combination of these media to achieve its advertising objectives.* The specific corporate advertising objectives, the target market, and the advertising budget—in combination with the characteristics of each medium—all affect the media plan.

Broadcast Media   Radio and television together accounted for about 28.5 percent of the total advertising mix in 1982. They have several advantages in common. First, they permit personalized presentations in which the human voice is the primary communicator of the advertising message. Second, companies can reach particular target markets through selective sponsorship, the timing of "spot" programming, and the choice of particular stations. Third, the advertising message is isolated from competitors' messages, at least to the extent that only one commercial is delivered at any given time. (Printed commercial media, on the other hand, may publish several ads on one page.) Finally, the highly verbal content of electronically transmitted commercials means that companies can reach less literate markets with ease, because all socioeconomic groups purchase radio and television receivers. The special features of radio and television follow.

Radio   There are over 6,400 commercial radio stations in the United States. The special advantages of radio are (1) its 24-hour programming in many areas, (2) its tremendous reach (Americans bought 60.6 million radios in 1982),[12] (3) its ability to appeal to very specialized target markets (due to the large number of stations in metropolitan areas, stations can specialize in rock, easy listening, news only, ethnic groups, and so on, and (4) its flexibility and timeliness (messages can be adapted quickly to current developments). Furthermore, radio advertisements may be heard by listeners who are driving, walking, working, or engaging in any number of other activities.

---

[12] *Radio Facts 1983,* (New York: Radio Advertising Bureau), p. 5.

Figure 16-4		
Top 25 Television Advertisers: 1983		
Rank	**Brand (Agency)**	**TV Spending***
1	Miller Lite (Backer & Spielvogel)	$50.1
2	Pepsi (BBDO)	74.1
3	Stroh's (The Marschalk Co.)	19.3
4	Federal Express (Ally & Gargano)	22.9
5	Burger King (J. Walter Thompson)	82.4
6	Coca-Cola (McCann Erickson)	40.1
7	McDonald's (Leo Burnett)	185.9
8	MCI Communications (Ally & Gargano)	26.9
9	Jell-O (Young & Rubicam)	31.3
10	Diet Coke (SSC&B)	20.4
11	Ford (J. Walter Thompson)	166.2
12	Levi's (Foote, Cone & Belding)	27.0
13	Budweiser Light (Needham Harper & Steers)	45.6
14	ATT Bell System (N.W. Ayer)	154.9
15	Calvin Klein Jeans (CRK Advertising)	5.0
16	Wendy's (Dancer Fitzgerald Sample)	49.7
17	Atari Video Games (Doyle Dane Bernbach)	45.9
18	British Airways (Saatchi & Saatchi Compton)	3.5
19	Polaroid (Doyle Dane Bernbach)	26.9
20	Shasta (Needham Harper & Steers)	5.7
21	American Express Credit Cards (Ogilvy & Mather)	20.5
22	Meow Mix (Della Famina Travisano)	7.6
23	Oscar Mayer (J. Walter Thompson)	9.2
24	Crest (Benton & Bowles)	32.4
25	Kibbles 'n Bits (J. Walter Thompson)	6.1
		*Millions

SOURCE: John Koten, "Creativity, Not Budget Size, Is Vital to TV-Ad Popularity," *Wall Street Journal,* March 1, 1984, p. 31.

Radio, however, lacks "visibility," which limits its usefulness in advertising products that are complicated or need demonstration to be fully understood and, therefore, need to be seen to be fully appreciated. Much radio advertising has been transferred to television, and expenditures for radio advertising are now less than one-third of those for commercial television time. "Immediate-response" advertising, too, is difficult to present through this medium, because many listeners do not have a pencil and paper handy with which to write down an advertiser's name and address and, of course, cannot clip out a coupon to return for more product information or to place an order.

Television   Because television commercials combine sound, sight, movement, and color, they tend to have a greater impact on the senses than radio or print commercials. For this reason television is a very valuable medium for products that need demonstrating or that require considerable persuasion to complete the sale. Although it is a comparatively new medium, television accounted for 21.5 percent of all advertising expenditures in 1982, or more than $14 billion. TV commercials have become quite sophisticated, and many are interesting and amusing, as well as informative. Figure 16-4 lists the 25 major television advertisers in the United States and the amounts of their television advertising expenditures for 1982.

A distinct disadvantage for many advertisers, however, is the high cost of both the production of commercials and television time. TV commercials may also take longer to prepare than ads for other media and, therefore, are less flexible and timely.

Other disadvantages of television are that, unlike radio, it requires the viewer's total attention to thoroughly perceive the message. Because it is oriented toward mass markets, television is largely unsuitable for industrial advertising, and even in consumer marketing often reaches many viewers who are not members of the target market.

Print Media   One basic advantage of print media is that a high degree of credibility is attributed to the written word. Print advertisements also have other advantages: (1) They have a comparatively long life (magazines may be kept around the house or office for weeks); (2) readers can absorb the messages at their own speed and refer to them at a later date; (3) return coupons may be used to stimulate sales and measure the success of the advertising; and (4) it is possible to reach very specific target markets, because there are newspapers or periodicals that cater to almost every group in our society. Newspapers can be used to reach neighborhood, metropolitan, state, and, in some cases, national markets. Nearly 250 national magazines offer regional editions for advertisers who wish to communicate their message to residents of a smaller geographic area. Newspapers and magazines accounted for approximately 32.2 percent of total advertising expenditures in 1982.

Newspapers   Despite the tremendous growth in popularity of radio and TV, Americans are still a newspaper-reading society. Almost as many promotional dollars are spent for newspaper advertising as for TV and radio combined. Nationwide there are approximately 1,700 daily and 6,800 weekly newspapers.[13] Because an estimated 89 percent of adult Americans read at least one newspaper each day, it is possible to reach both a large target market and a selected one simultaneously by placing advertising in sections devoted to sports, social activities, food, or business. Figure 16-5, a

---

[13] *Ayer Directory of Publications,* (Fort Washington, Pa.: IMS Press, 1982), p. 561.

Figure 16-5	
Largest U.S. Dailies	
Newspaper	**Circulation***
The Wall Street Journal	1,925,722
New York Daily News	1,544,101
Los Angeles Times	1,052,637
New York Post	960,120
New York Times	905,675
Chicago Tribune	758,255
Washington Post	726,009
Chicago Sun–Times	651,579
Detroit News	642,531
Detroit Free Press	631,989
Philadelphia Inquirer	553,582
San Francisco Chronicle	537,621
Long Island Newsday	515,728
Boston Globe	510,978
Cleveland Plain Dealer	487,672
Newark Star Ledger	424,224
Houston Chronicle	419,869
Miami Herald	397,953
Houston Post	376,455
Buffalo Evening News	330,694
Denver Rocky Mountain News	321,693
Dallas Morning News	317,279
Milwaukee Journal	307,112
Philadelphia Daily News	294,920
Kansas City Times	284,966
Total	15,879,364

* As of September 30, 1982
SOURCE: Audit Bureau of Circulation.

list of the 25 U.S. newspapers with the largest circulations, suggests the vast numbers of consumers who can be reached through newspaper advertising. Companies can direct advertising to the entire family or to people in selected age brackets. The comparatively low cost of space and ad preparation allows small firms to advertise with more frequency. Approximately 80 percent of newspaper advertising is by local concerns. Moreover, the ease with which ad copy can be inserted in a paper and the fact that most papers are published daily or weekly give the advertiser the advantages of flexibility, timeliness, and repetition.

One major disadvantage of newspapers is the poor quality of reproduction they provide, which contributes to the medium's relatively low prestige among advertisers. Another drawback is the fact that because newspapers usually carry a large number of advertisements, readers perceive only those that happen to attract their attention. Many newspaper advertisements are simply ignored by readers.

Magazines Industrial advertisers are particularly attracted to this medium, because it offers access to more specialized markets than any other vehicle except direct mail. Literally hundreds of magazines are published to reach different interest and occupational groups, income and educational levels, and geographic areas. Prominent magazines lend prestige to the ads they contain and often reinforce the ad's impact by providing excellent reproduction, color, and visual detail.

For advertising purposes, magazines are classified as (1) consumer, (2) farm, (3) business, or (4) professional publications. Large-circulation consumer magazines such as *Reader's Digest* and *Time* offer regional and international editions to encourage more advertising by both local and nationally known firms. Business periodicals such as *Forbes* and *Sales Management* reach a relatively specialized, homogeneous market of executive personnel. The business-publications category also includes trade papers such as *Women's Wear Daily* and *Footwear News* that, although not actually magazines, carry the news needed by decision-making management in the field for which they are published.

The *Journal of American Dentistry* and *Architectural Record* are examples of magazines through which advertisers may focus on highly specialized

Figure 16-6	
10 Leading American Magazines	
Magazine	**Circulation**
Reader's Digest	18,299,091
TV Guide	17,275,471
National Geographic	10,357,853
Modern Maturity	8,822,161
Better Homes & Garden	8,022,794
Family Circle	7,303,488
Woman's Day	6,949,344
McCall's	6,277,293
Good Housekeeping	5,420,830
Ladies' Home Journal	5,200,705
Total	86,625,542

SOURCE: Audit Bureau of Circulation.

professional markets. Other publications such as *Business Farming* and *Dairynews* are designed to supply information to the agricultural community. Figure 16-6 lists the average circulations per issue of the top 10 American magazines for the first six months of 1983.

Among the disadvantages of magazine ads is the fact that their content is rather inflexible once they are accepted for insertion. They are usually more expensive than newspaper ads, take longer to prepare, and because magazines are published only weekly or monthly, their repeated messages have a weaker impact. Costs, too, are often high in relation to circulation.

Direct Mail   Some advantages of printed commercial advertisements are enhanced by the use of direct mail. Mailing pieces may be designed for and directed to a more specialized market than ads in any other medium and can be personalized to a far greater extent. If a company uses zip codes to establish target mailing lists, mailing pieces may be prepared for specific demographic groups and sent out very quickly.

Flexibility and timeliness are among the strongest advantages of direct mail, and advertising performance can be measured against cost with comparative ease. Like most other media, however, direct mail has the disadvantage of competition with large amounts of other advertising. Although each mailing piece carries advertising for only one company, many consumers and industrial buyers receive a large amount of such mail, and the throwaway rate is high. Per-reader costs may be quite expensive compared to other media, and duplication of names on mailing lists often results in a high degree of wasted effort. Also, postal rates are increasing. Even a penny increase in the cost of first- or third-class mail may cost a large mail-order firm as much as $1 million. Finally, third-class mail also has the disadvantage of time delay in that a mailing may not be delivered for as long as three weeks.

Outdoor Advertising   Outdoor media such as billboards, posters, and signs serve principally to remind customers of products that are already well known or to direct them to a specific location where certain products or services are available. Because the advertising message must be brief and cannot fully inform the reader about a product, outdoor advertising is not suitable for the introduction of new products. Its impact is also lessened by competition for consumers' visual attention from traffic lights, automobiles, other outdoor advertising, and so on.

Billboards, signs, and posters depend on the mobility of the consuming public for their reach. Because they can be placed in high-traffic areas, often at or near the point of purchase, they are ideally suited for mass-circulation advertising. The per-capita cost of outdoor advertising is very low, and drivers and pedestrians who pass through an area frequently are exposed repeatedly to the message. A company may also combine billboards and signs with public service devices such as time and temperature indicators to help attract attention.

Despite its advantages, outdoor advertising has declined in importance. This form of advertising, in particular, has come under heavy attack in recent years as destructive of the natural beauty of the environment and a driving hazard. Over 700 outdoor sign and billboards operators do business in the United States. Demands for restrictions on the placement of signs and billboards on property bordering interstate highways have resulted in the passage of federal legislation to limit outdoor advertising. Although this is still a prevalent advertising medium, its use continues to be restricted legally.

Creating and Timing Advertisements

To create effective advertisements, the company must first determine its advertising campaign **theme**, that is, the aspect of the company it wishes to emphasize and the product attributes it wishes to communicate. The company aspect can be the corporation itself, one or more specific products, or the consumer's benefit from patronizing the company.[14] For example, when Philips Petroleum advertises the ways its products help society, its theme is that of a good corporate citizen. When Xerox advertises the high quality of its copiers, its theme is centered around the products' attributes. Finally, when Listerine advertises that its mouthwash prevents bad breath, its theme is oriented toward a consumer benefit.

Within the advertising theme, each advertisement has a **message** or **copy**. The message must be compatible with the corporate image, the theme, and the target market to be effective. More popular message approaches include information (basic product facts), arguments (attempts to persuade the customer), psychological motivation (for example, Luvs disposable diapers appeals to parents' love for their children), repeat-assertion (hard selling of a basic theme), commands (Drive 55!), and symbolic association (Prudential Insurance and the dependability of the Rock of Gilbraltar).[15]

Companies must time their advertisements to appear when the target market will view them. There are six basic types of media schedules[16]:

1. *Steady.* Advertisements are placed at an even rate throughout the year.
2. *Seasonal.* Advertising is increased at peak sales periods. Toy advertisements, for instance, increase in the pre-Christmas season.
3. *Periodic pulse.* Heavy advertising is purchased at regular intervals throughout the year.
4. *Erratic pulse.* Advertising is scheduled at irregular intervals.
5. *Start-up pulse.* Advertising is heaviest during a new product introduction or at the beginning of the selling season.
6. *Promotional pulse.* Advertising is heavy to support a specific sales promotion such as a contest.

In broadcast media marketing managers must be concerned not only with the time of year, but also with the time of day at which an advertisement is shown. If the ad is shown at a time when the target audience is not viewing, the commercial is wasted. For example, the most efficient time to reach the 33.2 million children in the U.S. is on television on Saturday mornings. Even though the networks (ABC, CBS, and NBC) have lost

[14] Julian L. Simon, *The Management of Advertising,* (Englewood Cliffs, N.J.: Prentice-Hall, 1971), pp. 174–206.

[15] Kenneth A. Longman, *Advertising* (New York: Harcourt Brace Jovanovich, 1971), pp. 371–72.

[16] Jules Backman, *Advertising and Competition* (New York: New York University Press, 1967), pp. 167–69.

Figure 16-7
Top 10 Advertising Agencies in U.S. Income (1982)

Agency	Gross Income (Millions)
Young & Rubicam	$246.7
Ted Bates Worldwide	233.4
Ogilvy & Mather	176.9
J. Walter Thompson Co.	167.2
BBDO International	155.0
Leo Burnett Co.	136.0
Doyle Dane Bernbach	129.0
Foote, Cone & Belding	126.8
Grey Advertising	109.0
Dancer Fitzgerald Sample	86.4

SOURCE: John O'Connor, "Agency Income Nears $6 Billion in 1982," *Advertising Age*, March 16, 1983, p. 1.

some of the children to video games and cable TV, in 1982 an average 23 million children watched the networks' Saturday-morning fare.[17] For advertisers of children's products, advertisement timing on Saturday morning television is critical. Much fewer children are reached if the same ad is scheduled to appear in midday during the week or after 10 PM.

The Advertising Agency

An **advertising agency**, which is a business organization established to render advertising services to its client-customers, assists most companies in the creation and timing of advertisements. The main work of an ad agency is to create, prepare, and place advertising that will achieve the client's promotional objectives. In addition to these three functions, agencies may also perform market research and render advice on packaging, pricing, and other marketing functions.

The first advertising "agents" were newspaper and magazine **space brokers**, people who bought advertising space from various print media and resold it to clients. Gradually, space brokers began to assist advertisers in the preparation of ads. Their functions continued to expand until they evolved into the advertising agencies we have today. Figure 16-7 lists the 10 largest agencies in the United States.

---

[17] Geoffrey Colvin, "Children Are Getting Hard to Find," *Fortune*, May 2, 1983, p. 125.

Today most large agencies are departmentalized. A **creative director** manages the development of advertising copy. An **art director** oversees layouts and illustrations. A **media director** supervises the purchasing of time and space. A specialized **production department** handles the technical production of advertisements. A **traffic director** keeps the work flowing between various departments and makes sure the campaign stays on schedule. Finally, a **research director** studies target markets and evaluates the effect of past or current advertising.

The key individual in the advertising agency, however, is the **account executive**, who serves as the liaison between the agency and the advertiser. Often the account executive is not creative in a literary or artistic sense, but specializes in diplomacy and coordination, interpreting the client's needs to agency personnel and the agency's suggested program to the client. The account executive secures the client's approval of the advertising budget and plans, then turns the actual creative work over to other agency personnel.

Although the number of agency job openings for novices is low in comparison to the number of young people who would like to enter this field, the rewards for those who succeed can be very great, financially and otherwise.

Agency Compensation   Traditionally, agencies receive a 15-percent commission from the media in which ads are placed, an outgrowth of the practices established when agencies were still space brokers. In recent years this commission system has come under heavy attack from both advertisers (which feel that because agencies are working for them, compensation by the media creates a conflict of interest) and many agencies (which, besides agreeing with this criticism, feel that their income should not depend on the amount of advertising a client places).

As a result, advertising agencies are now switching to a more realistic "commission plus fee" system. Because it may cost the agency almost as much to prepare an advertising campaign for a client with a $150,000 ad budget as for one with a $1,500,000 budget, production time and expenditures are normally billed to the client, as are creative fees and fees for research and other collateral services.

Choosing an Agency   Selecting an advertising agency is a critical decision for marketing managers. Among the points they must consider are (1) the track record, or reputation, of the agency; (2) the experience of the agency's personnel; (3) special additional services, such as marketing research, the agency may render; (4) the trial, or tentative, campaign developed by the agency to solicit the advertiser's account; and (5) the ability and temperament of the individual who will serve as the account executive. Agencies do not compete on a price basis, although they may of course differ in their recommendations as to how much the client should spend.

In-Company Advertising Departments   When a business retains the services of an advertising agency, someone in the firm must be responsible for approving its work. Even those advertisers that use an agency usually have their own advertising department. Its principal purpose is to explain the advertiser's marketing goals to the agency, approve or reject the agency's plans, and coordinate the work of the agency with the overall marketing program of the firm, especially the sales program.

The status of internal advertising departments varies widely. In companies that spend 10 percent or more of their total revenue on advertising, the advertising department is critically important and the company president may have to approve major campaigns. If advertising represents a small percentage of the firm's total revenue (well below 10 percent), the advertising department may be relatively unimportant.

Among the more important specific functions of the head of the advertising department are (1) to establish advertising goals, (2) to help select the advertising agency, (3) to explain management policies and philosophies to the agency, and (4) to allocate the advertising budget among various media. For example, even Ford and General Motors, which make their products very well known through advertising, each budget less than 1 percent of sales revenue for advertising. However, both have large internal advertising departments.

Evaluating Advertising Effectiveness

Evaluating the effectiveness of advertising is important for two major reasons. First, advertising represents an expenditure of money. Although overall advertising expenses are a small part of the total budget in specific companies, cost is a major consideration. For example, Miller Lite ads are generally considered the "best liked" ads on television. However, in terms of the number of prospects reached for dollars spent, they are not very cost efficient. A survey of 4,000 adults revealed that the cost per 1,000 impressions for Miller Lite was $29.86, much higher than the cost for many other companies. Coca-Cola, for example, only spent $8.96 for each 1,000 media impressions. Miller can, however, take comfort in the fact that Budweiser Light cost $41.67.[18]

Second, and more important than the cost factor, management wants to gauge the success of advertising in selling the product. Sales that are not made due to ineffective advertising obviously cannot contribute to profit goals. Knowing how effective an advertising program is suggests ways to make future advertising more effective.

---

[18] Bill Abrams, "Miller Lite's Ads Best Liked, but Aren't the Most Efficient," *Wall Street Journal,* March 3, 1983, p. 27.

Numerous people have said, in effect, "Develop a sure-fire way to evaluate the effectiveness of advertising, and you will make a fortune." It also has been said often, and not entirely in jest: "Half of our advertising expenditures are wasted. The problem is, we don't know which half." The basic difficulty in evaluating advertising is that so many other factors affect sales. Competitive actions, the economic climate, changes in price, and the cooperation of middlemen are just some of the elements that affect sales. During a deep recession, for example, an "excellent" advertising campaign is not likely to move durable products in the desired quantity. Assume a company significantly reduces the price of a product and at the same time launches a new advertising campaign. Sales go up significantly. Who can say which action played the larger role, the price reduction or the new advertising campaign? In addition it is difficult to determine exactly when an ad will affect sales. A consumer may see an ad and decide to buy, but the sale may not occur for several months. This "lagged effect" makes the relationship between advertising expenditures and sales very difficult to measure. Despite the difficulties, two general approaches, subjective and objective, are used to try to measure the effectiveness of advertising.

Subjective Evaluation   Subjective evaluation involves opinion. You often hear senior executives say something about their advertising such as, "It's doing a good job for us and we're going to spend more next year," or, "We're very disappointed—we're seriously considering changing agencies."

What executives—even those who have years of experience—think about an advertising campaign and the results achieved by it may differ greatly. The campaign built around the theme, "I can't believe I ate the whole thing," won a number of advertising awards, but sales were extremely disappointing. In this case there were no changes in price, product, or retail distribution, suggesting that the advertising campaign was basically a failure. There are many instances in which campaigns were judged successful by "experts," but the company went broke because the product did not sell.

Too often marketing people judge an advertising campaign on its likability, cleverness, or entertainment value. These are not true criteria of a good campaign. In the final analysis effectiveness of advertising is determined by its impact on sales.

Objective Evaluation   Objective evaluation of advertising uses facts developed through research as measures of value. This, however, is extremely difficult. Only two advertising situations lend themselves nicely to objective evaluation—direct mail and couponing. If one direct-mail advertisement sells more than another, we have objective evidence that it is the more effective of the two. If more coupons are returned from one advertisement than from another placed in the same medium, we can again reach an objective conclusion about their relative effectiveness.

Pre-testing Testing of advertising messages before they are projected to the general target market is called **pre-testing**. One method involves the use of a **consumer jury**—*a group of people selected to represent a cross section of the target market.* Their reactions to advertisements are studied and used to modify various elements of specific advertisements or the entire campaign.

Another pre-test technique is to place the advertisements in one or more test markets and, in the process, try to measure their impacts. As information develops, modifications can be made in the campaign before it is presented to the general target market.

Post-testing A number of research organizations (Hooper, Neilsen, and Starch, for example) specialize in measuring the impacts of specific advertisements. This information is then sold to subscribers, who may be advertisers, advertising agencies, or media companies. Although various research companies use different evaluation techniques and have different measures of effectiveness, in general they all try to determine the answers to the following questions:

1. How many people read, heard, or saw the advertisement?
2. How much of it did they read, hear, or watch?
3. How much of the message can they recall?
4. How many of those exposed to the advertisement can identify its sponsor?
5. How many of those exposed intend to buy the product?

The Future of Advertising Evaluation We probably will never learn how to evaluate advertising in a totally satisfactory way. There simply are too many variables to control, and too many factors other than advertising affect sales volume. However, the increasing emphasis on marketing research methodology and on understanding consumer behavior suggests that new, more sophisticated research devices will be implemented in the future and may make advertising evaluation less guesswork.

Criticisms of Advertising

Despite, or perhaps because of, its pervasiveness in our society, advertising is frequently attacked on economic, sociological, aesthetic, and even moral grounds. The following are some of the major criticisms.

Advertising Costs Too Much Much less is spent on advertising than most people realize. Various studies show that the public grossly overestimates the amount of money spent for advertising consumer products, in part because modern advertising techniques make it possible to make a relatively loud noise, figuratively speaking, with a comparatively small budget.

Advertising Adds Unnecessarily to the Cost of Products This long-standing argument against advertising loses some of its validity as the size of the market increases. Obviously, the price paid by the consumer must include all costs of doing business and advertising is certainly one of these costs, but to the extent that advertising stimulates demand and makes mass production more feasible, it may actually reduce the cost of products. Moreover, information provided by advertising is often directly useful to the consumer—for example, local supermarket ads, announcements of sales, and new product advertising. In spite of this fact many people still feel advertising costs too much and adds inordinately to product prices. A recent poll of 1,000 adults, for instance, found that 76 percent of the respondents thought advertising added to the cost of products. Only 4 percent thought it lowered prices.[19]

Much Advertising is Deceptive or Downright Dishonest   Unfortunately, this criticism is valid in many cases. Despite the efforts of Better Business Bureaus, trade associations, the Federal Trade Commission, and various consumer groups, much advertising remains just a come-on. In recent years the FTC has taken a stronger stance on deceptive advertising, and it is likely to take an even stronger one in the future as new laws increase the agency's enforcement responsibilities and as pressure from consumer groups continues.

Advertising Creates Discontent   Some critics claim that advertising overemphasizes the happiness people can obtain from material things and induces them to want what they really do not need—and, in the case of poor people, what they cannot realistically expect to acquire.

Some Advertising Insults Consumers' Intelligence   Some criticisms are directed not so much at advertising itself as at the quality of advertising. Observers point out that many ads are in bad taste and many others are simple minded and condescending. This criticism has been leveled most often at television commercials that picture homemakers ecstatic over detergents, members of the opposite sex overwhelmed by the appeal of users of various preparations, and similar exaggerated reactions to everyday products. Certainly some advertisements are either offensive and/or simple minded to some people, but other advertisements may be in excellent taste and carry a message that is both needed and appreciated.

Benefits of Advertising

Advertising has many faults, but it has advantages, too—and not only for the individual firm. Jules Backman's intensive study of the overall effect of advertising on our economy pointed out that advertising[20]:

---

[19] "Marketing," *Wall Street Journal,* March 24, 1983, p. 35.
[20] Jules Backman, *Advertising and Competition* (New York: New York University Press, 1967), pp. 167–69.

1. Contributes to economic growth and expands job opportunities.
2. Creates mass markets that encourage economies of scale in production.
3. Makes possible free radio and TV entertainment and lowers the prices of newspapers and magazines.
4. Reduces distribution costs by preselling goods.
5. Contributes to the maintenance of high-quality standards by making the public aware of the identity of the manufacturer.
6. Provides information about old and new products.

The implications of advertising, in short, are both far-reaching and complex. They merit thoughtful consideration by all of us, whether we are consumers or marketers.

PUBLICITY

All the demand stimulation devices discussed so far have had an obvious promotional objective. However, a firm may also use more subtle strategies as part of its long-range plan to maximize consumer patronage. These strategies, which make up its **publicity** or **public relations policy**, attempt to promote goodwill and understanding between the business and the general public.

Businesses, like individuals, develop a personality, or "image," over a period of time. The image a business has—that is, the way the public perceives or regards it—is important to marketing management, because it helps determine consumer acceptance of the firm's products. When consumers "like" a company, when they think of it as a "good citizen," or "friendly," they are more likely to buy its products or shop in its stores than if they think of it as a "profit gouger," "cold," "unconcerned," or "incompetent."

The image a business has affects all aspects of the company's operations. Good relationships with all the firm's "publics"—its employees, its shareholders, its suppliers, government agencies, educators, dealers, and labor unions—are helpful in winning greater acceptance in the marketplace.

Public Relations Goals

Large companies usually assign the responsibility for developing good relationships with various publics to a **public relations department**, or they retain an outside firm that specializes in this field. In organizations too small to afford this kind of specialization, much of the public relations function is assigned to the marketing department. Regardless of the place of public relations in the organizational structure, however, marketing management plays a large role in it. Public relations activities have five major objectives: (1) to obtain favorable publicity for the company, (2) to give the business a "good citizen" image, (3) to identify the firm with education, (4) to humanize the business, and (5) to counteract rumors or negative publicity. We will discuss each of these five objectives below.

Obtain Favorable Publicity A large part of the public relations program in many companies is designed to get maximum "good news coverage" in newspapers, magazines, and other media. Press releases about new or modified products, business expansion plans, personnel promotions, and "social contributions" are sent to editors in an effort to obtain favorable mentions. Many marketing managers feel that a good news story is more effective than regular advertising, because people are more inclined to believe statements that are not paid for.

A recent development to obtain favorable publicity is the company-sponsored magazine. Designed with the appearance of a consumer magazine and sent free to target markets, these publicity vehicles do a "soft sell" for the company. *Friendly Exchange,* a magazine published by Farmers Insurance Group, has articles on home repairs, ice cream, and babysitting. Says one receiver of this free magazine, "I couldn't believe it. It was terrific."[21] Other, similar magazines accomplish the same goal: subtly blow the company's horn and create good public relations. Airlines effectively use this concept, providing their own magazines as in-flight reading for their passengers.

"Good Citizen" Image Many firms consider it good public relations to develop community respect for the organization as a "good citizen." To achieve this objective, they may "lend" executives to community fund-raising drives, run training programs for handicapped people or for the hardcore unemployed, donate surplus products to charity, and take the lead in various civic improvement projects. The goal is, again, to achieve positive publicity and cast the company in a favorable light with its publics.

American Express used charitable giving as an effective method of enhancing its "good citizen" image. In Atlanta, for example, every time a customer uses an American Express credit card or traveler's checks, Atlanta's symphony, art museum, and repertory theater receive 5 cents. When a new card is issued, they receive 2 dollars. American Express spent $400,000 promoting the campaign in local television, newspaper, and point-of-purchase advertising. Was the effort successful? One company executive explains, "We were looking for a way to make our marketing more in tune with local communities, and donating to the arts appeals to the upscale, traveling market that we traditionally go after. At first we

---

[21] David Mills, "Publications at No Charge Are Subtle Ads," *Wall Street Journal,* August 5, 1983, p. 23.

didn't know whether we'd found a new philanthropic method or just a novel way to give away money, but increases in card usage and [issuance of] new cards in other cities where we've tried this show it to be as successful—if not more successful—as any marketing program we've ever done."[22]

Identify the Firm with Education   Because businesses that are conscious of public relations recognize that our society believes strongly in education, they often seek to develop goodwill in the educational community by providing scholarships, paying part or all of the costs of employees' education, offering films to schools, sponsoring open-house events for students, and providing speakers for special events. In a truly dramatic attempt to aid education, Apple Computer has proposed to give an Apple II to every public elementary and secondary school in the United States. The only stumbling block is obtaining a special tax break from Congress. If obtained, Apple will create considerable goodwill, ensure that children are trained on its computers, and spend little money in the process.[23]

"Humanize" the Business   To many customers large businesses seem aloof and too busy to care about the individual. To counteract this feeling, big companies sponsor an assortment of activities designed to convey the impression that they are just a large family of ordinary people.

The name "Betty Crocker," used on some General Mills products, is an example of a successful effort to give a business giant the human touch. "Betty Crocker" (actually a department of 50 people) receives several thousand pieces of mail daily, each of which is answered in a personal manner. Many businesses try to humanize their image by sponsoring events such as the Soap Box Derby (sponsored by the Chevrolet Division of General Motors) and the Punt, Pass, and Kick Contest (sponsored by Ford and participating dealers). They may also host open-house events and run plant tours.

Public relations activities are often the subject of institutional advertising. For example, a large company may show commercials or run print advertisements telling how its employees use their free time to do "good things" such as teaching deprived children how to read or working in clean-up campaigns. The rationale for this type of promotion is that if the public admires the people who work for a company, it will like the firm, too.

Counteract Rumors or Negative Publicity   Occasionally public relations campaigns are used to counteract rumors by clarifying the company's position on an issue or to win support for its stand in a public controversy. Public relations work may also be needed to offset negative publicity about

---

[22] "AmEx Shows the Way to Benefit from Giving," *Business Week,* October 18, 1982, pp. 44–45.
[23] "Apple Clears Hurdle on Its Plan to Send Computers to Class," *Wall Street Journal,* September 23, 1982, p. 10.

Figure 16-8

Positive and Negative Public Relations

The Situation	A Negative Approach	A Positive Approach
1. The company is ordered by the FDA to withdraw one of its food products from stores because it contains an unhealthy ingredient.	1. The company fights back with a court action. It launches an aggressive campaign to prove to the public that the product is really OK.	1. The company quickly removes the product and makes sure the offending ingredient is not in any of its other products.
2. A student writes to a large company requesting information about its advertising strategy. It happens that the information requested is confidential.	2. The company writes the student, curtly stating that such information cannot be made public.	2. The company thanks the student for his interest, but explains that the information cannot be released. It makes positive suggestions as to where similar non-confidential information might be obtained.
3. A customer calls a seller to inform her that he is short some of the merchandise he ordered.	3. The seller accuses the customer of sloppy receiving procedures. She is adamant in claiming that she couldn't have made a mistake and refuses to send the rest of the order or issue a credit.	3. The seller thanks the customer for making the complaint, but asks him to check his records and promises to check her own.
4. A wholesale customer is usually late in paying a manufacturer's invoices.	4. The manufacturer calls the customer and tells him that if future payments are not made by the deadline, either no more merchandise will be shipped or a penalty charge will be added to the invoice. The conversation ends with an implied threat.	4. The manufacturer calls the customer and sincerely thanks him for his business. He then explains his billing procedures and why it is necessary that payments be made by a certain date. He thanks him again for his past orders and ends the conversation cordially.
5. A motorist drives into a service station and asks for directions to Elm Street.	5. The attendant tells the motorist, "We're too busy to give directions," and walks away.	5. The attendant explains politely how the motorist can find Elm Street.
6. A major bank in a large city is displeased with a government agency's refusal to approve a plan to open up new branches.	6. The bank uses full-page newspaper ads to attack the "stupidity" of the government's decision. It attempts to turn public opinion against the government.	6. The bank makes a plea for reconsideration, then develops new data to support its position. It attempts to show how the plan for more branches will benefit the public.

some of the company's operations, such as the production of war-related goods, by playing up the firm's positive contributions to the community. A corporation may lose sales if it is accused of not employing a fair number of blacks or persons from other minority groups, creating excessive pollution, maintaining unsafe working conditions, earning excessive profits, or producing food products under unsanitary conditions. In such cases good public relations dictates that the firm explain its view of the situation, take steps to correct the problem (if the accusations are true or partly true), and explain what is being done as objectively as possible. Companies that say nothing or issue categorical denials when they are attacked by the media, consumerists, union spokespeople, or leaders of minority groups are often presumed to be guilty, or at least to have something to hide. Figure 16-8 describes the differences between positive and negative approaches to public relations in several typical business situations.

The Future of Public Relations

There is every indication that business, and marketing management in particular, will become increasingly sensitive to public opinion in the years ahead. This will mean more work for the firm's public relations department as (1) media coverage of business news expands, (2) more people are encouraged to speak out against business practices they consider unfair or "bad," (3) the consumerism movement grows, and (4) the pressure on corporations to behave in a socially responsible way increases. As a result we may expect professionalism in public relations to advance and job opportunities to increase. Marketing management will find positive attention to public relations a necessity in the future.

SUMMARY

- The primary objective of advertising is to increase sales. This may be done by introducing new products, counteracting competition, informing consumers about additional uses for the product, and maintaining brand loyalty. Advertising is also used to assist salespeople and secure leads to new customers and to convey a positive image of a firm or an industry.
- Pioneering advertising tries to create primary product demand. Competitive advertising attempts to create selective demand.
- Commercial advertising may be directed at ultimate consumers or busi-

ness buyers. Consumer advertising includes national (producer-sponsored) advertising and local (retailer-sponsored) advertising.

- Cooperative advertising occurs when producers and retailers share the expense of the advertising.
- Advertising directed at business buyers is classified as trade, industrial, farm, or professional advertising.
- Broadcast, print, direct mail, and outdoor advertising are the major media used by advertisers. Each has its advantages and disadvantages and should be evaluated carefully before a media mix is chosen.
- Creating advertisements concerns the theme and copy to be presented. Typical advertising timing schemes include steady, seasonal, periodic, erratic, start-up, and promotional patterns.
- Advertising agencies specialize in the creation and placement of advertising messages. Many companies that use the services of agencies, however, also maintain their own advertising departments.
- Although there are many criticisms of advertising's objectives, implementation, and cost, reviewing the benefits of advertising shows that it reduces distribution costs, contributes to economies of scale by creating mass markets, encourages higher quality by making the public aware of the product's identity, and provides product information.
- Advertising also reduces the cost of newspapers and magazines and pays for much of our television and radio entertainment.
- The goals of public relations are to obtain favorable publicity, give the firm a "good" corporate citizen image, identify the firm with education, humanize the business, and counteract negative publicity.
- Public relations will become more important in the future because of increasing media coverage of business, more people speaking out against bad business practices, the growth of consumerism, and increasing pressure for businesses to act in a socially responsible manner.

DISCUSSION QUESTIONS

1. Would a sophisticated marketer ever use advertising alone to promote a product? Why or why not?
2. What is advertising's chief objective? Name nine specific goals of advertising and give examples of how they may be achieved.
3. How is national advertising different from local advertising? What other names may be used for these kinds of advertising?

4. Define *cooperative advertising*. Give an example of a recent ad that appears to fall into this category.
5. What are the major advertising media? Are they equal in value to advertisers? Explain.
6. What is an advertising agency? What functions are performed by most agencies?
7. What is meant by "creativity" in advertising? Give examples of ads that could be described as creative.
8. What is the traditional method of compensating advertising agencies? What is the modern trend?
9. Why is it sometimes desirable for a company that uses the services of an ad agency to maintain its own advertising department?
10. List several criticisms of advertising. Are they justified? How could you answer them?
11. What are the benefits of advertising? What evidence is there that they outweigh its disadvantages?
12. Some people feel that public relations activities are designed to help a firm cover up its malpractices and misdeeds. Why does this feeling exist? How can public relations be given greater credibility?

APPLICATION EXERCISES

1. Select contemporary advertising themes or slogans that illustrate an attempt to achieve each of the following objectives: (a) to increase sales during an off season, (b) to increase the variety of product uses, (c) to increase the number of units purchased, (d) to introduce a new product, (e) to counteract competition, and (f) to maintain brand loyalty. Do most of these messages have more than one objective?
2. Contact the advertising departments of three consumer publications and ask for their advertising rate charts. Analyze them to account for the difference in rates and compare the number and types of consumers reached by each publication. Then, suggest five questions a media buyer should ask in selecting one or more of the publications for advertising purposes.
3. Assume you are the executive director of a national trade association of snack food manufacturers. The industry is under increasing attack by nutritionists, consumerists, and others who label snack foods as "junk foods." The executive committee of your association directs you to develop a public relations program to counteract the negative publicity the snack food industry is receiving. Prepare an outline of the plan you would submit to the executive committee.
4. What are some "public relations situations" you have encountered recently that were handled negatively? How do you feel toward the businesses that were involved?

CASE 16
American Greetings Goes After Hallmark[24]

For many years the two major U.S. marketers of greeting cards competed peacefully in the $2.1 billion industry. Hallmark, solidly number one with 40 percent of the market, was clearly the industry leader over American Greetings (35-percent market share). Over 100 companies compete for the remaining 25 percent.

Both companies started as one-person operations. Jacob Sapirstein founded American Greetings in order to market inexpensive cards for the masses. The company promoted heavily to retailers in the belief that consumers would buy whatever was available. Following this philosophy, American Greetings had never advertised on TV until recently.

Hallmark, founded by Joyce C. Hall, always produced high-quality cards and advertised heavily—it is well-known for its sponsorship of the award-winning "Hallmark Hall of Fame." Over the years Hallmark's advertising and its concentration in quality retail outlets led to its domination of the industry.

Recently, American Greetings has decided to go after Hallmark more aggressively. However, it faces a recognition problem. In an ad by American Greetings featuring a grandmother doting over cards from previous years, post-testing revealed that many viewers thought it was a Hallmark ad! The advertising theme was too close to the one traditionally used by Hallmark. To counteract this problem, American Greetings will now feature ads with humor as opposed to Hallmark's sweetness-and-light theme.

As an overall part of its strategy, American Greetings will also raise the quality of its cards, raise its prices to be compatible with Hallmark's, and emphasize its licensable characters: Ziggy, Holly Hobby, and Strawberry Shortcake. However, even here American Greetings has a problem typified by a comment from a customer who said she "often buys Hallmark's Peanuts and Ziggy cards." Ziggy cards are marketed by American Greetings!

Keeping creative pace with Hallmark may also be a problem. American Greetings has 225 artists developing cards, whereas Hallmark employs 640. However, American Greetings does invest heavily in consumer research to explore the reasons people buy cards and the kinds of artwork that fit with certain sentiments. This research helps determine the size, shape, and lettering of American Greeting cards. In addition the company chairman and a committee of older women (referred to by company artists as the "biddy committee") approve every card before it is marketed.

---

[24] Dean Rotbart, "American Greetings Cares Enough to Try Its Very Hardest," *Wall Street Journal,* March 17, 1982, pp. 1, 24; and Stephen Kindell, "New Markets, New Products," *Forbes,* July 30, 1984, p. 102.

Hallmark is struggling to develop licensed characters of its own. Although it uses (but does not own) the Muppets and Peanuts, it has no characters of its own to market—a competitive disadvantage. Meanwhile, American Greetings continues to wrestle with the thorny problem of getting people to recognize their TV ads as American Greetings, not Hallmark. The company's plans were expressed by one company official who hoped, "when you see [the comedy theme ads], you remember who paid for them."

Discussion Questions

1. What do you think of American Greeting's new advertising campaign?
2. Do you think the comedy theme is the best approach?
3. What advertising strategy would you recommend? What other changes in the overall marketing strategy would you suggest to support the advertising?

17 Personal Selling and Sales Promotion

STUDY OBJECTIVES

After studying this chapter, you should be able to

1. Outline the objectives of personal selling and explain why this method can achieve some objectives that other elements of the promotion mix cannot.
2. Describe the personal selling process, salesperson categories, and the various types of personal selling.
3. Describe the following functions of sales management: job analysis and description; recruitment, selection, training, and motivating of sales personnel; management of compensation programs; establishment of sales territories; and setting and evaluation of performance standards.
4. Explain the objectives of sales promotion.
5. Outline the techniques used in consumer-oriented sales promotion: sampling, contests, sweepstakes, games, premiums, coupons, product demonstrations, point-of-purchase advertising, and trading stamps.
6. Describe sales promotion aimed at business buyers.

I n this final chapter of Part Five we will examine the promotional
areas of personal selling and sales promotion. **Personal selling** *is the
face-to-face contact of company representatives with target customers.* **Sales promotion** *includes all promotional activities other than advertising, personal selling, or
publicity.*

PERSONAL SELLING

Personal selling is of critical importance to marketing. It is the focus of vast
expenditures of money, time, and talent. Its effectiveness may determine
not only the success of a firm's marketing program, but also the success of
the business itself.

Many people do not understand personal selling as a marketing function or an occupation. To some, it is merely an unnecessary adjunct to
advertising or order-taking. To others, it seems to have been made largely
obsolete by the self-service chains. The general public, because it is ac-
quainted almost exclusively with door-to-door salespeople and retail clerks,
tends to be unaware that most personal selling takes place behind the
scenes and that industrial users and buyers for resale are the major targets
for this kind of communication. Selling jobs held by college-educated people are frequently highly challenging and require above-average intelligence, initiative, and self-discipline.

To a marketer, **selling** *is the personal presentation of tangible and intangible
products—including ideas of commercial significance—to potential buyers.* If we
eliminated the words "of commercial significance" from this definition, we
would find our concept of selling greatly expanded. Many attribute the
success of most politicians, for example, to their ability to "sell themselves."
Certainly it is true that many of the skills that make for success in selling are
also useful in other professions such as law, politics, teaching, and even
medicine. The ability to (1) empathize with others, (2) persuade others to
adopt your point of view, (3) simplify complex ideas, and (4) exercise
initiative are very important in selling and in other occupations as well.

Differences in Emphasis on Personal Selling

The emphasis placed on personal selling depends on the industry and on
management's evaluation of the selling function. For makers of such products as industrial equipment, chemicals, apparel, furniture, and musical
instruments—and for life-insurance companies and real-estate firms—per-

sonal selling is of great significance. In other industries, such as nonprescription drugs, prepared foods, publications, and movies, relatively little emphasis is placed on personal selling.

There may be a great emphasis on personal selling at one level of distribution within an industry, whereas at another level the emphasis may be negligible. For example, it may take a great deal of personal persuasion to sell a new brand of coffee to a chain of supermarkets, but the food chain normally would not use personal selling to resell the coffee to consumers. A detergent manufacturer may do some very aggressive personal selling to get retail stores to stock its brand and let it set up attractive in-store displays. However, store personnel will probably make little if any effort to personally sell the detergent to the consumer. Similarly, a salesperson for a dairy may be very energetic in efforts to get the company's products into retail outlets, but once the goods are on the shelf, little or no personal selling takes place.

Regardless of the industry or level in the marketing channel, personal selling becomes more important when the product is more complex, is accompanied by many support services, or when extra persuasion or problem solving is necessary to complete the sale. In these situations the added explanatory and persuasive capacity of personal selling increases its effectiveness and, therefore, its emphasis.

Advantages of Personal Selling

Because, as its name indicates, personal selling is personal, it can accomplish certain objectives that the other forms of promotion cannot. First, personal selling is flexible; it can be adapted to the specific needs of the prospect. Many salespeople regard themselves as diagnosticians of prospective buyers' needs. Whereas advertising must be general enough to reach mass markets, personal selling can be tailored to the demands of specific buyers. In many cases a sales representative designs a specific selling strategy for each prospect.

Second, in many cases personal selling is intended to obtain immediate orders. Although advertising and sales promotion may plant in consumers the seeds of a desire to purchase, personal selling is designed to precipitate a decision to buy, often on the spot.

Third, because companies can use salespeople to collect information from customers and prospective customers about changing needs and styles, they operate as part of the marketing information system.

Finally, salespeople can often handle post-sale servicing and can follow up on other problems that may occur after the sale is made. Companies use personal selling, then, to perform functions that advertising and sales promotion cannot.

Does Personal Selling Create Demand?

In any discussion of the economic importance of personal selling, the question arises, "Does personal selling actually create demand?" Many marketing executives believe personal selling is at the very heart of the demand-stimulation process. They reason that people do not automatically buy what they need or want. Rather, they buy what they are persuaded to buy. Insurance executives recognize that most people, far from voluntarily seeking to buy life and medical insurance, are not even aware of their insurance needs until a sales representative explains them.

Executives who market customized factory installations and computers are also likely to feel that demand is created, not merely satisfied. Small retailers, for example, may be unaware of the economies of electronic data-processing services until a computer salesperson diagnoses their needs and persuades them to buy. For other products the demand stimulated by personal selling is even more obvious. One can only wonder, for example, how many sets of encyclopedias are "bought" each day and how many sets are "sold." Real estate and securities, too, are generally "sold" through personal contact.

Although we cannot always say with certainty that personal selling results in a net addition to total demand, it can be argued that, in competitive situations, the survival and profitability of a business are related directly to the success of its sales department. For example, many apparel firms compete for the clothing retailer's distribution facilities. Which firms receive the retailer's business depends basically on two factors: their product and the persuasiveness of their sales representatives. Normally, if two firms have reasonably similar merchandise, the manufacturer that has the most effective salespeople will get the most business.

Purpose of Personal Selling

Other than stimulating demand, what purpose does personal selling serve? Generally, personal selling efforts fall into three groups: (1) finding potential buyers, (2) convincing them to buy, and (3) keeping customers satisfied.

Finding Potential Buyers Advertising often is designed to encourage interested individuals to request additional information. However, the sales force is responsible for following up these information requests. Furthermore, a large number of corporate clients come from salespeople's efforts to search out new buyers. Because salespeople must perform much of this search process, it is important for them to be aware of all information defining the target market. Any available demographic, psychographic, or behavioral information may be helpful to salespeople in identifying potential buyers.

Convincing Potential Buyers Identifying potential buyers serves no purpose if they cannot be convinced to make a purchase. Salespeople must be adept at persuasion, information gathering, and problem solving to meet the needs of potential buyers and to persuade them to become buyers. Salespeople must be able not only to answer questions and handle objections from the potential buyer, but also know when to close the sale.

Keeping Customers Satisfied Selling to a customer the second time is much easier for a salesperson if the customer was satisfied with the first purchase. Thus, to encourage repeat sales, a salesperson must make the effort to keep customers happy after the sale. Follow-up calls and genuine efforts to handle any customer complaints are the primary methods of maintaining customer satisfaction.

The Personal Selling Process

Accomplishing the purposes of personal selling involves a number of activities. Specifically, the process of personal selling includes prospecting and evaluating, preparing, approach and presentation, overcoming objections, closing the sale, and a follow-up service.

Prospecting and Evaluating   *The effort to develop a list of potential customers is called* **prospecting**. Salespeople can find potential buyers' names in company records, customer information requests from advertisements, telephone and trade association directories, current and previous customers, friends, salespeople for noncompeting products, and newspapers. One method of locating potential buyers when no leads exist is the **cold canvas**. Under cold canvassing prospecting, a salesperson simply calls on every potential buyer in a certain category. For example, a salesperson for windshield sealant would call on all automobile assembly plants and car repair shops in the area in hopes of generating some interest. Although an expensive and inefficient method of pursuing contacts, it is useful when no alternatives exist. Furthermore, telemarketing (making initial contacts by phone) can substantially reduce its costs.[1]

Prospective buyers are determined by *evaluating* (1) their potential interest in the salesperson's products and (2) their purchasing power. The salesperson can often determine their product interest by evaluating other products they have purchased, and can often determine purchasing power from zip code records (for consumers) and corporate public records (for corporate customers).

Preparing   Before approaching the potential buyer, the salesperson should know as much as possible about the person or company. Again, zip code and other demographic sources may help in preparing to approach individuals. Annual reports, Dun & Bradstreet and other published business information, census material, magazines, and other salespeople may all be helpful in preparing for corporate contacts.

Approach and Presentation   During the **approach**, which constitutes the actual beginning of the communication process, the salesperson explains to the potential customer the reason for the sales call, possibly mentions how the potential buyer's name was obtained, and gives a preliminary explanation of what he or she is offering. The sales presentation is a detailed effort to bring the buyer's needs together with the product or service the salesperson represents. Whether it is putting together a life and health insurance package for a private individual or developing technical specifications on a piece of machinery for a large company, the salesperson in the personification of the company's marketing offering. The satisfaction of the customer's wants and needs is the guiding criterion. Therefore, the salesperson must not only present, but also listen. The salesperson can then make adjustments to the presentation based on the feedback received.

Overcoming Objections   One of the primary values of personal selling lies in the salesperson's ability to receive and deal with potential customers'

---

[1] Richard L. Benun, "Telemarketing: The Answer to Rising Cost of Cold Calls," *Direct Marketing,* December 1981, pp. 50–55.

objections to purchasing the product. Although advertising may stimulate potential customers' interest in buying the product, they may talk themselves out of purchasing it if there is no additional input from the advertiser. In a sales presentation many objections can be dealt with immediately. Others may take more time, but still may be overcome. This extra persuasive feedback makes personal selling an essential promotional tool for many companies.

Closing the Sale Many salespeople lose sales simply because they never asked the buyer to buy. At several times in a presentation the salesperson may try a **trial close** to gauge how near the buyer is to closing. In a trial close the salesperson asks questions that assume the buyer has agreed to close. For example, the potential buyer of a new stereo may be asked, "Do you want this with wood grain finish?" An industrial purchaser may be asked, "When do you want this delivered?" Answers to these questions indicate whether the potential buyer has decided to buy.

At several points in this presentation salespeople also should make an actual attempt to close the sale. Although they may not reach closure, the attempt to close often draws out hidden objections that the salespeople can address before trying again to close. It also gives the potential buyer ample opportunity to say yes.

Follow-Up To maintain customer satisfaction, the salesperson should follow up after a sale to be certain the product is delivered properly and the customer is satisfied with the result. Often everything goes as promised, but the customer is dissatisifed due to cognitive dissonance.[2] **Cognitive dissonance** *exists when the purchase decision has already been made and the buyer notices other products that are perceived to have advantages over the one purchased.* Salesperson follow-up that reemphasizes the advantages of the product purchased can reduce cognitive dissonance and increase customer satisfaction.

Salesperson Categories

Different individuals may be part of a company's personal selling effort and still have very different job tasks. Based on the tasks assigned, salespeople usually fall into the categories of order getters, order takers, or support personnel.

Order Getters What we typically think of as salespeople are order getters. Order getters are concerned primarily with selling to new prospects and getting established buyers to buy more, which requires the ability to prospect for new clients and to recognize new uses for company products

---

[2] Leon Festinger, *A Theory of Cognitive Dissonance* (Palo Alto, Calif.: Stanford University Press, 1957).

by present buyers. Order getters often explain new company products to established buyers, as well as how existing products can be used in other applications.

Order Takers   Order takers handle the majority of a company's repeat sales. As such, the order taker's time seldom is devoted to generating new sales, but rather is spent primarily in taking incoming orders. Although the job sounds mostly clerical, it should not be underestimated. Order takers write up the bulk of corporate sales, and if a company is without an efficient order-taking staff, buyers may take their repeat sales elsewhere. Clerks at retail counters and order-processing personnel in corporations are classified as order takers. Often order takers do generate sales by informing customers they need to reorder or by convincing buyers that they should also purchase other corporate products. However, theirs is mostly a job of processing orders that have already been closed.

Support Personnel   The salesperson does not always have enough time to complete all the tasks necessary to close a sale. Therefore, many companies have support personnel to perform specific functions to help the salesperson. The three primary types of support personnel are missionary salespeople, trade salespeople, and technical specialists.

Missionary salespeople *typically work for manufacturers and call on intermediaries.* Their job is to provide information, answer questions, and set the stage for later sales. Missionary salespeople usually do not try to close a sale, but rather try to create goodwill for the company and interest in the product.

For example, Neutrogena soap has a sales force of 66, but 16 of these people do nothing but drop in on 5,000 dermatologists. These missionary salespeople have a friendly visit with the doctor and staff and leave free samples of Neutrogena to be given to patients.[3] The result is that customers buy Neutrogena because, after all, the doctor gave it to them.

Trade salespeople *are often order takers, but also help channel members promote the product.* Used extensively by companies whose products sell through grocery stores, trade salespeople restock shelves, set up point-of-purchase displays, distribute samples, perform in-store demonstrations, and generally try to help the retailer with in-store promotions.

Technical specialists *are normally used in selling complex industrial products, especially those that must be adapted to the buyer's specific needs.* Technical specialists usually have a background in engineering or the physical sciences and function just as much as problem solvers as they do as true salespeople.

---

[3] William Harris, "If I have the Doctor . . . ," *Forbes*, March 30, 1981, pp. 63, 64, 67.

Types of Personal Selling

We can examine personal selling not only from the perspective of the tasks the salesperson performs, but from the institutions for whom they sell and the type of items they sell as well.

Selling for Manufacturers   Many salespeople work for the manufacturer of the product they sell. With consumer products, these salespeople typically have wholesalers and retailers as their clients, and emphasize not so much the product attributes as the desirability of the product for its profit margin and demand in the marketplace.

Manufacturers of industrial products utilize salespeople who call on other manufacturers. The product attributes and how it can assist the purchasing company are normally emphasized.

Selling for Wholesalers   Wholesalers employ thousands of salespeople who call on customers at regular intervals and are usually well known to buyers. In fact buyers often depend on them to evaluate the store's needs and even to keep inventory records. Many wholesalers' salespeople simply write up their own orders after inspecting the retailer's inventory. Because the wholesalers' salespeople often represent a full catalog of items, there is

Strategy

Avon Versus Mary Kay

"Avon calling" is probably one of the most familiar slogans used in advertising directed at ultimate consumers. Its friendly charm and familiar ringing doorbell are recognized by millions of women as the greeting of the lady who brings a selection of cosmetics, fragrances, jewelry, and other items for purchase in the home.

Yet all is not well with the world's number-one manufacturer and distributor of these products. Avon has encountered important changes in its marketing environment. How it responds to them can mean continuing success or accelerating decline in the 1980s.

Founded as the California Perfume Company in 1886 by David H. McConnell, the firm underwent several name changes before it became Avon Products in 1950. The fifties were a time of great growth for Avon. Post-war consumers had money to spend and wanted new products to buy. With the majority of women staying home to raise their families, Avon had a ready market for its goods. It also had a substantial supply of "representatives" for its line. Homemakers were naturals for selling to other homemakers, particularly when the work let them set their own hours and was less demanding than a full-time outside job.

In that era house-bound wives of blue-collar workers formed Avon's major market. They welcomed the opportunity to shop in the privacy and convenience of their homes. Avon successfully presented its approach as "a pleasant alternative to shopping in a retail store."

For more than 20 years the Avon formula advanced Avon's fortunes handsomely. Sales representatives were paid 25 percent on orders up to $100 and 40 percent above $100. They received no salary or fringe benefits. Low- and middle-level executives were paid low-level salaries. Advertising expenditures were kept to about 2 percent of sales, and there was little costly, risky pioneering in new products. Prices were set at a 65-percent markup over manufacturing costs. Representatives were given territories of about 150 families with saturation sales as their goal. All things combined, therefore, to provide a highly profitable operation.

Avon's last big growth year for domestic sales was 1974. That year Avon held 85 percent of the door-to-door cosmetic market and 20 percent of the $5 billion total cosmetics market. Since then sales have risen at a distinctly slower rate. Avon's formula, many say, became obsolete in the seventies. Cosmetics and related products are now available in outlets that the female shopper frequents most. As one veteran Avon representative put it, "Selling Avon may work just fine on farms or in the Dakotas where there is no competition, but now you can go down to the store and get the same thing for less without waiting two weeks."*

The increased number of women in the work force also contributed to Avon's decreasing profits. Fewer women were home during the day to receive their Avon representative and at night they could not spare the time. Increased job opportunities for women made it harder to recruit Avon ladies—other businesses offered better pay, regular hours, and fringe benefits.†

At this point Mary Kay Cosmetics entered the market. The company was not yet a major contender in the market, but it was a company with marketing ideas that met the challenges of the late seventies.

Mary Kay Ash started the company in 1963 with $5,000 from her savings and 10 other salespeople. She wanted to develop a company that would give women a chance to earn some good money by personally selling products.

Ash knew cosmetics through her association with a hide tanner who had applied his skill to the making of a skin-softening cream. She also knew about making sales through the home party plan from a previous employer. Putting the two together and imprinting the result with her own philosophy and innovation, Mary Kay saw her firm sell $198,000 worth of products in the first year.

Mary Kay consultants do not have assigned territories and typically do not sell door-to-door as Avon representatives do. Rather, they work with "hostesses" who invite up to six friends to attend an evening beauty show in their homes. The Mary Kay consultant gives a two-hour beauty plan and free makeup lessons to the guests, with the hope that each guest will buy the cosmetics she has just learned to use. Even though the customer tries before she buys, Mary Kay still prefers to maintain a policy of "satisfaction guaranteed or your money refunded."

Mary Kay Ash spends a great deal of time training and motivating those who sell her products. Mary Kay women are called "beauty consultants," not representatives. They are paid a 40-percent commission on orders between $50 and $100, 45 percent on orders between $101 and $500, and 50 percent on sales above $500. The consultants are encouraged to recruit additional women for the sales staff and earn an 8-percent commission on their recruits' wholesale orders for as long as the recruit sells at least $100 per month for a six-month period.

A consultant can earn an additional $700 per month with Mary Kay's volume bonuses. There are other luxurious rewards that act as incentives for the sales force. Diamond rings, pink Cadillacs, mink coats, fantasy vacations, and shopping sprees are some examples.

The products of the two companies are packaged differently. Avon has traditionally used theme packaging for its products. Mary Kay eschews this

Continued

"cutesy" packaging that has worked so well for Avon, preferring to rely on the recognition gained by standard packages. Mary Kay "thinks pink." Pink is the color for everything from the jars containing creams and makeup, to the Cadillacs she awards for one year's use to distributors who do an especially outstanding job, to the tractor-trailers used to deliver the products.

The two companies approach their product lines differently as well. Avon emphasizes variety. In one recent year the company offered 30 women's fragrances, six men's fragrances, and about 1,400 skin, makeup, bath, and hair-care items. Mary Kay, on the other hand, prefers to limit the line to a number that the beauty consultants can afford to stock (all items are paid for in advance by cash or money order) and be knowledgeable about with relative ease.

Despite its more lucrative incentive program, Mary Kay has also experienced a decline in recruitment. Its answer to the problem is to put all its 1984 promotion budget into a recruiting-oriented program. The money will be used to provide greater financial rewards for salespeople who are successful at recruiting new consultants.

Avon has developed its "Opportunity Unlimited" program to deal with declining recruitment. Avon finally will reward its salespeople on a cash basis for recruiting. Unfortunately, the extra incentives provided by "Opportunity Unlimited" result in the Avon representative's hourly wages averaging about $2.88. Avon still has a long way to go to match Mary Kay's incentives.

Another problem both firms are facing is contacting prospective customers. Avon reps find it difficult to catch people at home, and Mary Kay consultants are experiencing many "no-shows" at their parties. To combat this, both firms are increasing their product advertising to build product awareness and differentiate their product lines from those in retail outlets.

It was Mary Kay's incentive program that made it the fastest-growing cosmetics company in the seventies. The future success of these two firms rests in their ability to make both their products and sales opportunities attractive to potential representatives. Even though Mary Kay is smaller, it just may have the upper hand.

* Steven Minty, "Avon, You've Looked Better," *Sales and Marketing Management*, April 5, 1982, pp. 52–57.
† "Avon Tries a New Formula to Restore Its Glow," *Business Week*, July 2, 1984, pp. 46–47.

relatively little time for explaining the merits of individual products. More emphasis is placed on the reliability and reputation of the wholesaler as a whole than on each individual product offered.

In-Store Retail Selling   The main distinguishing feature of behind-the-counter retail selling is that the customer comes to the salesperson. Most in-store retail salespeople are paid relatively little because their job requires comparatively little skill or product knowledge, they need not be aggressive, hours are regular, and no travel is involved. However, effective sellers of large appliances, automobiles, furniture, and other large-ticket items can earn substantial incomes.

Direct-to-the-Consumer Selling   Although only a very small portion of total retail sales is accounted for by direct-to-the-consumer salespeople, this category is nevertheless important, especially as a training ground for salespeople who will ultimately sell other products and services. Many of America's top executives began their careers selling brushes, cookware, Bibles, dictionaries, magazines, or any one of hundreds of different products direct to the consumer.

For certain companies direct-to-the-customer selling is critically important, because it is the major or perhaps the only channel used. Avon cosmetics uses this as its principal method of distribution. Other companies that depend almost entirely on direct-to-the-consumer selling include Amway, Tupperware, Fuller Brush, and Sarah Coventry. Although direct-to-the-consumer salespeople can earn above-average incomes, their success requires an unusually high degree of initiative, persistence, and motivation. For example, Judy McCoy was at one time "looking to make $50 a week and get out of the house a bit." With a $300 bank loan her husband had to cosign, Judy became a door-to-door salesperson for Mary Kay Cosmetics in 1976. Today she makes an annual income in six figures, and her husband (and 225 other people) work for her as a Mary Kay sales director. How did she do it? She admits it was through hard work and "because I wanted to win."[4]

Selling Intangibles   One of the most rapidly growing fields for salespeople is in the area of intangibles—"products" that cannot be seen, touched, or felt. Insurance, securities, and bank services are among the leading intangibles being marketed today.

People who sell intangibles are frequently creative, polished, and articulate. They often work with prospects who occupy high executive positions in business. Most commercial banks have marketing departments, and their salespeople (sometimes called account service representatives) visit corporate customers regularly to describe bank services and obtain new business. Other types of intangibles include advertising, travel, and TV and radio time.

Selling Real Estate   The fields of industrial, commercial, and residential real estate provide thousands of selling jobs. The qualifications of real-estate personnel vary considerably, depending mainly on whether sales are

---

[4] Howard Rudnitsky, "The Flight of the Bumblebee," *Forbes*, June 22, 1981, pp. 104–06.

being made to consumers or to businesses. Real-estate selling can be complex. The dollar amount involved is usually significant and, because real estate cannot be mass-produced, each transaction is unique. Because no two parcels of land are identical, considerable imagination is often required to develop attractive selling points. Also, a considerable knowledge of real-estate law is usually required. Real-estate salespeople must be licensed and must pass an appropriate examination.

A Salesperson in Action

What, exactly, does a salesperson do? Although persuading someone to buy is a very important part of personal selling, salespeople also perform a number of other interesting activities, such as (1) exploratory research, (2) diagnostic interviews, (3) preliminary reports, (4) sales strategy development, (5) coordinative work with various departments in their organization, (6) formal presentations, (7) closures, and (8) post-sale account servicing. In effect the salesperson is what the customer sees of the overall marketing strategy. The following case history of a typical, if mythical, young salesperson provides some insight into what selling involves.

What a Salesperson Does   Maria Salazar graduated from college three years ago and now works as a sales representative for a well-known manufacturer of paper products, the Bigbox Corporation. She has just been given the responsibility of selling Bigbox's line to the Best Hamburger Company, a nationally known fast-food franchisor. All the activities described below are part of "making that sale."

Exploratory Research   Maria begins her assignment by asking Bigbox's marketing research people to put together as much background material as possible, as fast as possible, about (1) the paper product needs of fast-food franchises, (2) the Best Hamburger Company, and (3) the principal suppliers of paper products to fast-food companies. She studies this information in detail and develops a number of specific questions that can be answered only by a visit to Best.

A Diagnostic Interview   In its training program for sales representatives, Bigbox stressed the importance of diagnosing a prospect's needs before trying to sell. Thus, when Maria makes her first call on the Best executive charged with purchasing paper products, she frankly admits that she is there only to gather information, to see whether Bigbox might be able to do something for Best. By leading the conversation around to topics in which she is interested, Maria learns what general paper products Best uses and in what quantities, what Best pays for these items, and what its general attitude is toward its suppliers.

A Preliminary Report   Next, Maria sends a memo to her sales manager, stating what she has learned about Best Hamburger's paper product needs and how these needs are being satisfied. Later, she and her boss meet with several production people and Bigbox's chief cost accountant to determine whether they can compete on a price basis with Best's current suppliers. A careful examination of cost figures shows that Bigbox has a very strong advantage in the paper napkin field. Just recently the company acquired several new napkin-making machines that are the most advanced in the industry. After the meeting Maria's manager tells her to go ahead and "develop" the Best account.

A Second Visit to Best   Maria again calls on the Best purchasing executive, this time with three specific objectives in mind: (1) To obtain answers to a number of specific questions about the product quality, warehousing, and delivery requirements of Best; (2) to get the Best executive's general reaction to the price ranges for various Bigbox products; and (3) if the reaction is favorable, to arrange for a formal presentation to a senior executive at Best. Everything goes quite smoothly, and a meeting is arranged for two weeks later.

Developing a Sales Strategy   Based on what Maria has learned so far, she recommends that Bigbox initially attempt to sell only one product—paper napkins. Her argument is, first, that Bigbox has a strong competitive edge in making napkins because of its new machines; second, that at this stage it is better to concentrate all the sales effort on one target product than to try to appear to be experts on all paper products; and third, that she suspects, although she cannot prove it, that Best is somewhat dissatisfied with its present napkin supplier. Maria's manager agrees and tells her to develop a presentation based solely on paper napkins.

More Market Research   Maria now makes a hurry-up call on marketing research, asking them to: "Get all the facts you can about the paper napkins used in fast-food outlets. Try to pinpoint what consumers like and dislike about Best napkins compared to the competition." Marketing research works fast and has a report ready in less than a week.

Getting Help from Product Development   The marketing research director, product development specialists, and Maria meet to try to come up with a napkin that (1) feels better, (2) functions better, (3) looks better, (4) sets off the Best logo more effectively, and (5) can be sold for less than competing products.

Preparing a Formal Proposal   Based on her diagnosis of Best's needs for paper napkins and Bigbox's ability to meet those needs, Maria prepares a formal presentation. To make it as effective as possible, she asks the promotion department to develop visuals to go with it. The promotion department in turn consults the company's advertising agency. The final presentation is intended to provide Best executives with background information about Bigbox (its history, production capabilities, reputation, and so on) and specific information about the quality, design, and price of its paper napkins. Maria's manager looks the proposal over and sits through two dry runs.

Making a Formal Presentation   Working through Best's purchasing agent, Maria has arranged a meeting with a senior executive at Best. She arrives, ready to make her presentation and accompanied by her sales manager, a Bigbox production executive, a production technician, and a cost accountant, all of whom are prepared to answer technical questions that may come up. At the conclusion of the presentation an informal no-holds-barred discussion is held. Best is impressed with Bigbox and gives it an order for napkins worth $22,500 per month.

The Follow-Through   Maria's assignment now is to make sure that her new account is kept happy—that deliveries are handled properly and that Best is satisfied. At the next sales meeting she is praised publicly for her fine work and given an award. However, glory, too, is perishable. In a private interview with her sales manager the next day, she is chided for not making more of an effort to get the paper cup business from Best!

been amazed at the number of appointments I've been able to make with people when others haven't been able to get to see them."§

Although some buyers have been reluctant to deal with women salespersons and a few have flatly refused to do business with them, marketing managers repeat that such feelings are not widespread and, indeed, are diminishing.

Are women as good at selling as men? Dorise Mendelson, who covers her territory by flying from New York to Atlanta to Los Angeles, claims that in some industries there is no selling job a woman cannot do as well or even better than a man. The fact that the company she now represents asked her to represent it when she and her salesperson-husband divorced seems to support her assertion.

Even in industrial sales, traditionally a male bastion, women are experiencing significant sales success. Women have demonstrated a capacity equal to men in learning the often-complex product, organizational, and personal details involved in industrial selling and how to translate this knowledge into sales.

As more women enter business in general and marketing in particular, it is clear that women will continue to enter the sales force in increasing numbers. Given their past sales performance, this is a marketing milestone that should make any sales manager smile with visions of increased sales.

* U.S. Department of Commerce, Bureau of the Census, *Statistical Abstract of the United States,* 1984, p. 416.
† Joyce Winslow, "Heard the One About the Traveling Salesperson?" *Savvy,* October 1980, p. 58.
‡ "The Industrial Salesman Becomes a Salesperson," *Business Week,* February 19, 1979, p. 106.
§ "The Computer Field," *The Executive Female,* May/June 1980, pp. 23–24.

SALES MANAGEMENT

Although personal selling is an essential part of a company's promotional effort, little coordinated effort would be achieved without some provision for managing salespeople. **Sales management** includes those activities concerned with the planning, organizing, and controlling of all personal selling efforts. It involves job analysis and description, recruitment, selection, training, motivation, compensation, sales territory establishment, and salesperson evaluation.

Job Analysis

All sorts of people are engaged in personal selling. Their backgrounds and training vary with the products they sell and many other factors. Because of this variation the term "salesperson" means a wide variety of things to different people. Many companies, in an attempt to define more specifically the work their salespeople do, have adopted other titles for them (see Figure 17-1). Because the work performed by salespeople is so varied, the qualifications for sales jobs also differ considerably.

A very useful tool for sales managers is the job analysis, or careful study of the work their salespeople do. The job analysis is a big help in preparing a job description, which is the detailed explanation of the sales job.

Job analysis *is the systematic study of the activities of a selling position.* Informational inputs for the job analysis come from three main sources: (1) asking salespeople in personal interviews or by questionnaire to describe in detail the work they do, (2) observing what salespeople do and the way they do it, and (3) asking management what they want salespeople to do, especially regarding those activities that are often neglected.

The more comprehensive and thorough the job analysis is, the better equipped the sales manager will be to do his or her work—managing the sales force. All sales management functions are related directly to the work the salesperson does. If, for example, the job analysis shows that the sales job is relatively routine, the product is nontechnical, and the buyers are unsophisticated, the sales manager may decide to employ people without college training.

A large part of a sales manager's job consists of attempting to match the right people to the sales job. The job analysis, properly prepared, should reveal what type of person the company needs as far as intelligence, age, health, previous experience, technical or educational background, appearance, emotional maturity, and motivation are concerned.

Not all firms conduct formal studies of selling jobs. Some sales managers believe they know selling so well that a structured study is unnecessary. Others claim they do not have the time or the staff personnel to conduct job studies. Still others feel that sales jobs, even for the same product and same type of customer, are too varied to make a formal job study meaningful. However, an intensive appraisal of the work salespeople do—and are expected to do—is generally essential if sales management functions are to be performed with maximum effectiveness.

Job Description

The job analysis provides much of the information needed to prepare a **job description**, or detailed summary of the job to be done, the work environment, and related job factors. The major elements included in a job description are:

1. *Number, type, and location of assigned customers.* In most kinds of selling sales personnel assigned to a sales territory are given a certain number of established accounts. Who the accounts are, their demographic and psychological characteristics, and other pertinent information should be given to the salesperson.
2. *Territorial assignment.* The job description should define the territory assigned to the salesperson. When territorial boundaries are not made clear, several salespeople may solicit business from the same prospect, a wasteful and inefficient procedure that may confuse customers.
3. *Prospecting requirements.* Virtually all salespeople are expected to prospect for new customers. Emphasis placed on prospecting varies greatly depending on the type of sales job. The job description should spell out what the salesperson is expected to achieve in terms of new accounts.
4. *Explanation of sales tactics.* The "how" of selling—prospecting, making a sales approach, getting attention, creating interest, stimulating desire, and making a successful close—should be explained in as much detail as possible.
5. *Post-sale services.* In many kinds of selling post-sale services are part of the salesperson's job. These include installation, inspection of the product in use, and goodwill visits to the purchasers.
6. *Travel requirements.* Some sales jobs, especially those in major metropolitan areas, require no intercity travel. Other sales positions may require the salesperson to visit several states or much of the

nation. The amount of travel should always be stated in the job description.

7. *Physical fitness requirements.* Personal selling may make heavy demands on the physical capabilities of an individual, especially if heavy samples, extensive travel by automobile, and irregular hours are involved.

8. *Educational qualifications.* Technical and nontechnical educational requirements vary widely for different kinds of selling. In some situations products may be so complicated that extensive education in one or more of the sciences may be needed. In other cases sufficient product knowledge can be acquired on the job.

9. *Experience requirements.* Previous selling experience is specified in the job description when a firm cannot or chooses not to provide enough sales training to make new salespeople effective or when the job is highly complex.

10. *Reporting duties.* The job description should explain what kinds of reports salespeople must fill out, in addition to any meetings salespeople must attend or marketing research activities sales personnel may perform from time to time.

11. *Supervision and managerial support provided.* Although some sales personnel are very closely supervised, many salespeople function with very little management direction. The job description should explain what help management will give to the salesperson (such as helping to make presentations to key accounts; expediting critical orders; and informing the salesperson of changes in advertising, pricing, product modifications, and similar matters).

12. *Clerical support provided.* Some selling positions need strong clerical support in the form of telephone answering services, typing of letters and reports, and arranging of appointments. The job description should spell out what support the company will provide.

13. *Sales equipment.* Whether the salesperson will use his or her own automobile or a company car is an important consideration in many sales jobs. Practices vary widely, but for most salespeople who are employees—as contrasted with self-employed agents—the majority of companies provide an automobile allowance in one form or another.

14. *Financial responsibilities.* The job description should identify any money-handling responsibilities the salesperson may have. In some cases salespeople collect cash from buyers, a condition that may require bonding by an insurance company.

15. *Compensation arrangement.* Salespeople may be compensated by a straight salary, straight commission, or a combination of salary

and commission. Bonuses and other forms of incentive may also be provided.

Should Salespeople Set Prices?   Wide variations exist between industries and companies within industries regarding the delegation of pricing authority to salespeople. Some firms think it is essential that the salesperson, being on the spot where the transaction is to be made, have great flexibility in setting prices. Other firms require their salespeople to observe a strict one-price policy.

There is little evidence to indicate that either position is the better. One study, however, found that granting low-to-moderate pricing authority to salespeople is the most advisable course. It was concluded that "the strategy of delegating a high degree of pricing authority to the sales force is likely dysfunctional. It appears to produce relatively aggressive discounting behavior, resulting in lowered gross margin without any offsetting benefits. Sample firms that gave their sales personnel a high degree of price-setting authority had consistently poor performance. The sample firms that allowed moderate price latitude performed better on only one dependent variable—sales per sales representative."[5]

Recruitment

The first step in the hiring process is **recruitment**—*obtaining applicants for the sales job*. It can be a considerable headache. In some cases as many as 25 to 100 applicants must be screened to find one who satisfactorily fulfills all the qualifications. Recruitment procedures vary widely. Many companies use college placement offices to find job candidates; others use newspaper and trade magazine advertisements to attract applicants. A good deal of recruiting is done informally at trade association meetings, at conventions, or by encouraging present salespeople to recommend their friends for sales jobs.

Selection

Selection *is the process of choosing the applicant who will best fill a sales position*. A company may use a number of selection devices, such as psychological tests, physical examinations, interviews by executive personnel, credit reports, and references from former employers and educators. Many sales applicants are weeded out on the basis of their written applications.

---

[5] P. Ronald Stephenson, William L. Cron, and Gary L. Frazier, "Delegating Pricing Authority to the Sales Force: The Effects on Sales and Profit Performance," *Journal of Marketing,* Spring 1979, pp. 21–28.

The emphasis placed on selection varies widely, depending on the type of sales job. Some companies will give just about anyone who can buy a set of samples a chance at door-to-door selling. Firms that recruit on college campuses tend to be far more selective and may spend, in some instances, thousands of dollars to find one salesperson.

In the interviewing process the recruiter looks for both objective and subjective information. The recruiter will ask the applicant about courses taken in school, previous work experience, and so on. There also may be questions that require the applicant to reveal something about personality—questions designed to help the interviewer determine if the individual will fit into the organization, is management material, and projects the kind of image the firm wants. Recruiters are always looking for applicants who display sales ability in the interview. After all, applicants are in the job of selling themselves to the company.

A recent survey of 400 salespeople in the banking, chemical, communications, high technology, insurance, and pharmaceutical industries found that enthusiasm, maintaining good eye contact, knowing how to probe and close, and the ability to sell product features, advantages, and benefits were skills needed to be a good salesperson, but the survey found no exact success formula. The chairman of the group conducting the survey concluded, "While executives have a multitude of sophisticated systems and tools with which to run their businesses, the process of hiring and developing salespeople still is executed by trial and error."[6]

Training

The emphasis placed on training also varies widely. Most door-to-door organizations still use a sink-or-swim approach. Other organizations, especially those marketing industrial goods, may invest heavily in formal training programs. Again, the job analysis provides a guide to the amount and type of training needed.

Sales **training** *emphasizes three major areas: (1) product information*—how the product works, its applications, its advantages over competitive products, and similar information; *(2) selling techniques*—how to prospect for customers, buyer psychology, and specific strategies to use in making presentations; *and (3) company information*—facts about the firm's service facilities, history, productive capacity, credit policies, delivery policies, guarantees, and so on.

Companies employ many different training devices, such as lectures, role playing, slides, films, and videotapes. Probably the most important

---

[6] "Survey Identifies Traits of High-Performing Sales Reps," *Marketing News*, September 16, 1983, p. 14.

form of training is on the job. Often a new salesperson will accompany an experienced salesperson on rounds for several weeks or even months to learn firsthand how selling is done.

An example of a customized training program is furnished by Chesebrough–Ponds prior to its introduction of Rave hair spray. Sales manager Steve Phillos retained Management of Human Resources Development (MOHR) to design a behavior modeling program that would help the sales force "improve the quality and timing of orders, and retail positioning" of that particular product.

MOHR produced a film using Chesebrough–Ponds salespeople in role playing sessions showing the product coming up against real-life reactions, trained regional sales managers so they could train the salespeople, and had salespeople fill out "contracts" specifying a commitment to achieve specific results in contacts with customers.

In evaluating the program's results Phillos said, "We had 80 percent of our volume goals for the first two-month period when we started shipping. . . . The quality of distribution is better than ever."[7]

Motivating Salespeople

Even the most successful salesperson is frequently in stress-producing situations. He or she must put up with hostile reactions from buyers, with hearing "no" far more often than "yes" from customers, with time-wasting waits in reception rooms, complaints from customers about late deliveries and product breakdowns, the strain of travel, demands by the company for more sales, conflicts with the production department, and so on. All this tends to discourage a salesperson and results in lost business for the firm. According to one estimate 80 percent of "new business" is achieved after the fifth sales call, but only "two out of ten salespeople make the call."[8]

It is obvious, then, that motivation is a critical sales management function. The need for motivation is also evidenced by the fact that in many organizations 75 percent of the sales volume is accounted for by only 25 percent of the salespeople. This happens even when the same selection standards are used for all salespeople in the organization. Frequently, the question management must answer is not, "Does he or she have the ability?" but, "Does he or she have the ability and the motivation?"

Although compensation is an important motivation, sales managers also use many nonfinancial devices to get their people to try harder—pep talks, sales meetings, contests, various forms of recognition, and inspira-

---

[7] "Making Salespeople Behave," *Sales & Marketing Management,* July 9, 1979, pp. 16–17.

[8] Herbert L. Seeger, Jr., *Sales Promotion Planning: A Special Dartnell Sales and Marketing Service Report* (Chicago: Dartnell Corp., 1970), p. 5.

tional books, articles, bulletins, and tape cassettes. One study also found that aspects of the organization where the salespeople work affects motivation.[9]

A survey of sales executives revealed strong motivational factors for salespeople.[10] Ranked on a scale from one to ten, the five highest and lowest ranking motivators and their positions on the scale were:

High

Special recognition for outstanding performance	8.10
Opportunity for promotion and advancement	7.91
Encouragement and contact of supervisor	7.83
Individual incentive bonus	7.82
Commission incentive	7.73

Low

Sales meetings/conventions	6.78
Publicizing comparative performance	6.71
Assigned quotas other than dollar volume	6.16
Group incentive bonus	5.55
Merchandise-prize contests	5.40

Many companies use an incentive program of gifts and awards to motivate sales personnel. Marken suggested the following guidelines for a well-run incentive program.[11]

1. Award prizes immediately after the contest.
2. Design the program so individuals compete against their own past performance.
3. Make goals difficult, but attainable.
4. Display and promote performance during the contest.
5. Promote the contest to the sales staff and their families.
6. Set specific sales goals.
7. Present prizes at a meeting that maximizes peer recognition.
8. Make prizes something salespeople would not buy for themselves.

---

[9] Pradeep K. Tyagi, "Perceived Organizational Climate and the Process of Salesperson Motivation," *Journal of Marketing Research*, May 1982, pp. 240–54.

[10] "Those Inflation Blues," *Sales & Marketing Management*, November 12, 1979, p. 24.

[11] G. A. Marken, "A Well-Run Incentive Program is Best Sales Staff Motivator," *Marketing News*, October 15, 1982, p. 5.

Mary Kay Cosmetics has achieved sales volumes of over $100 million annually from motivating its housewife sales force with an incentive program of money, bonuses, fur coats, jewels, trips, and pink Cadillacs and Buicks—all awarded by Mary Kay herself at the annual inspirational sales meetings.[12] Notice that these gifts are ones most salespeople would not buy themselves and are presented in front of their peers.

Managing Compensation Programs

One of the basic functions of sales management is to design compensation programs that achieve four principal objectives: (1) to attract well-qualified people, (2) to reward salespeople for their performance, (3) to serve as a motivating force, and (4) to encourage salespeople to stay with the company.

Compensation plans should be tailored to the requirements of a particular selling job. An effective compensation program (1) is straightforward enough for salespeople to understand, (2) is fair, (3) provides enough income so that the salespeople will not be excessively worried about their private financial affairs, and (4) is easy to administer.

Straight Salary Plan   The simplest compensation plan is the **straight salary plan**. Under this system the salesperson receives a fixed sum at regular intervals. The pay is the same regardless of the volume sold. Because there is no direct incentive for the salesperson to improve performance, a company often uses this plan when it does not want the salesperson to resort to high-pressure tactics to make sales.

This plan is also used to compensate salespeople when little personal selling but considerable service and engineering are required. For example, public utilities salespeople who sell gas or electricity to industrial and commercial users are frequently paid a straight salary.

Straight Commission Plan   The **straight commission plan** is based on the concept that salespeople should be paid in direct proportion to their success in selling. Straight commission plans are common in selling securities, insurance, wholesale apparel, advertising, real estate, automobiles, and a number of other industries, as shown in Figure 17-2. The chief advantages of the straight commission plan are that, first, it provides the maximum monetary incentive; second, it makes all personal-selling costs variable (a highly desirable situation from management's standpoint, because only successful sales efforts are a cost of doing business); and third, it is easy to administer.

Straight commission plans have several disadvantages, however. First, management does not have tight control over a salesperson's activities.

---

[12] Rudnitsky, "The Flight of the Bumblebee."

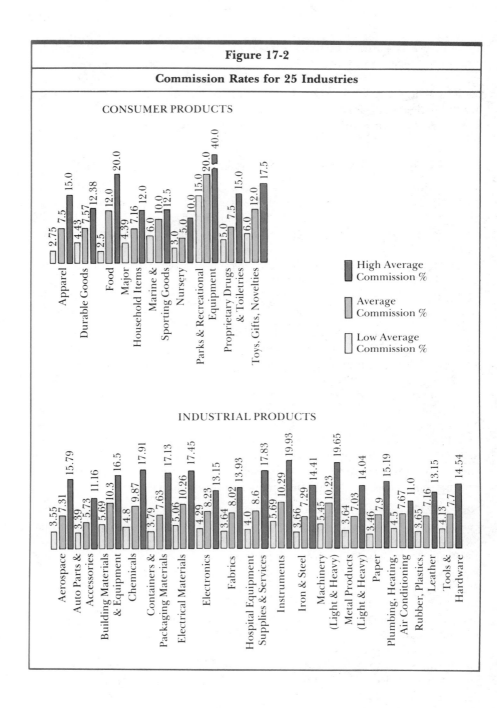

Figure 17-2

Commission Rates for 25 Industries

CONSUMER PRODUCTS

INDUSTRIAL PRODUCTS

- ■ High Average Commission %
- ▨ Average Commission %
- ☐ Low Average Commission %

People who are paid a straight commission are inclined to work when they want to work, call on accounts they prefer, and emphasize the products they like best. Second, many salespeople do not like the uncertain income provided by the straight commission plan. Third, salespeople compensated on a straight commission basis must have sufficient personal capital to finance themselves while they are building a clientele or developing a territory. Finally, salespeople on a straight commission are reluctant to perform any activities not directly related to making a sale (information gathering, for example).

Combination Plan   Most organizations provide salespeople with a combination salary and commission plan that has the advantages of both. The salesperson has the security of a fixed income and at the same time an incentive to work harder, because the more effectively he or she sells, the more he or she will earn overall. In addition many organizations also provide bonuses, profit sharing, paid life and health insurance, paid vacations, company cars, liberal expense accounts, and similar fringe benefits to help attract, motivate, and retain successful salespeople.

Establishing Sales Territories

One goal of sales management is to maximize sales volume within a given geographic area. A sales territory may be based on various geographic units such as states, counties, SMSAs, or determined in some other way— perhaps by the density of potential markets. For some sales jobs territories can be very large, perhaps covering an entire region of the United States. Other salespeople, such as those selling office equipment, may have territories that include only one or two large office buildings in a major city. The most common objectives in establishing sales territories are:

1. To secure maximum coverage of the market.
2. To control selling expenses.
3. To provide the best possible service for customers.
4. To equalize opportunities for all salespeople employed by the company.

Control and Evaluate

Sales management must set performance standards for salespeople, check whether the standards are being met, compare actual with anticipated or planned performance, and take corrective action.

Quantitative Evaluation   Some of the questions a sales executive asks in performing the control function are intended to evaluate quantitative performance: Is each salesperson achieving his or her share of the market potential? Is each territory providing sufficient sales volume? Are salespeople making an adequate number of calls per day? What is the average cost per call? What is the average order size? Sales reports may be required in order to obtain quantitative information as a basis for evaluating a salesperson. Reports are used to determine the number of calls made, orders obtained, miles traveled, selling expenses incurred, displays erected, and other work accomplished or problems encountered. Reports are also used to obtain information on competitors' activities and changes in business conditions.

Qualitative Evaluation   Other questions are intended to evaluate qualitative performance: Are the salespeople making headway in opening new accounts? Are they showing team spirit? What is their general attitude toward their work? Are customer complaints a major factor? These and many other questions on such issues as sales-force morale and customer satisfaction all constitute a sales manager's qualitative evaluation.

SALES PROMOTION

"One hundred stamps free with each purchase!" "Bonus coupon inside!" "Free T-shirt with $50 deposit." "Win an all-expense paid trip to Hawaii!" "Free demonstration—no obligation to buy!" "Free ten-day trial—return if not satisfied!" Promises such as these constitute a form of demand stimulation called sales promotion. The American Marketing Association defines **sales promotion** as *"activities other than personal selling, advertising, and publicity that stimulate consumer purchasing and dealer effectiveness such as displays, shows and exhibitions, demonstrations, and various nonrecurrent efforts not in the ordinary routine."*[13]

Sales promotion is sometimes thought of as a catchall term for miscellaneous unclassifiable methods of stimulating demand. Certainly, its boundaries are less clear-cut than those of, say, personal selling. Although an increasing number of companies have sales promotion departments and sales promotion managers, many organizations do not assign clear responsibility for this activity, and either sales management or the advertising department tends to take it over. However, sales promotion is becoming increasingly important in marketing as (1) a way of increasing the demand for new products, more of which reach the market each year; (2) a substitute for price competition; and (3) a way of differentiating similar products.

---

[13] Committee on Definitions, Ralph S. Alexander, Chairman, *Marketing Definitions* (Chicago: American Marketing Association, 1961), p. 20.

Sales Promotion Objectives

The basic goals of sales promotion are either identical or very similar to the objectives of advertising and personal selling: directly or indirectly, to promote the product. Six specific objectives of sales promotion follow.

Introduce New Products Sales promotions are often used to motivate consumers to try a new product or to induce business buyers to accept it for resale. Sampling, or the giving away of free samples, is a sales promotion technique frequently used to introduce new products to consumers. A company may offer money and merchandise allowances to induce business buyers to stock a new product. For example, when American Telecom Inc. (ATI) was trying to establish a dealer network for its telephone equipment, it hit on the sales promotion idea of sending all potential distributors a 3½-pound chocolate telephone with a sample of its distributor contract. Said the president of ATI's advertising agency, "Had we sent a telegram, brochure, or pamphlet, the response would have been much lower. Western Union told me the best response I could expect from a telegram would be 16%. Even by spending $50 per [phone], I never expected more than a 50% response." The cleverness of the sales promotion netted a 100-percent response, allowing ATI to pick the 60 best distributors for its channel.[14]

Attract New Customers Effective marketing executives are constantly on the lookout for ways to attract additional customers. In most cases new customers must be won away from other firms. Samples, premiums, contests, and similar devices are used to encourage consumers to try an unfamiliar brand or shift their patronage to a new retail outlet. The car-rental industry is constantly offering sales promotions to win customers from competitors. Avis has offered coupons for color televisions, National has given away alarm clocks or other electronic gadgets, Dollar gives sunglasses and umbrellas, and Budget has given luggage. Hertz, number one in the industry, has been reluctant to enter the sales promotion fray, but its chairman observed, "When a competitor buys away market share, it's okay to lose one share point. But when we lose three share points because of promotions, and the gap between us gets reduced, Hertz will not allow it; we will respond to protect our market share."[15]

Induce Present Customers to Buy More Producers of cake mixes and many other food products use promotions to encourage consumers to think of more ways and more occasions for using a product. The Pillsbury Annual Bake-Off, for example, with a top prize of $25,000, not only pro-

---

[14] "Sweet Sell Garners 100% Response for Phone Equipment Manufacturer," *Marketing News,* April 1, 1983, p. 3.

[15] Laura Landro, "Car-Rental Firms Slug It Out With Golf Bags and Tote Bags," *Wall Street Journal,* December 16, 1982, p. 33.

vides a wealth of new recipes, but ensures a great deal of publicity for the company as well. The intent is to display new recipes using Pillsbury products and to get customers thinking about baking.

Help the Firm Remain Competitive   Because virtually all companies marketing consumer goods and many firms courting industrial users conduct sales promotion activities, a company may have to engage in sales promotion simply to stay competitive. For example, when one major food chain in an area comes up with a new device, such as trading stamps, other chains in the area are almost compelled to follow suit with some sales promotion device.

Increase Sales in Off Seasons   Because many products have seasonal consumption patterns, an important aim of many sales promotion campaigns is to encourage the use of the product in off seasons. Campbell's Soup, for example, has conducted major campaigns to increase the variety of uses for soup and to encourage the consumption of soup, traditionally a cold-weather food, during summer months.

Increase the Inventories of Business Buyers   A key objective of many business sales promotions is to increase the size of retailers' inventories. Theoretically, the more units of a good a retailer has in stock, the more aggressive he or she will be in selling it to consumers. Moreover, a manufacturer that can sell in large quantities can usually reduce production and distribution costs. Therefore, money or merchandise allowances are used to encourage dealers to buy more. Special incentives to retailers may also help ensure better shelf positions for the firm's products inside the store.

Consumer-Oriented Sales Promotion

There are numerous sales promotion methods aimed at consumers. The major ones are sampling; contests, sweepstakes, and games; premiums; couponing; product demonstrations; point-of-purchase advertising; and trading stamps.

Sampling   Sampling, *the actual giving away of a product to the consumer,* is an old and widely used device for building consumer demand, especially when the product is new or has new feature. The cost of sampling can be high. For example, in 1969, in the laundry detergent field, housewives received so many free samples of new laundry brands that the effect on purchases was the same as if every homemaker in the United States had stopped doing laundry for nearly three weeks. Similarly, enough free toothpaste samples were distributed to cover the entire nation's toothbrushing needs for a full week.[16]

---

[16] "Soap, Toothpaste Sampling So Big It Cut into '69 Sales, Lever Says," *Advertising Age*, March 16, 1970, p. 1.

Sampling requires some distribution method to deliver samples to consumers. The most common methods are direct mail, door-to-door, point-of-purchase areas in stores, and attaching the sample to another product. Another problem is deciding the size of the sample. Retailers may object if the regular size is given away, because it subtracts from their sales.

Marriott solved the distribution problem by giving away samples to its hotel guests when they checked in. In an effort to draw attention to its gift shops, Marriott gave traveling businesswomen a packet containing 39 samples. A full-page advertisement in *Self* magazine announced the program and declared September of 1983 "National Traveling Businesswomen's Month." The samples were provided by *Self* advertisers. "Marketers are constantly seeking to reach upscale women with samples of their products," said *Self*'s creative/marketing director, Bill Abbott. "We created a package of surprise gifts that a traveler can take to her hotel room and examine at leisure. It's a bonus for the traveler, for Marriott, and for our advertisers."[17]

Sampling is not always a good marketing strategy. For example, sampling is not justified in the case of (1) a well-established product, (2) a product that is not superior in some way to competing products or whose points of superiority would not easily be recognized by the consumer, (3) a product with a slow turnover, (4) a product with a narrow profit margin, or (5) a highly perishable, fragile, or bulky product.

Sampling is an effective sales promotion device when the product is a frequently purchased convenience good such as coffee, cleaning agents, soaps, deodorants, and certain foods such as sausages and hot dogs.

Contests, Sweepstakes, and Games   A **contest** is a sales promotion device that offers prizes to consumers as a reward for analytical or creative thinking, usually about a product. For example, a contest may ask consumers to "Tell us in 25 words or less why you like brand X," or it may ask people to write a jingle about the product. A **sweepstakes**, which also offers prizes, usually requires only that the participant enter his or her name, which has a chance of being drawn from a "pot" containing all other consumer-entrant names. A sweepstakes is like a lottery except that no consideration is required to enter. To enter a sweepstakes, the consumer is not required to buy the product. A **game** is conducted over a longer period of time and is similar to sweepstakes in that pure chance determines the winners. Skill is not required. To the marketer, games have an advantage over sweepstakes and contests in that the consumer must often make repeat visits to the outlet that carries the firm's products to continue playing. The objective of contests, sweepstakes, and games is essentially the same—to encourage consumption of the product by creating consumer involvement.

---

[17] "*Self,* Hotels Reach Female Travelers with Sample Promo," *Marketing News,* October 14, 1983, p. 3.

Contests Although very popular in the past, the consumer-participation contest has lost much of its appeal in recent years. Not only have there been legal complications for various firms, but the fact that a true contest requires some expenditure of time and some exercise of mental skills apparently also makes them less attractive to consumers than sweepstakes or games.

Some contests have required considerable inventiveness on the part of entrants, but the prizes have also been quite worthwhile. For example, the Kentucky Club Tobacco Company once offered a grand prize of a race horse, a Kentucky Derby vacation for two, and $2,000 in spending money to the person who supplied the best name for the horse. The winning name was picked for its specific description of characteristics in the animal's lineage (the names of the horse's forebears were given), its creativeness, sparkle, and believability. Entrants were also required to a mail a box top from the pipe tobacco. Many contests require the entrant to complete a statement telling why he or she likes the product, to compose a jingle, or to suggest new product applications.

To support its selection as the official snack food of the 1984 Olympic Games, M&M sponsored a contest to guess the number of M&Ms in a 6 foot by 3 foot jar. The jar was a replica of the 20-ounce Olympic commemorative M&M jars on sale in stores. Expense-paid trips for four were awarded to the 10 people who came closest to guessing the correct number.[18]

Although the overall objective of a contest is to encourage people to buy the product, actual purchases are not required. Entrants are advised to submit evidence of a purchase (such as a label or box top), but they have the option of simply writing the product's name on a piece of paper. Occasionally consumers are told that they can obtain entry blanks only where the product is sold, an approach that at least gets them into the store.

Sweepstakes The objective of sweepstakes promotions is to encourage consumers to purchase a particular item. However, here again, legal considerations enter in. To avoid prosecution under lottery laws, sweepstakes sponsors no longer require entrants to actually purchase the product. Probably because they are so easy to enter, sweepstakes promotions have increased in importance in recent years as the popularity of contests has declined.

In a popular sweepstakes titled "Follow the Sun," the American Express Company offered the use of a Lear jet for two weeks as its number-one prize, along with the opportunity for the winner to pick his or her own vacation spot. The company offered a total of 1,335 other awards, with a money value of $150,000. The objective of the sweepstakes was to induce

---

[18] "Marketing Briefs," *Marketing News*, October 14, 1983, p. 2.

American Express cardholders to purchase *Venture*, a travel magazine. All the entrants had to do was detach a numbered circle from a mailing piece, insert it in a pocket provided, sign the card, and mail it to American Express, with or without a subscription order for the magazine.

In recent years there has been a movement to require fair play on the part of sweepstakes sponsors. It was discovered that many awarded no prizes if the numbers drawn were not entered by a participant. Thus, a sponsor promising $250,000 in prizes might give away only a small fraction of that amount. Under correct regulations sweepstakes sponsors must continue drawing numbers until they have awarded all prizes.

Games The chief objective of most games is to build store traffic and encourage repeat purchases. For example, Kroger once devised a simple Bingo-type game that it hoped would bring customers into its stores more often. Game materials and tickets were available on request from cashiers and store offices. Markers were to be peeled off the game ticket and placed in the appropriate spot on the Bingo card. The object, as in regular Bingo, was to fill any row of five squares. Cash prizes of $1 to $1,000 were awarded weekly. Because only one ticket was given for each visit to the store, anyone entering the contest would have to make a minimum of five trips to the store to win, thereby increasing store traffic.

The Federal Trade Commission requires companies that use games to adhere to certain rules. These include:

1. The sponsor may not misrepresent a participant's chances of winning.
2. The exact number of prizes and their value must be clearly stated.
3. The odds of winning a prize must be disclosed. (Figure 17-3 shows the odds for a game run by one retailer.)
4. The game sponsor must furnish a list of the names and addresses of winners of each prize.

Premiums A **premium** is a product usually offered free or at less than its usual price to encourage the consumer to buy another product. China or glass tumblers given away with detergent and toy whistles attached to tubes of toothpaste are examples of premiums. Frequently, cash is given as a premium. Consumers who send in a box top or label are offered a 25- or a 5-cent "refund." Premiums are used most often with small, frequently purchased products.

Wholesalers frequently use premiums to induce retailers to promote, or push, their products—called **push premiums**. Most premiums, however—called **pull premiums**—are used by retailers to induce consumers to purchase products.

For example, when the Credit Union National Association wanted to increase enrollments in its certified Credit Union Executive Program, it

Figure 17-3

Odds Chart

Odds vary depending on number of game tickets you obtain.
The more tickets you collect, the better your chances of winning.

ODDS CHART EFFECTIVE NOVEMBER 26, 1984

Prize Value	Number of Prizes	Odds for One Game Ticket	Odds for 13 Game Tickets	Odds for 26 Game Tickets Plus 10 Saver Chips
$2,500	52	1 in 328,846	1 in 25,296	1 in 9,135
100	2,067	1 in 8,273	1 in 636	1 in 230
10	3,875	1 in 4,413	1 in 339	1 in 123
5	7,750	1 in 2,206	1 in 170	1 in 61
2	30,998	1 in 552	1 in 42	1 in 15
1	199,028	1 in 86	1 in 7	1 in 2.4
Total No. Prizes	243,770	1 in 70	1 in 5.4	1 in 1.9

offered a premium of a specially designed wallet/calculator to all enrollers. The result of the direct-mail offering was an enrollment that was 10 percent higher than the program goal.[19]

Some premiums are **self-liquidating** (meaning that they pay for themselves). The consumer pays a small additional price to cover the cost of the premium and handling. The seller does not actually attempt to make a profit on the item, but tries to avoid a loss. When Budget Rent-A-Car, the offical rental agency for the 1984 Olympics, offered an Olympic warmup suit to customers, the cost was $39.95, just enough to cover Budget's cost of offering the premium.

What Constitutes a Good Premium?   The variety of items offered to manufacturers by the premium industry is almost endless. Some of the questions manufacturers ask in selecting premiums and retailers ask in accepting them as part of a promotional package are:

1. Does the item have strong appeal?
2. Will it increase sales?
3. Is it unusual—not on sale elsewhere?

---

[19] Ibid.

4. If a price is charged for the premium, does it represent a considerable savings over what the consumer would normally pay?

Couponing   A **coupon** is generally a certificate that, when presented to a retailer, entitles the holder to either a specified savings on a product or a cash refund. Most coupons are issued by manufacturers, and they are not only one of the most widely used sales promotion devices, but also one that is growing in popularity. In 1979, according to Nielsen studies, manufacturers distributed 81.2 billion coupons compared with 36.7 billion in 1975. Over half of all coupons are distributed in newspapers.[20]

Coupons may be distributed by mail or door-to-door, inserted in packages, or included as part of magazine or newspaper ads. When coupons are used to promote a product, caution must be exercised to prevent fraud, because in effect they function as cash.

Producers of consumer convenience goods such as detergents, cake mixes, coffee, soup, dog food—almost any item available in a food store—are likely to use coupons. One premise of couponing is that a change in attitude does not necessarily have to precede a change in behavior. A homemaker may be very loyal to one brand of detergent, but if a coupon for a competitive brand will save money, he or she may be induced to at least try it. Many customers are loyal to one product simply because they have never tried the competing product. Coupons are one way to change consumer habits.

An advantage of coupons is that no price reduction on the package is made. A problem in the use of coupons is inconvenience to the retailer—redeeming them takes employee time.

Product Demonstrations   Product demonstrations are used to some extent as a sales promotion device. Many manufacturers pay demonstrators to go from store to store instructing both sales personnel and customers about the uses of the product. A company may hire cosmeticians, for example, to provide free lessons on the proper use of makeup. Demonstrations are used to some extent in marketing apparel. Fashion shows are often staged at restaurants, department stores, and other locations where a reasonably affluent market can be reached.

Point-of-Purchase Advertising   Point-of-purchase advertising tells the consumer, "Here I am. Buy me now." The great variety of products retailed today, the continuing trend toward self-service buying, and increased competition among retailers have all helped to make point-of-purchase advertising a significant sales-promotion device.

In most stores selling space is at a premium. Installation of one display

---

[20] "Marketing Briefs," *Marketing News,* March 7, 1980, p. 13.

usually means that some other display must be removed. Retailers are not interested in simply exchanging one display for another unless the switch will produce more sales. They tend to favor displays that encourage impulse sales, sell related products, sell new products, and tie in with overall store promotions. Discount and self-service stores rely on point-of-purchase displays more than other retailers. Some of the more commonly used point-of-purchase materials are floor displays, stands, bins, end-of-counter displays, interior overhead signs, outside signs, wall signs, and posters. Some displays are illuminated, and some even have moving parts that add to their effectiveness.

To be effective, a point-of-purchase display should meet these criteria:

1. It is attractive and suits the decor of the store.
2. It shows the product off effectively.
3. It gives necessary information about the product.
4. It makes the product look valuable and worth at least the price charged.

Trading Stamps The various sales promotion techniques discussed to this point are sponsored mainly by manufacturers. Trading stamps are a retailer-sponsored sales promotion device. They are a bonus for purchasing goods in a particular retail store. The number of stamps given to a shopper is related directly to the size of the purchase. When the shopper has accumulated enough stamps, he or she may exchange them for merchandise (or cash) at redemption centers or through catalogs supplied by the stamp company. Some stamp companies report an over 90-percent redemption rate, although the rate is lower for smaller companies.

Normally a stamp company sells stamps to retailers on a semiexclusive basis—that is, it sells to only one retailer in each kind of business in a given area. Retailers pay from 2 to 3 percent of their total revenue for the stamps they give to customers.

The popularity of stamps rises and falls. There is little doubt that stamps add to the total cost of marketing. However, many consumers want them, and they may provide retailers, particularly those who are the first in an area to offer them, with a competitive edge.

Sales Promotion Aimed at Business Buyers

Up to this point we have examined consumer-oriented sales promotion techniques. Manufacturers also use a variety of sales promotion tactics to increase sales to business buyers, principally retail stores. These include discounts, advertising aids, direct compensation, contests, and advertising specialties.

Discounts   One very important form of sales promotion aimed at the trade consists of discounts on merchandise purchased. This is actually a form of pricing and will be discussed in Part Six. Another promotional device aimed at retailers is the promise of "free" goods—say, an extra dozen items if a retailer agrees to purchase a gross.

Advertising Aids   Advertising aids supplied to retailers are among the most important forms of sales promotion. Automobile manufacturers, for example, traditionally furnish their dealers with a variety of newspaper, radio, television, direct-mail, and billboard advertisements each quarter. All the local dealer need do is select the desired advertisements and supply them to local media.

Direct Compensation   Often a manufacturer will provide some type of direct compensation to stimulate retailers and their salespeople to push its product rather than that of a competitor. **Premium money**, or **push money**, acts as an incentive for middlemen to "push" the producer's line. Some retailers, however, object to this practice, feeling that it encourages their salespeople to promote some products and ignore others.

Contests   Manufacturers often sponsor contests to motivate wholesalers, retailers, or distributors to sell more aggressively. Producers commonly use free, all-expense-paid vacations to exotic places to reward middlemen who put forth an extra effort to move their lines.

Advertising Specialties   Still another sales promotion device is the advertising specialty, an item with a low unit cost that is given free to prospective customers of a company. Typically, it features the name, address, and logo of the firm and perhaps a brief sales message. Pencils, key chains, note pads, paperweights, ashtrays, rulers, and letter openers are some of the many advertising specialties in use.

An "ideal" advertising specialty is one that is used frequently and lasts for a reasonable length of time. A ballpoint pen meets both these criteria, and, in theory at least, the recipient will see the name of the company that distributed it hundreds of times before the pen is lost or wears out. It is very difficult to evaluate the effectiveness of advertising specialties, but they cost little and are given away on the premise that they will serve as frequent reminders to prospective customers that the business exists.

SUMMARY

- The chief characteristics of personal selling are that it can be adapted to the specific needs of the prospect; it can, in many instances, obtain an immediate order; and sales personnel can function as an "intelligence system" and handle post-sale servicing.
- The primary purposes of personal selling are to stimulate demand, to find potential buyers, to convince them to buy, and to keep them satisfied.
- The personal selling process entails prospecting and evaluating new clients, preparing, presenting, overcoming objections, closing the sale, and giving follow-up service.
- Salespeople can be classified as order getters, order takers, or support personnel.
- Major types of personal selling are selling for manufacturers, wholesalers, or retailers, and selling directly to consumers. Other important sales jobs are held by people who sell intangibles or real estate.
- Job analyses and descriptions are used by some sales managers to systematically study their sales personnel; manage the firm's compensation program for its salespeople; set up sales territories; and control and evaluate each salesperson's performance.
- Salespeople are paid according to a variety of compensation plans, including straight salary, straight commission, or a combination of the two. They may also receive other financial incentives such as bonuses, profit-sharing plans, and fringe benefits typical of other employees.

- Specific objectives of sales promotion include introducing new products, attracting new customers, inducing present customers to buy more, helping a firm remain competitive, increasing sales in off seasons, and increasing the inventories of business buyers.
- Sales promotion aimed at ultimate consumers includes a variety of devices such as free samples of the product, contests, games, sweepstakes, premiums, coupons, product demonstrations, point-of-purchase advertising, and trading stamps.
- Sampling is giving a product free to a consumer to encourage future sales.
- Contests offer prizes to consumers for creative or analytical thinking. Sweepstakes, on the other hand, are like lotteries except that those who enter do not pay an entry fee.
- A game is similar to a sweepstakes in that pure chance determines the winner. Games differ in that they take place over an extended period of time.
- A premium is a product offered free or at an unusually low price to induce consumers to buy another product.
- A coupon is a certificate that entitles its holder to a specified savings on a product or a cash refund.
- Trading stamps are a form of bonus for purchasing products in a particular store.
- Sales promotion techniques directed toward business buyers include discounts, advertising aids, direct compensation, contests, and advertising specialties.

DISCUSSION QUESTIONS

1. What are the purposes of personal selling? Explain the personal selling process.
2. What duties might a salesperson have other than face-to-face discussions with prospective customers?
3. Does personal selling "create" demand? What advantages does personal selling have over other forms of demand stimulation?
4. Name and define the major categories of salespeople and the types of personal selling.
5. What are the major sales management functions? What is a sales job analysis? How does it differ from a sales job description? How do these tools help sales management?
6. Name the basic sales compensation plans. What additional financial incentives may be offered to salespeople?

7. What are the differences between qualitative and quantitative evaluation of a salesperson's performance?
8. Under what circumstances might sampling work as a sales promotion tool? What kinds of products are frequently sampled?
9. Why are contests less popular than games and sweepstakes? Why do companies not require the consumer to buy a product to enter a sweepstakes?
10. "The use of coupons is very extensive and is growing." How do you account for this?
11. Trading stamps are not as popular a sales promotion device as they were a decade ago. Why? Are they likely to stage a comeback in the future?
12. Explain each of the leading sales promotion techniques aimed at business buyers.

APPLICATION EXERCISES

1. Interview three people who are knowledgeable about personal selling. Try to get them to talk to you objectively about it. Outline what you think are the pros and cons of selling as a career, and explain briefly why you would or would not like a career in personal selling.
2. Review the various job titles given salespeople, then read the job listings in a recent issue of your favorite metropolitan newspaper. Select two sales jobs you feel would be very appealing to a new college graduate and two that would be very unappealing. Explain the reasoning behind your selections in a brief report.
3. You are an assistant director of marketing for a savings bank. One of your key marketing objectives is to increase deposits by (a) attracting more new customers, (b) retaining present customers, and (c) increasing deposits per customer. Outline 10 sales promotion devices or techniques you would submit to the director of marketing for consideration. For each device, explain briefly why you recommend it.

CASE 17

Sales Force Problems for Brill

"Our new line of computers is just too advanced for our sales force to understand," John Wright, head of engineering complained to Bob Ross, sales manager. Both worked for Brill Enterprises, a $120-million-a-year conglomerate with growing pains.

Ross was fully aware that the company's 1501 series of in-home computers had been losing sales to its chief competitor, Oklahoma Calculators' OC 5000. He thought the reason, however, was that the OC 5000 could talk directly through telephone lines to utility-company computers, making the payment of electric, gas, and water bills much simpler than writing and mailing checks.

Wright conceded that the OC 5000 had the competitive edge on that feature. "But that isn't the basic problem," he insisted. "Even when we introduce our 2100 series, which will talk to computers and more, we'll still be in the same sales predicament. Our sales reps simply cannot convey the technological advantages of our product to the customers. How can they? They don't have any engineering background—just marketing."

"Wait a second," Ross warned. "Marketing majors are trained to sell all kinds of products. They learn selling techniques and psychology, not just product attributes. Why, our sales force has made us number two in this field!"

"But we ought to be number one," Wright said heatedly. "Except for that one telephone hookup feature, our 1501 is far superior to everything else on the market. But our people can't get maximum sales, because they don't know a remote job entry from a report generator. We ought to hire engineering graduates and send them out to sell these complex machines."

"But you're not talking about technology when you mention remote job entries and report generators," Ross interjected. "You're talking about applications of technology. And believe me, any marketing major can be taught to comprehend and describe all the functions, analyses, design features—even the software and hardware connected with the 1501. You're overestimating the amount of technical knowledge the sales team needs to have."

"On the contrary," Wright replied. "Our sales people frequently have to deal with industrial buyers who have engineering backgrounds. It's more effective to send people out to see them who talk their language. Engineering graduates could handle service and repair calls more efficiently as well."

"Don't sell marketing majors short," Ross retorted. "They understand buyer behavior and that means engineering buyers as well as buyers of consumer products. They're probably more sensitive to buyers' needs than engineers would be."

Discussion Questions

1. Is Wright perhaps just trying to build a larger franchise for engineers within the company? Is Ross, on the other hand, defending marketing majors because he's more familiar with their training and selling techniques?
2. Is there room for both marketing majors and engineering graduates on Brill's sales team? How could their assignments be separated? How might they dovetail?
3. What type of training program would you institute for marketing majors? For engineers?

P A R T

SIX

Price Decisions

18 Price Planning

STUDY OBJECTIVES

After studying this chapter, you should be able to

1. Define price.
2. Discuss nonprice competition and how it affects pricing.
3. List the various factors affecting pricing decisions.
4. Explain the law of demand and price elasticity.
5. Describe the difference between variable, fixed, total, marginal, assignable, and common costs and their effect on pricing.
6. Discuss various government restrictions on pricing practices.
7. Discuss the factors affecting the general price level.
8. Describe common pricing practices.
9. Explain quantity, trade, cash, seasonal, and promotional discounts; price promotions; cash rebates; and trade-in and damaged goods allowances.

With this part of the book we will conclude our discussion of the marketing controllable variables. It is appropriate that this part should concern price. In effect the price is a company's statement of its perceived value of the product, place, and promotional variables. Price is the concluding marketing controllable variable that brings the other three variables together.

The pricing decision can be quite complex and must consider many factors. In this chapter we will look at the many factors that affect price and pricing decisions. In Chapter 19 we will concern ourselves with how pricing decisions are actually made.

PRICE IS VALUE

What is a price? Basically, it is value expressed in terms of goods or money. From an economist's viewpoint all saleable goods have value. Under the barter system goods were valued in terms of other goods. A wheat farmer, for example, might agree to exchange a bushel of grain for five baskets of strawberries grown by a neighboring farmer. In this transaction, then, the strawberries constituted the value (the price) of the wheat.

Antiquated as it seems, barter is still used. PepsiCo, for example, in exchange for building two Pepsi-Cola plants in Bulgaria, accepted twice the value of the new operation in such Bulgarian products as mineral water, confectionery, forklift trucks, bottles, and wine. Said *Sales & Marketing Management* magazine, "It was a classic example of bartering, and few U.S. companies succeed at it the way PepsiCo does."[1] However, money and its present-day extensions—checking accounts and credit—are the most widespread mediums of exchange. Consequently, prices (called by a variety of names, as shown in Figure 18-1) are generally assigned to goods in terms of dollars (or some other monetary unit).

From an economics perspective **price** *is the amount of sacrifice you must incur to receive something of value.* Giving up dollars is a sacrifice to obtain a product. That product has a certain amount of utility for the customer. **Utility** *is the perception of how much satisfaction a consumer can receive from a certain product.* Generally, the more perceived utility a product has, the higher the price or sacrifice a consumer will be willing to pay.

Actually, consumers may treat the price not so much as a sacrifice but as a message about the product. If, for instance, we buy a new stereo system that is a source of pride for us, the fact that we paid a high price for the

---

[1] "S&MM Excellence Awards," *Sales & Marketing Management*, January 14, 1980, p. 38.

Figure 18-1

Price by Any Other Name Means Money Paid

Anything of commercial value has a price. Below are a number of different ways price is expressed in the marketplace.

Price is all around us. You pay RENT for your apartment, TUITION for your education, and a FEE to your physician or dentist.

The airline, railway, taxi, and bus companies charge you a FARE; the local utilities call their price a RATE; and the local bank charges you INTEREST for the money you borrow.

The price for driving your car on Florida's Sunshine Parkway is a TOLL, and the company that insures your car charges you a PREMIUM.

The guest lecturer charges an HONORARIUM to tell you about a government official who took a BRIBE to help a shady character steal DUES collected by a trade association.

Clubs or societies to which you belong may make a special ASSESSMENT to pay unusual expenses. Your regular lawyer may ask for a RETAINER to cover her services.

The "price" of an executive is a SALARY; the price of a salesperson may be a COMMISSION; and the price of a worker is a WAGE.

Finally, although economists would disagree, many of us feel that INCOME TAXES are the price we pay for the privilege of making money!

---

system may enhance the quality image and, thereby, add value. The price is augmenting the message we want to project about our purchase. Otherwise, why would so many people brag about how much they paid for certain items? The price is part of the product's value, not just a measure of sacrifice.[2]

In many situations sellers are able to adjust prices up or down by varying the amount of "value" added to their products. For example, in the case of a new automobile the dealer adds value in the form of an air conditioner, a tape deck, and other accessories and, therefore, can command a higher price for the car. If some of these extras are eliminated, less value is added to the basic car, and it can be sold at a lower price.

The **value-modification concept** has many applications in selling to commercial and industrial customers as well. A printing firm attempting to secure a contract will base its price on such factors as the quality of the paper, the quality and amount of artwork, the reproduction process used, and the delivery date. Similarly, a computer manufacturer can modify the

---

[2] For more discussion of the relationship between price, value, and benefits, see Irwin Gross, "Insights from Pricing Research," *Pricing Practices and Strategies,* Earl L. Bailey, ed. (New York: The Conference Board, 1978), pp. 34–39; John T. Mentzer and Kent B. Monroe, "Some Common Misconceptions About Pricing," *Working Paper,* Virginia Tech; and Benson P. Shapiro and Barbara B. Jackson, "Industrial Pricing to Meet Customer Needs," *Harvard Business Review,* November–December 1978, pp. 119–27.

value of a basic unit by offering the buyer different warranty and service arrangements.

PRICE AND NONPRICE COMPETITION

As we said, price brings together the other marketing controllable variables. Once the product has been designed, the distribution system established, and the promotional strategies implemented, price must put a value on the total effort. Typically, we think that competition causes at least some changes in price. In many cases, however, companies feel they cannot or should not change the price. For this reason much competition concentrates on holding price constant, but varying the other marketing controllable variables.

Bernardino he discovered the marketing strategy that would help make McDonald's a success.

The McDonald brothers, Richard and Maurice, had customers waiting in line to buy hamburgers, milkshakes, and french fries from six fast-food restaurants in the area. Kroc was inspired. He wanted to participate in this family's growth. The McDonalds did not want to expand, however. Eventually, Kroc bought the chain and its name for $2.7 million (plus $11 million in financing charges).

Kroc cleverly reduced McDonald's marketing strategy to the initials "QSC & V," meaning quality, service, cleanliness, and value. He set up Hamburger University to give intensive training courses to franchisees who purchase 20-year licenses to operate a McDonald's restaurant. He enforced stringent quality-control measures, emphasized new product development and advertised heavily.

He also encouraged his franchisees to be active in their communities. McDonald's franchisees frequently raise funds for worthy causes, stage carnivals to raise money for muscular dystrophy, and provide free food to disaster sites. One of Ray Kroc's favorite projects was the establishment of Ronald McDonald Houses to provide low-cost lodging to parents of critically-ill children being treated at nearby children's hospitals. On his seventieth birthday, Kroc donated $7.5 million to several service organizations. In celebration of his seventy-fifth birthday, the Ray A. Kroc/Ronald McDonald Children's Fund was established to complement the McDonald Houses.

Named Senior Chairman of the Board of McDonald's in 1977, Kroc never stopped working for McDonald's. Although Ray Kroc died in 1984, his effect on fast-food marketing will long be felt.

* "McDonald's Blends New Products, Savory Merchandising," *Business Week,* July 11, 1977, p. 56.
† "The Fast-Food War: Big Mac Under Attack," *Business Week,* January 30, 1984, pp. 44–45.

All of us are so frequently bombarded with advertising messages telling us that a certain store has "the lowest prices in town," "shop here and save," and "hear our price before you buy" that we probably overestimate the degree of price competition in our economy. Actually, competition based on nonprice product attributes is more common. Price differentials among such common products as gasoline, cigarettes, air travel, bread, and soft drinks are either very small or nonexistent. Even in the case of costly products such as automobiles, there is surprisingly little true price competition. Although price is often mentioned in manufacturer-sponsored advertising, the main promotional emphasis is on design, styling, quality, workmanship, and other nonprice considerations. Retailers may stress convenient location, trained personnel, and superior service more than price differences in their advertising.

Various other means are also used to deemphasize price competition or

avoid it altogether. Guarantees and warranties, "free" trading stamps, premiums, and redeemable coupons are just a few of the devices firms use to win customers away from competitors without lowering prices. Technically, even advertising and personal selling are forms of nonprice competition when they communicate data about product characteristics other than price.

Oneida, long a marketer of lower-priced tableware, now follows a nonprice strategy by presenting a superior product design. After conducting research to find patterns that customers would buy, Oneida introduced several higher-priced sets. As Oneida Chairman John Marcellus, Jr., sees it, "Your wife is the target we're after and for her $440 (the current price for a 40-piece set of Oneida Heirloom Ltd., the company's top stainless) is not a lot of money. She thinks it's cheaper than a $29.95 piece of junk. My wife thinks the same way. All she talks about is quality. It's the same way with me and boats. I look at a boat that used to cost $6,000 and costs $14,000 today. People won't pay exorbitant prices, but they will certainly pay to get good value. All you have to do is be fair with them."[3]

---

[3] Paul B. Brown, "Resetting the Clock in Oneida," *Forbes*, February 1, 1982, pp. 85, 89.

Superior design in distribution or promotion can also allow a nonprice strategy. Industrial marketers who guarantee order delivery in half the time as all competitors can probably charge a higher price to offset the higher costs. Chivas Regal Scotch is sold at a premium price mainly because of its superior promotional campaign. The extra profits from the higher price cover the promotional costs.

Whatever the reason, nonprice competition often allows a company to charge a higher price than the competition or to achieve a greater market share without changing price.

FACTORS AFFECTING PRICE

A company should consider numerous factors when making the pricing decision. These factors include the buyers, the competition, costs, the government, channel members, and factors that affect general price levels.

Buyers

When we discuss buyers and price, we are usually concerned with how price affects their *demand* for a product. The **law of demand** *states that more goods will be demanded at a lower price than at a higher one.* Thus, more loaves of bread will be sold at 69 cents each than at 89 cents each. This law holds true for most products.

The law of demand, expressed as a **demand curve**, is shown in Figure 18-2. This curve is drawn according to hypothetical estimates of the number of compact automobiles that would be sold at various prices.

To marketers **demand** *means the desire for a product, supported by the ability to purchase it.* In estimating the demand for its new models, for example, Cadillac's management will consider only those consumers who can afford to purchase a high-priced car. Therefore, regardless of their wish to own a Cadillac, consumers considered in Figure 18-2 do not constitute part of the demand for Cadillacs. They are not in the proper price range.

Price as a Market Equalizer   Not only are consumers willing to purchase different volumes of a product at various prices, but producers also will produce more of a product as the price rises. The **law of supply**—*supply will increase as price increases*—can be expressed as a **supply curve**. Figure 18-3 adds a supply curve to the automobile example of Figure 18-2.

When the price is too low (P_1), consumers demand more of a product than is supplied. Thus, consumers wanting the product offer more for it, and the price rises until supply equals demand. If the price is too high (P_2), consumers demand less than is supplied, and the producers lower their price to reduce excess inventory until supply equals demand. Therefore,

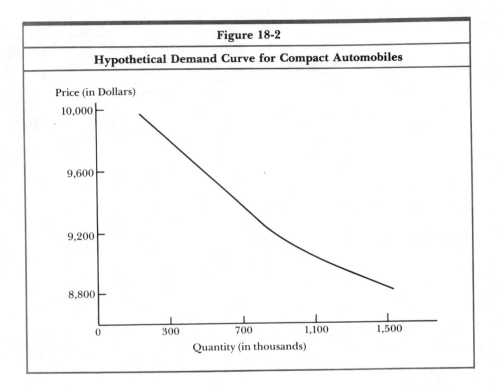

Figure 18-2

Hypothetical Demand Curve for Compact Automobiles

Price (in Dollars)

10,000

9,600

9,200

8,800

0   300   700   1,100   1,500

Quantity (in thousands)

price acts as a marketplace mechanism by which supply and demand are reconciled. Although the equilibrium price is never actually reached because of the other factors affecting price, price does have a tendency to equalize supply and demand.

Price Elasticity　All pricing managers are concerned with how sensitive consumers are to changes in price. This sensitivity is measured by price elasticity. **Price elasticity** *is defined as the relative change in quantity demanded caused by a relative change in price,* or

$$E_p = \%Q/\%P$$

where E_p = price elasticity; $\%Q$ = the percentage change in quantity demanded; and $\%P$ = the percentage change in price.

Demand for a product is said to be **elastic** if the percentage change in quantity is greater than the percentage change in price. Figure 18-4 illustrates that our hypothetical automobile demand is elastic. As price drops from $9,600 to $9,400, a 2-percent drop, quantity demanded increases from 500,00 to 700,000 units, a 40-percent increase, so that E_p equals +40/−2, or −20. Thus, demand is price elastic if E_p is between −1 and −∞. For

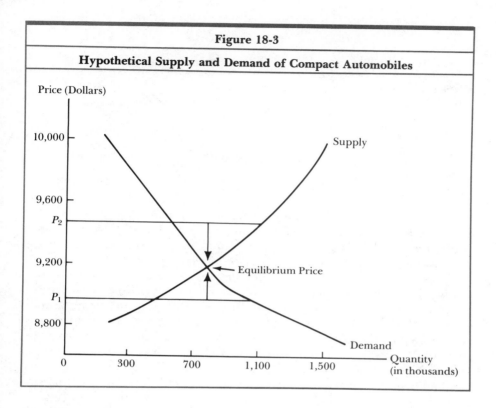

Figure 18-3

Hypothetical Supply and Demand of Compact Automobiles

Price (Dollars)

10,000 — Supply

9,600 —

P_2

9,200 — Equilibrium Price

P_1

8,800 —

Demand

0   300   700   1,100   1,500   Quantity
(in thousands)

price elastic demand, decreases in price increase total revenues (increases in quantity demanded more than make up for the price decrease). However, price increases decrease total revenue (see Figure 18-4).

Conversely, demand is said to be price **inelastic** if a percentage change in price causes a smaller percentage change in demand. Thus, E_p is between 0 and −1. Figure 18-5, a hypothetical demand for salt, illustrates

Figure 18-4

An Example of Elastic Demand: Automobiles

Price per Car ($)	Quantity Sold	Total Revenue ($)
10,000	100,000	1,000,000,000
9,800	300,000	2,940,000,000
9,600	500,000	4,800,000,000
9,400	700,000	6,580,000,000
9,200	900,000	8,280,000,000
9,000	1,200,000	10,800,000,000
8,800	1,650,000	14,520,000,000

Figure 18-5		
An Example of Inelastic Demand: Salt		
Price per Pound ($)	Quantity Sold (Lbs.)	Total Revenue ($)
0.28	5,000,000	1,400,000
0.24	5,250,000	1,260,000
0.20	5,500,000	1,100,000
0.16	6,000,000	960,000
0.12	6,250,000	750,000
0.08	6,500,000	520,000

inelastic demand. As the example demonstrates, total revenue for salt decreases as the price falls, because consumers do not buy enough additional salt to make up for price cuts. Thus, for price inelastic products, price decreases lower total revenues and price increases raise total revenues.

Most products, however, are not totally price elastic or inelastic. At any given price, products typically have different elasticities for price increases than for price decreases. It takes careful and involved marketing research to determine actual price elasticities at any given price. This research is complicated by the fact that consumers may not react immediately to price changes. *Business Week,* reporting on the declining consumption of gasoline due to higher prices, noted that "most studies of commodities such as gasoline, which enjoys a relatively inelastic demand, indicate that the biggest effect of price increases on consumption occur only after a year or two, [therefore] a more dramatic decline in demand may be on the horizon."[4]

Consumer price sensitivity, expressed as elasticity, is a factor of great concern for any marketing manager faced with a pricing decision. Whether the price is elastic or inelastic tells in which direction—raising or lowering the price—increased revenues lie.

Competition

Not only the consumer in the marketplace, but also the type of market (defined by the number of competitors) will affect pricing decisions. Before the question "What will competitors do?" is raised, the question "How many competitors are there?" should be asked. The answer often gives some general price guidelines.

Pure Competition   A perfectly elastic demand schedule occurs most often in the case of products sold in markets characterized by pure, or perfect, competition—when no one seller is able to influence price to an apprecia-

---

[4] "Economic Diary," *Business Week,* February 4, 1980, p. 20.

ble extent and there are many sellers whose products may easily be substituted for one another. Any attempt to raise prices above the industry level would cause consumers to switch to another, cheaper brand, and any attempt to lower prices would be pointless, because other producers would be forced to follow suit.[5]

Oligopoly   Industries in which there are a few large competitors are said to be **oligopolies.** Many large U.S. industries—automobiles, steel, and tires, for example—are oligopolistic. Usually, one of the firms has complete control over the prices it charges. Many simply follow the industry leader in setting prices and try to realize a profit by adjusting their costs accordingly. This practice tends to encourage price stability.

Monopolistic Competition   A product that the consumer views as clearly different in some way from all competing products has a market characterized by monopolistic, or imperfectly, competitive conditions. Pricing under conditions of imperfect competition extensively utilizes nonprice competition.

---

[5] Like all generalizations, this is not always true. A firm that could afford to take a loss might well adopt this strategy in order to force competitors out of business.

Product differentiation is one of the major strategies producers use to avoid pure competition and gain more control over price. For example, aspirin, according to the pharmaceutical code definition, is aspirin. Yet sellers of different brands differentiate their product as much as possible through advertising appeals and packaging, trying to create strong brand preference. As a result the price of aspirin varies widely depending on the brand name and the amount of brand loyalty.

Level of Competitive Intensity In making a pricing decision a company must be concerned with how intense the price competition is. The higher the level of competition, the harder it is to institute any price change. In pure competition price competition is typically so intense that no company can change price. Because oligopolies often have a price leader that all others follow, price competition is not very intense. Prices are changed with relative ease by the leader.

In a more general sense vigorous competition helps hold prices down. Because consumer dollars tend to move toward the seller with the lowest prices (for comparable products), there is great incentive for a business to charge less than other businesses in the same industry. This movement of consumer dollars toward the seller with the lowest prices affects competition between industries as well. Dollars spent for food cannot be spent for clothing, and money spent for automobiles cannot be spent for housing. Consequently, many industries make price a part of their attempts to compete successfully against other industries.

Costs

As we shall see in the next chapter, many companies base their pricing decisions entirely on costs. To ignore demand, competition, and many other factors is quite naive. Although costs should be understood and considered before pricing decisions are made, they should not be the *only* factor considered.

Costs are often viewed according to the way they relate to volume. Figure 18-6 demonstrates some of the costs related to volume. **Fixed costs** are items, such as rent, that are not affected by the volume produced. Whether a company produces one unit or one million units, for instance, has no effect on the annual cost of renting the manufacturing plant.

Variable costs are a direct function of volume. Direct labor and direct materials are both examples of variable costs. Because it takes the same amount of material and the same amount of labor to produce any unit of a product, the more units produced, the more total variable cost incurred. The sum of fixed and variable costs is **total cost**. Although we will discuss various methods of cost-based pricing approaches in Chapter 19, we will discuss one particular method—the economic pricing model—here.

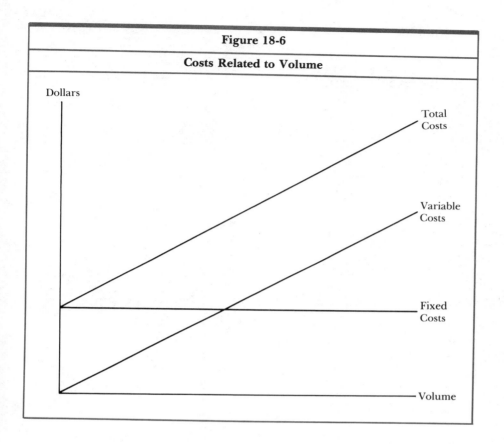

Figure 18-6

Costs Related to Volume

Dollars

Total Costs

Variable Costs

Fixed Costs

Volume

Economic Pricing Model   The traditional economic approach to pricing considers **marginal cost**, defined as *the amount total cost changes for each unit change in volume.* Remember, for each additional unit produced the fixed costs are spread over more units. Therefore, the average fixed cost per unit drops as volume increases. In addition, as a company produces more units, it often becomes more efficient at producing each unit (called the **Learning Curve Effect**), which lowers the variable cost per unit. However, as volume continues to increase, the company reaches the limits of capacity on its productive facilities and becomes less efficient, causing variable costs per unit to rise again. These factors combine to create a marginal cost function that decreases as volume rises to a point, and then starts to increase. Figure 18-7 illustrates all these functions.

   Marginal revenue *is the amount total revenue changes with each change in volume sold.* As we saw earlier, change in total revenue is a function of demand elasticity—the relative change in price and the relative change in quantity. Traditional economic theory states that the way to maximize profits is to price where *marginal revenue equals marginal cost.*

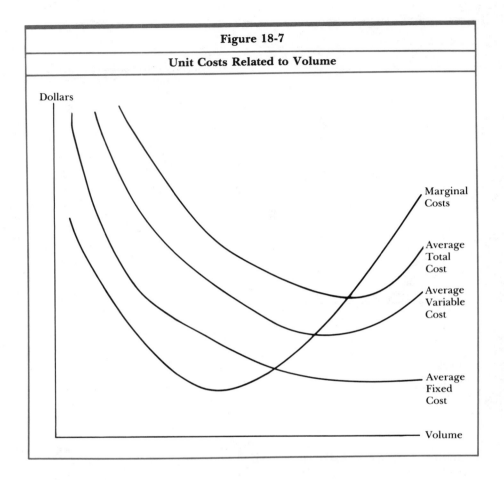

Figure 18-7

Unit Costs Related to Volume

Dollars

Marginal Costs

Average Total Cost

Average Variable Cost

Average Fixed Cost

Volume

An example should help demonstrate this point. Lowering the price of the product in Figure 18-8 from $100 to $90 raises demand enough that total revenue increases $700 (the marginal revenue). Because the total cost to produce 30 units as opposed to 20 units increases only $400, the company makes more profit. Profit continues to increase until 40 units are reached. Increasing to 50 units (dropping the price to $70) makes no more or less profit for the company. However, to go past 50 units, revenue will increase less than costs. Therefore, the maximum profit point is a price of $80, where marginal revenue equals marginal costs. To produce more or less would decrease profits.

Although this method works well in theory, it has many problems in actual pricing applications. First, the relationship between price and demand is often difficult to estimate. Second, companies often have goals

			Figure 18-8			
			Profit Maximization			
Price ($)	**Demand (Units)**	**Total Revenue ($)**	**Marginal Revenue ($)**	**Marginal Costs ($)**	**Marginal Profit/Loss ($)**	
100	20	2000 }				
90	30	2700 }	700	400	+300	
80	40	3200 }	500	350	+150	
70	50	3500 }	300	300	0	
60	62	3720 }	220	250	−30	
50	75	3800 }	80	150	−70	

other than profit maximization. Certainly nonprofit companies do. Even in profit-seeking companies profit maximization may not be the overriding goal. Losses incurred to gain market share, lower prices to better serve more of the community, and reaching higher sales volumes to impress stockholders are all common corporate goals that conflict with profit maximization.

A final problem with the economic model is how costs are assigned. Especially with fixed costs, many facilities that make up the fixed costs may be shared by several products. To price intelligently, we must be more concerned with what costs are assignable to particular products than arbitrarily assigning all costs to some product.

Assignable Costs   In pricing, we are much more concerned with whether costs are assignable or common than whether they are fixed or variable. **Assignable costs** *are expenditures incurred solely in the production and marketing of a particular product.* Direct materials, direct labor, and salesperson commissions are all examples of assignable costs. The acid test for whether or not a cost is assignable lies in the question "Would this cost cease if we stopped marketing this product?" For example, if we stop making a certain product, we would purchase no materials to produce it, no labor would be expended, and we would not pay sales commissions on something that was not sold. Therefore, all of these cost categories are assignable.

Common costs are expenditures incurred to operate the company or help produce and market numerous products. Because the costs are incurred to sell several products, those costs cannot be assigned to any one product. Examples of common costs include general administrative costs, research and development, general marketing research, and corporate (not product-specific) advertising.

When a company sets a price for any product, its first goal is to at least cover the assignable costs. If it does not cover these costs, then the company would have been better off not marketing the product. After all, income

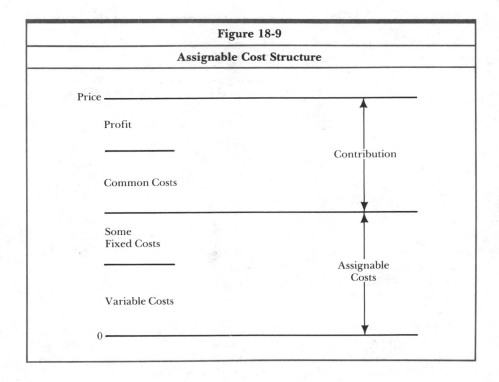

Figure 18-9

Assignable Cost Structure

Price

Profit

Common Costs

Contribution

Some
Fixed Costs

Assignable
Costs

Variable Costs

0

from the price is less than the costs assignable (costs that would not have occurred if the product was not marketed).

Any amount that the price exceeds the assignable costs is called **contribution**, because that money is excess over the assignable costs and can "contribute" to covering the common costs and profit. Figure 18-9 shows the relationship between assignable costs, common costs, and profit. As the figure demonstrates, assignable costs can be fixed or variable. For example, a plant that costs $100,000 per year to operate but is used solely to produce Product A is a fixed cost assignable to Product A. All common costs are those fixed costs that are shared by various products and, therefore, cannot be assigned.

Although a price that covers all assignable and common costs is most desirable, multiproduct companies are primarily concerned with each product covering its assignable costs and all products together contributing enough to common costs to cover them and leave some profit. Thus, the minimum price for any product is its assignable costs per unit. Below this price the product makes a negative contribution, and the company would be better off not marketing it. *The study of assignable costs, common costs, and prices that make a positive contribution to common costs and profits is called* **contribution analysis**.

Government

The government is a significant factor influencing the general level of prices in our economy and determining pricing policies in individual companies. The federal government and, to a lesser extent, state and local governments frequently take actions that are inflationary or deflationary in order to achieve the general objective of advancing the national economic welfare.

Fiscal and Monetary Policies Generally speaking, when the economy is operating near capacity and aggregate demand exceeds supply, the atmosphere is inflationary. In order to prevent prices from rising too much or too quickly, the government may adopt "tight" fiscal and monetary policies—restricting the amount of money in circulation, acting to raise interest rates (the price of money), cutting back on its own spending, imposing wage and price controls, and taking other actions that in effect slow the economy down.

To stimulate economic activity in times of recession, the government often takes action to reduce interest rates and make more money available to business and consumers. It may also engage in greater deficit spending, cut taxes, and increase government loans.

Regulated Industries Even in normal times marketing executives in many of our largest and most essential industries cannot change prices without government approval. When telephone, gas, electric power companies, and common carriers want to make a price change, representatives of the firm must appear before the appropriate state or federal regulatory commission to prove that the company needs a price change and that the proposed change will not adversely affect the public interest.

Pricing Restrictions In addition to overall economic policies on prices and regulated industries, the federal government restricts many of the pricing policies a company may practice.

The government places limitations on **price fixing**. The Sherman Antitrust Act and the Federal Trade Commission Act forbid **horizontal price fixing**, or *the practice of agreements on prices between competitors on the same level in a marketing channel.* For example, in 1976 70 percent of the manufacturers in the $1.5 billion corrugated cardboard industry were convicted of fixing prices on boxes and folding cartons. A federal judge set fines, probation, or jail terms for 47 executives in 22 companies.[6]

In order to avoid price fixing charges, a company should not (1) coordinate discounts, credit terms, or conditions of sale with competitors; (2) discuss prices, markups, or costs with competition; (3) issue new price lists

---

[6] Jeffrey Sonnenfeld and Paul R. Lawrence, "Why Do Companies Succumb to Price Fixing?" *Harvard Business Review*, July–August, 1978, pp. 145–57.

on the same date as competition; (4) rotate low bids on contracts; or (5) uniformly restrict production to maintain prices.[7]

Vertical price fixing *exists when one channel member tries to dictate prices to other channel members.* As we discussed in the Chapter 11 Marketing Milestone, the death of Fair Trade Laws eliminated the manufacturer's ability to control prices charged for its products by retailers. Manufacturers today can only control retail prices by (1) owning the retail stores, (2) selling on consignment, (3) suggesting prices, or (4) printing prices on the product.

Price discrimination *exists when a channel member sells "like quality" products to different buyers for different prices.* The Robinson–Patman Act prohibits price discrimination where the effect injures competition. To avoid price discrimination, such terms and conditions of sale as prices, discounts, rebates, premiums, guarantees, delivery, warehousing, and credit terms should be available to all buyers on a proportionately equal basis.[8] Although the Robinson–Patman Act restricts price discrimination, it does not apply if the products have substantial physical differences, if market conditions change, if the seller is meeting a competitor's price, if the difference can be justified by costs, or if competition is not injured. Therefore, most forms of price discrimination are legal.

Finally, the government sometimes institutes **price controls** to reduce inflation in certain industries. Such blanket measures are seldom used— President Nixon used mandatory controls in the early 1970s, and President Carter used voluntary controls in 1976—but they often affect pricing decisions. Fear of mandatory price controls during the Carter administration, for instance, caused many companies to raise their prices so they would be frozen at a higher level, bringing about exactly the opposite effect from the deflationary one hoped for.[9]

Whether government exercises heavy control, as in regulated industries, or light control, as when it merely oversees corporate pricing practices, it is a factor that a company should always consider in making its pricing decision. Without such concern, companies are open to lawsuits, criminal prosecution, and possibly further pricing regulation.

Channel Members

Because the final selling price of a product affects the success of all channel members, each member seeks input from other members on pricing decisions. Unfortunately, the differing goals of channel members can complicate this process. The manufacturer, for example, is concerned with its

---

[7] "Price Fixing Crackdown Under Way," *Business Week,* June 2, 1975, pp. 42–48.
[8] Kent B. Monroe, *Pricing: Making Profitable Decisions* (New York: McGraw-Hill, 1979), p. 253.
[9] Monci Jo Williams, "The No-Win Game of Price Promotion," *Fortune,* July 11, 1983, p. 93.

Figure 18-10	
Manufacturer Pricing Luggage Through the Channel	
Manufacturer's Cost	$15
Markup	5
Price	$20
Wholesaler's Cost from Manufacturer	$20
Markup	10
Price	$30
Retailer's Cost from Wholesaler	$30
Markup	20
Price	$50

price to the wholesaler and the price to the final consumer. The former determines the manufacturer's profitability, whereas the latter determines the product's acceptability in the target markets. In contrast, the wholesaler wants as low a price as possible from the manufacturer and as high a price as possible to the retailer. Finally, the retailer wants a low price from the wholesaler and may set prices to consumers high or low depending on its own objectives for the product. The price may be set low if the retailer wants high volume or set high if the retailer thinks it can gain a high profit from few sales. Often a retailer will *sell against the brand*. This practice involves setting the manufacturer's brand price high in an attempt to sell more of the retailer's brand. Obviously, manufacturers frown on such retailer pricing practices.

To set prices throughout the channel, a manufacturer must first determine the desired final selling price for its product. Figure 18-10 illustrates this process for a piece of luggage. The cost for the manufacturer to produce one unit of luggage is $15, to which a profit of $5 is added. This becomes the wholesaler's cost, to which a markup of $10 is added to cover the wholesaler's cost of doing business and to make a profit. The retailer, in turn, marks up its cost of $30 to a selling price of $50 to the final consumer. Presumably, the manufacturer determined the $50 selling price based on knowledge of its channel members' cost structure, its own volume goals, and knowledge of the expected demand generated by a $50 selling price. Its own price to the wholesaler was then set so that the final selling price would be $50.

To encourage retailers to stick to its pricing plan, manufacturers often sell to channel members at discounts from the suggested retail price. In our example, the manufacturer might issue prices as $50, 40/33⅓. This means the suggested retail price is $50, retailers can buy at a 40-percent discount from the price ($30), and wholesalers can buy at a 33⅓-percent discount from the $30 retailer price ($20). These discounts for specified members of the channel or trade are called **trade discounts** and are attempts to end up with a consumer price that the manufacturer wants and the desired compensation to the wholesaler and retailer for services performed.

Factors That Affect the General Price Level

Although the preceding considerations play a significant role in setting specific prices, other factors of a more general nature also affect prices. Among the most important of the forces that interact to establish the general price level are pressure for higher wages, business productivity, buyer resistance, seller resistance, speculation, and inflation.

Pressure for Higher Wages   One of the largest cost elements in the production and marketing of most goods is wages. Management is under almost constant pressure to pay higher wages to both organized and nonunion labor.

For example, double-digit inflation in early 1980 led to growing disregard for President Carter's request that employers raise wages no more than 7 percent. One study showed that union employees were gaining 7.4 percent in average increases. Michael Wachter, an economist at the Wharton School, theorized that nonunion workers were receiving even larger pay raises to keep them from job-hopping or joining unions.[10] Yet if the wage hikes obtained significantly exceed gains in productivity, the manufacturer's cost structure will increase and the general level of industry prices will also rise.

Business Efficiency   Business efficiency is a major factor influencing price. When costs go up without corresponding increases in efficiency or productivity, prices rise. Because sellers' prices are strongly influenced by what the competition is charging, there is continuing pressure on business management to produce goods and services more efficiently—that is, with a smaller input of human, financial, and material resources. There is a tremendous incentive, for example, for auto manufacturers to introduce more automated equipment as the price of labor goes up, primarily because other automakers are doing so. Much of the use of automated equipment in textile plants today is the result of increases in the minimum wage that were not accompanied by proportionate increases in productivity.

Buyer Resistance   Buyer resistance may result from (1) a feeling that prices are "too high," (2) a wish to save money by careful purchasing, or

---

[10] "Inflation is the Winner as Wages Catch Up," *Business Week*, November 19, 1979, p. 45.

		Average Price		Percent
Product	**1900**	**1950**	**1984**	**Increase Since 1900**
Newspaper	1¢	5¢	25¢	2,500
Eggs (1 dozen)	12¢	39¢	72¢	600
Bacon (1 pound)	12¢	35¢	$1.80	1500
Coffee (1 pound)	9¢	69¢	$4.00	4,000
Potatoes	5¢	5¢	15¢	300
Movie ticket	10¢	$1.10	$4.00	4,000

Figure 18-11

Price Changes for Reasonably Homogenous Goods and Services

(3) a reduction in income. Whatever the cause, such resistance dampens spending and may stop or slow price advances. Retailers experience buyer resistance when unemployment is high. When business activity slows, buyer resistance increases. Consumers tend to put more of their income into savings, and business buyers become more price sensitive.

McGraw-Hill's Laboratory of Advertising Performance found, as an example of price sensitivity, that 60 percent of 1,423 industrial purchasers surveyed during the recession of the late 1970s rated price as the major reason for not buying a product.[11]

Seller Resistance When sellers hold out for higher prices in a period of already rising prices because they expect that prices will continue to go up, prices do tend to advance. Consider, for example, a farmer who has an interstate highway routed through his property. The land surrounding the highway may become a prime location for service stations and motels because of the expected high traffic volume. The farmer may resist selling at what he formerly would have considered a "good" price and hold out for a very high price. This attitude, in turn, does cause prices to rise.

Speculation **Speculation** *is the buying or selling of goods in hopes of unusually large profits from an anticipated fluctuation in price.* The old rule, "Buy low and sell high fast," is still a fairly common business practice. After prices have advanced by an unwarranted amount as a result of speculation, a sharp sell-off may bring them down again. Therefore, the net result of speculation often is to destabilize prices.

Inflation It is clear from the data in Figure 18-11 that inflationary forces are stronger, in the long run, than forces that tend to hold prices down. Pricing policies are much more difficult to design, implement, and manage

---

[11] "That Old Devil, Price," *Sales & Marketing Management*, September 17, 1979, p. 28.

during periods of economic instability—especially during inflation—than during periods of price stability. This is true in part because the forecasting of costs and competitors' prices is more difficult, but also because psychological factors affect the implementation of policies, as do practical cost considerations.

Psychological Factors Continuous increases in prices produce an "inflationary psychology" that complicates demand anticipation. Buyer resistance, usually strengthened by high prices, may weaken under the expectation that further increases are inevitable. Consumers "buy now" as a hedge against even higher prices to come.

However, the purchase of high-priced items such as automobiles and major appliances, may be postponed as long as possible. Less money is put into savings (investments) by both consumers and businesses as rising costs absorb more of their income. The result is an unpredictable market for many goods. This makes it more difficult to project the types of products consumers will want to buy and the prices they will be willing to pay for specific items.

Industrial goods, however, are not always so price sensitive. Refuting the evidence of price as a factor in buyer resistance, IBM found that charging higher prices for its data and word processing equipment caused no disruptions in its sales. The company raised prices 5 to 7 percent on those products to compensate for having priced its 4300 series of computers too low.[12]

Cost Considerations The pricing function becomes more important than ever when economic conditions produce double-digit inflation. At such a time businesses, government, and consumers alike perceive that the battle for stable prices will not be easily won.

Uncertainty about future increases in the cost of everything from raw materials to finished goods requires a much more careful approach to pricing by marketing management. Marketers attempting to bid for long-term contracts, in particular, must consider probabilities that are rarely a factor in noninflationary times.

In recent years escalator clauses have been commonly used as producers seek to protect themselves against the possibility of continually rising costs. In the construction of a hotel, office building, or other project that requires months or years to complete, escalator clauses may provide automatic adjustments linked to the builder's actual rise in costs. A contract between Great Western, a hotel chain, and John Portman, architect, for example, contained numerous provisions of this nature. It was fortunate that it did. During the three years required to construct the Peachtree Plaza

---

[12] Robin Grossman, "Why IBM Reversed Itself on Computer Pricing," *Business Week,* January 28, 1980, p. 84.

Hotel in Atlanta, the cost of the completed building rose $4 million from its projected cost to $37 million.

Indexation and Price Stability   Some economists have proposed **indexation**, *the "widespread use of price-escalator clauses in private and governmental contracts,"*[13] as a means of reducing the ill effects of inflation or a sudden downturn, as in the case of a severe depression. Although its value is still a matter of controversy, Brazil, Canada, and Israel have adopted indexation to varying degrees. The United States has implemented it on a more limited scale, with escalators for Social Security payments, federal retirements benefits, and postal employees' wages. Several million U.S. workers are covered by union contracts that provide for automatic wage increases linked to increases in the cost of living. When a new home buyer takes out a variable rate mortgage, the buyer is agreeing to have the "price" of the mortgage (interest rate) indexed periodically based on the bank's cost of obtaining money.

COMMON PRICING PRACTICES

Several pricing practices are quite common today, especially in retailing. Often called **psychological pricing**, these practices attempt to influence a purchasing decision by using price to suggest either that the product is a bargain or that it is of high value.

Odd–Even Pricing

Sometimes even a minor modification in the price may cause the consumer to perceive a product's image as expensive or inexpensive. Many believe that to suggest a bargain, **odd pricing** should be used; for example, a product is marked $4.95 or $4.99 rather than an even $5.00. On the other hand, to suggest prestige, dollars only—no pennies—may be used. Expensive clothing, jewelry, and perfumes are frequently priced at an even dollar amount.

Although research has not shown any real effectiveness of odd–even pricing, it is a popular practice. Lawrence Friedman observed that over 80 percent of all retail prices end in a 9 or a 5.[14] Many believe that the more specific a statement is, the more inclined people are to accept it as fact. Thus, a new automobile price of $9,798.79—a very specific price state-

---

[13] Milton Friedman, "Using Escalators to Help Fight Inflation," *Fortune*, July 1974, p. 94.
[14] Lawrence Friedman, "Psychological Pricing in the Food Industry," in Almarin Phillips and Oliver E. Williamson, eds., *Prices: Issues in Theory, Practice, and Public Policy*, (Philadelphia: University of Pennsylvania Press, 1967), pp. 187–201.

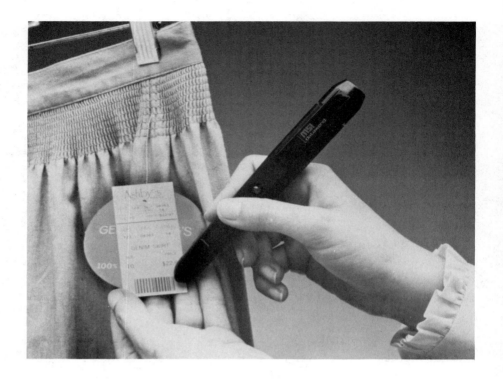

ment—is believed to be more suggestive of an honest effort to charge no more than necessary than a price of $9,800.00.

Bernard F. Whalen advises the general merchandise retailer to be very selective in assigning prices. "Every product which has an emotional or image factor attached to it should be given an even price ending, rounded upward. The rest of the products should have odd price endings."[15]

Despite such blanket statements, *research has shown no generalizable relationships between odd–even pricing and consumer reactions.*[16] Odd–even pricing seems to be a very widely accepted pricing practice with little basis in fact.

---

[15] Bernard F. Whalen, "Strategic Mix of Odd, Even Prices Can Lead to Increased Retail Profits," *Marketing News,* March 7, 1980, p. 24.

[16] Andre Gabor and Clive Granger, "Price Sensitivity of the Consumer," *Journal of Advertising Research,* December 1964, pp. 40–44; David M. Georgoff, "Price Illusion and the Effect of Odd–Even Pricing," *Southern Journal of Business,* April 1969, pp. 95–103; and Eli Ginzberg, "Customary Prices," *American Economic Review,* June, 1963, p. 296.

Prestige Pricing

Some products are priced high to enhance a prestige image. This practice of prestige pricing implies a *price–quality relationship* in the minds of consumers. That is, consumers perceive higher-priced products as higher in quality. Research into price–quality relationships has shown that when price is the only information consumers have with which to judge a product, a price–quality relationship does indeed exist. However, no such conclusive evidence of price–quality relationships exists when consumers have other factors besides price with which to judge (noticeable product attributes, for example).[17]

Despite this lack of a clear price–quality relationship, many companies have used prestige pricing successfully. Usually a company uses the higher price to augment an already quality image (IBM computers, for instance, always sell at a premium), or the higher price is supported by promotional messages reinforcing the price–quality relationship. L'Oreal used this tactic effectively with the theme, "It costs a little more, but I'm worth it." Curtis Mathes' theme of "The most expensive television sold in America, and darn well worth it" also supports prestige pricing with advertising messages.

Customary Pricing

In customary pricing, certain products are priced based on tradition. Customary prices usually are used when the sellers believe there is considerable buyer resistance to price changes and they try to compete on a nonprice basis. Candy bars offer an example of customary pricing. For more than half of the 20th century candy bars cost a nickel. Under inflationary pressures in the 1970s the price of these products rapidly rose to a quarter, but are now established at this new, higher customary price. When raw-material costs hurt manufacturer profitability, the size of the candy bars is changed to lower costs, but the 25-cent price remains unchanged. Consumers are actually paying a higher price (still 25 cents for less candy), but the price of the bar has remained stable.

Price Lining

Channel members, especially retailers, often establish several **price lines**, or categories, for the merchandise they carry. One successful apparel retailer, for example, uses price lines of $60, $75, and $90 for its dresses and

---

[17] Kent B. Monroe, "Buyers' Subjective Perceptions of Price," *Journal of Marketing Research*, February 1973, pp. 70–80.

MARKETING

Strategy

Apple Versus IBM

The two market leaders in the struggle for personal computer sales are IBM and Apple Computer, Inc. Despite IBM's relatively late entrance into the personal computer marketplace, it has surpassed Apple as the market leader. Recent figures show IBM with a 26-percent market share and Apple trailing at 21 percent.* What accounts for IBM's phenomenal performance?

IBM is an old established firm. The company began in 1911 when three companies, International Time Recording Company, the Computing Scale Company, and the Tabulating Company merged and became the Computing–Tabulating–Recording Company (C–T–R). In 1924 the company name of C–T–R was changed to International Business Machines. Three policies evolved that still form the basis for IBM's marketing philosophy: profit for customers, profit for employees, profit for stockholders.

Apple Computer has been in business since 1976. Two computer whiz kids, Steven P. Jobs and Steven G. Wozniak, founded the company in the now-famous Silicon Valley of California. The company introduced its Apple II in 1977. It was the first personal computer that was not a hobbyist's kit. Its unintimidating approach to computing and the 16,000 software programs developed for it enticed over 700,000 buyers.

The success of IBM's personal computer (PC) is the result of new strategies adopted by the very traditional firm. IBM took the advice of an outside software company and put a 16-bit microprocessor in their PC, double the capacity of any other personal computer on the market.

IBM published the software specifications for its PC to encourage other firms to develop applications software for the IBM machine. IBM realized it could not support the software needs of its PC users economically, but independent software houses could. The availability of good software packages for the IBM-PC helped increase sales tremendously.

Distribution channels are an important aspect of IBM's success. The company has its own giant sales force and product centers and 800 of the best computer retailers to handle the product. This use of independent retailers to distribute the PC is a departure from IBM's usual distribution methods, but has helped obtain quick exposure for its product.

IBM's ability to produce a high-quality machine at a relatively low cost is the result of the firm's vertical integration and production economies. Most industry spokespeople agree that to gain the pricing advantage inherent in high-volume production, a firm must manufacture its own semiconductor chips, which IBM does.

IBM's ability to manufacture computers at the least cost allowed it to adopt an aggressive pricing strategy. Soon after introduction, IBM cut the price of its PC by 20 percent and touched off a round of price cutting by a number of other firms. Despite lower prices on other personal computers, IBM still received most of the sales. Its well-established name and experience in the computing industry added an intangible value to its products. Thus, customers felt they were getting much more for their money with IBM's PC. More recently, IBM has introduced the PCJr to its distribution system. Priced for the low end of the personal computer market ($669), the PCJr was introduced to capture the individual purchaser who may be too price sensitive to buy the PC.

Apple is going through a complete overhaul of its operations in an attempt to keep up with IBM. Before 1981 when IBM introduced its PC, it was Apple's uniqueness of product and its strong market position that assured the company of continued sales. Not so anymore.

Apple's new approach is to assert itself as the technological leader in the field of personal computers. It realizes IBM has it beat in terms of price and distribution. So to assure its technological leadership, Apple is developing a company-wide focus on product planning. Its present concern is to promote the sale of its products to the small businessperson through retail outlets. Long-term success, Apple realizes, is based on its ability to sell machines to large corporations.

To cover both these objectives, Apple introduced the technologically advanced "Lisa." Small businesses and corporations are interested in "Lisa" because of the small amount of training needed to use the machine. A novice can learn to run Lisa in half a day compared to the 20 hours needed to learn how to operate the IBM-PC.

Originally, Lisa sold for $10,000, a price that drove many small companies and large-volume buyers to IBM's PC. Recently, however, Apple lowered the price to $8,190 to make Lisa more cost competitive. Even so, the price difference between the two machines is still about $6,000. Apple hopes to minimize this difference by stressing the lack of training needed to run Lisa and introducing lower-cost Lisa versions. More recently, Apple brought out the McIntosh, which maintains the same design philosophy as the Lisa, but at a list price of $2,495.†

If Apple is to succeed in competing with IBM, most industry sources say it must concentrate on the distribution and marketing of its products. Apple cannot rely on a tiny sales force and a network of independent retailers to sell Lisa, McIntosh, and its future variations to the same customers IBM's forces are able to reach. John Scully, Apple's new president, wants to promote the cultlike status of the Apple computer to help push sales into distribution channels that are not yet fully developed.

Continued

knit sportswear. Instead of pricing its clothing individually according to actual costs, the retailer selects its clothing to fit one of the three price lines. This policy assumes that customers perceive dresses priced between $90 and $76 as roughly equivalent. Thus, if price cuts within the range would not affect demand, why price a dress at $80 if the retailer can sell just as many at $90?

When retailers use price lining, they purchase their inventory with various price lines in mind. Once the lines are set, prices may be held constant over a period of time and adaptation to the market is accomplished by adjusting the quality of merchandise carried in each line.

Besides this ability to charge more and not affect demand, price lining has two other advantages. First, it is convenient, simple, and efficient. It is much easier to fit several hundred different garments into three price categories than to price each item individually. Second, price lining helps the merchant appeal to different target markets simultaneously; the low-, medium-, and high-priced lines will, hopefully, attract customers from different income levels.

Many producers develop products especially for different price lines. This policy, sometimes called **multiple pricing**, is widely used by makers of appliances, furniture, tires, and numerous other shopping goods.

DISCOUNTS

Although most products have a set price, a product often sells for less than that amount. This lower price is usually the result of various **discounts** available to buyers.

A variety of discounts and allowances are offered to make it appear to buyers that they are getting a "bargain." In some cases they actually are, but in most instances the discount or allowance is a trade-off for a relinquished service, guarantee, or other feature usually included in the full price.

Normally, the price of a product is designed to cover all the seller's production and marketing costs. These costs may be reduced, however, if the buyer purchases larger than normal quantities, performs some of the work of marketing the product, pays cash, buys during the off season, or accepts damaged goods.

Quantity Discounts

Quantity discounts based on either the dollar value or the number of units involved are found at all levels of distribution. Producers offer discounts to intermediaries to make buying in larger volume more attractive. Retailers urge ultimate consumers to buy "one for 79¢, two for $1.50."

The usual rationale for quantity discounts is that the per-unit cost of producing and selling several units is less than the cost of producing and selling one unit. Such expenses as factory setup costs and billing costs are fairly constant whether 1 or 1,000 units are involved. In addition transportation costs are lower (often cut in half) if quantities large enough to fill a truck or train car are ordered. Some of the savings realized by the seller in processing one large order rather than several small ones are passed on to the buyer. There are two types of quantity discounts: cumulative and non-cumulative.

Cumulative discounts are based on the total amount a customer purchases over a given period. The underlying reason for granting them is that a buyer is more likely to repeatedly patronize one seller if all of his or her purchases will be totaled at the end of the period (usually one year) and the discount based on this figure. Many daily newspapers offer a special cumulative-linage rate to encourage large-scale advertising. The price may be halved if the advertiser places more than a million lines during a 12-month period.

Noncumulative discounts make one-time purchases of larger lots more attractive. This type of discount is quite popular among some service establishments. A hotel with a daily room rate of $68 may price its rooms in blocks of 100 at a guaranteed rate of only $45 day to a group sponsoring a convention.

Banks customarily offer a prime (or lower) interest rate to borrowers of large sums who have excellent credit ratings. In similar fashion insurance companies may grant lower premium rates to holders of large policies, on the theory that the book work involved in administering a $250,000 policy is no greater than that required to administer a $1,000 policy.

Quantity discounts also enable certain sellers to pass on a portion of the

Figure 18-12	
Quantity Discount Example	
Seller's per-Unit Cost to Deliver One Unit:	
Transportation Cost	$5.00
All Other Costs	15.00
Total	$20.00
Price	$25.00
Profit per Unit	$5.00
Seller's per-Unit Cost to Deliver 1,000 Units:	
Transportation Cost	$3.00
All Other Costs	15.00
Total	$18.00
Price	25.00
Profit per Unit	$7.00
Buyer's per-Unit Cost of Storage:	
Less Than 1,000 Units Ordered	$4.00
1,000 Units Ordered	5.00
Extra per-Unit Cost to Order 1,000 Units	$1.00

storage function to the buyer and speed the flow of perishable goods. When a company offers a quantity discount, it must be certain the discount covers any additional costs the buyer may accrue in ordering in larger amounts. For instance, the buyer is not going to take advantage of a quantity discount that reduces the price $1 per unit if the cost of storing the extra units is $2 per unit. Sellers offering quantity discounts must first determine how much money they can save if buyers order in quantity. Next, the costs of the buyer for a quantity order should be estimated. The seller should only offer a quantity discount that saves the seller money and that saves the buyer more than the increase of his or her costs.

Figure 18-12 provides an example. If the seller can convince the buyer to order in quantities of 1,000 units, the seller's transportation cost decreases $2 per unit. However, the buyer's storage cost increases $1 per unit. For both to be better off, the seller must offer a discount of greater than $1 but less than $2 per unit. Suppose the seller offers a $1.75 discount. If 1,000 units are ordered, the seller's costs drop to $18.00 and the discounted price is $23.25. This leaves a profit of $5.25, $0.25 per unit more than before. The buyer's storage cost goes up by $1.00, but the purchase price drops by $1.75, lowering the buyer's total cost by $0.75 per unit. Thus, both buyer and seller are better off. Although this example is rather simplistic, far more complex quantity-discount analyses still follow this principle of making both the buyer and the seller better off.[18]

Trade Discounts

Many producers offer special discounts to the "trade" (wholesalers and retailers) in return for help in moving goods to industrial users or ultimate consumers. Because the intermediary in these cases performs portions of the marketing function, these reductions are also called **functional discounts**.

For example, a manufacturer might quote its retail list price as "$100, 40/10." The first figure represents the price to the consumer. The second figure (40, meaning 40 percent) is the trade discount to the retailer, and the third figure (10, meaning 10 percent) is the discount granted the wholesaler.

We would calculate the functional discounts (and prices) in this example as follows: Subtracting 40 percent of the $100 price leaves $60, which is the price to the retailer. The wholesaler's 10-percent discount is calculated on the retailer's price. Therefore, the wholesaler would purchase the product from the manufacturer for $54 ($60 minus $6) and resell it to the retailer for $60. The wholesaler would earn 10 percent to cover expenses and profit. The retailer would then sell the product to the consumer for $100, thereby earning 40 percent to cover expenses and profit.

The basic problem with this type of discount is that the producer has no assurance that the other channel members will actually perform marketing services equal in value to the discounts. Also, the rationale of a "discount granted for marketing services" becomes more questionable as the functions of middlemen increasingly overlap or duplicate each other.

Cash Discounts

Many firms offer cash discounts as a special inducement to buyers to pay for goods promptly. In some cases the savings can be significant. Many invoices offer a discount of "2/10, net 30." This means that 2 percent may be deducted from the invoice price if payment is made within 10 days. Otherwise, the full amount is due in 30 days after the purchase date.

There are several variations in dating procedures. Some firms give terms of "2/10, net 30 e.o.m." (end of month). This extends the beginning of the payment period until the month following the date of the invoice.

---

[18] John F. Crowther, "Rationale for Quantity Discounts," *Harvard Business Review,* March–April 1964, pp. 121–27; Mentzer and Monroe, "Some Common Misconceptions About Pricing"; and Kent B. Monroe and Albert J. Della Bitta, "Models for Pricing Decisions," *Journal of Marketing Research,* August 1978, pp. 413–28.

For example, the discount on an invoice issued July 16 would be good until August 10, and the full amount would not be due until August 30.

To accommodate buyers who do not wish to make payment before goods are received and inspected, some firms offer r.o.g. (receipt-of-goods) terms. An invoice carrying the phrase "2/10, net 30 r.o.g." would allow the buyer to take advantage of the discount up to 10 days after receiving the goods.

In most cases the buyer is foolish not to take advantage of a cash discount. Take 2/10, net 30, for example. The seller is offering a 2-percent discount to get the buyer to pay 20 days early. Because there are 18 periods of 20 days in a year, the annual percentage rate of such a discount is 36 percent ($18 \times 2\% = 36\%$)! Unless the buyer can invest the purchase price somewhere else at better than 36 percent (an unlikely event), it is better to pay in 10 days.

Suppose the price were $1,000. Even if the buyer had to borrow the $1,000 for 20 days at an annual rate of 18 percent in order to pay early, the interest would only be 1/18 (remember: 18 periods of 20 days in a year) of 18 percent, or 1 percent. Thus, the loan interest for 20 days would be 1 percent of $1,000, or $10. The cash discount would be 2 percent of $1,000, or $20. The buyer is $10 better off.

Although these percentage figures look attractive for the buyer, they can be a trap for the seller. A 2/10, net 30 discount says the seller can afford a 36-percent cost of money to receive payment 20 days early. Again, it is unlikely the seller can invest the early payment somewhere else at 36 percent. Therefore, the seller will make less money unless the cash discount generates more sales. Sophisticated models have been developed to determine how much sales have to increase for the cash discount to benefit the seller.[19] Suffice it here to state that sales have to increase from a cash discount for the seller to be better off.

Seasonal Discounts

The primary reason for granting seasonal discounts is to spread out production over the entire year and prevent expensive stockpiling of inventories. Numerous manufacturers are connected with products whose market is seasonal. Discounts enable the purchaser to make a better buy (provided it can economically absorb the cost of storage) and allow the producer to keep production lines running and to reduce inventory.

The hotel and travel industries also grant seasonal discounts in an effort to maximize use of facilities. Hotels and motels in Miami Beach, for example, are able to charge high prices in winter months, when their

---

[19] Mentzer and Monroe, "Some Common Misconceptions About Pricing."

facilities are most in demand, but have a substantially lower rate structure during the summer months.

A variation of the seasonal discount is the "off-hour" discount, a special rate used to stimulate sales in periods when demand is normally low. Airlines offer literally dozens of special-fare plans to attract customers during hours of the day and days of the week when flights are less in demand. Texas International Airlines (TIA), for example, doubled its volume by offering "Peanuts Fares"—discounts of 50 percent and more—on routes with low seat occupancy. Public utilities grant special rates to business customers during hours when normal energy consumption is below the daytime peak. Telephone companies offer special rates to consumers to encourage them to make calls during evening hours and on weekends.

Promotional Allowances

When buyers perform certain promotional functions for a product or service, special allowances may be granted to compensate them in whole or in part for the costs involved. Cooperative advertising is one type of promotional allowance. In this case the manufacturer pays some of the retailer's advertising costs in return for special featuring of its product. As a rule, allowances of this nature differ from discounts in that the intermediary bills the manufacturer for the costs incurred rather than deducting a percentage from the price on an invoice.

An example of highly organized cooperative advertising involves Associated Druggists (AD) of Wichita, Kansas. AD helps its clients—comprising 37 wholesale drug companies and 1,000 independent drugstores—pool their manufacturer co-op advertising allowances, featuring promotions in about 700 newspapers. AD is compensated by fees paid by wholesalers and retailers.[20]

Price Promotions

Also called **trade promotions**, price promotions are special discounts given by the manufacturer to the retailer to promote its product extra hard and to offer it as a sale item. Often used for new products and regularly used for such products as coffee, tuna, soft drinks, paper products, bake mixes, margarine, salad dressings, cooking oil, deodorants, and shampoo, price promotions are lower prices to retailers *only* if they lower the product's price to the consumer and feature it in their advertisements.

Although these discounts were started to stimulate sales, so many companies use them today that many manufacturers feel they must offer price

---

[20] "S&MM Excellence Awards," *Sales & Marketing Management,* January 1977, p. 36.

Milestone

Cash Rebates

Does a promise to return a portion of the purchase price directly to consumers who buy the manufacturer's goods have persuasive power in the marketplace?

The recession of the early 1970s prompted a surge of rebate programs, offered mostly by makers of small appliances and automobiles. Those who bought items that promised a rebate paid the regular price to the retailer, then applied directly to the manufacturer for the cash-back offer.

Although the issue has been argued from both sides, rebates are neither purely a pricing mechanism nor strictly a sales promotion tool. Elements of both work together to help users of rebates reduce their inventory and increase traffic in the outlets that carry their goods. Some marketers prefer rebates over price reductions because their effect is not as permanent as cutting prices and they increase the company's promotional options.

Some manufacturers offer rebates to their dealers, hoping the retailers will pass the saving on to the consumer. The Chrysler Corporation, for example, offered dealers rebates ranging from $200 to $500, depending on the model, on automobiles they bought and resold to auto leasing companies within 90 days. Chrysler's objective was to reduce its inventory of large cars in a period when consumers were turning more frequently to small automobiles.

Another rebate offered by Chrysler went directly to consumers. Those who test-drove certain models of Dodges were given a certificate to the effect that, if they bought a car within 30 days, even a car made by General Motors or Ford, Chrysler would "rebate" $50 upon presentation of the certificate and proof of purchasing an automobile. You may question whether such a device

promotions to maintain their market shares. Many manufacturers feel that price promotions lead to brand switching by consumers looking for bargains. Indeed, a 1983 survey by ad agency Needham Harper & Steers found brand-loyal shoppers had dropped from 77 to 59 percent.[21] Because manufacturers make less profit on price promotion sales, they have reason to worry.

---

[21] Williams, "The No-Win Game of Price Promotion."

can correctly be called a rebate if the recipient has not bought a Chrysler product.

Nevertheless, Chrysler's extensive use of rebates has produced some excellent results for the once trouble-ridden corporation. One $400 rebate offer, designed to boost model year-end sales in 1979, increased Chrysler's sales 23 percent above the level of the same period during 1978. Ford and GM sales declined 31.4 percent and 18.9 percent, respectively, during the same period.*

Why does Chrysler not simply lower the price? "[Rebates are] more flexible," explains Chrysler Vice Chairman Gerald Greenwald. "It's burdensome to reprice every time you see a change in the marketplace."†

Rebates have been offered by numerous other companies, including Sunbeam, Regal Ware, Norelco, Bristol–Meyers, Dr. Pepper, and Coca–Cola, but many companies are becoming disillusioned with cash rebate results. Since Gillette began rebates on hair dryers in the 1970s, sales have fallen 80 percent. Part of the problem is that any rebates are simply matched by competition.

General Electric, the largest rebater, cut back from 62 products with rebates in 1982 to less than 30 in 1983. Paul Van Orden, GE's Vice President of Hard Goods, explains, "We have reached the point where rebates are a hassle for us."‡ He says consumers are no longer responding to rebates and retailers do not like the paperwork.

Although cash rebates were certainly a marketing milestone in pricing and sales promotion, they probably will not be used as extensively by so many companies in the future. They will, however, continue to be a common practice in marketing, especially among companies that have used them effectively.

* "Chrysler Rebates Help 10-Day Sales Rise 23%," *New York Times*, September 6, 1979, p. D-1.
† "Why Detroit Can't Cut Prices," *Business Week*, March 1, 1982, pp. 110–11.
‡ Robert Johnson, "Rebating Rises, But Unhappy Firms Can't Think of a Good Alternative," *Wall Street Journal*, December 9, 1982, p. 31.

Cash Rebates

Sluggish sales in recent years have spurred many sellers to offer **cash rebates** to ultimate consumers. These refunds range from a few dollars for the purchase of some small appliances to several hundred dollars for buying certain automobile models. Typically, retailers charge regular prices for the goods. Purchasers then apply to the manufacturer, which rebates the designated amount directly to the consumer.

Although cash rebates ultimately do reduce the price of a product, the procedure by which they are paid makes them more closely akin to couponing methods than to pricing policies. As a promotional device, they stimulate sales, clear out accumulated inventory, and increase store traffic. The successful use of rebates in several industries has led some observers to predict that they will become a permanent sales stimulus.

Trade-in and Damaged Goods Allowances

Trade-in allowances for used goods are commonly employed to encourage consumers and industrial users to purchase items with a high unit value more frequently. Industrial buyers often trade in heavy equipment to take advantage of large allowances offered by sellers. Consumers often trade in their old cars to obtain a price reduction on a new model.

Damaged goods allowances are offered at all levels of the distribution channel, but are most common in retail transactions. Many grocery stores have a special basket of damaged goods, at discounted prices, available for customers to inspect. Although they are getting a lower price, consumers also are assuming the risk of possibly buying inferior goods.

Discounts Combined

Companies often qualify for numerous discounts on a single purchase. Take the wholesaler in Figure 18-13. With a single purchase of 1,000 units the wholesaler qualifies for three discounts. Because the consumer price of $100 is discounted 40 percent for retailers and an additional 10 percent for wholesalers ($100,40/10), the wholesaler's price is $54. The quantity discount lowers this price by 10 percent and the cash discount (2/10, net 30) lowers it an additional 2 percent if early payment is made. Thus, the final price for a wholesaler that orders 1,000 or more units and pays within 10 days is $47.63.

A Model of Pricing Procedures

In this chapter we have tried to discuss the various factors affecting the pricing decision. These factors include costs, demand, competition, channel members, government, and discounts. Figure 18-14 illustrates this process.

The lowest reasonable price for a product is one that just covers all assignable costs. To price below this amount means the company is spending more per unit than it is making. In effect, the product has a negative contribution, and it is creating a loss that other products will have to cover (along with common costs) before the company can make a profit.

The **price ceiling** *is the maximum price the target market would be willing to*

Figure 18-13

Wholesaler Discount Example

Terms of $100,40/10; 2/10,net 30; 10% off if 1,000 units or more

Wholesaler is offered a functional discount of $100,40/10:
$100 = Consumer Price
$100 − $40 = $60 = Retailer Price
$60 − $6 = $54 = Wholesaler Price

Wholesaler orders 1,000 units:
Bill = $54,000
$\underline{- 5,400}$ (10% quantity discount)
$48,600

Wholesaler pays within 10 days:
$48,600
$\underline{- \quad 972}$ (2% cash discount)
$47,628 Actual amount paid by wholesaler

Wholesaler Price per Unit = $47.63

Figure 18-14

Model of Pricing Procedure

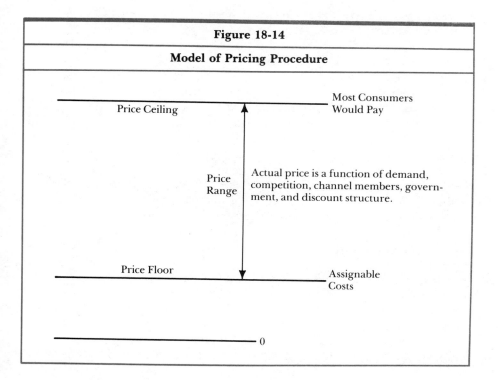

---

pay. In economic terms it is "what the market will bear." This price is often quite unrealistic and cannot actually be obtained because of the various factors we have discussed in this chapter.

The actual price a company charges will be based on the company's assessment of the marketplace. The company's volume goals and the price elasticity of demand will be considered. Reactions to prices by competitors and channel members also will influence the actual price. In addition, restrictions by various government agencies will have an effect. Finally, in actual sales the price may be adjusted by various discounts.

Therefore, the factors we have discussed will help determine where the actual price lies in the price range defined by the assignable costs and the price the market will bear. Wherever that actual price is, companies making pricing decisions must take demand, competition, channel members, government, and discounts into account to make an intelligent pricing decision.

SUMMARY

- Price is value expressed in terms of exchange for something of value (money or barter).
- Although economists see price as a measure of sacrifice, the price can also have value to the consumer.
- Nonprice competition emphasizes product, place, or promotional variables rather than price and often allows a higher price to be charged or greater market share to be achieved without changing the price.
- The law of demand says that more goods will be sold at lower prices than at higher prices.
- Price acts as an equalizer between supply and demand in the marketplace.
- Price sensitivity, measured by price elasticity, tells a marketing manager whether total revenue will increase or decrease with a price change.
- The number of competitors and competitive intensity affect pricing decisions.
- Variable, fixed, and marginal costs should be considered in setting prices.
- Although problems with the solution exist, the theoretical optimum price is where marginal revenue equals marginal cost.
- A more practical analysis of costs for pricing decisions is to consider assignable and common costs.
- Government actions with regard to fiscal and monetary policies; regulation; or the oversight of such activities as price fixing, price discrimina-

tion, or price controls largely influence the general level of prices and the price decisions companies can make.

- The cost structures, goals, and traditional markups of channel members all affect the final selling price.
- The general price level is affected by pressure for higher wages, business efficiency, buyer and seller resistance, speculation, and inflation.
- Although odd–even pricing is a widely accepted pricing practice, research has not shown it to have any real effectiveness.
- Prestige pricing uses a price–quality relationship to convince consumers that higher-priced products are of superior quality.
- Customary prices are used in industries in which manufacturers believe customers to be very sensitive to price changes. Often the quality or quantity of a product received at the customary price is altered to change the real price.
- Price lines are used when customers perceive no appreciable difference in quality within certain price ranges.
- Quantity discounts are designed to encourage buyers to purchase in larger quantities. The seller's savings from larger orders are shared with the buyer in the form of the discount.
- Although trade discounts are offered to channel members for performing certain functions, there is no way to guarantee these functions are actually performed.
- Cash discounts for early payment can afford the buyer substantial savings. Sellers, however, should offer cash discounts only if they will increase sales.
- Seasonal discounts encourage buyers to purchase products during slow sales periods.
- Promotional allowances, price promotions, cash rebates, and trade-in and damaged goods allowances are all special adjustments to the final selling price.
- Assignable costs establish the lower end of a pricing range, and "what the market will bear" establishes the upper end. The actual price within this range is determined by demand, competition, channel members, government, and the discount structure.

DISCUSSION QUESTIONS

1. Define *price*.
2. How can nonprice competition affect pricing decisions?
3. What is the law of demand? What exceptions to this law have you observed?

4. Explain the difference between elastic and inelastic demand.
5. Explain the difference between variable, fixed, marginal, assignable, and common costs. Can variable costs be common? Why?
6. What problems exist when a company follows a marginal revenue equals marginal cost pricing scheme?
7. Explain how each of the following affects prices:
   (a) Government
   (b) Channel members
   (c) Competition
   (d) Business efficiency
   (e) Buyer and seller resistance
   (f) Speculation
8. Define each of the following price practices:
   (a) Odd–even pricing
   (b) Prestige pricing
   (c) Customary prices
   (d) Price lines
9. Explain how quantity discounts, trade discounts, cash discounts, and promotional discounts work.
10. How is the price range for a product defined?

APPLICATION
EXERCISES

1. Document three examples of nonprice competition and three examples for which the law of demand does not hold true. For each, explain why this has occurred.
2. Wholesaler X places an order for 1,200 units of Product A on October 12. When the invoice is received on October 20, the pricing statement is "$120,35/15; 1/10,net 30 e.o.m.; 10 off if over 1,000 units; 5 off if ordered between July 1 and October 30." Which is the trade discount? The seasonal discount? Quantity discount? Cash discount? What was the final price per unit and the total dollar amount the wholesaler paid if the bill was paid on November 3?

CASE 18

Texas Instruments Gets Shocked by Its Own Electronics Price War[22]

With 20 percent of the home computer market, Texas Instruments (TI) became the major victim of a price war it started. TI's strategy of cutting prices to gain

[22] "How Texas Instruments Shot Itself in the Foot," *Business Week*, June 27, 1983,

market share and reduce its production costs through economies of scale and the learning curve effect worked well for it in hand-held calculators. However, when it followed the same strategy in the home computer market, TI's competitors quickly followed suit. TI's model 99/4A was introduced in 1981 at a suggested retail price of $525, but by 1983 its price, with rebates, had fallen to $100. Commodore's VIC-20 was introduced at $299, but fell to $90. Apple, Xerox, NCR, and IBM all dropped their prices by about 25 percent. Timex had the bottom of the price chain with its Timex 1000, introduced at $99.95 but eventually lowered to $49.95.

Certainly, improved technology and lower manufacturing costs helped drop prices, but most of the reductions were the result of "cutthroat" competition. As one industry retailer put it, "These prices are changing every day, but the one thing they don't do is go up."

All the price cutting started when TI slashed prices on the 99/4A and offered a rebate that brought the price to $199. Commodore countered with a price drop that forced TI to sell the 99/4A at $99, $15 to $20 below its estimated manufacturing costs. Thus, the 99/4A was not even covering its assignable costs in the short run. Commodore further heated the war by dropping the price of its software packages below $20. TI's were still at $30 to $40.

The result caused TI to announce a 1983 second-quarter loss of $100 million. The news made TI's stock price drop 39 points on June 13, 1983. Eventually, TI was forced to withdraw the 99/4A from the market.

The major question was whether TI could have recovered profitability at such low prices and held out until squeezed profits forced the rest of the industry to raise their prices. Apparently, TI did not feel it could.

Discussion Questions

1. To stay in the home computer market, should TI have kept its prices low, lowered them further to hurt competition, or raised them?
2. What information about costs and demand would you need in order to better answer Question 1?
3. Based on your answer to Question 1, what would your overall marketing strategy (product, place, and promotion) be to support your pricing decision if TI had stayed in the market?

p. 26; Laura Landro and James A. White, "Computer Firms Push Prices Down, Try to Improve Marketing Tactics," *Wall Street Journal*, April 29, 1983, p. 35; and Laura Landro and James A. White, "'Adam' Jolting Pricing Tactics in Computers," *Wall Street Journal*, June 9, 1983, p. 35.

19

Pricing Policy and Strategy

STUDY OBJECTIVES

After studying this chapter, you should be able to

1. Discuss sales-based, financial-based, competitive-based, and profit-based pricing objectives.
2. Explain pricing policy in terms of level and flexibility.
3. Describe the competition-based pricing strategies of pricing above or below competition, follower pricing, and price leadership.
4. Discuss the cost-based pricing strategies of cost-plus, markup, ROI, experience curve, and break-even point.
5. Explain how demand-based strategies are different from competition-based and cost-based strategies.
6. Discuss the principles behind product line pricing.
7. Explain the various forms of geographic pricing.
8. Describe negotiated and competitive bid pricing.
9. Discuss the factors to be considered in price changes.

I n the last chapter we concerned ourselves not only with the factors that affect pricing decisions but also with some common pricing practices. In this chapter we will build on that foundation to look at pricing objectives and policies, as well as strategies for accomplishing these objectives and policies. We will conclude with a look at pricing in some situations often faced by marketing managers and the issue of price changes.

PRICING OBJECTIVES

Price decisions are usually guided by one or more of several objectives set by corporate management. These are typically sales-, financial-, competitive-, or profit-based objectives.

Sales Objectives

A company will often follow a sales-based objective when larger unit sales lead to greater control of the market and lower unit costs. Also called a **market share objective**, this approach assumes a greater share of the market will lead to greater sales volume that will, in turn, lead to lower unit costs through the experience curve. The **experience curve** reminds managers that as sales volume increases, the company becomes more experienced, and hopefully more efficient, at producing and marketing a product. This combination of lower unit costs and higher volume should lead to higher profits.

However, the experience curve does not work for all companies.[1] For many companies higher volume means the same unit costs. The key to following an objective of gaining market share is to first determine whether the increased volume will decrease unit costs and increase corporate control of the market.

Companies following a sales-based objective typically practice penetration pricing. **Penetration pricing** *consists of setting the price as low as possible to capture a large share of the market.* Again, the assumption behind penetration pricing is that with a large share, unit costs will drop (increasing profits) or the company will control the market sufficiently to raise prices later (again increasing profits). The problem with penetration pricing is that customers accustomed to the lower price may resist later price increases.

---

[1] Walter Kiechel III, "The Decline of the Experience Curve," *Fortune*, October 5, 1981, pp. 139, 140, 144, 146.

When Sir Frederick (Freddie) Alfred Laker started a transatlantic airline with a no-frills $99 ticket price, he was following a penetration pricing policy. For Laker's airline to be successful, the high cost of flights had to be covered by many passengers, that is, full planes. Thus, rates were set low to encourage travel. Initially, the plan worked, with Laker making $700,000 in profit the first month and $3 million the first year.[2] However, to continue to be successful, Laker needed a large enough share to control the market. This was not achieved when competitive airlines simply matched his price. After a valiant effort, Laker's airline eventually went into bankruptcy. The competition was simply too large for Laker's penetration pricing to work in the long run.

Financial Objectives

Companies often have specific financial goals that influence pricing decisions. Although not strictly a financial objective, the common corporate objective of *survival* is often expressed in financial terms.

Survival   Companies that face overcapacity, changing customer wants, or intense competition may have an overriding goal of survival. Prices are set low to turn inventory fast, to keep operations at or near capacity, and keep customers interested. Profits in the short run are sacrificed to keep the company going. Chrysler and International Harvester both used large rebate programs to keep operating in the early 1980s. As long as prices covered assignable costs, the companies could operate in the short run. However, survival as an objective can only be a short-run reaction to environmental changes. Some fundamental changes in the marketing strategy (besides just price) must be made to meet changing competition, overcapacity, and customer wants.

Return on Investment   Pricing to obtain a predetermined **return on investment (ROI)** is a cost-based pricing objective and, at least partially, ignores demand. An ROI objective measures the costs involved in producing and marketing a product and sets the price at a level that returns a certain profit. For a long time General Motors, for example, had a return on investment objective of 40 percent before taxes.

This objective, however, assumes sufficient quantity can be sold at the determined price to meet ROI objectives. It also ignores the fact that the company might make more profit at a different (higher or lower) price.

Cash Flow   Companies that wish to quickly recover cash to cover the development and introduction costs of a new product follow a cash-flow

---

[2] "Laker Offers Plan to Cut Costs of Flights to Europe," *New York Times,* October 22, 1979, p. D-9.

objective. This objective, like ROI, partially ignores demand. A strategy used by some companies to meet this objective is **skimming pricing**.

Under a skimming strategy the company may set the price of a new product high in order to reap large unit profits on early sales from customers who will pay a high price (the "cream" that is being "skimmed"). Later, it will lower the price to reach more customers.

A cash-flow objective can be realistic when research has shown there is a group willing to pay a high price or when the product life cycle is expected to be short, that is, quick recovery of cash is necessary. Without such information, however, cash flow is a naive pricing objective.

Competitive Objectives

Often companies, especially oligopolies, have objectives based on their position relative to the competition. A company may be in a position that it considers favorable—whether first, second, or whatever in a particular industry—and may simply wish to maintain that position. In such a case pricing decisions will be largely influenced by what the competition does and adjusting accordingly to maintain the same position.

For example, Inco, the world's largest producer of nickel, once held prices constant while competitors undercut it. When market share and profits fell, Inco adopted a competitive objective of maintaining its position as number one. Now Inco is willing to slug it out in price wars with its competition. This has made smaller competitors reluctant to take on the giant and has stabilized prices. As Inco Vice President Robert G. Dunn explains, "A lot of people were bleeding during that time. Now there's a much more orderly market."[3]

Profit Objectives

Although all the objectives previously discussed are commonly used, profit objectives are the most realistic goals for both profit and nonprofit companies. After all, even nonprofit companies have a profit goal of zero—not negative—profits.

A profit objective recognizes that profits depend on three interrelated factors: (1) the price charged per unit, (2) the number of units that are sold at that price, and (3) the costs of producing and marketing this number of units. Thus, a profit objective recognizes the demand effect of prices and the cost effect of volume. The best price is one that strikes a reasonable balance between costs and revenue—one that is low enough to keep customers satisfied but high enough for the firm to make money.

---

[3] "Inco: Guarding Its Edge in Nickel While Starting to Diversify Again," *Business Week*, June 9, 1980, pp. 104, 106.

If the objective is profit maximization, the price should be set where marginal revenue equals marginal costs (see Chapter 18). Because that one price is difficult to find in reality, however, many companies follow a **satisfactory profit objective**. In this case a company first decides on what it believes to be a reasonable profit, then analyzes costs, volume, and demand, and finally sets a price to achieve this objective. Notice this is very similar to an ROI objective, but here a much more detailed analysis of demand—not just costs—is involved.

PRICE POLICY

Within the guidelines set by these objectives, marketing managers must determine price policy. **Price policy** *sets the general approach to be used in specifying individual product prices.*

Part of a price policy is the **price level**. The company must decide whether its products should be sold at a low price, as with most commodities; at a premium price, as with luxury goods; or somewhere in between. Rolex, long a marketer of prestige watches, has a high price policy (The lady's Rolex President sells for $6,000!) and certainly would not consider

instituting a discount policy.[4] The company can maintain this policy primarily because of the luxury image of its products.

Product brands that have a high price policy by virtue of their image include Mercedes-Benz, Cadillac, Chivas Regal, IBM, Xerox, and Sony. Companies marketing commodities such as gasoline, salt, or sugar have not been able to develop a prestige image and, thus follow more of a competitively priced policy.

Price policy is also defined by the degree of **price flexibility**. Companies may follow a one-price policy or flexible pricing.

Many companies, especially retailers, offer identical goods purchased at the same price to all customers. This called a **one-price policy**. Although

---

[4] Lawrence Minard, "The More It Costs, the Better It Sells," *Forbes,* December 22, 1980, pp. 59–62.

Early Quakers brought the one-price system to the United States, but it did not begin to gain wide acceptance until after the Civil War. F.W. Woolworth, Tiffany and Co., and John Wanamaker were among the nineteenth-century entrepreneurs who adopted the one-price policy. When J.L. Hudson founded his Detroit department store in 1881, he advertised a "strictly one-price policy," with the price plainly marked on all goods. The modern department store, because of its heavy dependence on a large volume of sales, probably could not function in the absence of a one-price system, which facilitates the speedy flow of products with comparatively few sales personnel.

Uniform prices eventually led to the development of the money-back guarantee and to the spread of catalog and mail-order selling. Modern accounting and budgeting techniques rely heavily on the one-price system, as does long-range planning, which is based on a forecast of earnings and cash flows and annual cost-price analyses.

Although some countries today still have negotiation as part of their buying process, most consumer items in the United States are retailed on a one-price basis, although there is some controversy as to whether quantity discounts, discounts on one-item purchases by mass merchandisers, and discounts to certain classes of people (such as ministers and teachers) constitute exceptions to this principle. The most notable exceptions to one-price selling occur in the marketing of automobiles, real estate, and costly industrial equipment, for which prices are usually negotiated. However, the major advantages of the one-price policy—speedy purchasing and equal treatment of all customers—have made it the rule rather than the exception in retailing most consumer products in the U.S.

prices of specific products may change daily (fresh produce is frequently marked down near the close of the day, and theater tickets are often higher priced for evening performances), at any given time all consumers are offered the products for the same price.

The one-price policy has two basic advantages for a firm. First, it is efficient, because it promotes fast handling of transactions. Second, the one-price policy helps to create confidence in the company.

A **flexible pricing policy** is followed when different, but similar buyers are charged a different price. Sales of automobiles are a good example of a flexible pricing policy. The price a customer pays depends on how good he or she is at bargaining with the salesperson. A flexible price policy is prevalent in any industry in which a great deal of bargaining accompanies the sale. For this reason, flexible pricing is especially prevalent in industrial marketing.

PRICE STRATEGIES

Within the guidelines of pricing objectives and the overall pricing policy, marketing managers must choose specific price strategies. Depending on the objectives of the company, strategies are either competition based, cost based, or demand based.

Competition-Based Strategies

Competition-based strategies are the result of a company's assessment of the other companies in an industry. This assessment leads to one of four competition-based price strategies: pricing below the competition, pricing above the competition, price follower, or price leader strategies.

Pricing Below the Competition   Some firms deliberately attempt to sell a product for less than the prevailing market price in an effort to gain patronage. Often, they will attempt to maintain profit margins by cutting down on services. There are, for example, petroleum retailers who charge lower prices to motorists who fill their own gasoline tanks. Discount houses sell below levels established by full-service department stores. They cut costs and maintain profits by concentrating less on providing a "comfortable" store environment and by stressing self-service.

Pricing Above the Competition   A business may sell a product that is distinctive or prestigious at a price above what the competition is charging. For example, in any large city some restaurants can command prices significantly higher than average. The difference may be in the reputation of the establishment, the decor, or the type of service. Jewelry stores with an excellent reputation can sell diamonds that are virtually identical to those in other stores at a higher-than-average price, because they have the confidence of the customer. Product characteristics need not be tangible to have value. A higher price by itself may connote value.

Price Follower   A **price follower strategy** is used when a company simply matches the price of a certain competitor or competitors. The company makes no effort to analyze its costs or demand; it simply assumes the competitor knows what it is doing and follows it. This is a very naive and dangerous pricing strategy. It is appropriate only if the follower is similar to the leader in terms of cost structure, volume, profit goals, competitive stature, and product/marketing quality.

Shapiro presented an example of a follower that produced a product that received further processing from customers before sale to final users. The competitor it followed was vertically integrated, that is, it produced the product, performed the final processing, and sold to the final consumers. The competitor priced the intermediary product high. Because the follower matched the competitor's price, all processors of the final product

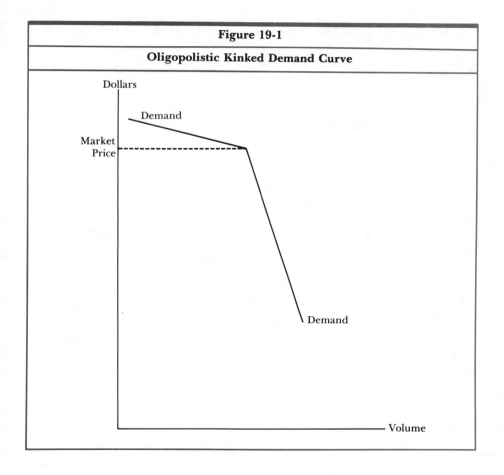

Figure 19-1

Oligopolistic Kinked Demand Curve

Dollars

Demand

Market
Price

Demand

Volume

paid the high price for the intermediary product. The competitor then
priced its final product low to remain competitive in the final consumer
market. Thus, its profits were reaped from the intermediary sales. Because
the follower did not sell the final product, it would have been smarter to
lower this price to increase industry consumption and its market share.[5]
Before adopting a follower strategy, a company must analyze its competitors to be certain they are very similar, and should periodically review the
similarities and the follower strategy.

Price Leader   The strategy of a **price leader** is usually found in oligopolistic industries. Oligopolies are characterized by **kinked demand curves**
(see Figure 19-1). Above the prevailing price, demand is very price elastic.

---

[5] Benson P. Shapiro, "Common Fallacies," in Earl L. Bailey, ed., *Pricing Practices and Strategies*
(New York: The Conference Board, 1978), pp. 29–33.

Any rise in price will not be matched by competition, and sales of the higher-priced competitor will fall drastically. Any price drop will be matched by competitors, thus having little effect on volume.

This situation leads to price stability, but it also makes any price changes necessitated by cost increases difficult. Therefore, one company establishes itself as the price leader, and others simply match its price. As we have already discussed, price following has its dangers, but it does allow an otherwise very price-competitive industry to make orderly price changes.

Price leaders are normally the result of industry tradition. U.S. Steel is the traditional price leader in the steel industry, as is General Motors in the auto industry. The leader must take not only its costs and demand structure into account, but also those of its competitors. Otherwise it may set prices that the competition will not follow, threatening its position as the leader and possibly starting a price war.

Price leaders often **signal** competitors by making price changes effective as of some date. This allows the competition time to analyze the price change and react. Chrysler often announces price changes ahead of General Motors but then adjusts them after GM announces its prices. Thus, Chrysler is still following the leader's decisions.

The fact that such similarities exist is not necessarily illegal. Under the Supreme Court rule of **conscious parallelism**, the FTC or the Justice Department must prove conspiracy to set prices before any illegality is found. Nonconspired, similar movement of prices is not illegal.

Cost-Based Strategies

Many companies set prices based largely on their costs and cost-based objectives. Many companies use cost-based strategies because they are easier to determine. Costs are simpler to estimate and use as a basis for prices than elasticity of demand or competitive reaction.

However, cost-based strategies are limited because they ignore market conditions, competition, the product life cycle, market share goals, and demand elasticity.[6] In spite of these limitations cost-based strategies are commonly used and, therefore, will be discussed here.

Cost-Plus Pricing   In the simplest method of cost-based pricing—**cost-plus pricing**—a predetermined profit is added to costs. The company estimates the number of units to be produced and adds estimated total variable and total fixed costs to total desired profit. Price is obtained by dividing this amount by the units expected to be produced, or

---

[6] Seymore E. Heymann, "Consider Other Factors Than Cost When Pricing Industrial Products," *Marketing News*, April 4, 1980, p. 11.

$$\text{Price} = \frac{\text{TVC} + \text{TFC} + \text{Total Profit}}{\text{Units Produced}}$$

where TVC = total variable costs and TFC = total fixed costs.

Although easy to compute, notice that the number of units produced (and assumed sold) has no relationship to price. We are assuming price does not affect demand! Further, no consideration is given to assignable and common costs. This strategy assumes that all fixed costs are assignable to the product. This may not be true. Finally, no incentive exists for controlling costs. If management believes that the company simply should raise the price whenever costs rise and that price does not affect output, there is no incentive to keep costs down.

Although this strategy is quite limited, it has some use in industries in which customers are not very price sensitive and the manufacturer can control prices. Monopolies and some prestige product manufacturers can use cost-plus pricing because customers will accept the price derived. However, it is always dangerous to set prices assuming demand will not be affected. For this reason, cost-based pricing should be used far less than it is.

Markup Pricing   A variation of cost-plus is **markup pricing**, typically used by wholesalers and retailers. The **markup** is a percentage added onto the purchase cost of the product to cover the channel member's costs and profit. We also can define markup indirectly by noting that the final price of the product is equal to the purchase cost for the company divided by 1 minus the markup percentage, or

$$\text{Price} = \frac{\text{Purchase Cost}}{(1 - \text{Markup})}$$

If, for example, a retailer purchases a shirt for $12 and feels a markup of 40 percent is necessary, the price will be:

$$\text{Price} = \frac{\$12}{1 - 0.40} = \$20$$

Thus, the purchase cost for the retailer is 60 percent of $20 or $12.

If this seems like a naive way of setting prices, remember that wholesalers and retailers often carry tens of thousands of products. They simply do not have the time to analyze the price sensitivity of demand for each product. Therefore, markup pricing has developed as a simple way of deciding how much markup must be added to a product's cost to make it profitable. If the product does not sell at that price, the wholesaler or retailer drops the product. Although it might sell equally well at a higher price, the wholesaler or retailer does not have the resources to analyze all its products and their price sensitivity to find out.

ROI Pricing   Still another variation of cost-plus is return on investment or **ROI pricing**. Instead of setting a predetermined profit, ROI pricing measures the money invested in a product and its costs, and sets a price that gives a profit equal to a predetermined return on the money invested, given a predetermined sales volume. For the return on investment to be reached, the entire planned sales volume must be sold at the planned price.

The method for setting price under an ROI strategy is

$$\text{Price} = \text{AVC} + \frac{\text{TFC}}{\text{PV}} + \frac{(\text{ROI})(\text{I})}{\text{PV}}$$

where AVC = average variable cost, TFC = total fixed cost, PV = planned volume, and I = investment.

Suppose a company has invested $1,000,000 in developing a new portable tape recorder. Variable cost per unit is $20, total fixed costs are $500,000, and the planned volume is 20,000 units. Management has decided an acceptable ROI is 25 percent. The price is

$$\text{Price} = \$20 + \frac{\$500,000}{20,000} + \frac{0.25\,(1,000,000)}{20,000}$$

$$= \$57.50$$

As a method of pricing, an ROI strategy is useful only if planned volume is achieved. For example, the United States auto industry successfully used ROI pricing until the 1970s. In the recessions of the 1970s and faced with increased foreign competition, however, the auto industry fell short of planned volume and consequently did not reach its desired ROI.

Given the cost orientation of this strategy and the assumption that demand is not affected by price, the solution was obvious. Raise prices! In fact, the auto industry has often raised prices in recessions. When no foreign competition existed, customers had to tolerate it. After 1970, however, buyers simply shifted to foreign cars, thus forcing American automobile manufacturers to either abandon this simplistic pricing policy or go out of business.

An ROI pricing strategy is still used in some regulated industries in which the regulatory body defines what is a fair ROI. Again, such a strategy works in these industries because all competitors use this pricing strategy, and customers, therefore, have no alternatives.

Experience Curve Pricing   As we discussed earlier in this chapter, many companies experience decreasing unit costs as sales volume increases. As more units are produced, workers become more experienced and more efficient, automated equipment can be used, and purchasing and distribution economies are realized.[7] Because of this lower cost structure at higher volumes, many companies follow a strategy of pricing low to gain market share and sales volume and to lower costs.

Two critical assumptions accompany this strategy. First, management is assuming that the target market is sufficiently price elastic for a lower price to create the necessary demand. Second, it also is assuming that the higher volume will lower costs enough to make the low price profitable. Although many companies follow experience curve pricing strategies, few actually analyze demand and costs to be certain both of these assumptions are true. In fact many products are price inelastic and a low price will only yield less total revenue.

Even for products that are price elastic, experience curve effects are not automatic. Often, substantially higher sales volume has little or no effect on costs. Therefore, the lower price will only yield lower profits. Companies should be very careful in following this strategy, and management must make a conscious effort to achieve experience curve results.

Break-Even Point Pricing   When introducing a new product, one of the first questions asked is, "Will we get our money back?" That is, "Will we break even?" **Break-even analysis** looks at the costs associated with a particular product and determines the sales volume necessary to recover all costs at a particular price. In essence the **break-even point (BEP)** is where total revenues equal total costs, or

$$\text{Price} \times \text{Quantity} = \text{TFC} + (\text{VC} \times \text{Quantity})$$

where TFC = total fixed costs and VC = variable costs.

If we solve this equation for quantity, the BEP in units is:

$$\text{BEP (units)} = \frac{\text{TFC}}{\text{Price} - \text{VC}}$$

In other words for each unit sold a certain amount of money is left over after variable costs are covered. This formula tells us how many of these units must be sold to cover total fixed costs and break even.

If we look at variable costs as a fraction of the price, then 1 minus that fraction is how much of each sales dollar is left over after variable costs are covered. Dividing this amount into total fixed costs tells us how much total dollar sales must be to break even:

---

[7] Robert D. Buzzell, Bradley T. Gale, and Ralph G.M. Sultan, "Market Share—A Key to Profitability," *Harvard Business Review*, January–February 1975, pp. 97–106.

$$\text{BEP (dollar sales)} = \frac{\text{TFC}}{1 - (\text{VC/P})}$$

where P = price.

Suppose our product is a calculator with a fixed cost of $1,000,000 and a variable cost of $7 per unit. Management is considering selling the product for $15. The break-even point is:

$$\text{BEP (units)} = \frac{\$1,000,000}{\$15 - \$7} = 125,000$$

or

$$\text{BEP (dollar sales)} = \frac{\$1,000,000}{1 - (\$7/\$15)} = \$1,875,000$$

At any sales level above 125,000 units the company would make a profit. This analysis is shown graphically in Figure 19-2.

As it stands, BEP analysis is limited. Similar to all the other cost-based strategies, it does not consider demand. In the preceding example there is no analysis to determine whether or not sales would actually be 125,000 or above at a price of $15. Further, BEP analysis assumes all costs are assignable to the product. What about common costs? Should they be included in this analysis or just ignored?

BEP analysis also assumes fixed costs do not change and variable costs stay the same per unit as quantity increases. However, companies that have experience curve effects actually exhibit decreasing variable costs. As volume increases, fixed cost often moves upward as more money is invested in plant and equipment.

All of the cost-based strategies exhibit the limitation of ignoring demand. However, when combined with demand-based strategies, some can be useful.

Demand-Based Strategies

Demand-based strategies guide pricing decisions with the realization that pricing will affect the quantity demanded. Whether it is a normal product and a higher price leads to lower sales or a prestige product and a higher price often leads to greater sales, price communicates a message to target customers and affects demand. Prestige pricing, odd–even pricing, price lining, and customary pricing are all attempts at demand-based strategies. A more fundamental guide to demand-based strategies is setting prices based on marketing research.

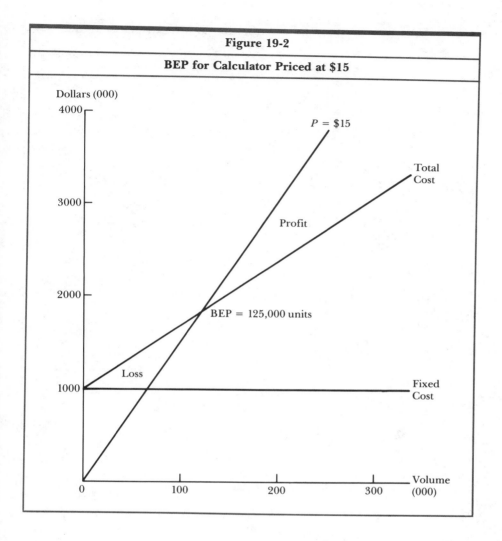

Figure 19-2

BEP for Calculator Priced at $15

Dollars (000)

P = $15

Total Cost

Profit

BEP = 125,000 units

Loss

Fixed Cost

Volume (000)

Before pricing decisions are made, it is valuable to determine how the target market will react. To illustrate, we will take our earlier BEP example. Figure 19-3 provides BEP schedules of five possible prices for our calculator. Notice the steeper slope for the higher prices—more revenue per unit. Because the cost structure is the same, higher prices lead to BEPs (marked by asterisks) at lower sales volumes.

Based on what we learned in Chapter 3, we now conduct marketing research to determine the expected sales level for the calculator at the various prices. These quantities are on line DD′ in Figure 19-3. Notice that the higher prices lead to lower sales volume, but higher profits per unit.

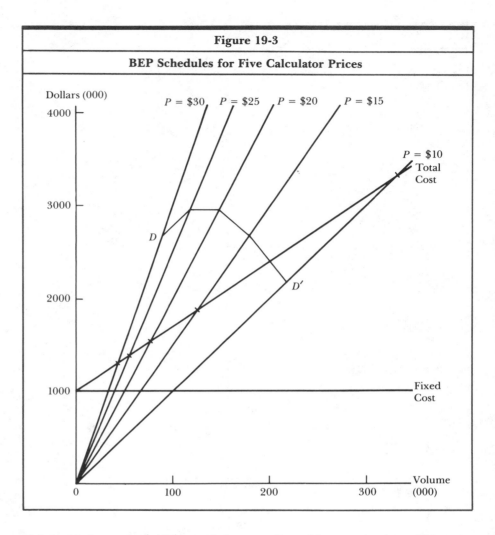

Figure 19-3

BEP Schedules for Five Calculator Prices

Figure 19-4 translates this graph into profit and loss projections. Not only do the prices $25 and $20 offer the greatest profit, but Figure 19-3 also shows that even if sales projections fall far below those determined by marketing research, either of these prices would still yield sales above break even. This gives marketing management a pricing "margin of safety" before a loss would occur.

Therefore, a cost-based strategy of BEP analysis can be very helpful when combined with demand-based research. In fact, any demand-based pricing strategy should use the pricing model at the end of Chapter 18 as a foundation. Costs, market conditions, and demand should all be factors in pricing strategies.

Figure 19-4				
BEP Calculations for Five Calculator Prices				
Price	**Demand**	**Revenue**	**Total Cost**	**Profit/(Loss)**
$30	90,000	$2,700,000	$1,630,000	$1,070,000
25	120,000	3,000,000	1,840,000	1,160,000
20	150,000	3,000,000	2,050,000	950,000
15	180,000	2,700,000	2,120,000	580,000
10	220,000	2,200,000	2,540,000	(340,000)

SPECIFIC PRICING SITUATIONS

There are several situations faced by marketing managers that require special pricing consideration. Because so many companies encounter at least some of these situations, they warrant special discussion.

Product Line Pricing

Companies normally market product lines rather than single products. Pricing decisions must be made on lines as a whole and on specific products as members of that line. In setting product line prices marketing managers must make decisions on the price of the most expensive and least expensive items in the line, how many products to include in the line, and the price differentials between each item in the product line.

Research has shown that consumers more readily remember end prices in a product line and make price/quality judgments about the entire line based on the highest and lowest prices.[8] In fact the lowest-priced product may affect the quantity sold of all products in the line more than any other product.[9] For example, the entire line of Sony tape decks is high priced. The highest priced and the lowest priced Sony are in the upper range of stereo equipment. This fact enhances the Sony image of high-priced, high-quality, prestige stereos. In contrast, the Panasonic line is in the middle of overall stereo prices and enhances its image of good but less expensive equipment.

End price decisions are critical. Too high a price may lead customers to buy more "reasonably" priced products. Too low a price may lead them to question quality. Would anyone look at a Sony tape deck for $25 and not

---

[8] Alfred Oxenfeldt, "Product Line Pricing," *Harvard Business Review*, July–August 1966, pp. 135–43.

[9] Kent B. Monroe, "The Information Content of Prices: A Preliminary Model for Estimating Buyer Response," *Management Science*, April 1971, B519–B532.

MARKETING
Strategy

Bic Versus A.T. Cross

The Bic and the A.T. Cross companies use price versus quality product decisions to guide the development of their marketing strategies. Their products are positioned at opposite ends of the price/quality spectrum, resulting in an entirely different marketing strategy for each.

Marcel L. Bich was born in Italy and lives in Paris where his company, Societe Bic, is headquartered. Bich founded his company in the late 1940s when he purchased a small pen-manufacturing company. He decided to concentrate on the production of the then new and revolutionary ballpoint pen. Bich decided to drop the last letter of his name because he thought a three-letter word was more marketable.

In 1958 Bich acquired the U.S. firm Waterman Pen Company, which was experiencing financial difficulties. The American company was named the Waterman–BIC Pen Company. In 1971 stock in this company, which was renamed BIC PEN CORPORATION, was sold to the public, with Bich retaining 60-percent ownership.

A.T. Cross was founded in 1846 by an English immigrant, Alonzo T. Cross. The company, like Societe Bic, is still closely held. Cross ran his company for 70 years until he sold it to Walter R. Boss in 1916. Boss' two grandsons, Brad and Russell, now run the business and have defined their target market as gift givers. Consistent with this definition, Cross also sells specialty products and leather goods.*

Bic's basic product strategy is to make and market only pens that can be produced cheaply, used for a relatively long time, and then be thrown away. Bich believes that even disposable products will not sell well unless the quality is high. "My personal marketing strategy," Bich says, "has been never to promote a product until it is equivalent in quality to the Number One product on the market. I continue to finance development of the product until I know that we can outdo the competition."†

question its quality? Further, the $25 item may cause customers to wonder if Sony was "cheapening" its entire line. Too low or too high an end price may hurt sales of the entire line.

Product line pricing decisions are influenced by the number of products in the line. The company should position each product to fulfill a

Bic pens come in a wide variety of styles and colors, but Bich is not an innovator. Instead, he concentrates on improving a product until he knows it can be marketed at a very low price.

A.T. Cross, on the other hand, markets only top of the line pens. The company benefited greatly from a major product strategy mistake of a competitor, The Parker Pen Company. After World War II, Parker, which had produced the prestigious Parker 51, decided to produce a cheaper pen. Because of the change in Parker's strategy, Cross was able to gain leadership in the high-priced pen market.

Bic zeroed in on the mass market, whereas Cross aimed at the gift market. Bic pens are the lowest priced available, beginning at 29 cents. A.T. Cross pens sell for about 20 dollars, although some cost a thousand dollars or more, depending on the metal case. Bic is a convenience product and is sold by drug, food, convenience, and mass merchandisers. Cross, on the other hand, is sold mainly in jewelry and department stores.

Bic is known for innovative promotion and makes extensive use of television. Bic sees itself as a mass marketer. (It sells over 3,000,000 pens a day in the U.S. alone). Bic marketing managers are very flexible and closely watch the impact of their promotion. If the product is moving well, they spend more. Conversely, if a product's sales are sluggish, promotion is cut back.

Cross spends only a small fraction of the amount spent on promotion by Bic. Cross began a modest once-a-week advertising campaign in the *Wall Street Journal* in the 1950s, aiming its ads at the executive market. It also advertises in *National Geographic, National Observer, The New Yorker,* and other publications that deliver a select affluent market.

The lifetime warranty offered by Cross is an important reason behind the product's success. Cross will repair any pen that malfunctions with no questions asked and no service charge. All the owner must do is return the pen to the factory.

Bic and Cross have proven that two companies can be equally successful in the same market by selecting different target markets and developing a marketing strategy catering to their particular targets.

* Martin Love, "Two Bosses, Two Crosses," *Forbes,* December 5, 1983, p. 66.
† *Business Week,* February 28, 1977, p. 61.

unique need in the line's market, so that, as such, it reaches a particular target market. Again, each more expensive item in Sony's product line may add special features that will appeal to different customers until the "delux," highest-priced item is reached. This item is aimed at the prestige-conscious customer.

Once the end prices and the number of products in the line are set, the price differentials between each product in the line must be determined. When noticeable differences exist between specific products in a line, the customer is confused if there is not also a noticeable difference in price. For example, if a basic tape deck and one with automatic shut-off, pause, and Dolby recording features are similarly priced, the customer may decide there actually is little difference between them (perhaps the item with more features is of lower quality). Thus, a noticeably different price reinforces the perception that the products are in fact different.

In product line pricing consumers are more affected by relative price differences than absolute differences.[10] For example, an extra $1,000 for a $9,000 Chevrolet automobile may seem like a big price change, but the same absolute extra price ($1,000) may not seem like much on a $45,000 Mercedes-Benz. The reason is that $1,000 is a lesser amount relative to $45,000 than it is relative to $9,000.[11]

Because of this phenomenon, different products in a product line should have the same relative price differences. Figure 19-5 provides an example. There are five models in this tape deck line. Each succeeding model has more desirable features than the preceding model. Marketing research determined the end prices of $135.00 and $279.94 to be consistent with the image marketing management wanted the line to present. The middle product prices of $162.00, $194.40, and $233.28 were determined by setting a constant relative price change (20 percent) from one model to the next. Thus, the three product line pricing decisions are resolved: end prices (consistent with the product line's image); number of items in the line; and the price of each (consistent with each specific product's image).

Geographic Pricing

Does a retailer in Florida pay the same price as a retailer in Ohio for merchandise produced in Chicago? Under some pricing policies the answer is yes, but the reasoning behind such a practice is not as unfair as it first seems.

Transportation costs are one of the largest costs for firms that market products over a wide geographic area. Efforts to simplify the enormous work of maintaining records of multiple freight rates and "averaging out" the cost of transportation have resulted in various geographic pricing systems.

---

[10] Kent B. Monroe, *Pricing: Making Profitable Decisions* (New York: McGraw-Hill, 1979), pp. 154–55.

[11] John T. Mentzer and Kent B. Monroe, "Some Common Misconceptions About Pricing," *Working Paper*, Virginia Polytechnic Institute, 1983.

Figure 19-5	
Tape Deck Product Line Prices	
Model	**Price**
A	$135.00
B	162.00
C	194.40
D	233.28
E	279.94

F.O.B. Origin Pricing   **Free-on-board origin pricing** *means that the pur-chaser pays all shipping costs, excluding loading charges.* Producers may desig-nate their factory as the origin, wholesalers may define it as their ware-house, and retailers as their store. P.O.E., or **port-of-entry pricing**, is a variant of F.O.B. often used by import firms. In this case the origin is the point where the shipment enters this country.

With F.O.B. origin pricing the transfer of title occurs when the goods are loaded onto the transporting vehicle. The buyer therefore assumes the risks of damage and loss during transit. Many marketers consider F.O.B. origin pricing the only fair method of allocating freight charges, because each purchaser picks up the entire tab for its shipment. The F.O.B. origin method may, however, limit the producer's or supplier's market: Buyers will tend to shop closer to home to save money on freight charges. If local shopping limits the market too much, a company may use one of several geographic pricing policies in which the seller absorbs some of the buyer's transportation cost.

F.O.B. Destination Pricing   If the seller is anxious to expand its geo-graphic market, **free-on-board destination pricing** may be used. Under this method the title to the goods is transferred at the buyer's destination. Thus, *the seller pays all transportation costs.* The price is the same to all cus-tomers anywhere in the country. This is also called **uniform delivered pricing**.

Zone Delivered Pricing   Under **zone delivered pricing** *the market is di-vided into geographic zones and all customers in any one zone are charged the same price.* The principal drawback of zone delivered systems is that some buyers actually pay less than the full cost of the shipments (**freight absorption** by the seller), whereas others pay for **phantom freight** (that portion of the shipping charges allocable to the distance the goods never traveled). Freight absorption and phantom freight are actually components of all geographic pricing systems, with the exception of F.O.B. pricing.

Basing-Point Pricing   *Sellers using* **basing-point pricing** *systems designate particular cities as the point from which all shipping charges are calculated.* Generally, entire industries, rather than individual sellers, adopt single or multiple basing-points to ease price competition over a wide market area.

Industries that use basing-point systems tend to have high freight costs and highly standardized products (such as chemicals, sugar, or cement). The classic example of this policy is provided by the steel industry. At one time Pittsburgh was the basing point for all transportation charges. It was chosen simply because, for many years, it was the nation's only steel center. Eventually, steel plants were established in other cities, and the industry was forced to adopt multiple basing points in response to customer dissatisfaction. No matter where the steel is produced, freight is charged from the basing point nearest the customer. If a customer in New Orleans orders steel, any manufacturer—regardless of its location—will charge freight from Birmingham, Alabama, the nearest basing point. In this manner all steel manufacturers can compete anywhere in the United States, without freight becoming a factor.

Negotiated Pricing

In our complex economy many marketing transactions involve products manufactured to the buyer's specifications. In these cases a policy of negotiated pricing is often followed.

For example, consider a major real-estate transaction involving a plant site near an interstate highway. The seller, usually acting through a real-estate broker, will set an asking price and specify the terms of sale. In all likelihood the prospective purchaser will submit a counter offer that differs in one or more important ways from the seller's offer. Some of the areas for negotiation may be (1) the price itself, (2) the down payment, (3) the length of the mortgage, (4) the interest rate, (5) zoning changes, and (6) the prorating of taxes.

Generally, negotiated pricing is much more important in marketing to industrial users and the government than to individuals. Most ultimate consumers come into contact with negotiated pricing only when they purchase very expensive products such as automobiles, houses, major appliances, or furniture. In negotiated pricing the final price and terms of sale are largely determined by the negotiating abilities of the buyer and seller.

Competitive Bidding

In large industrial marketing purchases and in many government purchases sellers are often asked to submit bids that give detailed product and service specifications at a stated price. The buyer then selects the bid that best satisfies its needs at the lowest price.

Competitive bidding is a challenging area of pricing in which the needs of the customer and the possible actions of the competition must be assessed. Too high a bid will mean losing the sale to the competition. Too low a bid may mean receiving the sale but making no profit.

Many companies use the expected profit model to aid in selecting a bid. The **expected profit model** *considers the cost of filling an order, various possible bid prices, and the probability of receiving the order at each price.* Figure 19-6 provides an example for a manufacturer of heavy machinery bidding on a U.S. Arsenal contract for a stamping machine.

According to the expected profit model example, the best bid is $55,000. This does not mean the company will win this particular contract or that $55,000 is the most money that could be made if the contract were assured. It means that in the long run this is the most profitable bid—one that compromises between profits and the probability of receiving the contract.

The difficult part of the expected profit model is estimating the probabilities. These estimates are often merely educated guesses, but they depend largely on the number of competitors, the likely bids of each competi-

			Figure 19-6		
Expected Profits for Stamping Machine Bids				
Bid (B)	Cost (C)	Profit (B − C)	Probability of Contract (P)	Expected Profit P(B − C)
$30,000	$45,000	$−15,000	1.00	$−15,000
35,000	45,000	−10,000	0.90	−9,000
40,000	45,000	−5,000	0.80	−4,000
45,000	45,000	-0-	0.65	-0-
50,000	45,000	5,000	0.55	2,750
55,000	45,000	10,000	0.40	4,000
60,000	45,000	15,000	0.25	3,750
65,000	45,000	20,000	0.10	2,000
70,000	45,000	25,000	0.00	-0-

tor (often determined by past bidding performance), and the quality of competitive products.[12]

PRICE CHANGES

Although much of the last two chapters has been devoted to setting prices, marketing managers often face the problem of raising or lowering established product prices. A company may *lower prices* to increase sales if it has excess productive capacity. It may also lower prices to meet price competition or to gain market share through price competition. For example, in recent years lower production costs and intensive price competition have brought about drastic price cuts in home computers.[13]

Prices may be *raised* because demand for the product is so large that the company cannot produce enough. Inflation—the continuing rise in the costs of producing a product—also creates a need to raise prices. Especially in inflationary price rises, the marketer must be careful to inform customers that its profits have not increased, that it is merely passing on its cost increases.

Marketers must be very careful in making any price change. Customers

---

[12] Franz Edelman, "Art and Science of Competitive Bidding," *Harvard Business Review*, July–August 1965, pp. 53–66; and Murphy A. Sewall, "A Decision Calculus Model for Contract Bidding," *Journal of Marketing*, October 1976, pp. 92–98.

[13] Laura Landro and James A. White, "Computer Firms Push Prices Down, Try to Improve Marketing Tactics," *Wall Street Journal*, April 29, 1983, p. 35.

may interpret a price rise or fall in a variety of ways.[14] A price drop may be interpreted as a signal that the company is lowering quality, offering a bargain, discontinuing the product, in financial trouble, or planning to reduce the price more later.[15] Price rises may be interpreted as the result of company efforts to improve quality, to price gouge, or to benefit from the great demand for an item, so buy now before it is out of stock. Whatever the interpretation, price changes are critical times in a product's marketing strategy and must be reinforced with considerable supportive communication between the company and its target markets.

SUMMARY

- A sales-based pricing objective assumes greater sales and market share will lead to lower unit costs and more market control. This is not always true.
- Companies following a sales-based objective typically use penetration pricing.
- Survival is a goal of all organizations. When survival is threatened, companies may cut prices in the short run to turn inventory fast, keep operating at or near capacity, or keep customers interested.
- A return on investment (ROI) pricing objective sets the price so that a predetermined return on investment is reached.
- Skimming pricing is used to recover cash from product development quickly. It usually follows a cash-flow objective.
- Both ROI and cash-flow objectives ignore target market demand.
- Some companies have a competitive objective of merely staying where they are relative to the competition.
- A profit objective recognizes the relationships between price, volume, and costs.
- Within the guidelines of objectives, price policy sets the general approach for specific product prices. Price policy can be defined in terms of price level and flexibility.
- Pricing strategies are competition based, cost based, or demand based.

---

[14] Kent B. Monroe, "Buyers' Subjective Perceptions of Price," *Journal of Marketing Research*, February 1973, pp. 70–80.

[15] Alfred R. Oxenfeldt, *Pricing for Marketing Executives* (San Francisco: Wadsworth, 1961), p. 28.

- Some companies follow a below-the-competition pricing strategy by cutting costs and services.
- Prestige companies or products are often marketed with an above-the-competition pricing policy.
- A price follower strategy can be dangerous if the price leader is not similar to the follower.
- Price leaders usually exist in oligopolistic industries to allow orderly price changes.
- Although easy to compute, cost-plus pricing assumes all units produced can be sold regardless of price.
- Due to the large number of prices they need to set, many wholesalers and retailers add a standard markup to costs to determine price. Although a simplistic pricing strategy, many channel members have too many products to use anything more sophisticated.
- Experience curve pricing assumes lower prices will lead to substantially higher sales which, in turn, will lower unit costs. This is not true for all products.
- Break-even point analysis looks at the costs associated with marketing a product to determine the sales volume at which total revenue equals total cost (the break-even point).
- Demand-based strategies use costs, marketing research information on demand, and knowledge of market conditions to set prices.
- Critical product line pricing decisions are the prices of the highest- and lowest-priced products in the line and the price differentials between each product in the line.
- With F.O.B. origin pricing the title to the goods is transferred at the seller's location. Therefore, the buyer pays all shipping charges.
- With F.O.B. destination pricing the title is transferred at the buyer's location. Thus, the seller pays all shipping charges.
- Under zone delivered pricing all customers in a given zone are charged one delivered price.
- Basing-point pricing charges customers freight from the nearest designated city (basing point), regardless of where the shipment actually originated.
- Negotiated prices are largely determined by the negotiating abilities of the buyer and the seller.
- Competitive bidding involves submitting detailed product and service specifications at a stated price.
- The expected profit model of competitive bidding is a compromise between profits and the probability of receiving the contract.
- Price changes are critical periods in a product's strategy and require special attention to communication between the company and its target markets.

DISCUSSION QUESTIONS

1. Explain penetration pricing and its relation to a sales-based objective. Explain skimming pricing and its relation to a cash-flow objective. When is each appropriate?
2. What is a one-price policy? What are its advantages?
3. Under what circumstances is it reasonable to price below the competition? Above the competition?
4. What is the rationale behind a price leader strategy? Price follower? Are they reasonable strategies?
5. Explain:
   - (a) Cost-plus pricing
   - (b) Markup pricing
   - (c) ROI pricing
   - (d) Experience curve pricing
   - (e) BEP pricing
6. How do demand-based pricing strategies differ from competition-based and cost-based strategies?
7. What are the critical decisions in product line pricing? How are they resolved?
8. Explain:
   - (a) F.O.B. origin pricing
   - (b) F.O.B. destination pricing
   - (c) Zone delivered pricing
   - (d) Basing-point pricing
9. Under what conditions might a price be negotiated?
10. Describe competitive bidding and the expected profit model.
11. What might be some customer reactions to a price decrease? A price increase?

APPLICATION EXERCISES

1. (a) As the new pricing manager for a small manufacturing concern, your first task is to set the price on a new product whose expected sales will be 10,000 units, total variable costs will be $15,000, and total fixed costs will be $25,000. Your boss (who did not read this chapter!) tells you she expects a profit of $20,000 and wants you to use cost-plus pricing. What is the selling price? What arguments would you give against using cost-plus?

   (b) Your boss now reminds you that $25,000 was invested in developing this product and the company expects a 30-percent ROI. Now what is the price? Again, what problems do you find with this method?

2. You go into a store and the retailer tells you a new suit costs $125, but the markup was 35 percent. What did the retailer pay for the suit?
3. You still work for the company in Exercise 1. Another new product is being introduced with fixed costs of $100,000 and variable costs of $11 per unit. Marketing research has shown the following relationship between price and expected sales:

Price	Expected Sales (Units)
$12	90,000
14	70,000
16	40,000
18	20,000
20	10,000

Prepare a BEP chart and table. What price would you recommend? Why?

CASE 19
IBM Makes Competitors Blue[16]

IBM, long nicknamed "Big Blue" by customers, is certainly making its competitors blue with anxiety. Throughout the 1960s and early 1970s IBM introduced new products at a leisurely pace. Deliveries took up to a year, and IBM made just enough computers to meet demand throughout the product life cycle. It leased computers to customers at 30-percent pretax profit margins and never cut prices until the machines were obsolete.

This created considerable opportunity for "plug compatible" competitors that made cheaper versions of equipment that worked with IBM systems. Giving lower prices and faster delivery, often of more technically advanced products, these competitors lowered IBM's market share from 60 percent in 1967 to 40 percent in 1980.

Since 1977, however, IBM has initiated a drive to once again be the price leader in the computer industry. Big Blue has spent over $10 billion on manufacturing plant and equipment to make it the lowest cost producer in the industry.

This strategy was adopted somewhat inadvertently in 1977 when IBM delayed introduction of its newest line of computers and was forced to extend the life cycle of its existing line by lowering prices. When prices on the IBM 370 were cut by one-third, demand increased more than corporate planners had imagined possible.

Today, following a new price-competitive strategy, IBM rapidly introduces technologically improved models to keep ahead of the plug compatibles. By the time

---

[16] Peter D. Petre, "Meet the Lean, Mean New IBM," *Fortune,* June 13, 1983, pp. 68–71, 74, 78, 82.

competition has had time to react, IBM cuts the prices on its older models. In 1981 IBM introduced the 3081 at an initial price of $4 million. However, by the time Amdahl (a major plug compatible manufacturer) could introduce a competitive product, the 3081 price had been cut $1 million! As a direct result Amdahl suffered its first operating loss in its seven-year history.

An additional tactic IBM now uses is offering special discounts to large customers. Justified on the basis of savings in selling costs, IBM offers large discounts on sizeable orders and "volume procurement amendments," which are additional discounts offered if a certain number of units is purchased by a set date. For example, AT&T received a $1-million-per-unit discount by purchasing 50 units of the 3081. Customers that buy a specific number of IBM 3380 disk drives in a two-year period even receive a discount on units they have already bought.

The effect of this aggressive pricing strategy has been to increase market share and profits for IBM and drive several of its weaker competitors out of the market.

Will the strategy work in the long run, or will it undermine Big Blue's profitability? Only time will tell.

Discussion Questions

1. What type of pricing strategy is IBM following? What was its strategy before 1977?
2. Do you think IBM should follow this price-cutting policy or stick to its old high-price approach? Why?
3. What form of discount is the "volume procurement amendment"?

P A R T

SEVEN

Other Marketing
Considerations

20 International Marketing

STUDY OBJECTIVES

After studying this chapter, you should be able to

1. Outline the main points in the theory of comparative advantage and describe U.S. comparative advantages and disadvantages.
2. Discuss the primary U.S. imports and exports.
3. Explain the environmental forces impacting on international marketing.
4. Discuss each international marketing controllable variable and the possible decisions under each.
5. Discuss the alternatives available for entering a foreign market.
6. Describe multinationalism and the various degrees of multinationalism.

To a significant degree, the European discovery of the New World was brought about through innovative international marketing practices. Spain funded Columbus' voyage of discovery in hopes of avoiding two of the more expensive marketing practices of the day—the costly and time-consuming overland transportation of spices and silk from the East and the "middleman's cut" demanded by the Arab traders who moved the goods through the Middle East to Europe. To the extent that Columbus did not find another route to the Far East, Queen Isabella's marketing venture was a failure. Obviously, however, the discovery of the New World provided a tremendous opportunity for expanded international trade. Although they had originally been motivated by the need for a sea route to the Far East, later European voyages of exploration were spurred by desires to exploit the gold and silver rumored to abound in the New World. Early explorers did not find gold in what is now the United States, but they almost immediately recognized the enormous potential of the new land as a source of raw materials. Once actual colonization was initiated, settlers began to export raw materials and agricultural products to Europe in exchange for manufactured products.

Gradually, as the United States developed a more industrialized economy, manufactured goods were exported along with the raw materials and food products. Although much of the world still relies on the United States for vast quantities of raw materials and agricultural products, the majority of our exports today consist of manufactured and semimanufactured products, as can be seen in Figure 20-1. Figure 20-2 compares total world exports and imports with those of the United States during selected years. In 1982, for example, the United States bought almost 13 percent of the world's exports. By itself, this figure may not seem particularly impressive. However, when we realize that the world population in 1981 was approximately 4.65 billion (compared to the U.S. population of 232 million), elementary mathematics leads us to the inevitable conclusion that 5 percent of the world population was buying nearly 13 percent of the world's exports. Moreover, although the percentage of world exports consumed by the United States is steadily growing, the percentage of U.S. products purchased by the rest of the world is rather steadily diminishing. Even though export revenues for the United States are a smaller percentage of the gross national product than they are for a number of other nations (including England, West Germany, and Japan) to whom international trade is relatively more important, marketers cannot ignore the profits to be derived from, say, the 9.2 billion dollars worth of computers or the over 87 billion dollars worth of machinery and transport equipment exported from this country in 1982.

Most developed companies, including the United States, are involved in international marketing. **International marketing** can be defined quite simply as *marketing across national boundaries.*[1] In this chapter we will examine this massive aspect of world trade: marketing to target markets in other countries.

THEORY OF COMPARATIVE ADVANTAGE

International trade is based on the theory of **comparative advantage** (or comparative cost). Essentially, the theory holds that *a nation should export those items it produces most efficiently (at the lowest cost) and import those it produces least efficiently (at the highest cost).* With some exceptions, most international trade follows this pattern. In the United States, for example, we are more efficient in the production of such goods as aircraft, agricultural machinery, and food stuffs (principally grain), than in production of goods such as motorcycles, small cars, and sewing machines, which we import. Although we can and do sometimes produce such items efficiently, our efficiency—and therefore our comparative advantage—is generally greater in the production of the products we export.

U.S. Comparative Advantages

Three characteristics of our economy explain the nature of the products we export in large quantities—advanced technology, a large supply of fertile agricultural land in the temperate zone, and large domestic markets.

Because of our advanced technology, we are able to export great amounts of industrial equipment, chemicals, aircraft, computers, and other products that require considerable engineering expertise. Over 27 percent of our labor force is engaged in manufacturing. However, because the superiority of American know-how is now being threatened by the rapidly expanding technologies of such countries as Japan and West Germany, advanced technology is the most volatile of our three comparative advantages.

Approximately 17 percent of the total U.S. land area is cropland. This land, combined with lands used for pasture and grazing, totals 59 percent of our land area devoted to farming and ranching. Yet less than 6 percent of the U.S. labor force works in agriculture. Our large acreage of productive farmland, together with our advanced farm technology, helps to explain our significant exports of grains and foodstuffs. (Approximately 38 percent of the cropland is devoted to corn and wheat, our largest agricultural exports.)

---

[1] Vern Terpstra, *International Marketing* (Hinsdale, IL: Dryden Press, 1978), p. 5.

Profile

Berry Gordy
(b. 1930)

Twenty-five years ago a prolific songwriter founded and became President of the Motown Record Corporation in Detroit, Michigan. Today Berry Gordy is Chairman of Motown Industries, a complete entertainment complex, recognized as the nation's "largest black-owned business corporation." The *New York Times* has described him as "the most influential black man in American pop-culture."

With talent from Detroit's inner city Gordy established the "Motown Sound," and within the past twenty-five years this music has become universally accepted as "the sound of young America."

The artists he discovered and developed have made musical history. Among them are Smokey Robinson and The Miracles (whose "Shop Around" brought Motown its first gold record), Stevie Wonder, Martha Reeves and the Vandellas, Diana Ross, The Supremes, The Temptations, Marvin Gaye, The Four Tops, Gladys Knight and the Pips, The Jackson Five, The Commodores, Rick James, High Inergy, and many, many others.

Significantly, Berry Gordy built Motown by building others. He stimulated the artistic talent of writers, producers, and corporate executives. One measure of his success is that during Motown's first decade roughly 75 percent of some 600 records released by the company landed on the national sales

Because our domestic market is so large, we can sometimes, through mass production, reduce per-unit costs enough to give us an advantage over other nations, even though we may not have a significant technological advantage for such products. Significantly, 26 percent of our gross national product is derived from manufacturing. Canada, for example, also has a highly advanced technology. However, because its population is only slightly more than 10 percent of our own, trade agreements have been formulated whereby American producers operating in Canada manufacture many products for both nations. American automakers, for example, operate plants in Canada which produce automobiles both for the Cana-

charts, a staggering figure compared to an industry-wide average of 2 to 5 percent.

While maintaining its excellence in the recording field, Motown, under Berry Gordy's personal guidance, expanded into other areas of the entertainment industry. Now based in Hollywood, Motown Industries includes music publishing companies; Motown Record Corporation, with labels such as Motown, Tamla, Gordy, Soul, and Black Forum; and Motown Productions, the television and movie arm of the complex.

Gordy's first venture into the motion picture field was *Lady Sings the Blues,* starring Diana Ross. A spectacular critical and box-office success, the movie earned five Academy Award nominations. Personally involved in the planning, production and promotion of the film, Berry Gordy turned director for the company's next movie project, *Mahogany.*

Other movies have followed, as well as TV specials and Motown-backed Broadway stage productions. Motown's involvement in all aspects of the entertainment industry is significant, not only because of the corporate profits gained, but also because of its leadership in providing career opportunities and valuable work experience for minority professionals. The motion pictures produced and/or directed by Berry Gordy and Motown have provided more employment for minorities than any other production organization in film history.

Berry Gordy's sense of social responsibility also is reflected in the creation of the Gordy Foundation, which administers the Lucy Gordy Wakefield Scholarship Fund and through which significant donations are made to selected human relations and charitable causes.

Berry Gordy once summed up his business philosophy in the following piece of advice: "Make your success work to help others achieve their measure of success, and hope they, in turn, will do likewise. This is the kind of chain reaction that is music to my ears."

dian market and for shipment to the United States, because there are no independent Canadian automobile manufacturers.

These three advantages, however, are clearly not static. As previously noted, other countries are making rapid technological gains. Some, in fact, already have technologies superior to our own in some respects. Although technology may permit the eventual agricultural use of 12 percent of our land area currently considered desert or swampland, we must expect increases in the percentage of land devoted to urban areas (currently approximately 7 percent), thereby diminishing the amount of land that can be devoted to agriculture. More importantly, as developing nations increase

Figure 20-1

U.S. Exports and Imports for Selected Years

GEOGRAPHIC AREAS

Exports (Millions of $)

	1970	1975	1982
Developed Countries			
Canada	9,079	21,744	33,720
Western Europe	14,463	29,945	60,054
Japan	4,652	9,563	20,966
Developing Countries			
20 American Republics	5,695	15,655	30,086
Other Western Hemisphere	837	1,444	3,506
Near East Asia	1,346	8,263	15,950
East and South Asia	4,030	10,095	24,962
Africa	1,580	4,949	10,271
Oceania	1,189	2,340	5,700
Communist Areas	354	3,092	3,610
Total	43,225	107,090	208,825

Imports (Millions of $)

	1970	1975	1982
Developed Countries			
Canada	11,092	22,151	46,477
Western Europe	11,169	20,892	52,346
Japan	5,875	11,425	37,744
Developing Countries			
20 American Republics	4,779	11,847	32,513
Other Western Hemisphere	1,057	4,210	5,477
Near East Asia	348	5,401	11,812
East and South Asia	3,397	10,267	33,328
Africa	1,113	8,299	17,770
Oceania	871	1,508	3,131
Communist Areas	227	891	1,067
Total	39,928	96,891	241,665

SOURCE: U.S. Department of Commerce, Bureau of the Census, *Statistical Abstract of the United States, 1984,* pp. 834–41.

SELECTED MERCHANDISE

Exports (Millions of $)

	1970	1975	1982
Food and Live Animals	4,356	15,484	23,950
Grains and Preparations	2,596	11,642	14,747
Wheat	1,112	5,293	6,869
Corn	824	4,448	5,683
Beverages and Tobacco	702	1,308	3,026
Crude Inedible Materials (non-fuel)	4,605	9,784	19,248
Mineral Fuels	1,595	4,470	12,729
Animal and Vegetable Oils	493	944	1,541
Chemicals	3,826	8,691	19,890
Machinery and Transport Equipment	17,882	45,668	87,148
Electronic Computers	1,236	2,228	9,159
Electrical Apparatus	119	359	673
Transport Equipment	6,197	16,452	26,668
Road Motor Vehicles and Parts	3,245	9,290	12,751
Aircraft, Parts and Accessories	2,656	6,136	11,775

Imports (Millions of $)

	1970	1975	1982
Food and Live Animals	5,375	8,503	14,453
Meat	1,014	1,141	2,075
Fish	794	1,356	3,143
Coffee	1,160	1,561	2,730
Beverages and Tobacco	855	1,419	3,364
Crude Inedible Materials (non-fuel)	3,307	5,566	8,589
Mineral Fuels	3,075	26,476	65,409
Chemicals	1,450	3,696	9,493
Machinery and Transport Equipment	11,172	23,457	73,320
Electrical Apparatus	224	899	4,524
Automobiles and Parts	5,068	9,921	29,218
Other Manufactured Goods	13,285	23,927	61,209
Paper	1,087	1,673	3,848
Metals	4,508	8,944	19,227
Textiles & Clothing	2,404	3,781	10,972
Footwear	629	1,275	3,437

			Figure 20-2			
			U.S. Share of World Trade: Selected Years			
			(millions of dollars)			
Year	Total World Exports	U.S. Exports	Percentage of Total	Total World Imports	U.S. Imports	Percentage of Total
1982	1,839,140	207,158	11.26	1,914,490	243,952	12.74
1980	1,990,000	216,668	10.89	2,054,000	244,871	11.92
1975	874,000	106,561	12.19	902,000	96,573	10.71
1970	314,000	42,590	13.56	329,000	39,952	12.14
1965	187,000	27,178	14.53	197,000	21,427	10.88

SOURCE: *Statistical Abstract of the United States, 1984*, pp. 838, 840, 879.

their literacy and technological abilities, our economies of scale (mass production, for example) may become less advantageous.

U.S. Comparative Disadvantages

For some kinds of goods domestic production is sufficiently expensive or limited that it is more efficient to import them. What we import is determined mainly by three comparative disadvantages—high wage rates, shortages of several basic products, and limited land in the tropical zone.

The high wage rates prevailing in the United States help to explain why we import such products as small automobiles, textiles, watches, and fine china. It should be noted, however, that "official" statistical comparisons of wage rates in the United States with those of other developed nations may be somewhat exaggerated. European nations and Canada, for example, generally provide more fringe benefits—longer paid vacations, superior sick benefits, and larger unemployment compensation—therefore incurring more indirect labor costs. Wage rates, of course, are directly related to the gross national product and indirectly related to the standard of living. Figure 20-3 compares the average individual gross national products per capita of selected nations throughout the world. Note that the United States no longer has the highest gross national product per capita.

Shortages of some products (or absolute cost disadvantages in production) are the basic reason we import large quantities of petroleum and some types of minerals. In some cases—and this applies at least partially to oil—it has been less expensive to import raw materials, even though we had the facilities to extract them domestically. It has been estimated that in 1984, for example, the United States imported at least 80 percent of the eight basic raw materials (aluminum, bauxite, coal, copper, crude oil, iron ore, tin, and zinc). Naturally, as developing nations enhance their own manu-

Figure 20-3

Gross National Product, Per Capita, for Selected Countries: 1980

Country	GNP Per Capita (dollars)
Switzerland	16,210
Sweden	13,032
France	10,709
United States	10,408
Austria	9,396
Canada	9,189
United Kingdom	7,210
Italy	5,855
Spain	5,276
Argentina	3,871
Yugoslavia	2,974
Venezuela	2,830
Mexico	1,901
Brazil	1,846
Turkey	1,546
Colombia	1,170
Thailand	592
Sri Lanka	250
India	208
Zaire	205

SOURCE: *Statistical Abstract of the United States, 1984*, p. 865.

facturing capabilities, the price of raw materials they export is likely to increase, because they will come to need these materials.

Finally, the fact that our tropical land is quite limited makes it necessary for us to import items such as rubber, sugar, and tropical fruit.

U.S. IMPORTS AND EXPORTS

Most nations have some flow of goods into the country (imports) and out of the country (exports). The ratio of imports to exports is called the **balance of trade**. If a country exports more than it imports, balance of trade is said to be positive—it is a net exporter. If imports exceed exports, balance of trade is negative (a net importer). A negative balance of trade means money flows out of the country in the form of payments for imports. Therefore, countries want a positive, or at least neutral, balance of trade.

For the past decade the United States has experienced a negative balance of trade. There are many reasons for this deficit, primarily:

1. Continued government spending to maintain a standing military force in foreign countries.
2. Vast capital investments made by U.S.-based corporations in foreign countries, particularly those located in Western Europe.
3. Price rises instituted by the Organization of Petroleum Exporting Countries (OPEC).
4. Expanded competition from foreign countries exporting to the U.S.

Why Import?

The United States imports goods for several reasons, most of them directly or indirectly related to the concept of comparative advantage:

1. *We lack the type of climate required to produce some products.* Coffee, bananas, cocoa beans, rubber trees, and cashew nuts do not grow well or cannot be grown in large enough quantities anywhere in the 50 states.
2. *Our cost advantage for certain products is marginal or nonexistent.* As other industrialized nations have developed their technologies, we have increasingly found it more advantageous to import large volumes of small cars, motorcycles, television sets, steel, textiles, tape recorders, musical instruments, and other manufactured goods, because these products can be sold at competitive prices in our domestic market. Moreover, as large agribusiness corporations have gained control over much of our agriculture, increasing amounts of foodstuffs have been imported. Up to 70 percent of the cost of growing fruits and vegetables goes to labor. Prior to 1975, for example, the Del Monte corporation paid American farmers 23 cents per pound for white asparagus. By switching its asparagus operation from California to Mexico, the company was able to buy the crop at only 10 cents per pound.
3. *The domestic supply of some minerals, fuels, and raw materials is insufficient.* We import vast quantities of petroleum products, metal ore, and chemicals, because our domestic supplies are inadequate to meet our needs, or as previously noted, because the domestic supply is too expensive.
4. *Some foreign nations have special production skills that make for higher quality.* Although "quality" is often measurable only subjectively, many consumers prefer imported beer, whiskey, cheese, watches, fancy goods, and automobiles. "Old country" production techniques also give some foreign-made products more status than domestic goods. Porsche and Rolls Royce automobiles, French wines, and Irish linen are prime examples of such products.

5. *Consumers want items that are unique.* A wide variety of products are imported to satisfy the consumer's desire to have something "different" from domestically made goods. This is particularly true for luxury items such as antiques, rugs, paintings, or jewelry, for which individual tastes and aesthetic preferences are the main criteria for buying. It is also evident in more ordinary items—such as Mexican pottery, Italian Amaretto liqueur, or Indian paisley bedspreads.

What Do We Import?

Figure 20-1 lists U.S. imports of principal commodities and selected merchandise for various years. Note that the dollar amounts spent for finished and semifinished goods (a total of over $134.5 billion) in 1982 is over two times as great as that spent for mineral fuels ($65.4 billion). The bulk of our remaining imports for that year consisted mainly of crude nonfuel materials and chemicals, meat, fish, and coffee.

From Whom Do We Import?

Figure 20-4 shows the percentages of U.S. imports from various areas of the world for 1982. Most of our imports come from highly developed nations, principally Canada, the countries of Western Europe, and Japan. Collectively, these countries accounted for more than 50 percent of our imports in 1982. The great majority of these imports were nonagricultural products. More specifically, in descending order of the dollar value of the imports, the eight countries from which the United States imported the largest amounts in 1982 were Canada, Japan, Mexico, the United Kingdom, West Germany, China (Taiwan), Saudi Arabia, and Nigeria.

Food products, minerals, and raw materials are imported in great quantities from Latin America. Noncontinental Asian countries other than Japan (chiefly Taiwan) are important sources of certain food products, crude materials, manufactured goods, metals, machinery, and clothing. Other major sources of imports are Africa (mainly food products, crude materials, and minerals); the Middle East (mostly petroleum products); and Australia and New Zealand (chiefly food products and minerals).

For long-standing political reasons we import very little from communist areas in Europe, even though some of these nations are well advanced technologically. Our imports from Southern Asia are also small. Almost at a standstill for 30 years after World War II, trade with the People's Republic of China has been enhanced since that country's entry into the United Nations and its reestablishment of political relations with the United States.

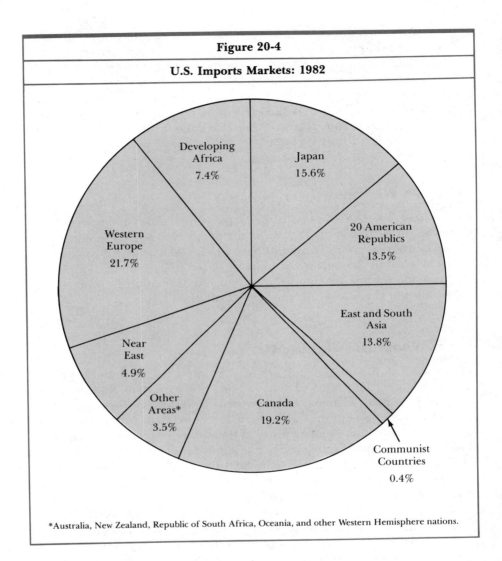

Figure 20-4

U.S. Imports Markets: 1982

Developing Africa 7.4%

Japan 15.6%

20 American Republics 13.5%

Western Europe 21.7%

East and South Asia 13.8%

Near East 4.9%

Other Areas* 3.5%

Canada 19.2%

Communist Countries 0.4%

*Australia, New Zealand, Republic of South Africa, Oceania, and other Western Hemisphere nations.

Why Export?

Basically, the reasons we export are the reverse of the reasons we import. We mainly export those items that we produce most efficiently due to our climate, technology, low costs, or other advantages that give us an edge over other nations. More specifically, we export for three main reasons:

1. *There is a great demand for products produced in the United States.* Many countries do not have the technological resources or the climate to

produce the manufactured goods or agricultural products that they need or want. In many instances the United States has been the only viable source for these products. In other instances international marketing practices have created markets for American goods, even though the country in question is perfectly capable of producing similar products. Virtually every country, for example, has its own soft drink and clothing industries, yet Coca-Cola and Levi's are often preferred over the domestically manufactured products.

2. *Markets for some products that have peaked within the United States are often in their initial stages of growth in foreign countries.* Large corporations such as Ford Motor Company, General Foods, and Nabisco, for example, can respond to a depressed home market by finding cheaper sources of supply in foreign countries and by expanding their marketing efforts into newer urban areas of Latin America, Africa, and the Far East.

3. *The United States is often in a favorable position to market surplus agricultural products,* which helps lend equilibrium to the balance of trade. The Russian wheat negotiations of the 1970s, for example, were in part motivated by the government's desire to balance the outflow

of U.S. dollars to OPEC with an inflow of Russian payments for grain.

Perhaps surprisingly, it has been estimated that approximately 95 percent of American manufacturers do *not* export anything. The principal reason for the lack of interest in foreign marketing appears to be that few firms know how to go about it.

What Do We Export?

Figure 20-1 lists the principal commodities and various kinds of merchandise exported by the United States during selected years. Our main exports are manufactured products, but we also sell other nations substantial quantities of crude nonfuel materials, chemicals, and food products. Specifically, our two largest export items are machinery and transportation equipment (electronic products, motor vehicles, and airplanes) and food and live animals.

To Whom Do We Export

Figure 20-5 shows the percentages of U.S. exports to principal areas of the world for 1982. Comparison of this chart to the one in Figure 20-4 reveals that our best international customers are also our best suppliers. Nearly 45 percent of our exports go to Canada and Western Europe. Although most of our trade is conducted with highly industrialized nations (approximately half of our international trade is with only five nations—Canada, Japan, Mexico, the United Kingdom, and West Germany), we export significantly more to developing nations than we import. The eight largest buyers of our exports in 1982 included the five nations already mentioned and, in descending order, Saudi Arabia, The Netherlands, and France.

In the future our exports to the developed nations will probably continue more or less along current lines. However, the export market to the less developed countries should increase substantially. U.S. marketers cannot long ignore a market of nearly 90 million Latin American consumers—perhaps 20 million in Brazil alone. In fact large corporations such as Coca-Cola, General Foods, General Motors, Nabisco, and PepsiCo are already expanding into the markets within developing nations. Coca-Cola, for example, has already captured nearly half of the Mexican soft-drink market.

INTERNATIONAL MARKETING ENVIRONMENTAL FORCES

Much like domestic marketing, international marketing is affected by uncontrollable environmental forces. Marketing to other nations would be

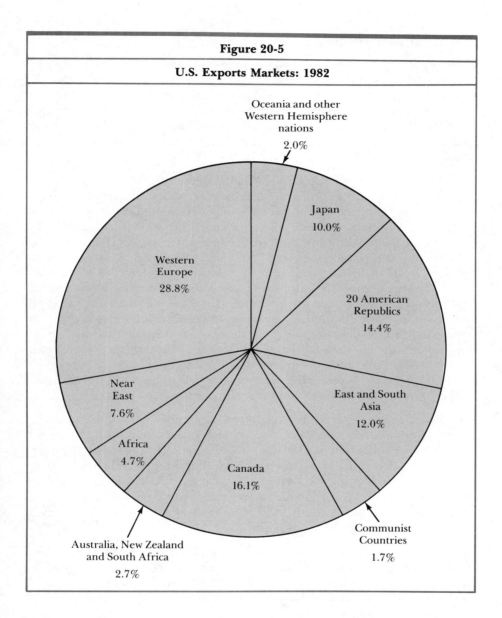

Figure 20-5

U.S. Exports Markets: 1982

Oceania and other
Western Hemisphere
nations
2.0%

Japan
10.0%

20 American
Republics
14.4%

Western
Europe
28.8%

East and South
Asia
12.0%

Near
East
7.6%

Africa
4.7%

Canada
16.1%

Communist
Countries
1.7%

Australia, New Zealand
and South Africa
2.7%

greatly simplified if the marketing strategy used to reach buyers in the United States could also be used to reach buyers abroad. Unfortunately, this approach generally does not work. Differences in the cultural, economic, technological, and political/legal environments of other countries usually necessitate adaptation of American marketing strategies to meet conditions in the host country.

Cultural Environment

Culture *is the total of a society's beliefs, art forms, morals, laws, and customs.*[2] It dictates the manner in which we consume, the priority of our wants and needs, and how those wants and needs should be satisfied. Because cultures can vary greatly from nation to nation, international marketers must adjust their marketing controllable variables to each particular culture. Specifically, they must consider differences in language, color connotations, and mores.

Language   There are thousands of languages and dialects in the world. Marketers, especially in promotional messages, must understand and properly use the language of the host country. To do otherwise invites true marketing blunders. For example, in Spanish the Chevrolet brand name "Nova" means "It does not go." In Cantonese the name "Philip Morris" sounds like the phrase meaning "No luck." In Japan, General Motors' phrase "Body by Fisher" translates to "Corpse by Fisher."

Language becomes a particular concern in countries that speak numerous languages. In India, for example, there are 203 dialects.[3] Even in countries that use the same language as the international marketer, communication problems can exist. Even though Great Britain and the United States both speak the same language, cultural differences exist. English homemakers hope furniture wax "will not tread off" and shoppers buy "tins" (rather than "cans") of grocery products. Such minor differences can make promotional messages sound foolish rather than persuasive.

Colors   Color is a large, though often subliminal part of a marketing effort. Colors in advertisements, on packages, and the product itself may communicate different impressions to different cultures. For example, blue is considered a warm color in Holland and a cold color in Sweden. White is for funerals and red is popular in China and Korea. Red, however, is not popular in Africa. Purple is associated with death in Brazil and in many Spanish-speaking countries. Yellow flowers are a sign of infidelity in France, but one of death in Mexico.[4]

Mores   **Mores** *are the customs and values of a culture.* Every nation has some unique behavior patterns. These may largely influence marketing strategies. For instance, Hindu cultures refuse to eat beef. These mores certainly hinder the strategies of McDonald's in India. The English and Japanese

---

[2] Clyde Kluckholm, "The Study of Culture," in Daniel Leiner and Harold D. Lassivel, eds., *The Policy Sciences* (Palo Alto, Ca.: Stanford University Press, 1951), p. 86.

[3] David J. Rachman and Elaine Romano, *Modern Marketing* (Hinsdale, IL: Dryden Press, 1980), p. 551.

[4] Bradley Hitchings, "Personal Business," *Business Week*, December 6, 1976, pp. 91–92.

drive on the left side of the road. Thus, cars marketed in England and Japan must have the steering wheel on the right side.[5]

Other examples of cultural mores include the fact that the average Frenchman uses almost twice as many beauty aids as his female counterpart. Pepsodent toothpaste was unsuccessful in Southeast Asia because it promised white teeth in a culture in which black or yellow teeth are symbols of prestige.[6] Maxwell House advertised itself as the "Great American Coffee" in West Germany, where the general populace has little respect for American coffee.[7]

Economic Environment

As with any other target market, a nation's population and the purchasing power of that population affect its viability as a market. When you consider

---

[5] Urban C. Lehner, "The Japanese Market, Once Hostile to U.S., Is Opening to Imports," *Wall Street Journal,* May 12, 1982, pp. 1, 24.

[6] David Ricks, Marilyn Y.C. Fu, and Jeffrey Arpan, *International Business Blunders* (Columbus, Ohio: Grid Publishing Company, 1974), p. 15.

[7] S. Watson Dunn, "Effects of National Identity on Multinational Promotional Strategy in Europe," *Journal of Marketing,* October 1976, p. 56.

that only 230 million of the world's more than 4 billion people live in the United States and the population growth rate of the rest of the world is 3 times that of the U.S., it is clear that considerable market opportunities exist outside the United States.

In size and degree of economic development, the nations of the world can be broken into three categories. The **developed nations** of Western Europe, the United States, Canada, and Japan have mixed economies with strong private enterprise and a definite consumer orientation. However, they all have large and growing public sectors. These are relatively stable and substantial economies that offer promising international marketing opportunities, which are augmented by the existence of sophisticated marketing infrastructures. That is, mass media, transportation, and production and distribution facilities are available on a similar level of sophistication.[8]

The **developing nations** (Australia, Israel, and Venezuela, for example) are economies moving from agricultural and raw-material production into industrial production. These countries enjoy an increasing standard of living and show prospects for increased economic growth.

The **less than developed countries** (Pakistan, Peru, and Sri Lanka, for instance) hold one-third of the world's population, with a low standard of living and little purchasing power. Not only do these countries lack economic development, but in many cases they also lack even the technological capabilities to begin economic development.[9] Although desperately in need of the products and services of the developed nations, they have difficulty paying for them.

A fourth sector of the international economy is the **communist nations**. Although they account for one-third of the world's population, political/legal difficulties have limited international marketing efforts to these nations. However, the population of these nations want the developed nations' products, and some companies have been quite effective in marketing to these countries. The U.S. Commerce Department, for instance, estimates that annual U.S. exports to mainland China could reach $4 billion by 1985.

The purchasing power of a particular nation is often measured by its gross national product and its per capita income. The **gross national product (GNP)** *indicates the value of goods and services produced by a nation in a year. The* **per capita income** *equals the GNP divided by the population.*

Observation of these two statistics can provide interesting insights into a nation's economy (see Figure 20-3). For example, the economy of Mexico is gradually improving, but its population is also growing. This limited its 1980 per capita income to only $1,901 (compared to a U.S. per capita

---

[8] John T. Mentzer and A. Coskun Samli, "A Model for Marketing in Economic Development," *Columbia Journal of World Business,* Fall 1981, pp. 91–101.

[9] Ibid.

income of $10,408). This was far superior, however, to the 1979 per capita income of Zaire ($205). International marketing opportunities do exist in Mexico, because a large portion of the national income is concentrated in one segment of the population. This target market has the purchasing power for such luxury goods as Omega digital watches and home computers.[10]

Regardless of the country under consideration, its economy should be analyzed to determine whether to market there, what marketing strategy to use, and how to enter the market. Without such analysis many international marketing efforts will (and do) fail.

Technological Environment

The state of a nation's productive and distributive technology affects the international marketing strategy a company should use. For instance, industrial marketers selling automated equipment have little success in countries in which production systems are labor intensive. Further, countries that have no rail system or a limited highway network have little use for railroad cars or luxury automobiles. Foreign workers often have no experience with machinery or technologically advanced systems and must undergo extensive training before they can deal with such technology.

Other seemingly minor technological differences may cause severe marketing problems. American small appliances, for example, will not work in Europe, because U.S. electric current is 110 volts but European voltage is 220. Many products produced in the U.S. cannot be repaired with other nations' tools, because most of the world uses metric-size tools whereas the U.S. still uses inches and feet as measurement standards in its appliances. Clearly, the level of technological development and the technological orientation of the society should be carefully studied in developing an international marketing strategy.

Political/Legal Environment

Not only do the laws and political systems of other countries differ from those of the United States, but the stability of those laws and politics often changes at an alarming rate. Companies that once invested in the seemingly friendly countries of El Salvador, Iran, and Grenada all found that the political environment could change extremely fast. In 1983, when U.S. Marines landed on Grenada to rescue U.S. citizens, this tiny Caribbean nation was still featured in several popular magazines as a recommended vacation spot.

---

[10] Susan Douglas and Bernard Dubois, "Looking at the Cultural Environment for International Marketing Opportunities," *Columbia Journal of World Business*, Winter 1977, p. 115.

Nationalism *is an attempt by a country to be self-reliant and raise its image in the international community.* Nationalism often leads to restrictive policies that favor native ownership of business. Many multinational companies have had their assets "nationalized" (a euphemism for taken over) or have been subjected to such tight restrictions that they were forced to sell their facilities to native buyers. These restrictions often involves prevention of the transfer of earnings from the country, increased taxes, unilateral changes in contracts, or even revocation of operating licenses.

An international marketer can protect itself from such political/legal pitfalls by measuring the political stability (riots, coups, mechanism for government transitions), military activity, and economic stability (amount of government intervention) before entering a foreign market.[11] Insurance against war and inconvertibility of earnings can also be obtained from the U.S. Overseas Private Investment Corporation or private insurance companies.

Nationalism also often forces international marketers into agreements that help promote the foreign country's products. Known as **countertrade**, such agreements force international marketers to take domestic goods as payment for imports. The international marketer must, in turn, sell these goods on the international market. In return for the right to import duty-free parts for their Brazilian plants, Brazil forced foreign-owned auto and truck makers to agree to export nearly $21 billion dollars worth of vehicles and other products by 1989. General Electric won a contract to supply engines to Sweden's JAS fighter only after it agreed to use the proceeds to buy Swedish products.[12] Such countertrades now account for an estimated 30 percent of international marketing. As Robert D. Schmidt, vice-chairman of Control Data Corporation, said, "Everybody is at it; more countries are demanding reciprocity."[13]

International marketers may also face trade restrictions when entering another country. **Tariffs**, *taxes placed on goods imported into a country*, are a common form of trade restriction. Tariffs are often designed to raise the imported good's price to a level equal to or greater than domestic products, thus limiting its competitive viability. **Quotas**, or *limits on the yearly amount of a product that may be imported*, may also be imposed on an importer. Finally, an international marketer may be completely eliminated from a market by an **embargo**, *a refusal to allow a product or a certain nation's products to be imported.*

To limit such trade restrictions, many companies enter into multilateral trade agreements. In 1948 the U.S. and 22 other nations signed the **Gen-**

---

[11] R. J. Rummel and David A. Heenan, "How Multinationals Analyze Political Risk," *Harvard Business Review*, January–February 1978, p. 71.

[12] "New Restrictions on World Trade," *Business Week*, July 19, 1982, pp. 118–22.

[13] Ibid.

eral **Agreement on Tariffs and Trade (GATT)**, which eliminated or reduced many trade restrictions. The most significant aspect of GATT was the **most-favored nation principle**. Most favored nations (all those covered by GATT) receive the best trade terms received by any nation. By 1979 the 99 members of GATT represented more than 90 percent of the total international trade volume.[14]

Trade restrictions are also reduced by regional trade associations or economic communities such as the European Economic Community (the Common Market), the Latin American Free Trade Association, the Asian Common Market, or the Caribbean Common Market. The Common Market is the most significant of these and consists of Belgium, Denmark, France, Great Britain, Greece, Ireland, Italy, Luxembourg, The Netherlands, Portugal, Spain, and West Germany. The Common Market agreement allows no tariffs between member nations; uniform tariffs with non-members; common standards on food additives, labeling, and packaging; and unrestricted flow of labor and capital.

THE INTERNATIONAL MARKETING CONTROLLABLE VARIABLES

An American firm that wants to develop international markets naturally seeks an approach that is both efficient and profitable. Discovering such an approach is seldom easy, because the American company must often compete with the other nation's domestic producers on their home ground. Moreover, various other nations may also be developing markets in the same target country, thereby intensifying the competition still further.

Nor is this all. Just as they must do to reach domestic consumers, astute international marketers must also consider all the varied demographic characteristics of the target market, the climate and political activities within the targeted country, and a host of other factors.

However, much like domestic marketing, the international marketing strategy is specified by decisions on the marketing controllable variables of product, place, promotion, and price. These decisions are largely dictated by the characteristics of the target market.

Target Markets

As with any other marketing strategy, the demographic and psychographic characteristics of each international market must be understood before the

---

[14] Hans Thorelli, "Gatt and The Tokyo Round: The Magna Charta of International Trade," in Hans Thorelli and Helmut Becker, eds., *International Marketing Strategy* (New York: Permagon Press, 1980), pp. 33–39.

marketing controllable variables can be specified. These characteristics, and consequently the marketing strategy, will differ for each country in which a company has a marketing offering. German buyers have different tastes and buying patterns from French or English buyers. Each is a unique target market.

Unfortunately, it is often much more difficult to obtain marketing information for international markets than for markets in the U.S. Secondary data that is routinely available for most U.S. markets may not even exist in many other countries. Cultural differences may also hamper the gather-

been reduced when Democrats come to power. President Dwight D. Eisenhower finally halted the tariff roller coaster as a partisan issue when he asked for "freer" trade legislation in 1955. Congress eventually authorized him to reduce duties by 20 percent in negotiating with the European Economic Community.

Today, tariffs range from 1.1 percent on imported soft wood to 130 percent for clocks and clock movements. They are enacted chiefly in response to pressure from "endangered" industries, rather than as a means for the government to collect revenues.

Quotas are of fairly recent origin. A quota limits the quantity of a product that may be brought into this country. Quotas are thought by many to control trade more effectively than tariffs do. Quotas were first introduced in the mid-1930s, but they have gained public notice only in recent years, probably because imports of two of the products dearest to American hearts—sugar and petroleum—are restricted.

Sugar quotas were imposed at the urging of America's sugar producers, following the typical pattern. Oil import quotas were another matter, however. In 1979 President Jimmy Carter ordered that imported oil could not exceed the level reached two years earlier. His action was taken as part of a comprehensive effort to reduce our country's dependence on foreign energy sources.

Advocates of protectionist measures believe that quotas protect both infant and established industries from unfair competition engendered by cheaper labor in other countries, provide more employment for Americans who make the products that are being imported, help reduce our balance of payments, and encourage foreigners who cannot sell their goods here to invest in the United States. Since 1980 the U.S. has imposed quotas on steel, textiles, apparel, and motorcycles; has negotiated steel import agreements with the European Economic Community; and has negotiated restrictions on Japanese imports, especially cars.* Many other countries have similar quotas with which international marketers must contend.

* "The Rising Winds of Trade War," *Business Week*, January 9, 1984, pp. 24–25.

ing of primary data. Mail surveys are difficult to conduct in many countries because the illiteracy rate is so high. Even in many of the developed nations only one-third of all households have telephones, making telephone surveys quite impractical. In Hong Kong, for instance, people simply will not take the time to fill out a long questionnaire.[15]

[15] Charles S. Mayer, "The Lessons of Multinational Marketing Research," *Business Horizons*, December 1978, pp. 7–13.

Despite these difficulties, target-market information is as critical as ever. Surveys designed to meet cultural characteristics should still be conducted, with native company representatives utilized to gather and interpret marketing information.

Additionally, some useful sources of secondary information do exist. The Department of Commerce is the most important public source of information about the "how" of international marketing. In many of our larger cities it maintains field offices that provide advice on international marketing opportunities. It also runs two agencies that directly assist the would-be exporter: the Bureau of International Commerce (BIC) and the Business and Defense Services Administration (BDSA).

BIC helps the American business to contact foreign businesses, display products in foreign markets, and obtain pertinent information about trade in other nations. BDSA helps business by screening information about specific marketing opportunities obtained from foreign-service posts around the world and by publishing regular foreign market surveys.

The United States operates permanent trade centers for product exhibitions in key cities such as Milan, Bangkok, Frankfurt, London, and Tokyo. The American exhibitor pays only a nominal sum for exhibit space.

Major commercial banks such as Morgan Guaranty, Chase Manhattan, and the Bank of America are excellent private sources of information on how to build foreign markets. Many such banks maintain international departments as well as branch offices in foreign countries.

Whatever the methods used, however, the gathering and interpreting of primary and secondary data are essential in international marketing—perhaps more so than in domestic marketing, because the marketer is less familiar with the market. Many have argued that the Japanese have been so successful marketing their products in the U.S. because they have effectively used U.S. sources of marketing information to increase their understanding of the American consumer. As always, this knowledge of the target market is vital to making decisions on the marketing conrollable variables.

Product Decisions

Product decisions in international marketing can be based on a product extension, product adaptation, backward invention, or forward invention strategy.[16] A **product extension strategy** is followed when a company offers the same products internationally that it markets domestically. No attempt is made to alter the product to fit local customs, technology, or purchasing patterns. This strategy is based on the belief that good products will sell anywhere. For most products it is a simplistic strategy that does not work well. For Coca-Cola, however, it has proven to be a very successful strategy worldwide.

Under a **product adaptation strategy** products are modified to meet local requirements. U.S. manufacturers of hand power tools, for example, modify their products to operate on the different voltage system when marketing in Europe. Other adaptations of domestic products are often used to meet local climate conditions, technological requirements, or purchasing behavior.

Invention strategies involve more fundamental product changes. Rather than using domestic products, a company designs products specifically for the host country. **Backward invention** is used to simplify products that a company wishes to market in developing nations. For instance, a marketer of electric tools may develop and market a line of manual tools to nations without widespread electricity. Similarly, several marketers of heavy farming machinery have developed lines of machinery designed to be pulled by oxen rather than heavy tractors. These simpler products are more affordable and practical in developing agricultural nations.

---

[16] Warren J. Keegan, "Multinational Product Planning: Strategic Alternatives," *Journal of Marketing*, January 1969, pp. 58–62.

Forward invention strategies involve attempts to develop new technologies for internationally marketed products. Typically aimed at developed nations, these products require considerable research and development investment and, therefore, can be quite a risky strategy for the international marketer.

Place Decisions

International marketers must make decisions on the number and types of intermediaries to have in their international channels and how to physically move their products. A company may elect either to sell its products through its own distributors in a foreign country or simply to sell the product to foreign companies and let them distribute the product. The more a product needs post-sale support and service, the more likely a company is to use its own distributors. Caterpillar sells better than half of its earthmoving equipment overseas. Because this complex equipment requires much technical information and post-sale service, Caterpillar has its own dealers in each foreign market.

The type of channel member will be determined by national characteristics. Many countries have few or no supermarkets, inadequate warehousing facilities, and a confusing array of wholesalers. Better than half of all fresh fish sold in Japan goes through three wholesalers before it reaches the retailer.[17]

Similarly, U.S. manufacturers marketing in Japan often make the mistake of expecting Japanese retailers to follow the same inventory standards as U.S. retailers. However, Japanese retailers face severe space limitations and require suppliers to keep inventories nearby and make fast, dependable deliveries. This is inefficient by U.S. standards, but a necessity for successful marketing channels in Japan.[18]

Foreign physical distribution facilities are often inadequate for efficiently moving and storing products. In Nigeria a 200-mile trip to the interior takes over two weeks in a four-wheel-drive truck because of inadequate highways. Perishable goods imported by this country simply cannot reach the interior market segment.[19]

Inadequate transportation, warehousing, and order processing systems should all be recognized in designing an international marketing strategy. Often the costs of compensating for these problems make marketing to such nations infeasible. At the very least, place decisions to less developed

---

[17] *Japan: A Growth Market for U.S. Consumer Products*, (Washington, D.C.: U.S. Department of Commerce, 1978), p. 16.

[18] William Lazer, "U.S. Sees Japan as Wealthy World Power; but, to Japanese, It's Small, Poor, Island Country," *Marketing News*, July 9, 1982, p. 10.

[19] Mentzer and Samli, "A Model for Marketing;" and Jonathan Kwitney, "Nigeria Faces Problems as Farm Output Lags," *Wall Street Journal*, September 26, 1980, pp. 1, 14.

nations require much more significant adjustment than when marketing to developed nations.

Promotion Decisions

International marketers must concern themselves with how much of the domestic promotional strategy they can use internationally and what aspects they must adjust to local markets. Certain parts of a promotional message may be used globally to maintain a consistent theme. The Marlboro ad with the western theme is used worldwide. Only the copy is translated into the appropriate language. This is a desirable approach, because little money is spent developing unique strategies for each country. Indeed, in some areas a consistent theme is necessary. For instance, in Western Europe the media in one country may be viewed by natives of other countries. Television stations are often viewed in several countries, and many magazines have multinational readership.

However, cultural differences often dictate different promotional themes in different countries. Earlier in the chapter we mentioned some examples of differing color perceptions. In some countries door-to-door selling is not accepted and consumers in different countries often respond to unique promotional messages. In addition some media simply are not available in certain countries. Many developing nations have few televisions or radios.

Because the number of movie theaters in Japan is limited, theater managers there can be very selective about the movies they show. Thus, managers insist on showing only movies that have had a large promotional budget, which must be spent over the six months before the movie is even released. These campaigns typically cost movie promoters several million dollars in advertising time alone—far more than is spent on the same movie in the U.S.[20] The promotional strategy differences lie entirely in the way Japanese, as opposed to Americans, expect movies to be promoted.

Price Decisions

Pricing decisions in international marketing should consider the same factors we discussed in Chapters 18 and 19, but these decisions are often confused by the **currency exchange rate**, that is, *the relationship between the currency in the marketer's home country and the currency in the nation in which the product is being marketed.* For example, when a U.S. firm determines that its price for a product sold in Great Britain should be $1 and the exchange rate with the British pound is 1.75 (1.75 dollars equals 1 pound), the price

---

[20] "What Makes a Film Fly in Japan," *Business Week,* June 29, 1981, p. 97.

Strategy

Volkswagen Rabbit Versus Ford Fiesta

Competition for the American consumer's automobile dollar has been keen enough to reduce the number of automakers to four domestic and a mere handful of foreign-based firms. The Detroit "big four"—General Motors, Ford, Chrysler and American Motors—traditionally enjoyed great success with large cars but have not been able to arouse equal consumer support for their various small car offerings.

Following the OPEC embargo on oil shipments to the United States in 1973, Americans experienced their first gasoline shortage since World War II. As a consequence consumer interest in small, energy-efficient automobiles increased sharply. However, domestic automobile manufacturers fared poorly in their attempts to market small cars. Americans favored imported models. Ford Motor Company, however, devised a marketing strategy that enabled it to compete favorably with Volkswagen, a major seller of automobiles in the United States. Ironically, Ford's strategy to achieve higher consumer respect and acceptance entailed importing an automobile from its West German plant. Ford began selling its Fiesta to the U.S. consumer in 1977.

Although Volkswagen had sold over five million "Beetles" in the United States over a 20-year period, sales began to decline during the early 1970s. The Beetle was replaced by the Rabbit, and Volkswagen took great care to present its new car as an even better, more refined automobile than the classic Beetle.

The innovative Rabbit was many things its predecessor was not. Its appearance was stylish, whereas the Beetle was homely. The Rabbit was faster, "hopping" from zero to 50 miles per hour in 8.3 seconds and attaining an optimum speed of between 75 and 80 miles per hour. A spacious interior was made possible by one of the Rabbit's most important innovations, the transverse engine. Mounting the engine sideways, Volkswagen found, nearly eliminated the transmission hump and the drive shaft tunnel, leaving a floor that is almost flat. Making the car taller increased the head room enough that seven-foot-tall basketball star Wilt Chamberlain could proclaim in television commercials that his Rabbit had more head room than his Rolls Royce. Better traction in bad weather conditions was provided by another innovation, front-wheel drive.

Consumer Reports rated the Rabbit first among subcompacts. Some of the advantages in product design cited by the magazine were the Rabbit's excellent fuel economy (it averaged 32 miles per gallon on regular leaded gasoline), comfortable front seats (though the back seats were said to be only moderately comfortable), safe handling, a superior repair record, large luggage area for its size, and well-placed gauges and controls. Some Rabbits featured an ingenious seat belt that closed around the driver automatically when the door was closed. Compared with Rabbits equipped with standard seat belts, the Department of Transportation found this system reduced deaths by two-thirds. The Rabbit was also the first automobile in its price category to offer a diesel engine to American car buyers.

Like the other Detroit-based automobile manufacturers, Ford Motor Company had never made a successful foray into the marketing of small cars in America. It had in Europe, however, where its Fiesta model was well-accepted and eventually attained 3.1 percent of the market for small cars. After a great deal of research and some product modifications, Ford decided to reach for a share of the U.S. small car market. To the nearly 20 percent of American car buyers who purchase imported autos, Ford offered a two-door hatchback with a four-cylinder engine, four-speed manual transmission and—a first for Ford—front-wheel drive.

Fiesta was *Consumer Reports'* second choice among subcompacts. The magazine listed its chief advantages as excellent fuel economy (36 mpg), quick acceleration, a low level of interior noise, and responsive steering.

Fiesta had an edge in pricing. Besides being several hundred dollars cheaper than the Rabbit, it offered more features—such as carpeting and radial tires—as standard equipment. To make Rabbit more competitive with the American cars, Volkswagen moved away from its traditional, simple pricing system and adopted four price lines with numerous options.

Advertising for both cars was well done and imaginative, aimed at the better educated, more affluent Americans who prefer imported cars. Ford called Fiesta "The European Success Car of the Year." Women were targeted by commercials showing women driving Fiestas over rough terrain, shifting the four-speed manual transmission with ease. Magazines got the lion's share of Fiesta's advertising, because Ford's research showed that Americans who buy foreign cars want information about the manufacturing and performance of automobiles.

The gentle humor that characterized Volkswagen's advertising for the Beetle ("Ugly is only skin deep," for example) was continued in ads for the Rabbit. One series of commercials was built around a restaurateur named Costello who delivered his pizzas in his automobile. They called it "Rabbit and Costello." Other commercials emphasized fuel economy, ease of handling, and quality (to compensate for the product's higher price).

Despite the many similarities in their products and the internationality of both companies, Volkswagen's Rabbit won and kept a decided lead over Fiesta. The reason, some say, was indifference on the part of Ford, which was struggling to meet fuel efficiency standards mandated by American law for all its vehicles. Perhaps Ford's first choice of media—high-quality magazines—was too limited in comparison to Volkswagen's use of celebrities to promote the Rabbit in television commercials.

Sadder and wiser, having lost the challenge to establish itself in an important American market, Ford still manufactures the Fiesta in Germany, but it is no longer sold in the United States.

in England is 0.57 pounds. If the exchange rate falls to 1.63 (the pound is *devalued,* that is, worth less dollars), the price *rises* in England to 0.61 pounds. The price in a foreign currency is largely determined by the exchange rate and, thus, uncontrollable by the international marketer.

Many marketers in developed nations follow a strategy of selling obsolete or excess production to foreign markets at lower prices. This strategy is called dumping and is often followed to keep prices in the home market stable or to underprice foreign competitors and establish a strong market share in the foreign market. **Dumping** has been defined as *selling a product in a foreign country at a price less than the prevailing foreign market price, less than the cost of production, or both.*[21] Dumping that hurts foreign competition is illegal in many countries.

INTERNATIONAL MARKETING ALTERNATIVES

Whether a foreign market will be profitable depends to a great extent on how a firm goes about entering it. No single approach is best for all companies or for all situations, and some companies may use several alternatives at one time or another.

Export Finished Products

The way most American businesses get started in international marketing is by selling their finished products directly to foreign customers. Compared with other approaches, this alternative has two basic advantages. It gives the firm more control over production, and it simplifies management. Eliminating the production problems associated with using foreign labor and facilities enables the company to concentrate more on marketing operations. Moreover, the additional production at the American plant may reduce per-unit costs, thereby adding to domestic profits. The capital requirements may also be less when the American firm manufactures domestically, provided that additional production facilities are not needed.

Export Components

Because of trade restrictions imposed by other nations, as well as comparatively high domestic production and transportation costs, it is often impossible for American firms to export finished products such as automobiles, appliances, electronic equipment, and drugs. However, when foreign manufacturers of such products find that they cannot efficiently produce certain highly sophisticated components or ingredients, they often elect to import them from the United States.

---

[21] Steven E. Plant, "Why Dumping is Good for Us," *Fortune,* May 5, 1980, p. 213.

When the People's Republic of China decided to construct and market paper copiers, it found it did not have adequate production and product design expertise. Therefore, it signed a 20-year contract with Clark Copy International, which will export 1,000 of its copiers to China, parts for 5,000 more copiers that will be manufactured in China, and other Clark products. Over a five-year period the profits for Clark should exceed $60 million.[22]

Export Through an EMC

The simplest way for a firm to export is to use the services of an export management company. An **export management company (EMC)** *is a company that specializes in marketing American-made products in foreign countries.* Usually, the EMC buys the product from the American firm and resells it to international buyers. The EMC handles the entire marketing program, including packaging, distributing, promoting, and pricing. Some EMCs function as sales agents and are compensated on a commission basis.

Licensing

Another approach to international marketing is to license the right to make and market the product to a foreign manufacturer for a specified percentage of sales revenue. In effect the foreign firm buys the reputation, skill, and processes of the American company for a certain period of time. One example of licensing is the sale of book publication rights by an American publishing company to a foreign publisher. Licensing may be a good alternative for marketing in foreign nations when the market is too small to justify setting up a sales organization, foreign competitors are strongly entrenched, and/or tariffs are unusually high. However, when a company licenses its product rights to a foreign marketer, it loses control over the quality of the product and the marketing strategy.

Joint Ventures

A company may form a partnership with a foreign company or government in order to enter that particular country's marketplace. This sharing of manufacturing and marketing expertise is often a valuable method of gaining the cultural and economic insights provided by the foreign partners' native management. Additionally, it can be a necessity in gaining the preferential treatment foreign governments often give native companies.

In May of 1983 American Motors signed an agreement to rebuild and jointly operate a Beijing (China) Jeep factory. After four years of negotiat-

---

[22] John Curley, "Small Firm Outmaneuvers Big-Time Rivals in Winning Copier Sales from the Chinese," *Wall Street Journal*, April 26, 1982, p. 29.

ing, AMC forged a deal whereby it will invest $8 million in cash and $8 million worth of technology for a 31.4-percent interest in a venture to produce and market a four-wheel-drive vehicle to China's massive domestic market. A condition of the agreement: AMC must plow all profits from domestic sales back into China.[23]

The disadvantage with such joint ventures is that the international marketer may not have as much control of the marketing effort as is desired. This is especially true in such countries as Mexico or Japan, where foreigners are restricted from having a majority ownership in any joint venture. With only minority ownership (such as the AMC–China arrangement), international marketers have little, if any, control over decisions.

Direct Ownership

Many American companies have learned that they can maximize their control over marketing in foreign countries if they begin by acquiring local firms that already have a foothold on the product line that they intend to market. Ralston–Purina, traditionally thought of as a supplier of animal foods, has interests in fast-service restaurants in Guatemala and Brazil, a cannery in Ecuador, and cookie plants in Mexico. Del Monte is involved with food growing and processing in Costa Rica, Guatemala, Kenya, and the Philippines. The fertilizer and shipping conglomerate, W.R. Grace, now owns a Guatemalan grain company. Standard Brands acquired Romix Foods (United Kingdom), Aurora desserts (Chile), and Rodrigues Pinto gelatins (Brazil). La-Z-Boy Chair Company acquired an interest in the operating assets of Deluxe Upholstering Ltd. (Canada) in 1979.

General Foods is an excellent case in point. The company successfully expanded its international market for processed foods by acquiring England's Alfred Bird and Sons frozen foods company. In Germany, however, the company attempted to start from scratch, without an acquired German company. In the words of General Foods former president C. W. Cook, the German operations turned out to be a "difficult experience." However, it was a learning experience as well. In 1956 the company acquired the Venezuelan seafood and chocolate processor, La India. This was followed, in 1960, by its acquisition of Brazil's largest ice cream manufacturer, Kibon. General Foods also employed the same strategy in the chewing gum markets of Europe and Brazil and the coffee and soup markets of Mexico.

By starting international marketing through acquisitions, American firms enjoy several advantages. Politically, the acquired company often retains its reputation as a domestic firm, rather than being viewed as an

---

[23] "How Jeep Hit the Road to China," *Business Week,* May 16, 1983, p. 26.

arm of an American conglomerate (even though the operation may receive U.S. government diplomatic aid and financial support in the form of government investment insurance). Starting costs, of course, are minimized as well, to the extent that it is possible for large companies to enter the markets of several countries at the same time. Moreover, once the local company has been acquired, it is much easier to recycle a successful marketing campaign that has already been at least partially paid for by sales in the American market.

American producers are obviously attracted to acquiring local companies to manufacture products for sale in foreign nations, especially when the foreign nation has considerable potential for long-term growth. A major disadvantage of this approach, however, is that the market in that nation may be too small to support efficient production. In such cases American firms may also try to export the products manufactured in foreign nations to other nations or even back to the United States. However— as American oil companies in Indonesia and Iran and American fertilizer and communications companies in Chile have discovered—the question of political stability can be extremely important with respect not only to expropriation, but also to controls on capital and profits, repatriation of profits, and so on. Naturally, there are less risky alternatives to international marketing.

MULTINATIONALISM

Traditionally, a firm that engages in international marketing makes a sharp distinction between its domestic and foreign markets and the strategies used to develop them. However, as international trade becomes increasingly important to a large firm, those distinctions tend to lessen. **Multinationalism** has come into wide use to describe *the policies of a business that operates both production and distribution facilities in many nations and makes extensive use of foreign labor and executive talent.*

The degree of multinationalism in firms engaged in international marketing varies considerably. Executives of such organizations tend, in the words of one observer, to be either **ethnocentric** *(home-country oriented)*, **polycentric** *(host-country oriented)*, or **geocentric** *(world oriented)*.[24] These orientations are compared in Figure 20-6.

Ethnocentrics see the home nationals of their company as superior to, more trustworthy than, and more reliable than foreigners. They are willing to build facilities in a country as long as their contacts in the host nation

---

[24] Howard V. Perlmutter, "The Tortuous Evolution of the Multinational Corporation," *Columbia Journal of World Business,* January–February 1969, pp. 11–12.

	Figure 20-6		
	Three Types of Orientation Toward Subsidiaries in International Enterprise		
Organizational Design	**Ethnocentric (Home-Country Oriented)**	**Polycentric (Host-Country Oriented)**	**Geocentric (World Oriented)**
Complexity of organization	Complex in home country, simple in subsidiaries	Varied and independent	Increasingly complex and interdependent
Authority; decision making	High in headquarters	Relatively low in headquarters	Aim for a collaborative approach between headquarters and subsidiaries
Evaluation and control	Home standards applied for persons and performance	Determined locally	Find standards which are universal and local
Rewards and punishments; incentives	High in headquarters, low in subsidiaries	Wide variations; can be high or low rewards for subsidiary performance	International and local executives rewarded for reaching local and worldwide objectives
Communication; information flow	High volume to subsidiaries; orders, commands, advice	Little to and from headquarters, little between subsidiaries	Both ways, and between subsidiaries; heads of subsidiaries part of management team
Identification	Nationality of owner	Nationality of host country	Truly international company, but identifying with national interests
Perpetuation (recruiting, staffing, development)	Recruit and develop people of home country for key positions everywhere in the world	Develop people of local nationality for key positions in their own country	Develop best people everywhere in the world for key positions everywhere in the world

SOURCE: Howard V. Perlmutter, "The Tortuous Evolution of the Multinational Corporation," *Columbia Journal of World Business*, January–February 1969, p. 12.

acknowledge the superiority of their methods and agree to run things their way.

Polycentrics realize that each host country has a different culture and that this fact should be given primary consideration in devising production and marketing strategies. They believe in "letting the nationals do it their way," even if they do not fully understand the reasoning behind an action. As long as the firm earns a profit, they will remain in the background.

Geocentrics, or truly multinational executives, take a world view. Their underlying philosophy as summed up by Jacques Maisonrouge, the French-born president of IBM World Trade:

> The first step to a geocentric organization is when a corporation, faced with the choice of whether to grow and expand or decline, realizes the need to mobilize its resources on a world scale. It will sooner or later have to face the issue that the home country does not have a monopoly of either men or ideas. I believe that the future belongs to geocentric companies. What is of fundamental importance is the attitude of the company's top management. If it is dedicated to geocentrism, good international management will be possible. If not, the best men of different nations will soon understand that they do not belong to the company, and will leave.[25]

SUMMARY

- Although the percentage of world exports consumed by the U.S. is steadily growing, the percentage of U.S. products purchased by the rest of the world is declining.
- International marketing consists of marketing across national boundaries.
- The theory of comparative advantage holds that a nation should export those items it produces most efficiently and import those it produces least efficiently.
- The main U.S. comparative advantages are (a) advanced technology, (b) a large supply of fertile land, and (c) a large domestic market.
- The main U.S. comparative disadvantages are (a) high wages, (b) shortages of several basic products, and (c) limited land in the tropical zone.

---

[25] Ibid, pp. 16–17.

- We import goods because (a) we lack the type of climate required to produce some products, (b) our cost advantage for a good is marginal or nonexistent, (c) our domestic supplies of some products are inadequate, (d) some foreign-made products are of higher quality, and (e) consumers want items that are unique.
- Most of our imports come from Canada, Japan, Mexico, the United Kingdom, West Germany, Taiwan, Saudi Arabia, and Nigeria.
- The main reasons we export are that (a) there is great demand for many products we produce, (b) markets for some products have peaked in the United States, and (c) the United States often has large agricultural surpluses.
- Most of our exports go to Canada, Japan, Mexico, the United Kingdom, West Germany, Saudi Arabia, the Netherlands, and France.
- Like domestic marketing strategy, international marketing strategy must take into account such uncontrollable environmental forces as culture, economy, technology, and political/legal issues.
- Cultural differences include differing languages, color perceptions, and mores.
- The economies of the world can be categorized as developed nations, developing nations, less than developed countries, and communist countries.
- The gross national product (GNP) indicates the value of goods and services produced by a nation in a year. The per capita income equals the GNP divided by the population.
- Technological differences can hamper or even prevent some international marketing efforts.
- Nationalism and trade restrictions may seriously constrain international marketing activities.
- The characteristics of the international target market help guide decisions on the marketing controllable variables.
- Product decisions often follow product extension, product adaptation, backward invention, or forward invention strategies.
- Place decisions concern the number and type of international intermediaries and how to move the product physically.
- Certain parts of a promotional message may be used to maintain a consistent theme, but other aspects must be adjusted to fit each nation.
- Pricing in international markets is complicated by the currency exchange rate.
- Dumping is the strategy of selling obsolete or excess production in foreign markets at lower prices.
- International marketing alternatives include exporting, licensing, joint ventures, or direct ownership.
- Multinational companies exhibit an ethnocentric (home-country), polycentric (host-country), or geocentric (world) orientation.

DISCUSSION
QUESTIONS

1. Of the factors cited as causes of our trade deficit, which do you feel is the most important? Why?
2. Explain the theory of comparative advantage and how it affects what we export and import.
3. "Our comparative trade advantages are not static." Explain.
4. What are our comparative disadvantages and how do they affect what we import?
5. Why is most of our international trade conducted with highly industrialized nations?
6. How can cultural factors affect international marketing strategy? Economic factors? Technological factors? Political/legal factors?
7. Why is it important for an international marketer to study target markets very carefully? Why is it difficult?
8. Explain the differences between production extension, product adaptation, backward invention, and forward invention.
9. Explain how place, promotion, and price decisions might vary from country to country.
10. Under what circumstances might an international marketer export finished products? Components? Use an EMC? License? Enter a joint venture? Use direct ownership?
11. Explain the meaning of ethnocentric, polycentric, and geocentric.

APPLICATION
EXERCISES

1. Suppose that all the nations of the world agreed today, with no advance notice, to remove all tariffs, quotas, and other trade restrictions. Prepare a report on the probable effects of such an agreement on domestic employment, purchasing power, and consumption patterns over the first several years. What industries would benefit most? Which would be most adversely affected? Overall, would the advantages outweigh the disadvantages?
2. Report briefly on the main arguments for and against the following proposition. Resolved: "American marketing would benefit from higher tariffs because American jobs and purchasing power would be protected." When you have completed your analysis, explain which side of the argument you feel is stronger.
3. Find three cases of American businesses paying bribes in countries where such a practice does not violate the native culture or laws. Do you think U.S. companies should be allowed to follow this practice?

CASE 20:
Mitsubishi Moves Into the "Foreign" U.S. Market

Although we often think of international marketing as the U.S. exporting to other countries, we must remember that other countries and their companies see the U.S. as a huge foreign market. Ironically, Japan's largest conglomerate, Mitsubishi, was relatively unknown in the United States in 1981. The $123 billion a year group had over $16 billion in annual sales in the U.S., but no one knew who they were, primarily, because their name was often obscured.[26] Mitsubishi sold cars in the United States in 1981 under the name of Dodge Colt and Plymouth Champ. Mitsubishi is the world's largest investment trader, but is known in the U.S. as MIC. Mitsubishi televisions were known as MGA.

To boost its reputation in the United States, it is entering many new businesses (primarily joint ventures or direct ownerships) and displaying the Mitsubishi name more prominently. Mitsubishi Electric entered a joint venture with Westinghouse to make semiconductors in the U.S. A joint venture with Kennecott mines copper in New Mexico and one with ATR Wire and Cable produces steel tire cords which are sold through Mitsubishi's existing channels to U.S. tire manufacturers.

A particularly difficult aspect of Mitsubishi's international marketing strategy concerns its exporting automobiles to the United States. Since 1971, Mitsubishi has manufactured cars and sold them through Chrysler's dealer network in the U.S. under the Chrysler name. The joint venture worked well for ten years. Mitsubishi needed Chrysler's dealer network and Chrysler needed Mitsubishi cars. However, financial crises at Chrysler prompted Mitsubishi to forge an interesting strategy. Not only will it sell cars under the Chrysler name, but it plans to develop its own dealer network for a line of (very similar) Mitsubishi cars. Many Chrysler dealers are scrambling to also be Mitsubishi dealers, especially since these cars are often their big sellers.

Mitsubishi also is annoyed that Chrysler has stepped up production of small cars and is pushing its own models at dealerships, to the detriment of Mitsubishi sales. However, even for giant Mitsubishi, the prospect of developing a dealer network for the entire U.S. is a huge and risky strategy. Even if many of their present Chrysler dealers also become Mitsubishi

---

[26] "Mitsubishi: A Japanese Giant's Plans for Growth in the U.S.," *Business Week*, July 20, 1981, pp. 128–32.

dealers, the cost of a failure could seriously damage the international marketer.

Discussion Questions

1. As a member of Mitsubishi America, what marketing research information would you want before you made a recommendation to corporate management on whether to develop its own dealership network?
2. What would you recommend? Should Mitsubishi start a national dealer network or begin with a regional one? In what part of the country should they start?
3. To what degree do you think Mitsubishi's decision is influenced by the fact that they are the only major Japanese producer of automobiles without an American dealer network? Is this a decision of marketing strategy or corporate pride?

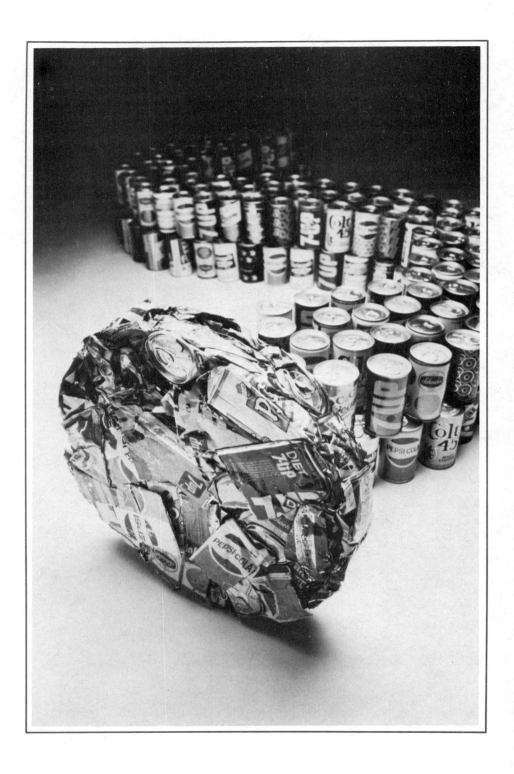

21 The Legal Environment and Social Responsibility of Marketing

STUDY OBJECTIVES

After studying this chapter, you should be able to

1. Explain why government regulation of marketing is necessary.
2. Briefly outline how the Clayton Act, Robinson–Patman Act, Federal Trade Commission Act, and the Wheeler–Lea Amendment define the basis for business competition in America.
3. Outline the powers and responsibilities of the Federal Trade Commission, the Justice Department, and six major federal agencies.
4. Discuss the roles of the Food and Drug Administration, Consumer Product Safety Commission, and Food Safety and Quality Service in the administration of federal consumer-oriented statutes.
5. Explain how the marketing concept relates to the social responsibilities of business.
6. Explain why certain historical and modern marketing practices resulted in the rise of consumerism.
7. List the major criticisms of marketing directed at deceptive packaging, pricing, personal selling, advertising, and warranties.
8. Suggest ways in which marketing could be made more socially responsible through additional legislation, consumer education, and self-regulation.

Throughout most of history a buyer was simply stuck if a product proved defective, injurious, short on weight, or in any other way unsatisfactory. The expression *caveat emptor* ("Let the buyer beware") was the rule governing sales transactions. Beginning early in this century and with exceptionally rapid acceleration, conditions changed. New laws, rules, and guidelines were set forth to combat the alleged misdeeds of marketers. Consumers began to demand—and receive—better treatment in the marketplace.

The change in the public's attitude toward the responsibilities of business has been so sweeping that some now feel the rule governing sales transactions is *caveat venditor,* meaning, "Let the seller beware."

Because a large part of the public's attitude has been manifested in the laws and regulations governing marketing, we will first revisit the legal environment briefly discussed in Chapter 2 and conclude this chapter with a broader discussion of marketing's social responsibilities.

THE LEGAL ENVIRONMENT

Virtually every marketing activity is subject to some form of government regulation. Product pricing, labeling and safety, dealer discounts, advertising strategies and claims, sales promotion, warranties, relationships with competitors, and customer relationships are only some of the areas in which legal considerations are very important. Various government agencies are becoming increasingly involved with marketing management in every industry. Each year new laws, regulations, and judicial rulings are enacted. Most of these come from the federal government, others from state and local governments. Before any discussion of a proposed change in a marketing program goes very far, some executive is bound to ask, "What is the opinion of our legal counsel?"

One of the Justice Department's longest-running and most renowned cases, for example, was pressed against IBM. The suit was filed in 1969, but the case was not resolved until 1983. The Justice Department charged IBM not only with creating a monopoly in data processing, but also with extending the monopoly by illegal means. Although the Justice Department eventually dropped the case, IBM submitted more than four million pages of documents in its defense, and the trial transcript came to more than 64,000 pages. Few marketers have the resources to conduct such a defense, but most must contend with lengthy, complicated regulations.

The Rationale for Government Regulation

Although it is extensive, government intervention in business and marketing activities is a relatively modern development. In the United States the period from 1776 to 1876 was dominated by the philosophy of **laissez-faire**, which holds that *market forces, by themselves, bring about the greatest economic good*. It was considered right for businesses to operate as they saw fit and run their companies in any way they chose in order to produce profits. As time went on, however, it became obvious that the public interest, even in a strictly economic sense, did not necessarily coincide with that of the industrial empires established by the Rockefellers, Morgans, Astors, and others. Near the end of the nineteenth century the government began to assert itself in an effort to curb the power of the oil and steel companies, the railroads, the banks, and the magnates who controlled them.

Two main premises underlie government's regulation of marketing: The public welfare is more important than the welfare of individual businesses or industries, and competition between businesses and industries should be encouraged.

Public Welfare Supersedes Business Welfare   Our society holds that if a business goal conflicts with a social goal, the latter is to be upheld. For example, it might be highly profitable for a meat processor to market wieners that contain an unusually large amount of cereal filler. If this practice were felt to conflict with the social demand for reasonably good nutrition, however, it would presumably be stopped, either by enforcing existing laws or by passing new ones.

There are many instances of conflict between business goals and social objectives. A railroad may want to terminate service to a certain city because there is too little freight to make the stop profitable. However, if the appropriate regulatory commission feels that the community would be adversely affected, it may deny the railroad's request. To cite another example, a business might find it profitable to market a potentially dangerous drug as a nonprescription item. Again, legislation designed to protect a social goal (public health) would be enforced. In our society today the prevailing view is that business has the right to operate and earn profits only as long as its activities do not injure or take unfair advantage of the public. Much of the work of lawmakers and enforcement agencies is aimed at upholding this premise.

Competition is Beneficial   Economic policy in the United States has long assumed that competition among businesses is the most efficient method of producing and marketing goods and services. (The notable exceptions to this premise are public utilities, which because normal benefits of competition do not apply to them, are not permitted to compete but are regulated instead.)

Proponents of competition contend that it results in maximum productivity, because it forces inefficient businesses to terminate their operations, reduces waste of human and other resources, gives the consumer an opportunity to choose from several vendors rather than buy from a monopolist, and stimulates creativity in seeking solutions to marketing problems.

If the national objective is to advance competition, why, when, do we regulate business? Don't regulations and controls inhibit competition? If we really believe in competition, why don't we pursue a policy of laissez-faire? Superficially, a policy of laissez-faire, which in the purest sense means no government intervention of any kind in business activities, might make good sense. In practice, however, there are several reasons why government regulation is necessary to maintain a competitive business environment.

Danger of Collusion In the absence of regulation there is a very real danger of collusion among businesses in the same industry. Two centuries ago Adam Smith made the observation, "People of the same trade seldom meet together but the conversation ends in a conspiracy against the public or in some diversion to raise prices."

If regulations prohibiting collusion did not exist, it would be all too easy for competitors to say to each other, in effect, "Look. Let's stop knocking ourselves out. Let's cooperate, raise our prices, cut our services, fence out other competitors, and keep this economic pie for ourselves." In fact collusion among competitors, chiefly the railroads, was the impetus for the first national legislation intended to prevent it. Despite such legislation instances of collusion still occur today.

Danger of Unfair Business Practices In the absence of regulation competition might result in unfair marketing practices. A financially strong firm, for example, might force suppliers to sell to it at a price below that charged other buyers so that it can undercut prices and force rivals out of business. Consumers may also be the victims of unfair marketing practices. In an intensely competitive environment in which the personal fortunes of executives rise and fall with the success of the business, there is a strong temptation to engage in practices that are harmful to customers. For example, a firm may (1) make false or misleading statements about a product to induce customers to buy it, (2) offer worthless guarantees for a product, or (3) use a package that makes the product look bigger or better than it really is.

Danger of Monopoly In the absence of regulation some firms might become monopolies even if they did not take unfair advantage of competitors or customers. Some economists believe monopoly is the end result of unregulated and unrestricted competition.

Observe for a moment what could happen in the airline industry if all regulations governing competition were eliminated. Conceivably, one airline (call it WIN) could hire the best possible management, develop attractive innovations in aircraft configurations, improve its schedules, project the friendliest image, create an unusually effective ad campaign, reduce its fares, eliminate all unprofitable routes, and take other actions that would help it grow at the expense of its competition. As time passed, it could acquire weaker competitors through mergers until, finally, only it remained. What would happen if WIN, now a monopolist in control of the skies, raised its fares, reduced the quality of its service, and in other ways began to exploit its monopoly power?

It could be argued that WIN would not behave this way. However, previous experience with monopolies in this and other capitalistic economies suggests that the potential danger of abusive practices is too great to allow monopolies to develop. Some economists, however, as well as other observers, believe that it would be a good idea to allow some industries— such as the airlines, railroads, and bus companies—to become monopolies and then regulate them as if they were in fact public utilities, like the telephone and electric-power industries.

Several pieces of federal legislation define the bases for competition among American businesses and foreign businesses operating in the United States. All such laws have the protection of the American citizen as their ultimate objective. In addition certain government agencies help administer these laws. For purposes of this discussion we will divide them into two categories: competitor-oriented legislation and agencies and consumer-oriented legislation and agencies.

Competitor-Oriented Legislation and Agencies

Competitor-oriented legislation is composed mainly of laws passed before World War II. Beginning with the Sherman Antitrust Act in 1890, Congress passed a series of laws that dealt with the dangers of the economic environment: the Clayton Act, the Federal Trade Commission Act, the Robinson–Patman Act, and the Wheeler–Lea Amendment. Together, these laws established guidelines for businesses to follow in competing with other businesses. We will discuss them individually below.

The Sherman Antitrust Act   Motivated by a public clamor against the tremendous growth of business monopolies and cartels toward the end of the nineteenth century, Congress instituted measures to control conspiracies that would tend to restrain trade. The Sherman Act of 1890 forbids "every contract [or] combination, in the form of trust, or otherwise, or conspiracy in the restraint of trade or commerce among the several states or with foreign nations."

One antitrust expert, Walter Guzzardi, Jr., comments, "The best scholars today agree that the intent of the Sherman Act was to protect competition, recognized as the regime most likely to bring the benefits of efficiency to the consumer. But in the 88 years since Benjamin Harrison signed the act, new statutes, amendments and a flock of court decisions have buried that intent under a silt of contradictory purposes."[1] Apparently, the Sherman Act's provisions were too broad to be effective for long in the rapidly expanding business community at the turn of the century.

The Clayton Act   By 1914 it was generally felt that more specific legislation was needed to combat the growth of monopolies and their negative effects on the economy. In that year the Sherman Act was supplemented by the Clayton Act. This legislation outlawed price discrimination and exclusive agreements between channel members when such practices tended to prevent competitors from entering the market. Also forbidden were interlocking directorates (in which the same people sat on the boards of directors of several, often competing, corporations) and the purchase of stock in a firm by its competitors.

The Federal Trade Commission Act   The powerful Federal Trade Commission was created in 1914 by an act of the same name. The FTC Act reinforces the Clayton and Sherman Acts' restraints against completely "free" competition. We will describe the activities of the FTC, which also administers other regulatory legislation, later in the chapter.

The Robinson–Patman Act   Possibly the most difficult law to interpret, and the one of most concern to marketing management, is the Robinson–Patman Act. It is the basis for federal regulation of pricing practices by firms engaged in interstate commerce.

The passage of the Robinson–Patman Act resulted from a scandal caused by some giant retail chains and mail-order houses that used their tremendous purchasing power to force suppliers to grant uneconomic price concessions. Passed in 1936 and administered by the Federal Trade Commission, Robinson–Patman amended the Clayton Act to render discounts, rebates, and other concessions made by producers to large purchasers illegal in cases in which such practices tended to lessen competition or to injure competing firms. It also introduced the concept of pricing based on products of "like grade and quality" and price differentials based on actual cost analysis.

Effect on Pricing   The Robinson–Patman Act makes price discrimination (charging different prices for products of like grade and quality to different similar buyers) illegal if the effect may lessen competition or tend to create a monopoly. These price differentials are legal if they can be cost justified or if the two buyers are not competitors (that is, if competition is not lessened). In addition it is illegal for buyers to willingly receive or induce a seller to offer a discriminatory price.

A case involving the Borden Company illustrates the varied and con-

---

[1] Walter Guzzardi, Jr., "A Search for Sanity in Antitrust," *Fortune*, January 30, 1978, p. 73.

fusing judicial interpretations of the Robinson–Patman Act and also shows its potentially far-reaching effects on pricing and related activities. Under the act a seller must charge identical prices for products of like grade and quality. However, in marketing, grades and quality are often determined by more than simple physical characteristics. Consequently, products that are physically the same are often priced differently because of the value added by the package or intangibles such as the brand name.

Some years back the Borden Company was charged with marketing canned milk under different labels at different prices. The Federal Trade Commission ruled that because the physical properties of the products were nearly identical, the prices should be the same. To the FTC the well-known Borden label made no difference. In 1966 the U.S. Supreme Court agreed, but remanded the case to an appeals court to decide the issue of injury to competition.

The appeals court ruled in Borden's favor on the issue of injury to competition (there was no evidence of this, it said), but by granting that the Borden label had "consumer appeal," confused the issue for other market-ers of products sold under two or more labels. The section of the Robin-son–Patman Act applied in this case could have extensive effects on busi-nesses that produce goods sold under several brand names. Apparently, the advisable course for a company is to emphasize product differentiation if it plans to charge different prices for basically similar goods.

Effect on Discounts   The price-discrimination provisions of the Robin-son–Patman Act also affect discounts. Under the act a producer may grant quantity discounts to large purchasers, but they must be based on actual cost differences related to the quantity sold. Calculating the actual costs of producing various numbers of the same item may seem simple in theory, but it can be difficult in some cases. Functional discounts granted to whole-salers and retailers for the marketing activities they perform are also within the bounds of legality, but they must be based on actual services. Under the provisions of the Robinson–Patman Act a retailer that buys directly from a producer cannot be granted the discount ordinarily given a wholesaler, for example, unless the retailer performs those services the wholesaler would have provided.

Effect on Promotional Allowances   Promotional allowances are also a bone of contention. Producers have frequently offered allowances, spe-cially priced "sale" merchandise, and other forms of support to their chan-nel members. Under the Robinson–Patman Act such promotional assis-tance must be offered to all buyers in proportion to the volume they purchase. The intent of this provision is to protect the small retailer, whose promotional needs may be ignored by firms that wish to cater to large retailers.

Three important observations should be made concerning the Robin-son–Patman Act. First, although it deals with price discrimination, it does not necessarily make all forms of price differentiation illegal. As the Borden case shows, the important matter is whether or not a price difference causes injury to competition. Second, the act makes the purchaser as well as the seller responsible for illegal price discrimination when the buyer knows he or she has been unfairly favored. Third, but not least, the general effect of the Robinson–Patman Act is to deemphasize competition on the basis of price.

The Wheeler–Lea Amendment   The Wheeler–Lea Amendment of 1938 was a forerunner of recent legislation designed to protect the consumer in today's extremely complex marketplace. It formed the basis for the prosecution of marketers engaging in "deceptive practices." An amendment to the FTC Act, it strengthened the price-discrimination provisions of the Robinson–Patman Act and opened the way to eliminating deception in both advertising and labeling. It expanded the powers of the FTC to regulate not only practices that tend to injure competition, but also those that hurt consumers. We will not discuss the specific provisions of the act here, because more recent legislation has expanded and underscored their importance.

Many violations of these antitrust laws can result in compensatory damage payments and punitive fines which may be *three times the actual damage.* For example, when a class action suit was brought against 38 plywood manufacturers for allegedly conspiring to fix prices, one manufacturer estimated the treble damage court settlement could be as high as $2 billion.[2] Understandably, most manufacturers settled out of court.

The Federal Trade Commission   The maintenance of a fair, competitive business environment is the basic objective of competitor-oriented regulation of marketing. The Federal Trade Commission (FTC), created in 1914, is the chief governmental agency responsible for regulating competitor-oriented marketing activity. The commission's original purpose was to halt the growth of monopolies as defined by the Sherman Antitrust Act, but since that time its authority has been expanded to include the prevention of deceptive practices (especially in advertising and labeling), concentration of power within a given industry, fixing of prices and quotas, and violations of product-safety requirements.

Until 1938 the FTC could act only on a complaint by a consumer, a competitor, or another branch of government, and only in cases in which injury to competition was involved. The Wheeler–Lea Amendment empowered the commission to issue its own complaints and to act in cases that did not necessarily involve injury to competition. The Wheeler–Lea

---

[2] Irwin Ross, "A Philadelphia Lawyer's Class-Action Gold Mine," *Fortune,* September 7, 1981, pp. 100–106.

Amendment also added specific bans against "unfair or deceptive acts or practices."

Additionally, the FTC is responsible for enforcing the Wool, Textile, Fur, and Flammable Fabrics Acts. In the field of food and drugs it shares enforcement responsibility with the Food and Drug Administration and the Meat Inspection Branch of the Agriculture Research Service (part of the Department of Agriculture).

Unfair Competition The principal methods of competition the FTC designates as unfair and as constituting a violation of the antitrust laws are:

1. Combinations among or agreements by competitors to raise or otherwise control prices, tamper with an industry's price structure, divide sales territories, or curtail other competitors' sources of supply.
2. Restriction by a seller of a customer's freedom to handle competing products.
3. The payment of excessive prices for raw materials for the purpose and with the effect of eliminating weaker competitors dependent on the same source of supply.
4. Boycotts or combinations to force sellers to give preferential treatment to certain firms.
5. Agreements among competitors to restrict exports or imports.
6. The knowing receipt of discriminatory allowances or unlawful payments by a customer from suppliers.
7. Preventing the advertising of competitive fees (by professional associations).
8. Inducing a breach of contract between competitors and their customers.
9. Secret bribery of buyers or other employees of customers.

Many deceptive or unfair practices continue, because "everybody does them," but they are nevertheless illegal, and the perpetrator will be prosecuted if caught by the FTC. To keep businesses up to date on changes in the law and to help them avoid litigation, the FTC:

- Holds Trade Practice Conferences that provide well-defined rules on the application of FTC-administered laws to specific industries.
- Issues *Industry Guides* that zero in on particular problems and are more limited in scope than Trade Practice Conference rules.
- In answer to requests by businesses, renders advisory opinions on whether a proposed action is acceptable.
- Issues *Trade Regulation Rules* after hearings have determined that such rules are needed. (All businesses affected by proposed rules are given an opportunity to participate in the hearings.)

Procedural Methods The FTC will accept complaints from almost any-one—injured individuals or businesses; Congress; federal, state, and local government agencies; trade associations; and its own staff. Each complaint is investigated to determine whether it concerns a matter of broad interest to the public welfare. At that point the FTC may decide to take one of three courses of action: (1) Close the case, (2) obtain voluntary compliance (agreement to stop violative activities), or (3) attempt to obtain a formal cease-and-desist order.

If the FTC decides to use the formal cease-and-desist procedure, it files a formal complaint against the offending person or company. The filing is followed by a period of private negotiation in an effort to settle the case out of court. If this does not work, or if the person or company (called the *respondent*) chooses to contest the charges, the matter goes into adversary litigation. Public hearings are held before an FTC hearings examiner for presentation of evidence by both FTC attorneys and legal counsel for the respondent. The hearing examiner's proposed order may be appealed to the five-member commission, with further appeal to a U.S. Court of Appeals. Once an FTC order is imposed, violations may result in civil penalties of $10,000 per day for each violation.

The Justice Department The assistant attorney general in charge of the Antitrust Division of the Justice Department is responsible for the enforcement of the federal antitrust laws. That division investigates possible antitrust violations, conducts grand-jury proceedings, prepares and tries antitrust cases, prosecutes appeals, and negotiates and enforces final judgments. The Justice Department routinely seeks jail terms in price-fixing cases, because that offense is a felony.

The Antitrust Division represents the United States in judicial proceedings to review certain orders of the Interstate Commerce Commission, the Federal Maritime Commission, and the Federal Communications Commission. In addition it directly represents the Secretary of the Treasury and the Civil Aeronautics Board in certain review proceedings. It also helps prosecute FTC cases before the Supreme Court. It is responsible for supporting competitive policies within federal departments and agencies and will advise other agencies on the competitive effects of activities within their jurisdiction.

Other Major Regulatory Agencies A number of other agencies regulate various aspects of marketing such as the level of service a firm must provide, the selling strategies it may use, and the territory or area it may cover. Pricing in particular is subject to regulation.

Interstate Commerce Commission (ICC) Broadly speaking, and within prescribed limits, the ICC is responsible for transportation economics and service. It regulates transportation economics by settling controversies over rates and charges among competing and like modes of transportation, shippers and receivers of freight, passengers, and others. It rules on applications for mergers, consolidations, acquisitions of control, and the sale of carriers and issuance of their securities to prevent unlawful discrimination, destructive competition, and rebating. It also has jurisdiction over the use, control, supply, movement, distribution, exchange, interchange, and return of railroad equipment. It regulates transportation service by granting the right to operate to trucking companies, bus lines, freight-forwarding agencies, water carriers, and transportation brokers. Additionally, it approves or disapproves applications to construct or abandon railroad lines or discontinue passenger train service.

The Motor Carrier Act of 1980 and the Railroad Act of 1980 have reduced the authority of the ICC significantly. The Motor Carrier Act gave trucking companies increased freedom in setting prices, choosing routes, and deciding on services to offer. The Railroad Act had similar effects for the railroads and also made mergers much easier. For all these sweeping changes, however, the ICC still remains a strong regulatory force.

U.S. Tariff Commission   The Tariff Commission is authorized to conduct investigations into alleged unfair methods of competition or unfair acts involving the importation of articles into the United States or their domestic sale. Such investigations are warranted if the effect of those methods or acts is to substantially injure or destroy an efficiently and economically operated domestic industry, to prevent the establishment of such an industry, or to restrain or monopolize trade and commerce in the United States. The commission reports such methods or acts to the President, who may prohibit the articles involved from entering the country.

Securities and Exchange Commission (SEC)   The SEC has very extensive authority to regulate the marketing of securities. Issuers of securities making public offerings in interstate commerce or through the mails must file registration statements containing financial and other data about the issuer and the offering. Companies whose securities are listed on the stock exchanges are required to file annual reports with the SEC. The commission is empowered to obtain court orders halting acts and practices designed to defraud investors; to revoke the registrations of brokers, dealers, and investment advisers who willfully engage in such acts and practices; to suspend or expel from national securities exchanges any member who violates any provision of the federal securities laws; and to prosecute persons who have engaged in fraudulent activities or other willful violation of those laws.

Federal Communications Commission (FCC)   The FCC regulates the rates, services, and accounting methods of interstate and foreign wire and radio communication services, and licenses radio and television facilities. It also administers and implements portions of the Communications Satellite Act of 1962.

Civil Aeronautics Board (CAB)   The CAB grants domestic air carriers authority to engage in interstate transportation and international air carriers authority to engage in air transportation between the United States and other countries. Until 1979 it had jurisdiction over the rates charged for air transportation. The CAB also sets the rates for mail carriage by air carriers and authorizes and pays subsidies to air carriers whose services are not self-sustaining, but are required by the public. In the interest of maintaining competition it authorizes mergers, agreements, acquisitions of control, and interlocking relationships involving air carriers. The board also has jurisdiction over unfair competitive practices by air carriers and ticket agents.

A landmark regulatory withdrawal occurred in 1979 when the Civil Aeronautics Board surrendered its authority to set the rates charged by domestic airlines. The immediate effect was a fierce price competition between the various carriers, who promoted dozens of different "fare saver" plans.

Federal Maritime Commission   The primary functions of the commission are to (1) regulate the services, practices, and agreements of common carriers by water; (2) approve or disapprove tariff filings of such common carriers engaged in foreign commerce; (3) regulate rates, fares, charges, classifications, tariffs, regulations, and practices of common carriers by water in the domestic offshore trade of the United States; and (4) investigate discriminatory rates, charges, classifications, and practices in water-borne foreign and domestic offshore commerce.

Consumer-Oriented Legislation and Agencies

The Federal Trade Commission exists primarily to maintain a competitive marketing environment among producers. Consumers, however, are protected from possible product-related hazards by three federal agencies—the Food and Drug Administration, the Consumer Product Safety Commission, and the Food Safety and Quality Service. These agencies work closely with each other and with two other agencies whose focus is primarily on safety in the workplace [the Occupational Safety and Health Administration (OSHA)] and the general environment [the Environmental Protection Agency (EPA)].

Food and Drug Administration (FDA)   The Food and Drug Administration was established in 1906 as a result of consumer complaints concerning the low quality of basic foods and the hazardous substances in many medicines. The Muckrakers, a group of journalists who publicized the appalling practices they found in the marketing of some consumer products (particularly processed foods), were highly influential in the founding of the FDA.

The broad purpose of the FDA has always been to ensure that consumers get safe, sanitary, properly labeled products. As a constituent agency of the Department of Health and Human Services, it employs approximately 7,500 people in 50 field offices throughout the country.

Legislation Enforced by the FDA   The FDA is responsible for enforcing four laws:

1. *The Food, Drug, and Cosmetic Act* of 1938 (and its several amendments) attempts to assure consumers that (a) foods are pure, safe to eat, and produced under sanitary conditions; (b) cosmetics are safe and properly labeled; and (c) packaging and labeling of these products is truthful and informative.
2. *The Public Health Service Act* of 1944 gives the FDA authority to regulate the safety of vaccines, serums, and blood in interstate commerce and to assure the safety of the food, water, and sanitary facilities for travelers on planes, buses, and trains.
3. *The Fair Packaging and Labeling Act* of 1966 requires that labels inform consumers of the ingredients and weight of packages containing food, drugs, medical devices, and cosmetics.
4. *The Radiation Control for Health and Safety Act* of 1968 gives the FDA authority to set standards to protect consumers from excessive radiation from electronic products such as X-ray machines, color television sets, and microwave ovens.

The FDA uses two methods to achieve the objectives of the Pure Food and Drug Act and the other laws it is responsible for: education and court procedures.

Education   The first method is to inform the regulated companies of the full requirements of the law. Seminars, correspondence, conferences, and individual counseling are all part of "preventative enforcement."

Court Procedures   The second method is enforcement. The FDA can take one of three legal steps when the law is violated. First, it can seize the product in question. This is an action against the product, not its manufacturer. If the manufacturer of the product fails to appear in court, the court may then order the product destroyed. If the problem is one of mislabeling (as opposed to dangerous quality), the court may sell the product or give it to charity.

If the manufacturer does appear in court and admits the product violates the law, the court may allow the product to be reconditioned for sale.

A firm found guilty of violating the Federal Food, Drug, and Cosmetic Act may be subject to criminal prosecution with a maximum fine of $10,000 and imprisonment of up to three years for the responsible official(s).

Probably the most hotly contested action of the FDA was its attempt to ban the use of saccharin from food products in 1977. Acting on its responsibility to prohibit the sale of cancer-causing products, the FDA announced the ban less than 48 hours after meeting with a Canadian researcher who found that saccharin could produce tumors in rats when consumed in extremely large quantities. Faced with overwhelming public clamor for the continued use of saccharin in products intended for use by diabetics and consumers interested in weight reduction, Congress eventually intervened to extend the length of time the noncaloric sweetener could be marketed. At stake was a $2 billion-plus industry which had already been hard hit by the FDA's earlier ban on cyclamates, another noncaloric sweetening agent deemed to be carcinogenic. As of this writing, saccharin was still being marketed, with labels carrying appropriate warnings that it could be a health hazard.

By 1984 over 70,000 different chemical compounds were in use and approximately 1,000 more are introduced each year for use in everything from meat to plastic. Protecting the public from such potentially harmful products is a primary responsibility of the FDA, the Consumer Product Safety Commission, and the Food Safety and Quality Service.

Consumer Product Safety Commission (CPSC)   Whereas the FDA was established in response to a wave of consumer complaints in the early 1900s, the Consumer Product Safety Commission was born of a later generation's frustration in the marketplace. Between 1906 and 1972 science and technology had revolutionized the growing and processing of food and simultaneously made possible the manufacture of innumerable items that could cause harm to consumers.

The primary goal of the CPSC is to substantially reduce injuries associated with consumer products in or around the home, schools, and recreational areas. Under a Congressional directive this agency sets and enforces safety standards for consumer products. In some cases, it has authority to ban hazardous products from the marketplace. Its responsibility extends to more than 10,000 consumer products.

Among the specific laws administered by the Consumer Product Safety Commission are the Federal Hazardous Substances Act, Flammable Fabrics Act, Poison Prevention Packaging Act, and Refrigerator Safety Act.

Food Safety and Quality Service (FSQS)   The Food, Drug and Cosmetic Act was accompanied by another major piece of legislation passed June 30, 1906—the Meat Inspection Act—which authorized the Department of Agriculture to protect consumers from unwholesome meat, poultry, and eggs. Some 70 years later the Food Safety and Quality Service was consolidated from among the various offices within the Department of Agriculture.

The FSQS sets standards for and certifies the quality of dairy products and fresh and processed foods in addition to meat, poultry, and eggs. It also purchases foods for schools and charitable organizations as needed by the federal food assistance programs. In addition to enforcing several laws dealing with the safety and labeling of meat and egg products, FSQS enforces legislation providing for the humane slaughter of livestock and poultry.

Government Regulation of Marketing in Perspective

Few, if any, informed people feel that the clock can be turned back to the days of laissez-faire. The complexities of modern society make some regulation imperative if our economy is to function. Debate continues, however, over the degree of regulation needed.

Arguments for Less Regulation   Marketing management contends that with consumer freedom of choice in the marketplace on the one hand and competition between businesses on the other, our economy requires little regulation. Businesses that do not provide the kind of products consumers want at a price they are willing to pay will lose out—in the normal course of events and without government intervention—to other businesses that do.

The following are some of the more common arguments against regulation:

1. Regulation often restricts competition rather than promoting it. Big businesses, for example, are sometimes forced to be less aggressive so that small businesses can survive. The net effect of this decrease in competition is to hurt the consumer.
2. Regulation may hamper marketing creativity. Package and product designers, for example, may come up with ideas that, if implemented, could sell more of a product. Yet such ideas may have to be shelved, because they could be considered "deceptive."
3. Under the present system virtually all responsibility for ensuring that the consumer gets his money's worth lies with the seller. The consumer should be protected through education rather than legislation.
4. Regulation is expensive, both for taxpayers and for businesses. Regulatory commissions spend large sums to make cases against businesses. To defend themselves, the accused firms must draw on their own resources, at the expense of shareholders, employees, suppliers, and consumers, to try to prove they are not violating the law.
5. Excessive and often arbitrary power is assigned to personnel of the regulatory commissions. Those responsible for administering and enforcing regulations do not always understand the law and may act highhandedly to promote their personal point of view.
6. Many forms of regulation are unnecessary, because it is advantageous for a business to put the consumer's interests first. Moreover, many businesses are becoming increasingly marketing- and consumer-oriented.

Arguments for More Regulation   Those who favor closer regulation of marketing may cite the following arguments:

1. The point of competition is to win. Because businesses are so concerned with earning a profit, they have few scruples when opportunities occur to take advantage of other businesses. Just as police are needed to protect citizens from one another, so too marketing regulations are needed to protect businesses from one another.
2. Businesses, if they are not regulated, will take advantage of consumers in order to increase their profits. The many instances of fraudulent warranties, misleading statements by salespeople and in advertisements, deceptive packages, unsafe products, and other marketing abuses prove the need for regulation.
3. Truly consumer-oriented firms are rare. To many marketing executives it is simply good public relations to say, "We put the consumer's interest first in everything we do." Logic suggests that, on the contrary, it is the law of self-interest that dominates the thinking of firms.
4. Often companies react slowly to market information when it is in their self-interest. Many argue that impartial agencies will act more expediently to critical information than the companies involved. For example, when a product is found to be potentially harmful, a company may advocate discontinuing the product only after inventories are used up. A government agency such as the FTC will be more likely to require immediate withdrawal, with the loss from obsolete inventory absorbed by the company.

Interestingly, most of those who advocate closer regulation of marketing do not find fault with the basic concept of a competitive, private-enterprise economy. Instead, they endorse a system in which businesses compete in the marketplace, but under rules that provide fair treatment for all concerned—consumers and businesses.

The arguments of consumer groups and others who feel that corporations should be more socially responsible have won widespread political support in recent years. Thus, regardless of the validity of the charges and countercharges and periodic trends toward deregulation, the demand for more regulation will probably continue.

SOCIAL RESPONSIBILITY OF MARKETING

Many consumers and businesspeople alike argue that marketing would not face so much regulation if it would live up to its social responsibilities. In a profit-directed society we can define **economic responsibility** as *the four-fold obligation of a firm to (1) produce and market products that meet the needs, wants, and desires of people; (2) provide employment; (3) earn profits needed to finance present and future business operations; and (4) pay the firm's proportionate*

share of taxes to help finance social programs. Meanwhile, we can define the **legal responsibility** of a firm simply as *the obligation to obey all applicable laws, regulations, and court orders voluntarily, conscientiously, and promptly.*

The social responsibility of business is more difficult to define than either economic or legal responsibility. For our purposes **social responsibility** means *the contribution a firm should make to society above and beyond meeting its economic and legal responsibilities.* Often, the distinction between the legal and social responsibilities of marketing managers is not clear. Certainly, it is the social responsibility of a firm not to make and market those items known to be dangerous, regardless of whether specific laws against such items have been enacted or not. After a product-safety law becomes operative, however, it is then also the legal responsibility of a firm to obey the law.

Social responsibility is intertwined deeply with ethics, which is the discipline that deals with what is "good or bad" or "right or wrong." Ethics is not a science, and there are a few universally accepted standards of ethical conduct. Nevertheless, over a period of time a general consensus may develop concerning whether certain marketing practices are responsible. For example, assuming a firm acts strictly within the law, is it demonstrating social responsibility when it (1) suggests through promotion that the product performs better than it really does, (2) promises something "free" with the purchase of another product when in truth nothing is actually free, (3) makes misleading comparisons of its products with those of a competitor, or (4) fails to tell consumers of the relatively low nutritional value found in some products, such as hot dogs, soft drinks, or many cereals?

Increasingly, consumers expect firms to do more than simply meet legal requirements. Ethics, morality, and fairness are also being used to appraise businesses in terms of social responsibility.

Criticisms of Marketing

Marketing has long been downgraded. Historically, business in general and marketing in particular have not had the respect accorded professions such as medicine, law, and education. Plato, for example, believed that the merchant class was inferior to all others. His protégé Aristotle felt that traders should be censured, because they profited at the expense of their fellow human beings. In Athens the word for retailer came to mean "trickster." The Old Testament contains many passages suggesting that merchants take advantage of people. A noted Roman statesman of the sixth century, Cassiodorus, made the pronouncement: *Nullus Christianus debet esse mercatur,* meaning, "No Christian should be a merchant." In more modern times, plays, books, and movies all have been used to describe marketing malpractices to the public. In this century we have had several periods of consumer protest, primarily prompted by the failure of marketing to live up to its social responsibility.

Consumerism   Consumer protest reached new heights in the 1960s and 1970s when the term **consumerism** came into widespread use to indicate *an attitude of dissatisfaction with marketing practices.* More specifically, the term indicates an organized effort by individuals, public and private agencies, and some businesses to protect consumers from marketing malpractices, such as inadequate product information, dishonest claims, and misleading warranties. The term is also associated with movements to correct other social problems, such as pollution and economic inequities. Its basic tenet, however, is fair play by business toward consumers.

As the consumer movement grew, reporters for the print and broadcast media made it a special point to investigate complaints by readers and viewers, usually involving the marketing side of business. Consumerists such as Ralph Nader appeared frequently on television to cite specific marketing malpractices. Many politicians, aware of voter interest in these issues, made legislative proposals designed to protect the consumer from alleged deceptive marketing techniques.

In examining the social responsibilities of marketing, we will attempt to evaluate objectively the criticisms directed at it—bearing in mind that any discussion of social responsibility is complicated by the subjectivity of the terms we must use. Words such as "ethics," "morality," "good," "bad," "right," and "wrong" are subject to considerably different interpretations by different individuals.

Economic Responsibilities of Marketing   Traditionally, marketers, as part of our economic system, have been expected to perform their functions so as to provide the maximum number of people with the maximum standard of living, measured quantitatively. Marketers have an obligation to maximize efficiency in the use of human, material, and financial resources.

Even among marketing's most outspoken critics, there is little question that it has played a key role in attaining a standard of living that, at least quantitatively, is the envy of many other nations. It is the way in which marketing seeks to provide a high quantitative standard of living that upsets many consumerists and social leaders. The emerging consensus, not only among marketing critics but also among many marketing practitioners, is that marketing has a responsibility beyond the mere attainment of a relatively high standard of living measured in quantitative terms.

Consumers Demand More Than Products   The feeling is growing that marketing must improve its conduct in dealing with consumers. Critics cite many abuses that must be corrected. Dishonest, distasteful advertising; misleading pricing policies; deceptive packaging; exaggerated product claims; the promotion of unsafe products; and worthless warranties are some of the practices that lower the quality of economic life. In addition some feel that it is the responsibility of marketing to contribute to a higher quality of life—for example, by providing recycling programs, by using less high-pressure selling, by stressing employee courtesy, and by putting less emphasis on planned obsolescence.

Many marketing leaders agree that more honesty, more "telling it like it really is," is needed in marketing. Moreover, they feel that adherence to a higher code of ethics will benefit not only the consumer, but business as well. Other statements by those who urge marketers to accept more responsibility for a higher qualitative standard of living are more controversial. For example, the argument that marketing should not try to make people want things they cannot afford is considered unjust by many businesses. Critics claim that influencing poor people to want costly goods results in social unrest and personal unhappiness. Most marketing people feel just the opposite—that making poor people want more and better quality products promotes initiative and self-advancement through education and hard work. Moreover, as long as society is upwardly mobile, providing incentives for self-advancement is good, not bad.

Social Responsibility and the Marketing Concept

The marketing concept is a policy of putting the consumer's needs and desires first. Logic suggests that if business truly put the consumer's interests first all the time, there would be no need for consumerism and the resulting deluge of laws, regulations, and criticisms of marketing.

Just as a strong case can be made to support the hypothesis that unions are the result of management's failings, an equally strong case can be made to support the contention that consumerism is the result of marketing management's failings. Deception and occasionally fraud in packaging, pricing, advertising, personal selling, warranties, and pricing are predicated, at least to some degree, on the assumption that the consumer can be fooled. To the extent that such practices exist, it is obvious that the marketing concept is not being practiced.

Most societies seem to have a saying similar to "honesty is the best policy." Yet no large society has ever been completely honest about all things in all situations. Deception is particularly noticeable in the marketplace, because this is where people surrender their money for products. Yet most of our successful businesses are honest in dealing with customers. Relatively few firms have succeeded by taking advantage of the consumer. Actually, more businesses have become successful in the style of the late J.C. Penney, who advocated doing business by following the Golden Rule, not by following a policy of "the public can be fooled."

Perhaps it is improper to blame business for all that is wrong—or said to be wrong—with marketing. Those who manage the marketing side of business had their attitudes toward competition, honesty, marketing responsibility, and ethics shaped largely by their experiences with other institutions—schools, churches, government at various levels, and the family. Business—particularly marketing—is a reflection of our culture. In the long run, the evolution of nonbusiness institutions within society largely determines how business is carried on.

The Consumer Movement

Various waves of consumer protest, alternating with periods of consumer indifference, have occurred during this century. During the 1930s many consumers were unable to buy what they needed and wanted because they had little purchasing power. During the early 1940s people sacrificed many of their desires for goods because of the war effort. It was not until the late 1940s and the 1950s that consumers had a chance to make up for all those postponed purchases. They did so by building and enjoying the most prosperous economy in world history. Great inputs of ingenuity and imagination were devoted to satisfying consumer wants, and many products never before dreamed of were created. The so-called affluent society came into being.

Preoccupation with fulfillment of human wants, however, eventually paved the way to an examination of the marketplace itself. Consumer discontent spread. A new generation had emerged whose members had known material comforts all their lives and had the leisure and motivation to observe and evaluate their world. After taking a closer look at long-established customs and practices, they laid the foundations of a new social conscience.

Yet another explanation of consumer discontent, and perhaps the most important one, concerns our ability to produce. Since the Industrial Revolution historians and sociologists have talked about a "cultural lag," meaning that our technological advances have outdistanced our ability to recognize and deal with the human problems they create. To many, this cultural lag seemed to become more pronounced with the outpouring of sophisticated products and the increase in productive capability that followed World War II.

President John F. Kennedy described some of the problems created for consumers by our booming technology in a special message to Congress in March of 1962:

> The march of technology—affecting, for example, the foods we eat, the medicines we take, and the many appliances we use in our homes—has increased the difficulties of the consumer along with his opportunities; and it has outmoded many of the old

MARKETING
Strategy

Beech-Nut versus Gerber

Gerber has long been the leader in the $500-million-a-year baby food industry, presently holding 70 percent of the market.* In recent years Beech-Nut Nutrition Corporation's advances into the market have caused Gerber to align its products and promotions with the current trends in infant nutrition.

Founded in 1928, Gerber produced only baby food in its early years. The basic strategy was "babies are our business." As the pioneer company in the industry Gerber had the lion's share of the market. Diversification seemed unnecessary. The market for baby food was expanding because of an increasing number of births as well as increasing consumer income after the Great Depression.

The downturn in the birth rate, as well as in the absolute number of births in the late 1950s and the 1960s, caused Gerber to reexamine its strategy of selling only baby food and a few baby-related nonfood products. The need to diversify seemed essential.

In the late 1960s Gerber attempted to market a number of foods aimed at adults. These ranged from catsup to convenience foods. Gerber ran into overwhelming competition from the big, well-established food companies and also found that a name so long associated with baby food was a handicap. No matter how it labeled any of its adult products, people still thought of it as baby food or as something for adults who could not eat regular adult food.

The desire to diversify induced Gerber to create two service businesses. In 1967 Gerber started selling mail-order life-insurance policies to young parents. In 1970 the company entered the day-care-center business. Both of these operations lost money for several years, and today are only marginally profitable.

Beech-Nut was comparatively unknown in the baby product market until 1973 when a group headed by Frank C. Nicholas acquired Beech-Nut and launched a major campaign to rejuvenate the sluggish baby food industry. For years both Gerber and Beech-Nut had advertised in print and TV, but not extensively. Gerber controlled most of the market, and Beech-Nut was too small to take on Number One. To do battle with Gerber, Beech-Nut decided to rely primarily on public relations, an element in the promotion mix that normally plays only a supportive role.†

In 1976 the company widely publicized its decision to change its baby food formula so that it contained no sugar or salt. The company's intent was to use public relations to impress consumers with the idea that it could change to meet current needs. The broad goal of the Beech-Nut public-relations program was to win consumer acceptance as a credible, trustworthy, and dynamic company producing healthy foods for babies.

One key element in the Beech-Nut public-relations effort was a consumer education program. Its goal was to persuade mothers that baby food without salt or sugar was good for babies, even though the food might not appeal to the mother's own taste.

Approximately 100 representatives of the print and broadcast media attended a luncheon in New York to hear Frank Nicholas announce that Beech-Nut would make baby food for the baby's taste, not for the mother's taste. The impact of this announcement was tremendous. All three TV networks carried it, and coverage in the press was extensive.

Beech-Nut management gives its public-relations campaign much credit for repositioning the company to be an important contender in the industry, introducing a new product, and improving the morale of company personnel.

At the moment Beech-Nut is beginning to seriously plunge into broadcast advertising. Its ad budget is now about $800,000, compared to a paltry $11,000 budgeted in years before.‡

Gerber had long contended that medical opinion about salt and sugar is divided, but the Beech-Nut campaign was so successful, Gerber followed suit and modified its formula. It has had to spend significantly more money on advertising to try to keep up with Beech-Nut's public-relations tactics. Its 1982 ad budget reached $4.5 million. The primary objective of these ads was to inform consumers that Gerber baby food also contains no salt or sugar.

Beech-Nut is still far behind Gerber in market share, but its move to meet a sensitive public issue about nutrition has paid off handsomely, putting it in second place in the baby food industry and shaking Number One.

* Cecelia Lentine, "Nutritional Concerns Feed an Industry," *Advertising Age*, March 15, 1982, pp M28–29.
† Jeanne Gunne, "Public Relations and the Marketing Mix," *Advertising Age*, February 6, 1978, p. 39.
‡ Al Urbanski, "Beech-Nut Reborn," *Sales and Marketing Management*, December 6, 1982, pp. 26–29.

The forefather of modern consumerism began around the turn of the century as an unorganized reform movement spearheaded by respected journalists. Although the earliest participants were sincere in their desire to bring abuses and problems to the attention of the public, other writers soon emerged who sought to exploit the movement for its sensationalism.

The emergence of big business during the 1890s had brought in its wake political, social, and economic problems. A corresponding growth in the publication of magazines and newspapers enabled journalists to attract a wide audience. As reader interest in the reform movement grew, few persons or institutions were excluded from criticism.

In the beginning it was the older and more respected magazines that catered to the people's awakening social consciousness. *Harper's, Scribner's,* and the *Atlantic Monthly* followed *McClure's* and *Collier's Weekly* as publishers of some of the earliest reform articles. Reputations were made and broken as Ida M. Tarbell exposed the internal operations of the giant Standard Oil Company, Lincoln Steffens publicized the questionable dealings of the mayor of Minneapolis, and E.H. Harriman brought to public view the names of 14 individuals and corporations that controlled 95 percent of the railroad and banking interests in the country. Even New York's Trinity Church came under attack by Ray Stannard for its ownership of income-producing tenements.

In April 1906 President Theodore Roosevelt applied the label of "muckrakers" to some members of the reform community as a way of protesting irresponsible mudslinging. Said the President,

laws and regulations and made new legislation necessary. The typical supermarket before World War II stocked about 1,500 separate food items—an impressive figure by any standards. But today it carries over 6,000. Ninety percent of the prescriptions written today are for drugs that were unknown 20 years ago. Many of the new products used every day in the home are highly complex. The housewife is called upon to be an amateur electri-

In Bunyan's *Pilgrim's Progress* you may recall the description of the man who could look no way but downward with the muckrake in his hands, who was offered a celestial crown for his muckrake, but who would neither look up nor regard the crown he was offered, but continued to rake to himself the filth of the floor.

Roosevelt was not unsympathetic to sincere attempts to institute reform, however. Following publication of Upton Sinclair's *The Jungle,* he began an investigation of the book's target—the Chicago meat-packing industry—which brought about the passage of both the Pure Food and Drug Act and the Meat Inspection Act in 1906. Both pieces of legislation were landmarks in the government regulation of marketing.

The muckrakers continued to batter the eyes and ears of the citizenry until, eventually, interest in their "sensational" exposés waned, even among the most enthusiastic supporters of social reform. With the coming of World War I the muckrakers quietly faded from the journalistic scene, but not, if must be said, before they helped bring about many needed reforms in government and business.

Although the term "muckraking" is seldom used today, the tradition of journalistic social reform with regard to marketing is still very much in evidence in such books as Ralph Nader's *Unsafe at Any Speed,* Rachel Carson's *Silent Spring,* Jessica Mitford's *The American Way of Death,* Dan Morgan's *Merchants of Grain,* Jim Hightower's *Eat Your Heart Out,* David Hapgood's *The Screwing of the Average Man,* and Jack Anderson's *Confessions of a Muckraker.*

Several periods of consumerism have existed in the twentieth century, and each has produced needed reforms in business and marketing. The increased and prolonged consumerism of the 1960s and 1970s may make more socially responsible marketing behavior a way of doing business in the future. Certainly, each previous consumer movement has helped increase the social responsibility of businesspeople.

cian, mechanic, chemist, toxicologist, dietitian, and mathematician—but she is rarely furnished the information she needs to perform these tasks proficiently.[3]

---

[3] "A Special Message on Protecting the Consumer Interest," speech delivered to Congress, March 15, 1962.

President Kennedy went on to list four basic consumer rights:

1. The right to be informed
2. The right to safety
3. The right to choose
4. The right to be heard

Marketing Practices Considered Most Irresponsible

No facet of marketing has completely escaped criticism in recent years. However, some tactics have come under hotter fire than others, primarily because of their high visibility. Despite efforts to legislate and regulate the functions of marketing and business, there are always enough unscrupulous practitioners around to arouse the public's suspicion of all marketers.

Most criticism of marketing is directed at

1. Misleading advertising
2. Deceptive packaging
3. Deceptive pricing
4. Defective products
5. Misleading warranties
6. Deceptive personal selling tactics

Misleading Advertising   Advertising is the most controversial of all demand-stimulation activities because it is so pervasive. Marketers use all sorts of media—television, radio, magazines, newspapers, billboards, public vehicles, and packages—to urge the consumer to buy. The pervasiveness of advertising in our society has led to obvious abuses. Advertisers have been charged, at the very least, with insulting the intelligence of their audience and at worst with intentionally misleading or deceiving the public.

Some progress, however, has been made toward greater social responsibility in marketing. The advertisements in Figure 21-1, for example, were typical of many used to promote products in the latter part of the nineteenth century. Devices were offered that would supposedly cure all kinds of ailments, from cancer to stuttering. Some cigarettes were even claimed to cure asthma, hay fever, throat diseases, and consumption. Figure 21-2 shows a 1930s advertisement for Lucky Strike cigarettes. Most tobacco companies used the smoking-is-good-for-your-health theme, a practice that today is both socially and legally irresponsible.

Some advertising techniques, such as **bait-and-switch advertising**, are obviously deceptive. In this case a retailer advertises a particularly desirable product at an especially attractive price. When customers arrive at the store, the retailer persuades them to switch to the purchase of more profitable items by pointing out heretofore-unmentioned drawbacks of the advertised good, by claiming to be out of stock, or by other high-pressure tactics.

Responsible advertisers sometimes get into trouble when they use mock-ups to represent products attractively in television commercials. Real ice cream, for example, will melt when exposed to the hot lights needed to film or videotape a commercial. Is using mashed potatoes, then, which are an acceptable substitute as far as the camera lens is concerned, unethical? Technically, under federal regulations, this sort of mock-up could be considered deceptive. Its intent, however, is not to deceive but to represent the product realistically.

Deceptive Packaging   The proliferation of odd package sizes and incomplete or misleading information on labels has caused concern in recent years. Opponents of packaging regulations have argued that the consumer is "too smart to be deceived." Those in favor of legislation, on the other hand, describe the consumer as "too overwhelmed" by the sheer numbers of products and package sizes offered to be able to make intelligent purchase decisions. The former argument was challenged by a test reported in the *Congressional Record* for June 2, 1966. Thirty-three young married women, all of whom had attended college for at least one year and had a year of regular shopping experience, were asked to choose the 20 "best" buys from items such as those carried by supermarkets. They were allowed two and one-half minutes per item to make a decision. When the results were tallied, it was found that the test groups had bypassed the "best" buys 43 percent of the time. Consumerists asked, "What degree of shopping expertise can be expected of less educated, less experienced consumers?"

The Fair Packaging and Labeling (Truth in Packaging) Act of 1966 attempts to standardize not only the contents statement, but also the way the product manufacturer is identified on the package. It also prohibits the practice of filling a package with considerably less than it can hold, unless the airspace is needed to preserve the contents.

Although academicians, legislators, and consumerists will debate marketing's responsibilities in the field of packaging and labeling for some time to come, some degree of standardization seems essential. When we consider that a supermarket, one of the many types of retailers with whom most consumers deal each week, stocks over 9,000 items, we see that the number of decisions forced on the consumer is staggering.

Deceptive Pricing   Theoretically, a misleading price should be much easier to detect than a misleading advertisement or package label. In truth, however, deceptive pricing is far more prevalent. Examples of intentional deceit abound in economic literature. They are found again and again in the sales of encyclopedias, magazines, automobiles, real estate, and many services. Deception in pricing is frequently hard to pin down. Sometimes it is all but inseparable from overly enthusiastic selling techniques, but no one is immune to injury from abuses in this area. For example, many shoppers assume larger retail packages are cheaper per ounce than smaller pack-

Figure 21-1

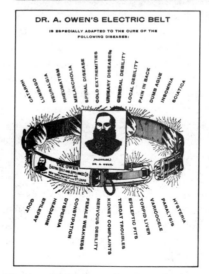

Source: All three from The Bettmann Archive.

Figure 21-2

"**I protect my voice with LUCKIES**"

"It's that delightful taste after a cup of coffee that makes Luckies a hit with me. And naturally I protect my voice with Luckies. No harsh irritants for me...I reach for a Lucky instead. **Congratulations on your improved Cellophane wrapper. I can open it.**"

Edmund Lowe

Who can forget **Edmund Lowe** as "**Sergeant Quirt**" in "**What Price Glory?**" That mighty role made Eddie famous in filmland—and he's more than held his own in a long line of talkie triumphs. We hope you saw him in the "**Spider.**" And be sure to see him in the **Fox** thriller, "**The Cisco Kid.**"

MOISTURE-PROOF CELLOPHANE
Sealed Tight Ever Right
THE UNIQUE HUMIDOR PACKAGE
Zip—
and it's open!

LUCKY STRIKE
IT'S TOASTED
CIGARETTES

"**It's toasted**"
Your Throat Protection — against irritation — against cough

And Moisture-Proof Cellophane Keeps that "Toasted" Flavor Ever Fresh

Copr., 1931,
The American
Tobacco Co.

★ **Is Mr. Lowe's Statement Paid For?**
You may be interested in knowing that not one cent was paid to Mr. Lowe to make the above statement. Mr. Lowe has been a smoker of LUCKY STRIKE cigarettes for 6 years. We hope the publicity herewith given will be as beneficial to him and to Fox, his producers, as his endorsement of LUCKIES is to you and to us.

Source: Life (November 23, 1936).

ages. However, a survey of 2,177 grocery brands found 400 brands for which the larger size cost more per unit (per ounce, for example) than the smaller size.[4]

Some so-called abuses are partly a result of custom in some industries. Moneylenders, for example, and those who sold goods on credit traditionally felt little or no guilt about not revealing the true cost of credit. Several years of investigation and discussion preceded the passage, in 1968, of the Consumer Credit Protection Act, more commonly known as the "Truth in Lending" Act. Thanks to this law, borrowers of money (whether from a retail store through credit purchases, from banks, or from consumer-finance firms) must be informed in detail about the full cost of the interest charged them. The percent-per-month financing fee charged by many retailers and credit-card companies, and its annualized equivalent, must be stated on credit agreements and monthly bills. Contracts between money-lenders and borrowers must show the actual dollar amount of interest to be paid, in addition to the percentage and the number of payments.

The intent of the truth-in-lending law was to provide the consumer with complete information concerning the cost of credit transactions, the rationale being that an informed customer will make sounder purchasing decisions. Certain limitations of putting so much emphasis on disclosure have been noted, however, both before and since the passage of the act. As Federal Trade Commission Chairman Paul Rand Dixon pointed out during prepassage congressional hearings, "Truth in lending is not going to reach the problem in the ghetto."

Defective Products   In recent years consumers have leveled numerous complaints against producers for failing to make products of the highest possible quality. Although quality is often a subjective term, the number of defective product recalls in the past 15 years bears evidence that many consumers are justified in their criticisms of product quality and performance.

Some states have even passed "Lemon Laws" in reaction to voter protests over product quality. Connecticut's law applies to automobiles and states that any dealer who cannot fix a defective car in four attempts or 30 days must give the owner a new car. California, New York, and New Jersey have similar laws, and 10 other states are considering them.[5]

Recalls are a prevalent method the government uses to force companies to fix defective products. No business is exempt from the possibility that some of its products will be recalled. A firm can take several steps to

---

[4] Stanley M. Widrick and Clint Tankersley, "Quantity Surcharge—Let the Buyer Beware," *Annual Conference Proceedings*, Vol. 2 (New Orleans, LA: American Institute of Decision Sciences, 1979), p. 245.

[5] William M. Bulkeley, "'Lemon Laws' Gaining Popularity Despite Auto Makers' Opposition," *Wall Street Journal*, July 12, 1983, p. 41.

minimize the potential damage to its reputation. First, it should exercise the closest possible quality control to reduce the chances of product recall. Second, if product recall is necessary, the firm should act to remove the product from the marketplace as quickly as possible. As a defensive measure, the firm should know where the potentially dangerous products are located (retailers, wholesalers, and ultimate consumers who may have purchased them). Third, necessary repairs to the recalled products should be made quickly, or, if this cannot be done, as in the case of food and drugs, middlemen and/or consumers should be compensated for their financial loss. Fourth, the recall program should be handled in a positive manner to protect the goodwill of the firm and keep the experience from becoming a cause célèbre.

Misleading Warranties In no area of marketing is there more misunderstanding between consumers and business people than in that of product warranties. Theoretically, a warranty should offer two-way protection. It should simultaneously protect the consumer against losses due to the purchase of a defective product and limit the manufacturer's liability to repair or replace the product.

Most of the confusion stems from the extensive use of "legalese" in warranty provisions. Because most consumers find it difficult, if not impossible, to decipher the warranty terms, they are often unable to take advantage of the protection the agreement offers.

Whirlpool is the acknowledged innovator in the field of warranty presentation. In the mid-1960s the company redesigned its appliance warranties as one-page letters to its customers. The letters stated clearly and simply the terms under which defective parts would be replaced and other repairs made. The consumer battle for more effective warranties is far from over, however. Numerous problems plague both the grantors and the receivers of warranties. One of the most prevalent problems is that many companies have too few trained repairpeople to carry out the terms of the warranty. Another disquieting problem is the high cost of product repair. A third is the inability of manufacturers and retailers to agree on how much responsibility each should have when a product proves unsatisfactory to the consumer.

Deceptive Personal Selling Tactics Most of the indignation over deceptive sales approaches is directed at door-to-door salespeople. Door-to-door selling tactics have perhaps always been considered "high pressure," and the consumer movement brought out numerous revelations of intentional deception on the part of unscrupulous marketers. One often-cited villain was a furnace manufacturer whose salespeople, sometimes posing as government inspectors, would advise homeowners that their heating systems were dangerous. One complaint against the company stated that a sales representative dismantled the furnace of a prospective customer, then refused to reassemble it, stating, "I wouldn't be a party to murder!"

Other complaints on file concerned tree "surgeons" who insisted on being compensated for felling perfectly healthy trees, pest-control inspectors who planted termites as proof of the need for their services, and aluminum-siding salespeople who made deals with the homeowners to allow visits by other prospects to view the firm's work (with a commission to be paid to the purchasers for each prospect who bought the siding) and then never sent anyone around to look.

Now purchasers of products or services sold door-to-door have a three-day "cooling off" period during which they may change their minds before a contract becomes valid. However, many unethical practices are next to impossible to stop. The FTC can step in only if the firm is engaged in interstate commerce, and state agencies often have neither the authority nor the facilities to handle complaints.

Causes of Irresponsible Marketing

Clearly, some marketing activities are irresponsible and certainly not in the best interests of the consuming public. Several explanations for such behavior have been suggested.

Plain Dishonesty Intentional fraud or deliberate, planned deception by unscrupulous marketers is probably relatively unimportant as a cause of irresponsible behavior, but it does take place. In order for it to command a higher price, wool is sometimes sold as virgin wool when in fact the seller knows full well that it is reclaimed wool. Some sellers of meat have deliberately put less in the package than the label indicates, and some automobile-repair shops have been known to charge motorists for parts never put into a vehicle. Some restaurants put turkey (it's less expensive than chicken) in chicken salad, the 12-ounce steak often weighs only 10 ounces, and the imported lobster sometimes comes from Florida.

A business may be able to survive for some time by deliberately cheating the consumer, but sooner or later, in most cases, either enough consumers will discover that they are being deceived and stop patronizing the business or a regulatory agency will appear on the scene to stop the fraud.

Tradition or Trade Customs A large number of what are now considered to be irresponsible marketing practices can be traced to long-standing trade customs. For generations bait-and-switch promotion was considered a fair ploy. For example, vendors of sewing machines believed that it was a legitimate sales tactic to advertise one machine at a ridiculously low price in order to sell another machine at a much higher price. If a salesperson actually sold the low-priced machine, he was fired. In recent decades it was not uncommon for automobile-repair shops to replace a damaged part with a used one and charge the insurance company the full price of a new part. Because this practice became so much a part of the industry's way of

operating, owners of repair shops that used these tactics apparently felt no guilt. Gross exaggeration of a product's benefits, now frowned upon, was once considered just "part of the game." Moral and ethical standards change, and what is considered ethical today may be a questionable practice in the future.

Ignorance or Carelessness on the Seller's Part   Some cases of what are now considered to be irresponsible marketing activities can be traced to ignorance on the part of the seller. It is hard to believe, for example, that cigarette advertising executives in the 1930s and 1940s knew they were selling a dangerous health hazard when they created such slogans as "Camels steady your nerves" and "Camels aid digestion." We can also cite ignorance as the probable cause for defects in many products, such as certain types of drugs, automobiles, lawn mowers, and unsafe toys. All too often, ignorance is compounded by negligence or insufficient testing of such products before they are marketed. Even when a company pretests a product, however, possibilities for consumer injury still exist.

Motor vehicles, for example, undergo extensive premarket testing. Consequently, the automotive world was shocked when the families of three teenaged girls charged Ford Motor Company officials with reckless homicide resulting from negligence in the design of its 1973 Pinto. Plaintiffs contended that the placement of the gasoline tank caused the car to catch fire after being hit from the rear. Ford, which was acquitted in March 1980 after a long and widely publicized trial, paid $22,500 to the victims' families (the upper limit allowed by Indiana law, scene of the trial).[6]

Competitive Pressures An important cause of irresponsible marketing behavior is related to the nature of our economic system. Executives in almost all industries are under heavy pressure to "win a larger share of the market," "beat last year's sales figures," or "exceed sales goals." As a result of this pressure some marketing managers yield to the temptation to deceive, exploit, or in some other way take advantage of consumers. Probably more irresponsible actions stem from competitive pressures than from a desire to defraud the consumer. Alterations in packages to suggest that they contain more than they actually do, exaggerated promises in advertising copy, deceptive pricing, and many other unethical practices often can be traced directly or indirectly to pressures for profit.

The same pressure for profit that results in some improper marketing activities produces positive results as well. Much, if not most, of the managerial energy created by this pressure results in genuine product improvements; cleaner, more attractive stores; more and better services; and other benefits for the consumer.

Making Marketing More Socially Responsible

It is reasonable to conclude that both the consumer and business want to eliminate abuses in the marketplace. There is considerable difference, however, in the way various groups want to see improvements brought about. Some favor more legislation. Others feel that the answer lies in consumer education. Still others support self-regulation by business.

More Legislation A record-breaking volume of consumer-oriented legislation was enacted during the 1960s and 1970s. Observing that consumers and voters are one and the same, politicians introduced laws at all levels of government designed to protect the public from "wrongdoing" by business. Many lawmakers, aware that new products and marketing techniques create new problems in the marketplace and that legislation sometimes creates new problems in interpretation and enforcement, call for still more legislation to protect consumers from newly discovered abuses and to plug loopholes in existing laws.

Those opposed to more consumer legislation argue that we should simply enforce the laws we already have. Requests for more legislation

---

[6] "Ford Pays $22,500 in Pinto Fire Deaths," *Business Insurance*, August 17, 1980, pp. 1–2.

presuppose obedience to legislation. Although many individuals and businesses will obey a law simply because it is a law, many others will not. All too often, laws are not backed up with adequate funds for enforcement.

Business also objects to more legislation because of the costly paperwork involved. Federally required paperwork is estimated to cost $100 billion per year or about $500 per capita. The work involved in filing reports to government agencies is staggering. For example, when Eli Lilly and Company applied to the Food and Drug Administration for the right to market a new arthritis drug, it submitted a report consisting of 120,000 pages.[7]

Opponents of more legislation feel that two other solutions to consumer abuse should be given more emphasis: consumer education and self-regulation by business.

Consumer Education   Most consumers receive little education or training in how to shop wisely or manage their money intelligently. Few public school systems require students to take courses that would prepare them to protect their own interests in the marketplace. Much free or inexpensive literature is available from both public and private sources, but the demand for these buying aids is not great. Surprisingly, few consumers subscribe to publications that provide objective information about how to shop wisely. *Consumer Reports,* the leading consumer publication, has a circulation of only 2,500,000 per month in a nation with more than 60 million households. Because of a lack of both appropriate education and inclination, typical consumers are buying amateurs in a marketing arena controlled by selling professionals.

Many business leaders and some educators, particularly home economists, support the view that in the long run consumer interests would be better served through education than legislation. They believe that if consumers were taught how to read labels, compare prices and quality, control their desire to buy too much on credit, and buy more rationally, they would need less legislation to protect them.

Critics of consumer education do not denounce it, but feel that it alone is not enough to achieve the desired result in our rapidly changing society. New products are introduced each day. They contend it is unrealistic to think that consumers have the time (or the interest) to become fully informed about everything they buy. This makes consumer-protection laws essential.

Self-Regulation   Many business leaders feel that self-regulation and self-policing by businesses within an industry is, overall, the best way to advance and protect the interests of consumers. The idea of self-regulation is not

---

[7] "Winning the War Against Paperwork," *Nation's Business,* January 1978, p. 72.

new, and it is in fact used extensively in our economy with varying degrees of effectiveness. One industry in which self-imposed regulation is effective is the broadcast industry. The Broadcasters' Code contains several provisions that relate to consumer protection. The complete code contains more than 6,000 words and covers a wide variety of matters.

Advocates of self-regulation point out that no one knows an industry and how it can benefit or take advantage of consumers better than the businesses in that industry. It makes sense, therefore, for an industry to set its own standards for dealing with consumers.

Critics of self-regulation agree that the concept of self-policing has considerable potential, but they point to several limitations. First, the agency doing the regulating, usually a trade association, has very limited power to enforce a "good-conduct" code. It can bring about compliance only through friendly persuasion. Second, competitors within the same industry will not share many of their promotional and merchandising plans. Third, the danger of collusion in pricing and restraints on trade is inherent in any system that brings competitors together to form their own rules. Thus, self-regulation could work against, not for, the consumer's interests.

Adapting Marketing to Consumerism

Precisely how a specific firm should modify its strategies to benefit from consumerism rather than be harmed by it will vary. However, a well-received six-point guideline was developed by Frederick E. Webster. In abbreviated form the guideline states:

1. The overriding objective of all company response should be to ensure a satisfied customer in a manner consistent with the public welfare. This is merely a restatement of the marketing concept, modified slightly to reflect a new awareness that individual consumer satisfaction sometimes detracts from the general welfare of all consumers.
2. The essential ingredients in consumer satisfaction are a product that works and an informed customer.
3. There are five mutually supporting ways of ensuring that a product works. These include (a) anticipating customer mistakes and designing them out; (b) developing the highest standard of quality control; (c) informing the consumer about proper product use and care through advertising, packaging, labeling, and other educational programs; (d) establishing warranty and guarantee provisions that are clear, complete, and honest; and (e) maintaining a

completely effective service organization, including quality control provisions, and backstopping the dealer organization.

4. An informed consumer has both good product information and expectations that are realistic. It therefore follows that: (a) All marketing communications should be truthful and informative in every respect, even for those consumers who are easily confused and misled; (b) marketing communications should not overpromise, creating expectations that the product cannot live up to; and (c) consumers must be educated with respect to their responsibility for the proper use and maintenance of the product, not simply held accountable in some way for failure to care for the product.

5. Consumers are more concerned about products and their performance than about companies per se. Companies become the focus of the consumer's attention only when products do not satisfy or necessary service cannot be obtained. To satisfy consumers, companies should devote their attention to improving product quality and customer service, rather than developing corporate advertising campaigns to improve company image.

6. The essence of effective response to consumerism is an integrated program of product quality, service, and customer information, supported by top management with high-level responsibility for consumer affairs.[8]

SUMMARY

- The two major premises underlying government intervention in business and marketing are that the public welfare supersedes the welfare of business and that competition between businesses and industries should be encouraged.
- Competitor-oriented and consumer-oriented federal legislation and agencies protect Americans from the dangers of unfair business practices, monopolies, and collusion between businesses.
- The Sherman Antitrust Act was the first federal statute aimed at curbing the growth of monopolies. It was supplemented by the Clayton Act, which outlawed price discrimination and agreements between channel members that would tend to keep competitors from entering the market.

---

[8] Excerpt from "Does Business Misunderstand Consumerism?" by Frederick E. Webster, Jr. (September–October 1973).

- Much federal regulation of pricing practices is based on the Robinson–Patman Act, which amended the Clayton Act and established many new provisions affecting discounts, promotional allowances, and variable pricing.
- The Wheeler–Lea Amendment to the Federal Trade Commission Act strengthened the Robinson–Patman Act and was the first government attempt to control advertising and labeling.
- The Federal Trade Commission is the largest of several federal agencies charged with maintaining fair competition among businesses. It also protects consumers through the enforcement of product-safety requirements and the prevention of deceptive advertising and labeling practices or the fixing of prices and quotas.
- In addition to the FTC, major federal regulatory agencies include the Justice Department, the Interstate Commerce Commission, U.S. Tariff Commission, Securities and Exchange Commission, Federal Communications Commission, Federal Maritime Commission, and the Civil Aeronautics Board.
- The FTC also administers consumer-oriented legislation and is joined in this endeavor by the Food and Drug Administration, the Consumer Product Safety Commission, and the Food Safety and Quality Service.
- The Occupational Safety and Health Administration focuses on safety in the workplace. Another agency—the Environmental Protection Agency—helps protect the quality of the general environment.
- Traditionally, the major social responsibility of marketers has been to raise our standard of living quantitatively by operating efficiently and increasing the supply of material goods.
- Today, marketers have a second social responsibility that is equally important—to raise the standard of living qualitatively by eliminating abuses in the marketplace and by considering the effects their marketing decisions will have on the public.
- The failure of some marketers to apply the marketing concept fully—putting the interests of consumers first—is one of the factors behind the consumer movement.
- Some specific marketing practices that are considered inimical to the best interests of buyers are (a) misleading advertising, (b) deceptive packaging, (c) deceptive pricing, (d) defective products, (e) misleading warranties, and (f) deceptive personal selling techniques.
- Irresponsible marketing actions are usually attributable to (a) plain dishonesty, (b) tradition or trade custom, (c) ignorance on the seller's part, or (d) the pressure for profits.
- Irresponsible marketing practices can be prevented by (a) increasing legislation to protect consumers, (b) increasing consumer education, and (c) increasing industry self-regulation.

DISCUSSION QUESTIONS

1. Virtually all marketing activities are subject to government regulation. What are some specific examples of marketing activities that are regulated?
2. How does the government's premise that public welfare takes precedence over business welfare affect the regulation of marketing?
3. What dangers does unregulated competition hold for businesses and consumers? Why would a system of laissez-faire not work today?
4. Describe the difference in intent between competitor-oriented legislation and consumer-oriented legislation.
5. What was the main purpose of the Sherman Antitrust Act? The Clayton Act? The Federal Trade Commission Act? The Robinson–Patman Act? The Wheeler–Lea Act?
6. Explain the objectives of the Federal Trade Commission and the procedural method its employs.
7. Briefly explain the marketing-related regulatory functions of each of the following agencies: the Interstate Commerce Commission, the U.S. Tariff Commission, the Securities and Exchange Commission, the Federal Communications Commission, the Civil Aeronautics Board, and the Federal Maritime Commission.
8. Describe the responsibilities of the Food and Drug Administration, the Consumer Product Safety Commission, and the Food Safety and Quality Service.
9. What are the principal economic responsibilities of marketing? What are the principal social responsibilities of marketing?
10. How are the social responsibilities of marketing related to the marketing concept?
11. Is consumerism partly a result of failures by marketing management? Explain.
12. In what ways do each of the following marketing practices injure consumers?: (a) misleading advertising, (b) deceptive packaging, (c) deceptive pricing, (d) defective products, (e) misleading warranties, and (f) deceptive personal selling techniques.
13. How does each of the following contribute to irresponsible marketing?: (a) dishonesty, (b) tradition or trade custom, (c) seller ignorance or negligence, (d) pressures for profit.
14. What is the best way to eliminate abuses in the marketplace—consumer legislation, consumer education, or industry self-regulation?

APPLICATION EXERCISES

1. Research current business periodicals to find three companies that have been charged with unfair trade practices by the Federal Trade Commission. Summa-

rize the circumstances surrounding these cases in a brief report. Conclude with your appraisal of whether the companies so charged should mount a defense or voluntarily cease the controversial activity.

2. "Resolved: We need more consumer-protection legislation." Develop five arguments for and five against this proposition. Describe your personal reaction to the statement.

3. The concept of a qualitative standard of living was discussed in this chapter. In a brief report summarize what you feel should be the minimum qualitative standard of living for Americans. (You may want to consider such things as products, stores, distribution facilities, packages, and advertising.) What changes in marketing would be required to achieve the goals you set?

4. In current business periodicals find examples of actions instituted by consumers against firms charged with deceptive or misleading marketing practices. Prepare a brief report in which you assess (a) the effectiveness of the various consumer groups involved and (b) the need for additional legislation to protect consumers from such practices.

CASE 21
Thompson Helps Fight Inflation

Between 1968 and 1981 scarcely a month passed that did not see a rise in the Wholesale Food Price Index. Increases in wholesale prices were passed on to the consumer through the retailer, of course. Continually rising prices made it difficult for many families to stay within their food budgets. There were various government programs to help low-income consumers use food stamps and food dollars wisely. Yet little was being done to help those in other income groups.

J.B. Thompson, Inc., a major food processor, saw an opportunity in this situation to show that a large corporation can be concerned about its customers. The president of the company, Edward Wilhoit, believes that in the future people will buy a company's philosophy, not just its products, so he is trying to help J.B. Thompson Foods build consumer goodwill now. One of the ways he has attempted to establish rapport with potential customers is through a computerized menu-planning program.

The Thompson company's kitchen staff spent over 700 hours preparing balanced menus based on various budgets. Data was accumulated on nutritional requirements, what foods were plentiful, food prices, and family characteristics. To prepare one 30-day menu plan alone, the firm tested over 900 recipes and 600 menus. Plans were created for families of from one to ten persons, with food budgets of from $25 to $70 per week.

In August of 1980 a program called "We'll Help You Win" was announced in newspapers and magazines. Readers were invited to send coupons accompanying the firm's ads to its meal-planning center in Chicago, Illinois. Space was provided for a description of the number of adults and children in the family and the weekly food budget.

At the center this information was fed into a computer geared to handle up to 30,000 coupons per day and programmed to select a month's menus tailored to each family. Each consumer received a 10-page printout giving the nutritionally balanced menus, as well as recipes for the major dishes and tips on shopping, food storage, and nutrition. A letter accompanying the printout contained additional tips as well as a description of the care that went into preparing J.B. Thompson products.

Over a million consumers responded to Thompson's invitation to send for their individual menu plan. In addition the firm received hundreds of letters praising the program.

Wilhoit felt the program had demonstrated to consumers that the company was truly concerned about their welfare and that it was sincerely trying to assist them with their problems. He began to meet resistance, though, from several members of the Board of Directors, who felt that generating "goodwill" did not justify the cost of the program. These directors contended that consumers would buy just as many J.B. Thompson products if the program were dropped and they promised to do everything in their power to have it stopped.

Discussion Questions

1. Do you agree that consumers are more likely to buy from firms that show socially responsible behavior? Why or why not?
2. How would you answer the dissenting directors who want to discontinue the program? Can you see logic in their arguments?
3. How would you revise the "We'll Help You Win" program in a period of low inflation (1983–85, for example)?

22 Strategic Marketing Planning

STUDY OBJECTIVES

After studying this chapter, you should be able to

1. Define strategic marketing planning, corporate mission, objectives, and strategies.
2. Explain the process of marketing opportunity assessment.
3. Discuss the Boston Consulting Group, General Electric, and PIMS approaches to marketing strategies.
4. Describe intensive, integrative, and diversified growth strategies.
5. Discuss function, product, region, and customer type marketing organizations.
6. Explain sales analysis, marketing cost analysis, and the marketing audit as methods of evaluating marketing performance.

Throughout this text we have addressed each marketing activity, its planning, and its operation. However, no marketing activity can be completely planned without also considering the other marketing controllable variables. In this final chapter we will discuss the development of an integrated marketing effort, often termed strategic marketing planning. **Strategic marketing planning** *is the process of developing and implementing an effort to fit the organization's marketing goals and capabilities to its marketing opportunities.* To develop a strategic marketing plan, the corporate mission, objectives, and strategies must first be addressed. Once these corporate-level decisions are input, the strategic marketing plan consists of assessing marketing opportunities, setting marketing objectives, developing a strategy to accomplish these objectives, and organizing and controlling the marketing organization to follow these strategies. Figure 22-1 illustrates this process.

CORPORATE MISSION

The **corporate mission** *is a statement of what the company wants to accomplish.* It involves an assessment of the company, its customers, and what both will be in the future. Corporate missions often contain statements concerning corporate products, technology, organization, personnel, customer needs, and target markets. For example, one company may have a corporate mission that could be stated as follows:

> Based on our strong technological foundation, high-tech personnel, state-of-the-art electronics products, contacts in the aerospace industry, and flexible organization, we are and will remain the number-one marketer of electronic subassemblies to the aerospace industry.

Notice that the corporate mission of this fictitious company not only takes a complete look at the company and its markets, but also states where the company is and where it wants to be. The specifics of how to get there are left to corporate strategies.

All companies have corporate missions, whether their personnel realize it or not. Some companies never bother to formally state their corporate mission and perform quite well. However, without a specified corporate mission, it is difficult to set corporate strategies and easy to lose sight of where the company is going.

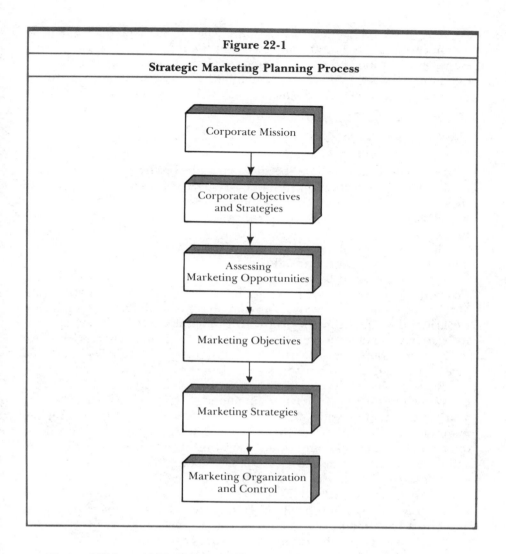

Figure 22-1

Strategic Marketing Planning Process

- Corporate Mission
- Corporate Objectives and Strategies
- Assessing Marketing Opportunities
- Marketing Objectives
- Marketing Strategies
- Marketing Organization and Control

From 1976 to 1978, for example, a loss of corporate mission netted Kentucky Fried Chicken (KFC) an annual 3-percent loss in per-store sales and an annual 26-percent decrease in pretax profits. However, in 1979 things changed. As Corporate Chairman Richard P. Mayer put it, "By moving through the strategies planning process with exhaustive analyses, we were able to realistically redefine our objectives and develop high-leverage strategies and action plans that changed our future." The result: KFC earnings tripled from 1979 to 1982.

As Mayer further explained, "The new mission—to become the strongest, most profitable, and fastest growing chain in the chicken segment of the quick service restaurant industry—set the tone and direction for the entire organization and required all efforts to focus on strategies needed to fulfill this mission."[1] Without such an intensive reexamination of its corporate image, Kentucky Fried Chicken may well have continued its decline.

CORPORATE OBJECTIVES

From the corporate mission, specific corporate objectives can be set. Every manager in the corporation should have specific objectives, derived from the corporate mission, which he or she is responsible for accomplishing. An **objective** *is a statement of what is to be accomplished.* A *corporate objective* may be to keep stockholders happy. A *financial objective* may be a 20-percent return on all investments. A *marketing objective* may be to achieve a 40-percent market share in a particular industry.

Objectives should be specific and realistic. A vague objective such as, "We want to do well in consumer durables," lends management little guidance in meeting the objective. Specific objectives refer to goals that are explicit and include time horizons. It is much more helpful for management to have an objective of "We want to obtain a 25-percent market share in the refrigerator market by 1990." This objective not only sets specific goals for management, but also states when the goals should be met.

Realistic objectives refer to goals that are obtainable. A goal for Toyota of "We will be the largest seller of automobiles in the United States by next year" is simply impossible. It ignores the power of domestic automobile manufacturers and the fact that the federal government would impose quotas before the company could meet this objective. Just because they should be obtainable objectives, however, does not mean they should be easy. Whereas unrealistic objectives may frustrate management, unnecessarily easy objectives will not challenge management. Good realistic objectives should be accomplishable goals, but ones that require commitment and effort from managers.

Unrealistic goals often cause serious management problems. For instance, Datapoint's objective of a continuing record of quarterly profit records forced marketing (under constant pressure to increase sales) into such questionable practices as shipping to customers who had not met company credit requirements, shipping distributors products for which they had no room, and even shipping to imaginary customers ("Joe Blow," in one instance) simply to move products and record sales. When the truth

---

[1] Richard P. Mayer, "Chain's Fortunes Improved When it Rearticulated Its Mission and Strategic Plan," *Marketing News,* July 9, 1982, p. 14.

came out, five marketing executives left the company, a director was demoted, and auditors were called to go over the corporate books. Corporate stock price fell from a high of $67.50 to $12.[2] All this because of management's attempts to meet unrealistic objectives.

CORPORATE STRATEGIES

Strategies *specify what activities need to be undertaken to accomplish the corporate objectives.* For example, an objective of increased profitability can be accomplished by holding sales levels constant and reducing costs or by increasing sales and keeping costs at the same percentage of sales. The first strategy involves efforts to lower marketing, production, and/or administration costs. Often described as an "austerity program," many companies follow this strategy from time to time. The second strategy involves more traditional marketing activities such as identifying new target markets, spending

---

[2] Brenton R. Shlender, "Datapoint Kept Trying to Set Profit Records Until the Bubble Burst," *Wall Street Journal,* May 27, 1982, pp. 1, 23.

more on distribution and promotion, or introducing new products. Which strategy a company follows depends largely on which is most feasible and most consistent with the corporate mission and objectives.

When faced with an objective to increase sales, Whirlpool took an approach that was consistent with its corporate mission to concentrate on the home appliance industry. Its strategy was to develop a loyal and successful dealer network and offer superior customer service—the company's 16-year-old Cool Line handles 250,000 calls a year from customers. The result of this strategy, which was consistent with the corporate mission and objectives, was a 23-percent share of the market in 1982—larger than its closest competitor, General Electric, with 22 percent.[3]

The corporate mission and the resulting objectives and strategies largely influence strategic marketing planning. Only after these corporate-level decisions have been made can marketing begin the process of determining its strategic marketing plans. As Figure 22-1 illustrated, the next step in this process is assessing marketing opportunities.

MARKETING OPPORTUNITY ASSESSMENT

A **marketing opportunity** *exists when the conditions in a particular target market fit the capabilities of a particular company.* **Marketing opportunity assessment** *is the process of searching for and evaluating marketing opportunities.* This ongoing search process is vital if a company wishes to recognize attractive marketing opportunities before it is too late to act on them. Many marketing opportunities exist only for a short period of time and if the company's actions are not timely, it may miss the opportunity. The term **strategic windows** is used to describe the fact that many marketing opportunities exist for a limited time.[4] If a company does not move through that "window," the opportunity is lost.

The process of searching for marketing opportunities is often termed **environmental monitoring**. Environmental monitoring should be an ongoing corporate endeavor to identify changes in the environment that create new corporate opportunities or change the viability of present opportunities. Without such an effort the company will be involved constantly in **crisis management**, that is, *dealing with situations management did not know would occur until it was too late.* Through environmental monitoring management can anticipate and manage many outside changes before they become critical. In this sense management is taking a proactive, rather than reactive, approach to its environment.

---

[3] Jeff Blyskal, "Diversification is for the Birds," *Forbes,* November 7, 1983, p. 132.
[4] Derek F. Abell, "Strategic Windows," *Journal of Marketing,* July 1978, pp. 21–26.

One company had the major position in branded, expensive men's clothing in the 1960s, but ignored environmental changes such as a shift to European styling, more casual clothing styles, sales shifts to suburban malls, and competitive brand building through advertising and promotion. The result by the late 1970s was a market-share slip from 90 percent to less than 50 percent.[5] This company's decline was largely the result of its lack of environmental monitoring.

Evaluation of marketing opportunities should involve an assessment of the market size and growth rate, market requirements, and actions of other companies.[6] Beyond the market size and growth rate, its potential is also affected by competitive, economic, technological, social, legal, and political factors.[7] Because these factors vary for each target market, their effect on market potential also varies.

Market requirements are related to the purchasing requirements of the target customers. Do they purchase in particular outlets? What promotional media and messages affect them? Are they product quality and/or price sensitive? Answers to these questions affect whether or not a particular target market matches the company's capabilities.

Finally, all marketing opportunities must be evaluated with reference to company characteristics. If the company has a reputation for fine quality, high-priced products, a marketing opportunity in discount channels probably will not fit the company mission. Management must evaluate all financial, productive, distributive, and technological capabilities and reputation before deciding on a specific marketing opportunity.

For example, Texas Instruments' efforts to take advantage of marketing opportunities in watches and home computers ignored the company's lack of consumer marketing capability. As the president of a competitor put it, "[TI] had the engineer's attitude. TI said, 'We'll educate the consumer to the benefits of our technology,' while Casio 'sets out to fill the consumer's wants.'"[8] The result of these misguided matches is that Texas Instruments has pulled out of both these marketing opportunities, the same opportunities that have been successful for companies such as Casio (watches) and Commodore (home computers), because their capabilities matched the marketing opportunities.

Once marketing opportunities are selected, marketing management can set specific marketing objectives and strategies. Again, these objectives

[5] C. Davis Fogg, "Anticipate Market Changes, Redefine Business, and Readjust Strategic Mix to Ensure Long-Term Success," *Marketing News*, March 18, 1983, Sect. 2, pp. 16–17.

[6] David Cravens, Gerald E. Hills, and Robert B. Woodruff, *Marketing Decision Making: Concepts and Strategy*, rev. ed. (Homewood, Ill.: Richard D. Irwin, 1980), p. 102.

[7] Derek F. Abell and John S. Hammond, *Strategic Market Planning*, (Englewood Cliffs, NJ: Prentice-Hall, 1979), p. 10.

[8] "When Technology Failed at Texas Instruments," *Business Week*, June 22, 1981, pp. 91–94.

and strategies must be realistic and consistent with the corporate mission and objectives.

MARKETING OBJECTIVES AND STRATEGIES

The setting of marketing objectives and strategies within the guidelines of corporate strategies is the essence of strategic marketing planning. Primarily, this process involves a matching of corporate strengths to market strengths. Four approaches to strategic marketing planning are most prevalent: the Boston Consulting Group approach, the General Electric approach, the PIMS approach, and growth strategies.

Boston Consulting Group Approach

The **Boston Consulting Group (BCG)**, or **product portfolio, approach** is based on an analysis of each product's market growth rate and its market share. The combination of these two factors provides some general strategic guidelines.

Much like investors with a number of investments of varying risks and returns, a company's product offering can be looked on as a "portfolio" of various risks and returns. In analyzing a corporate product portfolio, marketing managers should examine each product's competitive position and its profitability and cash flow potential.[9]

By developing a portfolio grid with market share on one axis and market growth rate on the other, a marketing manager can visualize specific categories of products and into which categories the company's product mix falls. Figure 22-2 illustrates this process.

Four categories of products are identifiable: stars, cash cows, dogs, and problem children.[10] **Stars** *are products that have a dominant share of a rapidly growing market.* Although stars often require large amounts of cash to finance their growth, they have a high probability of returning large profits over time.

Cash cows *are stars that have matured and have a dominant share of a stable market.* Because sales are high and little cash is invested for growth, cash cows return large sums of money to the corporation.

Dogs *are products that have a low share of a stable market.* They may generate enough cash to justify their continuance (though not always), but pro-

---

[9] Joseph P. Guiltinan and Gordon W. Paul, *Marketing Management: Strategies and Programs* (New York: McGraw-Hill, 1982), p. 31.

[10] George S. Day, "Diagnosing the Product Portfolio," *Journal of Marketing,* April 1977, pp. 29–38.

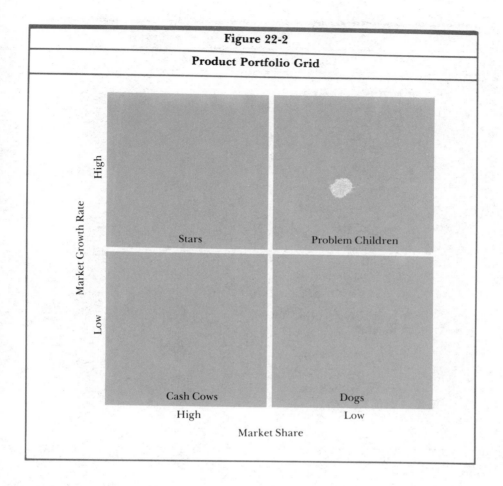

Figure 22-2

Product Portfolio Grid

Market Growth Rate

High

Low

Stars

Problem Children

Cash Cows

Dogs

High

Low

Market Share

vide little potential for large profitability. Companies cannot afford too many dogs.

Problem children *are products that have a low share of a high growth market.* Because they are not dominant products, there is some risk of their ever returning much cash to the company. A great deal of cash will be required to build them into stars or even maintain them. They are the riskiest products in which to invest corporate funds.

Figure 22-3 illustrates a portfolio grid for a particular company. Notice that the company has two cash cows (one large and one small), one star, three problem children, and three dogs. The size of the circles indicates the relative dollar sales of each product.

Although not in a bad position, this company's strategic marketing plans should address several potential problems. First, the company has

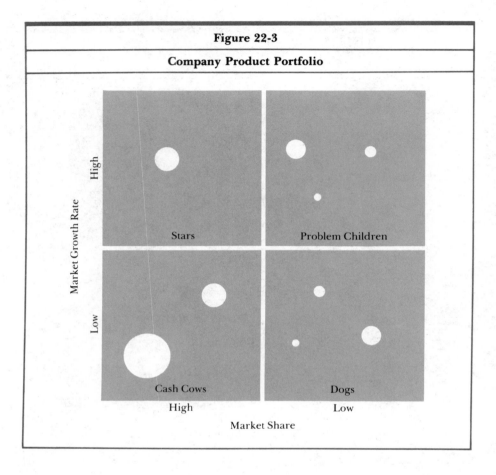

Figure 22-3

Company Product Portfolio

Market Growth Rate

High

Low

Stars

Problem Children

Cash Cows

Dogs

High

Low

Market Share

only one star. Even though its cash cows are quite healthy, they will fade eventually. Marketing needs to concentrate on developing more stars to eventually take the place of the present cash cows. Perhaps one of the problem children can be developed into a star. However, a careful analysis of each problem child should precede any large investment. Problem children are, by virtue of their market position, risky. Second, the company should give its dogs a critical examination. Two are quite small and may need to be eliminated. Often, the elimination of a weak product provides cash that a company can invest better in other areas.

A final point on the BCG approach is that the product portfolio analyzes the product mix at one point in time. The future potential for each product is only indirectly addressed. A company should use this analysis in conjunction with an appraisal of the future viability of each product, and should update the portfolio periodically to determine whether any products have moved from their previous positions in the grid. Many products start as problem children, move to stars and cash cows, and finally end up as dogs.

General Electric Approach

The management at General Electric Company developed an analysis similar to the BCG approach called the **market attractiveness/business position model**. It is illustrated in Figure 22-4. The *market attractiveness* on the vertical axis consists of an evaluation of market size and growth rate, potential profit margin, competitive intensity, business cycles and/or seasonality, potential economies of scale, and cost and feasibility of entering the market. The *business strength* on the horizontal axis consists of an appraisal of the company's market share relative to the competition, competitiveness of all four marketing controllable variables (product, place, promotion, and price), and knowledge of the market.

The three upper-left squares represent products with high overall attractiveness. These are strong products that are positioned in attractive markets. The three lower-right squares represent products with low overall attractiveness—the company's offering is weak, and the market is not very promising. Marketing should consider dropping or changing the marketing controllable variables and/or the target markets for these products.

The middle three squares represent promising products. Especially promising are products in the upper-right grid. The market is attractive, and through continued investment the company may improve its product position and move to the upper left. Again, this type of analysis can provide guidelines to management in strategic marketing planning.

PIMS Approach

In order to carry out research for its **Profit Impact on Marketing Strategy (PIMS)** program, the Strategic Planning Institute gathered information on 1,700 products offered by its member companies. Over 200 companies provided confidential information on their business environment, competitive position, production processes, budgets, strategic moves, and operating results.[11] Such information on member companies' experiences has allowed the institute to draw certain conclusions concerning strategies and profitability[12]:

---

[11] *The PIMS Program,* (Cambridge, Mass.: The Strategic Planning Institute, 1980).
[12] *The PIMS Letter on Business Strategy No. 1,* (Cambridge, Mass.: The Strategic Planning Institute, 1977), pp. 3–5.

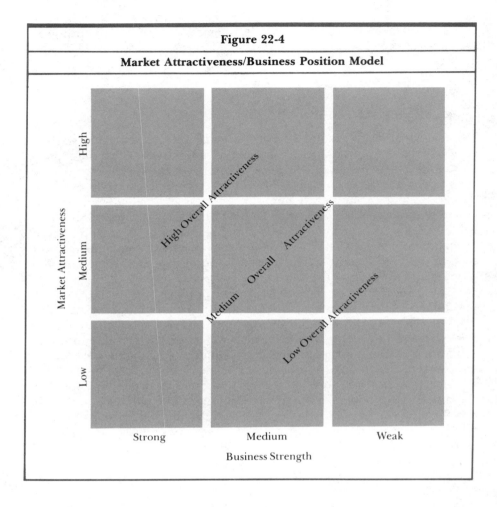

Figure 22-4

Market Attractiveness/Business Position Model

Market Attractiveness (High, Medium, Low)

Business Strength (Strong, Medium, Weak)

High Overall Attractiveness

Medium Overall Attractiveness

Low Overall Attractiveness

1. Companies that have high levels of investment generally show lower returns on investment and sales.
2. Companies with high productivity per employee are more profitable.
3. Market share has a positive impact on profit and cash flow.
4. Growth positively affects dollar profit, has no effect on percentage of profit, and negatively affects net cash flow.
5. Customer-perceived quality positively affects all measures of financial performance.
6. Innovation positively affects performance only if the company has a strong market position.
7. Vertical integration positively affects performance only in stable, mature markets.

Use of these conclusions, and others more specific to certain companies, may help guide strategic marketing planning and partially predict the outcome for particular companies.

Growth Strategies

Although it is important for a company to examine its current scope of operations, it should also develop some general strategies for future growth. Growth strategies can consist of one or more of three types: intensive growth, integrative growth, or diversification growth.[13]

Intensive Growth   When a company concentrates its growth strategy in its current products or markets, it is pursuing an **intensive growth strategy**. One possibility under this strategy is to increase sales of its present products in its current markets. Higher levels of advertising encouraging consumers to drink more Coca-Cola is an example of this strategy.

Another possibility is to increase sales of current products in new markets. Arm & Hammer Baking Soda followed this strategy when it sought to convince consumers that its product was also an air freshener.

Finally, new products can be marketed to present markets. When Arm & Hammer introduced its carpet freshener, the company was trying to market a new product to one of its present target markets.

Integrative Growth   A company usually follows an **integrative growth strategy** when it is a channel member in a strong, stable market and can grow by expanding its ownership of this channel.

Vertical integration *exists when a company acquires another company in the same channel. If the company acquires some of its supply sources, it is following* **backward integration**; *if it acquires some of its customers, it is following* **forward integration**. For example, if Coca-Cola buys a sugar plantation, it is following backward integration; if it buys one of its regional bottlers, it is following forward integration.

Horizontal integration *exists when a company acquires one of its competitors.* If Royal Crown Cola tried to buy Dr. Pepper, this would be an example of horizontal integration.

Whichever of these integrative approaches a company decides to take, it should do so based on its belief that the overall industry is healthy and stable. A company should not follow an integrative strategy in a declining industry.

Diversified Growth   When the main corporate products are in declining or uncertain markets, a **diversified growth strategy** will probably be most appropriate. Diversification does not mean the corporate mission is aban-

---

[13] Philip Kotler, *Principles of Marketing*, 2nd ed. (Englewood Cliffs, NJ: Prentice-Hall, 1983), pp. 522–24.

Strategy

Nike Versus Adidas

The race continues between Nike and Adidas for the dominant share of the lucrative athletic shoe market, in spite of the fact that the U.S. jogging boom is slowing down. Decreasing demand is spurring both manufacturers to make their marketing strategies as effective as possible.

Adidas is much the older and larger of the two companies. Worldwide sales for the West German firm topped $1 billion in one recent year, compared to $694 million for Nike in the same period. Nike is Adidas' most serious challenger in the United States, however, taking 33 percent of the market (compared to the larger company's 20 percent).

Three stripes and a flower identify Adidas shoes to America's 15 million runners, countless numbers of people who want to look like runners, and untold numbers of tennis, soccer, basketball, football, and racquetball players and fans. Adidas even makes footwear for boxers and sky divers. Clothing and other accessories round out the product line. More than 130 thousand pairs of shoes are produced each day in 17 countries. They are reputed to be of high quality and command top prices for their category.

The world's largest athletic shoe-making company was begun in 1920 by Adolph "Adi" Dassler. Gym shoes, the initial offering, were soon followed by soccer boots. A few years later, the multicolored training shoe became a very popular item.

Nike's founder, Phil Knight, first conceived the idea of a running shoe company in a paper written during the completion of his MBA from Stanford. He figured the low labor cost of Japanese manufacturers would overwhelm the European-dominated producers of athletic shoes. After graduation Knight went to Japan and struck a deal with Onitsuka, manufacturer of the Tiger running shoe, to be its sole distributor in the U.S. Knight soon was working nights and weekends peddling Tigers at track meets out of the trunk of his car. During this period Knight formed a partnership with former Oregon and Olympic track coach Bill Bowerman. For years Bowerman had been working on the development of a track shoe design. When Onitsuka abruptly discontinued Knight's exclusive dealership, Knight took Bowerman's designs to another Japanese manufacturer, and the Nike line was born. Nine out of ten Nikes are now produced in Asia, with only the most advanced designs produced at the company's two New England factories.

Like the company it challenges, Nike makes high-quality products and charges comparable prices for them. Both lines appeal to the sports enthusiast who wants the best available and the nonathlete who wants to sport the best-looking footwear around. To these consumers price is not an important factor. Both lines are retailed through department stores and specialty chains, rarely through mass merchandisers.

Though Adidas has been a substantial firm for many years, sales grew phenomenally after it stumbled onto a new promotional strategy in 1968. Actually, the step was taken to stay in competition with Puma, the highly successful athletic shoe-making firm founded by Adi Dassler's brother. Both gained tremendous attention by giving shoes and equipment to contestants in the 1968 Olympics. Adidas was in an excellent position to make the most of this new kind of promotion.

Nike also uses this publicity strategy. As Knight explains, "The secret to the business is to build the kind of shoes professional athletes will wear, then put them on the pros."* He contends the rest of the market will follow in a "trickle-down" effect. Nike has a number of pro athletes on contract. Some receive up to $100,000 annually for their continued brand loyalty. Nike cannot pay amateur athletes, but it can provide custom-crafted shoes, outfit an entire top college team, or sponsor sports clinics and events. Seventy-five percent of Nike's 20-million-dollar promotional budget is spent on such promotions.

Paid advertising is also important to the marketing of athletic shoes. Adidas' full-page, four-color ads in magazines catering to the runner tout the advantages of its shoes' design. Nike's approach is based on the self-involved, solitary spirit some associate with jogging. The ads show a lone runner in a beautiful natural setting over the headline, "There Is No Finish Line."† The copy continues, describing the "mystical experience" of running. The advantage of these large statement ads is that they appeal to huge audiences, ranging from the nonjogger to the serious runner.

For all their similarities, one difference between these companies seems to be increasing Nike's ability to compete successfully with Adidas. That is Nike's innovative spirit. Both make large investments in research and development, spending about $250,000 to bring a new shoe to market. Yet several major improvements in sports shoes that have won the respect of many major athletes are attributed to Nike. Their unsolicited endorsements, in turn, have won many new customers for Nike. Adidas, once the leader in new product development, is now perceived by many in the industry as the follower.

Both firms are aware that the recent decline in the U.S. jogging boom means they need new strategies. For Adidas, its apparel line will become its growth area. It presently accounts for 40 percent of company sales and Adidas is in the midst of beefing up the distribution of this line both in the U.S. and abroad.

Continued

Continued

Nike's strategy for continued growth in the American market is to diversify into children's, nonathletic leisure, and work shoes. Additionally, it is beginning to market its products on a worldwide basis, presently distributing its products in Europe and Japan, which both seem on the verge of a jogging craze. Currently, Nike's overseas sales account for only 16 percent of its total revenue.

The race for the foreign market is likely to be long, with Adidas holding more than half the world market. Nike may never take the lead, but as far as domestic sales go, Nike has that race already won.

* John Merwin, "Nike's Fast Track," *Forbes,* November 23, 1981, pp. 59–62.
† Myron Magnet, "Nike Starts the Second Mile," *Fortune,* November 1, 1982, pp. 158–67.

doned, merely that the company is pursuing new markets that are more promising and still in keeping with the corporate mission. For instance, Philip Morris has long been a marketer of cigarettes, but in a broader sense has a corporate mission of marketing consumer products. With the controversy over the health hazards associated with smoking increasing, Philip Morris has followed a diversified strategy into other consumer products (Seven-Up and Miller Beer are two examples). Thus, its diversification is into less risky, more promising markets that are still consistent with its corporate mission.

Combined Growth Strategies   Companies often follow a combination of growth strategies. Campbell Soup Company, for instance, has followed an intensive strategy by adding Swanson frozen foods, Pepperidge Farm bakery products, Vlasic Pickles, and Franco-American canned pasta to its soup line. In a diversified strategy it is also examining moves into proprietary drugs or household products.[14]

MARKETING ORGANIZATION

Although strategic marketing planning is of paramount importance, the best-laid strategies will not succeed without the support of the proper organization. In Chapter 2 we addressed the importance of marketing in the corporate organization. Our concern here is with the organization of marketing itself.

---

[14] "Campbell Soup: Widening Its Menu and Looking Beyond Food," *Business Week,* August 11, 1980, pp. 85–86.

Marketing is not organized by one universally accepted method. However, most marketing efforts are organized by functions, products, regions, or customer types.

Function Organization

The marketing departments of many small companies are organized by functions. Figure 22-5 illustrates a possible organization in which a marketing vice president coordinates the activities of managers of product development, advertising and promotion, sales, customer service, marketing research, and physical distribution. The advantages of this organizational form is that it is simple and each manager's responsibilities are clearly defined.

However, for companies with a large number of products and/or markets this type of organization can become hard to manage. With a large number of products, no one individual is responsible for any particular product, and therefore certain products may not receive sufficient attention. Although it may be appropriate for small companies, few large corporations find function organization viable.

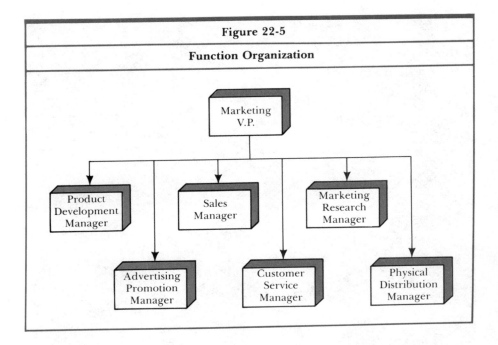

Figure 22-5

Function Organization

Marketing V.P.

Product Development Manager

Sales Manager

Marketing Research Manager

Advertising Promotion Manager

Customer Service Manager

Physical Distribution Manager

Product Organization

To overcome the problems inherent in function organization, companies with a large number of products and product lines often organize their marketing efforts around their products. Figure 22-6 presents such an organization. Notice that the product management does not eliminate the functional managers; it merely focuses them on specific products and draws on staff personnel when necessary.

In addition to the functional managers, each product line and each product has its own manager, who takes full responsibility for marketing the product and directs the functional managers under his or her control.

The main advantage of this organization is that each product has its own unique marketing strategy, coordinated by one individual. The product manager also can adjust this strategy quickly to changing conditions. Furthermore, no product is neglected (each has its own manager). Finally, product management is an excellent training ground for junior executives.

Product management does have its disadvantages. Primarily, it creates organizational conflict. Because each product manager is vying for the same corporate resources, they are often in competition with one another to accomplish their plans. A great deal of functional duplication can exist within product manager organizations, often making it an expensive method of organizing the marketing function.

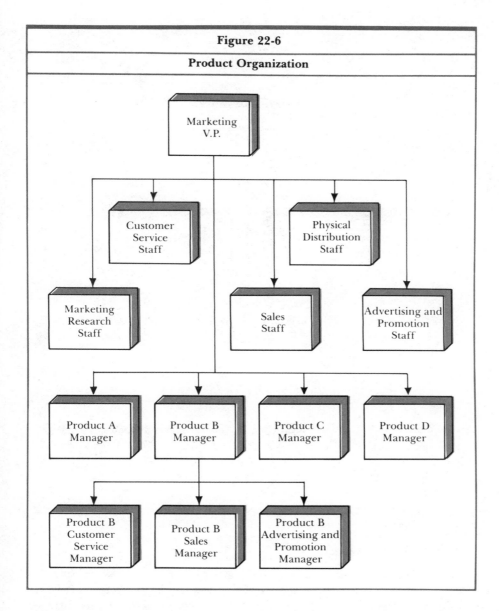

Figure 22-6

Product Organization

- Marketing V.P.
  - Customer Service Staff
  - Physical Distribution Staff
  - Marketing Research Staff
  - Sales Staff
  - Advertising and Promotion Staff
  - Product A Manager
  - Product B Manager
  - Product C Manager
  - Product D Manager
    - Product B Customer Service Manager
    - Product B Sales Manager
    - Product B Advertising and Promotion Manager

Still, numerous companies use product organizations. Procter & Gamble developed this form of organization in 1927 when it put a junior executive by the name of Neil H. McElroy (later president of the company) in charge of an ailing product, Camay Soap. After his success, the company added other product managers. Today, product managers are especially prevalent in companies marketing products sold in grocery stores.

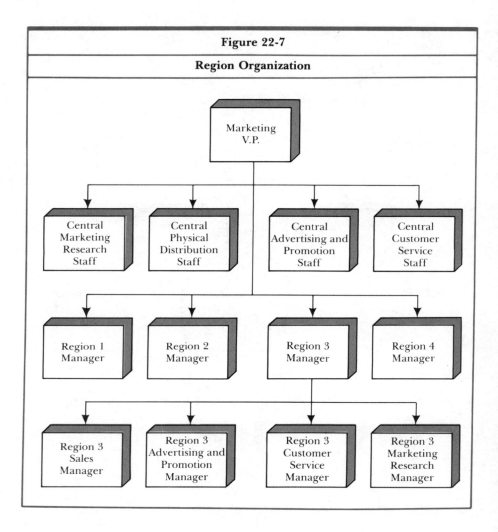

Figure 22-7

Region Organization

Marketing V.P.

- Central Marketing Research Staff
- Central Physical Distribution Staff
- Central Advertising and Promotion Staff
- Central Customer Service Staff

- Region 1 Manager
- Region 2 Manager
- Region 3 Manager
- Region 4 Manager

- Region 3 Sales Manager
- Region 3 Advertising and Promotion Manager
- Region 3 Customer Service Manager
- Region 3 Marketing Research Manager

Region Organization

When a company has many markets spread over the country and the world, it often becomes necessary for it to organize its marketing effort by geographic region. Figure 22-7 provides an example. Under this form of organization certain common marketing functions are performed centrally and other functions (especially sales) are developed for each region. These functions come under the control of the regional marketing manager. Region organization is effective when large differences exist between target markets in different regions. A disadvantage is the duplication of effort and, to some degree, the loss of a unified marketing effort.

Customer Type Organization

Many companies can group their customers by types, with the members of each particular type exhibiting similar requirements and characteristics. For instance, a manufacturer of refrigerators may sell to individual buyers, builders of homes, and builders of large apartment complexes. Each type of buyer may require a unique marketing strategy. Such companies may adopt an organization of the form shown in Figure 22-8. As was the case in the previous organization charts, certain functions may be performed by a general marketing staff, whereas others are performed by managers designated to serve particular customer groups. The advantage of this approach is that the marketing strategy is tailored to the unique needs of each group. Duplication of effort is the disadvantage.

A Combined Approach

If we examine Figures 22-5 through 22-8 closely, we can observe that each has some characteristic of other organizational approaches. The region organization, for example, still takes a functional approach within each region. Other companies might just as easily adopt a product organization within each region.

Because each organizational form has its own particular advantages and disadvantages, it is not unusual for companies to adopt a combination of these organizations in order to achieve the advantages of each. The particular products, markets, customers, and corporate characteristics of each company will determine which organization or combination of several is best.

MARKETING CONTROL

The process of controlling marketing activities involves three steps: First, standards or acceptable results must be established for various marketing activities. Standards indicate what the firm should be able to accomplish given certain resources and under assumed conditions. Second, actual performance should be measured against standards. Finally, action should be taken to correct any deviations of actual performance against the standard.

For example, market planners for the Always Open convenience food chain concluded that the firm should average 6-percent pretax profit per store. This became its profit standard. Planners in the company determined this standard by analyzing the historical profit statistics for the chain for the previous five years and comparing them with information supplied by a national trade association on the average profits for similar stores. However, because actual measurement of profits for Always Open showed

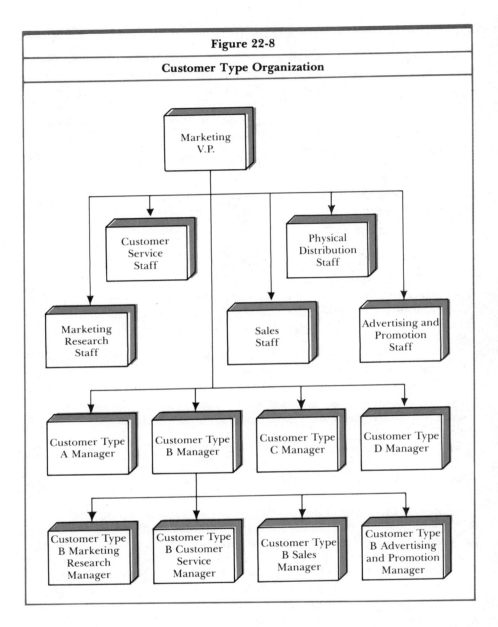

Figure 22-8

Customer Type Organization

```
                        Marketing
                           V.P.
```

- Customer Service Staff
- Physical Distribution Staff
- Marketing Research Staff
- Sales Staff
- Advertising and Promotion Staff

- Customer Type A Manager
- Customer Type B Manager
- Customer Type C Manager
- Customer Type D Manager

- Customer Type B Marketing Research Manager
- Customer Type B Customer Service Manager
- Customer Type B Sales Manager
- Customer Type B Advertising and Promotion Manager

that pretax profits are between four and two percent less than the standard management had set, management must now take corrective action—the third step in the control process. Corrective action may involve (1) changing the product mix to include more high-profit items, (2) modifying the promotion program, (3) closing marginal stores, (4) providing greater incentives for store managers, or (5) providing additional training for managers.

As suggested in the Always Open example, two sources of standards are the historical performance of the firm and information supplied by trade associations. Virtually all industries form trade associations; one of their most important functions is to collect and publish statistical information about member firms so that individual companies can compare their performance with industry averages.

There are other useful sources of standards. Business publications such as *Forbes, Fortune,* and *Business Week* frequently feature analyses of industry performance. *Advertising Age* publishes performance statistics of both major advertisers and ad agencies. The government is the largest supplier of statistical data about business. However, government data is often so generalized or so out of date that it has little value.

Three common methods of evaluating performance are sales analysis, marketing cost analysis, and the marketing audit.

Sales Analysis

Sales analysis involves comparing actual sales to sales goals. For example, if a company projected sales of a product for a given year to be $10,000 and at year end sales were only $8,500, clearly the marketing standard has not been met. However, further investigation is necessary. Suppose the marketing plan called for 1,000 units to be sold at $10 each and actual results indicated sales of 1,000 units, but the average price after sales-force discounting was only $8.50. Thus, the unit sales goal was achieved, but the dollar sales goal was not, because the sales force gave too large a discount. If the sales force gave such a large discount due to competitive pressures, its action may be justifiable and the company should revise its marketing plan. If competitive pressure is not the cause, perhaps the salespeople should have less pricing freedom.

This example illustrates the importance of examining both unit and dollar sales. Often, managers examine only dollar sales, because they are easily compared to expenses. If a company does not examine both dollar and unit sales, it may draw incorrect conclusions concerning necessary control actions.

Sales analysis should also consider market share. A company may experience a large sales gain but lose market share—the market is growing faster than the company. In this case the company is consistently losing part of its potential by being outmarketed by its competitors.

The opposite situation can also occur. Suppose a company plans for sales of 5,000 units, but sells only 4,000. The apparent conclusion is that the marketing plan is not being fulfilled. However, further analysis reveals that market share increased by 5 percent. That is, the market decreased

MARKETING
Milestone

The Trademark

With its roots in antiquity, the trademark is an important tool for both marketers and purchasers. Archaeologists have uncovered early trademarks in the debris of civilizations long buried, and trademarks still fulfill their original functions. Primarily, they distinguish the product they adorn, indicating the company that makes or markets them; assure that each product bearing the mark will be of a quality consistent with like-marked products; and help to promote the sale of the product.

As though establishing the vital link between maker and ultimate consumer, the first recorded trademark statute in English law required every baker in the land to use a personal mark for loaves he baked. That was in 1266, during the reign of Henry III.

In 1870 the U.S. Congress legislated America's first trademark law providing for the registration of trademarks. Authorization to grant such registrations was given to the Commissioner of Patents, who was also empowered to make appropriate rules and regulations for his new jurisdiction.

Within months the Averill Chemical Paint Company of New York City became the first to register a trademark in the United States. Eleven years later a law was enacted for the registration and protection of trademarks used in interstate and foreign commerce. More than 900,000 trademarks were registered by the end of 1984.

The Congress really got down to trademark cases in 1947 with the passage of the Lanham Act. This act defines a trademark as "any word, symbol, or

more than company sales. Although sales fell, the company has outmarketed its competitors and taken sales away from them. Because the market decrease is an uncontrollable variable, it cannot be changed but certainly should be considered in future strategic marketing plans.

Sales analysis also must involve a comparison of all expenses to sales. Appendix B illustrates a sample profit and loss statement with each expense expressed in actual dollar and percent-of-sales terms. This type of analysis allows management to evaluate whether any expense category is at variance with the performance standards.

For instance, if a company planned for advertising expenditures to be 2 percent of sales and found at the end of the year that advertising was

device or combination of any of these, used by a manufacturer or merchant to identify his goods and distinguish them from those of others." This definition distinguishes the trademark from a copyright, which deals with literary and other artistic creations. It also sets the trademark apart from a patent, which covers inventions. Trademarks used by services, such as Greyhound, are called service marks.

A marketer may seek to register a trademark only after using it—that is, after selling and shipping a product bearing the trademark across at least one state line. The United States Patent Office, to which the application is made, researches its records for possible duplication, checks the meaning and spelling of words used in the trademark and, finally, publishes the new trademark in a weekly bulletin, *Official Gazette.* Anyone having a similar trademark has the right to challenge. The Patent Office is the final arbiter of such disputes. The registration certificate is issued by the Commissioner of Patents, who has retained that authority since 1870.

The Lanham Act prohibits four classifications of trademarks: marks that run counter to public policy; could be confused with other marks; invade the right of privacy; or that contain descriptive words, words that mislead, geographical names, or surnames.

Though not governed by law, creativity and critical analysis are required to design a trademark that is distinctive yet can be easily read, pronounced, remembered, adapted to print and broadcast media, and easily translated into other languages for export. Some well-known trademarks that meet most or all of these criteria are

A.1.	Eveready	Scrabble
Band-Aid	Levi's	Technicolor
Chiclets	Playtex	Vaseline
Coca-Cola	Q-tips	Clorox

actually 3 percent of sales, initial indications are that the company is spending too much to advertise its products. This means that either (1) advertising is being spent inefficiently, (2) the market is saturated and will not respond to advertising as planned, or (3) production is at capacity and the advertising is creating demand the company cannot fill. If the first alternative is found to be the cause, corrective action to increase advertising efficiency and effectiveness is required. If the second alternative is true, the strategic marketing plan must be revised to reflect a more realistic appraisal of advertising effectiveness. If the third alternative is the cause, production capacity may be expanded or the strategic marketing plan revised to account for limited capacity. It is entirely possible that all three alternatives

contributed to the variance. The important point is that no investigation would have taken place if expense-to-sales percentages had not been investigated.

Finally, sales may be examined by market segments. *Market segments* may be customers, channels, geographic regions, products, or some other category management feels is appropriate. The advantage of segmental sales analysis lies in its determination of which segments contribute the most or the least to overall corporate sales. The company can use this information, in turn, to develop the strategic marketing plans for each segment.

Marketing Cost Analysis

Although it is valuable to analyze sales and costs as a percentage of sales, it is also vital to compare actual costs to actual dollar sales to determine profitability. **Marketing cost analysis** *is the process of classifying costs by specific marketing activities and examining their effect on profitability.*

For example, a firm may have sales of $10 million in the current year, which is a gain of $1 million over the previous year. On the surface the sales gain suggests that there has also been an increase in profits, but such is not necessarily the case. It does not follow automatically that the firm made any profit at all. It might have incurred a loss despite the larger volume. Only knowledge of total costs, including marketing expenses, will reveal the amount of profit or loss for the time period in question.

In this hypothetical case assume that total marketing costs were $3.6 million. This figure by itself, however, tells us little, if anything, that is useful to marketing managers in improving their productivity. Until marketing costs are allocated to specific products, territories, distributors, and personnel, marketing management does not have answers to questions such as: What was the contribution to profit (or loss) of various product lines and of the specific products within each line? What was the contribution to profit (or loss) of each territory? Which distributors performed satisfactorily and which ones did not? What was the contribution, when costs are considered, of each salesperson?

When marketing costs are properly allocated, management can compare sales results with the expenses incurred for the specific territories, products, individuals, and activities that were involved in the strategic marketing plan. These comparisons are a basic key to increasing productivity and provide the information needed to make numerous improvement decisions based on the answers to questions such as: Should some territories be eliminated? Do we need to modify our channels of distribution? Should some products be dropped? Should we realign our prices?

Figure 22-9 indicates some of the major decision areas in which marketing cost analysis is useful and indicates possible revelations of such analyses and possible remedial actions that managers may take.

Figure 22-9

**What Cost Analysis May Reveal in Specific Decision Areas
and Possible Remedial Actions**

Decision Area	What Cost Analysis May Reveal	Possible Remedial Actions by Marketing Management
1. Customer	Certain customers cost so much to service that they contribute nothing to profit. Some require a disproportionate share of service expenses.	Eliminate these customers. Or design plans that will make them profitable. (Perhaps the customers are fairly new and will become profitable in time.) Consider raising prices to these customers. Or consider assigning these customers to wholesalers.
2. Product	Certain styles, models or colors are unprofitable. Some products make a contribution to profit in some retail outlets, but not in others.	Eliminate unprofitable items from the line. Or give sales people extra incentive compensation to sell more profitable products. Or design new sales promotional materials to encourage ultimate consumers to buy. Conduct further analysis to determine why. Possibly adopt a policy of selective or exclusive distribution. Or use one channel of distribution to serve the outlets where the product is profitable and another channel for the outlet where the product is unprofitable.
3. Order size	Orders below a certain size are unprofitable.	Set a minimum order size for customers. Or provide a price reduction (quantity discounts) for orders of a profitable size.

Before marketing expenses can be allotted to elements in the marketing plan, they must be arranged into reasonably homogeneous classifications. Although there is no universal method, common classifications include:

Sales compensation	Transportation
Advertising	Order processing
Sales promotion	Marketing research
Travel	Credit
Storage	Overall administrative costs

Decision Area	What Cost Analysis May Reveal	Possible Remedial Actions by Marketing Management
4. Territory	Profits per order are significantly lower in certain territories than in others.	Eliminate the low-profit territories. Or use agent middlemen to serve them. Or use a different physical-distribution mix to deliver products. Or sell by telephone to accounts in low-profit territories.
5. Company-owned retail outlet	Some outlets are unprofitable or only marginal.	Consider closing or remodeling unprofitable outlets. Or replace managers in affected outlets.
6. Pricing	High-priced items in the product line sell poorly in some territories.	Revise product line in these territories and promote low and moderately priced items more aggressively.
7. Physical distribution	Turnover on certain products is so slow that carrying costs make the items unprofitable.	Remove these items from the product line. Or take action to speed turnover.
8. Promotion	Certain salespeople produce so little volume that the costs of maintaining them are excessive.	Provide extra training and motivation. Or terminate persons with disappointing sales records.

Marketing Cost Allocation   To determine the contribution to profit (or loss) of various components of the strategic marketing plan or operation, marketing costs must be assigned to the component under study. Allocating costs is never easy. Nor is cost allocation standardized among all firms, even in the same industry. Generally, however, costs can be allocated as direct, assignable, or nonassignable.

Direct Costs   Direct costs are those that can be assigned directly to a specific part of the strategic marketing plan—for example, to a product, territory, class of middlemen, or even a single customer. They may include salaries, commissions and travel expenses paid to sales personnel, transportation costs, and expenses incurred in post-sale servicing of the products. For example, sales commissions paid to a salesperson working in one sales territory are direct costs for that territory.

Assignable Costs   Assignable costs are not directly related to a particular segment, but can be assigned to that segment by some criteria. Suppose, for example, a company has a sales office with 2,000 square feet of floor space and pays rent of $500 per month. The salesperson for territory A uses 200 square feet or 10 percent of the facility. Therefore, territory A is assigned 10 percent of $500, or $50 per month of the rent expense.

Nonassignable Costs   Some costs are incurred to run the overall company and cannot logically be assigned to any segment. These nonassignable or **common costs** include the administrative staff, building, and equipment; institutional advertising; and staff marketing research.

Full Versus Direct Costing   Two methods are used to analyze market segments. The **full cost approach** *assigns all direct costs and some portion of all assignable and nonassignable costs to each market segment to determine a net profit by segment.* The danger in this approach is that costs are often assigned arbitrarily, resulting in unrealistic segmental net profit figures.

A much more useful approach is the **direct cost approach**, in which *only direct and assignable costs are assigned to a segment.* The resulting *sales minus direct and assignable costs is called* **segment contribution** and represents the amount that segment contributes toward covering common costs. Because only those costs over which the marketing manager of that segment has some control are assigned to the segment, the direct cost approach is a much more realistic evaluation of the segment and its manager.

The Marketing Audit

A **marketing audit** *is a comprehensive examination of a firm's total marketing effort.* If focuses on an in-depth review of each of the marketing controllable variables—product, place, promotion, and price—as well as the uncontrollable variables. Although a marketing audit usually is performed by people inside the organization, outside consultants are sometimes used, because they tend to be more objective and have more varied experience. The purpose of a marketing audit is to discover ways to improve marketing performance. Examples of questions a marketing audit attempts to answer are:

Product Questions
- Should certain products be added or deleted from the product line?
- What package modifications are needed?
- Does the product perform as its warranty suggests?

Place Questions

- Is the storage function performed as economically and effectively as possible?
- Should agents be added to our channel of distribution to reach new markets?
- Can transportation costs be reduced? If so, how?

Promotion Questions

- Should more or less money be spent on advertising?
- Can the telephone be used to greater advantage in selling to some customers?
- What revisions in the sales training program are needed?

Price Questions

- How would an increase in price affect sales?
- Should discounts to intermediaries be changed?
- How do our prices compare with competitors' prices?

Similar questions should be asked about the technological, economic, government, competitive, and social environments, the target markets, and their effect on strategic marketing plans. Figure 22-10 provides a more exhaustive list of questions to be asked in a marketing audit. Like any other audit, the marketing audit should be performed regularly to measure the overall performance of the corporate marketing activity. Although marketing audits can be expensive and disruptive to daily operations, they are an important part of the marketing control process and, therefore, are essential.

Qualitative Measures of Performance

To this point we have considered ways of measuring marketing performance quantitatively or objectively. Quantitative measures result in numbers such as percents or dollars. They have the advantages of simplicity and objectivity. Qualitative or subjective measures can also be used to appraise a firm's marketing efforts. Qualitative measures are judgmental and cannot be reduced to percents, dollars, or other kinds of numbers. Yet they can be useful if they are made by experienced people who have a good track record for evaluating conditions and people. Qualitative measures might be applied to such areas of marketing as:

1. Dealer willingness to cooperate with a sales promotion program.
2. Goodwill created by salespeople.

Figure 22-10
Marketing Audit Questions

MARKETING COMMITMENT: Corporate Culture

1. Does the chief executive believe in marketing planning, and is formal planning ingrained with all top managers?
2. Are plans prepared with the participation of functional managers, or dictated by the president?
3. Do you have a coordinated marketing program or an isolated sales department?
4. Are you using the computer as a marketing tool, and do your managers understand its capabilities?
5. Do you implement a marketing plan, measure performance, and adjust for deviation?
6. Are all marketing functions under the direction of one executive who reports to the chief executive officer?

PRODUCTS/SERVICES: The Reason for Existence

1. Is the product/service free from deadwood? Do you have a well-defined, continuous program to weed out unprofitable products and add new ones?
2. What is the life cycle stage?
3. How will user demands or trends affect you?
4. Are you a leader in new product innovation?
5. Do you have a systematic liaison with the research/development group?
6. Are inexpensive methods used to estimate new product potentials before considerable amounts are spent on R&D and market introduction?
7. Are new products introduced with forecasts and budgets?
8. Have you investigated possible advantages resulting from new materials or technology?
9. Do you have different quality levels for different markets?
10. Are packages/brochures effective salesmen for the products/services they present?
11. Do you present products/services in the most appealing colors (formats) for markets being served?
12. Are there features or benefits to exploit?
13. Has the safety of the product/service been brought to a satisfactory level?
14. Is the level of customer service adequate?
15. How are quality and reliability viewed by customers?

CUSTOMER: User Profiles

1. Who is the current and potential customer?
2. Are customers younger or older, on average, than those of competitors?
3. Are there geographic aspects of use: regional, rural, urban?
4. Why do people buy the product/service; what motivates their preferences?
5. Who makes buying decisions; when, where?
6. What is the frequency and quantity of use?

MARKETS: Where Products/Services Are Sold

1. How is the market shaped; where is the center of gravity?
2. Have you identified and measured major segments?

3. Are you overlooking small but profitable segments of the market in trying to satisfy the tastes of the majority?
4. Are the markets for the products/services expanding or declining?
5. Should different segments be developed; gaps in penetration?
6. Do segments require marketing differentiation?

SALES HISTORY: Previous Results

1. How do sales break down within the product/service?
2. Do you know where sales are coming from; segments and customer classification?
3. Are there abnormal cycles or seasonalities and, if so, how do you plan for them?
4. Do sales match previous forecasts?
5. Which territories/markets do not yield potential?
6. Are growth and profit trends reflected?

COMPETITORS: Their Influence

1. Who are the principal competitors, how are they positioned, and where do they seem to be headed?
2. What are their market shares?
3. What features of competitors' products/services stand out?
4. What are their strengths and weaknesses?
5. Is the market easily entered or dominated?

PRICING: Profitability Planning

1. What are the objectives of current pricing policy: acquiring, defending, or expanding?
2. Are price limitations inherent in the marketplace?
3. Are price policies set to produce volume or profit?
4. How does pricing compare with competition in similar levels of quality?
5. Do you understand how your prices are set?
6. Is the price list understandable and current?
7. Does cost information show profitability of each item?
8. What is the history of price deals, discounts, and promotions?
9. Are middlemen making money from the line?
10. Can the product/service support advertising or promotion programs?
11. Will size or manufacturing process require more volume?
12. Are there cost problems to overcome?
13. Are profitability and marketing cost known by the customer?

MARKETING CHANNELS: Selling Paths

1. Does the system offer the best access to all target markets?
2. Do product/service characteristics require special channels?
3. Have you analyzed each market with a view toward setting up the most profitable type of presentation: direct versus reps, master distributors or dealers, and so on?
4. What are the trends in distribution methods?
5. Do you provide cost-effective marketing support, selling aids, and sales tools?

(continued)

Figure 22-10

Marketing Audit Questions (*continued*)

SALES ADMINISTRATION: Selling Efficiency

1. Have you analyzed communications and designed paperwork or computer programs to provide meaningful management information?
2. Are customers getting coverage in proportion to their potential?
3. Are sales costs properly planned and controlled?
4. Does the compensation plan provide optimum incentive and security at reasonable cost?
5. Is performance measured against potential?
6. Are selling expenses proportionate to results and potentials within markets or territories?
7. Are there deficiencies in recruitment, selection, training, motivation, supervision, performance, promotion, or compensation?
8. Do you provide effective selling aids and sales tools?

DELIVERY/INVENTORY: Physical Peformance

1. Are adequate inventories kept in the right mix?
2. Is inventory turnover acceptable?
3. Do orders receive efficient, timely processing?
4. Are shipping schedules and promises kept?
5. Is the product/service delivered in good condition?
6. Are forecasts for production planning acceptable?
7. How does performance compare with competition?
8. Are warehouses and distribution points properly located?

ADVERTISING: Media Program

1. Are media objectives and strategies linked to the marketing plan?
2. What are the objectives of the ad program?
3. How is media effectiveness measured?
4. Is advertising integrated with promotion and sales activity?
5. Is the ad agency's effectiveness periodically evaluated?

---

3. Likely customer reactions to a change in product or package design.
4. Salesperson morale.
5. Value of a location under consideration for a retail outlet.

Qualitative evaluation of marketing performance plays an important part in planning future marketing activities. Until all marketing efforts can be appraised objectively (a situation that will probably never be true), qualitative evaluation will be needed.

6. Do you dictate copy theme and content to the agency?
7. Are you spending realistically, in relation to budget?
8. Do you use trade publications effectively?
9. How do you choose the ad agency?

PROMOTION: Sales Inducement
1. Does the promotion support a marketing objective?
2. Was it carefully budgeted?
3. Is it integrated with advertising and selling activity?
4. How is it measured for results?
5. What was the reason for its success or failure?
6. Are slogans, trademarks, logos, and brands being used effectively?
7. Is point-of-sale material cost-effective?
8. Do you have satisfactory displays of products/services?
9. Are you effectively using couponing, tie-ins, incentives, sampling, stuffers, combination offers?
10. How do you evaluate trade shows for effectiveness?

PUBLIC RELATIONS: Prestige Building
1. Do you have a clear idea of the type of company you want people to think you are?
2. Do you have a consistent communications program?
3. What kind of ideas and impressions have you created about your company?
4. Do you really know what your image is on a factual basis, or are you relying on customers' letters, salesmen's reports, and publicity in the press?
5. Do your company name, brand, and logo add to or conflict with the image you want?
6. Are you getting a share of favorable, unpaid publicity in editorials of the media?

SOURCE: Hal W. Goetsch, "Conduct a Comprehensive Marketing Audit to Improve Marketing Planning," *Marketing News,* March 18, 1983, Section 2, p. 14.

SUMMARY

- Strategic marketing planning is the process of developing and implementing an effort to fit marketing goals and capabilities to marketing opportunities.
- The corporate mission is a statement of what a company is and wants to be.

- An objective is a statement of what is to be accomplished. Objectives should be specific and realistic.
- Strategies are the specification of activities to accomplish objectives.
- Marketing opportunity assessment is the process of searching for and evaluating conditions under which a particular target market fits the capabilities of the company.
- Marketing opportunities are affected by market size and growth rate; market requirements; competition; and economic, technological, social, legal, and political factors.
- The Boston Consulting Group approach to strategic marketing planning is based on an analysis of each product's market growth rate and market share.
- The market attractiveness/business position model is similar to the Boston Consulting Group approach, but analyzes the attractiveness of markets and the company's strength in that market.
- Growth strategies can be intensive, integrative, or diversified.
- Marketing is typically organized by functions, products, regions, or customer types.
- Marketing control involves setting standards, measuring performance, and correcting performance deviations from standards.
- Standards are often developed from industry associations, business publications, and government sources.
- Sales analysis should examine dollar and unit sales, market share, and expenses as a percentage of sales.
- Marketing cost analysis classifies costs by specific marketing activities and examines their effect on profitability.
- Marketing costs can be divided into direct, assignable, and nonassignable costs.
- Marketing audits are regular, comprehensive examinations of the company's total marketing effort.

DISCUSSION QUESTIONS

1. Explain corporate mission, objectives, and strategies. Give an example of each.
2. What are strategic windows and how can environmental monitoring help identify them?
3. What factors should be considered in evaluating marketing opportunities?
4. Explain the difference between the Boston Consulting Group, General Electric, and PIMS strategic marketing planning approaches. What is the advantage of each? The disadvantages? Which do you prefer? Why?

5. Find an actual example of each of the following growth strategies:
   (a) intensive
   (b) integrative
   (c) diversified
6. Explain the advantages and disadvantages of each of the following kinds of marketing organizations:
   (a) function
   (b) product
   (c) region
   (d) customer type
7. Describe the marketing control process.
8. Explain the various forms of sales analysis.
9. What is a market segment?
10. What are direct, assignable, and nonassignable costs?
11. What is the difference between full and direct costing? What is a segment contribution?
12. What is a marketing audit? Why is it important?

APPLICATION EXERCISES

1. Pick a specific company and identify five possible marketing opportunities. Evaluate each opportunity with respect to your company. Which opportunities should the company pursue? Which should it discard? Why?
2. Select a company and prepare a list of all the questions that should be answered in its marketing audit. Justify your reasons for each question.
3. For three companies identify their corporate missions, objectives, and strategies. Do you believe the mission for each company is well-defined? Are its strategies working? Why?

CASE 22
Mattel Faces a Strategy Dilemma

Mattel has long been a name synonymous with toys. Its Barbie Doll was introduced in 1959 (company executives expected it to sell for one season) and is still a strong seller today. Overall toy and hobby sales contributed the largest share of corporate profits in 1982.[15]

---

[15] *Mattel Annual Report,* January 29, 1983, p. 2.

Keen knowledge of conventional toy markets and use of marketing research have largely contributed to Mattel's success in this huge industry. When Mattel was developing a new line of action toys for boys, its marketing research showed that a test group of boys preferred fantasy figures to army, spy, sports, or even space heroes. The result of this research was the development of the Masters of the Universe toys which proved a sellout for Mattel.

Mattel's problem, however, has been the preoccupation of children with electronic toys, which has forced Mattel to diversify into areas where it has less expertise. Ironically, Mattel pioneered electronic toys in 1976 with hand-held, video-sports games. However, misjudgment of consumer desires led Mattel to concentrate in these hand-held toys too long and allowed Atari to take the lead in home video game consoles.

In late 1980, Mattel temporarily caught up when it introduced Intellivision. In fiscal 1982, profits from Intellivision and its game cartridges were $73 million. However, in the last quarter of fiscal 1983, its Electronics Division lost almost $29 million, reflecting an apparent inability to keep up with swiftly changing events in the home computer/electronic toy markets.[16]

Sales by the Electronics Division were further hurt by such companies as Parker Bros., Imagic, and Activision marketing cartridges that are compatible with Intellivision. Trouble also developed in the slow introduction of Intellivision II and III models.

Mattel's entrance into the home computer market with the Aquarius came right at a time of severe price cutting in the industry. Introduced at $150, the Aquarius competed with the Texas Instruments 99/4A selling at $100 and the Commodore VIC-20 selling at $90. Mattel reacted by cutting the Aquarius price to $105. Critics, however, have observed that the Aquarius has no special edge over the competition.[17]

One strategy followed by Mattel to make the Electronics Division more viable has been to acquire a semiconductor manufacturer—reducing its dependence on components suppliers. Mattel also tripled research and development expenditures and quadrupled the Electronics work force.

Discussion Questions

1. What is Mattel's corporate mission? What do you think it should be?
2. How many different growth strategies of Mattel can you identify?
3. Use either the Boston Consulting Group or General Electric approach to analyze Mattel's products.
4. What strategic marketing plans would you recommend to Mattel?

---

[16] "Mattel Struggles to Fix Its Product Woes," *Business Week*, May 9, 1983, pp. 76, 78.
[17] *Ibid.*

A Careers in Marketing

O n completing this book you should have some idea of the activities involved in marketing. Marketing is a broad field which permeates virtually every organization. The career opportunities are almost limitless. If you enjoy working with people in a stimulating, challenging, constantly changing environment that offers considerable career advancement, marketing may be for you. This appendix is designed to acquaint you with the entry-level positions and career opportunities in marketing and how to market yourself for one of these positions.

MARKETING CAREER OPPORTUNITIES

Numerous career areas exist in marketing. This section describes the primary areas of marketing employment.

Marketing Research

Although numerous marketing research firms exist and many companies have their own marketing research staff, fewer positions exist in this area of marketing compared to other areas. Besides marketing research companies and "in-house" marketing research, advertising agencies, government agencies, and university research centers are the primary employers of marketing researchers.

In Chapter 3 we described the majority of a marketing researcher's responsibilities. However, a good researcher also needs an overall knowledge of marketing. Marketing researchers are basically problem solvers. A job in this area generally involves data gathering and analysis, interpretation of results, and making recommendations—in short, the marketing research procedure described in Chapter 3. To succeed in this area, certain quantitative and behavioral science knowledge is necessary. An understanding of statistics, computers, and certainly your marketing research courses is vital to being a good marketing researcher. If you are good with numbers, analytical by nature, and have a good understanding of people's attitudes, desires, and behavior, marketing research is probably a good field for you.

Entry-level marketing researchers will probably start as research assistants and perform primarily clerical functions such as coding and tabulating data and searching for secondary data sources. Along the way you will learn to design surveys and questionnaires, conduct interviews, analyze and interpret results, and write reports. Capable individuals in marketing research may rise to director of marketing research or other marketing managerial positions.

Product or Brand Manager

As we mentioned in Chapter 22, some companies assign one manager the responsibility for a particular product or brand. This manager acts much like a small company president, planning all marketing activities associated with that one product. This can be an exciting, but often frustrating career path. In many companies product managers are responsible for the success of a product, but are not given authority over such crucial decisions as production, inventory control, or budgeting. Product managers complain that much of their time is spent convincing other corporate managers to cooperate in marketing the product.

For these reasons individuals interested in product management should be well schooled in all aspects of marketing—especially product development—and possess considerable creative, communicative, and persuasive skills. Because your future career is often dependent on how well your product does, product management can be an excellent path for career advancement, but may also be extremely pressure-packed.

Entry-level positions are usually assistant product managers, with advancement to associate product managers and, finally, product manager. Although most companies prefer entrants in this area to have an MBA, some companies will hire assistant product managers with undergraduate degrees. Several companies that utilize product managers are Procter & Gamble, Du Pont, S.C. Johnson, and General Mills. Figure A-1 provides salary plus bonus figures for product managers and other marketing executives.

Figure A-1	
Marketing Manager Incomes	
Position	**Salary + Bonus**
Assistant/associate product manager	$30,100
(1–3 years' experience)	+ 3,000
Product manager	51,400
(3–5 years)	+10,000
Group product manager	55,800
(5–8 years)	+15,000
Marketing director	78,000
(8–10 years)	+25,000
Vice president—marketing	115,000
(10 years or more)	+40,000

SOURCE: Bill Abrams, "Financial-Service Advertisers Seen Neglecting Ad Research," *Wall Street Journal*, August 18, 1983, p. 25.

Figure A-2			
Average Annual Compensation in Distribution: 1983			
	Manager	**Director**	**Vice President**
Top quarter	$67,920	$79,800	$125,500
Second quarter	53,600	61,600	91,100
Third quarter	41,900	52,500	73,300
Lowest quarter	33,900	40,400	53,100
Average	49,300	58,500	85,600

SOURCE: Bernard J. LaLonde and David E. Lloyd, "Career Paths in Distribution: Profile 1983," *Annual Conference Proceedings* (Chicago: National Council of Physical Distribution Management, 1983), pp. 171–92.

Distribution Management

Numerous positions exist in distribution, including such titles as transportation manager, inventory control analyst, warehouse manager, customer service manager, and sales forecasting manager. Companies employing distribution managers consist of manufacturers, wholesalers, retailers, public warehouses, and transportation companies. Because much of distribution deals with quantitative analysis, distribution managers usually have considerable quantitative and analytical skills. If you are interested in a career in this area, it is wise to take as many marketing, computer, forecasting, and management science courses as possible. The largest percentage of distribution managers have undergraduate degrees in business administration.

Because distribution often represents such a large portion of a company's costs and has considerable customer service potential, successful distribution managers often are noticed quickly and promoted by upper management into higher distribution or other marketing management positions. Entry-level positions also pay quite well, as Figure A-2 illustrates.

Sales

Selling is probably the largest employer of marketing people, especially entry-level applicants. Every business has some form of sales force, whether that force works for the company or is an independent selling organization such as a manufacturer's agent. Retail salespeople typically work within one store or department, keep fairly regular hours, and do little traveling. Although little formal training is necessary to obtain an entry-level retail sales position, formal training in selling, retailing, and marketing in general may be necessary for any advancement in the retail organization to such positions as department or store manager or head of one of the administrative departments.

Wholesale selling responsibilities, training, and compensation vary widely, depending on the channel. Salespeople for grocery products often must travel to numerous individual stores and even stock shelves on a daily basis. These responsibilities are much different from those of a hospital supply salesperson, who may spend a month negotiating a major contract with one hospital. Salespeople for pharmaceuticals or electronics components normally need considerable technical training in the particulars of their product. However, any salesperson needs training in selling techniques and marketing in general.

The responsibilities, training, and compensation of manufacturers' salespeople also are affected largely by the industry. Regardless of the technical training necessary, a basic knowledge of marketing is still essential. Manufacturers' salespeople earn above-average income, which is typically a combination of salary and commissions. Figure 17-2 provides the average commission rates, and Figure A-3 the average experienced salesperson earnings for selected industries.

Entry-level salespeople ordinarily begin as sales trainees and work with an established salesperson to "learn the ropes." Successful salespeople can make outstanding incomes and often are afforded excellent opportunities

Figure A-3	
Average Annual Earnings of Experienced Sales Personnel: 1982	
Airlines	$25,000–28,400
Household appliances	23,000–30,500
Automotive parts and accessories	20,500–30,000
Building materials	20,000–30,000
Chemicals	20,000–29,500
Cosmetics and toilet preparations	21,500–23,100
Drugs and medicines	21,800–30,000
Electrical equipment and supplies	20,000–30,500
Electronics	21,200–30,400
Fabricated metal products	20,000–30,500
Food products	20,700–25,300
General machinery	20,000–30,900
Housewares	23,000–30,000
Instruments and allied products	20,000–28,900
Iron and steel	25,400–30,000
Office machinery and equipment	20,500–26,900
Paper and allied products	20,500–30,000
Petroleum and petroleum products	20,000–24,000

SOURCE: John W. Wright, *The American Almanac of Jobs and Salaries* (New York: Avon, 1982), p. 487.

for career advancement. Many companies see their sales force as executive training. After all, the salesperson is the personal representative of the entire marketing effort. To sell effectively, a salesperson must understand the entire marketing operation.

For a sales career, you should be comfortable working with different people, be a problem solver, enjoy some amount of travel, and want a constantly changing, challenging career environment.

Advertising

Many consider advertising to be a glamorous, pressure-packed career path. As the mass communication vehicle of marketing, advertisers often receive great credit or substantial blame based on the relative success of advertising campaigns. Although many companies have their own advertising departments, most job opportunities are in advertising agencies.

Copywriters are the individuals in ad agencies responsible for writing the message, or copy, in advertisements. Agencies typically want people with writing skills, often journalism majors, to fill these positions. Artists provide the visual aspect of advertisements and ordinarily have a creative arts education. Account executives are the liaisons between the agency and its clients. Usually, these individuals have business and marketing training because they are the agency's "salespeople." Finally, media buyers deal with the various advertising media to contract and schedule advertisements. These individuals are skilled in negotiating rates and in interpreting demographic media profiles. Figure A-4 lists salary ranges for these agency positions.

In hiring entry-level personnel agencies usually look for individuals with the training to fit one of these categories. Most agencies prefer to start new people in lower level positions and train them in the specifics of their approach to advertising. Career opportunities for those who are successful in advertising agencies are considerable. Often, promising account executives are hired by one of their clients for marketing executive positions.

Public Relations

Because public relations representatives deal on a daily basis with news agencies, their background is often in journalism or communications. Good communication skills are essential in public relations. The public relations representative must also have the ability to keep current on all aspects of the company's operations and often condense complex procedures to easily understood terms. Public relations representatives are the public's representation of a company and often are the recipients of considerable pressure and public displeasure with corporate actions.

	Figure A-4				
	Advertising Agency Salaries: 1983				
	High	**Low**		**High**	**Low**
Creative			**Account**		
Creative			Senior vice		
director	$150,000	$75,000	president—		
Associate			management		
creative			supervisor	$130,000	$40,000
director	85,000	65,000	Vice president—		
Copy			management		
supervisor	75,000	50,000	supervisor	75,000	45,000
Senior			Account supervisor	58,000	25,000
copywriter	75,000	50,000	Account executive	40,000	15,000
Copywriter	45,000	25,000	Assistant		
Junior			account		
copywriter	16,000	14,000	executive	29,000	14,000
Art			**Media**		
Executive			Senior vice		
art director	200,000	110,000	president—		
Group			media director	125,000	50,000
creative			Vice president—		
director	85,000	60,000	associate		
Art director	65,000	30,000	media director	100,000	32,000
Assistant			Media supervisor	35,000	20,000
art director	25,000	14,000	Media planner	30,000	12,000
			Media buyer	25,000	12,000

SOURCE: "Careers in Marketing," *Advertising Age*, January 2, 1984, p. M-17.

Entry-level positions take the form of public relations trainee—historically, a low paying job. Salaries for public relations directors vary widely by industry, with industrial marketers typically paying more.

HOW TO MARKET YOURSELF

The first marketing assignment you will have in your career is to market yourself to a target market of potential employers. Your task will be to convince these target customers you are a "product" they should "purchase," or hire. Therefore, let us take a marketing approach to your job search.

Marketing Research

Where are companies with available marketing positions? A good place to start is your college placement center. This facility usually has a list of corporate contacts and a schedule of on-campus visits in the near future.

Additionally, numerous professional organizations publish lists of their members, both in total and by state. Figure A-5 lists several of these by marketing areas.

Although this does not cover all marketing research efforts connected with a job search, we will address specific marketing research activities throughout this discussion.

Product

The product is you. You must decide exactly what you have to offer a potential employer by undertaking an honest self-evaluation before seeking any job opportunities. You should try to answer such questions as:

1. Do I want a job in marketing or a career with executive potential?
2. Do I have the ability to take the pressure and responsibilities of executive decision making?
3. Do I work better with numbers or people?
4. Am I primarily creative or analytical?
5. Am I highly motivated and want a job that is a challenge and takes a great deal of time, or am I more interested in a job only as a means of income?
6. For what types of jobs has my experience and schooling prepared me?
7. Do I want the structure of working for a large organization, or do I want a small company?
8. Do I need a lot of direction and feedback, or do I work best if left alone?

Answers to these questions should give you a good idea of the type of "product" you have to market. Be honest with yourself. It will save you a great deal of frustration later on.

Place

Where do you want to live? Is the Northeast of interest, or do you want to live in the Sun Belt? Perhaps you are getting married and your spouse has already accepted a job in Chicago. If you have a specific geographic preference, you should search for companies and positions solely in that area. Various library sources list companies by geographic region. *Thomas' Regis-*

Figure A-5
Professional Associations

Area	Association
Advertising	American Advertising Federation 1225 Connecticut Avenue, N.W. Washington, DC 20036
	American Association of Advertising Agencies 200 Park Avenue New York, NY 10017
	Association of Industrial Advertisers 41 East 42nd Street New York, NY 10017
Selling	Direct Selling Association 1730 M Street, N.W., Suite 610 Washington, DC 20006
	Sales & Marketing Executives, International 380 Lexington Avenue New York, NY 10017
Marketing	American Marketing Association 250 S. Wacker Drive Chicago, IL 60606
Distribution	National Council of Physical Distribution Management 2803 Butterfield Road Oak Brook, IL 60521
	American Society of Traffic and Transportation 327 S. La Salle Street Chicago, IL 60604
Public relations	Public Relations Society of America 845 Third Avenue New York, NY 10022
Wholesaling	National Association of Wholesaler–Distributors 1725 K Street, N.W. Washington, DC 20006
Retailing	National Retail Merchants Association 100 West 31st Street New York, NY 10001

ter lists manufacturers and their addresses by state. Various state and local Chambers of Commerce are quite willing to send lists of their members. As we already mentioned, most professional associations list their members alphabetically and by state.

Once you have a list of potential employers in your chosen geographic area, write to each and explain your decision to move to that area. Enclose a copy of your résumé and ask if you can arrange an interview at their location when you are in the area. Give specific times when you could be available. If you do not hear from the individual to whom you wrote after one month, call and inquire further.

Promotion

In promoting yourself the advertising aspect consists of your résumé. The job interview and on-site visit are personal selling. Your résumé should be a concise, yet complete statement of your qualifications and your goals. Figure A-6 presents an example. Notice that the address makes it easy for the company to reach (or leave a message) for the applicant at several locations. A picture is a good idea, because it allows the interviewer to associate the face from the interview with the face on the résumé at a later date.

A brief statement of immediate career goals is provided. If you are interested in several marketing areas, there is nothing wrong with having several résumés and providing each company with one tailor-made for the position they are trying to fill—as long as that position is truly one that interests you.

A brief summary of your education—school, degree, graduation date, and grade-point average—should be included. A chronological summary of your employment history is also good. Even if these seemed like menial jobs to you, it demonstrates you have the ambition to work. Finally, awards, hobbies, and school activities all show a well-rounded person and give topics to start the conversation in an interview.

The initial interview is an opportunity to sell yourself. You should prepare various points about yourself you wish to communicate to the interviewer, learn as much as possible about the company (annual reports and recent articles in the library are good sources), prepare a list of questions you wish to ask, and questions you expect the interviewer to ask. Such questions might include:

1. Why do you want to work for us?
2. What is your greatest weakness? Strength?
3. What position would you like in five years?
4. Why did you choose marketing?
5. Here is an object. Sell it to me.
6. Why should I hire you?

Figure A-6

RÉSUMÉ

Karen P. Marketing

SCHOOL ADDRESS

3547 Timberview Trail
Blacksburg, VA 24018
(703) 552-1111

PERMANENT ADDRESS

4132 Havenam Avenue
Roanoke, VA 24014
(703) 899-1111

OBJECTIVE

A challenging MANAGEMENT position in or related to MARKET-
ING

EDUCATION

June 1984
Virginia Polytechnic Institute and State University, Blacksburg, VA
B.S. Degree: Business Administration—Marketing Management
GPA = 3.56

Areas of Concentration:
Marketing Management, Industrial Marketing, Marketing Research,
Marketing Communications, Marketing Logistics

June 1981
Nassau Community College, Garden City, New York
A.S. Degree: Business Administration

HONORS   Dean's List, 1983

June 1979   Alfred G. Berner High School, Massapequa, New York

EXPERIENCE

1982–1983
THE EMPORIUM/MARY'S GIFT SHOP, INC., Blacksburg, VA
Position: Assistant Manager/Acting Manager

1980–1981
DEFENSE LOGISTICS AGENCY/STRATEGIC PETROLEUM RE-
SERVE, Alexandria, VA
Position: Cooperative Education Student—Procurement Agent Trainee
and assistant to the Deputy Program Manager

PART-TIME EMPLOYMENT

1981–1984
VIRGINIA TECH, WAR MEMORIAL GYM, Blacksburg, VA
Work Study Student Aide to the Dean of Education

1978–1981
FARRELL'S ICE CREAM PARLOUR & RESTAURANT, Massapequa,
New York
Waitress and cook—Kitchen Supervisor

ACTIVITIES

Nassau Community College: Kickline-Lionettes, Work Study, Orientation Committee

Virginia Tech: Cooperative Education Program, Member of The
American Marketing Association Marketing Club, DLA's Softball
Team, Den Mother for Underprivileged, Ballet

Community: Birthright Volunteer

HOBBIES

Music, Reading, Tennis

REFERENCES

Furnished on request

It may help to practice your interview strategy with a friend.

At the end of the interview ask what you can do to further your chances with the company. After the interview write down your impressions of the key points of discussion and write a follow-up letter to thank the interviewer for his or her time, to reiterate some of the high points from the interview, and to offer to provide any additional information if needed. If you do not hear from the company in a month, call the interviewer and inquire about your status.

Price

The salary you request and eventually receive is the price. What is a reasonable salary to expect? The answer to this question can be partially answered by asking your friends what offers they have received. Ask recent graduates what salary range you should expect. Many professional associations publish surveys of salaries at different management levels. Finally, the company will probably give you some idea of the salary range during an on-site interview. All these will provide general guidelines. Only you can decide whether or not a specific offer is sufficient or whether you should ask for more.

Summary

As with any marketing effort, your job search requires planning and coordination of the marketing controllable variables. Without such planning you may miss attractive employment opportunities or, worse yet, end up in a job you do not like.

Whatever approach you take, good luck in your job search and your future marketing career!

B Marketing Math

T hroughout this text we have referred to certain financial information as it pertains to marketing. Understanding the relationships between sales, expenses, and certain financial ratios is crucial to many marketing decisions. For this reason we will examine two aspects of marketing math: the operating (or profit and loss) statement and selected financial ratios.

THE OPERATING STATEMENT

The two primary financial documents of a company are the balance sheet and the operating statement. The **balance sheet** *is a summary of the company's assets and liabilities at a given* point *in time.* The **operating statement** *is a summary of the company's performance in terms of sales and costs over a given* period *of time.* By examining sales and costs in an operating statement and comparing statements from one time period to the next, marketing managers can identify any cost problems or unfavorable sales or cost trends. The operating statement follows the basic format of:

Gross Sales	$70,000
Returns	5,000
Net Sales	$65,000
Cost of Goods Sold	30,000
Gross Margin	$35,000
Operating Expenses	31,000
Profit	$ 4,000
Taxes	1,500
Net Profit	$ 2,500

The cost of goods sold represents the cost of readying products to sell. For a retailer, this component is the price paid to its supplier. For a manufacturer, it is the cost of the raw materials plus manufacturing costs.

To understand the operating statement more fully, let us examine the detailed statement for a retailer shown in Figure B-1. The difference between net and gross sales is the value of those items returned by customers and allowances given on damaged goods sold. Cost of goods sold during the year starts with the value of inventory on hand at the beginning of the year, adds to this amount all goods purchased for resale during the year, and subtracts the value of any inventory left at the end of the year. Notice that cost of goods sold for this company constitutes less than 50 percent of the sales level and is less than half of all expenses.

Figure B-1

Retailer Operating Statement

			Percentage of Sales*
Gross Sales		$70,000	
Less: Returns and Allowances		5,000	
Net Sales		$65,000	100.00
Cost of Goods Sold:			
Beginning Inventory	$36,000		
Purchases	29,000		
Cost of Goods Available for Sale	$65,000		
Less: Ending Inventory	35,000		
Cost of Goods Sold		30,000	46.15
Gross Margin		$35,000	53.85
Operating Expenses:			
Marketing Expenses:			
Salaries and Commissions	$5,000		7.69
Advertising	4,000		6.15
Delivery	1,000		1.54
Marketing Research	500		0.77
Total Marketing Expenses		$10,500	16.15
Administrative Expenses:			
Salaries	$6,000		9.23
Supplies and Equipment	2,000		3.08
Miscellaneous	500		0.77
Total Administrative Expenses		8,500	13.08
General Expenses:			
Insurance	$3,500		5.38
Utilities	750		1.15
Telephone	750		1.15
Rent	7,000		10.77
Total General Expenses		12,000	18.45
Total Operating Expenses		31,000	47.68
Profit		$ 4,000	6.15
Taxes		1,500	2.31
Net Profit		$ 2,500	3.85

* Percentages have been rounded off to the nearest hundredth of a percent, so there may some minor disagreement among totals.

Examination of the operating expenses and their percentage of sales reveals several interesting points. First, a manager might question what is included in the miscellaneous category, which is listed under administrative expenses. Almost 1 percent of sales is a large amount to be lumped under miscellaneous. More significantly, why does this small retailer incur larger administrative salary expense than marketing salaries and expenses? A small retailer is primarily a marketing organization and should have little administrative overhead. This expense seems out of line. Such analysis is a primary value of the operating statement to all managers.

Regardless of their type or size, all corporations have operating statements. Although usually more complicated than our example, operating statements follow the basic format shown in Figure B-1. In-depth analysis of expenses and their percentage of sales are crucial for understanding, controlling, and managing marketing operations.

SELECTED FINANCIAL RATIOS

The operating statement gives managers a view of how the company performed in the last period. Certain ratios derived from the operating statement, termed operating ratios, point out key information to the manager. **Operating ratios** *are selected items expressed as a percentage of net sales.* The most popular operating ratios are gross margin percentage, returns and allowances percentage, operating expense percentage, and net profit percentage. The formulas for each are given below, and the actual percentages for our example are in Figure B-1:

Gross Margin Percentage = Gross Margin/Net Sales
Returns and Allowances Percentage = Returns and Allowances/Net Sales
Operating Expense Percentage = Total Operating Expenses/Net Sales
Net Profit Percentage = Net Profit/Net Sales

These ratios are particularly useful for comparing performance from one year to the next. For example, suppose management noticed that the net profit ratio for 1984 was 3.85 percent and for 1983 it was 6.24. Management would want to know why the net profit percentage dropped by almost one-half. Further analysis might reveal that the gross margin percentage for 1984 was 53.85 percent and for 1983 it was 53.26 percent. Therefore, the problem was not in the amount paid for products to sell (gross margin percentage had changed only slightly). However, the 1984 operating expenses percentage was 47.68 percent, whereas for 1983 it was 30.10 percent. Thus, the profit problem lies somewhere in the operating expenses. In fact investigation reveals that the cause of the profit erosion was primarily due to the increase of annual rent from $3,500 in 1983 to $7,000 in 1984. To restore old profit levels, management must lower other expenses, renegotiate the lease, or move to a less expensive store.

Another useful ratio is the stock turnover, or inventory turns, rate. *The* **stock turnover rate** *measures the amount of inventory that was carried to generate a given level of sales.* The more popular methods of calculating this ratio are:

$$\text{Inventory Turns} = \frac{\text{Net Sales}}{\text{Average Inventory Units} \times \text{Unit Price}}$$

$$\text{Inventory Turns} = \frac{\text{Cost of Good Sold}}{\text{Average Inventory Units} \times \text{Unit Cost}}$$

$$\text{Inventory Turns} = \frac{\text{Unit Sales}}{\text{Average Inventory Units}}$$

Average inventory is usually derived by adding the ending inventory to the beginning inventory and dividing by 2.

If we use the second formula, the inventory turns for our example in Figure B-1 is:

$$\frac{\$30,000}{(\$36,000 + \$35,000)/2} = 0.845$$

or we turned our inventory less than one time during the entire year. Because the more times we can turn our inventory, the more efficiently we are using our inventory investment, management would have to conclude that we are carrying too much inventory for the sales we are achieving.

Finally, managers are often faced with the decision of investing a certain amount of money to make money. The ratio of money made to money invested is called the **return on investment (ROI)** or:

$$\text{ROI} = \text{Income/Investment}$$

Many companies have ROI guidelines that state any company investment must return higher than a certain ROI or the money would be better used elsewhere. This minimum ROI is often called the corporate **hurdle rate**.

Suppose marketing wants to spend (invest) $10,000 on a one-time advertising campaign which they believe will increase sales, resulting in $1,000 higher annual profits. Thus, the ROI is $1,000/$10,000, or 10 percent. If the corporate hurdle rate is 20 percent (money can be invested elsewhere at 20 percent, as no investment less than this will be accepted), the marketing proposal would be rejected.

To analyze overall corporate return on investment, a more general ROI model is used:

$$\text{ROI} = \frac{\text{Net Profit}}{\text{Net Sales}} \times \frac{\text{Net Sales}}{\text{Investment}}$$

This two-step formula is used to illustrate the relationship between the net profit percentage and the ratio of sales-to-investment on overall ROI.

In our example from Figure B-1 investment is the $35,000 in personal finances that the retail store owner has put into the company. (Investment also may be the value of all assets held by the company, or it may be inventory investment. For a larger company it may be total stockholders' equity.) Thus, for our example the ROI is:

$$\frac{\$2,500}{\$65,000} \times \frac{\$65,000}{\$35,000} = 3.85 \times 1.86 = 7.16$$

or a 3.85-percent net profit ratio and a 1.86 sales-to investment ratio return 7.16 percent on corporate investment. How can this investment be improved? The formula provides the answer. Higher sales on the same investment, the same sales on a lower investment, or higher profits with sales and investment the same will all improve the ROI.

The objective of ROI calculations is to determine how effectively the company is using its resources. Resources can be defined in whatever way management feels is relevant.

Glossary

Adoption process. The steps consumers are believed to go through in making a decision to try a new product.

Advertising. Any paid form of impersonal presentation of products or ideas of commercial significance to prospective buyers.

Advertising specialty. An item with a low unit cost given free to prospective customers. Such items typically feature the name and address of the company and a brief sales message about the firm or a product. Ballpoint pens, key chains, and paperweights are frequently used as advertising specialties.

Agent middleman. A wholesale middleman that negotiates sales or purchases or both, but does not take title to the goods in which it deals.

Allowances. Compensation by a wholesaler or manufacturer for services such as advertising or in-store displays provided by a retailer or wholesaler. Allowances often take the form of a percentage reduction in the purchase price.

Automatic merchandising. The sale of products through vending machines; also called *automatic selling.*

Backward invention strategy. An international marketing approach followed when a company develops less complicated products to fit the needs of developing nations.

Bait-and-switch advertising. An alluring but insincere offer to sell merchandise at a lower-than-normal price, usually made in order to increase store traffic.

Balance of trade. The relationship of cash flow in and out of a country, including government, corporate, and individual transactions. A deficit balance of trade suggests that the country in question imports more than it exports.

Basing-point pricing. Calculating transportation costs on the basis of the destination's distance from a selected production center, regardless of whether the goods are actually shipped from that center. Basing-point pricing is used mostly by producers of commodities such as steel and cement.

Brand. The name, term, symbol, design, or combination of these that identifies a product.

Break-even point. A level of sales at which revenues and costs are equal. A combination of sales and costs at which the firm neither makes a profit, nor suffers a loss.

Buying power. (1) The ability to buy in large quantities and thereby obtain a special price or other concessions. (2) Income available for the purchase of consumer goods. (*See also* Purchasing power.)

Capital investment goods. Products, such as manufacturing plants, installations, tools, and computers, used to produce other products.

Captive market. The potential clientele of monopolies such as utilities; of firms that are the only source of supply in a given geographic area for a given product or service; or of retail or service businesses located in hotels, airports, railroad stations, or other facilities where consumers do not have reasonable alternative sources of supply.

Cash-and-carry wholesaler. A limited-function merchant wholesaler that does not sell on credit or make deliveries.

Central buying. A purchasing procedure by which one division is authorized to act for several store units in selecting merchandise for resale.

Channel management. The effort to select the most effective, efficient, and profitable channel of distribution.

Channel of distribution. Also called a marketing channel, this is the path a product takes as it moves from the producer to the user. The path includes all intermediaries who facilitate the movement of the product to the user.

Close-out. An offer to sell slow-moving merchandise, an incomplete assortment of goods, or the remainder of a line of merchandise that is to be discontinued at reduced prices to ensure an immediate sale.

Collusion. A secret, illegal agreement between two or more businesses to defraud competitors or customers, usually by fixing prices or market shares.

Commission merchant. A non-title-taking agent middleman that supplies space for goods, acts as a contact between producers and buyers, and is generally empowered to conclude a sale. Commission merchants are particularly important in the sale of agricultural products.

Commodity exchange. An organization, usually owned by member-traders, that provides facilities for bringing together buyers and sellers of specified standard commodities (or their agents) and conducting business in accordance with set rules.

Common carrier. A business that offers to transport goods under the same conditions for all shippers. Common carriers are closely regulated by federal and state governments.

Common market. A union of various countries, usually in the same geographic area, for the purpose of reducing or eliminating tariffs, quotas, and other restrictions on trade. There is usually a free flow of capital and labor between member nations, and a common tariff may be imposed on all nonmember countries.

Concept testing. A new-product testing approach where a prototype is shown to groups of potential customers for their reactions.

Consignment. An agreement by which products are supplied for future sale or other purposes. The receiver (consignee) becomes responsible for the goods upon receipt of the shipment, but title to them remains with the sender (consignor). The consignee may eventually purchase the goods, act as an agent for their sale to others, or otherwise dispose of them in accordance with the terms of the arrangement.

Consolidated metropolitan statistical area (CMSA). A geographic unit used by the Department of Commerce in making statistical analyses. CMSAs are major urban areas.

Consumer cooperative. A marketing organization owned by, and operated for the mutual benefit of a voluntary group of consumer-owners.

Consumer credit. The ability to buy now by promising to pay later. *Installment credit* involves a promise to pay fixed amounts at regular intervals. *Noninstallment credit* involves payment in full at a specified future date. Consumer credit is an important factor in determining purchasing power.

Consumerism. A loosely organized but highly vocal movement by consumers to protest unfair marketing practices such as false advertising, deceptive pricing, and inadequate product warranties.

Containerization. In transportation, the practice of consolidating a number of packages into one container, sealed at its point of origin. The container remains sealed until it reaches its destination.

Contract. An agreement enforceable by law, characterized by (1) a lawful promise, (2) competent parties, (3) an offer and an acceptance, (4) legal consideration, (5) a meeting of minds of the parties, and (6) a written document, if the agreement involves more than a certain amount ($50 in most states) or runs for more than a year.

Contract carrier. A transportation company that provides service to one or more shippers on a contract basis, does not operate on a regular schedule, and has rates more easily adapted to specific situations than those of common carriers.

Convenience goods. Consumer products, such as bread, razor blades, or gasoline, that are usually low in cost and purchased with little if any deliberation on the part of the buyer.

Cooperative. An organization of independent channel members joined together contractually to act as one company.

Cooperative advertising. An arrangement in which manufacturers and retailers share the cost of local advertising, usually on a 50-50 basis. Since the retailers, who purchase the advertising, can do so at lower rates in local media, this arrangement in effect stretches the advertising dollar.

Corporate mission. A statement of what the company wants to accomplish.

Cost-plus pricing. Pricing an item by computing its cost and adding a certain amount to that figure.

Culture. All the tangible and intangible aspects of our environment that are created by people.

Deceptive packaging. The use of packages whose size or construction suggests that they contain more of the product than is actually present.

Demand schedule. An estimate of the number of units of a product that would be sold at each of a series of prices.

Demographics. Statistics which can be gathered and used to describe a population.

Department store. A retail organization that carries several lines of merchandise, such as women's ready-to-wear clothing, fashion accessories, men's and boy's clothing, piece goods, and home furnishing, all of which are handled by separate departments.

Depreciation. The reduction in potential usefulness, and hence value, of a fixed asset due to wear and tear or the passage of time.

Derived demand. Demand for a product that stems, directly or indirectly, from the demand for another good. Thus the demand for steel is derived, in part, from the demand for automobiles.

Diffusion process. The stages of a new product's movement from introduction to acceptance.

Discretionary personal income. That portion of disposable personal income not needed for necessities or contracted payments.

Disposable personal income. Income available for spending or saving, calculated by subtracting personal taxes from personal income.

Distribution center. A modern storage facility equipped to take orders and deliver merchandise. Such centers are frequently operated by major chain department stores.

Distribution channel. The route taken by a product as it passes from the original owner or maker to ultimate consumers or industrial users.

Drop shipper. A limited-function merchant wholesaler that sells merchandise to a customer and then arranges for the producer or manufacturer to deliver it directly (drop ship) to the buyer.

Durable goods. Products such as washing machines that have a relatively high unit value and a long life; sometimes called *hard goods*.

Elastic demand. Demand that is sensitive to changes in price.

Environmental monitoring system. That part of a marketing information system dealing with information about marketing's uncontrollable environment.

E.O.M. (end-of-month) dating. A billing system in which the cash-discount and net-credit periods begin on the first day of the following month rather than on the date of the invoice. Thus if the terms of sale are "2/10, net 30, E.O.M." and an order is filled on June 16, the cash discount may be taken any time through July 10 and the net amount is due on July 30.

Exclusive distribution. A policy of intentionally limiting, usually to only one, the number of retailers that handle an item in a market area.

Exempt carrier. A transportation business excluded from much federal regulation of the transportation industry by virtue of the products carried.

Experimental method. In marketing research, the testing of a product or an idea in the marketplace to determine if it is suitable for a specific purpose or will bring about a desired result. Such testing is used frequently to measure the popularity of product designs, packages, and prices.

Fixed cost. An operating expense, such as rent, that does not vary with the volume of business.

F.O.B. (free-on-board) pricing. An arrangement in which all shipping costs from a specified point are paid by the purchaser.

Franchise. A right or license, granted by a franchisor, to do business under a certain name.

Free trade. Trade between nations with no tariff or other restrictions.

Freight forwarder. An organization that consolidates less-than-carload shipments from several manufacturers, distributors, or other shippers into carload lots.

Full-function wholesaler. Also called a *full-service wholesaler*. A merchant middleman that performs all the functions normally associated with the term *wholesaler.* That is, it buys, sells, assembles, and divides merchandise; delivers and warehouses goods; extends credit; assumes risk; and gives information and advice.

General line wholesaler.   A merchant wholesaler that carries a complete supply of one product line such as drugs, hardware, or food.

General merchandise wholesaler.   A merchant wholesaler that carries a broad assortment of unrelated or loosely related products such as hardware, drug sundries, and groceries.

Gross national product.   Commonly abbreviated as GNP; the total national output of goods and services valued at market prices for a given period, usually one year.

Guarantee, guaranty.   Assurance, express or implied, of the quality of goods offered for sale. An express guarantee with a definite promise of a refund in the event of poor performance or some other specific assurance is often used as a sales aid, especially by mail-order firms whose merchandise cannot be inspected before purchase. (*See also* Warranty.)

Imperfect competition.   Sometimes called *monopolistic competition.* A situation in which there are relatively few producers of a given product and, as a result, some firms have a degree of control over price.

Impulse goods.   Consumer products usually purchased without prior deliberation.

Indexation.   The use of escalator clauses, usually linked to a cost-of-living index, throughout a society or by a large portion of it.

Industrial consumers (users).   All businesses, government agencies, and nonprofit organizations that consume, or use, products to (a) make a profit or (b) help meet a social need.

Industrial goods.   Products intended for use by industrial consumers.

Inelastic demand.   Demand that is comparatively insensitive to changes in price.

Inflation.   An increase in the volume of money and credit relative to the supply of available goods, resulting in a rise in the general price level.

Intensive distribution.   A policy of using the maximum number of retailers to distribute a product.

Internal data.   Generally, operational data such as sales, credit, and inventory statistics generated within the company.

Internal information system.   That part of a marketing information system dealing with internal sources of information.

Inventory.   A supply of raw materials, work-in-process, or finished goods being held for further processing or sale.

Jobber.   Generally, a full-function or full-service wholesaler.

Law of demand.   An economic law which states that more goods will be sold at lower prices than at higher prices.

Lead time.   The number of days between the placement of an order and its arrival.

Learning curve effect. Occurs when a company experiences lower variable cost per unit as volume produced increases. The effect is caused by more efficient operations.

Leased department. A department of a retail business managed and operated by an outside person or organization rather than by the store of which it is a physical part. Drug departments, beauty salons, and restaurants are frequently leased operations.

Life cycle analysis. The study of age-related changes in demand.

Limited-function wholesaler. A merchant wholesaler that does not perform all the functions normally associated with the term *wholesaler*. The most important are cash-and-carry wholesalers, drop shippers, and truck distributors.

Limited-line retailer. A retailer that carries a slightly more varied product mix than single-line stores. Sometimes called a *specialty store*. Apparel, shoe, and gift shops are limited-line retailers.

Manufacturer's agent. Also called a *manufacturer's representative*. A non-title-taking agent middleman, authorized by his principal (a manufacturer) to sell all or part of the principal's line in a clearly defined territory. The manufacturer, not the agent, controls the price of the goods and the terms of sale.

Manufacturer's sales branch. A wholesale establishment that is owned and operated by a manufacturer and carries an inventory of the manufacturer's product.

Manufacturer's sales office. A wholesale establishment owned and operated by a manufacturer that does *not* carry an inventory of the product.

Manufacturer's salesperson. A salesperson hired by a manufacturer to call on wholesalers, retailers, industrial buyers, ultimate consumers, or other manufacturers.

Marginal cost. The cost of producing and selling one additional unit of a good.

Marginal revenue. The income derived from selling one additional unit of a good.

Mark-down. A reduction in the original or previous retail price of an item, often stated as a percentage of the selling price.

Marketing. The activities performed by individuals or organizations, for commercial or noncommercial objectives, aimed at satisfaction through the exchange process of buyers' demand for products, services, people, or ideas.

Marketing audit. A comprehensive examination of a firm's total marketing effort.

Marketing controllable variables. The product, place, promotion, and price decisions that make up the total marketing mix.

Marketing information system. A complex of people, machines, and procedures to generate an orderly flow of information from internal and external sources for use in marketing management decision making.

Marketing management. The planning, organization, direction, and control of the marketing activities of a firm or division, including the formulation of marketing objectives, policies, and programs.

Marketing mix. The combination of marketing controllable variables performed by a firm. It differs from company to company depending on the degree of emphasis placed on particular activities such as advertising or personal selling.

Marketing opportunity assessment. The process of searching for and evaluating marketing opportunities.

Marketing research. The systematic gathering, recording, and analyzing of data related to marketing.

Market-segmentation analysis. The division of the total market for a product into reasonably homogeneous segments on such bases as age, occupation, income, and geographic location.

Mark-up. The percentage added onto the purchase cost of a product to cover a channel member's costs and profits.

Mass market. The total number of prospective customers for products in our economy.

Mass merchandiser. Generally, a large retail store with a policy of charging lower prices for merchandise than "conventional" department stores, rendering only limited services to its customers, and charging extra for those services it does perform.

Merchandise broker. A non-title-taking agent middleman that buys or sells for its principal on a one-time or sporadic basis. Merchandise brokers have little control over the price of the goods they handle or the terms of sale.

Merchant middleman. A middleman that takes title to the merchandise it handles.

Metropolitan statistical area (MSA). A geographic unit used by the Department of Commerce in making statistical analyses. MSAs are urban areas which are not part of a consolidated metropolitan statistical area and stand alone.

Missionary salesperson. A type of manufacturer's salesperson who places little emphasis on personal selling, concentrating instead on giving advice on store layouts, displays, advertising, pricing, and special promotions. In the drug industry, a missionary salesperson is called a *detailer*.

Monopoly. A single seller of a product for which there is no close substitute.

Multinationalism. A policy, followed by some businesses engaged in international trade, of operating many of their production and distribution facilities abroad and making extensive use of foreign labor and executive talent.

Multiple channels. Distributing the same product through two or more separate channels.

National income. The sum of the total amount earned by employees, proprietors' income, corporate profits, rental income, and net interest for a given year.

Negotiated price. A price worked out during discussions between the seller and buyer. Often the terms of sale (the size of the down payment, credit arrangements, delivery dates, and so on) will also be negotiated.

Nonprice competition. Competition based not on the price of the product, which is about the same everywhere, but on such factors as the services provided by the seller, the style of the product, the terms of sale, packaging, or the reputation or location of the maker or seller.

Nonprofit marketing. Pursued by organizations which seek to serve some aspect of what the organization perceives to be the public interest rather than seek financial profits.

Nonstore retailer. A retailer that does not maintain stores in the conventional sense, for the public to visit. Mail-order houses, vending-machine companies, and door-to-door sales organizations are nonstore retailers.

Non-title-taking agent middleman. A wholesale middleman that does not take title to the merchandise it handles. This category includes manufacturer's agents, selling agents, merchandise brokers, commission merchants, import and export agents, auction companies, and purchasing agents or resident buyers.

Observational method.   In marketing research, the viewing of an action or an event in order to develop solutions to marketing problems. The researcher may obtain data from trained observers, or he may use cameras or other mechanical devices.

Oligopoly.   An economic or marketing situation in which a few sellers control the supply of a product, and hence its price.

One-price policy.   A policy of offering identical products to all buyers at the same price at any one point in time.

Operating supplies.   Industrial products, such as cleaning aids, fuel, paper clips, and lubricating oils, used in the normal operation of a business.

Patronage motive.   The reason a consumer purchases a product from one retailer rather than another. A store's pricing policies, its location, and the friendliness of its service are often patronage motives.

Penetration pricing.   Setting the price as low as possible to capture a large share of the market.

Perception.   The interpretation of the sensory input of hearing, seeing, tasting, smelling, and feeling.

Perfect competition.   A situation in which there are many producers of identical or nearly identical products, and no one firm or group of firms has any appreciable control over price.

Personal income.   National income *minus* corporate income taxes, retained earnings, and contributions for social insurance *plus* interest paid by the government and business and government transfer payments such as social security benefits, veterans' pensions, relief payments, and unemployment compensation.

Personal selling.   The personal presentation of products or ideas of commercial significance to prospective buyers.

Phantom freight.   The amount by which the allowance for freight delivery costs in a seller's delivered-price quotation exceeds that actual cost. It is commonly associated with basing-point pricing systems.

Physical distribution.   All the activities required to physically move the product from the manufacturer to the final customer. These activities include order processing, transportation, inventory control, warehousing, and materials handling.

Physical distribution service.   Providing the right product at the right place at the right time.

Piggyback service.   A form of coordinated motor and rail transportation in which loaded truck trailers are hauled on specially designed rail flatcars.

Pilferage.   Thefts, usually small, by employees.

Place utility.   The value added to a product by making it available to the consumer at a convenient location.

Planned obsolescence.   Sometimes called *managed obsolescence*. The intentional production of products that will wear out, break down, or go out of fashion in a relatively short time in order to assure a large replacement market.

Planned shopping center. A geographic cluster of stores whose location, number, and type, as well as the architecture, parking facilities, and other features of the center as a whole, were planned by the developer.

Point-of-purchase advertising. A sale-promotion strategy, usually implemented through window or counter displays in retail stores.

Premium. A product offered free or at less than its usual price to encourage the consumer to buy another product. Water glasses given away by a service station in return for the purchase of a certain amount of gas and toys enclosed in cereal packages are typical premiums.

Price controls. Limits imposed by the federal government on the prices firms can charge for their products.

Price discrimination. Charging different prices to different customers under similar conditions of sale. Such actions may violate the antitrust statutes if they tend to create a monopoly or substantially lessen the competition and if the buyers are on the same level of the distribution chain.

Price elasticity. The relative change in quantity demanded caused by a relative change in price.

Price lining. The establishment of a limited number of predetermined prices at which merchandise will be offered for sale. Thus a manufacturer of ladies' slacks may elect to price each pair at $4.95, $9.95, or $14.95, regardless of minor variations in the quality or cost of production of garments in each category.

Price-quality relationship. A perception by customers that a higher price means higher quality.

Primary data. Data gathered directly by a marketing research project.

Primary metropolitan statistical area (PMSA). A geographic unit used by the Department of Commerce in making statistical analyses. PMSAs are major urban areas contained within consolidated metropolitan statistical areas.

Principle of diminishing utility. An economic law which states that the more units we have of something, the less each additional unit means to us.

Private carrier. A carrier that avoids most forms of government regulation because (a) it owns the commodities it transports, (b) these commodities are related to its principal business, (c) it employs its own drivers, and (d) it owns or leases the equipment it uses.

Product adaptation strategy. An international marketing approach followed when a company modifies its domestic products to meet the requirements of other nations.

Product differentiation. An attempt to establish in consumers a preference for one company's product although the product may be physically similar to the competition's product.

Product extension strategy. An international marketing approach followed when a company offers the same products internationally that it markets domestically.

Productivity. The ratio of output, or production results, to the corresponding input of economic resources during a given period.

Product life cycle. The patterns of competition, profitability, and marketing strategies over the life of a product. The product life cycle begins at introduction and concludes with the withdrawal of the product from the market.

Product mix. The range of products offered for sale by a firm or a business unit.

Product position. The consumers' perception of the product relative to other product offerings. Products can be positioned by features, benefits, or comparison to other products.

Promotion. All communication activities undertaken by the company to inform people about its products, services, corporate image, or social intent.

Promotional allowance. A special price reduction given by sellers to retailers to compensate them for money spent in advertising an item in local newspapers or giving preferred display space to the sellers' products.

Publicity. Any nonpaid impersonal communication about a company or its products appearing in the media as news.

Public relations. The promotion of goodwill toward a business among its various "publics" (customers, dealers, employees, suppliers, labor unions, and the general community) through programs designed to create for it a positive image.

Public warehouse. A storage facility, usually privately owned, whose operators do not take title to the goods they handle and whose receipts can be used as collateral for loans.

Purchasing power. Sometimes called *buying power*. The ability of an individual buyer, a group of buyers, or the total market to finance purchases using current income, savings accounts or other forms of wealth, or credit.

Quantity discount. A reduction in the per-unit price of an item based on the number of units purchased. *Cumulative quantity discounts* are based on the total volume a customer purchases in a given period. *Noncumulative quantity discounts* are based on the volume purchased at any one time.

Rack jobber. A wholesale middleman that supplies certain classes of merchandise not handled by a retailer's regular suppliers. Rack jobbers commonly set up display racks in stores, provide an opening inventory on consignment or on a guaranteed-sale basis, periodically check the stock, and replenish inventories. They operate principally in the food trade.

Raw material. Unprocessed material used in the production of other goods.

Real income. Income measured in terms of what it will buy. During periods of inflation prices rise faster than wages, thereby reducing real income. In periods of deflation, the reverse is true.

Rebate. A refund, usually in cash, of a portion of the price paid by an ultimate consumer for a product.

Reorder point (ROP). The amount of inventory that is on hand when a new order is placed.

Resale price maintenance. A policy of allowing the manufacturer of an item to set the price at which it will be sold by wholesalers or retailers.

Research design. A procedure for gathering data and determining who should be studied and how to study them.

Resident buyer. A non-title-taking agent middleman that purchases merchandise for its principals. Resident buyers are most common in the apparel industry, where they may purchase identical merchandise for stores in widely separated areas.

Retailing. Selling directly to the ultimate consumer.

Safety stock.   Inventory in excess of what is expected to sell during the lead time. It is carried as insurance against uncertainty.

Sales forecast.   An estimate of the sales, in dollars or physical units, that will result from a proposed marketing plan or program during a specified future period.

Sales promotion.   Activities other than advertising, personal selling, and public relations that stimulate consumer purchases and increase dealer effectiveness. Displays, demonstrations, coupons, and samples play a frequent part in sales promotions.

Sampling.   In sales promotion, the actual giving away of a product to a consumer to help build consumer demand. In marketing research, the selection of a representative portion of a universe.

Scrambled merchandising.   A deviation from traditional merchandising that involves the sale of items not usually associated with a retail establishment's primary lines (e.g., the sale of hardware items in drugstores and nonfood products in supermarkets).

Seasonal discount.   A price reduction granted to retailers who place orders for seasonal merchandise well in advance of the normal buying period.

Seasonal goods.   Products such as antifreeze, bathing suits, or lawnmowers for which the demand is much higher at certain times of year.

Secondary data.   Information previously published or collected, and not the result of primary research.

Secondary shopping district.   An unplanned collection of retail stores away from the downtown area and close to residential neighborhoods. Such districts are characterized by on-street parking and consist mainly of stores that retail convenience goods.

Selective distribution.   A form of market coverage where only specific outlets, each of which meets certain corporate criteria, are allowed to stock the product.

Selective perception.   The individual's mechanism for blocking out stimuli which are not thought to be important.

Selling agent.   A non-title-taking agent middleman that normally handles the entire output of its principal, is not restricted to a territory, and has considerable authority from its principal to negotiate prices, delivery dates, and other terms of sale.

Semimanufactured goods.   Products that have undergone some processing but are incomplete in themselves, such as sheet steel, fibers, and plastics.

Shopping goods.   Consumer products that are purchased only after the buyer has compared them to competing products. Automobiles, apparel, and furniture are frequently shopping goods.

Single-line retailer.   A retailer, such as an automobile dealer or an appliance store, that specializes in one product line.

Skimming.   A pricing approach where the price is set as high as possible to recover development costs of a new product. It is often followed by the intention to drop the price when competition enters the market.

Social class.   A group of people with similar rankings of social position of respect.

Social responsibility.   The contribution a firm should make to society above and beyond meeting its economic and legal responsibilities.

Sorting process.   A function all channels perform, it is the activities that take heterogeneous natural supply and turn it into the type of heterogeneous supply that consumers desire.

Specialty goods. Consumer products that ultimate consumers will go considerably out of their way to buy. Most specialty goods have either unique features or a well-known brand name.

Specialty wholesaler. A merchant wholesaler that handles only a segment of a broad product line. A food wholesaler that deals only in frozen foods, for example, is a specialty wholesaler.

Speculation. The buying or selling of products with the intention of profiting by fluctuation in their price.

Stagflation. The simultaneous occurrence of inflation and recession.

Standard industrial classification (SIC). A system used by the Department of Commerce to segment companies by their primary economic activity.

Standard metropolitan statistical area (SMSA). A geographic unit formerly used by the Department of Commerce in making statistical analyses. Each SMSA contains one city with 50,000 or more inhabitants or a city with at least 25,000 inhabitants, which, together with contiguous places (incorporated or unincorporated) having population densities of at least 1,000 persons per square mile, has a combined population of 50,000 and constitutes for general economic and social purposes a single community, provided that the county (or counties) in which the city and contiguous places are located has a total population of at least 100,000 (75,000 in New England).

Stock-turnover rate. An index of the velocity with which merchandise moves into and out of a store or department; the number of times during a period that the average inventory on hand has been sold and replaced.

Straight-commission plan. A method of compensation whereby salespeople are paid solely on the basis of the volume of business they produce.

Straight-salary plan. A method of compensation whereby salespeople are paid a fixed sum at regular intervals. It is used when individual performance is difficult to measure with precision.

Strategic marketing planning. The process of developing and implementing an effort to fit the organization's marketing goals and capabilities to its marketing opportunities.

Strategy. The specification of the activities to be undertaken to accomplish the corporate objectives.

Supermarket. A large departmentalized retail establishment offering a broad stock of dry groceries and produce, plus a variety of nonfood convenience goods.

Survey method. Sometimes called the *questionnaire method.* A marketing-research technique based on actual interviews with people, either in person, by mail, or on the phone.

Target market. The most likely purchasers of a product.

Target-return pricing. Pricing products in such a way as to produce a predetermined percentage or dollar return on the firm's investment.

Testimonial. A product endorsement, usually paid for and often from a prominent personality.

Test marketing. The limited introduction of a new product in selected markets that are believed to be representative of the overall market.

Trade association. A nonprofit organization, local or national, that serves the common interests of firms in the same business. Its functions generally include research, education, and working for the enactment of legislation favorable to the industry.

Trade discount. Sometimes called a *functional discount*. A reduction in the list price of a product granted to a class of customers (manufacturers, wholesalers, retailers) on the assumption that they will perform part of the marketing function.

Trademark. A distinguishing word, emblem, or symbol, or any combination of these things used to identify a manufacturer or distributor of a particular product.

Trading up. (1) Handling and promoting more expensive or higher-quality merchandise in order to elevate the prestige of the firm. (2) Attempting to interest customers in better, more expensive goods than they expect to buy.

Truck distributor. A limited-function merchant wholesaler that performs the selling and delivery functions at the same time.

Ultimate consumer. One who buys products for personal, family, or household use.

Uniform delivered pricing. A policy of regarding the entire nation as one physical zone and charging all purchasers, regardless of their location, the same delivered price.

Value. The power of a product to command other goods in exchange.

Value added. In marketing, an increase in the monetary worth of a product as a result of the functions performed by each link in the distribution chain. In production, the value added by each physical change in the product.

Variable cost. An operating expense, such as labor costs, that varies with the volume of business.

Vertical marketing system. A type of channel in which everything from production to retailing is owned by one company.

Warranty. A subsidiary promise or collateral agreement, a breach of which entitles the buyer to make certain claims for damages against the vendor. A warranty may be express (deriving from a specific agreement) or implied (deriving from the operation of law).

Wealth. Property that has a monetary value. Wealth constitutes potential purchasing power.

Wholesaler. A business that specializes in performing some or all of the wholesaling functions—assembly, breaking bulk, selling, delivery, credit extension, etc.

Zone delivered pricing. A policy of charging all purchasers within a geographic area the same price regardless of differences in transportation costs.

Credits and Acknowledgments

AMERICAN MARKETING ASSOCIATION. Figure 4–5, from the *Journal of Marketing Research*, November 1966; Figure 22–10 from *Marketing News*, March 18, 1983; Case 3, from *Marketing News*; Marketing Strategy (Ch. 15), from *Fortune, Business Week, Wall Street Journal, Forbes,* and *Marketing News*; and Adapted material for Ch. 9, from *Wall Street Journal* and *Marketing News*. Reprinted by permission.

AUDIT BUREAU OF CIRCULATIONS. Figures 16–5 and 16–6, from FAS-FAX, June 30, 1984. Reprinted by permission.

BUSINESS WEEK. Figure 2–4. Reprinted from the January 27, 1975 issue of *Business Week* by special permission. Copyright © 1975 by McGraw-Hill, Inc.

ROBERT J. COEN, MCCANN-ERICKSON, INC. Figure 16–1, from *Advertising Age*. Reprinted by permission.

TRUSTEES OF COLUMBIA UNIVERSITY IN THE CITY OF NEW YORK. Figure 20–6, from the *Columbia Journal of World Business*. Reprinted by permission.

CRAIN COMMUNICATIONS. Figures 3–5, 3–6, 16–2, 16–3, and 16–7, from *Advertising Age*. Reprinted with permission from the October 15, 1979, March 16, 1983, and September 8, 1983 issues of *Advertising Age*. Copyright © 1979 by Crain Communications, Inc.

FORTUNE. Case 12, from *Fortune*, Bill Saporito; Marketing Strategy (Ch. 12), from *Fortune*, Anne B. Pillsbury; and Case 19, from *Fortune*, Peter D. Petre. Adapted by permission. Copyright © 1980, 1983. All rights reserved.

HANDLING & SHIPPING. Case 14. Adapted by permission.

HOLT, RINEHART AND WINSTON, CBS COLLEGE PUBLISHING. Figure 5–2, from *Consumer Behavior*, 3rd edition, by James F. Engel, Roger D. Blackwell, and David T. Kollat. Copyright © 1978 by the Dryden Press. Reprinted by permission.

NEWSWEEK. Epigraph, from "To Market, To Market." Adapted by permission.

UNESCO. Figure 5–5, from "Some Applications of Behavioral Research." Copyright © Unesco 1957. Reproduced by permission.

WALL STREET JOURNAL. Figure 16–4, adapted material for Ch. 9, and Cases 10, 13, and 16. Reprinted by permission of the *Wall Street Journal*. Copyright © Dow Jones Company, Inc. 1982, 1983. All rights reserved.

Table of Contents Photo Credits

Page i © Karen Kent. **vi** (left) © 1984 George E. Jones/Photo Researchers, Inc.; (right) General Electric. **vii** (left) © G. Gladstone/The Image Bank West; (right) © Ken Sherman/ Bruce Coleman, Inc. **viii** (left) Safeway Stores, Inc.; (right) National Medical Enterprises. **ix** (left) Mary Kay Cosmetics; (right) General Motors. **x** (left) © Michael Melford 1980/Peter Arnold, Inc.; (right) © Gary Burke. **xi** (left) Pepsi-Cola Company; (right) © Edward L. Miller/Stock Boston. **xii** (left) Safeway Stores, Inc.; (right) © Peter Menzel/Stock Boston. **xiii** (left) D. P. Hershkowitz/Bruce Coleman, Inc.; (right) © Joachim Messerschmidt/Bruce Coleman, Inc. **xiv** (left) Mary Kay Cosmetics; (right) ITT Corporation. **xv** (left) © Burt Glinn/Magnum Photos, Inc.; (right) © Stuart Cohen/Stock Boston. **xvi** (left) © Jay Freis 1982/The Image Bank; (right) © Four By Five, Inc.

Photo Credits

Page 1, © Bruce Coleman; **2**, © Barbara Alper, Stock, Boston; **6**, Benihana of Tokyo; **17**, © Judy Gelles, Stock, Boston; **18**, © Peter Mentzer, Stock, Boston; **32**, HBJ Photo; **40**, Edward C. Topple, NYSE Photographer; **58**, Merck and Co.; **64**, HBJ Photo; **79**, Du Pont Company; **90**, Courtesy, France Actuelle; **103**, State of California, Department of Public Works; **104**, Magnum Photos, Inc.; **108**, Courtesy of George Gallup; **110**, David Moskowitz; **114**, Courtesy of Johnson and Johnson Co.; **121**, © Peter Mentzer; **136**, James H. Karales: Peter Arnold, Inc.; **155**, Courtesy, I Ski; **160**, © Hazel Hankin, Stock, Boston; **169**, Harry Wilkes, Stock, Boston; **176**, Mobil Oil; **180**, © Hazel Hankin; **199**, William N. Bereck, Frederick Lewis; **210**, Stock, Boston; **214**, © Don Smetzer, Click/ Chicago; **216**, © Don Smetzer, Smetzer Stock Studio; **223**, © John Maher, EKM-Nepenthe; **229**, A. T. Cross Company; **237**, Alton Box Board Company; **238**, © Michael Heron, Woodfin Camp & Assoc.; **240**, General Motors; **242**, Courtesy of Diane Von Furstenberg; **247**, Merck and Co.; **254, 259**, © Hazel Hankin; **267**, Crane; **274**, General Motors; **282–83**, Pennzoil Co.; **297**, HBJ Photos; **302**, Danskin; **312**, Houston Grand Opera; **321**, Qantas, the Australian Airline; **329**, American Cancer Society; **334**, USDA Photo by Larry Rana; **341**, Arthur Grace, Stock, Boston; **342**, Peter Southwick, Stock, Boston; **346**, Shelley Katz; **354**, Pepsi Cola Co.; **366**, © Sepp Seitz, Woodfin Camp & Assoc.; **378**, NYSPIX-Commerce; **384**, Courtesy of IBM Corporation; **389**, © Gabor Demjen, Stock, Boston; **406**, Leo Vals, Frederick Lewis; **413**, The Grand Union Company; **416**, Courtesy of the Southland Corp.; **430**, Mike Mazzaschi, Stock, Boston; **440**, © Baron Wolman, Woodfin Camp & Assoc.; **449**, Ellis Werwig, Stock, Boston; **453**, HBJ Photo, Ewing Galloway; **458**, Joe Jedd; **477**, George Jones, III, Photo Research; **478**, © Jose A. Fernandez, Woodfin Camp & Assoc.; **482**, Executive Vice President, Carl Byoir and Association, Inc., Chairman, Media Communications Training, a Byoir Subsidiary; **484**, Goodyear; **491**, Courtesy of American Home Products; **496**, The Stockmarket; **510**, © Bruce Kliene, Jeraboam; **521**, Wendy's International, Inc. © 1984; **525**, Coca Cola; **527**, Courtesy of Nabisco Brands, Inc.; **534**, HBJ Photo; **552**, Mary Kay Cosmetics; **556**, HBJ Photo, Ken Karp; **561**, Owen Franken, Stock, Boston; **595**, Jeff Smith, The Image Bank; **596**, © Sepp Seitz, Woodfin Camp & Assoc.; **600**, McDonald's Corporation; **602**, HBJ Photo; **607**, Peter LeGrand, Click/ Chicago; **620**, MSI Data Corp.; **638**, Courtesy Gentech, Inc.; **643**, © Earl G. Graves Publishing Co.; **661**, Sam Pierson/Photo Researchers, Inc.; **669**, EKM Nepenthe; **670**, HBJ Photo, Barbara Salz; **674**, Courtesy of Motown Records; **683**, Coca Cola; **687**, Burton Wilson; **694**, © Peter Arnold; **710**, American Can Co.; **718–19**, HBJ Photos; **729**, McDonald's Corporation; **743**, © Jack Thomas; **752**, Click/Chicago; **757**, Way Vanden Busshe; **769**, HBJ Photo; **778**, © Dean Abramson, Stock, Boston.

Illustration Credits

Figure 2.8, Reprinted by permission of The Wall Street Journal, © Dow Jones & Co., Inc., December 12, 1982. All rights reserved. **2.9**, Reprinted by permission of The Wall Street Journal, © Dow Jones & Co., Inc. January 10, 1983. All rights reserved. **4.3**, U.S. Government Census Bureau. **8.2**, Reprinted by permission of The Wall Street Journal, © Dow Jones & Co., Inc., March 22, 1984. All rights reserved. **9.2**, Booz, Allen and Hamilton, Inc. **11.3**, Ronald L. Ernst, Marketing News, March 7, 1980, "Distribution Channel Detente Benefits Suppliers, Retailers, Consumers." **14.2**, Adapted with permission of Macmillan Publishing Company from *Logistical Management* by Donald J. Bowersox. **15.4**, *Promotional Strategy,* fourth edition, (1979) by Engel, Warshaw, and Kinnear, Richard D. Irwin, Inc.

Name Index

Subject Index

A 5
B 6
C 7
D 8
E 9
F 0
G 1
H 2
I 3
J 4